ASP.NET Bible

ASP.NET Bible

Mridula Parihar *et al.*

Hungry Minds™

Best-Selling Books • Digital Downloads • e-Books • Answer Networks • e-Newsletters • Branded Web Sites • e-Learning

New York, NY ✦ Cleveland, OH ✦ Indianapolis, IN

ASP.NET Bible

Published by
Hungry Minds, Inc.
909 Third Avenue
New York, NY 10022
www.hungryminds.com

Library of Congress Control Number: 2001093388

ISBN: 0-7645-4816-6

Printed in the United States of America

10 9 8 7 6 5 4 3 2 1

1B/SQ/QS/QS/IN

Distributed in the United States by Hungry Minds, Inc.

Distributed by CDG Books Canada Inc. for Canada; by Transworld Publishers Limited in the United Kingdom; by IDG Norge Books for Norway; by IDG Sweden Books for Sweden; by IDG Books Australia Publishing Corporation Pty. Ltd. for Australia and New Zealand; by TransQuest Publishers Pte Ltd. for Singapore, Malaysia, Thailand, Indonesia, and Hong Kong; by Gotop Information Inc. for Taiwan; by ICG Muse, Inc. for Japan; by Intersoft for South Africa; by Eyrolles for France; by International Thomson Publishing for Germany, Austria, and Switzerland; by Distribuidora Cuspide for Argentina; by LR International for Brazil; by Galileo Libros for Chile; by Ediciones ZETA S.C.R. Ltda. for Peru; by WS Computer Publishing Corporation, Inc., for the Philippines; by Contemporanea de Ediciones for Venezuela; by Express Computer Distributors for the Caribbean and West Indies; by Micronesia Media Distributor, Inc. for Micronesia; by Chips Computadoras S.A. de C.V. for Mexico; by Editorial Norma de Panama S.A. for Panama; by American Bookshops for Finland.

For general information on Hungry Minds' products and services please contact our Customer Care department within the U.S. at 800-762-2974, outside the U.S. at 317-572-3993 or fax 317-572-4002.

For sales inquiries and reseller information, including discounts, premium and bulk quantity sales, and foreign-language translations, please contact our Customer Care department at 800-434-3422, fax 317-572-4002 or write to Hungry Minds, Inc., Attn: Customer Care Department, 10475 Crosspoint Boulevard, Indianapolis, IN 46256.

For information on licensing foreign or domestic rights, please contact our Sub-Rights Customer Care department at 212-884-5000.

For information on using Hungry Minds' products and services in the classroom or for ordering examination copies, please contact our Educational Sales department at 800-434-2086 or fax 317-572-4005.

For press review copies, author interviews, or other publicity information, please contact our Public Relations department at 317-572-3168 or fax 317-572-4168.

For authorization to photocopy items for corporate, personal, or educational use, please contact Copyright Clearance Center, 222 Rosewood Drive, Danvers, MA 01923, or fax 978-750-4470.

Hungry Minds™ is a trademark of Hungry Minds, Inc.

Credits

Acquisitions Editor
Sharon Cox

Project Editor
Sharon Nash

Development Editor
Nancy D. Warner

Technical Editor
Michael MacDonald

Copy Editor
Bill McManus

Editorial Manager
Mary Beth Wakefield

Vice President and Executive Group Publisher
Richard Swadley

Vice President and Publisher
Joseph B. Wikert

Project Coordinator
Bill Ramsey

Graphics and Production Specialists
Sean Decker
Melanie DesJardins
Joyce Haughey
Barry Offringa
Betty Schutte

Quality Control Technician
Laura Albert
David Faust
John Greenough
Andy Hollandbeck

Proofreading and Indexing
TECHBOOKS Production Services

About the Authors

Mridula Parihar has a master's degree in Applied Operations Research from Delhi University. She is a Microsoft Certified Solution Developer (MCSD) and has worked approximately 2½ years with NIIT Ltd. Mridula spent her first year in the Career Education Group (CEG) of NIIT, in which she taught NIIT students and was involved in scheduling and managing resources. For the past 1½ years, she has been working in the Knowledge Solutions Business (KSB) group of NIIT, in which she has had the opportunity to work on varied technical projects. Mridula has been involved in design, development, testing, and implementation of instructor-led training courses. Her primary responsibilities include instructional review, technical review, and ensuring ISO compliance. For the past six months, Mridula has been involved in textbook writing on varied technical subjects such as TCP/IP and .NET.

Essam Ahmed is an accomplished developer with more than 10 years of professional programming and design experience. Essam enjoys writing — his publications include *JScript .NET Programming* (published October 2001 by Hungry Minds), more than 50 book reviews at codeguru.com, and various articles at asptoday.com and thecodechannel.com. Essam's professional affiliations include the IEEE Computer Society (http://computer.org), the Association for Computing Machinery (http://acm.org), and the Worldwide Institute of Software Architects (www.wwisa.org), in which he is a practicing member. Essam was a speaker at VSLive 2001 in Sydney, Australia. Essam's Web site is www.designs2solutions.com.

Jim Chandler is an independent consultant with extensive experience in architecting and developing custom, integrated software solutions for small to medium-sized businesses in the Midwest. Before focusing his career on the Windows platform, Jim was a Graphics Partner at Digital Equipment Corporation, evangelizing X11 and Motif. Jim is also a co-author of the *Visual Basic.NET Bible* and an active member of the St. Louis .NET Users Group. He has delivered presentations on such topics as ASP.NET, XML, and Web services to the St. Louis developer community. His research interests include everything .NET as well as COM+ and developing mobile applications for the Pocket PC. Outside the daily challenges of developing applications and fulfilling his research interests, Jim shares his spare time with his wife, Rhonda, and their two sons, Sam and Thomas.

Bill Hatfield is the best-selling author of several computer books, including *ASP.NET For Dummies,* two editions of *Active Server Pages For Dummies* (on Classic ASP), *Visual InterDev For Dummies,* and *Creating Cool VBScript Web Pages* (all from Hungry Minds). He is also the editor of three monthly publications from Pinnacle Publishing on .NET technologies: *C# Developer, .NET Developer,* and *ActiveWeb Developer.* He's an independent corporate trainer and maintains a Web site (www.edgequest.com) dedicated to helping developers solve problems. He works from his home in Indianapolis, Indiana, where he and his wife have celebrated the birth of their first child, Bryce Christopher. Of course, now that he has a real baby, he can stop dressing up the cat in little outfits.

Richard Lassan is a Senior Consultant with GA Sullivan in Nashville, TN. He is currently involved in learning and writing about .NET. Richard can be reached at rickl@gasullivan.com.

Peter B. MacIntyre lives and works in Charlottetown, Prince Edward Island, Canada (the home of the fictional Anne of Green Gables). Peter and his wife, Dawn, are trying to raise four kids: Daniel (14), Charity (12), Michael (12), and Simon (11). He has been in the software development industry for over 12 years and has seen many changes in technology in that time frame. Peter can be reached at petermac@isn.net and is available for small to midsized consulting projects.

Dave Wanta has been working in Web development since the mid-1990s. His Microsoft-centric Web technology has led him to develop a number of large e-commerce and B2B applications. His love for ASP.NET has led him to build the largest online ASP.NET directory, at www.123aspx.com. You can usually find Dave online discussing ASP.NET topics at the lists found at www.aspfriends.com.

About the Series Editor

Michael Lane Thomas is an active development-community and computer-industry analyst who presently spends a great deal of time spreading the gospel of Microsoft .NET in his current role as a .NET technology evangelist for Microsoft. In working with over a half-dozen publishing companies, Michael has written numerous technical articles and written or contributed to almost 20 books on numerous technical topics, including Visual Basic, Visual C++, and .NET technologies. He is a prolific supporter of the Microsoft certification programs, having earned his MCSD, MCSE+I, MCT, MCP+SB, and MCDBA.

In addition to technical writing, Michael can also be heard over the airwaves from time to time, including two weekly radio programs on Entercom (www.entercom.com/) stations, most often in Kansas City on News Radio 980KMBZ (www.kmbz.com/). He can also occasionally be caught on the Internet doing an MSDN Webcast (www.microsoft.com/usa/webcasts/) discussing .NET, the next generation of Web application technologies.

Michael started his journey through the technical ranks back in college at the University of Kansas, where he earned his stripes and a couple of degrees. After a brief stint as a technical and business consultant to Tokyo-based Global Online Japan, he returned to the States to climb the corporate ladder. He has held assorted roles, including those of IT manager, field engineer, trainer, independent consultant, and even a brief stint as Interim CTO of a successful dot-com, although he believes his current role as .NET evangelist for Microsoft is the best of the lot. He can be reached via e-mail at mlthomas@microsoft.com.

First and foremost, I want to dedicate this book to my Supreme Guide who has always guided me in the right direction. Then, I would like to dedicate this book to my Mom and Dad, without whose support I could have never completed this book. My Mom and Dad have always been a constant source of energy and encouragement for me. Also, I must thank my brothers, Amit and Abhay, who have always given their constant support to me. — ***Mridula Parihar***

For my sons, Vikranth and Siddharth — ***Essam Ahmed***

I'd like to dedicate this book to my family, whose love and support mean everything to me. I love you all. And, finally, the answer to the question posed by my sons, Sam and Thomas, who asked: "Dad, will our name be in the book, too?" You bet! — ***Jim Chandler***

To my lovely wife Melanie for the patience, kindness, and love she shows to our child every hour of every day. Bryce couldn't have picked a better mom! — ***Bill Hatfield***

To my parents, William and Eleanor, for always being there. — ***Rick Lassan***

I would like to dedicate the chapters that I wrote to my lovely wife, Dawn Etta Riley. Without your patience and understanding, I would not have been able to pull this off! I know it has been hard sometimes, but reward comes with hard work. I love you very much and appreciate all that you do for me and all that you are to me. — ***Peter MacIntyre***

To my Parents, Roy and Terry, and my Brother Bob for being the coolest brother someone could have. — ***Dave Wanta***

Preface

Introduction of the Microsoft .NET platform has begun a new era in the field of application development that will drive the next-generation Internet. ASP.NET, a part of the Microsoft .NET platform, is a revolutionary programming framework that enables the rapid development of enterprise-class Web applications. It provides the easiest and most scalable way to develop, deploy, and run Web applications that can target any browser or device. In fact, these features are only a few of several that make ASP.NET developers' first choice for creating Web applications.

ASP.NET makes application development much easier than it was with classic ASP, and hence it has dramatically improved developers' productivity. ASP.NET enables you to provide richer functionality to your Web applications by writing the least amount of code. The best part is that ASP.NET enables you to select any of the available .NET programming languages. So, unlike classic ASP, in which you had to depend on interpreted VBScript and JScript languages, ASP.NET provides a wide choice of programming languages.

In addition to the usual Web applications, ASP.NET allows you to create other types, which enables you to extend your applications' reach to new customers and business partners. For example, XML Web services enable sharing of data across the Internet regardless of the operating system and the programming language — this certainly widens the reach of your applications. Also, ASP.NET provides you with mobile controls that enable your applications to target a large number of mobile Web devices.

Deploying server applications has always been a pain for developers. With ASP.NET, however, developers do not need to worry on this front at all, because ASP.NET has dramatically simplified the deployment process. Deploying a Web application simply requires you to copy it to the Web server.

In addition to providing a rich developer experience, ASP.NET provide a rich user experience. ASP.NET Web applications are faster than the classic ASP applications. The reason is quite obvious. Unlike classic ASP, in which you relied only on interpreted languages, ASP.NET enables you to use compiled programming languages. Thus, ASP.NET applications do not require an explicit compilation step and, in turn, execute faster. Additionally, ASP.NET has rich caching and state-management features that add to the improved performance of ASP.NET Web applications. In addition to providing high performance and scalability, ASP.NET applications are highly reliable and secure. The greater reliability and security features enable your application users to build more confidence in using them.

This book seeks to provide to all Web-application developers a greater understanding of ASP.NET. This book covers ASP.NET from its basic features to its advanced features, such as application configuration, caching, security, localization, XML Web services, and deployment.

Icons Used in This Book

Each icon used in this book signifies a special meaning. Here's what each icon means:

Note icons provide supplemental information about the subject at hand but generally something that isn't quite the main idea. Notes are often used to elaborate on a detailed technical point.

Tips provide special information or advice. They indicate a more efficient way of doing something or a technique that may not be obvious.

Caution icons warn you of a potential problem or error.

Cross-Reference icons direct you to related information in another section or chapter.

How This Book Is Organized

The basic aim of this book is to provide Web-application developers with insight into ASP.NET features and to enable them to develop rich, secure, and reliable Web applications. The book begins by introducing the basic features of ASP.NET and then moves on to explore the advanced ASP.NET features.

This book is divided into five parts.

Part I: ASP.NET Basics

This part presents the salient features of the .NET Framework and introduces you to the relationship of the .NET Framework with ASP.NET. This part covers the basic features of ASP.NET, including the Web controls, Rich Web controls, and Validation controls. In addition, this part discusses how to create custom Web controls and to use various ASP.NET debugging techniques to debug Web applications.

Part II: ASP.NET Database Programming

This part provides an overview of the ADO.NET technology. It discusses how to use SQL Server with ASP.NET applications to access and manipulate server-side data.

This part also covers data binding with ASP.NET server controls and discusses how to work with Data Grids. Also, it discusses working with XML. Finally, it presents you with Web-server control templates to customize the look and layout of server controls.

Part III: Advanced ASP.NET

This part covers the advanced features of ASP.NET, such as application configuration, caching, and security. This part discusses how to develop business objects (the .NET components), build HTTP handlers, and develop wireless applications using mobile controls. It also discusses how to develop localized ASP.NET applications. Finally, this part presents you with the deployment of ASP.NET applications.

Part IV: Building Web Services

This part gives you an overview of Web services, the Web services infrastructure, and the Simple Object Access Protocol (SOAP). It then discusses how to build and deploy Web services. Finally, this part discusses how to find and consume Web services.

Part V: Building ASP.NET Applications

The Web services section covers the foundational technologies of Web services (such as XML and SOAP) as well as detailed information on how to develop, debug, and consume ASP.NET Web services using the Microsoft .NET Framework and ASP.NET.

Appendixes

This section of the book provides an overview of Visual Basic .NET and C#. Use this section as a reference for these programming languages. In fact, this section provides an easy way for beginners to get started with ASP.NET by introducing the salient features of Visual Basic .NET and C#.

Companion Web Site

This book provides a companion Web site from which you can download the code from various chapters. All the code listings reside in a single WinZip file that you can download by going to www.hungryminds.com/extras and selecting the ASP.NET Bible link. After you download the file (ASPNETBible.zip), and if you have WinZip already on your system, you can open it and extract the contents by double-clicking. If you don't currently have WinZip, you can download an evaluation version from www.winzip.com.

When extracting the files, use WinZip's default options (confirm that the Use Folder Names option is checked) and extract the ASPNETBible.zip file to a drive on your system that has about 3MB of available space. The extraction process creates a folder called ASPNETBible. As long as the Use Folder Names option is checked in the Extract dialog box, an entire folder structure is created within the ASPNETBible folder. You'll see folders arranged by chapter number, and some of those chapter folders will contain subfolders.

If you'd rather download just the code you need from a particular chapter — when you need it — simply click the separate chapter link on the Web site instead of downloading the entire WinZip file.

Acknowledgments

It's a great feeling to acknowledge the efforts and contributions of each one of those who were involved in the development of this book. I would like to acknowledge the time and effort put in by the teams at both ends, NIIT and Hungry Minds. At NIIT, I would like to convey my special thanks to Ms. Anita Sastry, the Project Manager, and Sunil Kumar Pathak, the Graphics Designer. Without their valuable contributions, this book wouldn't have been possible. Also, I would like to thank Namrata, Rashim, Meeta, Ashok, Nitin, and Yesh for their timely help. Thank you once again for giving a helping hand when it was needed the most.

At Hungry Minds, my special thanks go to the Acquisitions Editor, Sharon Cox, and the Project Editor, Sharon Nash, who gave me the opportunity to write this book. Also, I would like to acknowledge the Technical Editors, Ken Cox and Michael MacDonald, and the Copy Editor, Bill McManus, for their valuable input and constant support. Thank you all for your valuable contributions, without which this book wouldn't be possible. — **Mridula Parihar**

Tom Archer — for helping me get my writing career off the ground. Sharon Cox — a great acquisitions editor to work with! Sharon Nash — thanks for your patience. My family — for their ongoing support in all of my endeavors. — **Essam Ahmed**

I would like to thank Bill Evjen for giving me the opportunity to fulfill the lifelong goal of becoming a published author as well as his dedication to the St. Louis .NET Users group — it is an outstanding organization due in large part to his efforts. I would also like to thank Craig Smyth, whose support and encouragement have contributed much to the career success I enjoy today. I am also grateful to Bob Hundman at Novus International for allowing me to "disappear" when I needed to while writing for this book. And, of course, a special thank you to my wife, Rhonda, who was patient and supportive while I worked into the wee hours of many nights and during our family vacation in order to meet the book's deadlines. — **Jim Chandler**

Thanks to Chris Webb, Sharon Cox, Sharon Nash, and everyone else at Hungry Minds who helped put this together. You guys are great to work with! — **Bill Hatfield**

I would like to give thanks and praise to God above for giving me the talents and skills that it takes to be both a computer specialist and an author. Of course, the great people at Hungry Minds who gave me this opportunity need to be mentioned as well, namely Sharon Cox and Sharon Nash. Their attention to detail and occasional prodding are what helped make this project a success! — **Peter MacIntyre**

To my Wife, my "Best Friend" (Karen), for all of her encouragement while I contributed to this book. — **Rick Lassan**

Contents at a Glance

Contents

● ●

Chapter 12: Using SQL Server with ASP.NET 225

Chapter 13: Advanced Data Binding and XML 249

Part III: Advanced ASP.NET   269

Chapter 14: ASP.NET Application Configuration 271

Chapter 23: Web Services Infrastructure 473

Chapter 24: Understanding SOAP 495

Chapter 25: Building a Web Service 521

Part V: Building ASP.NET Applications 605

Chapter 29: ASP.NET Blackjack 607

Chapter 30: Chatty Discussion Forum 643

ASP.NET Basics

Understanding the .NET Framework

The Internet revolution of the late 1990s represented a dramatic shift in the way individuals and organizations communicate with each other. Traditional applications, such as word processors and accounting packages, are modeled as stand-alone applications: they offer users the capability to perform tasks using data stored on the system the application resides and executes on. Most new software, in contrast, is modeled based on a distributed computing model where applications collaborate to provide services and expose functionality to each other. As a result, the primary role of most new software is changing into supporting information exchange (through Web servers and browsers), collaboration (through e-mail and instant messaging), and individual expression (through Web logs, also known as Blogs, and e-zines — Web based magazines). Essentially, the basic role of software is changing from providing discrete functionality to providing services.

The .NET Framework represents a unified, object-oriented set of services and libraries that embrace the changing role of new network-centric and network-aware software. In fact, the .NET Framework is the first platform designed from the ground up with the Internet in mind.

This chapter introduces the .NET Framework in terms of the benefits it provides. I present some sample code in Visual C# .NET, Visual Basic .NET, Visual Basic 6.0, and Visual C++; don't worry if you're not familiar with these languages, since I describe in the discussion what each sample does.

Benefits of the .NET Framework

The .NET Framework offers a number of benefits to developers:

✦ A consistent programming model

✦ Direct support for security

✦ Simplified development efforts

✦ Easy application deployment and maintenance

Consistent programming model

Different programming languages offer different models for doing the same thing. For example, the following code demonstrates how to open a file and write a one-line message to it using Visual Basic 6.0:

```
Public Sub testFileAccess()
    On Error GoTo handle_Error

    ' Use native method of opening an writing to a file...
    Dim outputFile As Long
    outputFile = FreeFile
    Open "c:\temp\test.txt" For Output As #outputFile
    Print #outputFile, "Hello World!"
    Close #outputFile

    ' Use the Microsoft Scripting Runtime to
    ' open and write to the file...
    Dim fso As Object
    Set fso = CreateObject("Scripting.FileSystemObject")
    Dim outputText As TextStream
    Set outputText = fso.CreateTextFile("c:\temp\test2.txt")
    outputText.WriteLine "Hello World!"
    outputText.Close
    Set fso = Nothing
    Exit Sub

handle_Error:
    ' Handle or report error here
End Sub
```

This code demonstrates that more than one technique is available to create and write to a new file. The first method uses Visual Basic's built-in support; the second method uses the Microsoft Scripting Runtime. C++ also offers more than one way of performing the same task, as shown in the following code:

```
#include <fstream>
#include <iostream>
#include <cstdlib>
#include <stdio.h>
```

```cpp
using namespace std;

int main(int argc, char* argv[])
{
    // Use the C Runtime Library (CRT)...
    FILE *testFile;
    if( (testFile  = fopen( "c:\\temp\\test3.txt",
      "wt" )) == NULL ) {
        cout << "Could not open first test file!" << endl;
        return 1;
    }
    fprintf(testFile,"Hello World!\n");
    fclose(testFile);

    // Use the Standard Template Library (STL)...
    ofstream outputStream("c:\\temp\\test4.txt");
    if(!outputStream) {
        cout << "Could not open second test file!" << endl;
        return(1);
    }
    outputStream << "Hello World!" << endl;
    outputStream.close();
    return 0;
}
```

What both code listings demonstrate is that when using different programming languages, a disparity exists among the techniques that developers use to perform the same task. The difference in techniques comes from how different languages interact with and represent the underlying system that applications rely on, thereby increasing the amount of training that developers need. The following code demonstrates how to perform the same tasks in Visual Basic .NET and Visual C# .NET.

```vbnet
Visual Basic .NET:Imports System.IO
Imports System.Text

Module Demo

  Sub Main()
    Dim outputFile As StreamWriter = _
      New StreamWriter("c:\temp\test5.txt")
    outputFile.WriteLine("Hello World!")
    outputFile.Close()
  End Sub

End Module
```

```csharp
Visual C# .NET:
using System.IO;
using System.Text;

class Demo {
  static void Main() {
```

```
        StreamWriter outputFile =
          new StreamWriter("c:\\temp\\test6.txt");
        outputFile.WriteLine("Hello World!");
        outputFile.Close();
    }
```

The preceding code demonstrates, apart from slight syntactical differences, that the technique for writing to a file in either language is identical — both listings use the StreamWriter class to write the "Hello World!" message out to the text files. In fact, unlike the Visual Basic and Visual C++ listings, which demonstrate that there's more than one way to do something *within* the same language, the preceding listings show that there's a unified means of accomplishing the same task by using the .NET Class Library.

The .NET Class Library is a key component of the .NET Framework — it is sometimes referred to as the Base Class Library (BCL). The .NET Class Library contains hundreds of classes you can use for tasks such as the following:

✦ Processing XML

✦ Working with data from multiple data sources

✦ Debugging your code and working with event logs

✦ Working with data streams and files

✦ Managing the run-time environment

✦ Developing Web services, components, and standard Windows applications

✦ Working with application security

✦ Working with directory services

The functionality that the .NET Class Library provides is available to all .NET languages, resulting in a consistent object model regardless of the programming language developers use.

Direct support for security

Developing an application that resides on a user's desktop system and uses local resources is easy, from a security point of view, because security simply isn't a consideration in this scenario. Security becomes much more important when you create applications that access data on remote systems or applications that perform privileged tasks on behalf of nonprivileged users, because systems may have to authenticate users, and encryption (scrambling to avoid eavesdropping) may be necessary to secure data communications.

Windows NT, Windows 2000, and Windows XP have a number of security features based on Access Control Lists (ACLs). An ACL contains a number of entries that specify which users may access, or are explicitly denied access, to resources such as files and printers. ACLs are a great way of protecting executable files (applications) from unauthorized access, but they do not secure all parts of the file. The .NET Framework enables both developers and system administrators to specify method-level security. Developers (through easy-to-use programming language constructs called attributes) and systems administrators (by using administrative tools and byediting an application's configuration file) can configure an application's security so that only authorized users can invoke a component's methods.

The .NET Framework uses industry-standard protocols such as TCP/IP and means of communications such as the Extensible Markup Language (XML), Simple Object Access Protocol (SOAP, a standard application messaging protocol), and HTTP to facilitate distributed application communications. This makes distributed computing more secure, because .NET developers cooperate with network connectivity devices as opposed to attempting to work around their security restrictions.

Simplified development efforts

Two aspects of creating Web-based applications present unique challenges to Web developers: visual page design and debugging applications. Visual page design is straightforward when creating static content; however, when you need to present the result of executing a query in a tabular format using an ASP page, page design can get rather involved. This is because developers need to mix traditional ASP code, which represents the application's logic, and HTML, which represents the presentation of the data. ASP.NET and the .NET Framework simplify development by allowing developers to separate an application's logic from its presentation, resulting in an easier-to-maintain code base. ASP.NET can also handle the details of maintaining the state of controls, such as the contents of text boxes, between calls to the same ASP.NET page, thereby reducing the amount of code you need to write. Visual Studio .NET, which is tightly integrated with the .NET Framework, assists developers as they create ASP.NET and other applications by providing visual designers that facilitate visual drag and drop editing, making page layout and form layout a breeze.

Another aspect of creating applications is debugging. Developers sometimes make mistakes; systems don't behave as you expect them to, and unexpected conditions arise — all of these issues are collectively referred to as, using the affectionate term, "bugs." Tracking down bugs — known as "debugging" — quickly and effectively requires developers to be familiar with a variety of tools, sometimes available from a third party, and techniques — a combination of programming techniques and techniques for using a particular tool. The .NET Framework simplifies debugging with support for Runtime diagnostics.

Runtime diagnostics not only help you track down bugs but also help you determine how well your applications perform and assess the condition of your application. The .NET Framework provides three types of Runtime diagnostics:

✦ Event logging

✦ Performance counters

✦ Tracing

Event logging

Windows 2000 and Windows XP have a feature called an Event Log _ a database containing information about important hardware or software events. The Event Log is useful for recording information about the status of your applications and provides systems administrators a means of diagnosing problems, since they can review Event Log entries using the Event Viewer (supplied with Windows and available in the Administrative Tools group in the Control Panel). There are three types of Event Log events:

✦ **Informational events:** Usually contain basic information, such as an application starting or shutting down

✦ **Warning events:** Usually provide information about unusual conditions that have the potential to become errors

✦ **Error events:** Represent critical errors in an application that prevent it from executing normally

Events are stored in Event Logs — Windows supports three types of Event Logs:

✦ **Application:** Contains messages that applications such as Microsoft SQL Server log

✦ **System:** Contains messages that device drivers and system services log.

✦ **Security:** Contains system-generated messages about events that occur when security auditing is enabled

The .NET Framework makes it easy to work with the Event Log as shown in the following code:

```
Imports System
Imports System.Diagnostics

Module eventLogDemo

   Sub Main()
     If Not EventLog.SourceExists("ASPnetBible") Then
       EventLog.CreateEventSource( _
         "ASPnetBible", "Application")
       Console.WriteLine( _
         "Created new EventSource 'ASPnetBible'")
     End If

     Dim evLog As New EventLog()
     evLog.Source = "ASPnetBible"

     ' Note: this listing does not show the
     ' complete message for brevity
     evLog.WriteEntry( "...starting")
     Console.WriteLine("Wrote 'starting'...")
```

```
        evLog.WriteEntry("... exiting")
        Console.WriteLine("Wrote 'exit'...")
        End Sub

    End Module
```

This code is a Visual Basic .NET console application that creates an Event Source called ASPnetBible and logs the application's starting and exiting events to the system's Application event log — although the listing doesn't show it, both messages are informational.

Performance counters

Performance counters are useful for monitoring the health and performance of an application. You can chart the value of performance counters using the Performance applet in the Administrative Tools folder of the systems Control Panel. The .NET Framework makes it easy for you to read the value of existing performance counters, such as the system's percent CPU Utilization, as well as create your own application-specific performance counters. The following code demonstrates how to work with performance counters in a simple Windows Forms application:

```
' Create a new performace counter
Dim counterCollection As New CounterCreationDataCollection()
Dim couterItem As New CounterCreationData()

counterName = "demoCounter"
perfCatName = "ASPnetBible"

couterItem.CounterName = counterName
couterItem.CounterType =
    PerformanceCounterType.NumberOfItems32
counterCollection.Add(couterItem)
PerformanceCounterCategory.Create(perfCatName, _
"sample counter", counterCollection)

' ...elsewhere in the application - Increment the counter
Dim perfCounter As PerformanceCounter
perfCounter = New PerformanceCounter()
perfCounter.CategoryName = perfCatName
perfCounter.CounterName = counterName
perfCounter.ReadOnly = False
perfCounter.IncrementBy(50)
System.Threading.Thread.Sleep(2000)
perfCounter.IncrementBy(-50)

'...elsewhere in the application - Delete the sample counter
PerformanceCounterCategory.Delete(perfCatName)
```

This code demonstrates how to create a new performance counter category and counter using the `CouterCreationDataCollection` and `CouterCreationData` classes — the fragment shown is from the sample application's `Load` event handler. In the next section of the code, from a button's `Click` event handler, the code creates an instance of the sample performance counter, increments it, and waits two seconds before decrementing the counter. The last part of the code shows how to delete the performance counter when the form closes.

Tracing

Debugging an application by using the Visual Studio .NET debugger is a great way to track down problems; however, there are many scenarios in which things happen too quickly to follow interactively or in which you simply need to know the sequence of events that lead to a problem before the problem occurs.

Tracing is an alternative to using a debugger to step through each line of code as your application executes. You can configure ASP.NET tracing by using two methods: page-level tracing and application-level tracing. Both types of tracing provide similar results; however, the difference is in how you access the results for each approach. Page-level tracing provides trace details on the ASPX page when it completes executing, and application-level tracing stores the details of the trace in a file called (by default) `trace.acx`, which is located in the same directory as the ASP.NET application—you can view the file by using your browser.

When you enable tracing, which is disabled by default, ASP.NET records detailed information about the page request, trace messages, control information, cookies, header information, the contents of any form fields, and a raw output of the contents of server variables (like `CONTENT_TYPE` and `HTTP_REFERRER`). Table 1-1 shows a fragment of a trace output from a simple ASP.NET page.

Table 1-1
Fragment of an ASP.NET Page Trace

Category	Message	From First(s)	From Last(s)
aspx.page	Begin Init		
aspx.page	End Init	0.000096	0.000096
aspx.page	Begin LoadViewState	0.000189	0.000092
aspx.page	End LoadViewState	0.000308	0.000119
aspx.page	Begin ProcessPostData	0.000393	0.000085
aspx.page	End ProcessPostData	0.000551	0.000158
	Page_Load event handler started	0.000647	0.000096
	Page_Load event handler exit	0.000729	0.000082

The last two entries in Table 1-1 are custom Trace messages written using the
`Page.Trace.Write(...)` method.

Easy application deployment and maintenance

Applications are often made up of several components:

✦ Web pages

✦ Windows forms-based components

✦ Web services

✦ Components housed in DLLs

The .NET Framework makes it possible to install applications that use some or all of
these components without having to register DLLs (using `regsvr32.exe`) or to create Registration Database (also known as the system Registry) entries.

The .NET Framework makes it easy to deploy applications using zero-impact installation — often all that's required to install an application is to copy it into a directory
along with the components it requires. This is possible because the .NET Framework
handles the details of locating and loading components an application needs, even if
you have several versions of the same component available on a single system. All of
this is possible because the .NET Framework records extra information about an
application's components — the extra information is called metadata. A component
of the .NET Framework, the Class Loader, inspects an application's metadata and
ensures that all of the components the application depends on are available on the
system before the application begins to execute. This feature of the .NET Framework
works to isolate applications from each other despite changes in system configuration, making it easier to install and upgrade applications.

Once an application is running on a system, it is sometimes necessary to change
certain traits of the application, such as its security requirements, optional parameters, and even database connections. .NET Framework applications use a configuration model based on application-configuration files. A configuration file is a text file
that contains XML elements that affect the behavior of an application. For example,
an administrator can configure an application to use only a certain version of a
component the application relies on, thereby ensuring consistent behavior regardless of how often the component is upgraded. The following code shows an
ASP.NET's basic configuration file; the file is called `web.config`:

```
<configuration>
  <system.web>
    <pages
      buffer="true"
      enableSessionState="true" />
```

```
            <appSettings>
              <add key="dsn" value="localhost;uid=sa;pwd="/>
            </appSettings>
        </system.web>
    </configuration>
```

This code shows that the ASP.NET application will have page buffering on (pages will be sent to clients only when the page is completely rendered), and that ASP.NET will track individual clients' session information (as shown in the `pages` tag). This code also demonstrates how to define a custom configuration key, called `dsn`—within the `appSettings` section, which applications have access to through the `TraceSwitch` class.

Elements of the .NET Framework

The .NET Framework consists of three key elements (as shown in Figure 1-1):

✦ Common Language Runtime

✦ .NET Class Library

✦ Unifying components

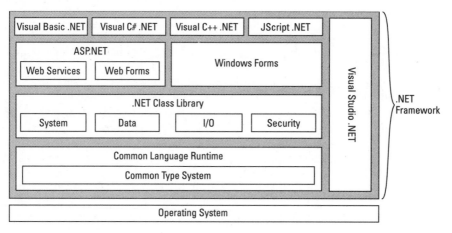

Figure 1-1: Components of the .NET Framework

Common Language Runtime

The Common Language Runtime (CLR) is a layer between an application and the operating system it executes on. The CLR simplifies an application's design and reduces the amount of code developers need to write because it provides a variety of execution services that include memory management, thread management, component lifetime management, and default error handling. The key benefit of the CLR is that it transparently provides these execution services to all applications, regardless of what programming language they're written in and without any additional effort on the part of the developer.

The CLR is also responsible for compiling code just before it executes. Instead of producing a binary representation of your code, as traditional compilers do, .NET compilers produce a representation of your code in a language common to the .NET Framework: Microsoft Intermediate Language (MSIL), often referred to as IL. When your code executes for the first time, the CLR invokes a special compiler called a Just In Time (JIT) compiler, which transforms the IL into executable instructions that are specific to the type and model of your system's processor. Because all .NET languages have the same compiled representation, they all have similar performance characteristics. This means that a program written in Visual Basic .NET can perform as well as the same program written in Visual C++ .NET. (C++ is the language of choice for developers who need the best possible performance a system can deliver.)

Common Type System

The Common Type System (CTS) is a component of the CLR and provides a common set of data types, each having a common set of behaviors. In Visual Basic, for example, the String data type maps to the CTS `System.String` class. Therefore, if a JScript .NET client needs to communicate with a component implemented in VB .NET, the client doesn't have to do any additional work to exchange information because it's using a type common to both JScript .NET and VB .NET. The CTS eliminates many interoperability problems that exist outside .NET.

.NET programming languages take advantage of the CTS by enabling developers to use their language's built-in data types — the .NET compilers convert the native data types' into their equivalent CTS types at compile time. Developers can also use CTS types directly in their code if they wish. Table 1-2 describes each standard CTS data type.

Table 1-2
Common Type System Data Types

Complete Name	Description
System.Byte	Unsigned 8-bit integer ranging in value from 0 to positive 255
System.Int16	Signed 16-bit integer capable of holding values from negative 32,768 to positive 32,767
System.Int32	Signed 32-bit integer having a range from negative 2,147,483,648 to positive 2,147,483,647
System.Int64	Signed 64-bit integer ranging from negative 9,223,372,036,854,755,808 to positive 9,223,372,036,854,755,807
System.Single	Single-precision 32-bit floating-point number
System.Double	Double-precision 64-bit floating-point number
System.Decimal	Signed 96-bit floating-point value with up to 28 digits on either side of the decimal
System.Char	16-bit Unicode character (unsigned values)
System.String	Sequence of Unicode characters with a capacity of about two billion characters
System.Object	32-bit address, referencing an instance of a class
System.Boolean	Unsigned 32-bit number that may contain only 0 (False) or 1 (True)

You can use other non-CTS-compliant data types in your applications and components; you're free to use non-CTS-compliant data types, but they may not be available on other implementations of the .NET Framework for other operating systems (see Table 1-3).

Table 1-3
Non-CTS-compliant Data Types

Complete Name	Description
System.SByte	Signed 8-bit integer ranging from negative 128 to positive 127
System.UInt16	16-bit unsigned integer ranging from 0 to positive 65,535
System.UInt32	32-bit unsigned integer ranging from 0 to positive 4,294,967,295
System.UInt64	64-bit unsigned integer ranging from 0 to positive 184,467,440,737,095,551,615

.NET Class Library

In an earlier section, "Consistent programming models across programming languages," the .NET Class Library was described as containing hundreds of classes that model the system and services it provides. To make the .NET Class Library easier to work with and understand, it's divided into *namespaces*. The root namespace of the .NET Class Library is called System, and it contains core classes and data types, such as Int32, Object, Array, and Console. Secondary namespaces reside within the System namespace.

Examples of nested namespaces include the following:

✦ **System.Diagnostics**: Contains classes for working with the Event Log

✦ **System.Data**: Makes it easy to work with data from multiple data sources (System.Data.OleDb resides within this namespace and contains the ADO.NET classes)

✦ **System.IO**: Contains classes for working with files and data streams

Figure 1-2 illustrates the relationship between some of the major namespaces in the .NET Class Library.

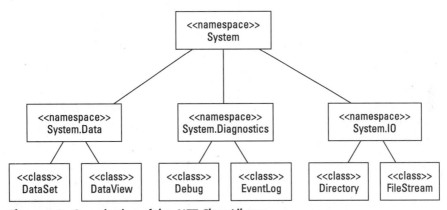

Figure 1-2: Organization of the .NET Class Library

The benefits of using the .NET Class Library include a consistent set of services available to all .NET languages and simplified deployment, because the .NET Class Library is available on all implementations of the .NET Framework.

Unifying components

Until this point, this chapter has covered the low-level components of the .NET Framework. The *unifying components*, listed next, are the means by which you can access the services the .NET Framework provides:

✦ ASP.NET

✦ Windows Forms

✦ Visual Studio .NET

ASP.NET

ASP.NET introduces two major features: Web Forms and Web Services.

Web Forms

Developers not familiar with Web development can spend a great deal of time, for example, figuring out how to validate the e-mail address on a form. You can validate the information on a form by using a client-side script or a server-side script. Deciding which kind of script to use is complicated by the fact that each approach has its benefits and drawbacks, some of which aren't apparent unless you've done substantial design work.

If you validate the form on the client by using client-side JScript code, you need to take into consideration the browser that your users may use to access the form. Not all browsers expose exactly the same representation of the document to programmatic interfaces. If you validate the form on the server, you need to be aware of the load that users might place on the server. The server has to validate the data and send the result back to the client. *Web Forms* simplify Web development to the point that it becomes as easy as dragging and dropping controls onto a designer (the surface that you use to edit a page) to design interactive Web applications that span from client to server.

Web Services

A *Web service* is an application that exposes a programmatic interface through standard access methods. Web Services are designed to be used by other applications and components and are not intended to be useful directly to human end users. Web Services make it easy to build applications that integrate features from remote sources. For example, you can write a Web Service that provides weather information for subscribers of your service instead of having subscribers link to a page or parse through a file they download from your site. Clients can simply call a method on your Web Service as if they are calling a method on a component installed on their system—and have the weather information available in an easy-to-use format that they can integrate into their own applications or Web sites with no trouble.

Windows Forms

Windows Forms is the name of a unified set of classes that provides support for creating traditional desktop applications — applications that have a graphical user interface (GUI). Windows Forms make it easy to develop end-user applications using any .NET programming language. Furthermore, through Visual Studio .NET, developers can easily design forms by using drag-and-drop editing.

Visual Studio .NET

Visual Studio .NET fulfills the promise of a single development environment for all languages. Visual Studio .NET simplifies development in a mixed-language environment through features such as support for end-to-end debugging across all programming languages; visual designers for XML, HTML, data, and server-side code; and full IntelliSense support (statement completion). Visual Studio .NET replaces the Visual Basic 6, Visual C++, and Visual InterDev development environments.

Visual Studio .NET is able to provide this level of integration because it relies and builds on the facilities of the .NET Framework. Designers for Web forms and Windows Forms enhance developer productivity during the development cycle. Integration of deployment features enhances productivity during post-deployment debugging. Table 1-4 summarizes Visual Studio .NET's major features.

Table 1-4
Visual Studio .NET's Major Features

Feature	Benefit
Single IDE	Simplifies mixed-language development with support for Visual Basic, C++, C#, and JScript .NET
Task List	Organizes tasks and manages errors and warnings in a single place. Tasks are read from specialized comments in source code and are presented in a tabular format. Double-click the task to jump to the section of source code where the task was entered.
Solution Explorer	Provides a hierarchical view of a solution organized into projects. Allows the management of related projects within a single solution.
Server Explorer	Manages your computer and other computers on the network, including resources such as SQL Server, message queues, services, and so on. Integrates performance and event monitoring and Web services.
Multi-Monitor support	Makes the best possible use of available screen space

Continued

Table 1-4 *(continued)*	
Feature	*Benefit*
IntelliSense	Ensures consistent statement completion across all supported languages
Dynamic Help	Makes reference documentation available based on what you're working on
End-to-end debugging	Facilitates cross-language, process, and system debugging through the Visual Studio .NET debugger; the learning curve is reduced, and developers are better able to take advantage of the debugger's features.
Deployment support	Integrates deployment into each solution (project); as changes are made in the solution, deployment information is updated. You can deploy your solution using traditional setup (install on a single system), Web setup, and Web download. This feature also facilitates deployment for debugging across systems.

Summary

This chapter introduced you to the .NET Framework and its components in the context of the problems and the benefits the .NET Framework provides. The next chapter discusses setting up the development environment for creating ASP.NET applications, creating a simple ASP.NET application using both VB and C#, and deploying an application on a Web server.

✦   ✦   ✦

Getting Started with ASP.NET

The Microsoft .NET Framework provides a powerful platform for the development of applications for both the desktop and the Internet. The .NET Framework allows you to develop Internet applications with an ease that was never provided before. To develop Internet applications, the .NET Framework is equipped with ASP.NET. ASP.NET is a powerful programming framework for the development of enterprise-class Web applications.

This chapter introduces you to the .NET Framework and ASP.NET. You'll learn to set up the development environment for creating ASP.NET applications. You'll also learn how to create an ASP.NET application by using Visual Basic .NET and C#, and deploy the application.

Introducing the .NET Framework

Since 1995, Microsoft has been constantly making efforts to shift focus from the Windows-based platforms to the Internet. Microsoft introduced Active Server Pages (ASP) as an endeavor toward Internet programming. However, writing ASP script, an interpreted script, was a traditional way of programming as compared to the existing structured object-oriented programming. Moreover, it was very difficult to debug and maintain the unstructured ASP code. Definitely, you could combine the code written in structured object-oriented languages, such as Visual Basic, with ASP code. However, you could combine the VB code only as a component. Moreover, the software integration for the Web development was quite complicated and required an understanding of a host of technologies and integration issues on the part of the developers. Therefore, an architecture was needed that would allow the development of Web applications in a more structured and consistent manner.

Recently, Microsoft introduced the .NET Framework with a vision for developers to create globally distributed software with Internet functionality and interoperability. The .NET Framework includes multiple languages, class libraries, and a common execution platform. In addition, the .NET Framework includes protocols that allow developers to integrate software over the Internet and the .NET Enterprise Servers, such as SQL Server 2000, Commerce Server 2000, and BizTalk Server. Thus, the .NET Framework provides the richest built-in functionality for software integration ever provided by any platform. Also, with the .NET Framework, developing the Internet applications is as easy as developing desktop applications.

The .NET Framework frees the software developer from most of the operating system specifics, such as memory management and file handling, because the .NET Framework covers all the layers of software development above the operating system. Figure 2-1 describes the different components of the .NET Framework.

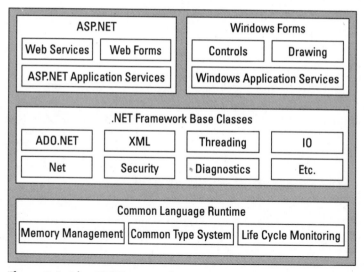

Figure 2-1: The .NET Framework

The top layer represents user and program interfaces, and includes Windows Forms, Web Forms, Web Services, and Application Services. Windows Forms provide a Win32-based user interface. Web Forms provide a Web-based user interface. Web Services are the most revolutionary program interfaces because they allow programs to communicate over the Internet. The Internet-based program interfaces, which include Web Forms and Web Services, are implemented by ASP.NET, which is a built-in component of the .NET Framework.

The middle layer represents the .NET Framework classes, which are universally available across multiple languages. The usage of these classes is consistent across all languages included in the .NET Framework.

The base layer represents the common execution platform called the Common Language Runtime (CLR). This is the most important component of the .NET Framework. The CLR provides support for multiple languages and allows cross-language inheritance. For example, you can inherit a class written in Visual Basic from a class written in Visual C++. Thus, with .NET, the choice of a programming language simply depends on the user's choice. With .NET, it is possible to create applications by using multiple languages. The multiple-language support is possible because the CLR provides a common system of data types. In addition, the CLR performs the memory management and monitors the complete life cycle of objects, while it tracks objects and handles garbage collection.

Visual Studio .NET (VS.NET) is the first release of the products based on the .NET Framework. It includes Visual Basic, Visual C++, and C#. VS.NET provides a common Integrated Development Environment (IDE) for all languages. Therefore, developers always work in a consistent environment irrespective of the language they use.

With that basic understanding of the .NET Framework, you are ready to look at the basic features of ASP.NET.

Introducing ASP.NET

ASP.NET, the next version of ASP, is a programming framework that is used to create enterprise-class Web applications. The enterprise-class Web applications are accessible on a global basis, leading to efficient information management. However, the advantages that ASP.NET offers make it more than just the next version of ASP.

ASP.NET is integrated with Visual Studio .NET, which provides a GUI designer, a rich toolbox, and a fully integrated debugger. This allows the development of applications in a What You See is What You Get (WYSIWYG) manner. Therefore, creating ASP.NET applications is much simpler.

Unlike the ASP runtime, ASP.NET uses the *Common Language Runtime (CLR)* provided by the .NET Framework. The CLR is the .NET runtime, which manages the execution of code. The CLR allows the objects, which are created in different languages, to interact with each other and hence removes the language barrier. CLR thus makes Web application development more efficient.

In addition to simplifying the designing of Web applications, the .NET CLR offers many advantages. Some of these advantages are listed as follows.

✦ **Improved performance:** The ASP.NET code is a compiled CLR code instead of an interpreted code. The CLR provides just-in-time compilation, native optimization, and caching. Here, it is important to note that compilation is a two-stage process in the .NET Framework. First, the code is compiled into the Microsoft Intermediate Language (MSIL). Then, at the execution time, the MSIL is compiled into native code. Only the portions of the code that are actually needed will be compiled into native code. This is called Just In Time compilation. These features lead to an overall improved performance of ASP.NET applications.

✦ **Flexibility:** The entire .NET class library can be accessed by ASP.NET applications. You can use the language that best applies to the type of functionality you want to implement, because ASP.NET is language independent.

✦ **Configuration settings:** The application-level configuration settings are stored in an Extensible Markup Language (XML) format. The XML format is a hierarchical text format, which is easy to read and write. This format makes it easy to apply new settings to applications without the aid of any local administration tools.

✦ **Security:** ASP.NET applications are secure and use a set of default authorization and authentication schemes. However, you can modify these schemes according to the security needs of an application.

In addition to this list of advantages, the ASP.NET framework makes it easy to migrate from ASP applications.

Before you start with your first ASP.NET application, take a quick look at how to set up the development environment, described next.

Setting Up the Development Environment

ASP.NET is based on the CLR, class libraries, and other tools integrated with the Microsoft .NET Framework. Therefore, to develop and run the ASP.NET applications, you need to install the .NET Framework. The .NET Framework is available in two forms:

✦ .NET Framework SDK (Software Development Kit)

✦ Visual Studio .NET (VS.NET)

You can install the .NET Framework SDK or VS.NET on a machine that has one of the following operating systems:

✦ Windows 2000

✦ Windows NT 4.0

✦ Windows Me

✦ Windows 98

✦ Windows XP Professional

Installation of the .NET Framework SDK is very simple — just run the Setup program and follow the onscreen instructions. However, the development machine must have Internet Explorer 5.5 or higher available before the installation. Otherwise, you will be prompted to download it before you install the .NET Framework SDK.

To develop any Web application, you need Internet Information Server (IIS) configured on either the development machine (in the case of Windows 2000 or Windows NT 4.0) or another machine on the network. In the latter case, the .NET Framework must be installed on the machine on which IIS is configured.

Note   In the case of Windows 2000 Server, the IIS server is automatically installed.

In addition to installing IIS, you need to install SQL Server 7.0 or higher to develop ASP.NET database applications. You can install SQL Server on the development machine or any other machine on the network.

You can create ASP.NET applications by just installing the .NET Framework SDK and configuring an IIS server. In this case, you need to use a text editor, such as Notepad, to write the code. Therefore, if you do this, you'll have to work without the IDE and other integrated tools that come with VS.NET. Hence, installing VS.NET is recommended, to get the full benefit of the .NET features.

VS.NET Beta 2 comes with four CD-ROMs:

✦ Windows Component Update CD

✦ VS.NET CD1

✦ VS.NET CD2

✦ VS.NET CD3

When you run the Setup program from VS.NET CD1, a dialog box appears that prompts you for the following three options:

✦ Windows Component Update

✦ Install Visual Studio .NET

✦ Check for Service Releases

If you have not run the Setup program from the Windows Component Update CD, only the first of the preceding three options will be available. In this case, you need to insert the Windows Component Update CD in the CD-ROM drive of the machine and click the first link, Windows Component Update, to begin the update. This option updates Windows with the components that are required to install .NET. Some of the components include Microsoft Windows Installer 2.0, Setup Runtime Files, and Microsoft Data Access Components 2.7. Then, follow the onscreen instructions. In the process, you'll need to reboot the machine several times. After the Windows Component Update is complete, you can use the second link to install VS.NET. After VS.NET is installed, you can click the third link to check for any updates.

When you start Visual Studio .NET, the Start Page is displayed prominently in the window. Figure 2-2 displays the Visual Studio .NET window.

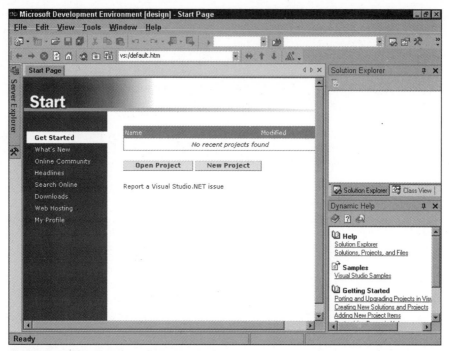

Figure 2-2: The Visual Studio .NET window

The VS.NET window contains the Solution Explorer window to the right. This window displays the projects that are created. The Toolbox and Server Explorer windows can be seen hidden at the extreme left. When you point to the Toolbox or Server Explorer, the corresponding window opens. You use the Toolbox to create the user interface for an application. The Server Explorer window is used to add any Web server or database connection.

The main Start Page window is the central location from where you can perform several tasks, such as create a new project, open an existing project, and get the latest news and recent articles at the MSDN online library. The different options available on the Start Page and what they enable you to do are described as follows:

✦ **Get Started:** Create a new project or open an existing project.

✦ **What's New:** Identify the new features of Visual Studio .NET.

✦ **Online Community:** Contact other developers online. To do this, you must have a newsgroup reader configured on your machine.

✦ **Headlines:** Get the latest news from the MSDN online library.

✦ **Search Online:** Search the Web.

✦ **Downloads:** Get the latest product updates, SDK releases, and sample code from the Internet.

✦ **Web Hosting:** Post your Web applications and Web services created in Visual Studio .NET directly to the Internet.

✦ **MyProfile:** Set the IDE-specific preferences.

Creating an ASP.NET Application

After you've set up the development environment for ASP.NET, you can create your first ASP.NET Web application. You can create an ASP.NET Web application in one of the following ways:

✦ **Use a text editor:** In this method, you can write the code in a text editor, such as Notepad, and save the code as an ASPX file. You can save the ASPX file in the directory C:\inetpub\wwwroot. Then, to display the output of the Web page in Internet Explorer, you simply need to type `http://localhost/` `<filename>.aspx` in the Address box. If the IIS server is installed on some other machine on the network, replace "localhost" with the name of the server. If you save the file in some other directory, you need to add the file to a virtual directory in the Default WebSite directory on the IIS server. You can also create your own virtual directory and add the file to it.

✦ **Use the VS.NET IDE:** In this method, you use the IDE of Visual Studio .NET to create a Web page in a WYSIWYG manner. Also, when you create a Web application, the application is automatically created on a Web server (IIS server). You do not need to create a separate virtual directory on the IIS server.

From the preceding discussion, it is obvious that the development of ASP.NET Web applications is much more convenient and efficient in Visual Studio .NET.

ASP.NET Web pages consist of HTML text and the code. The HTML text and the code can be separated in two different files. You can write the code in Visual Basic or C#. This separate file is called the *code behind file*. In this section, you'll create simple Web pages by using VB as well as C#.

Cross-Reference For more information on code behind files, refer to Chapter 3.

Before you start creating a Web page, you should be familiar with basic ASP.NET syntax. At the top of the page, you must specify an @ Page directive to define page-specific attributes, such as language. The syntax is given as follows:

```
<%@ Page attribute = value %>
```

To specify the language as VB for any code output to be rendered on the page, use the following line of code:

```
<%@ Page Language = "VB" %>
```

This line indicates that any code in the block, `<% %>`, on the page is compiled by using VB.

To render the output on your page, you can use the `Response.Write()` method. For example, to display the text "hello" on a page, use the following code:

```
<% Response.Write("Hello") %>
```

> **Note** The syntax used in the block, `<% %>`, must correspond to the language specified in the `@ Page` directive. Otherwise, an error is generated when you display the page in a Web browser.

You can use HTML tags in the argument passed to the `Response.Write()` method. For example, to display the text in bold, you use the following code:

```
<% Response.Write("<B> Hello </B>") %>
```

For dynamic processing of a page, such as the result of a user interaction, you need to write the code within the `<Script>` tag. The syntax of the `<Script>` tag is given as follows:

```
<Script runat="server" [language=codelanguage]>
    code here
</Script>
```

In this syntax . . .

✦ `runat="server"` indicates that the code is executed at the server side.

✦ `[language=codelanguage]` indicates the language that is used. You can use VB, C#, or JScript .NET. The square brackets indicate that this attribute is optional. If you do not specify this attribute, the default language used is VB.

After gaining an understanding of the basic ASP.NET page syntax, you can now create a simple ASP.NET Web application. In the following sections, you'll create a simple Web application by using VB and C#. To do so, you'll use the VS.NET IDE.

Creating a Visual Basic Web Application

You can create an ASP.NET application using Visual Basic by creating a Visual Basic Web Application project. To do so, complete the following steps:

1. Select File ➪ New ➪ Project. The New Project dialog box appears.

2. Select Visual Basic Projects from the Project Types pane.

3. Select ASP.NET Web Application from the Templates pane. The Name box contains a default name of the application. The Location box contains the name of a Web server where the application will be created. However, you can change the default name and location. In this case, the name of the sample application is SampleVB. The New Project dialog box now appears as shown in Figure 2-3.

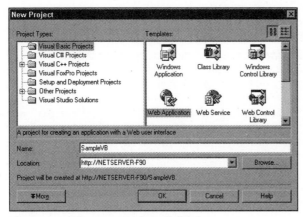

Figure 2-3: The New Project dialog box

4. Click OK to complete the process.

VS.NET displays the application, as shown in Figure 2-4. By default, the file WebForm1.aspx is selected and displayed. In addition to several other files, WebForm1.vb is also created. You can write the page logic in this file. This file is the *code behind file*.

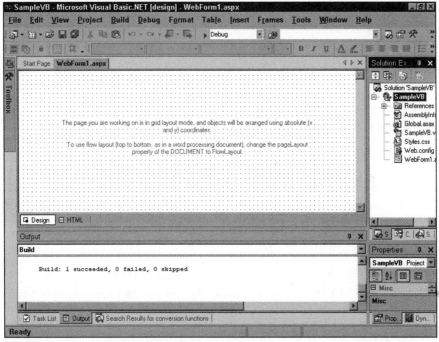

Figure 2-4: The VS.NET window with a new project

The WebForm1.aspx file is displayed in Design mode by default. To view the file in HTML mode, click HTML at the bottom of the WebForm1.aspx file window.

As you can see in HTML view, the language to be used on the page is VB. Any HTML text or code (in the `<% %>` block) within the `<Body> </Body>` block is rendered on the page when it is displayed in a Web browser.

The default background color of a page is white. You can change the background color of a page by setting the `bgcolor` attribute of the `<Body>` element. When you set this attribute, you are prompted to pick the color, as shown in Figure 2-5.

Figure 2-5: Setting the `bgcolor` attribute

When you select a color from the color palette, the corresponding color code is set as the value of the `bgcolor` attribute. A sample of such code is given as follows:

```
<Body bgcolor="#ccccff">
```

Write the following code within the `<Body> </Body>` element to display the text "Hello World":

```
<% Response.Write(" <Font Size=10> <Center> <B> Hello World </B> </Center>
</Font>") %>
```

After you complete writing the code for your application, you need to build your application so that you can execute it on a Web server. To build the project, choose Build ➪ Build.

Tip   You can also build a project by pressing Ctrl + Shift + B.

When you build a project, the Web Form class file is compiled to a Dynamic Link Library (DLL) file along with other executable files in the project. The ASPX file is copied to the Web server without any compilation. You can change the ASPX file (only the visual elements of the page) without recompiling, because the ASPX file is not compiled. Later, when you run the page, the DLL and ASPX files are compiled into a new class file and then run.

The output of the page that you developed is displayed in Figure 2-6.

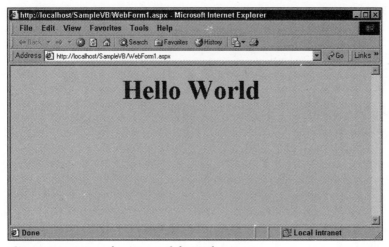

Figure 2-6: A sample output of the Web page

Creating a C# Web Application

In addition to Visual Basic, you can also use C# to create ASP.NET Web applications. To do so, you need to create a Visual C# Web application project as follows:

1. Select File ➪ New ➪ Project. The New Project dialog box appears.

2. Select Visual C# Projects from the Project Types pane.

3. Select Web Application from the Templates pane. The Name box contains a default name of the application. The Location box contains the name of a Web server where the application will be created. However, you can change the default name and location. In this case, the name of the sample application is SampleCSharp.

4. Click OK to complete the process.

When you switch to HTML view of the WebForm1.aspx file, you'll notice that the language specified in the @ Page directive is C#. To create a Web page that displays "Hello World," you simply need to write the following code in the `<Body> </Body>` block of the page:

```
<% Response.Write("<Font Size=10> <Center> <B> Hello World </B> </Center>
</Font>"); %>
```

Notice that the code in the `<% %>` block is terminated with a semicolon. This difference in syntax is due to the fact that the language for this page is C# and not VB.

When you build the application and execute it, a Web page appears in the browser displaying the text "Hello World."

Deploying an ASP.NET Web Application

After creating and testing your ASP.NET Web applications, the next step is deployment. *Deployment* is the process of distributing the finished applications (without the source code) to be installed on other computers.

In Visual Studio .NET, the deployment mechanism is the same irrespective of the programming language and tools used to create applications. In this section, you'll deploy the "Hello World" Web application that you created. You can deploy any of the application that was created by using VB or C#. Here, you'll deploy the application created by using VB. To do so, follow these steps:

1. Open the Web application project that you want to deploy. In this case, open the SampleVB project.

2. Select File ⇨ Add Project ⇨ New Project to open the Add New Project dialog box.

3. From the Project Types pane, select Setup and Deployment Projects. From the Templates pane, select Web Setup Project.

4. Change the default name of the project. In this case, change it to "SampleVBDeploy."

5. Click OK to complete the process. The project is added in the Solution Explorer window. Also, a File System editor window appears to the left, as shown in Figure 2-7. The editor window has two panes. The left pane displays different items. The right pane displays the content of the item selected in the left pane.

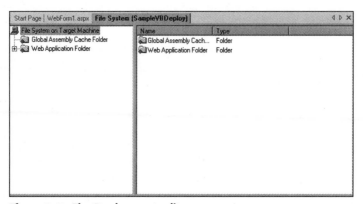

Figure 2-7: The Deployment editor

6. Select Web Application Folder in the left pane of the File System editor window. Then, from the Action menu, select Add ⇨ Project Output to open the Add Project Output Group dialog box, shown in Figure 2-8.

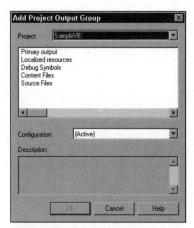

Figure 2-8: The Add Project Output Group dialog box

7. Verify that SampleVB is selected in the Project drop-down list. Then, select Primary Output and Content Files from the list.

8. Click OK. The output files and content files of the SampleVB project are added to the solution.

9. Select Web Application Folder in the File System editor and select Properties Window from the View menu to open the Properties window.

10. Set the `VirtualDirectory` property to a folder, <folder name>, that would be the virtual directory on the target computer where you want to install the application. By default, this property is set to `SampleVBDeploy`, which is the name of the Web Setup project that you added. In this case, set the property to `DeployedApplication`.

Caution The <folder name> should be a new folder name and should not already exist on the target machine. Otherwise, the contents in the folder will be overwritten.

11. In the same Properties window of the Web Application Folder, set the `DefaultDocument` property to WebForm1.aspx. This property is used to set the default Web Forms page for the application.

12. Build the solution by selecting Build Solution from the Build menu.

13. After the solution is built successfully, a SampleVBDeploy.msi file is created in the Debug directory of the Web Setup project. The default path is \documents and settings\<*login name*>\My Documents\Visual Studio Projects\SampleVB\ SampleVBDeploy\Debug\SampleVBDeploy.msi.

14. Copy the SampleVBDeploy.msi file to the Web server computer (c:\inetpub\ wwwroot) where you want to deploy the application.

15. Double-click the SampleVBDeploy.msi file on the target computer to run the installer.

Note   To run the installer, you must have the install permissions on the computer. And, to install to the Web server, you must have IIS permissions.

After the installation is complete, you can run your application on the target computer. To do so, start Internet Explorer and enter `http://<computer name>/ DeployedApplication` in the address box. The "Hello World" page that you developed is displayed.

Summary

In this chapter, you learned how to set up the development environment for creating ASP.NET applications. Then, you learned how to create a simple ASP.NET application by using both VB and C#. Finally, you learned how to deploy an application on a Web server.

✦   ✦   ✦

Building Forms with Web Controls

The increased use of the Internet in the business scenario has shifted focus from desktop applications to Web-based applications. Because of this shift in focus, a Web development technology is needed that can combine the capabilities of different languages and simplify application development. Microsoft's response to this need is the release of ASP.NET, which provides a common Web development platform.

ASP.NET is a powerful programming platform that is used to develop and run Web-based applications and services. ASP.NET provides improved features, such as convenient debugging tools, over the earlier Web development technologies. ASP.NET provides a rich set of controls to design Web pages. Visual Studio .NET provides visual WYSIWYG (What You See Is What You Get) HTML editors. Therefore, you can design Web pages by simply dragging and dropping the controls. ASP.NET supports the C#, Visual Basic .NET, and JScript .NET languages, all of which you can use to build programming logic for your Web pages. You can choose which one of these languages to use based on your proficiency on a particular language. One of the most important features of ASP.NET is that it provides separate files for page presentation and programming logic, which simplifies Web application development. This chapter introduces you to designing simple Web pages by using basic Web controls. You'll also learn how to handle various events of these controls.

Introducing ASP.NET Web Forms

The ASP.NET Web Forms technology is used to create programmable Web pages that are dynamic, fast, and interactive. Web pages created using ASP.NET Web Forms are called *ASP.NET Web Forms pages* or simply *Web Forms pages*.

ASP.NET uses the .NET Framework and enables you to create Web pages that are browser independent. In addition to being browser independent, the following are some of the features that may lead you to select Web Forms over other technologies to create dynamic Web pages:

✦ Web Forms can be designed and programmed using Rapid Application Development (RAD) tools.

✦ Web Forms support a rich set of controls and are extensible, because they provide support for user-created and third-party controls.

✦ Any of the .NET Framework language can be used to program the ASP.NET Web Forms pages.

✦ ASP.NET uses the Common Language Runtime (CLR) of the .NET Framework and thus benefits from its features, such as type safety and inheritance.

Web Forms components

An ASP.NET Web Forms page consists of a user interface and programming logic. The user interface helps display information to users, while the programming logic handles user interaction with the Web Forms pages. The user interface consists of a file containing a markup language, such as HTML or XML, and server controls. This file is called a *page* and has .aspx as its extension.

The functionality to respond to user interactions with the Web Forms pages is implemented by using programming languages, such as Visual Basic .NET and C#. You can implement the programming logic in the ASPX file or in a separate file written in any CLR-supported language, such as Visual Basic .NET or C#. This separate file is called the *code behind* file and has either .aspx.cs or .aspx.vb as its extension depending on the language used. Thus, a Web Forms page consists of a page (ASPX file) and a code behind file (.aspx.cs file or .aspx.vb file).

Web Forms server controls

You can design a Web Forms page by using controls called *Web Forms server controls*. You can program the functionality to be provided for the server controls. The server controls are different from the usual Windows controls because they work within the ASP.NET Framework. The different types of server controls are described as follows:

✦ **HTML server controls:** These controls refer to the HTML elements that can be used in server code. The HTML elements can be converted into HTML server controls. To do so, you need to use attributes, such as ID and RUNAT, in the tags that are used to add the HTML controls. You can also add these controls to the page by using the HTML tab of the toolbox. The different tabs of the toolbox are shown in Figure 3-1.

✦ **ASP.NET server controls:** These controls do not map one-to-one to HTML server controls. ASP.NET server controls include traditional form controls, such as text boxes and buttons, and complex controls, such as tables.

✦ **Validation controls:** These controls are used to validate users' input. Validation controls can be attached to input controls to check the values entered.

✦ **User controls:** These controls are created from the existing Web Forms pages and can be used in other Web Forms pages.

Figure 3-1: The Visual Studio .NET toolbox

Creating Web Forms Application Projects

Before you use any server control to design a Web Forms page, you need to create an ASP.NET Web Application project. You can create either a Visual Basic .NET or a C# Web Application project, depending on the programming language you want to use. A Web Application project is always created on a Web server.

Note   A Web server must be installed on the development computer to create a Web Application project.

The steps to create an ASP.NET Web Application project are as follows:

1. Select Start ➪ Programs ➪ Microsoft Visual Studio .NET 7.0 ➪ Microsoft Visual Studio .NET 7.0 to start Visual Studio.NET.

2. Select File ➪ New ➪ Project to open the New Project dialog box.

3. Select Visual Basic Projects or Visual C# Projects in the Project Types pane.

4. Select ASP.NET Web Application in the Templates pane.

5. Specify the project name in the Name box, if necessary.

6. Specify the name of the computer where you want to create the application, in the Location box if necessary, and click OK. The name of the computer should be in the form http://*computer name*. A new Web Application project is displayed in the designer window, as shown in Figure 3-2.

Note By default, the Name and the Location boxes contain a project name and the computer name, respectively. However, you can change the default names.

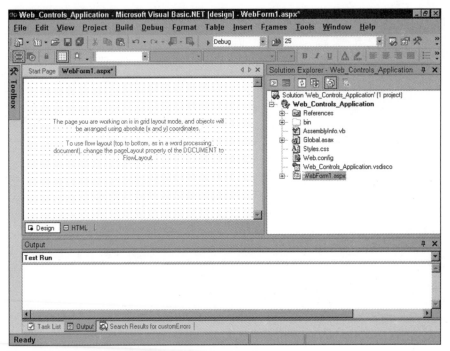

Figure 3-2: A Web Application project

When you create a Web Application project, the Application Wizard creates the necessary project files along with the page file and code behind class file as described:

✦ **WebForm1.aspx:** This page file consists of the user interface for the visual representation of the Web Forms page. The file has two views, Design and HTML. The default view is Design view.

- **Design view:** This view represents the user interface for the Web Forms page. You can place controls directly from the toolbox to the Web Forms page in Design view. By default, the page layout of the Web Forms page is GridLayout. This layout enables you to accurately position controls on the page by using the absolute coordinates (X,Y) of the page. In addition to GridLayout, ASP.NET provides another page layout, which is called FlowLayout. In FlowLayout, you can add text to the page directly in Design mode. You can change the page layout from the default GridLayout to FlowLayout. To do so, right-click the page in Design view and select Properties from the context menu. Next, in the DOCUMENT Property Pages dialog box, from the Page Layout list box, select FlowLayout.

- **HTML view:** This view represents the ASP.NET code for the Web Forms page. To open HTML view, click the HTML tab in the designer. When the Web Application project is a Visual Basic project or a C# project, the scripting language used in the HTML page is Visual Basic or C#, respectively.

✦ **WebForm1.aspx.cs or WebForm1.aspx.vb:** This file consists of the code to implement programming logic in the Web Forms page. You can view the code file by using the Show All Files icon in the Solution Explorer window. If the Web Application project is a Visual Basic project, you use Visual Basic .NET to implement the programming logic and the code file is called the *WebForm1.aspx.vb* file. Conversely, if the Web Application project is a C# project, you use C# to implement the programming logic and the code file is called the *WebForm1.aspx.cs* file. The code file (WebForm1.aspx.vb) appears within the WebForm1.aspx node as shown in Figure 3-3.

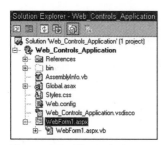

Figure 3-3: The Solution Explorer window showing all the files

Using Web Controls

You can add ASP.NET server controls to a Web Forms page by using either of the following two features:

✦ The Web Forms section of the toolbox

✦ The ASP.NET code

You add controls from the toolbox in Design view of the Web Forms page (the ASPX file). The toolbox categorizes the different types of controls in separate tabs, such as Web Forms, HTML, Components, and Data. You can use the HTML tab to add HTML controls and use the Web Forms tab to add the ASP.NET server controls to Web Forms. However, to make the HTML controls available for coding at the server end, these controls need to be converted to server controls. To do so, right-click the HTML control on the page and select Run As Server Control from the context menu. While selecting between HTML and Web server controls, using Web server controls is preferred, because they provide a rich object model and are adaptable to multiple browsers depending on browser capabilities. However, HTML server controls are preferred when migrating from the existing ASP pages to ASP.NET pages, because, unlike Web server controls, HTML server controls map directly to HTML tags.

You can also add a Web control to a page by using the ASP.NET code. You can access the ASP.NET code in the HTML view of the page (ASPX file). The actual syntax depends on the type of control that you want to add. The syntax used to add an HTML TextBox control is given as follows:

```
<input id="Text1" Type=text runat="server">
```

You can add ASP.NET server controls by using an Extensible Markup Language (XML) tag referenced as asp. When you add an ASP.NET TextBox control, the following syntax is generated for you:

```
<asp:TextBox id="TextBox1" runat="server"></asp:TextBox>
```

 Note   When you use the toolbox to add Web controls in Design view, the corresponding ASP.NET syntax is automatically generated.

In the preceding code, the XML tag asp maps to the System.Web.UI..WebControls namespace. This is different from the HTML server controls where the input tag lacks any such mapping. However, the Web server controls use the runat=server attribute, which is similar to the HTML server controls.

You can also programmatically add a control at run time. The following VB.NET code snippet demonstrates how to add a TextBox control at run time:

```
Dim TextBox1 as New TextBox()
Controls.Add(TextBox1)
```

Every control has specific properties and methods. You can set control properties to modify the appearance or behavior of controls. For example, you can set the font, color, and size of a control. You can use the control methods to perform a specific task, such as moving a control. You can set control properties at design times by using the Properties window or at run time by using the code. Every control has a property called ID that is used for the unique identification of the control. You can set the property of a control at run time by using the following syntax:

```
ControlID.PropertyName=Value
```

In this syntax:

- ✦ ControlID represents the ID property of the control.
- ✦ PropertyName represents the control property.
- ✦ Value represents the value assigned to PropertyName, which is a control's property.

Figure 3-4 displays a Web Forms page that contains almost every basic Web control. You can see that the Web Forms page is a user registration form. The form is designed to accept user input through various controls. After filling out the form, a user may click the Register button to complete the registration process. Alternatively, a user may click the Reset button to clear the values entered in the form. Table 3-1 lists the IDs of the different controls used in the form. The section that follows describes some of the basic Web controls in detail.

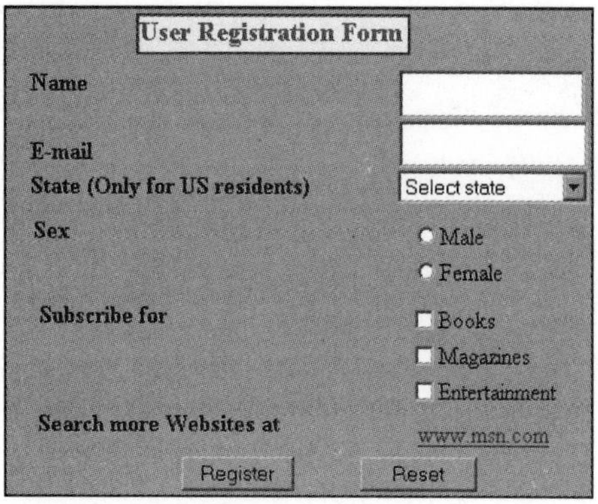

Figure 3-4: A Web Forms page

<table>
<tr><th colspan="3" align="center">Table 3-1
IDs of different controls</th></tr>
</table>

Control	Contains	ID
TextBox	Name	UserName
TextBox	E-mail	Email
DropDownList	State	USStateList
RadioButtonList	Sex	SexOption
CheckBoxList	Subscriptions	SubscriptionOption
HyperLink	Search	SearchLink
Button	Register	RegisterButton
Button	Reset	ResetButton

Label control

You use the Label control to display static text in a Web Forms page that users cannot edit. When you add a Label control, the text "Label" appears as its caption. However, you can use the Text property to modify the caption. Table 3-2 lists some of the properties of the Label control.

<table>
<tr><th colspan="2" align="center">Table 3-2
Properties of the Label control</th></tr>
</table>

Property	Description
Text	Represents the caption of a label
BackColor	Represents the background color of a label
ForeColor	Represents the font color of a label
Visible	Indicates whether or not a label is visible

You can also change the text of a label by using the following code:

```
Label1.Text="Welcome"
```

In this code, Label1 is the ID of the Label control for which you want to change the state. You can use the Visible property of the Label control to make it visible or not. For example, in the following code, the `Visible` property is set to False, making the label invisible:

```
Label1.Visible=False
```

TextBox control

You use the TextBox control to get information, such as text, numbers, and dates, from users in a Web Forms page. You can set the `TextMode` property of a TextBox control to set the type as a single-line, password, or multiline TextBox control. By default, a TextBox control is a single-line text box that allows users to type characters in a single line only. A password TextBox control is similar to the single-line text box, but masks the characters that are typed by users and displays them as asterisks (*). A multiline TextBox control allows users to type multiple lines and wrap text.

The appearance of the TextBox control can be modified by using properties such as `BackColor` or `ForeColor`. Table 3-3 lists some of the properties of the TextBox control.

Table 3-3
Properties of the TextBox control

Property	Description
Text	Represents the text to be displayed in the TextBox control. Also, you can use this property to set or retrieve the text to or from a TextBox control at run time.
MaxLength	Represents the number of characters that a user can type in the TextBox control.
Width	Represents the width of a TextBox control. This property takes value in pixels.
Columns	Represents the width of a TextBox control in characters. If you set both the Width and Columns properties, the Width property takes precedence over the Columns property. The default value is 0.
TextMode	Represents the behavior of the TextBox control, such as single-line, multiline, or password. By default, the control is a single-line text box. To set a password text box, set this property to TextBoxMode.Password. To set a multiline text box, set this property to TextBoxMode.MultiLine. The values SingleLine, MultiLine, and Password are part of an enum called TextBoxMode. You cannot specify it directly.

Continued

	Table 3-3 *(continued)*
Property	**Description**
Height	Represents the vertical size of the TextBox control and takes value in pixels.
Rows	Represents the vertical size of the MultiLineTextBox control and takes value in number of rows The default value is 0.
Wrap	Represents the word wrap behavior in a multiline TextBox control. The text wraps automatically if the value is set to True. However, a user must press a carriage return to move to a next line if the value is set to False. The default value is True.

Note   The Height and Width properties do not work in browsers that do not support Cascading Style Sheets (CSS). The CSS is a list of CSS styles that is used to apply a general rule to attributes of a set of elements.

CheckBox and CheckBoxList controls

Check boxes provide you with independent choices or options that you can select. You can add check boxes to a Web Forms page by using either the CheckBox control or the CheckBoxList control. The CheckBox control is a single check box that you can work with. On the other hand, the CheckBoxList control is a collection of several check boxes. After you add the CheckBoxList control, you need to add a list of items to it. To do so:

1. Display the Properties window of the CheckBoxList control.

2. Click the ellipsis button for the Items property of the CheckBoxList control.

3. In the ListItem Collection Editor dialog box, click Add to create a new item. A new item is created and its properties are displayed in the Properties pane of the dialog box.

4. Verify that the item is selected in the Members list, and then set the item properties. Each item is a separate object and has following properties:

   • Text: Represents the text to be displayed for the item in the list.

   • Value: Represents the value associated with the item without displaying it. For example, you can set the Text property of an item as the city name and the Value property to the postal code of the city. Thus, you can keep the Text and Value properties different when you do not want the actual value to be displayed to the user.

   • Selected: A Boolean value that indicates whether or not the item is selected.

In addition to adding the CheckBoxList control and the member items at design time, you can programmatically add them at run time. To do so, you use the following VB.NET code:

```
Dim CheckBoxList1 As New CheckBoxList()
Controls.Add(CheckBoxList1)
CheckBoxList1.Items.Add("Check1")
```

The Add() method of the Items class can take either a string argument or a ListItem object. This code snippet uses the Add() method that takes one string argument to represent the text of the item.

The Add() method can also take a ListItem object as an argument. The ListItem constructor can take one argument (one string to represent the text of the item) or two arguments (one string for the text and another string for the value of the item). The following code snippet explains the usage of the ListItem object in the Add() method:

```
Dim ListItem1 as New ListItem("Check1","check")
CheckBoxList1.Items.Add(ListItem1)
```

The following VB.NET code snippet assumes that the Web Forms page contains a TextBox control and a Button control. The following code is also associated with the Click event of the button. When the user enters a number in the text box and clicks the button, the specified number of check boxes is added to the CheckBoxList control:

```
'Create a CheckBoxList object
Dim CheckBoxList1 as New CheckBoxList()
'Adding the CheckBoxList control to the page
Controls.Add(CheckBoxList1)

'Declare the total number of items
Dim ChkCount as Integer

'Declare the current number of items
Dim ChkCtr as Integer

'Accept the total number of items
ChkCount = Val(TextBox1.Text)

For ChkCtr = 0 To ChkCount-1
    CheckBoxList1.Items.Add("Check" & ChkCtr)
Next ChkCtr
```

The choice between using the CheckBox control and the CheckBoxList control depends on application needs. The CheckBox control provides more control over the layout of the check boxes on the page. For instance, you can set the font and color of the check boxes individually or include text between different check boxes. On the other hand, the CheckBoxList control is a better choice if you need to add a series of connected check boxes, such as check boxes to represent areas of interest.

You can identify whether a check box is checked or not by using the `Checked` property of the CheckBox control. The `Checked` property returns a Boolean value, as indicated in the code that follows. If the control is checked, it returns True; otherwise, it returns False.

```
Dim CheckBox1 as New CheckBox()
Dim IsChk as Boolean
IsChk=CheckBox1.Checked
```

If you have a CheckBoxList control and you want to identify the item that has been checked, you use either the `SelectedIndex` or `SelectedItem` property of the control. The `SelectedIndex` property returns an integer value indicating the index (the first item has an index 0) of the selected item. This property returns -1 if nothing is selected.

```
Dim i As Integer
i=CheckBoxList1.SelectedIndex()
```

The `SelectedItem` property, on the other hand, returns the selected item:

```
Dim ListItem1 As New ListItem()
ListItem1=CheckBoxList1.SelectedItem()
```

You can also access the `Text`, `Value`, or `Selected` property of the item. For example, the following code retrieves the `Text` property of the selected item:

```
Dim CityName as String
CityName=CheckBoxList1.SelectedItem.Text
```

When you add a CheckBox control to a page, you can set the caption of the check box by setting the `Text` property. Then, you can change the orientation of the caption by setting the `TextAlign` property. Table 3-4 describes some of the properties of the CheckBox and CheckBoxList controls.

Table 3-4
Properties of the CheckBox and CheckBoxList controls

Property	Available with	Description
`Text`	CheckBox	Represents the caption of the CheckBox control.
`TextAlign`	CheckBox and CheckBoxList	Represents the text orientation of the CheckBox and CheckBoxList controls.
`Items`	CheckBoxList	Represents the collection of individual check boxes in the CheckBoxList control. Each item has three properties, `Text`, `Value`, and `Selected`, associated with it.

RadioButton and RadioButtonList controls

Radio buttons provide a set of choices or options that you can select. You can add radio buttons to a Web Forms page by using either the RadioButton control or the RadioButtonList control. The RadioButton control is a single radio button. On the other hand, the RadioButtonList control is a collection of radio buttons. Radio buttons are seldom used singly. Usually, you use radio buttons in a group. A group of radio buttons provides a set of mutually exclusive options — you can select only one radio button in a group. You can group a set of radio buttons in two ways:

✦ Place a set of RadioButton controls on the page and assign them manually to a group. To do so, you can use the GroupName property.

✦ Place a RadioButtonList control on the page; the radio buttons in the control are automatically grouped.

After you add a RadioButtonList control, you need to add the individual radio buttons. You can do so by using the Items property in the same way as you do for the CheckBoxList control.

You add the items to a RadioButtonList control at run time in the same way as you add items to a CheckBoxList control. The following VB.NET code snippet demonstrates how to add items to a RadioButtonList control programmatically:

```
Dim RadioButtonList1 As New RadioButtonList()
Controls.Add(RadioButtonList1)
RadioButtonList1.Items.Add("Radio1")
```

You can use the Checked property of the RadioButton control to identify whether or not the control is selected. For the RadioButtonList control, you can access the index of the selected item by using the SelectedIndex property and access the selected item by using the SelectedItem property of the control.

Table 3-5 describes some of the properties of the RadioButton and RadioButtonList controls. Like the CheckBox control, the RadioButton control offers more control over the layout of the radio buttons on the page.

Table 3-5
Properties of the RadioButton and RadioButtonList controls

Property	Available with	Description
Text	RadioButton	Represents the caption of the RadioButton control.
TextAlign	RadioButton and RadioButtonList	Represents the text orientation of the RadioButton and RadioButtonList controls.
Items	RadioButtonList	Represents the collection of the individual radio buttons in the RadioButtonList control. Each item has three properties associated with it: Text, Value, and Selected.

ListBox control

The ListBox control is a list of predefined items and allows users to select one or more items from the list. The ListBox control is a collection of items. The individual list items can be added by using the Items property of the ListBox control.

You can add list items to the ListBox control in the same way you add items to the CheckBoxList and RadioButtonList controls. You can access the index of the selected item by using the SelectedIndex property and access the selected item in the list by using the SelectedItem property of the control.

Table 3-6 describes some of the properties of the ListBox control.

Table 3-6
Properties of the ListBox control

Property	Description
Items	Represents the collection of list items in the ListBox control. Each list item has three properties associated with it: Text, Value, and Selected.
Width	Represents the size of a ListBox control and takes value in pixels.
Height	Represents the vertical size of the ListBox control and takes value in pixels.
Rows	Represents the vertical size of the ListBox control and takes value in number of rows. If the control contains more than the specified number of items, the control displays a vertical scroll bar.
SelectionMode	Represents the number of items that can be selected. To allow users to select only one item, set the SelectionMode property to ListSelectionMode.Single. To allow users to select multiple items, set the SelectionMode property to ListSelectionMode.Multiple. ListSelectionMode is the enum that allows you to specify the selection mode. To select more than one item, users can hold the Ctrl or Shift key while clicking multiple items. This is possible only when you set the SelectionMode property to ListSelectionMode.Multiple.

DropDownList control

The DropDownList control allows users to select an item from a set of predefined items — each item is a separate object with its own properties, such as Text, Value, and Selected. You can add these predefined items to a DropDownList control by using its Items property. Unlike the ListBox control, you can select only one item at a time, and the list of items remains hidden until a user clicks the drop-down button.

You can add list items to the DropDownList control in the same way you add items to the CheckBoxList, RadioButtonList, and ListBox controls. You can access the index of the selected item by using the SelectedIndex property and access the selected item in the list by using the SelectedItem property of the control.

Table 3-7 describes some of the properties of the DropDownList control.

Table 3-7
Properties of the DropDownList control

Property	Description
Items	Represents the collection of items in the DropDownList control. Each item has three properties associated with it: Text, Value, and Selected.
Width	Represents the width of a DropDownList control and takes value in pixels.
Height	Represents the vertical size of the DropDownList control and takes value in pixels.

HyperLink control

The HyperLink control creates links on a Web page and allows users to navigate from one page to another in an application or an absolute URL. You can use text or an image to act as a link in a HyperLink control. When users click the control, the target page opens. Table 3-8 describes some of the properties of the Hyperlink control.

Table 3-8
Properties of the HyperLink control

Property	Description
Text	Represents the text displayed as a link.
ImageUrl	Represents the image displayed as a link. The image file should be stored in the same application project.
NavigateUrl	Represents the URL of the target page.

Note   The `ImageUrl` property takes precedence when both the `Text` and the `ImageUrl` properties are set.

The following code illustrates how to set the `NavigateUrl` property programmatically:

```
Dim HyperLink1 as New HyperLink()
HyperLink1.NavigateUrl="http://www.msn.com"
```

Table control

A table is used to display information in a tabular format. A table consists of rows and columns. The intersection of a row and a column is called a cell. You can add a table to a Web Forms page by using the Table control. This control displays information statically by setting the rows and columns at design time. Also, you can program the Table control to display information dynamically at run time.

You can add rows at design time by setting the `Rows` property, which represents a collection of TableRow objects; a TableRow object represents a row in the table. You can add cells to a table row by setting the `Cells` property of the TableRow object. The `Cells` property represents a collection of TableCell objects; a TableCell object represents a cell in a table row. Thus, to set rows and columns of a table at the design time, you first add the Table control to the form. Then, set the `Rows` property of the Table control to add TableRow objects. Finally, set the `Cells` property of the TableRow objects to add TableCells objects. The steps are given as follows:

1. Display the Properties window of the Table control.

2. Click the ellipsis button for the Rows property of the Table control.

3. In the TableRow Collection Editor dialog box, click Add to create a new row. A new row is created and its properties are displayed in the Properties pane of the dialog box.

4. Verify that the row is selected in the Members list, and then click the ellipsis button for the Cells property to add a cell for the row.

5. In the TableCell Collection Editor dialog box, click Add to create a new cell. A new cell is created and its properties are displayed at the right side of the dialog box. Table 3-9 describes some of the properties of the TableCell object.

You can also add the rows and columns (cells) to a table at run time programmatically. To do so, you first need to create the TableRow and TableCell objects:

```
Dim Table1 as New Table()
Dim TableRowObj As New TableRow()
Dim TableCellObj As New TableCell()
```

Then, you need to add the TableCell object to the TableRow object:

```
TableRowObj.Cells.Add(TableCellObj)
```

Finally, you need to add the TableRow object to the Table control. If the ID of the Table control is Table1, use the following code to add the TableRow object to the Table control:

```
Table1.Rows.Add(TableRowObj)
```

Table 3-9 **Properties of the TableCell object**	
Property	**Description**
ColumnSpan	Represents the number of columns that the cell spans. By default, this property is set to 0.
RowSpan	Represents the number of rows that the cell spans. By default, this property is set to 0.
VerticalAlign	Represents the vertical alignment, such as top and bottom of the cell.
HorizontalAlign	Represents the horizontal alignment, such as left and right of the cell.
Text	Represents the text contents of a cell.

The following Visual Basic .NET code snippet demonstrates how to add rows and cells (columns) at run time. Assume that the Web Forms page contains a Table control, a Button control, and two TextBox controls (to accept the number of rows and cells that need to be added to the table). The following code is also associated with the Click event of the Button control:

```
' Declare the total number of rows
Dim RowCnt As Integer
'Declare the current row counter
Dim RowCtr As Integer

'Declare the total number of cells
    Dim CellCtr As Integer
'Declare the current cell counter
Dim CellCnt As Integer

'Accept the total number of rows and columns from the user
RowCnt = Val(TextBox1.Text)
CellCnt = Val(TextBox2.Text)

For RowCtr = 1 To RowCnt
    'Creating a TableRow object
    Dim TableRowObj As New TableRow()
```

```
        For CellCtr = 1 To CellCnt
          'Creating a TableCell object
          Dim TableCellObj As New TableCell()
          TableCellObj.Text = RowCtr & "Row, " & CellCtr & "
Cell "
          'Add the new TableCell object to row
          TableRowObj.Cells.Add(TableCellObj)
        Next
        'Add new row to table
         Table1.Rows.Add(TableRowObj)
     Next
```

Image control

The Image control allows users to display images in a Web Forms page and manage them at design time or at run time. After you add an Image control to a Web Forms page, you need to set the image to be displayed in the control. You can do so by using the ImageUrl property. Table 3-10 describes some of the properties of the Image control.

Table 3-10
Properties of the Image control

Property	Description
ImageUrl	Represents the URL of the image to be displayed in the control.
ImageAlign	Represents the alignment of the image with respect to the other controls in the page and not just the text.
AlternateText	Represents the text that is displayed as a tooltip or when the image cannot be loaded.

Consider the following code that is used to set the ImageUrl property of the Image control in the Page_Load event:

```
Dim Img1 as New Image()
Img1.ImageUrl="Rose.gif"
```

Button, LinkButton, and ImageButton controls

The Button control on a Web Forms page is used to perform an event, such as form submit, on the server. You can create three types of server control buttons:

✦ **Button:** Represents a standard button.

✦ **LinkButton:** Represents a button that can act as a hyperlink in a page. However, a LinkButton control causes the page to be submitted to the server.

✦ **ImageButton:** Represents a graphical button to provide a rich button appearance. You can set the `ImageUrl` property to point to a specific image.

Table 3-11 describes some of the properties of the server control buttons.

Table 3-11
Properties of the button server control

Property	Available with	Description
Text	Button and LinkButton	Represents the text to be displayed on the Button and the LinkButton controls.
Enabled	Button, LinkButton, and ImageButton	Represents whether or not the button is available at run time. By default, this property is set to True, indicating that the button is available at run time.
ImageUrl	ImageButton	Represents the URL of the image to be displayed in the control.
AlternateText	ImageButton	Represents the text that is displayed as a tooltip or when the image cannot be loaded.

Working with Events

A Web Forms application provides fast, dynamic, and user-interactive Web Forms pages. When users interact with different Web controls on a page, events are raised. In the traditional client forms or client-based Web applications, the events are raised and handled on the client side. However, in Web Forms applications, the events are raised either on the client or on the server, but are always handled on the server. ASP.NET server controls support only server-side events, while HTML server controls support both server-side and client-side events.

Round trips

Most Web pages require processing on the server. For example, consider an Orders Web page used to receive orders on the Web. When a user enters a value for the quantity of a product to be bought, the page must check on the server to see whether or not the quantity requested is available. This type of dynamic functionality is accomplished by handling server control events. Whenever a user interaction requires some kind of processing on the server, the Web Forms page is submitted to the server, processed, and then returned to the browser (client). This sequence is called a *round trip*. Figure 3-5 describes round trips.

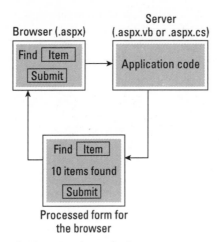

Figure 3-5: A round trip

Most of the user interactions with the server controls result in round trips. Because a round trip involves sending the Web Forms page to the server and then displaying the processed form in the browser, the server control events affect the response time in the form. Therefore the number of events available in Web Forms server controls is limited, usually to Click events. The events that occur quite often, such as the OnMouseOver event, are not supported by server controls. However, some server controls support events that occur when the control's value changes. Table 3-12 describes the events associated with different ASP.NET server controls.

Table 3-12
Events associated with ASP.NET server controls

Control(s)	Event	Description
TextBox	TextChanged	Occurs when the content of the text box is changed.
RadioButton and CheckBox	CheckedChanged Checked	Occurs when the value of the property changes.
RadioButtonList, CheckBoxList,ListBox, andDropDownList	SelectedIndexChanged	Occurs when you change the selection in the list.
Button, LinkButton, and ImageButton	Click	Occurs when you click the button. This event causes the form to be submitted to the server.

By default, only the `Click` event of the Button, LinkButton, and ImageButton server controls causes the form to be submitted to the server for processing—the form is said to be *posted back* to the server. The `Change` events associated with other controls are captured and cached and do not cause the form to be submitted immediately. When the form is posted back (as a result of a button click), all the pending events are raised and processed. No particular sequence exists for processing these `Change` events, such as `TextChanged` and `CheckChanged` on the server. The `Click` event is processed only after all the `Change` events are processed.

You can set the change events of server controls to result in the form post back to the server. To do so, modify the `AutoPostBack` property to True.

Event handlers

When the events are raised, you need to handle them for processing. The procedures that are executed when an event occurs are called *event handlers*. An event handler is associated with the corresponding event by using the `WithEvents` and `Handles` keywords. The `WithEvents` keyword is used to declare the control generating an event. For example, when you declare a control, say `Image1` as 'Protected WithEvents Image1 As System.Web.UI.WebControls.Image', the `WithEvents` keyword specifies that `Image1` is an object variable used to respond to events raised by the instance assigned to the variable. The `Handles` keyword is used to associate the event handler with the event, which is raised by the control. The control in turn is declared by using the `WithEvents` keywords.

Event handlers are automatically created when you double-click the control in Design mode of the form. For example, the following code is generated when you double-click a Button control whose ID is RegisterButton. You can then write the code in the event handler to perform the intended task.

```
Public Sub RegisterButton_Click(ByVal sender As System.Object,
ByVal e As System.EventArgs) Handles RegisterButton.Click

End Sub
```

In this code:

✦ The procedure `RegisterButton_Click` is the event handler for the `Click` event of the button with ID RegisterButton. The `Handles` keyword associates the event with the event handler.

✦ The procedure takes two arguments. The first argument contains the event sender. An *event sender* is an object, such as a form or a control, that can generate events. The second argument contains the event data.

Implementing the events and event handlers

After discussing the events and event handlers in detail, we'll now implement them for the Web Forms page shown in Figure 3-3, earlier in the chapter.

In Figure 3-3, when you click the Register button, another page should open displaying a relevant message along with the username entered in the UserName TextBox control. Before you can proceed to write the event handlers, you need to add another Web Forms page (the target page) to the Application project. To do so:

1. Select Project ➪ Add Web Form. The Add New Item dialog box opens.

2. Specify the name of the Web Forms page and click Open. In this case, leave the default name of the Web Forms page, WebForm2.aspx.

Tip   When you add a Web Forms page to a project, the name of the Web Forms page automatically takes the next number. For example, if WebForm1 already exists in the project, the default name of the new Web Forms page would be WebForm2.

Because the target page (WebForm2) should display a message, you need to add a Label control to this page. Set the ID property of this Label control to MessageLabel.

To implement this functionality, you need to write the following code in the Click event of the Register button (in the WebForm1 page):

```
Response.Redirect("WebForm2.aspx?strTextValue=" & "Hi," & UserName.Text & ", You
have been successfully registered")
```

In this code, the Response.Redirect method takes the URL of the target page. The URL specifies another form named WebForm2.aspx (that you added) and passes a text string along with the value in the TextBox control whose ID is UserName in a variable called strTextValue.

After passing the text in the strTextValue variable, the Label control in the target form, WebForm2, must be initialized in the Init procedure of the form as follows:

```
MessageLabel.Text = Request.QueryString("strTextValue")
```

In this code, the value stored in the strTextValue is set as the caption of the label with ID MessageLabel in WebForm2.

The Web Forms page displayed in Figure 3-3 also contains a Reset button. When you click the Reset button, all the controls should be empty. To implement this functionality, use the following code:

```
UserName.Text = ""
Email.Text = ""
```

```
USStateList.ClearSelection()
SexOption.ClearSelection()
SubscriptionOptions.ClearSelection()
```

In this code:

✦ The `Text` property of the TextBox controls with IDs UserName and Email are set to a null value.

✦ `ClearSelection` is a method of the list controls, such as ListBox, DropDownList, CheckBoxList, and RadioButtonList controls. The method is used to clear any selection made in the list.

Handling post back

As mentioned earlier, the Web Forms page is posted back to the server only when a Button, LinkButton, or ImageButton ASP.NET server control is clicked. After the page is posted to the server, it is processed there. You can respond to a button event in one of the following ways:

✦ Write an event handler for the `Click` event of the button.

✦ Write the event handler for the `Load` event of the Web Forms page. The `Load` event is generated when the form is loaded from the server to the client (browser). You can use the `IsPostBack` property in the `Load` event to determine whether the page has been processed for the first time or by a button click. To understand the `IsPostBack` property better, consider the following code in the `Page_Load` event of the WebForm1 page. The following code checks whether the `IsPostBack` property is True. If it is, the `Visible` property of the Register button is set to False.

```
Private Sub Page_Load(ByVal sender As System.Object, ByVal e
As
System.EventArgs) Handles MyBase.Load
    If ResetButton.Page.IsPostBack = True Then
        RegisterButton.Visible = False
    End If
End Sub
```

Using the view state

In all Web applications, whenever a Web page is processed at the server, the page is created from scratch. In traditional Web applications, the server discards the page information after processing and sending the page to the browser. Because the page information is not preserved on the server, the Web pages are called *stateless*. However, the Web Forms framework works around this limitation and can save the state information of the form and its controls. To implement this, the Web Forms framework provides the following options:

✦ **The ViewState:** The framework automatically saves the state of the page and its current properties, and the state of the server controls and their base properties, with each round trip.

✦ **The State Bags:** Every page has a state bag that stores values to be restored in the next round trip.

The framework automatically stores and restores page information with each round trip. So, you do not need to worry about storing and restoring the page information with each round trip.

The ViewState contains the state of all the controls on a page between requests sent to the server. The state information is stored as hidden form fields as name-value pairs in the System.Web.UI.StateBag object. When you view an ASP.NET page in a browser, you can see the ViewState for this page by displaying the source code of the page. To do so, select View ⇨ Source in the browser in which the ASP.NET page is displayed. The ViewState thus is stored in a page rather than in the server. For complex pages that contain many controls, the ViewState information is too large to be stored in a page and might affect the performance of the page. This is the only disadvantage with ViewState.

By default, the ViewState is enabled for all the server controls. All the server controls have the `EnableViewState` property set to True by default. Therefore, to take advantage of the ViewState, you do not need to do anything explicitly. However, as already mentioned, due to performance issues, you can set the `EnableViewState` property to False to disable the ViewState. If you do not want to maintain the state of any of the server controls on an ASP.NET page, you can set the `EnableViewState` property of the page to False:

```
<%@ Page EnableViewState="false" %>
```

Summary

This chapter served as a foundation for creating Web Forms applications. This chapter introduced you to the basic Web controls used for designing Web Forms pages. You learned the basic steps to create a Web Application project. Then, you learned the usage and properties of Web controls. The chapter also introduced you to events. You learned how to handle server-side events. Finally, you learned to handle post back and use the view state.

✦   ✦   ✦

Using Rich Web Controls

ASP.NET has brought about a complete change in the way controls are used in Web applications. In addition to the client-side rendering of controls, ASP.NET provides controls that can be rendered on the server side. This allows server-side processing, and thus provides dynamic Web pages resulting in a rich and improved user experience.

The previous chapter discussed the basic Web controls. In addition to these Web controls, there are specific Web controls that have more complex and rich functionality. These controls are called Rich Web controls, examples of which are the AdRotator and Calendar controls. Some of the Rich Web controls include:

✦ TreeView

✦ TabStrip

✦ MultiPage

✦ Toolbar

In this chapter, you will learn about the functionality of these Rich Web controls and learn how to work with them in ASP.NET.

Using the AdRotator Control

The AdRotator control is used to display flashing ads, such as banner ads and news flashes on Web pages. The control is capable of displaying ads randomly, because the control refreshes the display every time the Web page is refreshed, thereby displaying different ads for different users. Also, you can assign priorities to the ads so that certain ads are displayed more frequently than others.

You can add the AdRotator control in an ASP.NET Web page by using the following syntax:

```
<asp:AdRotator
propertyname = propertyvalue
propertyname = propertyvalue
>
</asp:AdRotator>
```

Alternatively, you can use the toolbox provided with VS.NET to add the control to the page. When you do so, the code is automatically generated and can be seen in the HTML view of the ASPX file.

Properties of the AdRotator control

Along with the properties that are inherited from the System.Web.UI.Control base class, the AdRotator control has three additional properties:

✦ AdvertisementFile

✦ KeywordFilter

✦ Target

This section describes these properties in detail.

AdvertisementFile

The AdvertisementFile property represents the path to an Advertisement file. The *Advertisement file* is a well-formed XML document that contains information about the image to be displayed for advertisement and the page to which a user is redirected when the user clicks the banner or image. The following is the syntax of the Advertisement file:

```
<Advertisements>
  <Ad>
    <ImageUrl>
      URL of the image to display
    </ImageUrl>
    <NavigateUrl>
      URL of the page to navigate to
    </NavigateUrl>
    <AlternateText>
      Text to be displayed as ToolTip
    </AlternateText>
    <Keyword>
      keyword used to filter
    </Keyword>
    <Impressions>
      relative weighting of ad
    </Impressions>
  </Ad>
</Advertisements>
```

Note   The Advertisement file must be a well-formed XML document, as the AdvertisementFile property of the AdRotator control needs to be set to an XML file.

The following are the different elements used in the Advertisement file:

✦ ImageUrl: Specifies an absolute or relative URL to an image file that presents the image for the advertisement. This element refers to the image that will be rendered in a browser.

✦ NavigateUrl: Specifies the URL of a page to navigate to, if a user clicks the advertisement image. If this parameter is not set, the ad is not "live." Although this parameter is optional, it must be specified, because the ad must direct clients to a target URL when it is clicked.

✦ AlternateText: Is an optional parameter that specifies some alternative text that will be displayed if the image specified in the ImageUrl parameter is not accessible. In some browsers, the AlternateText parameter appears as a ToolTip for the ad.

✦ Keyword: Is an optional parameter that specifies categories, such as computers, books, and magazines that can be used to filter for specific ads.

✦ Impressions: Is an optional parameter that provides a number that indicates the weight of the ad in the schedule of rotation relative to the other ads in the file. The larger the number, the more often the ad will be displayed.

KeywordFilter

The KeywordFilter property specifies a category filter to be passed to the source of the advertisement. A keyword filter allows the AdRotator control to display ads that match a given keyword. This enables the AdRotator control to display more context-sensitive ads, where the context is specified in the ASPX page containing the AdRotator control. When you use a keyword filter, three conditions arise:

✦ Both the KeywordFilter and AdvertisementFile properties are set. In such a case, the AdRotator control renders the image that matches the keyword specified.

✦ The AdvertisementFile property points to a valid Advertisement file, and the KeywordFilter property specifies a keyword that matches no images. In such a case, the control renders a blank image, and a trace warning is generated.

✦ The KeywordFilter property is empty. In such a case, keyword filtering will not be used to select an ad.

Target

The Target property specifies the name of the browser window or frame in which the advertisement needs to be displayed. This parameter can also take any of the HTML frame-related keywords, such as the following:

✦ _top: Loads the linked document into the topmost window.

✦ _blank: Loads the linked document into a new browser window.

✦ _self: Loads the linked document in the same window.

✦ _parent: Loads the linked document in the parent window of the window that contains the link.

After looking at the properties, let's understand the events associated with the AdRotator control.

Events of the AdRotator control

The AdRotator control supports the adCreated event that you can handle to monitor the activities of a user or a session. The adCreated event is generated with every round trip to the server, after the AdRotator control is created but before the page is rendered in the browser. The event handler for the adCreated event is OnAdCreated and has the following syntax:

```
OnAdCreated (sender as Object, e as AdCreatedEventArgs)
```

The event handler takes two parameters. The first parameter represents the object that raises the event. The second parameter represents the AdCreatedEventArgs object that contains the data related to this event. The AdCreatedEventArgs object has a set of properties that provide information specific to the AdCreated event:

✦ AdProperties: Is an IDictionary type object that provides all the advertisement properties that have been set for the currently selected advertisement.

✦ AlternateText: Is a String type value that sets the ALT property of the image that is sent to the browser. In some browsers, this text is displayed as a ToolTip when the mouse cursor hovers over the image.

✦ ImageUrl: Is a String value that sets the URL of the image that is displayed in the AdRotator control.

✦ NavigateUrl: Is a String type value that specifies the URL of the Web page to navigate to when a user clicks the advertisement.

The OnAdCreated event handler can be used to select ads in a local code or to modify the rendering of an ad selected from the Advertisement file. If an advertisement file is set, the parameters of the AdCreated event handler are set to the selected ad when the event is generated. The source image that is specified by the Advertisement file is sized by the browser to the dimensions of the AdRotator control, regardless of the image's actual size. The ad is selected based on impressions weighting from the file.

If the values are not set in the Advertisement file, the developer can modify the values in the ImageUrl, NavigateUrl, and AlternateText properties to modify the rendering of the AdRotator control. A very common use of this is when developers need to populate the event arguments with values pulled from a database.

Rendering ads to client browsers using AdRotator

The following code uses the AdRotator server-side control to render ads to the client browsers. The AdRotator control uses an Advertisement file named Ads.xml.

```
<%@ Page Language="VB" %>
<html>
    <head>
    </head>

    <body>
     <form runat="server">
       <h3><font face="Verdana">AdRotator Example</font></h3>
       <asp:AdRotator id="AdRotator1" runat="server"
AdvertisementFile="Ads.xml"/>
    </form>

    </body>

</html>
```

The following code describes the Ads.xml file that is used by the AdRotator control. The file contains two advertisements that will be dynamically shown to different users. The first ad points to an image file named Saturn.gif. When users click this image, they are directed to the Saturn Web site. The second ad points to the image named Moon.jpg. When users click this image, they are directed to the Moon Web site.

```
<Advertisements>
  <Ad>
    <ImageUrl>
       saturn.gif
    </ImageUrl>

    <NavigateUrl>
       http://www.saturnrings.com/
    </NavigateUrl>

    <AlternateText>
     Saturn Rings Web Site
    </AlternateText>
    <Impressions>
       1
    </Impressions>
    <Keyword>
       Saturn
    </Keyword>
  </Ad>
```

```
<Ad>
  <ImageUrl>
    Moon.jpg
  </ImageUrl>
  <NavigateUrl>
    http://www.moon.com
  </NavigateUrl>
  <AlternateText>
    Moon Explorers Web Site
  </AlternateText>
  <Impressions>
    1
  </Impressions>
  <Keyword>
    Moon
  </Keyword>
</Ad>
</Advertisements>
```

Figure 4-1 shows the output of the preceding code.

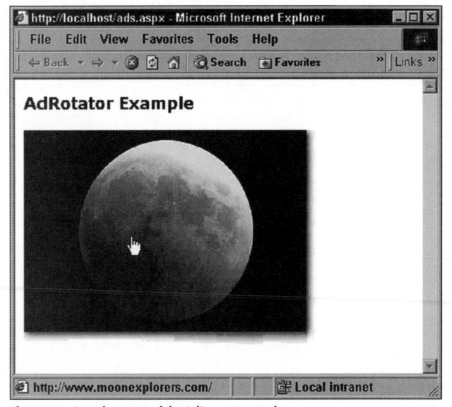

Figure 4-1: Sample output of the AdRotator control

Using the Calendar Control

The Calendar control is used to display a one-month calendar. Users can use this control to view dates or select a specific day, week, or month.

The following is the syntax to add the Calendar control:

```
<asp:Calendar id="Calendar1" runat="server"
    propertyname = propertyvalue
    propertyname = propertyvalue
/>
```

Properties of the Calendar control

The Calendar control has properties that you can set when you add the control to your page. Table 4-1 describes some of the properties of the Calendar control.

Table 4-1
Properties of the Calendar control

Property	Description
CellPadding	Specifies the space between cells.
CellSpacing	Specifies the space between the contents of a cell and the cell's border.
DayNameFormat	Specifies the format of the day name.
FirstDayOfWeek	Sets a value for the day of the week that will be displayed in the calendar's first column.
ShowNextPrevMonth	Takes a Boolean value and specifies whether or not the calendar is capable of displaying next and previous month hyperlinks.
NextMonthText	Shows the HTML text for the "Next Month" navigation hyperlink if the ShowNextPrevMonth property is set to true.
NextPrevFormat	Specifies the format of the next month and previous month hyperlinks.
PrevMonthText	Shows the HTML text for the previous month hyperlink if the ShowNextPrevMonth property is set to true.
SelectedDate	Represents the date selected in the Calendar control.

Continued

Table 4-1 *(continued)*

Property	Description
SelectedDates	Specifies a collection of DateTime objects representing days highlighted on the calendar. This is a read-only property.
SelectionMode	Specifies whether the user can select a day, week, or month. The default is Day.
SelectMonthText	Shows the HTML text for the month selection in the selector column if the SelectionMode property is set to DayWeekMonth.
SelectWeekText	Shows the HTML text for the week selection in the selector column if the SelectionMode property is set to DayWeek or DayWeekMonth.
ShowDayHeader	Specifies whether or not to display the names of the days of the week.
ShowGridLines	Specifies a value that determines whether or not the days in the calendar should be displayed with gridlines around them. However, even if the property specifies to display lines around the calendar days, not all browsers can display the gridlines.
TitleFormat	Specifies the format of the month name in the title bar of the calendar.
TodaysDate	Specifies the current date.
VisibleDate	Specifies the month to be displayed in the calendar. The property is updated after the VisibleMonthChanged event is raised.

In addition to the properties in Table 4-1, the Calendar control has certain style objects associated with it. The style objects are used to set the appearance of the individual elements, such as the appearance of the day and week values of the control. Some style objects are described in Table 4-2.

Table 4-2
Style objects

Property	Description
DayHeaderStyle	Sets the appearance of the days of the current month.
DayStyle	Sets the appearance of the row above the calendar where the day names appear.
NextPrevStyle	Sets the appearance of the sections at the left and right ends of the title bar.

Property	Description
OtherMonthDayStyle	Sets the appearance of the days that are not in the displayed month.
SelectedDayStyle	Sets the appearance of the day selected by the user.
SelectorStyle	Sets the style properties for the week and month selector.
TitleStyle	Sets the appearance of the title bar at the top of the calendar containing the month name and month navigation links. If the value for NextPrevStyle is set, it overrides the extreme ends of the title bar.
TodayDayStyle	Sets the appearance of the current date.
WeekendDayStyle	Sets the appearance of the weekend days.

Events of the Calendar control

The Calendar control supports certain events that make the control interactive on the Web page. The supported events include the DayRender, SelectionChanged, and VisibleMonthChanged events. This section covers these events in detail.

DayRender event

The DayRender event is generated when a day cell is rendered. You can trap this event to modify the format and content of a particular day cell before the cell is rendered. The event handler for this event is OnDayRender and has the following syntax:

```
OnDayRender (sender as Object, e as DayRenderEventArgs)
```

The DayRenderEventArgs parameter contains data pertaining to this event. This object has the following properties that can be used to make changes to the appearance of the day cell:

✦ Cell: Refers to a TableCell object that represents a table cell into which the day is rendered. A TableCell object has the following properties:

- RowSpan: Represents the number of rows in the table that the cell spans.

- ColumnSpan: Represents the number of columns in the table that the cell spans.

- HorizontalAlign: Controls the horizontal alignment of the cell contents.

- VerticalAlign: Controls the vertical alignment of the cell contents.

- Wrap: Determines whether or not the contents wrap to fit the contents in the cell.

✦ Day: Refers to a `CalendarDay` object that represents the day being rendered. A `CalendarDay` object has the following properties:

- `Date`: Represents the date, such as 15 July 2000, being rendered.

- `DayNumberText`: Is a String that in turn represents the number of the day. For example, "15" is the `DayNumberText` for 15 July 2000.

- `IsOtherMonth`: Is a Boolean value that returns True if the day cell being rendered is in the Calendar control's currently displayed month.

- `IsSelectable`: Returns a Boolean value indicating whether or not the day cell being rendered can be selected.

- `IsSelected`: Returns a Boolean value indicating whether or not the day cell being rendered is selected.

- `IsToday`: Returns a Boolean value indicating whether or not the day cell being rendered is today's date.

- `IsWeekend`: Returns a Boolean value indicating whether or not the day cell being rendered is a Saturday or Sunday.

SelectionChanged event

The `SelectionChanged` event is generated when a user selects a day, week, or month by clicking the Calendar control. You can handle this event to validate against business logic the date selected by users. The event handler for this event is `OnSelectionChanged` and has the following syntax:

```
OnSelectionChange(sender As Object, e As EventArgs)
```

The `sender` parameter points to the control that generated this event, and any event-specific values are stored in the `EventArgs` object.

MonthChanged event

The `MonthChanged` event is generated when a user clicks the next or previous month navigation controls on the title heading of the Calendar control. The event handler for this event is `OnVisibleMonthChanged` and has the following syntax:

```
OnVisibleMonthChanged(sender  as Object, e as
MonthChangedEventArgs)
```

The `MonthRenderEventArgs` parameter contains data pertaining to this event. This object has the following properties that can be used to make changes to the appearance of the month:

✦ `NewDate`: Is a `DateTime` object that represents the new month that is selected.

✦ `PreviousDate`: Is a `DateTime` object that represents the previous month selected.

Rendering a Calendar to client browsers using the Calendar control

The following code uses the Calendar control to render a calendar in the client browsers:

```
<%@ Page Language="VB" %>
<html>
  <head>
   <script runat="server">
    Sub OnSelectionChanged (sender as Object, e as EventArgs)
      lblSelDate.Text = Calendar1.SelectedDate
    End Sub
   </script>
  </head>
  <body>
   <h3><font face="Verdana">Calendar control demo</font></h3>
   <form runat="server">
   <asp:Calendar id="Calendar1" runat="server"
     SelectionMode="DayWeekMonth"
     Font-Name="Verdana;Arial" Font-Size="12px"
     Height="180px" Width="230px"
     TodayDayStyle-Font-Bold="True"
     DayHeaderStyle-Font-Bold="True"
     OtherMonthDayStyle-ForeColor="gray"
     TitleStyle-BackColor="#3366ff"
     TitleStyle-ForeColor="white"
     TitleStyle-Font-Bold="True"
     SelectedDayStyle-BackColor="#ffcc66"
     SelectedDayStyle-Font-Bold="True"
     NextPrevFormat="ShortMonth"
     NextPrevStyle-ForeColor="white"
     NextPrevStyle-Font-Size="10px"
     SelectorStyle-BackColor="#99ccff"
     SelectorStyle-ForeColor="navy"
     SelectorStyle-Font-Size="9px"
     SelectWeekText = "wk"
     SelectMonthText = "month"
     OnSelectionChanged="OnSelectionChanged"
    />
    <BR>
    <asp:label style="font-name:Verdana;font-
  size:12px;forecolor:gray" id="lblSelDate" runat="server"/>
   </form>
  </body>
</html>
```

Figure 4-2 shows the output of the preceding code. When you select a date, the date is displayed on the label.

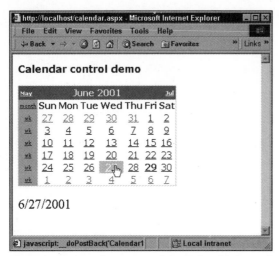

Figure 4-2: Sample output of the Calendar control

Using the TreeView Control

The TreeView control is used to present hierarchical data to users in the Windows Explorer–style format, wherein the items can be expanded and collapsed. This control, like the other ASP.NET Server controls, is rendered as an HTML 3.2-compatible tree in older browser versions, such as Microsoft Internet Explorer 3.0. In newer browser versions, such as Microsoft Internet Explorer 5.5 and higher, this control is rendered by using the Dynamic HTML (DHTML) behaviors. Hence, compared to the older browser versions, the user experience is richer in the more recent browser versions.

Unlike the standard ASP.NET controls, TreeView and the other controls discussed in the sections to follow are not shipped as part of the ASP.NET Framework. These are additional controls that must be installed separately. Therefore, when you want to use these controls in an ASP.NET page, you must explicitly import the assemblies containing these controls. To import the assemblies, use the following code:

```
<%@import namespace="Microsoft.Web.UI.WebControls"%>
<%@Register TagPrefix="tp" Namespace =
"Microsoft.Web.UI.WebControls"
Assembly="Microsoft.Web.UI.WebControls"%>
```

The import directive causes ASP.NET to import the contents of the specified namespace. The Register directive causes ASP.NET to identify all the controls in the specified assembly with the tag prefix "tp."

To add a TreeView control to the page, use the following syntax:

```
<tagprefix:TreeView runat="Server">
   <tagprefix:treenode text=".." DefaultStyle="  " HoverStyle="
"
SelectedStyle="  ">
<tagprefix:treenodetype Type="  " ChildType="  ">
      <tagprefix:treenode text="  "/>
<tagprefix:treenode text="  ">
</tagprefix:treenode>
</tagprefix:treenodetype>
```

The elements used in the preceding code are explained as follows:

✦ TreeView: Defines a TreeView control. It acts as a container for the nodes of the tree. The TreeView control is made up of various elements, every one of which is referred to as a *node*. Some nodes contain other nodes called *child* nodes. The container nodes are called *parent* nodes.

✦ TreeNode: Represents the node in the TreeView control.

✦ TreeNodeType: Defines the type of a node. A single TreeView control can have different types of nodes, such as a folder or any custom type.

Properties of the TreeView control

In addition to the properties that are inherited from the System.Web.UI.Control base class, the TreeView control has properties that can be used to control the behavior of the control. Some of these properties are described in Table 4-3.

Table 4-3
Properties of the TreeView control

Property	Description
AutoPostBack	Takes a Boolean value and indicates whether or not the control posts back to the server on each client request.
AutoSelect	Takes a Boolean value and indicates whether or not a tree node can be selected by simply pointing the mouse to the node, without having to click the node.
DefaultStyle	Sets a default style for the elements in the tree.
ExpandedImageURL	Sets an image to be displayed when a node is expanded.
HoverStyle	Sets a style, such as "font-family:Verdana;font-size:12pt; color:black," for the elements in the tree when the mouse hovers over them.

Continued

Table 4-3 *(continued)*	
Property	**Description**
ImageURL	Sets an image to be displayed to represent a node.
Indent	Sets the number of pixels by which the child nodes need to be indented.
ShowLines	Takes a Boolean value and indicates whether or not lines are used to connect the nodes in the tree.

Events of the TreeView control

The events supported by the TreeView control include Collapse, Expand, and SelectedIndexChanged. The sections that follow look at each of these events in detail.

Collapse event

The Collapse event is generated when a user clicks a tree node to collapse it. You can trap this event to control the format and decide the contents of a particular node and its child nodes. The event handler for this event is OnCollapse and has the following syntax:

```
OnCollapse(sender As Object, e As TreeViewClickEventArgs)
```

As you can see, the event handler takes two arguments. The first argument, As Object, represents the object that generated the event. The second argument is the object of the TreeViewClickEventArgs class. This object contains the node information pertaining to this event. A Node object refers to the index of the node that was clicked, and has the following properties:

✦ Expandable: Sets or retrieves a value that indicates whether or not a plus-sign image is displayed with the node. A plus-sign image indicates that the node is expandable.

✦ Expanded: Indicates whether or not the node is expanded.

✦ Level: Returns the level of the node; level 0 refers to the root.

✦ Text: Returns the text of the selected node.

Expand event

The Expand event is generated when a user clicks a tree node to expand it. You can trap this event to control the formatting and decide the contents of a particular node and its child nodes. The event handler for this event is OnExpand and has the following syntax:

```
OnExpand(sender As Object, e As TreeViewClickEventArgs)
```

The second parameter is an object of the `TreeViewClickEventArgs` class and contains the data pertaining to the `Expand` event.

SelectedIndexChanged event

The `SelectedIndex` event is generated when a user clicks the TreeView control to change the active tree node. This causes the TreeView control to move the highlight from the node that was selected earlier to the newly selected node. You can trap this event to control the formatting and decide the contents of the selected node. The event handler for this event is `OnSelectedIndexChanged` and has the following syntax:

```
OnSelectedIndexChanged(sender As Object, e As
TreeViewSelectEventArgs)
```

The second parameter is the `TreeViewSelectEventArgs` object and contains the data pertaining to the `SelectedIndexChanged` event. This object has the following properties that can be used to make changes to the appearance of the selected node:

✦ `NewNode`: Refers to a `Node` object that represents the tree node that has been selected.

✦ `OldNode`: Refers to a `Node` object that represents the tree node that was previously selected.

Rendering a TreeView control

The following code renders a TreeView control in a page:

```
<%@ Page Language="VB" %>
<%@import namespace="Microsoft.Web.UI.WebControls"%>
<%@Register TagPrefix="mytree" Namespace =
"Microsoft.Web.UI.WebControls"
Assembly="Microsoft.Web.UI.WebControls"%>
<html>
    <script language="VB" runat="server">
    Sub OnCollapse( sender as Object, e as
TreeViewClickEventArgs)
      'append node index to the label control when tree is
      'collapsed
      mylabel.Text += "<BR>Collapsed (Node Index = " &
e.Node.ToString() + ")"
    End Sub
```

```
    Sub OnExpand (sender as Object , e as
TreeViewClickEventArgs )
        ' append node index to label control when tree is
        'expanded
        mylabel.Text += "<BR>Expanded (Node Index= " &
e.Node.ToString() + ")"
    End Sub

    Sub OnSelectedIndexChanged ( sender as Object,  e as
TreeViewSelectEventArgs)
        ' append node index to label control when a new node is
        'selected in the tree
        mylabel.Text += "<BR>Selected " & e.NewNode.ToString() &
" (oldNode Index=" + e.OldNode.ToString()+")"
    End Sub
    </script>
<head>
</head>

<body>

    <h3><font face="Verdana">TreeView control demo</font></h3>
    <form runat="server">

    <!—render tree view control, setup event handlers for
collapse, expand and selectedindexchanged events -->

    <mytree:TreeView runat="server" AutoPostBack="true"
DefaultStyle="font-name:Verdana;font-size:12pt;color:black;"
SelectedStyle="font-face:Verdana;font-size:12pt;color:white;"
OnCollapse="OnCollapse" OnExpand="OnExpand"
OnSelectedIndexChanged="OnSelectedIndexChanged">
        <mytree:treenode text="Asia">
            <mytree:treenode text="China"/>
            <mytree:treenode text="India"/>
        </mytree:treenode>
        <mytree:treenode text="Africa">
            <mytree:treenode text="Zaire"/>
            <mytree:treenode text="Zambia"/>
        </mytree:treenode>
        <mytree:treenode text="North America">
            <mytree:treenode text="Canada"/>
            <mytree:treenode text="United States"/>
        </mytree:treenode>
    </mytree:treeview>
<br>
    <asp:label id=mylabel runat="server">Event Log: </asp:label>
    </form>
</body>
</html>
```

Figure 4-3 shows the output of the preceding code.

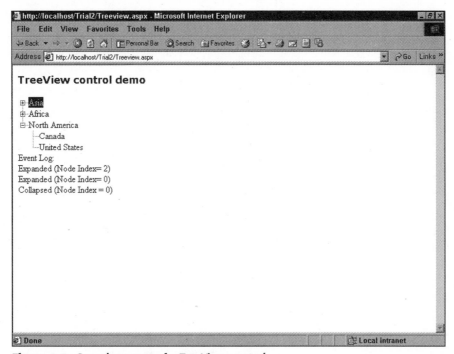

Figure 4-3: Sample output of a TreeView control

Using the TabStrip and MultiPage Controls

The TabStrip control is used to present tabbed controls, which can be used along with the MultiPage control to display varied information in a given space. The TabStrip control renders tabs that users can click to switch between the different tabs. The MultiPage control is used to display multiple pages of data in a given screen area. This control is typically used with the TabStrip control.

TabStrip control

You use the following syntax to add a TabStrip control to a page:

```
<tagprefix:TabStrip runat="Server" TabDefaultStyle=".."
TabHoverStyle=".." TabSelectedStyle=".." SepDefaultStyle="..">

    <tagprefix:Tab text=".." >
      <tagprefix:Tab text="Node1.1"/>
      <tagprefix:Tab text="Node1.2">
    </tagprefix:Tab>
</tagprefix:TabStrip>
```

The TabStrip control uses the following elements to define the tabbed interface to be rendered:

✦ `TabStrip`: Defines a TabStrip control, which acts as a container for the tabs and tab separators.

✦ `Tab`: Defines a tab element in the TabStrip control, which is rendered on the client browser as tabs on top of the tab strip.

✦ `TabSeparator`: Represents the separator bars between the tabs.

Table 4-4 describes some of the properties of the TabStrip control.

	Table 4-4 **Properties of the TabStrip control**
Property	*Description*
`AutoPostBack`	Specifies whether or not the control posts back to the server on every client request.
`DefaultStyle`	Specifies the default style of the TabStrip control.
`Orientation`	Specifies the orientation of the tabs, which can be horizontal or vertical.
`SelectedIndex`	Returns the index of the selected tab.
`SepDefaultStyle`	Specifies the default style for the tab separators.
`SepHoverStyle`	Specifies the style to be applied to the tab separators when the mouse hovers over the separators.
`TargetID`	Specifies the name of the MultiPage control to which the tabs will be linked automatically.

The TabStrip control supports the `SelectedIndexChanged` event, which is fired when a user shifts from one tab to another. This event can be trapped to control the formatting and decide the contents of a particular tab. The event handler for this event is `OnSelectedIndexChanged` and has the following syntax:

```
OnSelectedIndexChanged(sender As Object, e as EventArgs)
```

The second parameter is the `EventArgs` object and contains data pertaining to this event.

MultiPage control

The MultiPage control is a container control that contains a set of PageView elements, which are used to render different pages in a given screen space. The PageView elements contain the visible part of the MultiPage control. The MultiPage control is typically used with the TabStrip control to give users the ability to navigate from one page to another.

The following code segment creates a MultiPage control with two PageView elements:

```
<tagprefix:MultiPage runat="server" selectedindex="1">
   <tagprefix:PageView>
     <P> Data for page view <B>1</B> </P>
   </tagprefix:PageView>

   <tagprefix:PageView>
     <P> Data for page view <B>2</B> </P>
   </tagprefix:PageView>

</tagprefix:MultiPage>
```

Just like the TabStrip control, the MultiPage control supports the `SelectedIndex` property, which indicates the selected PageView.

Using MultiPage and TabStrip controls together

As mentioned, the TabStrip control provides navigation capabilities and the MultiPage control provides the ability to view multiple pages in the same screen area. The two controls typically are used in combination.

To actually combine the MultiPage control with the TabStrip control, you need to set the `TargetID` property of the TabStrip control to the ID of the MultiPage control. This enables the TabStrip control to automatically switch from one PageView element to another when a user clicks a tab.

The following code renders the TabStrip and MultiPage controls on the page:

```
<%@ Page Language="VB" %>
<%@import namespace="Microsoft.Web.UI.WebControls"%>
<%@Register TagPrefix="myts" Namespace =
"Microsoft.Web.UI.WebControls"
Assembly="Microsoft.Web.UI.WebControls"%>
```

```
<html>
<head>
</head>
<body>
    <h3><font face="Verdana">TabStrip and MultiPage control
demo</font></h3>

    <!—render the TabStrip control and set the TargetID to point
to the multipage control-->

    <form runat="server">

    <myts:TabStrip id="ts1" runat="server"
TabDefaultStyle="background-color:lightgrey;font-
family:verdana;font-weight:bold;font-size:8pt;color:blue;width:
79;height:21;text-align:center"
TabHoverStyle="background-color:#777777"
TabSelectedStyle="background-color:darkgray;color:#000000"
SepDefaultStyle="background-color:#FFFFFF;border-
color:darkblue;border-width:3px;border-style:solid;border-top:n
one;border-left:none;border-right:none" TargetID="mymultipage">

        <myts:Tab Text="Home" />
        <myts:TabSeparator/>
        <myts:Tab Text="About us" />
        <myts:TabSeparator/>
        <myts:Tab Text="Products" />
    </myts:TabStrip>

    <!—render the MultiPage control and notice that the id of
the control has been set as the targetID of the TabStrip
control-->

    <myts:MultiPage id="mymultipage" runat="server">
        <myts:pageview><P><H3 style="font-family:verdana">
Welcome to our Home page! </H3> <br> Click on the tabs on top
to switch to other pages in our web site.</P></myts:pageview>

        <myts:pageview><P><H3 style="font-family:verdana"> About
Us  </H3></P></myts:pageview>

        <myts:pageview><P><H3 style="font-family:verdana">
Product Information here
</H3></P></myts:pageview></myts:multipage>
    </form>
</body>
</html>
```

The output of the preceding code is shown in Figure 4-4.

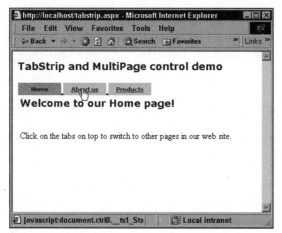

Figure 4-4: Sample output of the TabStrip and MultiPage controls

Using the Toolbar Control

The Toolbar control is used to render a toolbar in the client browsers. At the simplest level, a toolbar is a collection of graphical buttons. The Toolbar control is typically used to provide the commonly used functionality to users in a graphical form.

To add the Toolbar control to a page, use the following syntax:

```
<tagprefix:Toolbar ..>
  <tagprefix:ToolbarButton Text=".." ImageUrl=".." />
  <tagprefix:ToolbarSeparator />
  <tagprefix:ToolbarButton Text=".." ImageUrl=".."/>
  <tagprefix:ToolbarButton Text=".." ImageUrl=".."/>
</tagprefix:Toolbar>
```

As you can see in the preceding syntax, the Toolbar control is a container control that contains elements to define a toolbar. These elements are described as follows:

✦ ToolbarButton: Defines a button on the toolbar.

✦ ToolbarCheckButton: Defines a check button on the toolbar.

✦ ToolbarCheckGroup: Defines a group of check buttons on the toolbar.

✦ ToolbarLabel: Defines a label to display plain text on the toolbar.

✦ ToolbarSeparator: Defines a separator on the toolbar, which is useful in identifying the separate groups of toolbar buttons.

✦ ToolbarTextBox: Defines a text box on the toolbar.

Properties of the Toolbar control

In addition to the properties that are inherited from the System.Web.UI.Control base class, the Toolbar control has additional properties. Table 4-5 describes some of these properties.

Table 4-5 Properties of the Toolbar control	
Property	**Description**
AutoPostBack	Specifies whether or not the control posts back to the server on every client request.
DefaultStyle	Specifies the default style of the toolbar.
HoverStyle	Specifies the style to be applied when the mouse hovers over the toolbar.
SelectedStyle	Specifies the style to be applied when the toolbar items are selected
Orientation	Specifies the orientation of the toolbar, which can be horizontal or vertical.

Note   Every button on the toolbar has three states — Default, Selected, and Hover. You can define appropriate CSS styles for each of the three states. Then, ASP.NET will apply the appropriate style when rendering the button.

Events of the Toolbar control

The Toolbar control supports the ButtonClick and CheckChange events, which make the control interactive when rendered on a page. The following sections look at each of the events in detail.

ButtonClick event

The ButtonClick event is generated when a user clicks a toolbar button. The event handler for this event is OnButtonClick and has the following syntax:

```
OnButtonClick(sender As Object, e As EventArgs)
```

The second parameter is the EventArgs object and contains the data pertaining to this event. To retrieve the toolbar data in the event handler, the sender variable must be converted into a variable of type ToolbarButton. To see how the data is converted, see the example of the toolbar control in the upcoming section "Rendering a toolbar."

CheckChange event

The `CheckChange` event is generated when the state of a ToolbarCheckButton changes. This event is trapped to respond to any change in the state of a ToolbarCheckButton. Here is the event handler for this event:

```
OnCheckChange(sender As Object, e As EventArgs)
```

The `EventArgs` parameter contains data pertaining to this event. To retrieve the toolbar data in the event handler, the `sender` variable must be converted into a variable of type ToolbarButton. The syntax for the same is given as follows:

```
Dim tb as ToolbarButton
tb=CType(sender,ToolbarButton)
```

Rendering a toolbar

The following code example renders a toolbar on the page:

```
<%@ Page Language="VB" %>
<%@import namespace="Microsoft.Web.UI.WebControls"%>
<%@Register TagPrefix="ie" Namespace =
"Microsoft.Web.UI.WebControls"
Assembly="Microsoft.Web.UI.WebControls"%>
<html>

    <script runat="server" language="VB">
       sub OnButtonClick(sender as object, e as EventArgs)
          Dim sMsg as String, tb as ToolbarButton
          'convert from Object type to ToolbarButton type
          tb=CType(sender,ToolbarButton)
          sMsg="<BR>You chose to : <B>" & tb.Text & "</B>"
          lblMessage.Text = sMsg
       End Sub
    </script>

<head>
</head>
<body>
    <h3><font face="Verdana">ToolBar control demo</font></h3>
    <!—display toolbar control, setup event handler for
Buttonclick Event-->
    <form runat="server">
    <ie:Toolbar id="tb2" runat="server" BorderColor="Gray"
Font-Name="Tahoma" Font-Size="8pt" BackColor="#CCCCCC"
Width="75%" OnButtonClick="OnButtonClick">
       <ie:ToolbarButton Text="Manage" ImageUrl="mmc.gif"
Tooltip="Manage Server"/>
       <ie:ToolbarSeparator />
       <ie:ToolbarButton Text="Browse" ImageUrl="web.gif"
Tooltip="Browse Info" selectedstyle="color:red;font-size:12pt;"/>
```

```
        <ie:ToolbarButton Text="Print" ImageUrl="print.gif"
Tooltip="Print Document" />
        <ie:ToolbarSeparator />
        <ie:ToolbarButton Text="Help" ImageUrl="help.gif"
Tooltip="Get Help" />
    </ie:Toolbar>

    <asp:label id=lblMessage runat="server" style="font-
family:verdana"/>
    </form>
</body>
</html>
```

Figure 4-5 shows the output of the preceding code.

Figure 4-5: Sample output of the
Toolbar control

Summary

In this chapter, you learned about the functionality of the Rich Web controls. First, you learned the properties, methods, and events associated with the AdRotator and Calendar controls. Then, you learned how to create and use the additional Rich Web controls, such as TreeView, TabStrip, MultiPage, and Toolbar. You learned how to set their properties and handle the events raised by them.

✦   ✦   ✦

Creating and Using Custom Controls

Visual Studio .NET provides a rich set of standard controls, which are also called intrinsic controls. These standard controls provide a wide range of functionality and allow you to design and develop a user-friendly interface for your applications. Additionally, Visual Studio .NET provides you custom controls that you can use if the existing controls do not meet your requirements. For example, consider a Web application that needs to have multiple Web Forms and most of the Web Forms need a calculator. In this case, instead of adding standard controls to each Web Form for implementing the calculator, you can create one custom control to represent a calculator and use it across the Web Forms in your application. Thus, custom controls allow reusability. This chapter describes the procedure to create and use custom controls.

Introduction to Custom Controls

You can create the following types of custom controls in Visual Studio .NET:

+ **User control:** A Web Forms page that can be used as a control on other Web Forms pages. Thus, if you already have a Web Forms page and you need to construct a similar one, you can use the existing page as a user control.

+ **Composite control:** A combination of existing controls that is used as a single control. You can create a composite control in any .NET programming language and use it on an ASP.NET page. For example, you can create a composite control comprising a button and a text box in C# and use it on an ASP.NET page.

In addition to the custom controls discussed, you can perform the following actions with controls:

✦ Extend the functionality of the existing Web Form controls to meet your requirements. For example, consider a situation in which an existing Web Forms control meets almost all of your requirements, but you need some additional features in the control. In such a situation, you can add more features to your Web Form and customize the control. This can be done by inheriting from the control and overriding its properties, methods, or events.

✦ Develop a custom control by inheriting directly from one of the Control base classes. You'll need to do this when none of the existing Web Forms controls meets any of your requirements. The benefit of using the existing classes to create custom controls is that they provide the basic framework needed by a Web Forms control. This way, you can concentrate more on programming the features that you want to incorporate.

Before you create your own custom controls, let us examine the base classes used by the controls.

Basic Structure of Web Forms Controls

This section equips you with the basic understanding of the elements involved in developing a Web Forms control. We will first discuss the classes that are used to create Web Forms. This is followed by a discussion of the interfaces that can be implemented in Web Forms controls.

Classes used for Web Forms controls

Each Web Forms control is a class that inherits from the System.Web.UI. Control class directly or indirectly. Therefore, in this section, we examine the System.Web.UI.Control class and its inherited classes that are used to create a Web Forms control.

The System.Web.UI.Control class

The System.Web.UI.Control class defines all the properties, events, and methods that are common to all the Web Forms controls. You need to inherit your control from this class in the following cases:

✦ When your control does not have a user interface

✦ When your control includes other controls that render their own user interface

Some of the properties, methods, and events of the Control class are described in Table 5-1, Table 5-2, and Table 5-3 respectively.

Table 5-1
Control properties

Property	Description
ID	Represents the control identifier to refer to the server control in programs.
Parent	Represents the parent control in the server control hierarchy.
Visible	Indicates whether or not a server control should be rendered on the page.

Table 5-2
Control methods

Method	Description
Dispose	Causes a server control to perform final cleanup.
Equals	Used to check whether or not an object is the same as the current object. This method is overloaded.
FindControl	Used to search a container for a specified server control. This method is overloaded.
ToString	Used to return the string representation of the current object.

Table 5-3
Control events

Event	Description
Init	Is fired when a control is initialized. This is the first step when a page needs to be displayed in a browser.
Load	Is fired when the control is loaded in a page.
Unload	Is fired when a control is unloaded from the memory.

The System.Web.UI.WebControls.WebControl class

The System.Web.UI.WebControls.WebControl class is the base class for all Web controls. This class provides properties and methods to implement user interface functionality. It is inherited from the Control class. Some of the properties that are used to render additional user interface functionality are ForeColor, BackColor, BorderStyle, Width, and Height. Web controls, such as Label, TextBox, Button, Table, and Calendar, all inherit from the WebControl class. Therefore, if you have a control that has a user interface, it should inherit from the WebControl class.

The System.Web.UI.HtmlControls.HtmlControl class

The HtmlControl class is the base class for all HTML controls in Web Forms. This class inherits from the Control class. The controls provided by this class map directly to HTML elements. Therefore, these controls are useful for migrating ASP applications to ASP.NET.

Interfaces used for Web Forms controls

Several interfaces are available that you can implement depending upon your requirements. For example, if your control provides data binding, you need to implement the INamingContainer interface. In this section, we examine the interfaces that you might need to implement when you create controls.

Note   Interfaces are the collection of properties, methods, and events that are implemented through classes.

INamingContainer interface

This interface is used when you need to create controls that satisfy any of the following conditions:

✦ Provides data binding

✦ Is a templated control

✦ Routes events to its child controls

The INamingContainer interface doesn't have methods. When this interface is implemented by a control, the ASP.NET page framework creates a namespace for the control and ensures that each child control in the parent control has a unique ID.

IPostBackDataHandler interface

A control should implement the System.Web.UI.IPostBackDataHandler interface when it needs to update its state or raise events on the server after examining the postback data.

For example, the data sent to a TextBox control might result in the text box changing its text, as determined by its `Text` property. When the text changes, the text box also raises a `TextChanged` event. Thus, this control is examining the data, changing its state, and raising events.

IPostBackEventHandler interface

The IPostBackEventHandler interface is implemented in a control when you want to transfer events that are generated on the client side to the server. Events generated on the client side are postback events, hence the interface name.

An example of implementing this interface is when a user submits a form on the client side. In this case, the server does not know that the form is submitted unless the IPostBackEventHandler interface generates the `Click` event on the server when the form is submitted. This ensures that the server is in sync with the events that occur at the client end.

Creating Custom Controls

In this section, you'll create a custom control that represents a product form. The form provides text boxes to enter the product ID and product name of a specific product. You can reuse this control in the pages that need user input for any product. Figure 5-1 displays a sample user control.

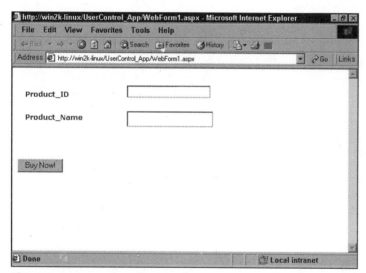

Figure 5-1: A sample user control

Let us now create this sample control.

Creating and using a user control

You can create a user control by creating a Web Forms page and excluding its `<HTML>`, `<HEAD>`, `<BODY>`, and `<FORM>` elements in the page. Let us now create a Web Forms page and convert it into a user control. The Web Forms page that you convert to a user control can be designed in either Visual Basic or C#.

Creating a user control

Creating a user control involves designing a Web Forms page to work as a control and then modifying the extension of the Web Forms file to .ascx. The steps are described in the sections that follow.

Step 1: Add a Web Form to the existing project

The first step involves adding a Web Form to the existing project. To do so:

1. Select the Add Web Form option from the Project menu. The Add New Item dialog box appears.

2. Type the name of the Web Form (for example, MyWebForm) in the Name box.

Note The Add New Item dialog box already displays a default name for the Web Form. You can modify it, if necessary.

3. Click Open. This will open a new Web Form.

Step 2: Convert your Web Form to a user control

This step involves converting your Web Form to a user control. You can do so by adding the controls to the form using the Toolbox and then editing the HTML code of the ASPX file. In our example of the Web Form displayed in Figure 5-1, the Toolbox has been used to add controls to the Web Form. As you can see, the Web Form has two text boxes, labeled Product_ID and Product_Name. The HTML code is automatically generated when you add these text boxes and labels.

After creating the visual interface for the user control, you need to edit the HTML file. As discussed earlier, the user control HTML file cannot contain the HTML tags that include the <HEAD>, <BODY>, <HTML>, and <FORM> tags. Therefore, you need to remove these tags from the HTML file. Additionally, you also need to change the @ Page directives to @ Control directives.

After you remove the HTML tags, your HTML file should look like this:

```
<table height=90 cellspacing=0 cellpadding=0 width=361 border=0
ms_2d_layout="TRUE">
  <tr valign=top>
    <td width=14 height=15></td>
    <td width=188></td>
    <td width=159></td></tr>
  <tr valign=top>
    <td colspan=2 height=9></td>
    <td rowspan=2>
<asp:TextBox id=Product_ID
runat="server"></asp:TextBox></td></tr>
  <tr valign=top>
    <td height=37></td>
    <td>
```

```
<asp:Label id=Label1 runat="server" font-bold="True" font-
names="Verdana"
font-size="Smaller">Product_ID</asp:Label></td></tr>
  <tr valign=top>
    <td colspan=2 height=4></td>
    <td rowspan=2>
<asp:TextBox id=Product_Name runat="server" Width="158"
Height="28"></asp:TextBox></td></tr>
  <tr valign=top>
    <td height=25></td>
    <td>
<asp:Label id=Label2 runat="server" Width="133" Height="19"
font-bold="True" font-names="Verdana" font-
size="Smaller">Product_Name</asp:Label></td></tr></table>
```

Note The table elements will appear only if the layout of the page is changed to GridLayout.

After editing the code, save and close the file.

Step 3: Change the extension of the file to .ascx

This step involves changing the extension of the file to .ascx. To rename the file, you need to follow these steps:

1. Right-click the user control Web Form file in the Solution Explorer window and select Rename from the shortcut menu.

2. Change the extension of the file to .ascx.

Note Do not leave the user control file open while renaming it. If the user control file is open, you will not be able to rename the file.

Using a user control in a Web Forms page

After you create a user control, you can use it on another Web Forms page. To do so, you need to register the control and then add it to your Web Forms page. The steps are described as follows.

Step 1: Register the user control

This step involves registering the user control that you created. To do so, you'll need to follow these steps:

1. Open the Web Forms page in which you want to add your user control. Open the WebForm1.aspx file that was created by default when you created the Web application project.

2. Write the following code:

```
<%@ Register TagPrefix="Acme" TagName="Product"
Src="MyWebForm.ascx" %>
```

This code will register the MyWebForm.ascx file. `TagPrefix` is an alias name that is used to identify the namespace on the Web Forms page to which it is added. The `TagName` tag contains the alias name for the class that represents the user control. `Src` is the name of the file that has the user control to be registered. The user control file can be within the same project or another project.

Step 2: Add the user control to your Web Forms page

This step involves adding the user control to your Web Forms page. To do so, use the following code:

```
<Acme:Product id="MyProduct" runat="Server"/>
```

The code given needs to be placed in the script where you want the control to appear on the page. In most cases, the code is placed in the `<BODY>` region of the page within the `<FORM>` element. In this code:

✦ Acme is the `TagPrefix` for your user control.

✦ `MyProduct` is the ID of your user control. You'll use this ID to refer to the control in programs.

Your Web Forms page will display the user control when you run the program.

Developing a composite control

You can create new controls using one or more existing controls. Such controls that aggregate a number of controls are referred to as composite controls. The primary difference between composite controls and user controls is that composite controls are compiled into assemblies and the compiled file is included into the project in which you want to include the control. In this section, we will create a composite control in C# and use it on an ASP page.

Concepts involved in creating a composite control

When you create a composite control, you need to do the following:

✦ Define the class that implements the composite control. The class needs to inherit from the Control class and, optionally, the INamingContainer class.

✦ Optionally override the `CreateChildControls` method of the Control class. The `CreateChildControls` method creates any child controls that need to be drawn on a page. This method is used in composition-based rendering, wherein child controls are instantiated and rendered on the page.

✦ Optionally implement the `Render` method of the Control class. You need to implement this method when you use the rendering logic instead of composition to render the ASP page. When you render controls, the performance overhead is less because controls need not be instantiated. Instead, the page is rendered as defined by the `Render` method. The Render method controls the output of the page at run-time.

Creating the control

You have examined the basic concepts to create a control. Let us now create a composite control. We will create the control in C#. The same programming logic can be used in VB.NET as well, except that the syntax will change.

The control that we will create comprises a Calendar control, a TextBox control, a Submit button, and a Label control. The user is expected to select his or her date of birth from the calendar, specify their work experience in years, and click the Submit button to ascertain whether he or she is eligible for a job.

To create the custom control project, create a new Class Library project in C#.

The controls that you need to use on the form are in the System.Web namespace. Therefore, include a reference to the System.Web.dll file. To include the reference, you need to perform the following steps:

1. Select the Add Reference option from the Project menu. The Add Reference dialog box appears.

2. In the Add Reference dialog box, from the .NET tab, select System.Web.dll and click Select.

3. The component moves to the Selected Components list. Click OK to add the reference.

After you add a reference to the System.Web.dll file, you can write the code for the control. To code the control, select the class module from the Solution Explorer. In the class module, declare the namespaces that are used by the control by specifying the following statements:

```
using System;
using System.Web;
using System.Web.UI;
using System.Web.UI.WebControls;
```

Next, declare the namespace for the control and declare a public class in the namespace. You should also declare the properties that you need to expose for the control. In the following code, we have declared the namespace, class, and a Text property for an EmpElg label. Additionally, we have also left placeholders for the CreateChildControls method and the Click event of the Submit button.

```
namespace CalcControl
{
    /// <summary>
    /// This class is used to establish if an applicant is
    ///eligible for job
    /// </summary>
    public class CalcClass : Control, INamingContainer
    {
```

```
        private Label EmpElg;
        public string Text
        {
            get
            {
                EnsureChildControls();
                return EmpElg.Text;
            }
            set
            {
                EnsureChildControls();
                EmpElg.Text=value;
            }
        }
        protected override void CreateChildControls()
        {
        }
        protected void Submit_Click(object sender,
    System.EventArgs e)
        {
        }
    }
}
```

The following is the code for the CreateChildControls method. In this code, we are declaring a few controls for the form and we are also using literal controls to display plain text on the form.

```
protected override void CreateChildControls()
{
    Controls.Add(new LiteralControl("<h3>Select date of birth :
"));
    Calendar Cal1 = new Calendar();
    //Cal1.TodaysDate();
    Controls.Add(Cal1);
    Controls.Add(new LiteralControl("<h3>Work Experience (Years)
    :
            "));
    TextBox WorkEx = new TextBox();
    WorkEx.Text="0";
    Controls.Add(WorkEx);
    Controls.Add(new LiteralControl("</h3>"));
    Button Submit = new Button();
    Submit.Text = "Submit";
    Controls.Add(new LiteralControl("<br>"));
    Controls.Add(Submit);
    Submit.Click += new System.EventHandler(this.Submit_Click);
    Controls.Add(new LiteralControl("<br><br>"));
    EmpElg = new Label();
    EmpElg.Height = 50;
    EmpElg.Width = 500;
    EmpElg.Text = "Check your eligibility.";
    Controls.Add(EmpElg);
}
```

Finally, the code for the Submit button, which is used to check the eligibility of an employee, is as follows:

```
protected void Submit_Click(object sender, System.EventArgs e)
{
    EnsureChildControls();
    if (Int32.Parse(((TextBox)Controls[3]).Text)>=5)
    {
        if ((((Calendar)Controls[1]).SelectedDate.Year) <= 1975)
        {
            EmpElg.Text = "You are eligible to apply for a job in
our
                company!!";
        }
        else
        {
            EmpElg.Text = "You are NOT eligible to apply for a job
in
                our company!!";
        }
    }
    else
    {
        EmpElg.Text = "You are NOT eligible for applying for a
job in
                our company!!";
    }
}
```

When the user clicks Submit, this code checks whether the work experience of the user is more than five years. It also checks whether the user is born in or before 1975. When both the conditions are satisfied, the user is considered eligible for the job.

 Note You can find the complete code for creating a composite control on the companion Web site for this book.

Compile the application to create the DLL file for the composite control. After compiling the file, you can proceed and include the file on an ASP page and check whether the control works as desired.

Adding the composite control to a page

After you have compiled the composite control into a DLL, you can include it in a Web application. The steps to include the control into a Web application are given as follows:

1. Create a new ASP Web application or open an existing project.

2. Add a reference to the custom control that you created in the previous step. To add a reference, in the Add Reference dialog box, select the Projects tab and browse to the DLL file of your custom control.

3. In the HTML source file, specify the @ Register directive to register the control. For example, if the name of the control namespace is CalcControl and the name of the class library project is CustomControls, you can register the control by specifying the following statement:

```
<%@ Register TagPrefix="Custom" Namespace="CalcControl"
Assembly =
      "CustomControls" %>
```

4. Include the control on the page by using the tag name with which the control was registered. For example, in the preceding case, the tag name is Custom. Therefore, to include the control in the <BODY> region of the form, write the following code:

```
<form id="Form1" method="post" runat="server">
   <Custom:CalcClass id="CalcClass" Text="Select options and
             click Submit" runat="server" />
</form>
```

After you have included the control, it appears as displayed in Figure 5-2.

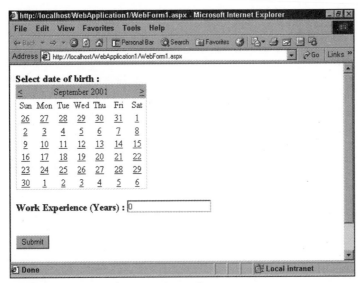

Figure 5-2: Composite control on a form

You can check whether the control is functioning correctly by selecting a date less than 1975 and specifying the work experience of more than five years. The output after you specify the aforesaid values is given in Figure 5-3.

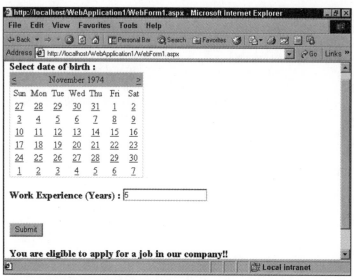

Figure 5-3: Data validation by the composite control

Adding Properties and Methods

After creating a custom control, you can add properties and methods to it and obtain the functionality you want in your control.

Properties are specifications that qualify the appearance and behavior of controls. In the case of standard controls, you can specify the property values either at design time or run time. At design time, the properties can be specified using the Toolbox. At run time, the implemented code sets the properties. If a property has a set accessor, the syntax to set a property would be as follows:

```
control.property = value
```

In this syntax:

- ✦ `control` signifies the name of the control.
- ✦ `property` signifies the property that you want to set for the control.
- ✦ `value` is the value that you specify for the property.

Methods are functions or procedures that provide a specific functionality to a control. Each Web Forms control has a set of methods associated with it. You can call a method of a control by using the following syntax:

```
control.method
```

In this syntax, `control` represents the name of the control and `method` represents the method associated with the control.

You can add properties and methods to custom controls also. To add a property to a user control, you need to write the code in the ASCX file of the control. Consider the example wherein you created a user control earlier in the chapter. To add properties, `ProductID` and `ProductName`, you need to add the following code in the class that implements the control:

```
<script language="C#" runat="server">

    public String ProductID
  {
   get
     {
      return Product_ID.Text;
     }
   set
     {
      Product_ID.Text = value;
     }
  }

    public String ProductName
  {
   get
     {
      return Product_Name.Text;
     }
   set
     {
      Product_Name.Text = value;
     }
  }
</script>
```

In this code, the `get` and `set` properties have been used. The `get` property is used to retrieve the value associated with the property. The `set` property is used to assign a value to a property.

Handling and Exposing Events

Each control has events associated with it. Events are generated as a result of user interaction or can be raised from other procedures. In Web Forms controls, the events are raised and handled on the server. An action is requested from the client side to the server with the help of a Web request. Then, the control raises an event on the server as a response to the client action. After the page or controls handle the event, the response is sent back to the client. This results in user experience similar to a desktop application.

Note Only the postback event can be posted to the server. User interface events that occur on the client side, such as mouse clicks or key presses, can only be communicated to the server by using postback events.

You can associate custom events with your controls. Handling user control events is more or less the same as handling events in any other Web Forms control. You need to decide whether to use the event handler in the containing Web Forms page or the user control. Writing event handlers in either of the cases is similar. However, you need to take some precautions if you decide to include the event handler in the user control. For example, if you have included the properties for the control in the existing Web Forms page, the properties will not be accessible from the user control unless you add functionality within the user control.

Let us create a button and add an event handler to it. Consider the user control that you created earlier in the chapter. You can add an event in such a way that whenever you write a value in the Product_ID text box and click a button labeled "Buy Now!," the name of the product will automatically appear in the Product_Name text box. To add the button to the control, add the following code:

```
<asp:Button id=Buy runat="server" Text="Buy Now!"
        OnClick="Buy_Click"></asp:Button>
```

The ID of the Button control is Buy. The button can achieve the desired functionality by the following code:

```
<script language="Vb" runat="server" ID=Script1>
  Sub Buy_Click (Src As Object, E As EventArgs)
    If MyProduct.ProductID="P001" Then
      MyProduct.ProductName="Toys"
    End If
  End Sub
</script>
```

This code is executed when a user clicks the button "Buy Now!" After a user clicks this button, the value of the TextBox labeled Product_Name is set to "Toys" if a user enters the product code as "P001."

Summary

In this chapter, you learned the basic structure of Web Forms controls and looked at the classes used for them. You explored the custom controls in detail. First, you learned how to create and use user controls. Then, you learned how to create and use composite controls. In this process, you learned how to use events, methods, and properties with custom controls.

✦   ✦   ✦

Validating User Input

This chapter covers the validation controls used in ASP.NET. These controls make page validation much easier and reduce the amount of code that the developer must write to perform page validation. The ASP.NET team reviewed numerous Web sites to determine the most common types of validation that were taking place on the Web. Most developers were reinventing the wheel to perform validation, so the ASP.NET team decided that Web developers needed a set of validation controls to add to their toolbox. From the start, these controls were designed to detect the version of the browser when used in client-side validation and then render the correct version of HTML for that client browser.

These research efforts lead to the development of the six controls covered in this chapter. The examples in this chapter will take a look at each control and explain the most commonly used properties for each control. However, keep in mind that all of the controls share basic properties, such as font, fore color, back color, and so on, so this chapter won't discuss those properties in detail. After you have read this chapter, you will have a firm understanding of validation controls and will be ready to use them in your own Web applications.

Understanding Validation Controls

Everything in the .NET Framework is a class, and the validation controls are no exception. All validation controls in the .NET Framework are derived from the BaseValidator class. This class serves as the base abstract class for the validation controls and provides the core implementation for all validation controls that derive from this class. Validation controls always perform validation checking on the server. Validation controls also have complete client-side implementation that allows browsers that support DHTML to perform validation on the client. Client-side validation enhances the validation scheme by checking user input as the user enters data. This allows errors to be detected on the client before the form is submitted, preventing the round trip necessary for server-side validation. In addition, more than one validator may be used on a page to validate different aspects.

Before you look at the validation controls, step back in time before .NET and take a look at a simplified example of performing validation with ASP. Launch your browser and run the BeforeDotNet.asp code. A screen similar to Figure 6-1 should be displayed.

Figure 6-1: BeforeDotNet.ASP

The following ASP code generated Figure 6-1, which is one example of how validation might be performed on the server using "classic" ASP:<%@ Language=VBScript %>

```
<html>
  <head>
    <title>When dinosaurs roamed...</title>
    <%
     '-- perform server side validation
     If Request.Form("Submit") <> Empty Then
        If Len(Request.Form("First")) = 0 Then
           Response.Write("Please enter your first name.")
        Else
           Response.Write("Hello, " &
CStr(Request.Form("First")))
```

```
        End If
     End If
   %>
  </head>
  <body>
<h3><b>Hungry Minds<b></h3><hr><br>
 <form method="post" action="BeforeDotNet.asp" name="OldStyle">
First<br>
   <input name="First" maxlength="15">
   <br><hr>
   <input name="Submit" type="submit">
   <br><br>
 </form>
 </body>
</html>
```

This style of validation has a few drawbacks. First, if you have several more controls on this page to validate, the validation routine will become quite lengthy and
prone to errors. Second, if you delete or rename your controls on the page, you
need to update your validation routine. Also, you may want to perform several
different types of validation on the same control's value. As you can see, this adds
to your validation routine and requires a fair amount of code to implement. Finally,
you have your validation code mixed with the presentation code. As you will soon
see, .NET's validation controls overcome all of these limitations.

Note You could just as easily have used client-side validation with JScript to save a round
trip to the server. However, it is always good practice to validate the values again on
the server to prevent any unwanted values from being passed to your server.

Using the RequiredFieldValidator Control

Use the RequiredFieldValidator control when a value is required for an input element on the Web page. This control checks whether the value of the associated
input control is different from its initial value. You can easily convert the previous
sample ASP code into .NET with the RequiredFieldValidator control. Take a look at
the following code fragment:

```
<!-- Required Field Validator -->
First<br>
<asp:textbox id="First" maxlength="20" runat="Server"/>
<asp:requiredfieldvalidator
id="rfvFirst"
   controltovalidate="First"
   display="dynamic"
   errormessage="Please enter your first name."
   runat="Server">
</asp:requiredfieldvalidator>
<br>
```

Launch your browser and navigate to Required.aspx code. A screen similar to Figure 6-2 should be displayed.

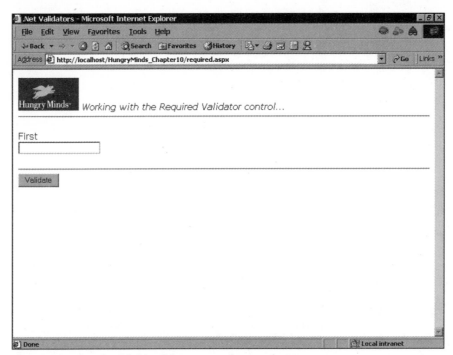

Figure 6-2: Required field validator control example 1

Before entering a First name, click the Validate button. A screen similar to Figure 6-3 should be displayed.

If all went well, you should see the validation message "Please enter your first name." on the page. Now enter your name and click the Validate button again. This time you should see the message, "Hello, *your name*" displayed on the page, as shown in Figure 6-4.

Figure 6-3: Required field validator control example 2

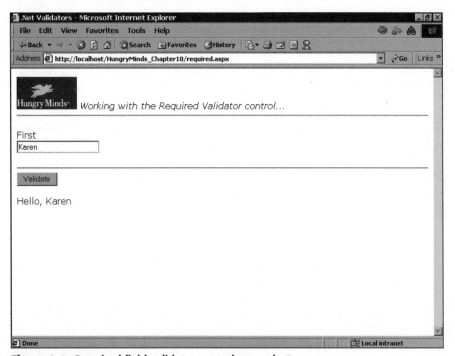

Figure 6-4: Required field validator control example 3

Figure 6-4 looks just like the example for "Classic ASP" in Figure 6-1, but underneath the covers, ASP.NET has written the validation code for you.

Now that you have looked at a quick example of using .NET validation, Table 6-1 gives you a more detailed description of the properties for the RequiredFieldValidator control.

Table 6-1
Properties of the RequiredFieldValidator control

Property	Definition
ID	This property gets or sets the identifier for the control. This identifier is used via programming to access the control's properties. If an identifier does not exist, then you cannot write handlers for this control.
ControlToValidate	Gets or sets the name of the control to validate.
Display	Gets or sets the display appearance of the validator control on the Web page.
ErrorMessage	Gets or sets the error message displayed for this control.
RunAt	Specifies that this control runs on the server.

The ControlToValidate and Display properties from Table 6-1 are explained in more detail in the following sections.

ControlToValidate property

Set this property's value to the name of the control to validate. If you refer to the code listing, this property was set to First to indicate that a value is required for this control.

Display property

You can set this property to one of three values to determine how the error message is displayed on the page if validation fails:

✦ Dynamic: The validator is displayed inline on the Web page if validation fails. The validator only takes up space on the page when the validator is visible. This allows multiple validators to occupy the same physical location on the Web page when those validators become visible. To avoid the Web page layout changing the validator becomes visible, the HTML element containing the validator must be large enough to accommodate the size of the validator.

✦ Static: The validator is displayed inline on the Web page if validation fails. Also, if the validator is hidden and becomes visible, the page layout does not change.

✦ None: The validation contents are not displayed inline on the Web page, the error message is displayed in the ValidationSummary control.

Using the CompareValidator Control

Use the CompareValidator control to make sure that a value matches a specified value. This control compares the value of an input control to another input control or a constant value using a variety of operators and types. You can also use this control to make sure that your input value is of a specific type: integer, string, and so on. Table 6-2 lists the commonly used properties for the CompareValidator control.

Table 6-2	
Properties of the CompareValidator control	
Property	**Definition**
ID	This property gets or sets the identifier for the control. This identifier is used via programming to access the control's properties. If an identifier does not exist, then you cannot write handlers for this control.
ControlToValidate	Gets or sets the name of the control to validate.
ControlToCompare or ValueToCompare	Gets or sets the identifier of the control on the Web page to compare with. Gets or sets a specific value that is used to compare against.
Display	Gets or sets the display appearance of the validator control on the Web page.
ErrorMessage	Gets or sets the error message displayed for this control.
RunAt	Specifies that this control runs on the server.

A good example for the CompareValidator control would be to compare passwords the first time a user creates an account in your Web application. The following code fragment shows the code for the CompareValidator control:

```
<!-- Compare Field Validator -->
Password:<br>
<asp:textbox id="Password" maxlength="16" runat="Server"/><br>
```

```
Confirm:<br>
<asp:textbox id="Confirm" maxlength="16" runat="Server"/>
<asp:comparevalidator
id="cvPasswords"
    controltocompare="Password"
    controltovalidate="Confirm"
    display="dynamic"
    errormessage="Passwords do not match, please try again."
    runat="Server">
</asp:comparevalidator>
```

Launch your browser and navigate to Compare.aspx. Figure 6-5 should be displayed.

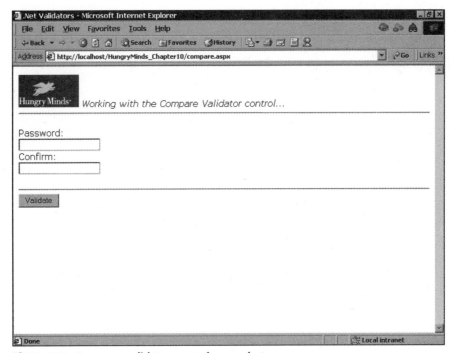

Figure 6-5: Compare validator control example 1

Click the Validate button. Why did the CompareValidator control fail to display your error message? Simple; even though you specified the CompareValidator control, you did not specify the RequiredValidator control, meaning that neither Password nor Confirm is a required value. So blank passwords would compare. Keep this in mind when using the CompareValidator control.

This time enter a value for the Password field, press the Tab key, enter a different value for Confirm (for testing purposes), and then press the Tab key again. A screen similar to Figure 6-6 should be displayed, depending on the values that you entered.

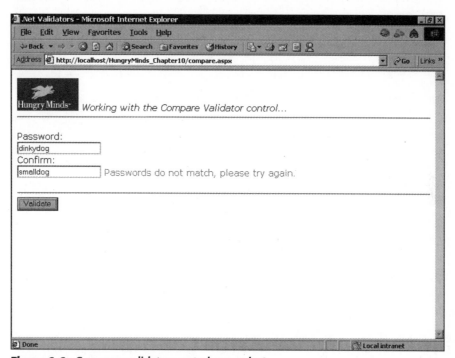

Figure 6-6: Compare validator control example 2

This time the validator works as intended and displays the error message that the Password and Confirm TextBox controls do not match.

Now, enter the same values for the Password and Confirm fields and click the Validate button. Because the passwords match, the error message should not be displayed and you should see your message displayed on the page, as in Figure 6-7.

This is just one example of using the CompareValidator control. As shown earlier in Table 6-2, you could specify the `ValueToCompare` property instead of the `ControlToCompare` property. Try it! Delete the `ControlToCompare` property, add the `ValueToCompare` property, and set its value to some test value. Then run the Compare.aspx sample again. Validation will fail if the value entered in the `ControlToValidate` field does not match the value in the `ValueToCompare` property.

Note   This control is case-sensitive. For instance "RICK = Rick" will not compare as being equal.

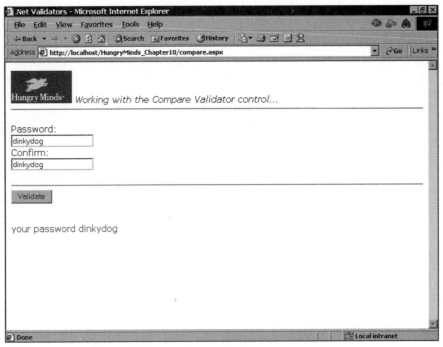

Figure 6-7: Compare validator control example 3

Using the RangeValidator Control

Use the RangeValidator control to determine whether a value falls within the specified range. It checks whether the value of the associated input control is within some minimum and maximum, which can be a constant value or the value of another control. Table 6-3 lists the properties commonly used with the RangeValidator control.

Table 6-3	
Properties of the RangeValidator control	
Property	**Definition**
ID	This property gets or sets the identifier for the control. This identifier is used via programming to access the control's properties. If an identifier does not exist, then you cannot write handlers for this control.
ControlToValidate	Gets or sets the name of the control to validate.
MaximumValue	Gets or sets the maximum value of the validation range.

Property	Definition
MinimumValue	Gets or sets the minimum value of the validation range.
MaximumControl	Gets or sets the ID of the control that specifies the maximum value of the validation range.
MinimumControl	Gets or sets the ID of the control that specifies the minimum value of the validation range.
Display	Gets or sets the display appearance of the validator control on the Web page.
ErrorMessage	Gets or sets the error message displayed for this control.
Type	Gets or sets the data type to determine how the values should be compared. For instance, string to string or int to int.
RunAt	Specifies that this control runs on the server.

Type property

You can set the Type property to one of the following values, which determines the type of values in the range:

*Currency: The data type is Currency.

*Date: The data type is DateTime.

*Double: The data type is Double.

*Integer: The data type is Integer.

*String: The data type is String.

MinimumValue and MaximumValue properties

The RangeValidator control is useful when you need to make sure that a value falls within a specified range of values. Take a look at the code fragment that follows for the RangeValidator control:

```
<!-- Range Validator Control  -->
Number of tickets:<br>
   <asp:textbox id="Tickets" maxlength="2" columns="2"
runat="Server"/>
   <asp:rangevalidator
      id="rvTickets"
      controltovalidate="Tickets"
      minimumvalue=1
      maximumvalue=4
      type="Integer"
```

```
        display="dynamic"
        errormessage="You can only purchase 1 to 4 tickets,
please try again."
        runat="Server">
    </asp:rangevalidator><br>
```

Launch your browser and navigate to Range.aspx. A screen similar to Figure 6-8 is displayed.

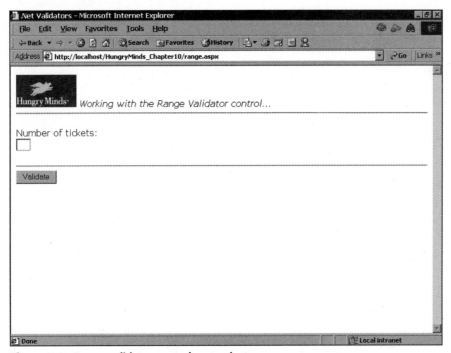

Figure 6-8: Range validator control example 1

As you can see from the code fragment, the `MinimumValue` property is set to 1 and the `MaximumValue` property is set to 4. Now, enter a value less than 1 or greater than 8 in the Number of tickets field and then press the Tab key. A screen similar to Figure 6-9 should be displayed.

Because you specified a range of 1 to 8, any other value will fail validation and your error message will be displayed. Enter a value within the range and then click Validate. A screen similar to Figure 6-10 is displayed.

Figure 6-9: Range validator control example 2

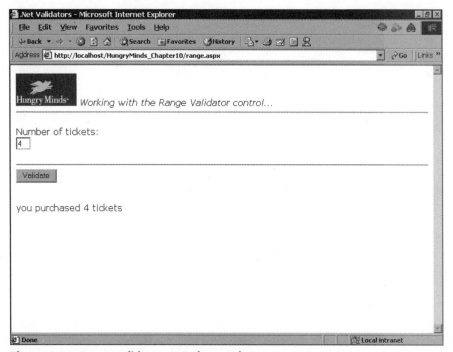

Figure 6-10: Range validator control example 3

MinimumControl and MaximumControl properties

As mentioned in the previous section, the RangeValidator control is useful when you need to make sure that a value falls within a specified range of values. You can specify values for the `MinimumControl` and `MaximumControl` properties for the range just as easily as you did for the `MinimumValue` and `MaximumValue` properties previously. Try it! Add two controls to the form and then set the `MaximumControl` and `MinimumControl` properties to these new controls. Make sure that you remove the `MinimumValue` and `MaximumValue` properties.

Using the RegularExpressionValidator Control

Use the RegularExpressionValidator control to check a value against a regular expression. It checks whether the value of the associated input control matches the pattern of a regular expression. Table 6-4 lists the properties commonly used with the RegularExpressionValidator control.

Table 6-4	
Properties of the RegularExpressionValidator control	
Property	*Definition*
`ID`	This property gets or sets the identifier for the control. This identifier is used via programming to access the control's properties. If an identifier does not exist, then you cannot write handlers for this control.
`ControlToValidate`	Gets or sets the name of the control to validate.
`ValidationExpression`	Gets or sets the regular expression that is used as the validation criteria.
`Display`	Gets or sets the display appearance of the validator control on the Web page.
`ErrorMessage`	Gets or sets the error message displayed for this control.
`RunAt`	Specifies that this control runs on the server.

This control allows you to check for known sequences in characters, such as phone numbers, social security numbers, and so on. Take a look at the following code fragment for the Regular ExpressionValidator control:

```
<!-- Regular Expression Validator Control  -->
Phone:<br>
```

```
<asp:textbox id="Phone" maxlength="12" columns="12"
runat="Server"/>
<asp:regularexpressionvalidator
id="revPhone"
      controltovalidate="Phone"
      display="dynamic"
      validationexpression="[0-9]{3}\s[0-9]{3}-[0-9]{4}"
      errormessage="Phone number format must be xxx xxx-xxxx,
please try again."
      runat="Server">
    </asp:regularexpressionvalidator><br>
```

Note that the string assigned to the ValidationExpression property uses JScript regular expression syntax. Regular expressions are beyond the scope of this book, but the following explanation will help. The ValidationExpression property in the preceding code fragment means the following:

✦ First sequence

   [0-9]: Any digit from 0 to 9

   {3}: Three digits are required for this first group of numbers

   \s: A space is required

✦ Second sequence

   [0-9]: Any digit from 0 to 9

   {3}: Three digits are required for this first group of numbers

   -: A dash is required

✦ Third sequence

   [0-9]: Any digit from 0 to 9

   {4}: Four digits are required for this first group of numbers

Note   For more help on JScript regular expression, visit the Microsoft MSDN Web site on scripting at http://msdn.microsoft.com/library/en-us/script56/html/js56reconIntroductionToRegularExpressions.asp.

Run the sample for this control by launching your browser and navigating to Regular.aspx, shown in Figure 6-11.

Because the format in your ValidationExpression is xxx xxx-xxxx, enter some other phone sequence to test the validation control. After you enter the value, press the Tab key, and Figure 6-12 displays.

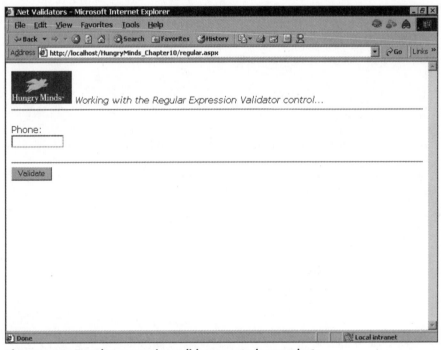

Figure 6-11: Regular expression validator control example 1

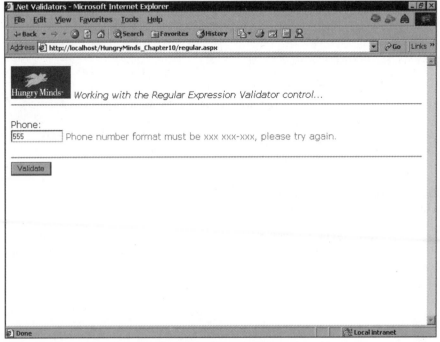

Figure 6-12: Regular expression validator control example 2

Because the phone number is not in the expected format, validation fails and your error message is displayed. This time, enter the correct phone number format and then click the Validate button. The validation message is cleared from the page and your message is displayed. Your screen should look like Figure 6-13.

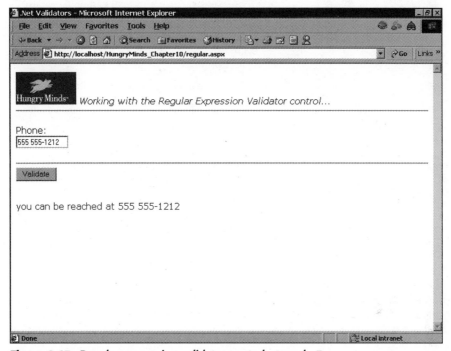

Figure 6-13: Regular expression validator control example 3

With the RegularExpressionValidator control, you can verify known sequences of characters without building your own validation routines from scratch. However, you can create custom validation routines, as well, which is the purpose of the next validation control in ASP.NET, CustomValidator.

Using the CustomValidator Control

Use the CustomValidator control to perform user-defined custom validation. This control allows custom code to perform validation on the client and/or server. Table 6-5 lists the properties commonly used with the CustomValidator control.

Table 6-5
Properties of the CustomValidator control

Property	Definition
ID	This property gets or sets the identifier for the control. This identifier is used via programming to access the control's properties. If an identifier does not exist, then you cannot write handlers for this control.
ControlToValidate	Gets or sets the name of the control to validate.
ClientValidationFunction	Indicates the client script function to call for validation.
OnServerValidate	Indicates the name of the event to raise on the server.
Display	Gets or sets the display appearance of the validator control on the Web page.
ErrorMessage	Gets or sets the error message displayed for this control.
RunAt	Specifies that this control runs on the server.

Because the client validation function runs on the target browser, the function needs to be written using a scripting language supported by the browser, such as JavaScript or VBScript. The CustomValidator control also has an event that can be set for server-side validation.

 Note   When using server-side events, remember to always prefix the event name with the word *on*. For instance, onServerValidate, which is the required syntax for this event.

Take a look at the code fragment for the CustomValidator control:

```
<!-- Custom Validator Control  -->
Credit card number:<br>
    <asp:textbox id="CardNumber" maxlength="16" columns="16"
runat="Server"/>
    <asp:customvalidator
        id="cvCardNumber"
        controltovalidate="CardNumber"
        ClientValidationFunction="IsCardValid"
```

```
        display="dynamic"
        errormessage="Invalid credit card number, please try
again."
        runat="Server">
    </asp:customvalidator><br>
```

By now, you should be familiar with most of the properties when wiring up the validation controls. However, for the CustomValidator control, you are interested in the `ClientValidationFunction` or the `OnServerValidate` event. In the example, you are going to concentrate on the `ClientValidationFunction` event. Here, this property points to the `IsCardValid` function, which must be a valid function defined as JScript or VBScript on the client. Take a look at the code for this function:

```
<script language="javascript">
//--- source is the name of control that is being checked
    //--- value is actual value that is entered into the control
    function IsCardValid(source, value) {
    if (value != "5555555555555555" )
        return false;
    else
        return true;
    }
    </script>
```

The `ClientValidationFunction` event expects two parameters:

✦ `source`: The name of the control that is being validated, pointed to by the `ControlToValidate` property

✦ `value`: The actual value entered by the user

Keep in mind that you can use whatever name you prefer; you don't need to use `source` and `value`. The `ClientValidationFunction` event must return a `True` or `False` condition to indicate whether validation succeeded for failed.

Run the example by launching your browser and navigating to Custom.aspx, shown in Figure 6-14.

Figure 6-14: Custom validator control example 1

For this example, the IsCardValid function expects the credit card number to be a string of all 5s. In a real-world application, you might want to add the logic to validate the credit card so that you can make sure an individual's credit card number is valid.

Enter a value that is not valid as per the IsCardValid function and then press the Tab key; your screen should appear similar to Figure 6-15.

Because the value you entered does not match the value in the IsCardValid function, the function returns False and your error message is displayed.

Next, enter all 5s and click the Validate button. This time, IsCardValid returns True and your message is displayed as shown in Figure 6-16.

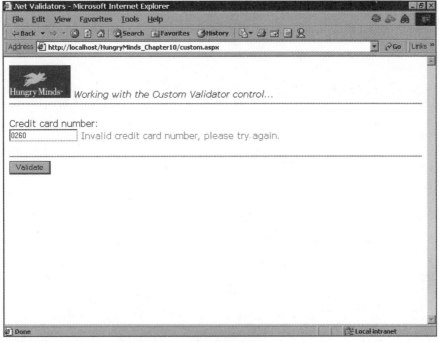

Figure 6-15: Custom validator control example 2

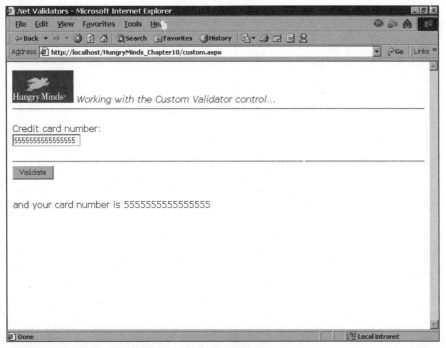

Figure 6-16: Custom validator control example 3

As you can see, the CustomValidator control is really the catchall for all the other validation controls. When one of the other controls does not fit the bill, you can customize your validation control to roll your own validation.

Using the ValidationSummary Control

Use the ValidationSummary control to capture all the validation errors from the other controls and display them on the page as a list, a bulleted list, or in single paragraph format. The errors can be displayed inline and/or in a pop-up message box. Table 6-6 lists the properties commonly used with the ValidationSummary control.

Table 6-6 Properties of the ValidationSummary control	
Property	**Definition**
ID	This property gets or sets the identifier for the control. This identifier is used via programming to access the control's properties. If an identifier does not exist, then you cannot write handlers for this control.
DisplayMode	Indicates the display mode on the page for the validation summary.
HeaderText	Indicates the text heading to display at the top of the validation summary.
ShowMessageBox	Indicates whether the validation summary should be displayed in a client side message box.
ShowSummary	Indicates if the validation summary should be displayed inline.
RunAt	Specifies that this control runs on the server.

The ValidationSummary control gathers and displays all `ErrorMessage` objects of validators of the same page. At the same time, any validator can display its own error message if you put the message in the control's inner content. This control allows you to group all of your messages in a convenient spot on the page in the style of your choosing.

Look at the following code for the ValidationSummary control:

```
<!-- Validation Summary Validator -->
<asp:validationsummary
id="vsAll"
```

```
    headertext="<i>The following errors occurred, please correct
and try again.</i><br><hr>"
    displaymode="list"
    runat="Server">
</asp:validationsummary><br>
```

Put all of this together and use all the validation controls discussed so far with the ValidationSummary control by launching your browser and navigating to Summary.aspx, shown in Figure 6-17.

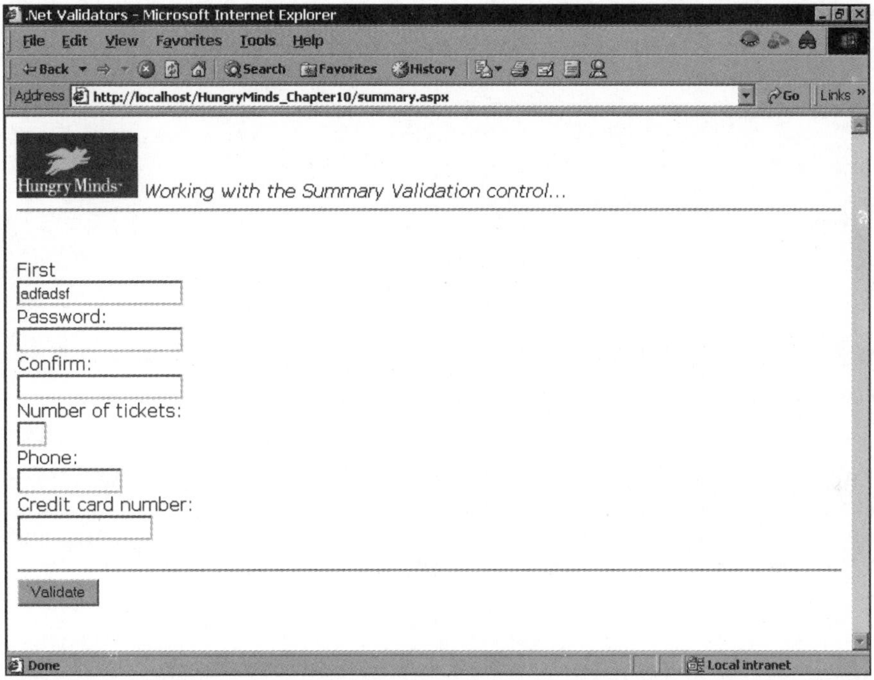

Figure 6-17: Validation summary control example 1

To demonstrate the ValidationSummary control, enter invalid values for each of the controls on the page. Keep in mind the validation rules for each control, because you want to make sure validation fails. Also, keep in mind the empty values are valid. After you have entered your values, click the Validate button. A screen similar to Figure 6-18 should appear.

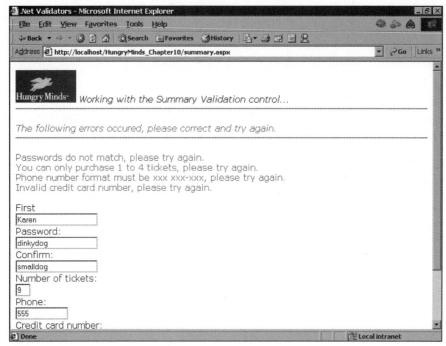

Figure 6-18: Validation summary control example 2

As you can see, all the validation messages are displayed at the top of the page instead of inline after each control. The ValidationSummary control provides you with a clean way to display error messages and inform the user simultaneously. Whether you use inline validation or the ValidationSummary control is a matter of preference.

Validation Events

Up to this point, you have looked at the common properties of each control, learned how to wire them up on the page, and reviewed examples of the code running in the browser. The .NET Framework also exposes some common events for these controls that give the developer more options over the controls. Take a look at Table 6-7.

Table 6-7 Public Instance Events	
DataBinding	The event occurs when the control binds to a data source.
Init	The event occurs when the control is initialized; this is the first event in the page lifecycle. The control can perform any initialization steps that are required for the Web page.

Load	The event occurs when the control is first loaded to the `Page` object.
PreRender	This event occurs when the control is about to render the HTML to the page. Controls should perform any pre-rendering steps before saving the view state and before rendering content to the `Page` object.
Unload	This event occurs when the control is about to be unloaded from memory. The control should perform any cleanup code in this Unload event.

The developer can also wire up these events to further control what happens when the control is loaded, unloaded, and so on from the page. These events would be used when the Web developer wants to initialize values before the page is loaded and to perform any cleanup code before the page is destroyed.

Multiple Validation Controls and Code Behind

In this section we are going to take a quick look at how we can use the Validator controls in a "Code Behind" Web page. The concept of "Code Behind" is new to .NET allowing us to separate our presentation HTML from the code logic. Figure 6-19 is displayed when the "Code Behind" example is executed in the browser.

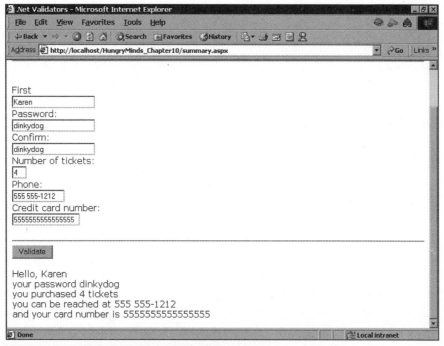

Figure 6-19: Validation with code behind example 1

When using the validation controls, keep in mind that you should use the RequiredField validator along with the other controls to perform validation. As you saw in an earlier example using the CompareValidator control, blank passwords will match. If you had also used the RequiredFieldValidator control, the Password and Confirm fields would need a value, and then those values would be compared before determining whether validation fails. Keep in mind that you can use more than one validation control with a specified control on the page.

Also, consider the differences in using client- versus server-side validation. With client-side validation, the user gets immediate feedback as to whether the value entered is valid. Using client-side validation also prevents a round trip to the server. However, when using server-side validation, you can move the code to the server and encapsulate your logic in a code behind page. For instance, your IsCardValid function could be moved to a code behind page to separate the presentation code from the business rules for performing validation.

Using Code

To demonstrate using validation from a code behind page, take a look at the following code fragment for Codebehind.aspx:

```
<%@ Page Language="C#" Src="codebehind.cs"
Inherits="HungryMinds.Validation"%>
...
```

The page directive informs the ASP.NET parser to look in the Src attribute for the code to compile and in the Inherits attribute for the code behind class to inherit. In the preceding example, the Src attribute points to the following code behind page listing:

```
namespace HungryMinds {
    using System;
    using System.Web.UI.WebControls;
    //--- we could also wire up the page_load, page_init, etc.
events here also
    //--- inherit from the page class
    public class Validation : System.Web.UI.Page {
        //-- we need to reference the controls on the .ASPX
page
        protected System.Web.UI.WebControls.TextBox CardNumber;
        protected System.Web.UI.WebControls.Label Message;
        //--- this is our validation function that we set in
the onServerValidate
        //--- property of the Custom Validator
        protected void IsCardValid(object sender,
ServerValidateEventArgs e) {
            //--- do some type of validation and return either
true or false
        if (e.value != "5555555555555555" )
```

```
            e.IsValid = false;
        else
            e.IsValid = true;
        }

        protected void ShowMessage(Object sender, EventArgs
    e) {
        String Msg;
        if (Page.IsValid) {
            if (CardNumber.Text.Length > 0) {
                Msg ="<br>and your card number is  " +
    CardNumber.Text;
                Message.Text = Msg;
            }
        }
    }
   }
  }
}
```

The first line in your code listing defines the namespace for this class. Next, you import the required class libraries: System and System.Web.UI.WebControls. You next define your class, which is inherited from the ASPX page. This class must be derived from the Page class in the .NET Framework. The next lines declare references to your controls on the ASPX page, the TextBox control and the Label control, which are defined in the System.Web.UI.WebControls class. You next define the functions used by the ASPX page. By using this implementation, you are able to separate the presentation code from the business logic code.

Summary

This chapter has explored each of the validation controls and provided examples of how to use each one with its commonly used properties. In this chapter, we covered: the RequiredFieldValidator control (which requires a field on the Web page to have value); the CompareValidator control (which allows us to compare values in one control to another control on the page, or a specified minimum and maximum value); the RangeValidator control (which allows us to compare the value of a control on the Web page to a range of values); and the RegularExpression Validator control (which we can use to validate a value against regular expressions). Also, we have the CustomValidator control, so that if none of the other validation controls fit our needs, then we can write our own validation routine. Finally, we discussed the ValidationSummary control, which allows us to accumulate all of the error messages from the other controls and display them as a list on the Web page.

As you can see, the .NET Framework provides Web developers with a great set of controls for doing page validation, instead of spending time writing validation code. This chapter also looked at how to implement code behind validation in ASPX pages to separate the presentation code from the business logic.

✦   ✦   ✦

Debugging ASP.NET Pages

In the previous chapters, you saw how to design and develop an ASP.NET application by using Web Forms. After designing and developing the application, it becomes critical to check it for the desired functionality.

While you are developing the application, the code editor catches most syntax errors. However, the errors that cannot be caught during application development cause the application to display error messages at run time. The errors that occur while the application is running are called *run-time errors*. On the other hand, if there is a problem in the programming logic, the application would run without errors, but it will not provide the desired functionality. Such errors are called *logical errors*. The process of going through the code to identify the root cause of an error in an application is called *debugging*.

This chapter introduces you to error handling and using the different debugging tools. You'll also learn the guidelines to writing good ASP.NET code.

Error Handling

ASP.NET provides rich support for handling and tracking errors that might occur while applications are running. When you run an ASP.NET application, if an error occurs on a server, an HTML error page is generated and displayed in the browser. While displaying error messages to users, ASP.NET takes care of the security issues by default, which makes it a reliable development tool for Web applications. ASP.NET ensures that no secure information, such as the remote machine compiler messages, configuration settings, filenames, stack traces, or source code, is revealed on the client machine. When an error occurs, a generic error message, "Application Error Occurred," is displayed to users. To see the error details, one of the following needs to be done:

✦ Access the page again from the local server.

✦ Modify the configuration settings of the computer.

✦ Modify the configuration settings of the application's Web.config file to enable remote access.

Following is a sample of the Web.config file that you can modify:

```
<configuration>
    <system.web>
        <customErrors mode="Off" />
    </system.web>
</configuration>
```

In this code, the `<customErrors>` tag has an attribute `mode` whose value is set to `"Off"`. This value indicates that the remote users always see the original error message that is generated on the server.

Using custom error pages

As mentioned earlier, an HTML error page is displayed to a user in case an error occurs on a server. These error messages are secure, because they do not leak any secret information. However, these pages are not pretty to see. You can create custom error pages that can be displayed in case errors occur. For example, you can create an error page that displays the company's brand and some error messages that you want to display. To implement the custom error pages:

1. Create a Web page that you want to display as an error message page. This can be a page with an .html or .aspx extension.

2. Modify the Web.config file of your application to point to the custom page in the event of any error. The configuration settings, shown here, point to a file called MyError.aspx:

```
<configuration>
  <system.web>
    <customErrors mode="RemoteOnly"
defaultRedirect="MyError.aspx"/>

    </system.web>
</configuration>
```

The `mode` attribute of the `<customErrors>` tag can take three values:

✦ On: Indicates that the custom error messages are always sent to users and that the detailed ASP.NET error page is never shown.

✦ Off: Indicates that only original error messages are sent to users even if a custom error page is available.

✦ RemoteOnly: Indicates that the custom error messages are displayed only to remote users accessing the site. If no custom error page is available, remote users simply see a message indicating that an error has occurred.

When you modify the Web.config file to set the defaultRedirect attribute, the user is directed to the same custom error message irrespective of the type of the error. The type of the error is identified by the HTTP status code. You can specify specific error messages, such as "Page not found" or "server crash" for specific status codes, as shown in the following code:

```
<configuration>
<system.web>
<customErrors
 defaultRedirect="http://host1/MyError.aspx"
mode="RemoteOnly">
    <error statusCode="500"
           redirect="http://host1/pages/support.html"/>
    <error statusCode="403"
           redirect="http://host1/pages/access_denied.html"/>
</customErrors>
</system.web>
</configuration>
```

In this code, the error tag takes two attributes, statusCode and redirect. The statusCode attribute represents the value of the HTTP status code. The redirect attribute points to the error message file.

Tracking errors

In an earlier section, you saw how to display custom error messages to users in case errors occur on a server. In addition to displaying error messages to users, you should ensure that the administrators and developers are also able to track errors. This would allow them to identify and solve the problems associated with the code.

You can implement error tracking by handling the Application_Error event, an application-level event that is generated when an exception occurs during the processing of a Web request. The developers can use this event handler to obtain information, such as the page URL, the query string arguments, and cookie values. With this information, developers can write the code to track the problem or notify administrators and developers about the problem. The errors can be tracked by using the Event Log, sending e-mail to administrators, or writing to a database etc.

You can write to the NT Event Log by adding code in the Application_Error event handler in the Global.asax file of your application. You can write to the NT Event Log only after you've imported the System.Diagnostics namespace.

To implement error tracking, create a Visual Basic ASP.NET Web Application project. In this project, import the System.Diagnostics namespace in the Global.asax file:

```
Imports System.Diagnostics
```

Then, write the following code in the event handler for the Application_Error event (in the Global.asax file). This code demonstrates how to write an Event Log to track errors related to page URL. The Event Log is named MyLog.

```
Sub Application_Error(ByVal sender As Object, ByVal e As
EventArgs)
        ' Fires when an error occurs
        'Retrieving the request URL

        Dim pageUrl, message, logName as String
        Dim event_log1 as New EventLog

        pageUrl = Request.Path

        'Creating error message to write to Event Log
        message = "Page URL: " & pageUrl

        'Specifying the Event Log name
        logName = "MyLog"

        'Creating Event Log if it does not exist
        If (Not EventLog.SourceExists (logName)) Then
            EventLog.CreateEventSource (logName,logName)
        End If

        'Writing to the log
        event_log1.Source = logName
        event_log1.WriteEntry ("Application error occured. " +
message,EventLogEntryType.Error)
End Sub
```

The application project contains a default Web Form, WebForm1.aspx. Rename this file to read "MakeEvent.aspx." Open the code behind file of this page and write the following statement to import the System.IO namespace:

```
Imports System.IO
```

Finally, in the Page_Load method, write the following code:

```
Sub Page_Load(Sender As System.Object, e As System.EventArgs)
Handles MyBase.Load
    'Cause the event log entry to be made
    throw New FileNotFoundException("test exception")
End Sub
```

When the MakeEvent.aspx page is executed, it generates an exception called `FileNotFoundException`. This exception will fire the `Application_Error` event in the Global.asax file, which in turn will record a log of this error in the Windows Event Log. You will be able to see the errors using the Windows Event Log Viewer. To do so:

1. Select Start ➪ Programs ➪ Administrative Tools ➪ Event Viewer.

2. Click the Event Log node to open the log. In this case, the name of the log is MyLog. You need to select the log file from the \winnt\system32\config folder. The file will be named MyLog.evt.

Using Debugging Tools

A chef, while demonstrating to his students the preparation of a new dish, makes sure that all the students write down the instructions or important points in their description manual so that they can easily refer to their manual if they encounter problems while preparing the dish on their own.

In the creation process, writing or drawing an outline plays a major role, because in case of a failure, you do not need to waste your time scratching your head. Instead, you can refer to the outline to solve the problem. In any kind of development, if the developer starts logging the steps involved, debugging or finding errors and fixing them becomes very systematic and easy.

In programming, logging of the process usually refers to the ability of an application to incorporate the use of debugging, code tracing, performance counters, and event logs. In this section, you'll learn to use the different debugging tools.

Visual Studio .NET Debugger

Visual Studio has always provided the developer with very powerful GUI debuggers, and Visual Studio .NET is no exception to this tradition. The debugger built into Visual Studio .NET is powerful and has a lot of new features compared to the debugger that was available with Visual Studio 6.0. Features that were previously available to the developers of Visual Basic only, like the Immediate window, are now common to all the .NET languages. So, irrespective of the language that is used to create a Web application, the debugging tools remain the same, thereby delivering a better developer experience. You can use the Visual Studio .NET debugger to debug applications in one of the following two ways:

✦ By using the Debug menu

✦ By manually attaching the debugger to a running application

The debugger provides many options that allow you to check for any errors by running through the code step by step, skipping a code routine, or placing a breakpoint. A *breakpoint* marks a point in the code at which the application halts and enters a mode called *Break mode*. The different options available in this mode help a developer to trace the source of an error in an application.

Using the Debug menu

To debug an application, select Debug ➪ Start. This option starts the application and attaches a debugger to it. The different Debug menu options are described in Table 7-1.

	Table 7-1 Debug options	
Option	**Description**
Start	Used to start the application execution.
Continue	Used to continue the application execution after the application enters a break mode.
Restart	Used to restart the debugging process.
Step Into	Used to transfer the control to a called procedure in the application.
Step Out	Used to transfer control from the called procedure (without proceeding further) back to the calling procedure.
Step Over	Used to skip a called procedure.
Run To Cursor	Used to execute the code until it reaches the line where the cursor is placed, or until a breakpoint is reached, whichever occurs first.
New Breakpoint	Used to set a breakpoint on any line of code. Using the New Breakpoint dialog box (Ctrl+B) provides a lot of options, such as to specify additional conditions that must be met for a breakpoint to be hit, and when the breakpoint will be hit.
	An alternative way to set a breakpoint is to click the left margin of the line where you want to set a breakpoint.

Note   The Step Into and Step Over options perform the same operation until the code reaches a calling statement to call a procedure. The Step Into option causes you to enter the called procedure and run through it, whereas the Step Over option causes you to skip any called procedure.

Let us look at a step-by-step approach to debug an ASP.NET Web page. Consider a simple Web page that provides users with the functionality of adding two numbers. The code of this Web page is given as follows:

```
<%@ Page Language="vb"%>
<!DOCTYPE HTML PUBLIC "-//W3C//DTD HTML 4.0 Transitional//EN">
<HTML>
 <HEAD>
```

```
<TITLE></TITLE>
</HEAD>

  <Script runat="server">

    Sub DoArithmetic(Src As Object, E As EventArgs)
        lblResult.Text = txtNum1.Text + txtNum2.Text
    End Sub

  </Script>

<Body>
 <Form id="Form1" method="post" runat="server">
  <P>
    <asp:Label id="lblNumber1" runat="server">Number
1</asp:Label>
    <asp:TextBox id="txtNum1" runat="server"></asp:TextBox>
  </P>
  <P>
    <asp:Label id="lblNumber2" runat="server">Number
2</asp:Label>
    <asp:TextBox id="txtNum2" runat="server"></asp:TextBox>
  </P>
  <P>
    <asp:Button id="cmdCalculate" runat="server"
Text="Calculate" onclick="DoArithmetic" />
  </P>
  <P>
    <asp:Label id="lblResult" runat="server" Width="270px"
Height="31px"></asp:Label>
  </P>
 </Form>
</Body>
</HTML>
```

When you browse this Web page in Internet Explorer, and enter two numbers, say 5 and 5, in the two text boxes, and then click the Calculate button, you'll notice that the result that is displayed is 55 instead of 10.

Let us see how you can use the Visual Studio .NET debugger to debug the preceding code. Before browsing the page in Internet Explorer, the first thing that you need to do is to set a breakpoint on the line from where debugging should start. Typically, the line on which the debugger should break will be the one that the developer suspects as a source of malfunctioning. In our case, the breakpoint should be on the Sub procedure named DoArithmetic. Note that a breakpoint can also be conditional; the debugger will break on the breakpoint only if a given condition evaluates to True or False as defined on the breakpoint. Figure 7-1 shows the New Breakpoint dialog box.

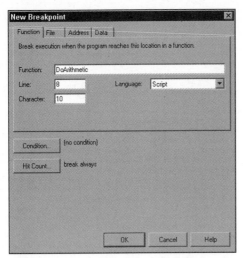

Figure 7-1: The New Breakpoint dialog box

Note   You can also add a breakpoint by clicking the left margin of the line on which you need to set the breakpoint or by pressing the F9 key while the cursor is on the line. Then, to remove a breakpoint, press F9 or click the left margin of the line at which the breakpoint was set.

To debug the current page, you need to mark the page as the startup page of the project. This can be done by right-clicking the ASPX file in the Solution Explorer window and choosing the Set As Start Page option from the context menu.

After you have set the breakpoint and set the Web page as the startup page of the project, you can start debugging your page. To start debugging the page, select Start from the Debug menu. This will start a new instance of Internet Explorer, and load the current page in it.

When you enter numbers in the Number1 and Number2 text boxes, say 5 and 5, respectively, and click the Calculate button, the debugger enters Break mode. In this mode, you can see the line at which you set the breakpoint being highlighted. You can check the values of the various variables and controls for correctness in Break mode.

You'll now run through the procedure in a stepwise manner to identify the source of the problem. To do so, select Debug ➪ Step Into. You'll notice that the next line (this is the only code line in the procedure) gets highlighted. Select Debug ➪ Step Into once more to execute this line of code. At this stage, the next line (End Sub) gets highlighted. This is the time when you should check the value in each text box and thus conclude the source of the problem. The Immediate window can be used for ad-hoc querying of variable and control property values. You can open the

Immediate window by selecting Debug ⇨ Windows ⇨ Immediate. In the Immediate window, type the following statement:

```
?lblResult.Text
```

After typing the preceding statement, press Enter. The Immediate window displays "55." The Result "55" gives an indication that the result is a string and not a number. This is enough to identify that the problem was due to the datatype. The numbers entered in the two text boxes were set in the `Text` property of the text boxes. In the `DoArithmetic` procedure, when you added the two numbers by accessing the `Text` property of the text boxes, the "+" operator worked as the concatenation operator to concatenate two strings rather than adding two numbers. Therefore, the values entered in the text boxes must be converted to a numeric datatype before adding them.

After you've found the actual error, you can stop debugging and correct the code. To stop the debugging process, select Debug ⇨ Stop Debugging.

Next, remove the breakpoint (Press F9 at the line at which the breakpoint was set). Modify the line in the `DoArithmetic` procedure to read:

```
lblResult = Cint(txtNum1.Text) + Cint(txtNum2.Text)
```

After you fix the code and run the application, you'll notice that now the page gives the correct output.

Attaching a Debugger

In addition to attaching a debugger to an application when you start it, you can attach a debugger while an application is already running. To do so, complete the following steps:

1. Open the application in Visual Studio .NET.

2. Select Debug ⇨ Processes to open the Processes dialog box.

3. Ensure that the "Show system processes" option is selected.

4. In the Available Processes pane, all the processes are listed. Scroll through the list to select aspnet_wp.exe.

5. Click Attach to open the Attach To Process dialog box. From the available choices, select Common Language Runtime and Script.

6. Click OK and then click Close.

After you've attached the debugger to your running application, you can debug the application to trace the source of error.

Note   You can attach a debugger to a running Web page only if it is running in Internet Explorer. If you are viewing the page within the IDE, you will not be able to attach a debugger with your page.

The ASP.NET Trace functionality

In ASP.NET, the trace feature ensures that the programmers are able to log their applications by providing the means to monitor and examine program performance either during development or after deployment. ASP.NET allows tracing at two levels:

✦ Page-level tracing

✦ Application-level tracing

Trace capability of ASP.NET is declared in the TraceContext class. To enable the Trace Page, the `Trace` directive must be set to True. The `Trace` property is exposed as a public property within ASP.NET pages. The `Trace` property refers to the TraceContext of the ASP.NET page.

The TraceContext class is a noninheritable public class of the .NET Framework that is used for capturing the execution details of a Web request and presenting the data on the page. For developers to include messages for specific Trace categories, this class can be a good utility. You need to include the System.Web namespace in your Web project to be able to use this class.

The class has certain properties and methods that provide the functionality for enabling the debugging of the ASP.NET pages.

Table 7-2 and Table 7-3 list the properties and methods exposed by the TraceContext class.

Table 7-2 Properties of the TraceContext class	
Property	*Description*
IsEnable	Indicates whether tracing is enabled for the current Web request. Allows browsers to determine the state of tracing for the current Web request for the page or the application. You can use this property to check whether or not the page or application should include the tracing information before writing anything to the trace log. You can set this property for the page by including a trace="true" attribute in the @ Page directive as the first element on the page. To set this property for the entire application, use the application's Web.config file.
TraceMode	Indicates the sequence in which the trace messages should be displayed to the requesting browser. The sequence of the trace messages can be sorted alphabetically or in the order in which they were processed by using user-defined categories.

Note When the IsEnable property is set to True for the entire application, it is mandatory to exclusively set the property to False for any page that needs to be restricted from displaying the tracing information.

Table 7-3
Public instance methods of the TraceContext class

Method	Description
Equals	Used to check whether or not the instance of an object equals the current object.
GetHashCode	Used for hashing algorithms and data structure, such as a hash table.
ToString	Used to return a string that represents the current object.
GetType	Used to return the type of the object passed.
Warn	Used to write the trace information along with the optional exception data in the Trace log. The warnings that are written into the Trace log appear as red text.
Write	Used to write to the Trace log.

After discussing the TraceContext class properties and methods, let us now understand the two levels of tracing.

Page-level tracing

ASP.NET makes it easy to debug and test applications by providing a trace capability. After the trace capability is enabled, ASP.NET provides the following functionalities automatically:

✦ Creates and appends a table called the table of performance data to the end of the ASP.NET page.

✦ Allows a developer to add custom diagnostic messages in the code wherever required.

Basically, the following are the two ways to generate trace statements in a page:

✦ Use the code written within a file.

✦ Use an HTML editor.

While generating the trace statements, you can include custom trace messages to the Trace log. Then, with the help of an HTML editor, you can present those messages and other trace information in a better manner.

You'll now write an ASP.NET page that generates the trace statements. Both Visual Studio .NET and Notepad can be used for writing the code. In this case, Notepad is used to create the ASPX file. The steps involved in writing the code for the page are described as follows:

1. Open Notepad and type the following code:

```
<%@ Page Language="VB" Trace="False"%>
 <html>
  <head>
   <title> Trace Demo </title>
  </head>

   <Script runat="server">
      Public Function Addition(FNum As Integer, SNum As
Integer) As Integer
         Trace.Write("Inside Addition() FNum: ",
FNum.ToString())
         Trace.Warn("Inside Addition() SNum: ",
SNum.ToString())
         return FNum + SNum
      End Function
   </Script>

  <body>
   Calling the Addition Function: 10 + 5 =
<%=Addition(10,5)%>
  </body>
</html>
```

2. Save the file as an ASPX file in a Web directory on the Web server. In this case, the file is named TraceStat.aspx.

3. Execute the TraceStat.aspx file. Figure 7-2 shows the output as shown in the browser when the ASP.NET page (TraceStat.aspx) is executed.

In this code, the Trace.Write statements generate the trace statements. The Addition function takes two integer values and returns an integer value as the sum of the two numbers taken as parameters. In the Calling statement, the Addition function is called by using the <% and the %> delimiters used for specifying the ASP code.

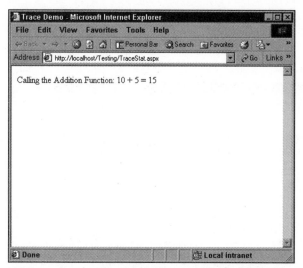

Figure 7-2: An example of the Trace.Write() method

Using the same code that generated the trace statement, you'll now look at the steps involved in presenting the statements generated in the ASP.NET page itself. The steps involved are described as follows:

1. Open the file TraceStat.aspx in Notepad and add the following directive as the first element in the file:

```
<%@ Page Trace="true" %>
```

2. Save the file in the same location with the same name.

3. Reexecute the TraceStat.aspx file. Figure 7-3 shows the output as displayed in the browser when the ASP.NET page (TraceStat.aspx) is executed.

In Figure 7-3, the trace information has been appended at the end of the ASP.NET. Looking at the output, the trace statements are as follows:

✦ Inside Addition() Fnum:
✦ Inside Addition() Snum:

Note @Page directives are special instructions that ASP.NET uses when processing a request for an ASP.NET resource. @Page directives can be used to override or apply configuration settings for an ASP.NET page. A directive must be the first element on a page.

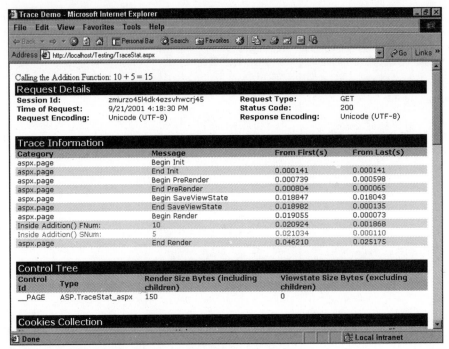

Figure 7-3: The output with Tracing enabled

Application-level tracing

Application-level Tracing is enabled by using the Web.config file. This file is also used to enable the ASP.NET framework to gather the HTTP request information for the entire application.

Unlike page-level Trace statements, application-level Tracing does not present the Trace information in a browser unless specified, but the information can be displayed in a Web-based Trace viewer application. The Trace viewer displays trace information for a sequence of requests to the application, thus making it mandatory to store the matrix for each request in memory until tracing is enabled. This can be done by including a TraceContext class that participates in the HTTP execution of each request for the application.

By opening the root Web.config file and looking at the tracing section, the following code can be seen:

```
<configuration>
  <system.web>
    <trace enabled="false" requestLimit="10" pageOutput="false"
traceMode="SortByTime" />
  </system.web>
</configuration>
```

The Trace element has four attributes. These attributes are described in Table 7-4.

Table 7-4
Attributes of the Trace element

Attribute	Description
enabled	Indicates whether or not the application-level Tracing is enabled. This attribute can take one of the two values, True or False. By default, the value is set to False.
requestLimit	Takes an integer value that specifies the total number of trace requests to keep cached in memory on a per-application basis. By default, the value is set to 10.
pageOutput	Indicates whether or not the Trace information would be presented on the ASP.NET page. This attribute can take one of the two values, True or False. By default the value is set to False.
traceMode	Indicates the mode in which the Trace information is presented. The information can be sorted by time or category.

Note   Sorting by category is used to differentiate between the settings made by the system and the `Trace.Write()` settings enabled by the developer. On the other hand, sorting by time sorts the information by the amount of time spent in the call.

You'll use the same sample code as used for the page-level Tracing to implement the application-level Tracing. However, you need to remove the @ Page directive to implement the application-level Tracing. Then, modify the Web.config settings as follows:

```
<configuration>
  <system.web>
    <trace
        enabled="true"
        requestlimitrequestLimit="10"
        pageoutputpageOutput="false"
        tracemodetraceMode="SortByTime"
    />
  </system.web>
</configuration>
```

Figures 7-4 and 7-5 show the output when the pageOutput attribute in the Web.config file is set to False and when the attribute is set to True, respectively. Do remember to remove all tracing directives from the @ Page directives that you may have declared in the individual ASPX pages. Controlling trace behavior of an ASP.NET Web site becomes easier using the Web.config file, because it is the only file that is used to enable or disable the tracing ability of the Web site. For large Web sites, it is recommended that trace mode be controlled using the Web.config file rather than from the individual pages.

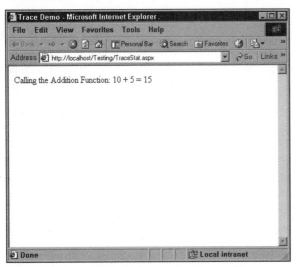

Figure 7-4: Output with the pageOutput attribute set to False

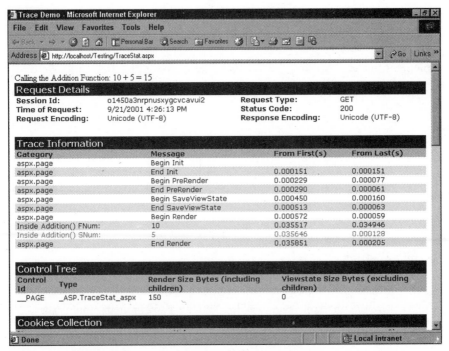

Figure 7-5: Output with the pageOutput attribute set to True

Writing Good ASP.NET Code

Good programming practices make it easy to understand, debug, and maintain code. Poorly written programs lead to confusion while debugging. The developer who has written the code might find himself in a situation where he cannot tell what the code is doing. Therefore, every developer should follow good programming practices. The same applies for an ASP.NET developer. While developing an ASP.NET application, a developer must keep in mind certain guidelines with respect to form designing, naming variables and objects, designing and implementing programming logic, and using coding style.

Form design

The form design should be visually appealing. It should be simple and neat. Although Web pages use bright colors and lots of images to make them attractive, this type of design takes a longer time to load the pages. Therefore, while designing pages, you should keep the following guidelines in mind:

✦ The controls that need user input should have the correct tab order and should be grouped and arranged in an order that makes sense while entering data.

✦ The controls should be properly aligned.

Variables and objects

While naming variables and objects, keep the following guidelines in mind:

✦ Use a proper naming notation, such as Hungarian or camel-casing notation, to name variables and objects. Hungarian notation enables you to identify the datatype of the variable from the name of the variable. So, a variable storing the first name of an employee will be declared as sFirstName. In camel-casing notation, the variable names take the form sfirstName, with the second part of the variable, which is a noun, capitalized.

✦ Name the variables and objects meaningfully. Meaningful names combined with Hungarian notation make the purpose and type of the variables clear. This results in a self-documented code, which is easy to understand and maintain.

✦ Declare the variables and objects in the beginning of a procedure. Declaration in the beginning makes the code execution more efficient, besides making it easy to understand by someone looking at the code text.

✦ Always initialize variables to certain default values before using them, to avoid any type conversion issues.

✦ Always rely on explicit conversion functions to eliminate confusion.

Programming logic

While implementing the programming logic, you should do a good chunking of the code. The chunking helps you to maintain the code and speed up debugging. Keep the following guidelines in mind:

✦ If you want to implement a programming logic that returns a single result, use a function.

✦ If you need multiple arguments to be passed without expecting a return value, use a procedure.

✦ If you want to create a reusable piece of code, use functions or Sub procedures or put the code in a separate class (if the code can be logically grouped).

Coding style

The program should be easy to read and to understand when you need to refer back to it. Follow these guidelines while coding:

✦ Always use "Option Explicit" to catch any undeclared or misspelled variables. Also, the use of "Option Explicit" makes the Web pages run fast. The "Option Explicit" option forces the explicit declaration of variables.

✦ Declare one variable per line. This avoids confusion about datatypes.

✦ Use comments wherever possible to document a difficult code section.

✦ Use blank lines in the code for clarity.

✦ Use proper code block indenting.

Summary

This chapter explored error handling and debugging tools for ASP.NET applications. First, you learned how to display custom error messages to users. You saw how to log errors in the NT Event Log. Then, you learned the concept of debugging and its importance. You learned to use the Visual Studio .NET debugger. You saw the properties and methods of the TraceContext class and @ Page directive. You also examined the Web.config file for setting the application-level Tracing. You learned to enable the Tracing functionality at the page level as well as the application level. Finally, you learned how to write good ASP.NET code.

✦   ✦   ✦

ASP.NET Database Programming

Introducing ADO.NET

As more and more companies are coming up with *n*-tier client/server and Web-based database solutions, Microsoft with its Universal Data Access (UDA) model, offers high-performance access to diverse data and information sources on multiple platforms. Also, UDA provides an easy-to-use programming interface that works with practically any tool or language, leveraging the technical skills developers already have.

The Microsoft UDA model is a collection of Data Access Components, which are the key technologies that enable Universal Data Access. The Data Access Components include ActiveX Data Objects (ADO), Remote Data Service (RDS), formerly known as Advanced Data Connector (ADC), Object Linking and Embedding Database (OLE DB), and Open Database Connectivity (ODBC).

Microsoft is targeting many more such Data Access components that offer easy-to-maintain solutions to organizations. Such solutions are aimed at allowing organizations use their own choice of tools, applications, and data sources on the client, middle tier, or server. One of the emerging components within the UDAs collection is ADO.NET. This chapter introduces you to ADO.NET.

ADO.NET Basics

Microsoft ADO.NET is the latest improvement after ADO. ADO.NET provides platform interoperability and scalable data access. In the .NET Framework, data is transmitted in the Extensible Markup Language (XML) format. Therefore, any application that can read the XML format can process data. It is not necessary for the receiving component to be an ADO.NET component at all. The receiving component might be a Microsoft Visual Studio–based solution or any application running on any other platform.

Although ADO.NET preserves some of the primary concepts from previous ADO models, it has been chiefly stretched to provide access to structured data from diverse sources. ADO.NET provides access to diverse data sources by using a consistent and standardized programming model. ADO.NET is upgraded to offer several advantages over previous versions of ADO and over other data access components.

ADO.NET builds the foundation of data-aware .NET applications. ADO.NET brings together all the classes that allow data handling. Such classes represent data container objects that feature typical database capabilities — indexing, sorting, and views. While ADO.NET offers a solution for .NET database applications, it presents an overall structure that is not as database-centric as the ADO model.

The ADO model uses the concept of recordsets, which are the ADO representation of tables and views from a database. Although these recordsets are very flexible to use and allow access to data even when disconnected from data sources, they suffer from a major drawback. In the case of distributed and Web applications, data needs to be exchanged among different components at different tiers, which might be running on variety of platforms. Of course, the format of the data being exchanged should be understood by all components. This transmission of data requires the conversion of data types of values to some data types that are recognized by the receiving components. This conversion is called COM marshalling. Thus, the interoperability is limited when using ADO recordsets. So, the concept of ADO recordsets fails when we look at the Internet interoperability.

Like ADO, ADO.NET also allows you to access data when disconnected from actual data sources. However, unlike ADO, ADO.NET uses XML as the data format. Because XML is a universal data format being used, ADO.NET expands the boundaries of interoperability to the Internet. In addition, instead of recordsets, ADO.NET uses the DataSet and DataReader objects to access and manipulate data. You'll learn about these objects later in the chapter. Thus, ADO.NET is designed to perform better and be more flexible than ADO. However, to support ADO objects, the corresponding equivalents exist in ADO.NET.

Note   Data container objects are the objects that contain data to be transmitted to the receiving components.

To take full advantage of ADO.NET, you should put some effort into understanding the concept itself, rather than simply figuring out the fastest way to port your code. Whatever .NET programming model you might choose — Windows Forms, Web Forms, or Web Services — ADO.NET will be there to help you with data access issues. The workings of ADO.NET are shown in Figure 8-1. Let us now look at the key features offered by ADO.NET.

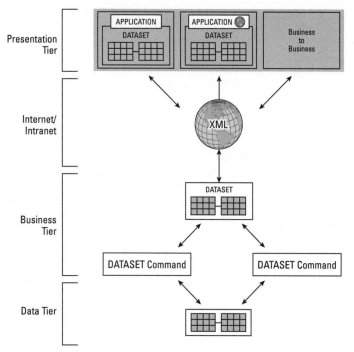

Figure 8-1: The workings of ADO.NET

Interoperability

The ADO.NET model is designed to take maximum advantage of the flexibility provided by the large industry acceptance of XML. ADO.NET uses XML for transmitting datasets among components and across tiers. Any component that is capable of reading the XML format can process the data. It is not necessary for the receiving component to be an ADO.NET component. The component that is sending or transmitting the dataset can simply transmit the dataset to its destination without bothering with how the receiving component is implemented. The component asking for the dataset, the destination component, can be implemented as a Visual Studio application or any other application. However, the important point to be considered is that the receiving component should be capable of accepting the XML file formatted as a dataset.

Maintainability

After an application is deployed, there might be a need for changes in the application. For example, the application might need substantial architectural changes to improve its performance. As the performance load on a deployed application server grows, system resources can become inadequate, resulting in higher response times. As a solution to these problems, the application might need to undergo architectural changes by adding tiers. Here, the problem is not the multi-tier application design, but rather the problem lies in increasing the number of tiers after an application is deployed. This transformation becomes easier if the original application is implemented in ADO.NET using datasets. In ADO.NET, the communication between tiers is relatively easy, because the tiers can transmit data through XML-formatted datasets.

Programmability

The ADO.NET model uses typed programming to manipulate objects. In *typed programming,* the programming environment or programming language itself recognizes the types of things that are important to users. To take full advantage of typed programming, you must know the things that are of interest to programmers and to end users. Consider the following code using typed programming in ADO.NET:

```
If TotalQty > DataSet1.ProductInfo("Baby Food").QtyAvailable
```

This code is equivalent to a line using non-typed programming and is easier to read by end users. An end user who has little or no programming experience can easily grasp the meaning of the condition being tested. Also, in non-typed programming, if the developer makes a spelling mistake by chance (for example, ProductInfo is spelled as ProdcutInfo), a run-time error will get generated. On the other hand, in typed datasets, errors in the syntax caused by misspellings are detected at compile time rather than at run time.

Performance

In ADO, while transmitting data across tiers using COM marshalling in the form of disconnected RecordSets, the values must be converted to data types that are recognized by COM. This results in poor performance. On the other hand, ADO.NET is designed to use disconnected data architecture, which in turn is easier to scale because it reduces the load on database (does not require any data type conversions). Thus, in the ADO.NET model, everything is handled at the client side, which in turn improves performance.

Scalability

The Web-based, data-centric applications require multiple users to access data simultaneously. This increases the demand on data to be accessed, making scalability one of the most critical features. Applications that use resources, such as database connections and database locks, cannot support more users to access data simultaneously, because eventually the user demand for the limited resources will exceed their supply. Because ADO.NET uses disconnected data access, applications do not retain database locks or active database connections for long durations. Hence, ADO.NET accommodates scalability by encouraging programmers to conserve limited resources, and allows more users to access data simultaneously.

ADO.NET Object Model

The .NET Framework is designed to change dramatically the developer's current style of developing applications, including the data access features. For the .NET applications, the primary data access technology to be used would be ADO.NET — the latest addition to the ADO model.

The ADO.NET Object Model is primarily divided into two levels:

✦ **Connected Layer:** Consists of the classes that comprise the Managed Providers

✦ **Disconnected Layer:** Is rooted in the DataSet

This section describes both the Managed Providers and the DataSet.

Managed Providers

Managed Providers are a collection of classes in the .NET Framework that provide a foundation for the ADO.NET programming model. The .NET Framework allows you to write language-neutral components, which can be called from any language, such as C++ or Visual Basic. In the .NET Framework, the OLE DB and ADO layers are merged into one layer. This results in high performance, and at the same time allows components to be called from any language. The Managed Data Providers include classes that can be used for the following:

✦ Accessing data from SQL Server 7.0 and later

✦ Accessing the other OLE DB providers

The Managed Provider for ADO.NET is the System.Data.OleDb namespace, which allows you to access OLE DB data sources. This namespace includes classes that are used to connect to OLE DB data sources and execute database queries to access and manipulate data. Some of the classes included in the namespace are described in Table 8-1.

Table 8-1
ADO.NET classes for OLE DB data sources

Class	Description
OleDbConnection	Represents an open connection to a data source.
OleDbCommand	Represents a SQL query to be executed against the data source.
OleDbDataReader	Corresponds to a forward-only, read-only RecordSet. It is a highly optimized and nonbuffering interface for getting the results of a query executed against the data source.

Continued

Table 8-1 *(continued)*

Class	Description
OleDbDataAdapter	Represents a set of data commands and a database connection that are used to fill the DataSet and update the data source.
OleDbParameter	Represents a parameter that is passed with an OleDbCommand object.
OleDbError	Represents the errors that are generated by the data source.

The Managed Provider for the ADO.NET classes to access and manipulate data stored on a SQL Server is the System.Data.SqlClient namespace. Table 8-2 describes some of the classes in this namespace.

Table 8-2
ADO.NET classes for SQL Server

Class	Description
SqlConnection	Represents an open connection to a SQL Server data source.
SqlDataAdapter	Represents a set of data commands and a database connection to populate the ADO.NET DataSet object. The SQLDataAdapter class corresponds to the OleDbDataAdapter class.
SqlCommand	Represents a T-SQL statement or stored procedure that SQL Server will execute. The SqlCommand corresponds to the ADOCommand class.
SqlParameter	Used for passing parameters to the SqlCommand object. When the SqlParameter object of ADO.NET is used to pass a parameter to the SqlCommand object, the parameter represents a T-SQL statement or stored procedure. When SqlParameter object is used to pass a parameter to the SqlDataSetCommand object, the parameter represents a column from a result set. SqlParameter corresponds to the ADOParameter class.
SqlError	Collects information about run-time warnings and error conditions that an ADO.NET application encounters. SqlError corresponds to the ADOError class.

To demonstrate how to open a connection to a SQL Server database and fill the DataSet (discussed later in this section) with a database query result, consider the following code:

```
Dim connection As New
SqlConnection("server=localserver;uid=sa;pwd=;database=Sales")

Dim command As New SqlDataAdapter("SELECT * FROM Products Where
ProductID=@ID", connection)

Dim param1 As New SqlParameter("@ID", SqlDbType.Int)
param1.Value = 1

command.SelectCommand.Parameters.Add(param1)

Dim dataset As New DataSet()
command.Fill(dataset, "Products")
```

In this code:

- ✦ `connection` is a SqlConnection class object that represents a connection to the SQL Server database.
- ✦ `command` is a SqlDataAdapter class object that represents a set of data commands and a database connection.
- ✦ `param1` is a SqlParameter class object that represents the parameter to be passed in the T-SQL command.
- ✦ `dataset` is a DataSet class object that represents the DataSet that is filled by the query results.

DataSet class

The DataSet comprises the Disconnected Layer of ADO.NET. The DataSet consists of a local buffer of tables and relations. As shown in Figure 8-2, the DataSet object model consists of Tables, Columns, Relations, Constraints, and Rows. A DataSet contains a collection of DataTables (the Tables collection). A *DataTable* represents one table of in-memory data. A DataTable consists of the following:

- ✦ A collection of columns (the Columns collection) that represents the table's schema.
- ✦ A collection of rows (the Rows collection) that represent the data held by the table.

A DataTable remembers the original state along with the current state, tracking the kinds of changes that have occurred. The data access classes are included in the System.Data namespace. Table 8-3 lists some of these classes along with their descriptions.

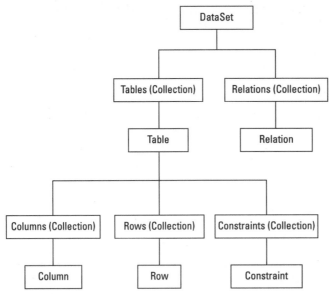

Figure 8-2: The DataSet object model

	Table 8-3 The data access classes of ADO.NET	
Class	*Description*
DataSet	Represents a complete collection of tables, relationships, and constraints. Both the System.Data.OleDb and the System.Data.SqlClient namespaces share this object of ADO.NET, making it the core component of the ADO.NET architecture.
DataAdapter	Represents a database query or stored procedure that is used to populate the DataSet object.
DataTable	Represents a data source that stores data in row and column format.
DataColumn	Represents a column in a DataTable.
DataRow	Represents a row in a DataTable.

Unlike RecordSets, which are equivalent to tables in ADO, DataSets keep track of the relationships between tables if any. The DataSet is designed with a rich programming model. The following code creates a new DataTable with the name ProductInfo:

```
Dim dset As DataSet = New DataSet("ProductInfo")
```

Later, you can add columns to the DataTable. The columns are added to the DataTable by using the Add method on the Columns collection, and the column is assigned a name and a datatype. Finally, data is added to the table by calling the NewRow method on the DataTable and storing the column values in each DataRow.

Changes from ADO

ADO.NET is an evolutionary improvement over ADO. Some of the improvements are described in Table 8-4.

	Table 8-4 **Feature changes in ADO.NET**	
Feature	*ADO*	*ADO.NET*
Memory-resident data representation	Uses the RecordSet object, which looks like a single table.	Uses the DataSet object, which contains one or more tables represented by DataTable objects.
Relationship between multiple tables	Requires a JOIN query to combine data from multiple tables in a single result table.	Provides the DataRelation object for combining data from multiple DataTable objects without requiring a JOIN query.
Data navigation	Scans the rows sequentially.	Uses a navigation model for nonsequential access to rows in a table. Tracks relationships to navigate from rows in one table to corresponding rows in another table.
Disconnected access	Supports the connected access, which is represented by the Connection object. To communicate with a database, ADO first makes a call to an OLE DB provider. However, ADO also supports the disconnected data access by the RecordSet object although it is not designed for it.	ADO.NET uses standardized calls for the DataSetCommand object to communicate with a database, which in turn communicates with the OLE DB provider. Sometimes, the DataSet object directly communicates with the APIs provided by a database management system.

Continued

	Table 8-4 *(continued)*	
Feature	*ADO*	*ADO.NET*
Programmability	Uses the Connection object to transmit commands for mapping a data source that has an underlying data construct.	Uses the typed programming characteristic of XML. Data is self-describing because names for code items correspond to the "real-world" problem solved by the code. The underlying data constructs, such as tables and rows, do not appear, making code easier to read and write.
Sharing disconnected data between tiers or components	Uses COM marshalling to transmit a disconnected RecordSet. Only those data types that are defined by COM standards support the feature to share disconnected data between tiers or components. Therefore, ADO needs to perform the data type conversions, which require system resources, resulting in low performance.	Transmits a DataSet with an XML file. The XML format places no restrictions on data types. Therefore, ADO.NET requires no data type conversions, resulting in improved performance.
Transmitting data through firewalls	Problematic, because firewalls are typically configured to prevent system-level requests, such as COM marshalling.	Supported because ADO.NET DataSet objects use XML for representing data. Using HTTP as the transport, XML data can pass through firewalls.
Scalability	Database locks and active database connections for long durations result in limited database resources, allowing fewer users to access data simultaneously.	Disconnected access to database data without retaining database locks or active database connections for lengthy periods does not limit the database resources. This allows more users to access data simultaneously.

Communicating with OLEDB Data Sources Using ADO.NET

Every application that needs to retrieve data from a database needs to establish a connection to the database. In ADO, this was achieved using the Connection object. In ADO.NET, the classes to be used for establishing the connection depend on the data source being used. For instance, to connect to SQL Server databases, the classes in the System.Data.SqlClient namespace are used. To connect to OLE DB data sources, you need to use classes in the System.Data.OleDb namespace. It must be noted that both the SQL Server and OLE DB providers are managed providers. These providers act as a thin layer that connects the application to the database without adding any unnecessary overhead, such as converting from OLE DB-compatible data types to native SQL Server data types and vice versa when communicating between the client and the server. The SQL Server data provider, for example, does not depend on OLE DB/ODBC. Instead, it uses the Tabular Data Stream (TDS) protocol of SQL Server to natively communicate with the SQL Server. The use of the TDS provides a tremendous performance boost to applications.

Let us now look at the classes required to establish a connection to a Microsoft Access database using the OLE DB-managed data provider.

System.Data.OleDb.OleDbConnection class

This class encapsulates the connection to an OLE DB data source. Applications that need to use an OLE DB provider to connect to the data source should use this class, because not all data sources will have managed .NET data providers. When the .NET Framework is shipped by Microsoft, it provides managed data providers for some of the popular DBMSs like MS Access and SQL Server. But, the data providers for the other DBMSs will be developed by the respective vendors. To avoid waiting for the availability of managed data providers, ADO.NET has the option of connecting to any OLE DB-compliant data sources. The OLE DB provider makes it easier for the application to be migrated to ADO.NET. All the features of ADO.NET can be readily used in an application without having to depend on the availability of a managed .NET data provider.

Here is sample code that connects to an Access database:

```
<%@ Page Language="VB"%>
<%@ Import Namespace="System.data.oledb"%>
<html>
<head>
  <title> ADO.NET Demo </title>
</head>
<Script runat="server">
    Public Sub DBConnect()
        dim cnAccess as OleDbConnection
        'construct the OleDbConnection object
        cnAccess = new
OleDbConnection("Provider=Microsoft.Jet.OLEDB.4.0;Data
Source=C:\ADODemo\Employee.mdb")
        'Open the database connection
        cnAccess.Open()
        Response.Write("Connection established!")
```

```
      End Sub
</Script>

<body>
<%DBConnect()%>
</body>
</html>
```

Figure 8-3 shows the output of the page.

Figure 8-3: Output of the page demonstrating the usage of the OleDbConnection class

System.Data.OleDb.OleDbCommand class

This class encapsulates the commands that need to be sent to the OLE DB data source. Applications use the OleDbCommand class to create select, insert, update, and delete commands that need to be sent to the data source. Also, this class can be used to execute stored procedures besides sending input parameters to the stored procedure and retrieving output parameters from the stored procedure.

Here is sample code that inserts data using an insert command into an Access table:

```
<%@ Page Language="VB"%>
<%@ Import Namespace="System.Data.OleDb"%>
<html>
  <script language="VB" runat=server>
    Sub Insert_Click(Src As Object, E As EventArgs)
```

```
      ' Connect to Database
      dim cnAccess as New
OleDbConnection("Provider=Microsoft.Jet.OLEDB.4.0;Data
Source=C:\ADODemo\Employee.mdb")
      cnAccess.Open()

      dim sID, sFName, sLName, sAge, sInsertSQL as string
      sID = eID.Text
      sFName = FName.Text
      sLName = LName.Text
      sAge = Age.Text

      'Make the insert statement
      sInsertSQL = "insert into employees values(" & sID & ",'"
& sFName & "','" & sLName & "'," & sAge & ")"

      'Make the OleDbCommand object
      dim cmdInsert as New OleDbCommand(sInsertSQL,cnAccess)

      ' This not a query so we do not expect any return data so
use
      ' the ExecuteNonQuery method
       cmdInsert.ExecuteNonQuery()

      response.write ("Data recorded!")
    End Sub
  </script>

  <body>

    <form runat=server>
      <h3><font face="Verdana">Enter Employee
Details</font></h3>
      <table>
        <tr>
          <td>ID:</td>
          <td><asp:textbox id="eID" runat="server"/></td>
        </tr>
        <tr>
          <td>First Name:</td>
          <td><asp:textbox id="FName" runat="server"/></td>
        </tr>
        <tr>
          <td>Last Name:</td>
          <td><asp:textbox id="LName" runat="server"/></td>
        </tr>
        <tr>
          <td>Age:</td>
          <td><asp:textbox id="Age" runat="server"/></td>
        </tr>
      </table>
      <asp:button text="Insert" OnClick="Insert_Click"
runat=server/>
      <p>
```

```
          <asp:Label id="Msg" ForeColor="red" Font-Name="Verdana"
    Font-Size="10" runat=server />
      </form>
    </body>
</html>
```

Figure 8-4 shows the output of the page.

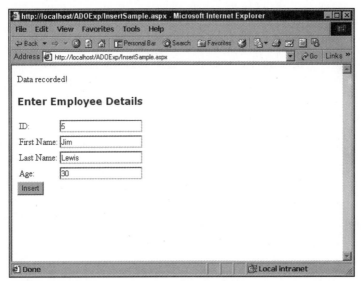

Figure 8-4: Output of the page demonstrating the usage of the OleDbCommand class

System.Data.OleDb.OleDbDataReader class

This class is equivalent to a forward-only, read-only Recordset object in classic ADO. This class is very useful to all applications that want to retrieve data returned from a query to the database and want to process one record at a time. A classic example for this would be to populate a list box with values retrieved from, say, a master table. The OleDbDataReader is independent of the OLE DB data source from which the data is retrieved. The process of reading data using the OleDbDataReader object is similar to reading data from any stream.

The following code retrieves a list of all the employees from an Access database:

```
<%@ Page Language="VB"%>
<%@ Import Namespace="System.Data.OleDb"%>
<html>
```

```
<script language="VB" runat=server>
  Sub Page_Load()
    ' Connect to Database
    dim cnAccess as New
OleDbConnection("Provider=Microsoft.Jet.OLEDB.4.0;Data
Source=C:\ADODemo\Employee.mdb")
    cnAccess.Open()
    dim sSelectSQL as string

    'Make the select statement
    sSelectSQL = "select * from employees"

    'Make the OleDbCommand object
     dim cmdSelect as New OleDbCommand(sSelectSQL,cnAccess)

    ' This query should return an OleDbDataReader so we use
the
    ' ExecuteReader method
    dim drEmp as OleDbDataReader, sbResults as new
StringBuilder()
    drEmp = cmdSelect.ExecuteReader()
    sbResults.Append ("<Table>")
    do while drEmp.Read()
      sbResults.Append ("<TR><TD>")
      sbResults.Append ( drEmp.GetInt32(0).ToString())
      sbResults.Append ("</TD><TD>")
      sbResults.Append ( drEmp.GetString(1))
      sbResults.Append ("</TD><TD>")
      sbResults.Append ( drEmp.GetString(2))
      sbResults.Append ("</TD><TD>")
      sbResults.Append ( drEmp.GetInt32(3).ToString())
      sbResults.Append ("</TD><TR>")
    loop
    sbResults.Append ("</Table>")
    lblResult.text = sbResults.ToString()
  End Sub
</script>

<body>
    <h3><font face="Verdana">Employee Details</font></h3>
    <p></p>
    <asp:label id="lblResult" runat="server" text=""/>
</body>
</html>
```

Figure 8-5 shows the output of the page.

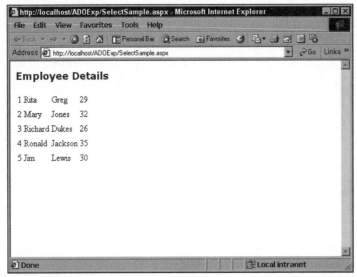

Figure 8-5: Output of the page demonstrating the usage of the OleDbDataReader class

System.Data.OleDb.OleDbDataAdapter class

The data adapter acts as the conduit between the client application and the database connection, command objects. The data adapter represents the command and connection that are used to populate the client dataset. In case of a disconnected client, the data adapter has the responsibility of firing the appropriate `insert`, `update`, or `delete` commands onto the database to synchronize the changes that are recorded in the client dataset.

The OleDbDataAdapter class has three command properties that are used to update the database:

✦ `InsertCommand`: Represents the query or stored procedure that is used to insert new records into the data source.

✦ `SelectCommand`: Represents a SQL statement used to select records in the data source.

✦ `DeleteCommand`: Represents a SQL statement for deleting records from the data set.

System.Data.DataSet, System.Data.DataTable, System. Data.DataRow, and System.Data.DataColumn classes

The DataSet is a generic class provided by the .NET Framework. This class is very useful on the client side to store data in a manner that is much more functional and powerful than the ADO Recordset object. Moreover, the data in a DataSet is in XML format, and therefore is readily accessible and manageable. The XML format makes it very well suited to Web applications, and makes cross-platform access possible. The DataSet in memory is quite similar to a full-blown, in-memory DBMS in that it has the ability to store data from multiple tables and the relationships between them. The tables are stored in DataTable objects, and DataRelation objects represent the relationship between tables. The rows and columns in a table are stored in DataRow and DataColumn objects, respectively.

Let us look at an example that lists all the employees from an Access database by using a DataSet in a Web page:

```
<%@ Page Language="VB"%>
<%@ Import Namespace="System.Data"%>
<%@ Import Namespace="System.Data.OleDb"%>
<html>
  <script language="VB" runat=server>
    Sub Page_Load()
      ' Connect to Database
      dim cnAccess as New
OleDbConnection("Provider=Microsoft.Jet.OLEDB.4.0;Data
Source=c:\ADODemo\Employee.mdb")
      cnAccess.Open()

      dim sSelectSQL as string
      ' Make the select statement
      sSelectSQL = "select * from employees"

      'Make the OleDbCommand object
      dim cmdSelect as New OleDbCommand(sSelectSQL,cnAccess)
      dim daEmp as new OleDbDataAdapter(cmdSelect)
      dim dsEmp as new DataSet
      dim sbResults as new StringBuilder()

      ' Fill the data with the output of the cmdSelect command. Note
      ' that the dataadapter is associated with the command. We use
      ' the dataadapter to fill the dataset.
      daEmp.Fill(dsEmp, "Employees")
      PrintRows(dsEmp)
    End Sub

    Sub PrintRows(ByVal myDataSet As DataSet)
      Dim dtEmp As DataTable
      Dim drEmp As DataRow
      Dim dcEmp As DataColumn, sbResult as new stringbuilder()
      ' Iterate through all the DataTables in the DataSet
      For Each dtEmp in myDataSet.Tables
        sbResult.Append("<Table>")
          ' Iterate through all the DataRows in the DataTable
```

```
            For Each drEmp In dtEmp.Rows
              sbResult.Append("<TR>")
                 ' Iterate through all the DataColumns in the
DataRow
                For Each dcEmp in dtEmp.Columns
                  sbResult.Append("<TD>")
                  sbResult.Append(drEmp(dcEmp))
                  sbResult.Append("</TD>")
                Next dcEmp
              sbResult.Append("</TR>")
              Next drEmp
          sbResult.Append("</Table>")
          Next dtEmp

    lblResult.Text = sbResult.ToString()
        End Sub

    </script>

    <body>
        <h3><font face="Verdana">List of Employees</font></h3>
        <p></p>
        <asp:label id="lblResult" runat="server" text=""/>
    </body>
</html>
```

Figure 8-6 shows the output of the page.

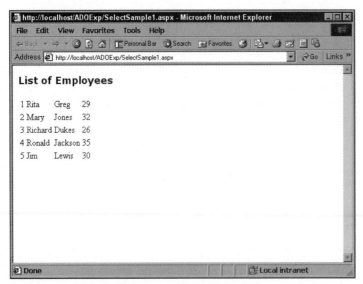

Figure 8-6: Output of the page demonstrating the usage of the DataSet, DataTable, DataRow, and DataColumn classes

Summary

This chapter introduced you to the new data access technology ADO.NET. First, you learned the basic features of ADO.NET. Then, you learned some of the most important ADO.NET objects. Here, you learned the objects to access OLE DB data sources as well as SQL data sources. To understand the advantages of ADO.NET over ADO, the features, such as disconnected data access, scalability, and interoperability of ADO and ADO.NET were compared. Finally, you learned to implement ADO.NET objects, such as OleDbConnection, OleDbCommand, OleDbDataReader, OleDbDataAdapter, and DataSet to access and manipulate data from OLE DB data sources.

✦   ✦   ✦

Understanding Data Binding

ASP.NET provides a rich set of controls that enable you to display information to users as well as accept information from users. You can display information in controls from a wide variety of data stores, such as properties, arrays, data structures, or databases. Some of the data stores are static, whereas others are dynamic. You usually use static data stores to display information for user reference. In addition to displaying static information in controls, there are situations that require you to display information dynamically. For example, you might need to display the discount based on the quantity purchased for a product. Also, you might need a control to display information from a database whose data keeps changing constantly. In such situations, ASP.NET provides a solution by providing a feature that allows data binding to controls.

This chapter introduces you to data binding with the ASP.NET server controls.

Introduction to Data Binding

Data binding means binding controls to information stored in a data store. Here, the term "data" is used in a very broad sense. When we talk about data binding, it implies binding any control property to almost any kind of data store. A data store can be as simple as a public property on a page, or as complex as a database stored on a server. This broad choice among data stores provides high flexibility, and thus enables you to bind a control to any data store based on your need.

The Web Forms controls that are bound to a data store access data through the properties of specific classes, categorized as *data classes*. Data classes typically include methods that can be used for updating the underlying data stores. Because the term "data" is used in a broad sense, the class category "data classes" is also used in a generic, broad sense. These classes differ depending on the data store. Some data classes provide more functionality than others—you can use any one of these classes depending on your need.

You can bind a control to different data stores, such as properties, methods, or collections. These different data stores can be bound to a control property by using *data binding expressions*. While binding, the data is always bound to a particular property of the control (the property name might differ for various controls). When a data binding expression is evaluated, the resulting value is loaded in the control's bound property. You can bind simple controls to public properties. A public property can be of a control on a page or the page itself.

Note Simple controls are the controls that can bind only to a single value. Some simple controls include Label, TextBox, and Button controls.

You can bind complex controls to any structure by using a data class that implements the ICollection interface, which ensures that the data classes provide the basic functionality of data access and navigation. For example, you can bind a DropDownList control to an array by using the ArrayList class, which implements the ICollection interface.

Note Complex controls are the controls that contain embedded controls. Some complex controls include DataList, Repeater, and DataGrid controls.

When you bind a control property to a data store, the Web Forms Framework cannot evaluate data binding expressions automatically. To display the evaluated value in the control's bound property, you need to call the DataBind() method explicitly. The page and each control on the page support this method. When you call the DataBind() method for a control, it is cascaded to all its child controls. For example, if you call the DataBind() method for the page control, the method is automatically called for all the controls on the page.

The explicit method for data binding enables you to control when to load the bound controls with data. Therefore, calling the DataBind() method explicitly should not be seen as a disadvantage. You can load the bound controls with data in one of the following situations:

✦ When you need to display data in the bound controls as soon as the page is loaded. In such a situation, you can call the DataBind() method at the Page_Load stage. You can call the DataBind() method for the page or for a specific control, depending on your requirement.

✦ When data in the dataset is updated and you want to display the updated data in the bound controls. In such a situation, you need to call the DataBind() method in the event-handling methods that resulted in the change to the dataset. Again, you can call the DataBind() method for the page or for specific controls depending on whether you want to refresh the complete page or specific controls.

Data Source Binding

You can use the ASP.NET syntax to bind data to the ASP.NET server controls. To bind these controls to data, you first need to open the ASPX file for the Web Forms page. Then, you can use the appropriate syntax for data binding for different controls. To bind a property of a control to some data represented by an expression, use the following tag:

```
<% # expression %>
```

When the expression is evaluated, the value is loaded in the control's bound property. For example, you can bind the Text property of a Label control to a public property called ProductID of the page. To do so, use the following code:

```
<asp:Label ID = "ProdID" runat = "Server" Text = '<% #
ProductID %>' />
```

In this code, the <% # ProductID %> tag is used to bind the Text property of the Label control to the ProductID property of the page.

Caution   You should be careful while using quotation marks in the expression. If the expression contains quoted strings, you should use single quotation marks.

As mentioned earlier, the control property will not display the bound data until the DataBind() method is called explicitly. You can call the DataBind() method for the page by using the following statement:

```
Page.DataBind()
```

Alternatively, you can simply use the following statement to call the DataBind() method for the page:

```
DataBind()
```

To call the DataBind() method for a specific control, use the following syntax:

```
ControlID.DataBind()
```

In this syntax, ControlID refers to the ID of the control for which you want to call the DataBind() method. For example, to call this method for a DataList control whose ID is DataList1, use the following statement:

```
DataList1.DataBind()
```

The topics that follow implement data binding of control properties to page properties, control properties, methods, collections, and lists. However, before implementing data binding, you need to create an ASP.NET Web Application project. You can choose Visual Basic .NET or C#, depending on your language proficiency. In your Web application, design a form as shown in Figure 9-1.

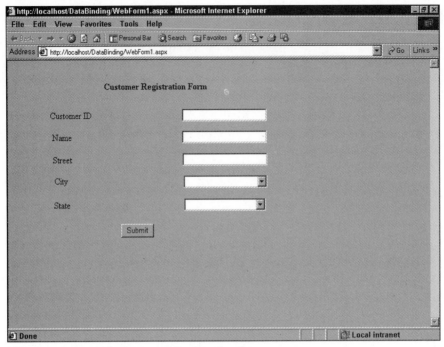

Figure 9-1: A sample Customer Registration form

Table 9-1 describes the properties for different controls used in the form.

Table 9-1		
Form control properties		
Control Type	**Contains**	**Control ID**
TextBox	Customer ID	CustID
TextBox	Customer name	CustName
TextBox	Customer street	CustStreet
DropDownList	Customer city	CustCity
DropDownList	Customer state	CustState
Button	Submit button	SubmitButton

In addition to the controls that you see in Figure 9-1, add a Label control below the button. Set the ID of this label to "DisplayLabel." Also, set the Visible property of this label to False. You can make it visible through programming, whenever required.

Binding data to page properties

In this section, you'll bind a simple property, CustomerID, of the page to the Text property of the TextBox control with ID CustID. To implement this data binding, follow these steps:

1. In the ASPX file of the Web Forms page, in the <HEAD> element, write the following code to create a read-only property called CustomerID:

```
<Script Language = "VB" runat = "Server">

    ReadOnly Property CustomerID() As String
            Get
                CustomerID = "C001"
            End Get
    End Property

</Script>
```

2. Edit the ASP code for the TextBox control with ID CustID to include the data binding expression as follows:

```
<asp:TextBox ID="CustID" runat="Server" Text='<% # CustomerID
%>' />
```

3. Call the DataBind() method in the Page_Load method. This is the most critical step, because the data-bound TextBox control will not display data until the DataBind() method is called explicitly. Therefore, write the following code in the <Script> tag:

```
Sub Page_Load(Sender As System.Object, e As System.EventArgs)
Handles MyBase.Load
        If Not IsPostBack Then
            Page.DataBind()
        End If
End Sub
```

When you execute the application, you'll find that the CustID TextBox control displays the value stored in the property CustomerID, as shown in Figure 9-2.

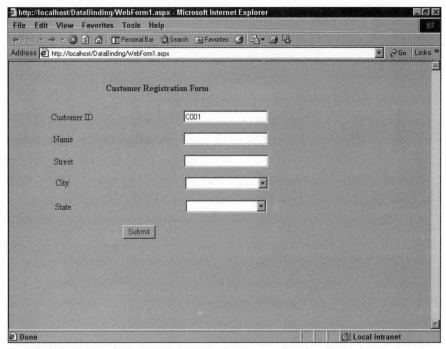

Figure 9-2: Output of the application implementing data binding to page properties

Binding data to control properties

In this section, you'll bind the Text property of the Label control with ID DisplayLabel to the text entered in the TextBox control with ID CustStreet. When a user clicks the Submit button, the Label control should display the street entered in the CustStreet text box. To implement this functionality, follow these steps:

1. In the `<Script>` tag, write an event handler for the Click event of the Button control whose ID is SubmitButton. This method calls the DataBind() method for the Label control with ID DisplayLabel and set its Visible property to True, as shown in the following code:

```
Sub SubmitButton_Click(Sender As System.Object, e As
System.EventArgs)

    'Calling the DataBind() method for the Label control
    DisplayLabel.DataBind()

    'Setting the Visible property of the Label control to
True
    DisplayLabel.Visible = True

End Sub
```

2. Edit the ASP code for the Label control with ID DisplayLabel to include the data binding expression. The expression combines a string and the `Text` property of the TextBox control with ID CustStreet.

```
<asp:Label ID = "DisplayLabel" runat = "Server" Text = '<%
#("The street that you entered is: " + CustStreet.Text)%>' />
```

3. Edit the ASP code for the Button control with ID SubmitButton to add the SubmitButton_Click event handler for the `Click` event:

```
<asp:Button ID="SubmitButton" runat="Server" Text="Submit"
OnClick="SubmitButton_Click" />
```

Figure 9-3 displays the output when you enter the name of the street and click the button at run time.

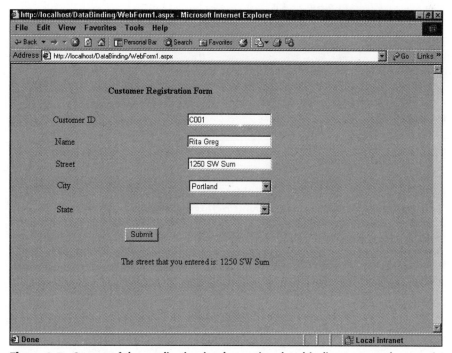

Figure 9-3: Output of the application implementing data binding to control properties

Data binding to an ArrayList

As mentioned earlier in the chapter, the controls, such as DropDownList, ListBox, and DataGrid, can be bound only by using the data classes that implement the ICollection interface. In this section, you'll bind the ArrayList class to the `DataSource` property of the DropDownList with ID CustState. To implement this data binding, write the following code in the Page_Load event handler.

```
Sub Page_Load(Sender As System.Object, e As System.EventArgs)
Handles MyBase.Load
     If Not IsPostBack Then
        'Creating an object of the ArrayList class
        Dim objArrayList as ArrayList= new ArrayList()

        'Adding items to the object of the ArrayList class
        objArrayList.Add ("New York")
        objArrayList.Add ("California")
        objArrayList.Add ("Oregon")
        objArrayList.Add ("Illinois")
        objArrayList.Add ("Texas")
        objArrayList.Add ("None")

        'Binding the DropDownList control with ID CustState to
the object of the ArrayList class

        CustState.DataSource = objArrayList

'Calling the DataBind() method for the State1 Drop Down control

        CustState.DataBind()
     End If
End Sub
```

In this code:

✦ objArrayList is an object of the ArrayList class.

✦ The Add() method of the ArrayList class is used to add items to the object.

✦ The DataSource property of the DropDownList control with ID CustState has been bound to the object of the ArrayList class.

After binding the State DropDownList control to the object of the ArrayList class, you can bind the Text property of the Label with ID DisplayLabel to the selected item in the DropDownList control with ID CustState. To do so, edit the ASP code for the Label control with ID DisplayLabel to include the data binding expression:

```
<asp: Label ID="DisplayLabel" runat="Server" Text='<% #("The street that you
entered is: " + CustStreet.Text + " and the state that you selected is: " +
CustState.SelectedItem.Text)%>' />
```

At run time, when you enter the name of a street, select a state, and click the button, the label with ID DisplayLabel becomes visible and displays the text as shown in Figure 9-4.

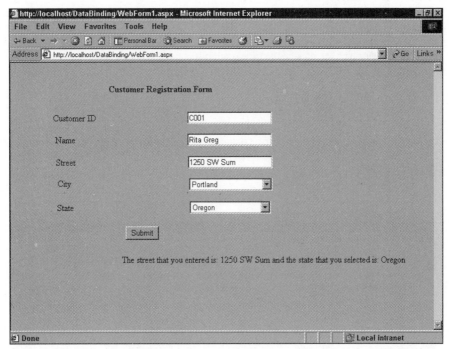

Figure 9-4: Output of the application implementing data binding to an ArrayList

Binding methods

Binding methods is similar to binding any other expression. In this section, you'll create a method to return a string based on the value selected from the DropDownList control with ID CustState. Then, you'll bind the Text property of the Display Label to this method. To implement this binding, write the following code in the <Script> tag to create a method called StateValue:

```
Function StateValue() As String

    If CustState.SelectedItem.Text="None" Then
        StateValue="Not a US resident"
    Else
        StateValue="Selected state: " +
CustState.selectedItem.Text
    End If

End Function
```

The StateValue method returns a string, "Not a US resident", if a user selects None from the DropDownList control with ID CustState. If the user selects any other value, the method returns the selected state. Next, you need to bind this method to the Text property of the Label control with ID DisplayLabel. To do so, edit the ASP code for this Label control to include the data binding expression:

```
<asp:Label ID="DisplayLabel" runat="Server" Text='<%
#StateValue%>' />
```

At run time, when you select None from the State DropDownList control and click the Submit button, the label shows the text "Not a US resident." Otherwise, if a user selects a state and clicks the Submit button, the selected state is displayed on the label as shown in Figure 9-5.

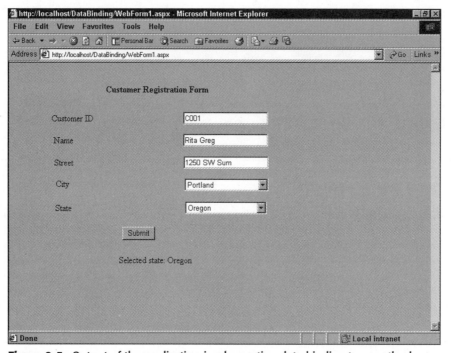

Figure 9-5: Output of the application implementing data binding to a method

Binding to a DataView

The DataView class represents a custom view of a data table. This class is a member of the System.Data namespace, and to use this class in your page, you need to import the System.Data namespace. Before you can implement binding to a data table, add a new Web Forms page to your ASP.NET Web Application project. In this form, add a DataGrid control. Then, to implement the functionality of the DataView class in this new form, you'll need to import the System.Data namespace. To do so, write the following statement in the ASPX file of the new Web Forms page:

```
<%@import Namespace="System.Data"%>
```

You can bind a DataView object to a DataGrid control. A DataGrid control displays information in row and column format. In this section, you'll create an object of the DataView class. This object represents a data table that displays cities and their respective states. Then, you'll bind this DataView object to the DataSource property of the DataGrid control. To implement this functionality, write the following code in the Page_Load method:

```
Sub Page_Load (Sender As System.Object, e As System.EventArgs)
Handles MyBase.Load
    If Not IsPostBack Then
        'Declaring objects of the DataTable and DataRow classes
        Dim DataTable1 As DataTable
        Dim DataRow1 As DataRow

        'Initializing the DataTable object
        DataTable1 = New DataTable()

        'Adding columns to the DataTable object
        DataTable1.Columns.Add(New DataColumn("City",
GetType(string)))
        DataTable1.Columns.Add(New DataColumn("State",
GetType(string)))

        'Creating arrays to store cities and their respective
states
        Dim strCity(5) as String
        Dim strState(5) as String
        Dim I as Integer
        strCity(0)="Chicago"
        strCity(1)="Hampstead"
        strCity(2)="Houston"
        strCity(3)="New York"
        strCity(4)="Portland"

        strState(0)="Illinois"
        strState(1)="New York"
        strState(2)="Texas"
        strState(3)="New York"
        strState(4)="Oregon"

        'Adding rows in the DataTable object
        For I=0 To 4
            DataRow1 = DataTable1.NewRow()
            DataRow1(0) = strCity(I)
            DataRow1(1) = strState(I)
```

```
        DataTable1.Rows.Add(DataRow1)
    Next

    'Setting the DataSource property of the DataGrid control to
the
    'DataView representing the DataTable object
    DataGrid1.DataSource=New DataView(DataTable1)

    'Calling the DataBind() method for the DataGrid control
    DataGrid1.DataBind()
    End If
End Sub
```

When you execute the application, the output appears as shown in Figure 9-6.

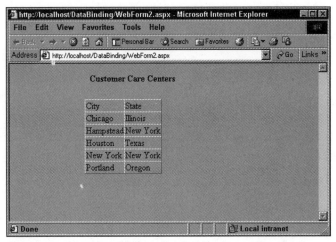

Figure 9-6: Output of the application implementing data binding to a DataView

Handling PostBack Data

When a form is submitted to a server, the postback event is generated. You might need to process the form data at the server during the postback. The System.Web.UI namespace contains an interface called IPostBackDataHandler that you can use for handling the postback data.

The IPostBackDataHandler interface has two member methods, `RaisePostDataChangedEvent()` and `LoadPostData()`. These methods are described as follows:

✦ `RaisePostDataChangedEvent`: This method draws attention of the control to inform any listener about the control's state change. In Visual Basic, the syntax of the method is as follows:

```
Sub RaisePostDataChangedEvent()
```

✦ `LoadPostData`: This method handles the postback data of a specific control by processing its postback data. The method returns True if the postback results in state change. On the other hand, if the state does not change after the postback, the method returns False. The method takes two arguments:

  • `postDataKey`: This is a String argument that represents the key identifier of the specified control.

  • `postCollection`: This argument is an object of the NameValueCollection in the System.Collections namespace. The argument represents all the incoming name values. In Visual Basic, the syntax of the method is given as follows:

```
Function LoadPostData( _
    ByVal postDataKey As String, ByVal postCollection As
NameValueCollection) As Boolean
```

After understanding the methods of the IPostBackDataHandler interface, let us see how the postback data is handled. You can handle the postback data only for those server controls that implement the IPostBackDataHandler interface. When you submit a Web Forms page to the server, the Page Framework searches the content that is posted, for the unique names of the server controls that implement the IPostBackDataHandler interface. Then, for each control that implements this interface, the `LoadPostData` method is invoked. This method returns True if the state of the control changes. Otherwise, this method returns False. For all the controls for which the `LoadPostData` method returns True, the `RaisePostDataChangedEvent` method is invoked. This method, then, raises the `Change` events, if any, for the control.

Summary

This chapter introduced you to the basic concepts of data binding to the Web Forms server controls. To bind a control property to a data store, you need to use a data binding expression and then call the `DataBind()` method for the control. You learned how to implement data binding to properties, ArrayList objects, methods, and DataView objects. Finally, you learned how to handle the postback data.

✦　　✦　　✦

Working with Data Grids

he DataGrid control is a bound data control that displays items from the selected data source in a grid or spreadsheet-like fashion. This was possible before .NET, but it required a fair amount of code if you wanted to implement more than a read-only grid. This new server control, along with the Repeater and DataList controls, makes it a snap to wire up to a data source and display columnar data using a minimal amount of coding. New to the DataGrid control is paging. You no longer have to be concerned with writing code to handle the paging of data in the grid. For anyone who has written this type of code in the past, this is a welcome relief.

This chapter also takes a look at sorting, editing, and selecting items located in the DataGrid. Also, since the `DataSource` property of the DataGrid control expects the source of data to be derived from the System.Collections.IEnumerable class, you don't have to bind to just SQL or ODBC data. You can also use arrays and collections as the data source for the DataGrid control.

Using a Data Grid Example

Before getting into the details of the various properties and events available to developers, take a look at a simple example of using the DataGrid control. The following code shows the minimal amount required to wire up and use the DataGrid control:

```
<html>
  <head>
    <title>Hungry Minds Chapter 9...</title>
    <script language="C#" runat="server">
```

```
    void Page_Load(Object sender, EventArgs e) {

        //-- create a data source
        String[] items = {"Rick", "Billy", "Ed", "Steve"};

        //-- bind the data source
        simple.DataSource = items;
        simple.DataBind();
    }
  </script>
  </head>
  <body>
  <img src="logo.gif">
  <br>
  <font face="verdana" size="5">DataGrid Grid Body Formatting
Example...</font>
  <hr>
   <form method="post" runat="server">
  <asp:DataGrid
     ID="simple"
     BorderColor="#6699cc"
     BorderWidth="1"
     CellPadding="1"
     Font-Name="verdana"
     Font-Size="10pt"
     HeaderStyle-BackColor="#6699cc"
     AutoGenerateColumns="true"
     Runat="server">
  </asp:DataGrid>
   </form>
  </body>
 </html>
```

At this point, all you need to focus on are the page load event and the DataGrid control itself. First, take a look at the line that starts with asp:DataGrid located within the body element. All that has to be done is to specify the ID of the control, set the AutoGenerateColumns property to true, and set the RunAt attribute to server. Next, in the Page_Load event, the data source is created as a simple one-dimensional array, and then the BindData method of the DataGrid control is called. That's it! The output in Figure 10-1 is displayed when this ASPX page is executed.

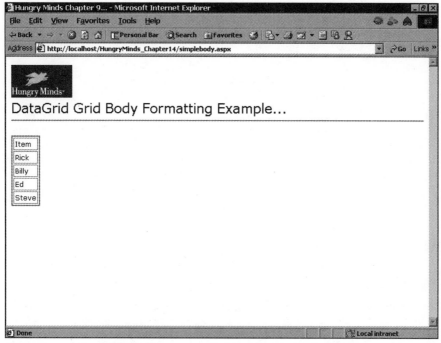

Figure 10-1: SimpleDataGrid.aspx, as displayed in Internet Explorer

The following HTML fragment is the source code generated from the DataGrid control after it is executed on the server and returned to the client browser:

```
<table cellspacing="0" cellpadding="1" rules="all"
bordercolor="#6699CC" border="1" id="simple" style="border-
color:#6699CC;border-width:1px;border-style:solid;font-family:v
erdana;font-size:10pt;border-collapse:collapse;">
  <tr style="background-color:#6699CC;">
    <td>
       Item
    </td>
  </tr><tr>
    <td>
       Rick
    </td>
  </tr><tr>
    <td>
       Billy
    </td>
  </tr><tr>
    <td>
       Ed
```

```
        </td>
    </tr><tr>
        <td>
            Steve
        </td>
    </tr>
</table>
```

For each item in this simple array, the DataGrid control generated a `tr` and `td` tag within the `table` tag. This may seem trivial, but it saves you from writing and maintaining a loop in the script that would need to iterate through each item in the array and generate the appropriate HTML output. Also, you don't need to be concerned with the number of items in the array or setting up the table, because the DataGrid controls handle this for you.

Additional Capabilities when Designing ASPX Pages

Now that you have seen a simple example of using the DataGrid control, you are ready to learn about some of the other capabilities that are available to you when designing ASPX pages:

✦ Controlling the header and footer

✦ Determining the "look and feel" of the grid

✦ Controlling the columns in the grid and specifying what type of column you want to use

✦ Paging

✦ Sorting

As you can see, you have quite a bit of flexibility with the DataGrid control — not only where you get the data, but also how you display that data within your Web pages. Each of these points will be discussed in the sections that follow, with examples of how they work.

Header and Footer

To change the style of the header and footer when the grid output is written to the page, you control the various properties of the `HeaderStyle` and `FooterStyle`. If you want to set the header background to gray and the header font to Verdana, you only need to insert the following HeaderStyle code:

```
<asp:DataGrid
    ID="simple"
    BorderWidth="1"
    CellPadding="1"
```

```
    HeaderStyle-BackColor="#6699cc"
    HeaderStyle-Font-Name="verdana"
    HeaderStyle-Font-Size="10pt"
    FooterStyle-BackColor="#6699cc"
    FooterStyle-Font-Name="verdana"
    FooterStyle-Font-Size="10pt"
    AutoGenerateColumns="true"
    Runat="server">
</asp:DataGrid>
```

When you launch your browser and navigate to HeaderFooter.aspx, the screen should look like Figure 10-2.

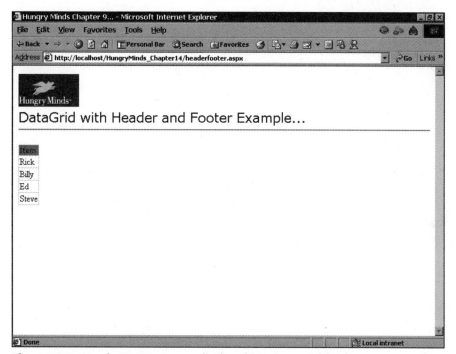

Figure 10-2: HeaderFooter.aspx, as displayed in Internet Explorer

The table heading should now have a steelblue background with a bold Verdana font. The same technique is used when formatting the footer for the DataGrid.

Instead of specifying HeaderStyle properties, take a look at the following code from HeaderFooter.aspx:

```
    FooterStyle-BackColor="#6699cc"
    FooterStyle-Font-Name="verdana"
    FooterStyle-Font-Size="10pt"
```

You can also enclose the Header and Footer sections of the DataGrid as elements within the <ASP:DataGrid> tags. You can then specify the properties for each section and control whether or not to display the header and footer (see Figure 10-3).

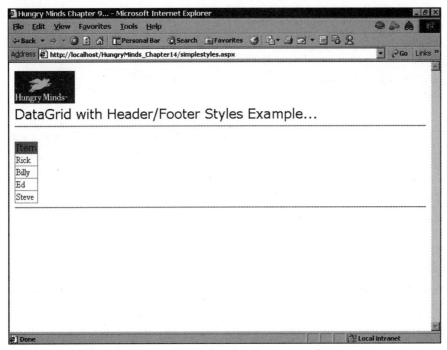

Figure 10-3: SimpleStyles.aspx, as displayed in Internet Explorer

The following code shows how to use the DataGrid with the HeaderStyle and FooterStyle properties:

```
<html>
   <head>
     <title>Hungry Minds Chapter 9...</title>
     <script language="C#" runat="server">
       void Page_Load(Object sender, EventArgs e) {

            String[] items = {"Rick", "Billy", "Ed", "Steve"};

            simple.DataSource = items;
            simple.DataBind();
        }
     </script>
   </head>
   <body>
   <img src="logo.gif">
   <br>
```

```
    <font face="verdana" size="5">DataGrid with Header/Footer
Styles Example...</font>
    <hr>
     <form method="post" runat="server">
    <asp:DataGrid
        ID="simple"
        BorderColor="#6699cc"
        BorderWidth="1"
        CellPadding="1"
        AutoGenerateColumns="true"
        ShowHeader=True
        Runat="server">
        <HeaderStyle
            BackColor="#6699cc"
            Font-Name="verdana">
        </HeaderStyle>
        <FooterStyle
            BackColor="#6699cc"
            Font-Name="verdana">
        </FooterStyle>
    </asp:DataGrid>
    <hr>
     </form>
   </body>
 </html>
```

Remember when using the style sections that they are elements within the DataGrid, not attributes. When using the Header or Footer style, make sure that you set the `ShowHeader` and `ShowFooter` properties to `true`. The `HeaderStyle` property is inherited from the `ControlStyle` property. Why is this important? If you can define your "look and feel" in the `ControlStyle` property and then inherit from it, this will provide you a common appearance for your page.

Controlling the appearance of the Grid Body

If you want to format the body of the grid so that your Web page has a specific look and feel, you need to set the properties of the `asp:DataGrid` element. To change how the grid is displayed, take a look at the following code:

```
<html>
    <head>
     <title>Hungry Minds Chapter 9...</title>
     <script language="C#" runat="server">
       void Page_Load(Object sender, EventArgs e) {

           //-- create a data source
           String[] items = {"Rick", "Billy", "Ed", "Steve"};

           //-- bind the data source
           simple.DataSource = items;
           simple.DataBind();
       }
    </script>
```

```
        </head>
        <body>
        <img src="logo.gif">
        <br>
        <font face="verdana" size="5">DataGrid Grid Body Formatting
    Example...</font>
        <hr>
         <form method="post" runat="server">
         <asp:DataGrid
             ID="simple"
             AutoGenerateColumns="true"
             BorderColor="#6699cc"
             BorderWidth="2"
             GridLines="Both"
             CellPadding="2"
             CellSpacing="2"
             Font-Name="verdana"
             Font-Size="10pt"
             Runat="server">
        </asp:DataGrid>
         </form>
      </body>
    </html>
```

When you launch your browser and navigate to SimpleBody.aspx, the screen should look like Figure 10-4.

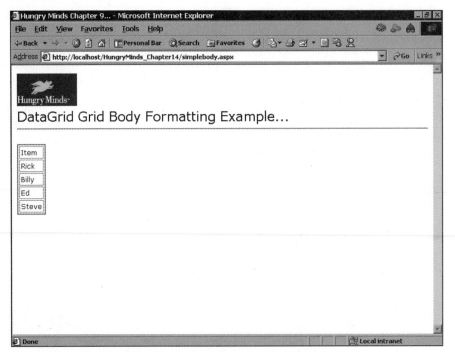

Figure 10-4: SimpleBody.aspx, as displayed in Internet Explorer

The following code is a fragment of the HTML source generated on the server and returned to the browser when SimpleBody.aspx is executed:

```
<table cellspacing="2" cellpadding="2" rules="all"
bordercolor="SteelBlue" border="2" id="simple" style="border-
color:SteelBlue;border-width:2px;border-style:solid;font-family
:verdana;font-size:8pt;">
   <tr>
      <td>
         Item
      </td>
   </tr><tr>
      <td>
         Rick
      </td>
   </tr><tr>
      <td>
         Billy
      </td>
   </tr><tr>
      <td>
         Ed
      </td>
   </tr><tr>
      <td>
         Steve
      </td>
   </tr>
</table>
```

Notice how the property settings are generated into HTML code. The appropriate attributes of the table element are set and the rest of the properties are transformed into the style element tag. The point here is that the .NET Framework runtime will recognize the level of the browser requesting the page and generate the supported level of HTML required by the browser. This architecture frees the Web page developer to determine the look and feel of the Web page and not be concerned with the version of the browser that requested the page.

Using the Columns Property

The discussion up until this point has addressed how to control the appearance of the grid by setting the various style properties. Also, the examples thus far have let the DataGrid control determine how the columns are generated and in what order. This section looks at how to control what columns are displayed and the type of columns displayed.

When the AutoGenerate property is set to True, the DataGrid control automatically reads the fields from the data source and generates a BoundColumn type for each field. This is useful if you only want to have a quick display of the data; however, to gain control over what fields are displayed and what type of column to display, you need to set the AutoGenerate property to False. Then, you need to define the type of columns to display within the Columns property. The Columns property is in the following format:

```
<columns>
...
</columns>
```

This property is contained within the <asp:DataGrid> </asp:DataGrid> elements. The following are the column classes that can be defined in the Columns property:

✦ BoundColumn: Displays a column bound to a field in a data source; each item from the data source is displayed in the grid as text. The BoundColumn is the default column type for the DataGrid control.

✦ ButtonColumn: Displays a command button for each item in the column; this control will let you create a column of custom button controls, such as the OK or Cancel button.

✦ EditColumn: For each item in the grid, displays a column that contains editing commands.

✦ HyperLinkColumn: Each item in the column is displayed as a hyperlink; the column contents can be bound to a field in a data source or static text.

✦ TemplateColumn: Each item in the column can be displayed with a specified template; this will allow you to provide custom controls in the column.

The sections that follow look at the first four column types.

BoundColumn Class

The following code shows the syntax required to use the BoundColumn column type in the DataGrid control:

```
<form method="post" runat="server">
<asp:DataGrid
     ID="Custom"
     AutoGenerateColumns="false"
     ShowHeader="True"
     RunAt="server">
  <HeaderStyle
     BackColor="#6699cc" />
  <Columns>
     <asp:BoundColumn
        HeaderText="String"
        DataField="String" />
  </Columns>
  </asp:DataGrid>
</form>
```

To use the BoundColumn type, you first need to set the AutoGenerate property to False and then specify asp:BoundColumn as the type. Next, you need to set the HeaderText, but only if you wish to display a header, and then set the DataField property. The DataField must be set to a field defined in the data source. When the above code is executed in the browser the screen shown in Figure 10-5 is displayed.

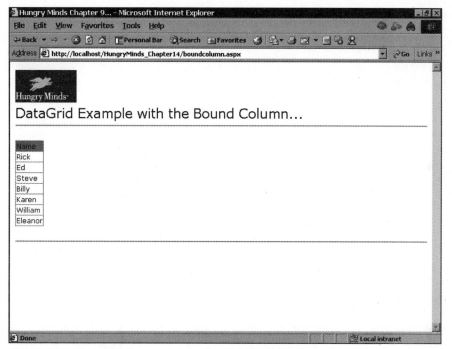

Figure 10-5: BoundColumn.aspx, as displayed in Internet Explorer

You can also specify the style formatting and the format for the data field when it is displayed in the grid. If the data field that you are binding to is a currency or number field, you can use the DataFormatString property to set the display format. For instance, in the BoundColumn2.aspx shown in Figure 10-6, the HeaderText and DataField properties have been changed to "Integer", which is the second field defined in your data source. Also, the DataFormatString has been added with the following value:

```
DataFormatString="{0:d2}"
```

Execute BoundColumn2.aspx, and this time the Integer data field is displayed with a leading zero, as shown in Figure 10-6.

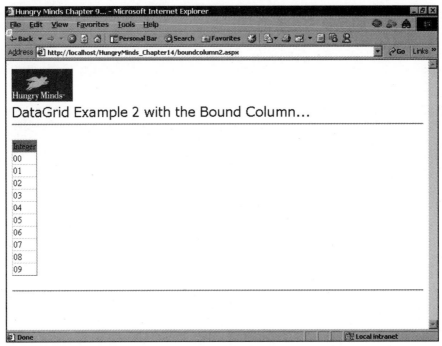

Figure 10-6: BoundColumn2.aspx, as displayed in Internet Explorer

Before moving on to the HyperLink column type, one more property is worth mentioning: the ReadOnly property of the BoundColumn type. This is set to False by default when using the BoundColumn type; editing of the data is allowed when set to True.

ButtonColumn Class

The following code shows the syntax required to use the ButtonColumn column type in the DataGrid control:

```csharp
<%@ Import NameSpace="System.Web.UI.WebControls" %>
<%@ Import NameSpace="System.Data" %>
<html>
  <head>
    <title>Hungry Minds Chapter 9...</title>
    <script language="C#" runat="server">
      void Page_Load(Object sender, EventArgs e) {

        //-- create a data source
        DataTable dt = new DataTable();
        DataRow dr;

        //-- randomly generate some test data
```

```
        dt.Columns.Add(new DataColumn("String",
typeof(string)));
        dt.Columns.Add(new DataColumn("Integer",
typeof(Int32)));

        for (Int32 i = 0; i < 10; i++) {
            dr = dt.NewRow();
            dr[0] = "Button " + i.ToString();
            dr[1] = i;
            dt.Rows.Add(dr);
        }

        //-- bind the data source
        Custom.DataSource = dt;
        Custom.DataBind();
    }
  </script>
</head>
<body>
<img src="logo.gif">
<br>
<font face="verdana" size="5">DataGrid Example with the
Button Column...</font>
<hr>
 <form method="post" runat="server">
<asp:DataGrid
    ID="Custom"
    AutoGenerateColumns="false"
    ShowHeader="True"
    RunAt="server">
    <HeaderStyle
        BackColor="#6699cc" />
    <columns>
        <asp:ButtonColumn
            ButtonType="PushButton"
            DataTextField="String"
            HeaderText="String" />
    </columns>
</asp:DataGrid>
 </form>
 <hr>
</body>
</html>
```

To use the ButtonColumn type, you first need to set the AutoGenerate property to False and then specify asp:ButtonColumn as the type. You can specify the ButtonType property as one of the following:

✦ PushButton: A column of push buttons

✦ LinkButton: A column of hyperlink-buttons

In the preceding example, you set the property to PushButton, set the HeaderText if you wish to display a header, and then set the DataField property. The DataField must be set to a field defined in the data source. When the DataGrid is bound to the data source in the previous example, Figure 10-7 is displayed when executed in the browser.

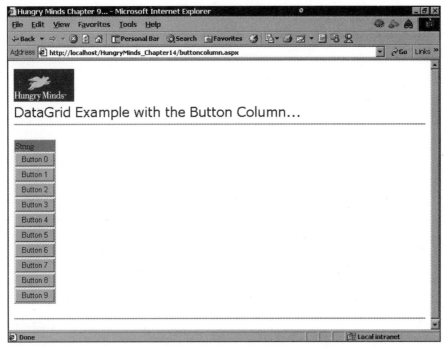

Figure 10-7: ButtonColumn.aspx, as displayed in Internet Explorer

You could just as easily have specified the LinkButton property to display a column of hyperlinks from your data source. If you click one of the buttons, the form is posted back to itself. Take a look at the following HTML fragment from ButtonColumn.aspx:

```
<td>
<input type="submit" name="Custom:ctrl2:ctrl0" value="Button 0"
/>
</td>
```

When the ButtomColumn type is rendered on the browser, each td element in the table is generated as a Submit button. What if you want to add an event handler for each button that performs some type of action when the button is clicked? You can do that by adding the OnItemCommand event handler to the CommandName property of the button. The following code demonstrates how to wire up the OnItemCommand event for the DataGrid control:

```
...
protected void Custom_Click(Object sender,
DataGridCommandEventArgs e) { Msg.Text = "You clicked Integer "
+ e.Item.Cells[1].Text; }
...

<form method="post" runat="server">
<asp:DataGrid
      ID="Custom"
      AutoGenerateColumns="false"
      ShowHeader="True"
      OnItemCommand="Custom_Click"
      RunAt="server">
   <HeaderStyle
      BackColor="#6699cc" />
   <columns>
      <asp:ButtonColumn
         ButtonType="PushButton"
         Text="Click"
         HeaderText="Action"
         CommandName="PushButton" />
      <asp:BoundColumn
         DataField="Integer"
         HeaderText="Integer" />
      </columns>
   </asp:DataGrid>
   <br>
   <asp:Label ID="Msg" text="Click a column button."
Runat="server" />
</form>
```

The script code defines the `Custom_Click` event, which is called every time a button on the grid is clicked. This event takes two arguments: the Sender parameter, which is of type Object, and the `DataGridCommandEventArgs` as the second parameter.

The `DataGridCommandEventArgs` argument has the following properties that can be inspected:

✦ `CommandArgument`: This property gets the argument passed from the command.

✦ `CommandName`: This property gets the name of the command.

✦ `CommandSource`: This property gets the source of the command.

✦ `Item`: This property gets the item that is selected in the DataGrid control.

In the preceding example, the `CommandName` is `"PushButton"` and the `Item` is a `DataGridItem` that represents the selected item in the control. It is also used to access the properties of the selected item.

The second code fragment has the HTML to set up the button to handle the click event. The only line you are concerned with here is the `CommandName` property, which identifies the button that is clicked and is passed to the `CustomClick` event in the `DataGridCommandArgs` event.

When you launch your browser and execute the ButtonColumn2.aspx page, your page should look like Figure 10-8.

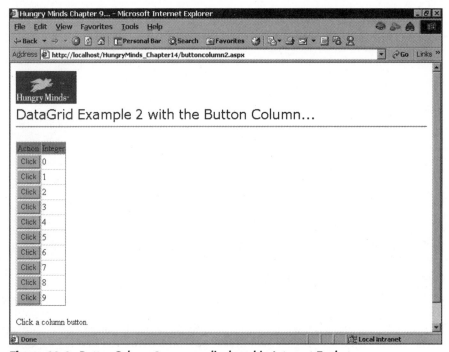

Figure 10-8: ButtonColumn2.aspx, as displayed in Internet Explorer

Click any one of the buttons, and a message displays in the Label control at the bottom of the page.

EditColumn Class

Next on the list is the `EditColumn` class. When used in the DataGrid control, the Web page developer can perform any type of editing on any data item within the grid. This is a powerful addition to the Web developer's toolbox. In the past, this type of editing would require a great deal of code to accomplish. With .NET, you only need to wire up the `Cancel`, `Edit`, and `Update` events and set the appropriate properties. In this example, you are going to read in some data from an XML file and then allow the user to edit the data. Launch your browser and navigate to EditColumn.aspx; your screen should look like Figure 10-9.

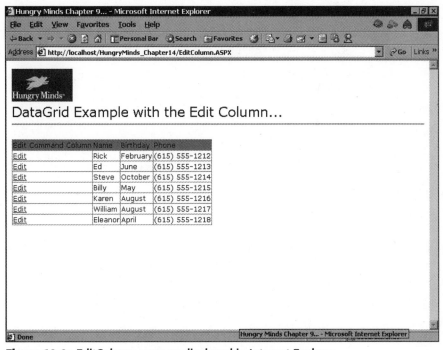

Figure 10-9: EditColumn.aspx, as displayed in Internet Explorer

Before you review the code, walk through editing one of the items in the grid. Click Edit on any of the rows in the grid. Notice that the other columns change to TextBox controls so that you can edit the data. Also, the Edit button changes to the Update and Cancel buttons. At this point, you can change the data in any of the TextBox controls and then choose to update or cancel the changes. If you have any columns that are ReadOnly, you can flag that column, and editing will not be allowed on that data item.

Note   In this example, you are not going to save the changes back to the XML file to preserve the integrity of the XML file.

The EditColumn.aspx file is generated by the following code:

```
<%@ Import Namespace="System.Data" %>
<html>
<head>
<script language="C#" runat="server">

    DataSet ds = new DataSet();

    void Page_Load(Object sender, EventArgs e) {

        ds.ReadXml(Page.MapPath("data.xml"));
        if (!IsPostBack)
```

```
        BindData();
    }

    void EditColumn_Edit(Object sender, DataGridCommandEventArgs
e) {
        EditColumn.EditItemIndex = e.Item.ItemIndex;
        BindData();
    }

    void EditColumn_Cancel(Object sender,
DataGridCommandEventArgs e) {
        EditColumn.EditItemIndex = -1;
        BindData();
    }

    void EditColumn_Update(Object sender,
DataGridCommandEventArgs e) {

        String Name = e.Item.Cells[1].Text;
        TextBox Birthday = (TextBox)e.Item.Cells[2].Controls[0];
        TextBox Phone = (TextBox)e.Item.Cells[3].Controls[0];

        ds.Tables[0].DefaultView.RowFilter = "Name='" + Name +
"'";

        if (ds.Tables[0].DefaultView.Count > 0 )
            ds.Tables[0].DefaultView.Delete(0);

        ds.Tables[0].DefaultView.RowFilter = "";

        DataRow dr;
        dr = ds.Tables[0].NewRow();
        dr[0] = Name;
        dr[1] = Birthday.Text;
        dr[2] = Phone.Text;
        ds.Tables[0].Rows.Add(dr);

        EditColumn.EditItemIndex = -1;
        BindData();
    }

    void BindData() {
        EditColumn.DataSource = ds;
        EditColumn.DataBind();
    }
</script>
</head>

<body>
    <img src="logo.gif">
    <br>
    <font face="verdana" size="5">DataGrid Example with the Edit
Column...</font>
    <hr>
```

```
<form runat="server">
    <asp:DataGrid id="EditColumn" runat="server"
        BorderColor="#6699cc"
        BorderWidth="1"
        CellPadding="1"
        Font-Name="verdana"
        Font-Size="10pt"
        HeaderStyle-BackColor="#6699cc"
        OnEditCommand="EditColumn_Edit"
        OnCancelCommand="EditColumn_Cancel"
        OnUpdateCommand="EditColumn_Update"
        AutoGenerateColumns="false">
    <Columns>
        <asp:EditCommandColumn
          ButtonType="LinkButton"
          EditText="Edit"
          CancelText="Cancel"
          UpdateText="Update"
          ItemStyle-Wrap="false"
          HeaderText="Edit Command Column"
          HeaderStyle-Wrap="false"/>
        <asp:BoundColumn
          HeaderText="Name"
          ReadOnly="true"
          DataField="Name"/>
        <asp:BoundColumn
          HeaderText="Birthday"
          DataField="BirthDay"/>
        <asp:BoundColumn
          HeaderText="Phone"
          DataField="Phone"/>
    </Columns>
    </asp:DataGrid>
</form>
</body>
</html>
```

The presentation code will be discussed first, followed by the event handlers. Like the other column classes discussed, the EditColumn class is enclosed within the <columns> </columns> tags of the DataGrid control. Next, you need to specify which button type to use; the ButtonType property can be set to PushButton or LinkButton. The EditText, CancelText, and UpdateText properties can be set to any string value that you choose. These string values are displayed either as hyperlinks or as push buttons, depending on the setting of the ButtonType property. Most of the other properties for the EditColumn class are for formatting the display output.

Now that the properties are set, turn your attention to wiring up the event handlers for the Edit, Cancel, and Update buttons. When the user clicks the Edit button on the grid, it raises the EditCommand event, which then passes the DataGridCommandEventArgs class as a parameter. From there, you can extract which item was selected in the grid and then set the `EditItemIndex` to the selected item. Look at the following line of code:

```
EditColumn.EditItemIndex = e.Item.ItemIndex;
```

After you set this property, you call the `BindData` method to rebind your data and display the text boxes for editing.

The `CancelCommand` event is raised when the user decides to cancel the edits and return the grid to its previous values. Once again, this event takes the `DataGridCommandEventArgs` class as a parameter. You only need to set the `EditItemIndex` to -1 to flag that you are aborting all edits on the grid.

Most of the code that you need to write is for the `UpdateEvent`. You need to take several steps, each of which is described next. First, you need to extract the values from the grid, as in the following lines of code:

```
String Name = e.Item.Cells[1].Text;
TextBox Birthday = (TextBox)e.Item.Cells[2].Controls[0];
TextBox Phone = (TextBox)e.Item.Cells[3].Controls[0];
```

You extract the name to a string value for a couple of reasons. Because the Name field is flagged as ReadOnly in the `columns` tag, you can't edit this field. In addition, you are going to use this value as the filter in the data table to find the selected row. The next two lines of code extract the values from the grid and cast them to TextBox controls. You need to save these values because you are going to be deleting the selected row from the grid. In the following lines of code, you filter the data table for the selected row and then delete it (we are not actually deleting the row from the DataSource):

```
ds.Tables[0].DefaultView.RowFilter = "Name='" + Name + "'";
if (ds.Tables[0].DefaultView.Count > 0 )
ds.Tables[0].DefaultView.Delete(0);
ds.Tables[0].DefaultView.RowFilter = "";
```

Notice that you check to make sure the `Count` property of the `DefaultView` is greater than zero before you delete the row. Then, you set the `RowFilter` property back to an empty string. Finally, you add the new values to a new data row and then add this row to the data table. Call the `BindData` method to refresh the grid and display your new values.

Note   Since you are not saving the changes back to the XML file, if you edit the grid again, the original values will be displayed.

HyperLinkColumn Class

The last column class to discuss is the `HyperLinkColumn` class. This column type is rendered as an `anchor` tag by the browser. Use the HyperLink control to create a link to another Web page. The HyperLink control is typically displayed as text specified by the Text property. It can also be displayed as an image specified by the ImageUrl property.

The following are the commonly used properties of the HyperLink control:

✦ DataNavigateUrlField: Indicates the field name to set or get from a data source to bind to the URL

✦ DataNavigateUrlFormatString: Indicates the string to get or set that specifies the display format for the URL

✦ DataTextField: Indicates the a field from the data source that is used as the text caption of the hyperlinks

✦ DataTextFormatString: Indicates the string to get or set that specifies the display format for the text caption of the hyperlinks

Take a look at the following code in the HyperLink column example:

```
<%@ Import NameSpace="System.Data" %>
<html>
  <head>
   <title>Hungry Minds Chapter 9...</title>
    <script language="C#" runat="server">

      DataSet ds = new DataSet();

      void Page_Load(Object sender, EventArgs e) {

         ds.ReadXml(Page.MapPath("data.xml"))    ;
         BindData();

if (Request.QueryString["birthday"] != null ) msg.Text = "Your
birthday is in " + Request.QueryString["Birthday"];
}

      void BindData() {
         HyperLink.DataSource = ds;
         HyperLink.DataBind();
       }
    </script>
  </head>
  <body>
  <img src="logo.gif">
  <br>
  <font face="verdana" size="5">DataGrid Example with the
HyperLink Column...</font>
   <hr>
   <form method="post" runat="server">
   <asp:DataGrid
      ID="HyperLink"
      AutoGenerateColumns="false"
      ShowHeader="True"
```

```
        RunAt="server">
        <HeaderStyle
            BackColor="#6699cc" />
        <columns>
            <asp:HyperLinkColumn

DataNavigateUrlFormatString="HyperLinkColumn.ASPX?Birthday={0}"
                DataNavigateUrlField="Birthday"
                DataTextField="Name"
                HeaderText="Name" />
        </columns>
    </asp:DataGrid>
    <asp:Label ID="msg" Runat="server" />
     </form>
     <hr>
   </body>
</html>
```

In the preceding code, the `DataNavigateUrlFormatString` is where you specify what URL to navigate to when the user selects an item. You can also add parameters to the query string. Notice that the syntax for specifying the `Birthday` parameter is enclosed in parentheses. If you had other arguments to pass on the query string line, you would use a comma-separated list. The next property is the `DataNavigateUrlField`, which indicates the specific field in the DataSource to use as the parameter in the query string. In the preceding example, this field is the Birthday field. Next is the `DataTextField` property, which is the actual field that is displayed as the data item in the grid column. This can be any field from the specified DataSource. Finally, the `HeaderText` property sets the column heading in your grid.

Launch your browser and navigate to HyperLinkColumn.aspx; the screen should look like Figure 10-10.

Click one of the names in the list, when the form is reloaded we check the `Request.QueryString` for the `Birthday` parameter. If the birthday parameters exist, the birthday message is displayed in the `asp:Label` control.

As you can see from the examples, the .NET DataGrid server control brings a lot of functionality to the table for the Web page developer. Instead of being concerned with writing the application logic, the Web developer can concentrate on the presentation of the page. The previous sections have looked at the most commonly used properties of each of the column controls that can be used in the DataGrid control so that you can get up to speed quickly using them in your own code. Before you wrap up this chapter on the DataGrid control, the following sections walk you through a few examples for sorting and paging data in the grid.

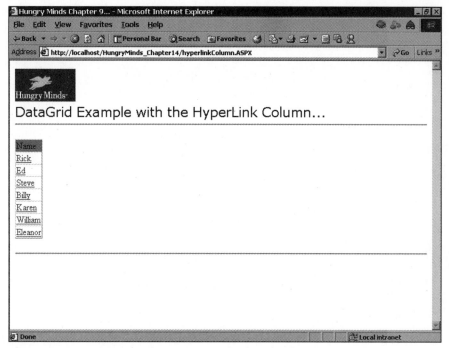

Figure 10-10: HyperLinkColumn.aspx, as displayed in Internet Explorer

Paging Grid Data

Paging came along with the introduction of the DataGrid control. This simple event actually involves quite a bit of work behind the scenes. When the user requests the next page of data, the browser makes a round trip to the server to determine the next page of data, and then renders the next page of data on the client. With .NET, this is now a trivial task, requiring only that you set a few properties and wire up one event. If you want to handle your own paging, you can do that by setting the CustomPaging property.

The following code automatically generates the data items from the data source and then sets the style of paging:

```
<%@ Import NameSpace="System.Data" %>
<html>
  <head>
    <title>Hungry Minds Chapter 9...</title>
      <script language="C#" runat="server">

        DataSet ds = new DataSet();

        void Page_Load(Object sender, EventArgs e) {
```

```
        if (!IsPostBack)
            BindData();
    }

    void LoadDataSource() {
        ds.ReadXml(Page.MapPath("data.xml"))    ;
    }

    void BindData() {
        LoadDataSource();
        Paging.DataSource = ds;
        Paging.DataBind();
    }

        void PageIndexChanged(Object sender,
DataGridPageChangedEventArgs e) {
        Paging.CurrentPageIndex = e.NewPageIndex;
        BindData();
        }
    </script>
    </head>
    <body>
    <img src="logo.gif">
    <br>
    <font face="verdana" size="5">DataGrid Paging
Example...</font>
    <hr>
    <form method="post" runat="server" ID="Form1">
    <asp:DataGrid
        ID="Paging"
        AutoGenerateColumns="true"
        OnPageIndexChanged="PageIndexChanged"
        ShowHeader="True"
        BorderColor="#6699cc"
        BorderWidth="1"
        CellPadding="1"
        Font-Name="verdana"
        Font-Size="10pt"
        HeaderStyle-BackColor="#6699cc"
        AllowPaging="true"
        PageSize="4"
        PagerStyle-NextPageText="[Next Page]"
        PagerStyle-PrevPageText="[Previous Page]"
        PagerStyle-HorizontalAlign="center"
        RunAt="server">
    </asp:DataGrid>
    </form>
    <hr>
    </body>
</html>
```

Launch your browser and navigate to DataGridPaging.aspx; the screen should look
like Figure 10-11.

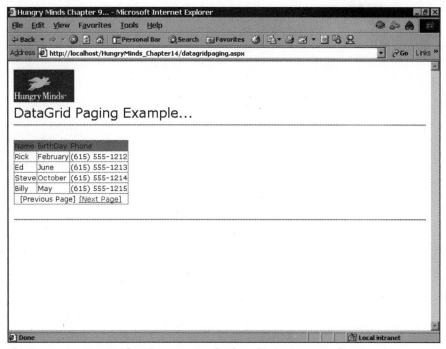

Figure 10-11: DataGridPaging.aspx, as displayed in Internet Explorer

Select the Next or Previous hyperlink at the bottom of the data grid. The next or previous page of data is fetched from the data source and displayed in the grid. You can adjust the number of pages to display, the style of the paging buttons, and determine the number of pages in your data source. With the Data Grid control, you have complete control over paging. If you prefer, you can enable the CustomPaging property and implement your own paging logic.

To enable paging, you must first turn it on by setting the Paging property to True (by default, this is turned off). So, if your data source has many rows, it will appear as one long continuous list of tabular data on your page. Once Paging is set to True, you can set the other paging properties to control the display and the type of paging. You also need to code the PageIndexChanged event to handle when the user selects a new page of data. Typically, in this event, you need to set the CurrentPageIndex to the index of the page you want to display, and then call the DataBind method to rebind the data to the grid. The PageIndexChanged event takes the DataGridPageChangedEventArgs object as a parameter. This object has the following properties:

   ✦ CommandSource: Indicates the source of the command

   ✦ NewPageIndex: Gets the index of the page selected by the user from the page selection element of the control

You can also set the paging mode property `PagerMode` to one of two values:

✦ `NextPrev`: Displays Previous and Next buttons to access the next and previous pages

✦ `NumericPages`: Displays numbered buttons to access pages directly

By default, when paging is turned on, the Next and Previous links are displayed as less than (<) and greater than (>) symbols. As in the DataGridPaging.aspx code example, the links are displayed as `"[Next Page]"` and `"[Previous Page]"`. The `NextPageText` and `PrevPageText` can be set to any string value you choose. If you set the `PagerMode` to `NumericPages`, the links at the bottom of the grid for paging are displayed as numbers from 1 to *n*. Try it! Insert the `PagerStyle-Mode=` `"NumericPages"` in the DataGrid.

Sorting Grid Data

One last important feature of the DataGrid control is sorting. Just like paging, you only need to set a few properties and then handle the `Sort` event.

Launch your browser and navigate to DataGridSorting.aspx; the screen should look like Figure 10-12.

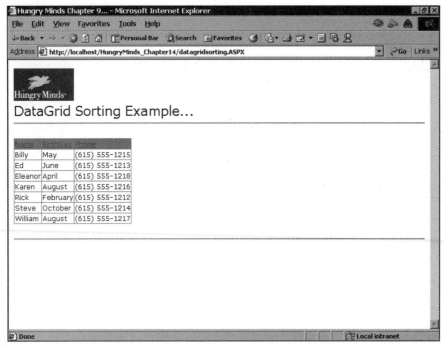

Figure 10-12: DataGridSorting.aspx, as displayed in Internet Explorer

Take a look at the following code:

```csharp
<%@ Import NameSpace="System.Data" %>
<html>
  <head>
    <title>Hungry Minds Chapter 9...</title>
     <script language="C#" runat="server">

       String SortOrder;

       void Page_Load(Object sender, EventArgs e) {

          if (!IsPostBack) {
             if (SortOrder == null)
                SortOrder = "name";
             Paging.DataSource = LoadDataSource();
             Paging.DataBind();
          }
       }

       ICollection LoadDataSource() {
          DataSet ds = new DataSet();
          ds.ReadXml(Page.MapPath("data.xml"))    ;
          if (SortOrder != null)
             ds.Tables[0].DefaultView.Sort = SortOrder;
          return ds.Tables[0].DefaultView;
       }

          void Sort_Grid(Object sender,
DataGridSortCommandEventArgs e) {
          SortOrder = e.SortExpression.ToString();
          SortMsg.Text = "<br>Grid sort order is <b>" +
SortOrder + "</b>";
          Paging.DataSource = LoadDataSource();
          Paging.DataBind();
          }
     </script>
   </head>
   <body>
   <img src="logo.gif">
   <br>
   <font face="verdana" size="5">DataGrid Sorting
Example...</font>
   <hr>
    <form method="post" runat="server" ID="Form1">
   <asp:DataGrid
        ID="Paging"
        AutoGenerateColumns="true"
        OnSortCommand="Sort_Grid"
        ShowHeader="true"
```

```
            BorderColor="#6699cc"
            BorderWidth="1"
            CellPadding="1"
            Font-Name="verdana"
            Font-Size="10pt"
            HeaderStyle-BackColor="#6699cc"
            AllowSorting="true"
            RunAt="server">
    </asp:DataGrid>
    <asp:Label ID="SortMsg" Runat="server" />
    </font>
     </form>
     <hr>
    </body>
  </html>
```

To enable sorting, you set the `AllowSorting` property of the DataGrid to `True` and set the `OnSortCommand` to point to the name of your sorting event. When sorting is enabled, the grid header columns are displayed as "clickable" links, allowing you to sort by any data column in the grid. In the DataGridSorting.aspx code, the `Sort_Grid` takes either of the following as a parameter:

✦ `CommandSource`: Gets the source of the command

✦ `SortExpression`: Gets the expression used to sort the DataGrid control

In the previous example, you extract the `SortExpression` into your `SortOrder` string variable and then use this value in your `LoadDataSource` routine. In the DataGridSorting.aspx code, you set the `Sort` property of the `DefaultView` in your data set and then call the `DataBind` method of the DataGrid to sort and redisplay the grid data.

Summary

This chapter covered how to format the grid using different styles. It also looked at using the `Columns` property of the DataGrid control to display data items as different column types. In addition, you saw how to enable paging and sorting in the DataGrid. With the help of the DataGrid and all of its built-in functionality, you can display, page, and sort your data with a minimal amount of coding.

✦   ✦   ✦

Using Templates

ASP.NET provides a rich set of Server controls that you can use in your Web Forms pages. When you drag Server controls to a Web Forms page, the controls have a default set of properties and styles already applied to them. These default properties and styles provide a specific look and layout to the controls. You can customize the look and layout of the controls by setting properties and styles according to your requirements. However, there might be situations when you cannot customize the controls by using the properties and styles. In such situations, ASP.NET allows you to create templates for some Server controls. *Templates* are used to customize the look and layout of Server controls according to your requirements.

This chapter introduces you to templates. You'll also learn how to create templates and combine them with the Repeater, DataList, and DataGrid controls.

Introduction to Templates

Templates consist of HTML elements, controls, and embedded Server controls that allow you to customize and manipulate the layout of a particular control. For example, you can customize the layout of the individual rows, alternating rows, or selected rows of a DataList or DataGrid ASP.NET Server control by defining different templates. Then, at run time, instead of the default HTML, the contents of the templates are rendered on the page.

You can define templates to control the layout of different portions — such as header item, footer item, edit item, selected item, alternating item, or separator — of a control according to your requirements. Different types of templates are available depending on the portion of the control for which the template is defined. For example, the template defined for the header of a control is called HeaderTemplate. However, not all the Server controls support templates. The Server controls that support templates are Repeater, DataList, and DataGrid. Also, not all types of templates are supported by all the controls that support templates. Table 11-1 lists the different types of templates and the controls that support them.

Table 11-1
Templates and the supporting controls

Template	Description	Supported by
ItemTemplate	The set of elements and controls that are rendered once for each row in the data source.	Repeater, DataList, and DataGrid
AlternatingItemTemplate	The set of elements and controls that are rendered once for every alternating row in the data source.	Repeater and DataList
SelectedItemTemplate	The set of elements and controls that are rendered when an item is selected in the control.	DataList
EditItemTemplate	The set of elements and controls that are rendered when an item is in Edit mode.	DataList and DataGrid
HeaderTemplate	The set of elements and controls that are rendered once before all the items in the control.	Repeater, DataList, and DataGrid
FooterTemplate	The set of elements and controls that are rendered once after all the items in the control.	Repeater, DataList, and DataGrid
SeparatorTemplate	The set of elements that are rendered between each row.	Repeater and DataList
PagerTemplate	The set of elements and controls that are rendered while paging the information.	DataGrid

Again, you can manipulate the look and layout of individual controls by using styles; however, you should not confuse styles with templates. Styles are used to specify the appearance of controls by setting specific properties, such as color, font, and width. On the other hand, templates are sets of HTML elements and controls that provide a specific layout to specific portions of a control. You can use styles with the controls that do not have templates defined for them. Also, you can use styles with the controls that have templates defined. For such controls, you can use styles to specify the appearance of the elements that define the template.

Before proceeding to create templates for the Repeater, DataList, and DataGrid Server controls, you need to understand the basic features of these controls, described next.

Repeater control

The Repeater control allows you to create custom lists to display data from different data sources. Unlike other Server controls, such as TextBox and ListBox, the Repeater control does not have a default look and layout. You need to provide the layout to the Repeater control by creating templates. Because it is you who provides the layout to the control, you can create any kind of list for the control, depending on your requirements. Some of the lists that you can create include tables or grids, comma-separated lists, and bulleted or numbered lists.

After you drag a Repeater control on a form, you can set the base control properties by using the Properties window. Then, you need to create templates to provide the layout to the control. Of all the templates supported by the Repeater control, you must create at least one template, ItemTemplate, to provide a basic layout to the control. Then, you can create other templates to enhance the look and layout of the control. To render a Repeater control on a page, you must bind the control to a data source and create ItemTemplate.

The Repeater control supports two events:

✦ `ItemCreated`: Enables you to customize the way items are created. One way to customize the item-creation process is to set certain properties while the items are being created.

✦ `ItemCommand`: Generated when users click one of the buttons included in the Repeater control items. These buttons could be the usual Button controls or the LinkButton controls.

DataList control

The DataList control enables you to display rows of data from a data source in a list. Each row of data displayed in the DataList control is an item. To create items, you must create at least one template, ItemTemplate. By default, the items in a DataList control are displayed in a single vertical column. However, you can provide a custom layout to the items in the control by using templates.

In addition to specifying the layout of controls and the data to be displayed in individual items, the DataList control enables you to specify how the individual items are laid out with respect to each other. The options that you can choose from are the following:

✦ **Vertical/horizontal:** The default layout is a single vertical column. However, you can specify more than one column for the control. If you've specified a multiple-column layout for the control, you can also specify the ordering of items as vertical or horizontal.

✦ **Number of columns:** You can specify the number of columns that the list will have irrespective of the ordering of items as vertical or horizontal. In this manner, you can control the rendered width of the Web page.

✦ **Flow/table:** You can choose either flow layout or table layout for the control. The flow layout presents the list items in a format like a word-processing document, while the table layout presents the list items in an HTML table.

The DataList control supports many styles and templates that you can use extensively to customize the layout of the control. You can use the autoformat feature to customize the appearance of different elements of the control. In addition to the styles, you can create the templates to customize the control. For example, you can create EditItemTemplate to allow item editing in the control. The DataList control also enables you to have a multiple-column layout. Also, you can customize the control to allow multiple-item selection.

In addition to the `ItemCreated` event, the DataList control supports five more events that are generated when buttons are clicked in the list items. The type of the event generated depends on the `CommandName` property of the button that is clicked. The DataGrid control has a generic event called `ItemCommand`. This event is generated when a user clicks a button that has no predefined command. Table 11-2 shows the different events that are generated.

Table 11-2	
The DataList events	
Command	**Event**
Edit	EditCommand
Update	UpdateCommand
Cancel	CancelCommand
Delete	DeleteCommand

 Caution   The `CommandName` property of a button is case-sensitive and takes values in lower-case. Therefore, be sure to assign lowercase values to the `CommandName` property.

DataGrid control

The DataGrid Server control is a multicolumn, data-bound grid that enables you to define different types of columns. These columns not only provide layout to the grid contents, but also add functionalities to select, edit, sort, and page the data. Also, the DataGrid control provides functionality for full customization of the output through the use of specific columns called *TemplateColumns*.

When you add a DataGrid control to a form, the control will be rendered only if it is bound to a data source. A data source can be created by using Visual Studio Data Designer or any database on a server. It can also be a simple structure, such as an array of type ArrayList. When you bind a DataGrid control to a data source, the columns are generated automatically based on the fields in the data source. However, you can specify the columns in different ways. The different types of columns that you can create are described as follows:

✦ **Bound columns:** Used to specify the database fields that need to be displayed in the columns along with the order, format, and style of the display.

✦ **Hyperlink column:** Used to display information as hyperlinks that users can click to navigate to different pages. For example, you can display product names as hyperlinks. When users click these hyperlinks, they are directed to product details in a separate page.

✦ **Button columns:** Used to display buttons for each item in the grid and add custom functionality to the buttons. For example, you can add a button labeled Query and associate logic with it. When users click the button, the logic is executed.

✦ **Edit command columns:** Used to allow in-place editing of items. In-place editing allows users to edit the items in the grid only. To implement this editing, you need to add a special column in the grid that contains buttons labeled Edit. When users click this button, the current row is displayed again with editable fields for all columns. Also, the column with the Edit button is redisplayed with the Update and Cancel buttons.

Cross-Reference

For more information on Button columns and Edit command columns, refer to Chapter 10 and Chapter 12.

✦ **Template columns:** Used to create a custom layout for a column by using a combination of HTML text and Server controls. The controls in the Template column can be bound to display data from a data source. This column provides you complete flexibility for customization. With the template columns, you can create custom-editing layout. This approach enables you to manipulate the columns that can be edited and the way users can edit data.

The DataGrid control supports multiple events that are raised from the controls in the grids. In addition to the `ItemCreated`, `ItemCommand`, `EditCommand`, `UpdateCommand`, `CancelCommand`, and `DeleteCommand` events, the control supports these two events:

✦ `PageIndexChanged`: Generated when a page selection element is clicked.

✦ `SortCommand`: Generated when a column is sorted.

Comparing the Repeater, DataList, and DataGrid controls

As mentioned, the Repeater, DataList, and DataGrid controls are used to display data in the form of lists on the Web Forms pages. All of these controls are bound to some data source and display each row in the data source as an entry called *item*.

All three controls must be bound to a data source by the `DataSource` property so that they can be rendered on a page. Even if the `DataSource` property is set, the controls will not display the data from the data source until the `DataBind()` method is called for the control. The `DataSource` property is set for the control. For the individual controls in the templates, you can use the container data.

For more information on data binding, refer to Chapter 9.

Table 11-3 compares the Repeater, DataList, and DataGrid controls.

		Table 11-3	
	Comparison of the Repeater, DataList, and DataGrid controls		
Feature	**Repeater**	**DataList**	**DataGrid**
Default layout	No default layout	The default layout is a single vertical column layout	The default layout is a grid layout
Autoformatting	No options for autoformatting	Provides options for autoformatting	Provides options for autoformatting
Item selection and editing	Items are read-only; no inherent support for selecting and editing items	Provides options for editable contents and single- and multiple-item selection	Provides options for editable contents; also supports single- and multiple-item selection
Paging	Does not support default paging, and all data is displayed in a single list	Does not support default paging	Provides support for paged output

Creating Templates

You can create templates by using the Web Forms Designer in a WYSIWYG (What You See Is What You Get) way or by using the ASP.NET syntax in the ASPX file. This section explores both of these methods.

The method to create templates by using the Web Forms Designer is very convenient to use:

1. Right-click the control and choose Edit Template from the shortcut menu. Then, choose the type of template to edit. For example, to edit Item templates, such as ItemTemplate, AlternatingItemTemplate, SelectedItemTemplate, or EditItemTemplate of a DataList control, choose Item Templates. The control

appears in the template-editing mode. Figure 11-1 displays the DataList control in the template-editing mode for the Item templates.

Figure 11-1: The DataList control in the template-editing mode

2. In the template-editing mode, add the HTML text and drag controls from the Toolbox onto the template. For example, you can drag Label or TextBox control to the Item template.

3. Edit the properties of the controls that you have added as you would do for any other control.

4. After you have added all the controls that you need to the template and edited their properties and styles, you need to end the template editing. To do so, right-click the control and choose End Template Editing.

Note The WYSIWYG template editing is not supported by the Repeater control.

You can also create a template by directly editing the ASPX file in the HTML view. For example, if you want to create ItemTemplate for a DataList control, type the following code:

```
<asp:DataList ID=DataList1 runat="Server">
    <ItemTemplate>
    </ItemTemplate>
</asp:DataList>
```

You can then add the controls that you want to include in the Itemtemplate. Also, you can set the properties for the embedded controls and data-bind them. To do so, add the code for the embedded elements inside the <ItemTemplate> and </ItemTemplate> element. For example, to add a Label control to the ItemTemplate in the DataList control, use the following syntax:

```
<ItemTemplate>
    Name: <asp:Label ID=Label1 runat="Server" Text='<%# data binding
expression %>'/>
</ItemTemplate>
```

In this syntax, `data binding expression` represents the data binding expression for the Label control of the template. The data binding expression is evaluated at run time.

As mentioned earlier, the Server control for which the template is created must be bound to a data source. Otherwise, it will not be rendered on the page. Then, the controls within the template can be bound to the container data. The `DataBinder.Eval()` method provided by the .NET Framework evaluates the late-bound data binding expression and eliminates the explicit casting of the bound data to the desired data type .The `DataBinder.Eval()` method takes three arguments and has the following syntax:

```
<% # DataBinder.Eval(NamingContainer,DataFieldName,[FormatString])>
```

In this syntax:

+ `NamingContainer`: Represents the naming container for the data item. The `Page` object can be one of the containers for data items. For the Repeater, DataList, and DataGrid controls, this argument is always `Container.DataItem`.

+ `DataFieldName`: Represents the name of the data item field.

+ `[FormatString]`: Represents the format string, which determines the format of the bound data item. This is an optional argument. If this argument is not specified, the data item is automatically formatted to a value, which is of object type.

Combining templates with the Repeater control

The templates that the Repeater control supports include ItemTemplate, AlternatingItemTemplate, HeaderTemplate, FooterTemplate, and SeparatorTemplate. To render the Repeater control on a page, you must bind the control to a data source and create at least ItemTemplate. The controls within the templates can be bound to the container data.

This section implements creating templates for the Repeater control. First, create an ASP.NET Web application project. You can create a Visual Basic or C# application. The example in this section creates a Visual Basic Web application. After you create the application, add a Repeater control to the form. In the example that follows, the Repeater control is bound to a `DataView` object, and the individual items are bound to the individual fields in the data source. To use the `Data` objects, you need to import the `System.Data` namespace. To do so, write the following statement in the HTML view of the ASPX file of the form:

```
<%@ Import Namespace="System.Data" %>
```

You need to create a `DataView` object that represents a data source. The `DataView` object created here represents a data source that contains products and their quantities. Write the following code in the `<Script>` tag to create the `DataView` object and bind the Repeater control to it:

```
<Script Language = "VB" runat="Server" ID=Script1>
        Sub Page_Load(ByVal sender As System.Object, ByVal e As
System.EventArgs) Handles MyBase.Load
                If Not IsPostBack Then
                        Dim DataTable1 As DataTable
                        Dim DataRow1 As DataRow
                        Dim strProd(5) as String
                        Dim intQty(5) as Integer
                        Dim I as Integer

                        strProd(0)="Cinnamon"
                        strProd(1)="Basil Leaf"
                        strProd(2)="Anise Seeds"
                        strProd(3)="Annatto Seeds"
                        strProd(4)="Asafoetida Powder"

                        intQty(0)=300
                        intQty(1)=500
                        intQty(2)=150
                        intQty(3)=250
                        intQty(4)=350

                        'create a DataTable
                        DataTable1 = New DataTable
                        DataTable1.Columns.Add(New
DataColumn("ProdName", GetType(String)))
                        DataTable1.Columns.Add(New
DataColumn("ProdQty", GetType(Integer)))

                        'Create rows and put in sample data
                        For I=0 To 4
                            DataRow1 = DataTable1.NewRow()
                            DataRow1(0) = strProd(I)
                            DataRow1(1) = intQty(I)
                            DataTable1.Rows.Add(DataRow1)
                        Next

                        Repeater1.DataSource = new DataView(DataTable1)
                        Repeater1.DataBind()
                End If
        End Sub
</Script>
```

After you have created the data source and bound the Repeater control with it, you can create templates. As mentioned before, you must create at least ItemTemplate to render the control on the page. Use the following code to create ItemTemplate:

```
<asp:Repeater ID=Repeater1  runat="Server">

    <ItemTemplate>
```

```
      <tr>
        <td>
          <%# DataBinder.Eval(Container.DataItem, "ProdName") %>
        </td>
        <td> <%# DataBinder.Eval(Container.DataItem, "ProdQty")
%>
        </td>
      </tr>
    </ItemTemplate>

</asp:Repeater>
```

In the preceding code, the item is bound to the ProdName and ProdQty fields of the data source. Because the Repeater control has no layout of its own, the bound data appears in a row, as shown in Figure 11-2.

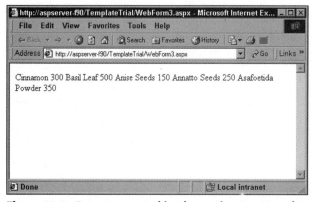

Figure 11-2: Repeater control implementing ItemTemplate

You can create HeaderTemplate to render text or controls before data item fields. The following code creates a table with two columns with the headings "Product" and "Quantity":

```
<HeaderTemplate>
<table border=1>
      <tr>
        <td>
          <b>Product</b>
        </td>
        <td>
          <b>Quantity</b>
        </td>
      </tr>
</HeaderTemplate>
```

In the preceding code, the `<table>` element has not been closed, because the HeaderTemplate elements are rendered even before the ItemTemplate elements, which use the `<tr>` and `<td>` elements that need to be displayed within the table. You can close the `<table>` element in FooterTemplate as follows:

```
<FooterTemplate>
</table>
</FooterTemplate>
```

You can apply special formatting to the alternating items by creating AlternatingItemTemplate. The following AlternatingItemTemplate sets the background color of the alternating rows to light blue:

```
<AlternatingItemTemplate>
    <tr>
       <td bgcolor="lightblue">
          <%# DataBinder.Eval(Container.DataItem, "ProdName") %>
       </td>
       <td bgcolor="lightblue">
          <%# DataBinder.Eval(Container.DataItem, "ProdQty") %>
       </td>
    </tr>
</AlternatingItemTemplate>
```

After creating all the previous templates, the Repeater control is rendered on the page, as shown in Figure 11-3.

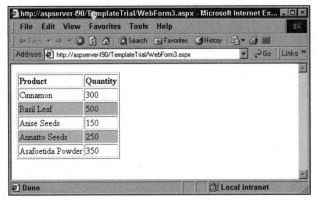

Figure 11-3: A Repeater control after implementing the templates

Combining templates with the DataList control

The DataList control supports two more templates in addition to the templates supported by the Repeater control:

✦ **SelectedItemTemplate:** Enables users to select items

✦ **EditItemTemplate:** Enables users to edit items

You must bind the DataList control to a data source and create at least ItemTemplate to render the control on a page. To understand templates with the DataList control, you'll use the same data source as you used for the Repeater control. First, you need to add a DataList control to a form.

Note   You can add the DataList control in the same form, or you can add another Web form and add the control in the new form.

In the HTML view of the ASPX file, you need to import the `System.Data` namespace, and bind the DataList control with the `DataView` object in the `Page_Load` method. After you've bound the DataList control to the `DataView` object, you need to create ItemTemplate and bind to the individual data fields in the data source. You can create a similar ItemTemplate for the DataList control, as follows:

```
<ItemTemplate>
    <tr>
     <td>
       <%# DataBinder.Eval(Container.DataItem, "ProdName") %>
     </td>
     <td>
       <%# DataBinder.Eval(Container.DataItem, "ProdQty") %>
     </td>
    </tr>
</ItemTemplate>
```

By default, the DataList control displays data items in a single vertical column, as shown in Figure 11-4.

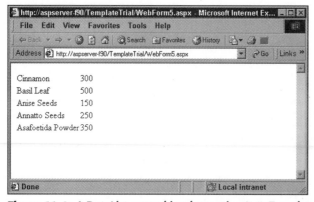

Figure 11-4: A DataList control implementing ItemTemplate

You can override the default single vertical column layout. To do so, create HeaderTemplate, AlternatingItemTemplate, and FooterTemplate in the same way you created them for the Repeater control. After you create these templates, the DataList control appears similar to the Repeater control.

Implementing item selection functionality

You can also add the functionality to allow users to select and edit items. To implement the functionality of item selection, you need to follow these steps:

1. Create SelectedItemTemplate. You can add text, elements, and controls to be rendered on the page when an item is selected.

2. Add a Button or LinkButton Server control in ItemTemplate. Using the following code, set the `CommandName` property of the Button or LinkButton control to "`select`":

```
<asp:LinkButton ID=LinkButton1 runat="Server" Text="Select"
CommandName="select" />
```

3. Rebind the list when an item is selected. To do so, create an event handler for the control's SelectedIndexChanged event. The complete code is given as follows:

```
Private Sub DataList1_SelectedIndexChanged(ByVal sender As
System.Object, ByVal e As System.EventArgs) Handles
DataList1.SelectedIndexChanged
    DataList1.DataBind()
End Sub
```

4. You can unselect an item by setting the control's SelectedIndex property to -1. To do so, you can add a Button control in the SelectedItemTemplate of the DataList control and set the CommandName property to unselect. Then, add the event handler for the ItemCommand event of the DataList control. The complete code is given as follows:

```
Private Sub DataList1_ItemCommand(ByVal source As Object,
ByVal e As
System.Web.UI.WebControls.DataListCommandEventArgs) Handles
DataList1.ItemCommand
    If e.CommandName = "unselect" Then
        DataList1.SelectedIndex = -1
    End If
    DataList1.DataBind()
End Sub
```

Implementing item editing functionality

To implement the functionality of item editing, follow these steps:

1. Add a Button or LinkButton Server control in ItemTemplate. Using the following code, set the `CommandName` property of the Button or LinkButton control to "`edit`":

```
<asp:LinkButton ID=LinkButton3 runat="Server" Text="Edit"
commandName="edit"/ >
```

2. Create EditItemTemplate. You can add text, elements, and controls to be rendered on the page when an item needs to be edited. The template should contain the controls for all the values that need to be edited, along with two buttons. Both the buttons are either Button or LinkButton controls. One button should have the Text property set to "Update" and the CommandName property set to "update". This button is used to implement the functionality of saving the changes to the data source. The other button should have the Text property set to "Cancel" and the CommandName property set to "cancel". This button is used to implement the functionality of quitting without saving the changes to the data source. The following code snippet shows a typical EditItemTemplate that displays the Update and Cancel buttons and other controls to display the bound data in Edit mode:

```
<EditItemTemplate>
    <tr>
        <td>
        <asp:LinkButton ID=LinkButton1 runat="Server"
Text="Update" CommandName="update" />
        </td>
        <td>
        <asp:LinkButton Id=LinkButton2 runat="Server"
Text="Cancel" CommandName="cancel" />
        </td>
        <td>
<!   Other controls go here    >
        </td>
</EditItemTemplate>
```

3. Create an event handler for the EditCommand event of the control to implement item editing. In this event handler, set the EditItemIndex property of the control to the index of the item to be edited. Also, call the DataBind() method of the control, using the following code:

```
DataList1.EditItemIndex = e.Item.ItemIndex
DataList1.DataBind()
```

4. Create an event handler for the UpdateCommand event of the control to update the data source with the edited values. In the event handler, after you update the data source, you need to come out of the Edit mode and bind data to DataList:

```
DataList1.EditItemIndex = -1
DataList1.DataBind()
```

5. Create an event handler for the CancelCommand event of the control to cancel the changes in the edited values. In this event handler, you simply need to come out of the Edit mode and bind data to DataList.

Combining templates with the DataGrid control

The DataGrid control usually has bound columns. However, different types of columns, such as Hyperlink columns, Button columns, and Template columns, can provide additional functionality. Template columns enable you to create many templates, such as ItemTemplate, HeaderTemplate, FooterTemplate, and EditItemTemplate. Therefore, Template columns provide complete flexibility to present data.

You can create different types of columns by using the DataGrid Properties window. In the Properties window, click the ellipsis in the Columns property to open the Properties dialog box, as shown in Figure 11-5.

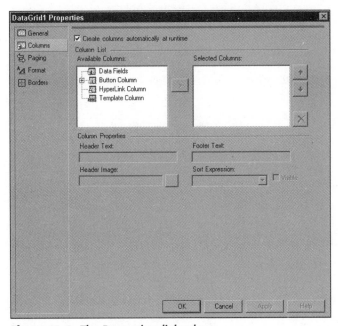

Figure 11-5: The Properties dialog box

Button columns provide functionality for selecting, editing, and deleting items. You can create three types of Button columns: Select, Edit, and Delete. If you create the Edit button column, the Edit button is created in each row. To add the functionality to the Edit button, create the event handler for the `EditCommand` event of the DataGrid control in the same way you created the event handler for the `EditCommand` event of the DataList control. Then, to update the changes in the data source, you need to create the event handler for the `UpdateCommand` event. And, to cancel any changes made by users, you need to create the event handler for the `CancelCommand` event of the DataGrid control.

For information on button columns, refer to Chapter 12.

Template columns provide complete flexibility to give a custom layout to the column. When you add a Template column, you can specify the header and footer text, and a header image in the Properties dialog box. You can also specify a sort expression. After adding a template column, when you switch to the HTML view, the following code automatically appears in the file:

```
<asp:TemplateColumn> <asp:/TemplateColumn>
```

You can create HeaderTemplate, FooterTemplate, ItemTemplate, and EditItemTemplate in the TemplateColumn element. To display values in the Template column, you must create at least the ItemTemplate.

You'll implement the same example that you implemented for the Repeater and DataList controls. First, you need to add a DataGrid control to the form.

You can add the DataGrid control in the same form, or you can add another Web form and add the control in the new form.

After adding the DataGrid control to the form, follow these steps to add the Template column:

1. Display the Properties window for the DataGrid control by right-clicking the control and choosing Properties from the shortcut menu.

2. Display the Properties dialog box by clicking the ellipsis in the Columns property.

3. Click Columns in the left pane.

4. Select TemplateColumn from the Available Columns list and click the > button to add TemplateColumn to the Selected Columns list.

5. In the Header Text box, enter Product Category and click OK.

You can also specify the header image, footer text, and a sort expression.

After adding the Template column to the DataGrid control, you can create templates. To do so, switch to the HTML view of the ASPX file. Because you'll be using the DataView object to bind data to the DataGrid control, import the System.Data namespace in the page using the following code:

```
<%@ Import namespace="System.Data" %>
```

Then, in the Page_Load method, write the code to create the DataView object and bind the DataGrid control with it. To create the DataView object, use the same code you used for the Repeater and DataList controls.

Finally, create the ItemTemplate in the Template column as follows:

```
<asp:TemplateColumn HeaderText="Product Category">

    <ItemTemplate>
        <asp:Image ID=Image1 runat="Server"
ImageUrl="category.tif" />
    </ItemTemplate>

<asp:/TemplateColumn>
```

Note   Because the image file Category.tif has been added to the project, the `ImageUrl` property is set to the filename instead of the complete URL.

In the preceding code, an Image control is created as an item in the Template column. The `ImageUrl` property of the Image control is set to the image to be displayed in the column. Figure 11-6 shows the DataGrid control after creating the ItemTemplate for the Template column.

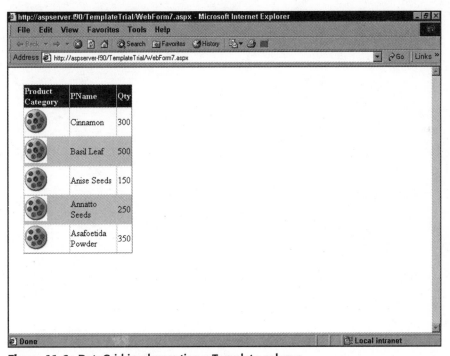

Figure 11-6: DataGrid implementing a Template column

Summary

This chapter introduced you to the ASP.NET Server control templates. First, you learned the different types of templates that can be created. You identified the Server controls that support templates. Then, you learned the basic features of the Repeater, DataList, and DataGrid controls and identified the templates that each of these controls supports. Finally, you learned how to create templates for the Repeater, DataList, and DataGrid controls to customize their look and layout.

✦   ✦   ✦

Using SQL Server with ASP.NET

CHAPTER

12

In This Chapter

Introduction to Server-Side Data Access

Stored Procedures

Adding, Modifying, and Deleting Data

Using the ADO Extensions (ADOX)

With more and more applications shifting to the Internet, e-business is booming. To conduct business on the Internet, Web applications need to access data stored on a server. Thus, data access is most critical to real-world applications.

Visual Studio .NET provides Web Forms controls, such as the DataGrid control that you can use to access data from various data sources, such as a SQL server or a Jet database. This chapter introduces you to the Structured Query Language (SQL), which is used to access data stored on a SQL server through Web Forms. You'll also learn how to use ADO Extensions to create and manage different schema objects, such as databases and tables.

Introduction to Server-Side Data Access from a SQL Server

Server-side data access is critical to all real-world applications. Therefore, these applications must address server-side data access to implement business solutions. This section introduces you to the SQL server data access through Web Forms.

Microsoft SQL Server is a Relational Database Management System (RDBMS) that is used to store and organize related data — the collection of related data is called a *database*. Microsoft SQL Server is based on the *client/server architecture*, in which data is stored on a centralized computer called a *server*. Other computers, called *clients*, can access the data stored on the server through a network. The client/server architecture prevents data inconsistency.

You can access data stored on a SQL server through Web Forms. To do so, you can create Web applications that have data access controls. These data access Web controls present the data in a consistent manner irrespective of the actual source, such as Microsoft SQL Server or MS Access. Therefore, while creating a Web application, you do not need to worry about the format of the data. However, before you can access or manipulate data from a SQL server, you need to perform the following steps in the specified sequence:

1. Establish a connection with the SQL Server.

2. Write the actual command to access or manipulate data.

3. Create a result set of the data from the data source with which the application can work. This result set is called the *data set* and is disconnected from the actual source. The application accesses and updates data in the data set, which is later reconciled with the actual data source.

To achieve this functionality, you first need to import two namespaces, System.Data and System.Data.SqlClient, into your Web Forms page. The syntax is given as follows:

```
<%@ Import Namespace="System.Data" %>
<%@ Import Namespace="System.Data.SqlClient" %>
```

The two namespaces are described as follows:

✦ **System.Data:** A collection of classes that are based on the ADO.NET architecture. The ADO.NET architecture allows for efficient data management and manipulation from multiple data sources. ADO.NET provides tools to request and update data in a data set, and reconcile data in the actual data source. Some of the classes included in this namespace are described as follows:

   • **DataSet:** Represents the data set cached in memory with which applications work.

   • **DataTable:** Represents a table of data in a data set.

   • **DataRow:** Represents a row of data in a data table.

   • **DataColumn:** Represents a column of data in a data table.

✦ **System.Data.SqlClient:** A collection of classes that are used to access SQL server data sources. Some of the classes are listed as follows:

   • **SqlConnection:** Represents a connection with a SQL server data source. The first step to access data from a SQL server database is to create an object of this class.

   • **SqlDataAdapter:** Represents a set of data commands and a database connection that are used to access or manipulate data. After creating a SqlConnection object, you need to create an object of the SqlDataAdapter class to populate the data set and update the data source.

   • **SqlCommand:** Represents the SQL command to perform data operations in a SQL server data source.

You use the following code to import the two namespaces if you want to use the Visual Basic code file instead of the ASPX file:

```
Imports System.Data
Imports System.Data.SqlClient
```

You can use the different classes to create and manipulate database objects. For example, the following code illustrates how to create a table called "Products" in a SQL server database "Sales."

```
Dim MyCommand As SqlCommand
Dim MyConnection As SqlConnection

MyConnection = New
SqlConnection("server=localhost;uid=sa;pwd=;database=Sales")
Dim CreateCmd As String = " Create Table Products (ProductID
VarChar (4) Primary Key, ProductName VarChar (20), UnitPrice
Money, QtyAvailable Integer)"

'Passing the SQL query in the SQLqlCommand object

MyCommand = New SqlCommand(CreateCmd, MyConnection)

'Opening the active connection

MyCommand.Connection.Open()

'Executing the command

MyCommand.ExecuteNonQuery()
'Closing the connection

MyCommand.Connection.Close()
```

Before delving into the details of implementing the different ADO.NET classes in your Web applications, let's have a recap session for T-SQL.

Revising T-SQL

A SQL database stores data in *tables*, which consist of rows and columns. A column stores the information regarding properties of an item, while a row stores the complete information of an item. For example, consider a Products table. The columns store information, such as product identification number, product name, and quantity available. The rows store information about different products. Each column stores data of a specific type. Therefore, each column has a specific data type. Table 12-1 describes some of the SQL data types.

Table 12-1 SQL data types	
Data Type	**Description**
Integer	Used to store whole numbers.
Float	Used to store decimal numbers.
Char(*n*)	Used to store character data that can be letters, numbers, or special characters such as #, %, or $, or a combination of letters and characters. Char stores a single character of data. To store more than one character, you use Char(*n*), where *n* refers to the number of characters you want to store.
VarChar(*n*)	Used to store character data, where *n* refers to the number of characters you want to store, but the length of the column depends on the actual number of characters entered.
DateTime	Used to store date and time data.
Money	Used to store monetary data values.

Each table must have at least one column that uniquely identifies each row in the table. Such a column is called a *primary key*. For example, the ProductID column in a Products table identifies each row uniquely and is therefore a primary key.

Note   A primary key must be unique. No two values in a primary key column can be identical.

The client programs can access data from the tables stored on a SQL server or communicate with a SQL server by using a form of SQL called Transact SQL (T-SQL). You can create a table by using the `Create Table` statement, shown as follows:

```
Create Table Products
(
ProductID VarChar (4) Primary Key,
ProductName VarChar (20),
UnitPrice Money,
QtyAvailable Integer
)
```

The next two sections give a brief overview of the T-SQL statements to retrieve, insert, modify, and delete data in tables.

Retrieving data from a SQL database

You can retrieve information stored in tables by using the `Select` statement. The syntax is as follows:

```
Select Column1, Column2,..., ColumnN
From Table
```

In this statement:

- ✦ ColumnN: Represents the name of a column in the table from which the information needs to be retrieved. A comma separates the different column names.
- ✦ Table: Represents the name of the table.

You can also retrieve information from all the columns of a table by using the following statement:

```
Select *
From Table
```

In the preceding statement, * represents all the columns of the table.

If you want to retrieve only specific rows from a table, you need to specify a condition in the Select statement. You can specify a condition by using the Where clause, as follows:

```
Select *
From Table
Where ColumnN="Value"
```

In this statement, only those rows will be retrieved where the column has a specific value. For example, to retrieve the information from the Products table for a product called "cinnamon," use the following statement:

```
Select *
From Products
Where ProductName = "cinnamon"
```

Inserting, updating, and deleting data in a SQL database

You might need to add a new row to a table in a SQL database. For example, suppose you need to add to the Products table a new row for a new product. To add a row to a table, use the following statement:

```
Insert Into Table
Values (Column1_Value, Column2_Value, ..., ColumnN_Value)
```

In this syntax:

- ✦ Table: Represents the table in which the row needs to be inserted.
- ✦ Values: Takes the column values for the new row as parameters.

✦ ColumnN_Value: Represents the value to be inserted in the column with name ColumnN.

The values must be supplied in the same order as the columns in the table. Also, if the data type of a column is Char, VarChar, or DateTime, you need to specify values in quotes.

For example, to insert a row in the Products table, write the following statements:

```
Insert into Products
Values ('P001', 'Baby Food', 2.5, 1200)
```

Here, it is important to note that for every row that you want to insert in a table, you need to use a separate insert statement. So, to insert another row in the Products table, write the following statements:

```
Insert into Products
Values ('P002', 'Chocolate', 4.5, 1000)
```

In addition to adding a row to a table, you might need to modify the value in a specific column of a row. For example, you might need to modify the price of a specific product in the Products table. You use the Update statement to modify specific column(s) of a specific row of a table as follows:

```
Update Table
Set ColumnN="Value1"
Where ColumnM="Value2"
```

In this statement, the Set clause is used to set the value of a column named ColumnN to "Value1" where the column named ColumnM has a value "Value2". For example, to update the price of a product whose ID is P001, use the following statement:

```
Update Products
Set UnitPrice=25
Where ProductID="P001"
```

You might also need to delete a specific row in a table. For example, you might need to delete a specific product in the Products table. To do so, you use the Delete statement as follows:

```
Delete From Table
Where ColumnN="Value"
```

Stored procedures

A *stored procedure* is a set of SQL statements used to perform specific tasks. A stored procedure resides on the SQL server and can be executed by any user who has the appropriate permissions. Because the stored procedures reside on the SQL server, you do not need to transfer SQL statements to the server each time you want to perform a task on the server. This reduces the network traffic. When you want to execute a procedure, you only need to transfer the name of the procedure. However, if the procedure takes any parameters, you also need to transfer the parameters along with the procedure name.

You can create a stored procedure by using the `Create Procedure` statement as follows:

```
Create Procedure ProcName
As
SQL statements
Return
```

In this statement:

- ✦ `ProcName`: Represents the name of the stored procedure.

- ✦ `SQL statements`: Represents the set of SQL statements in the stored procedure.

- ✦ `Return`: Represents the end of the procedure. Each stored procedure must end with a `Return` statement.

After the stored procedure is created, the SQL server scrutinizes it for any errors. The procedure can be executed by using the `Execute` or `Exec` keyword, as follows:

```
Execute ProcName
```

You can also pass parameters or arguments to a stored procedure to perform a specific task based on the parameter. For example, consider the following procedure that displays the price of a product whose ID is passed as a parameter:

```
Create Procedure ProductPrice (@id char (4))
As
Select UnitPrice
From Products Where ProductID=@id
Return
```

This procedure takes a parameter, `@id`, at the time of execution. To display the price of the product whose ID is "P001", execute this procedure using the following code:

```
Execute ProductPrice "P001"
```

Implementing T-SQL in Web Applications

Many situations require Web applications to retrieve, add, modify, and delete data stored in a database on a server. For example, consider a Web application that enables users to register as customers. When a customer fills out the Registration form and submits it, the customer registration information must be stored in a database on a server so as to maintain the registered customer's records. After the registration, the customer might need to change their customer details, such as telephone number or address. Later, the customer might want to discontinue purchasing from the same store. In such a situation, the Web application must take care of addition, modification, and deletion of data in the respective database on a server.

In this section, you'll create a Web application to retrieve, add, modify, and delete data in a table stored on a SQL server. You can choose to use either Visual Basic or C# to do so. In the following example, you'll create a Visual Basic Web application project. Figure 12-1 displays the schematic diagram of the tables used to illustrate the server-side data access from a Web application.

Figure 12-1: A schematic diagram of the Sales database

Before you start implementing T-SQL in your Web application, create the tables as shown in the preceding schematic diagram. Also, add records in the Products and Customers tables. You can refer to Figure 12-2 and Figure 12-3 to add records in the Products and Customers tables.

After creating the ASP.NET Web Application project, design two Web Forms as shown in Figure 12-2 and Figure 12-3. The Order form will enable customers on the Web to place orders for products. Refer to Table 12-2 to specify IDs for the controls (that are used in code examples) on the Order form. In this form, you'll implement the functionality to view the complete product list or to view the details of a specific product. For this to happen, you'll access data from the Products table in a database called "Sales" stored on a SQL server.

Table 12-2
IDs of the Controls on the Order Forms

Control	ID
Order ID TexBox	Order_ID
Customer ID TextBox	Customer_ID
Product ID TextBox	Product_ID
Quantity TextBox	Order_Quantity
Order Date TextBox	Order_Date
Data Grid	MyDataGrid

The Customer form will enable users to register themselves as customers. Table 12-3 shows the IDs of the controls (that are used in code examples) on the Customer form. This form uses the Customers table in the "Sales" database stored on a SQL server.

Table 12-3 IDs of the Controls on the Customer Form	
Control	**ID**
Customer ID TextBox	Cust_ID
Customer Name TextBox	Cust_Name
Address TextBox	Cust_Address
City TextBox	Cust_City
State TextBox	Cust_State
Zip TextBox	Cust_Zip
DataGrid	MyDataGrid
Label next to the Add button	LblMessage

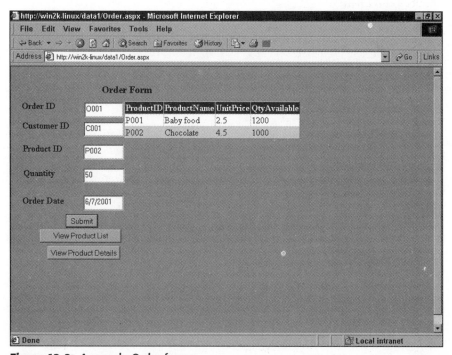

Figure 12-2: A sample Order form

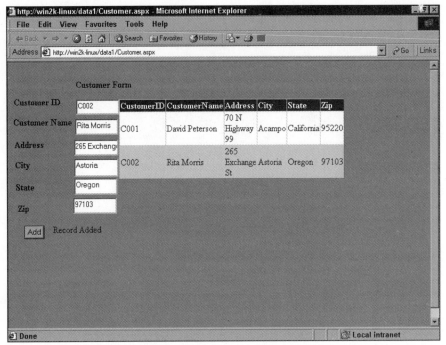

Figure 12-3: A sample Customer form

The sample forms use a DataGrid control to display records from the tables stored in a SQL database on a SQL server. A DataGrid control enables a form to display data bound to a data source.

Accessing data

After designing the forms, you'll add the desired functionality to them. First, you'll add the functionality to the Order form. The form should enable customers to view the complete product list by clicking the View Product List button. Also, the form should enable customers to view the details of a specific product by clicking the View Product Details button.

To implement this functionality, open the code behind file (with .vb extension) of the Order form. At the top of the Order form, import the two namespaces as follows:

```
Imports System.Data
Imports System.Data.SqlClient
```

Next, in the Click event of the button labeled View Product List, enter the following code:

```
'Declare the objects of the SqlConnection,
'SqlDataAdapter, and DataSet classes
```

```
Dim DS As DataSet
Dim MyConnection As SqlConnection
Dim MyCommand As SqlDataAdapter

'Initializing the SqlConnection object

MyConnection = New SqlConnection
("server=localhost;uid=sa;pwd=;database=Sales")

'Initializing the SqlDataAdapter object with the SQL
'query to access data from the Products table

MyCommand = New SqlDataAdapter("select * from Products",
MyConnection)

'Initializing the DataSet object and filling the data set with
the query result

DS = new DataSet()
MyCommand.Fill(DS,"Products")

'Setting the DataSource property of the DataGrid control

MyDataGrid.DataSource=DS.Tables("Products").DefaultView

'Binding the DataGrid control with the data

MyDataGrid.DataBind()
```

In this code, the comments provide explanation for the statements that follow.
However, some statements need more explanation:

✦ When initializing the SqlConnection object, the constructor takes four
   parameters:

   • The first parameter, which represents the SQL Server, is localhost,
      indicating that the server resides on the local computer. However, if the
      SQL server resides on a network, you need to give its complete address.

   • The uid and pwd parameters represent the User ID and Password on the
      SQL Server.

   • The database parameter represents the name of the SQL database that
      you want to access. In this case, the database is "Sales."

✦ When initializing the SqlDataAdapter object, the constructor takes two
   parameters:

   • The first parameter represents the SQL query. In this case, the query is
      used to retrieve all the records from the Products table.

   • The second parameter represents the SqlConnection object.

✦ The `Fill` method of the SqlDataAdapter class is used to fill the DataSet object with the data. This method takes two parameters:

- The `DataSet` object
- The identifier for the `DataTable`

✦ When setting the `DataSource` property of the DataGrid control, the default view of the Products table in the DataSet object is used.

After you write the respective code, save the project and execute it. When you click the button with the "View Product List" caption, the product details are displayed in the DataGrid control.

Now, you'll implement the functionality to display the product details of only that product whose ID is entered in the Product ID text box. To do so, write the following code in the `Click` event of the button labeled "View Product Details":

```
Dim DS As DataSet
Dim MyConnection As SqlConnection
Dim MyCommand As SqlDataAdapter

'Initializing a String variable with the SQL query to be passed as a
'parameter for the SqlDataAdapter constructor

Dim SelectCommand As String = "select * from Products where
ProductID = @prod"

MyConnection = New
SqlConnection("server=localhost;uid=sa;pwd=;database=Sales")

MyCommand = New SqlDataAdapter(SelectCommand, MyConnection)

'Creating a SQL parameter called @prod whose data type is
VarChar with size 4

MyCommand.SelectCommand.Parameters.Add(New
SqlParameter("@prod", SqlDbType.NVarChar, 4))

'Setting the SQL parameter @prod with the value of the text box
displaying Product ID

MyCommand.SelectCommand.Parameters("@prod").Value =
Product_ID.Text

DS = New DataSet()
MyCommand.Fill(DS, "Products")

MyDataGrid.DataSource = DS.Tables("Products").DefaultView
MyDataGrid.DataBind()
```

After you've written this code, save the project and execute it to check the desired functionality.

Adding data

You'll implement the functionality to add data in the Customer form shown earlier in Figure 12-3. The form should enable a user to add the customer registration information upon clicking the Add button.

To implement this functionality, add the following code at the top of the code behind file of the Customer form:

```
Imports System.Data
Imports System.Data.SqlClient
```

Tip   As a good programming practice, the objects that are shared across the form are declared globally. Also, the code that implements data binding to the DataGrid control has been segregated in a separate procedure, which can be called whenever required.

In the Declaration section of the form class, declare the object of the SqlConnection class as follows:

```
Dim MyConnection As SqlConnection
```

Next, create a procedure called BindGrid to bind data from the Customers table to the DataGrid control. To do so, write the following code in the form class:

```
Sub BindGrid()
    Dim MyCommand As SqlDataAdapter = New
    SqlDataAdapter("select * from Customers", MyConnection)

    Dim DS As DataSet = New DataSet()

    MyCommand.Fill(DS, "Customers")

    MyDataGrid.DataSource = DS.Tables("Customers").DefaultView
    MyDataGrid.DataBind()
End Sub
```

Then, in the Click event of the Add button, write the following code:

```
Dim DS As DataSet
Dim MyCommand As SqlCommand

'Checking for the customer details. If the values are not
entered, an
'error is displayed

If Cust_ID.Text = "" Or Cust_Name.Text = "" or
Cust_Address.Text="" or Cust_City="" or Cust_State="" Then

    lblMessage.Text = "Null values not allowed in these fields "
    BindGrid()
End If
```

```
'Defining the SQL query for inserting data into the Customers
table

Dim InsertCmd As String = "insert into Customers values (@CID,
@Cname,@Caddress,@Ccity,@Cstate,@Czip)"

'Passing the SQL query in the SqlCommand object

MyCommand = New SqlCommand(InsertCmd, MyConnection)

'Adding the SQL parameters and setting their values

MyCommand.Parameters.Add(New SqlParameter("@CId",
SqlDbType.NVarChar, 4))
MyCommand.Parameters("@CId").Value = Cust_ID.Text

MyCommand.Parameters.Add(New SqlParameter("@Cname",
SqlDbType.NVarChar, 20))
MyCommand.Parameters("@Cname").Value = Cust_Name.Text

MyCommand.Parameters.Add(New SqlParameter("@Caddress",
SqlDbType.NVarChar, 20))
MyCommand.Parameters("@Caddress").Value = Cust_Address.Text

MyCommand.Parameters.Add(New SqlParameter("@Ccity",
SqlDbType.NVarChar, 20))
MyCommand.Parameters("@Ccity").Value = Cust_City.Text

MyCommand.Parameters.Add(New SqlParameter("@Cstate",
SqlDbType.NVarChar, 20))
MyCommand.Parameters("@Cstate").Value = Cust_State.Text

MyCommand.Parameters.Add(New SqlParameter("@Czip",
SqlDbType.NVarChar, 20))
MyCommand.Parameters("@Czip").Value = Cust_Zip.Text

'Opening the connection

MyCommand.Connection.Open()

'Executing the command

MyCommand.ExecuteNonQuery()
lblMessage.Text = "Record Added successfully"

'Closing the connection

MyCommand.Connection.Close()

'calling the BindGrid method to reflect the added record in the
DataGrid control

BindGrid()
```

When you run this application, you'll notice that the customer details are reflected in the DataGrid control after you enter the data in the respective text boxes and click the Add button.

Modifying and deleting data

The DataGrid control enables users to modify and delete records. To allow rows to be edited, the EditItemIndex property of the DataGrid control is used. By default, this property is set to -1, indicating that no rows are editable.

The DataGrid control has a property called Columns that you can use to add buttons to allow user interaction with individual data rows. To add a button column, follow these steps:

1. Open the Property Window of the DataGrid control.

2. Click the ellipsis in the Columns property to open the Properties dialog box, as shown in Figure 12-4.

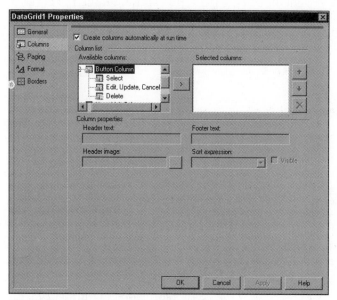

Figure 12-4: The Properties dialog box

3. In the left pane, click Columns.

4. In the right pane, under the Available Columns list, under Button Columns, select Edit, Update, Cancel and click the > button to add this button column to the control.

5. Click OK to close the dialog box.

The DataGrid control can have three types of button columns, described as follows:

✦ The Select button column renders a Select link button used to access a specific row.

✦ The Edit, Update, Cancel button column renders three link buttons: Edit, Update, and Cancel. The Edit button is used to display the row in Edit mode. After the row switches to Edit mode, the column displays Update and Cancel buttons, which are used to update or cancel the changes made to the row.

✦ The Delete button column renders a Delete button that enables users to delete a specific row.

To add the update functionality, add the Edit, Update, Cancel button column to your DataGrid control. When the Edit button is clicked, the EditCommand method of the DataGrid control is called. The UpdateCommand method is called when the Update button is clicked. And, when the Cancel button is clicked, the CancelCommand method is called. Therefore, you need to write appropriate code in these methods to implement the desired functionality.

In the EditCommand method of the DataGrid control, set the EditItemIndex property as follows:

```
Public Sub MyDataGrid_EditCommand(ByVal source As Object, ByVal
e As System.Web.UI.WebControls.DataGridCommandEventArgs)
Handles MyDataGrid.EditCommand

'Setting the EditItemIndex property of the DataGrid control to
indicate the row to be edited

   MyDataGrid.EditItemIndex = e.Item.ItemIndex

End Sub
```

In this code:

✦ The EditCommand method takes two arguments:

• source: Represents the object that generates the event. In this case, the source is the DataGrid control.

• e: Represents the object of the DataGridCommandeventArgs class. This argument represents the event information of the source.

✦ Item indicates the item that generated the event. In this case, it is the DataGrid control.

✦ ItemIndex represents the row number for the item.

After you've written this code, you need to use the following SQL statement as a String variable in the UpdateCommand method to modify the customer address based on a customer ID:

```
Dim UpdateCmd As String = "Update Customers Set Address =
@Address Where CustomerID = @CID"

MyCommand = New SqlCommand(UpdateCmd, MyConnection)
```

Now, let us discuss how we can implement data deletion in a SQL table. The first step is to add a Delete button column to the DataGrid control. Then, in the `DeleteCommand` method of the DataGrid control, add the code to delete a customer record. The following SQL statement needs to be used as a String variable to delete a customer record based on a customer ID:

```
'Defining the SQL query to delete a record from Customers table

Dim DeleteCmd As String = "Delete from Customers where
CustomerID = @CID"

MyCommand = New SqlCommand(DeleteCmd, MyConnection)
```

After understanding how to update and delete data in a SQL Server database, let us now see how to use stored procedures through your Web applications.

Using stored procedures

As mentioned earlier, stored procedures perform database operations more efficiently than the ad hoc SQL queries, because stored procedures are stored on the SQL Server. You simply need to write the procedure's name and the procedure parameters, if any, to execute the stored procedure. When using stored procedure, the traffic is less as compared to passing the complete set of SQL queries to the server. Therefore, the performance is greatly improved.

If a stored procedure already exists on a SQL Server, use the following syntax to create the SqlDataAdapter object:

```
MyCommand = New SqlDataAdapter("Procedure_Name", MyConnection)

MyCommand.SelectCommand.CommandType =
CommandType.StoredProcedure
```

In this syntax:

- ✦ `MyCommand` is the object of the SqlDataAdapter class.
- ✦ `MyConnection` is the object of the SqlConnection class.
- ✦ `Procedure_Name` represents the name of the procedure to be called.
- ✦ The second statement specifies that the command passed in statement1 is a stored procedure.

Stored procedures can also take parameters that need to be passed while executing them. Parameters make the stored procedures more flexible because they return results based on user input. For example, you can create a stored procedure that takes a product name as a parameter and displays the product details for the specified product. To use stored procedures that take parameters, use the following syntax:

```
MyCommand = New SqlDataAdapter("Procedure_Name", MyConnection)

MyCommand.SelectCommand.CommandType =
CommandType.StoredProcedure

'Adding a SQL parameter with SQL data type

MyCommand.SelectCommand.Parameters.Add(New
SqlParameter("@Parameter_name", SqlDbType.datatype, size))

'Setting the value of the SQL parameter

MyCommand.SelectCommand.Parameters("@Parameter_name").Value =
TextBox1.Text
```

In the last statement, the value of the parameter is initialized. Here, the value is initialized by a value entered in a text box at run time.

Before you can use a stored procedure in your Web application, create a procedure named "DisplayCustomer." The code for the same is given as follows:

```
Create Procedure DisplayCustomer (@CustID Varchar(4))
As
Select * from Customers
Where CustomerID=@CustID
Return
```

Next, you'll extend the functionality of the Customer form shown in Figure 12-3.

Add a button with ID and text as "Query." In the `Click` event of this button, write the following code:

```
Dim DS As DataSet
Dim MyConnection As SqlConnection
Dim MyCommand As SqlDataAdapter

MyConnection = New
SqlConnection("server=localhost;uid=sa;pwd=;database=Pubs")

'Calling the DisplayCustomers stored procedure

MyCommand = New SqlDataAdapter("DisplayCustomers",
MyConnection)
```

```
MyCommand.SelectCommand.CommandType =
CommandType.StoredProcedure

'Adding the SQL parameter

MyCommand.SelectCommand.Parameters.Add(New
SqlParameter("@CustID", SqlDbType.NVarChar, 4))

'Specifying the parameter value

MyCommand.SelectCommand.Parameters("@CustID").Value =
Customer_ID.Text

DS = New DataSet()
MyCommand.Fill(DS, "Customers")

MyDataGrid.DataSource = DS.Tables("Customers").DefaultView
MyDataGrid.DataBind()
```

When you run the application, you can test the code for its functionality. To do so, enter a customer ID in the Customer ID text box and click the Query button. The DataGrid control now displays only one record with the specified customer ID.

Using ADO Extensions (ADOX)

Data is stored and maintained in different data sources. Some data source applications include MS-Access, SQL Server, Oracle, and Sybase. Each data source uses its own native syntax. Therefore, when you need to manage data stored in data sources from your applications, you would prefer to use standard objects and syntaxes irrespective of the data sources. It is inconvenient to use different objects, methods, and syntaxes to manage different data sources. ADOX provides a set of standard objects that you can use to manage data stored in different data sources.

ActiveX Data Objects Extensions (ADOX) is an extension of the ADO objects and programming model that allows creation, modification, and manipulation of schema objects, such as databases, tables, and columns. ADOX also includes security objects that enable you to maintain users and groups that access the schema objects. ADOX security objects can be used to grant and revoke permissions on objects that are accessed by different users and groups.

ADOX is part of the Microsoft Data Access Components (MDAC) SDK. When you install Visual Studio .NET, the Windows Component update installs MDAC 2.7. You can visit the http://www.microsoft.com/data/download.htm site to get the latest release of MDAC SDK.

Standard ADOX objects

ADOX objects are a set of standard objects that are used to create and manipulate data stored in different data sources irrespective of their native syntaxes. Table 12-4 describes the ADOX objects.

Table 12-4 ADOX objects	
Object	**Description**
Catalog	Represents the collections that describe the schema catalog of a data source.
Table	Represents a table stored in a database. This object includes columns, indexes, and keys.
Column	Represents a column that might be from a table, index, or key.
Index	Represents a table index.
Key	Represents a key field: primary, foreign, or unique.
View	Represents a view, which is a set of filtered records from a table.
Procedure	Represents a stored procedure in a database.
User	Represents a user who has access to a database.
Group	Represents a group that has access to a database.

The different ADOX objects can be grouped together in *ADOX collections*. For example, Tables is an ADOX collection that represents all the Table objects in a catalog. The other ADOX collections are Columns, Indexes, Keys, Views, Procedures, Users, and Groups.

The different ADOX objects share a set of common properties and methods. Table 12-5 describes some of the ADOX properties.

Table 12-5 ADOX properties	
Property	**Description**
ActiveConnection	Represents the ADO Connection object.
Count	Represents the number of objects in an ADOX Collection.
Name	Represents the name of an ADOX object.

Property	Description
PrimaryKey	Used to indicate whether or not the index represents a primary key.
Unique	Used to indicate whether or not the index represents a unique key.
Type (Column)	Represents the data type of a column.
Type (Key)	Represents the data type of the key.
Command	Represents the ADO Command object that is used to create or execute a procedure.

Table 12-6 describes some of the ADOX methods.

Table 12-6 **ADOX methods**	
Method	**Description**
Create	Used to create a catalog.
Delete	Used to delete an object from an ADOX Collection.
Append	This is a common method shared among different objects and is used to add a new ADOX object to an ADOX Collection. For example, when used with Tables object, the method is used to add a Table object to a Tables Collection.
GetObjectOwner	Used to get the name of the owner of an object in a catalog.
SetObjectOwner	Used to specify the owner of an object.
GetPermissions	Used to get the permissions for a user or a group on an object.
SetPermissions	Used to specify permissions for a user or a group on an object.
ChangePassword	Used to change the password of a user.

Using ADOX objects

You can use ADOX objects in your Web applications to manage data stored in different data sources. However, before you can use ADOX objects, you need to establish a reference to the ADOX type library. The name of the ADOX library is Msadox.dll. To establish a reference to this type library, select Add Reference from the Project menu. Then, you can specify the path for the library.

Note ADOX requires an interop assembly. When you add reference for the ADOX library, a dialog box appears asking you if you want to generate an interop wrapper. At this stage, click Yes to add the ADOX reference.

After adding the reference to the type library, you can go ahead and write the code to create databases, tables, or columns in a table.

To create a database, use the following syntax:

```
Dim ObjectName as New ADOX.Catalog
ObjectName.Create "Provider = Name of the provider; Data Source
= Path of the database"
```

In this syntax:

✦ `ObjectName` refers to the instance of the ADOX `Catalog` object.

✦ The `Create` method takes two parameters:

   • **Provider:** Specifies the name of the database provider. The different providers include Microsoft OLE DB Provider for ODBC, Microsoft OLE DB Provider for the Microsoft Jet Database Engine, Microsoft OLE DB Provider for Oracle, and Microsoft OLE DB Provider for SQL Server.

   • **Data Source:** Specifies the path where you want to create the database.

The following code snippet illustrates how to create a table called "Products" in a database called "Sales.mdb" stored in MS Access:

```
Dim table1 as New Table
Dim catalog1 as new ADOX.catalog

'Setting a connection with the Sales database

catalog1.ActiveConnection = "Provider =
Microsoft.Jet.OLEDB.4.0; Data Source = C:\Sales\Sales.mdb"

'Specifying the name of the table

table1.Name = "Products"

'Adding columns in the table. Notice that the column name along
with its data type is specified as arguments to the Append
method.

table1.Columns.Append "ProductID", adVarWChar, 4
table1.Columns.Append "ProductDescription", adVarWChar, 20
table1.Columns.Append "Price", adInteger
```

```
table1.Columns.Append "Quantity", adInteger

'Adding the table in the Tables collection. Notice that the
Table object is specified as an argument to the Append method.

catalog1.Tables.Append table1
```

In addition to managing data with ADOX objects, you can set the security options associated with different schema objects. Before you can use the ADOX objects to set user or group permissions, you must open the connection with the system database that stores all security information. Then, you can use the `GetPermissions` and `SetPermissions` functions to grant and revoke user or group access permissions on an object.

Summary

This chapter explored the server-side data access by using SQL Server from your Web applications. First, you learned the SQL basics. You learned how to retrieve, add, modify, and delete data in SQL tables. You also learned how to create and execute stored procedures. Then, you learned how to implement the retrieval, addition, modification, and deletion of server-side data from your Web applications. You also learned to implement stored procedures in your Web applications. Finally, you learned how to use ADOX objects to create and manipulate schema objects.

✦　　✦　　✦

Advanced Data Binding and XML

Thee World Wide Web and its rapid growth in the 1990s revolutionized the methods of accessing information and conducting commerce. Numerous companies use the Web as a powerful tool to advertise and sell their products. This has led to an increase in the number of Web applications and their requirements in terms of payment handling, data access, and security. As a result, various new technologies have evolved.

One of the most important requirements of Web applications, especially B2B e-commerce applications, is the ability to interchange data in a standard format that can be understood by any hardware and software platform. Enterprises having similar business interests may need to share data, which may be stored on disparate platforms. This need for a common interface for exchanging data resulted in the evolution of Extensible Markup Language (XML), which is the latest and the most hyped Web technology.

What is XML? How does it allow data interchange in Web applications? These are the questions that need to be answered before you look at its use in ASP.NET. In this chapter, you will learn about XML and its related specifications. You will also learn to use XML documents in ASP.NET.

Introduction to XML

XML is the World Wide Web Consortium's (W3C) specification for interchanging structured data in Web applications. An XML document enables you to store data in the same way a database enables you to store data. However, unlike databases, an XML document stores data in the form of plain text, which can be understood by any type of device, whether it is a mainframe computer, a palmtop, or a cell phone. Thus, XML serves as a standard interface required for interchanging data between various Web applications.

Note   W3C (www.w3c.org) is a consortium that ensures the growth of the Web by developing common protocols for the Web. It also ensures that various Web technologies are interoperable. W3C has more than 500 organizations as its members.

XML is a markup language that enables you to enclose data within tags. So how is it different from HTML? The difference lies in the fact that HTML has a set of predefined elements that concentrate on the appearance of the contents within the document. For example, when you enclose the data within the <I> and </I> tags, the browser interprets these tags and displays the content enclosed within the tags in italics. The browser is not concerned about the contents within the tags.

Conversely, XML concentrates on the content in the document and is not concerned with how the contents should appear. For example, if you are creating a document that stores the data about the products offered by your company, you can create a tag called <ProductDescription> and enclose the description of a product within this tag. Thus, tags in XML serve the purpose of structuring the content within the XML document. No presentation or appearance is associated with any of the XML tags. XML does not provide any predefined set of tags. Rather, it enables you to create your own tags. In that sense, XML can be called a meta-markup language, which enables you to create your own markup or vocabulary. In fact, many existing markup languages have been derived from XML. Some examples of markup languages that are based on XML are Wireless Markup Language (WML), which is used to create Web applications that can be accessed using a cell phone, and MathML, which is used to represent mathematical equations.

An example will help you to understand the difference between XML and HTML. Consider the following HTML document that displays a list of items and their prices:

```
<HTML>
<HEAD> <TITLE> Items Data </TITLE> </HEAD>
<BODY>
<OL>
     <LI> Item Name : Chocolate  Price: 1 </LI>
     <LI> Item Name: Cadbury Price: 2.5 </LI>
</OL>
</BODY>
</HTML>
```

When you open this HTML document in a browser, such as Internet Explorer 5.0, it will look like Figure 13-1.

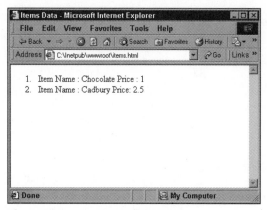

Figure 13-1: An HTML document

Now, let's create an XML document that represents the same information:

```
<?xml version="1.0"?>
<ITEMS>
    <ITEM>
            <NAME> Chocolate </NAME>
            <PRICE> 1 </PRICE>
    </ITEM>
    <ITEM>
            <NAME> Cadbury </NAME>
            <PRICE> 2.5 </PRICE>
    </ITEM>
</ITEMS>
```

In this code, the first statement, `<?xml version="1.0"?>`, is called *XML declaration*. It informs the browser that the document being processed is an XML document.

Note   XML documents have the extension .xml.

When you open the preceding XML document in Internet Explorer 5.0, it will look like Figure 13-2.

As can be seen from the figure, the XML document is displayed in the form of a tree view, which can be expanded and collapsed. Any XML document that you open in Internet Explorer 5.0 will be displayed in a similar format.

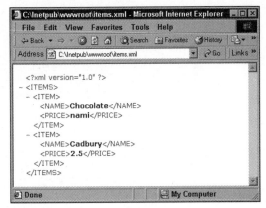

Figure 13-2: An XML document

While creating an XML document, you must remember some basic rules:

✦ All tags must be closed. In HTML, even if you don't close a tag, it does not give you any errors. However, in XML, all opening tags must have corresponding closing tags; otherwise, the browser displays an error message.

✦ All empty tags must include a / character before the closing angular bracket (>). For example, in HTML, you have the ⟨IMG⟩ tag for inserting an image in a Web page. This tag does not require any closing tag because the tag itself contains all the relevant information, such as the image source and its position. Therefore, ⟨IMG⟩ is an empty tag. If you want to use an empty tag called ⟨Image⟩ in XML, you must include a / character before closing the angular bracket of the tag as follows:

```
<Image src="tree.gif" />
```

✦ All attributes of an element must be enclosed within quotes.

✦ Tags should not overlap; that is, the innermost tag must be closed before closing the outer tags. Consider the following code:

```
<FirstName> James <LastName> Ford </FirstName> </LastName>
```

This statement would result in an error because the outer tag, ⟨FirstName⟩, has been closed before the inner tag, ⟨LastName⟩.

✦ Tags are case-sensitive. Therefore, the case of the closing tag should match the case used in the opening tag.

An XML document that conforms to these rules is called a *well-formed* XML document.

An Overview of XML-Related Specifications

XML does not exist all by itself. Numerous additional XML-related specifications provide guidelines for working with XML documents. Before discussing the implementation of XML in ASP.NET, it is important to understand these XML-related specifications. Therefore, this section looks at some of the important XML-related W3C specifications.

Document Type Definition

A Document Type Definition (DTD) enables you to specify the structure of the content in an XML document. Creating a DTD is similar to using a `CREATE TABLE` statement in SQL, in which you specify the columns to be included in the table and whether they can hold null values. In a DTD, you can specify the elements that can be used in an XML document and specify whether it is mandatory to provide values for the elements.

When you include a DTD in an XML document, software checks the structure of the XML document against the DTD. This process of checking the structure of the XML document is called *validating*. The software that performs the task of validating is called a *parser*. The following are the two types of parsers:

   ✦ **Nonvalidating parser:** Checks whether an XML document is well formed. An example of a nonvalidating parser is the *expat* parser.

   ✦ **Validating parser:** Checks whether an XML document is well formed and whether it conforms to the DTD that it uses. The MSXML parser provided with Microsoft Internet Explorer 5.0 is an example of a validating parser.

An XML document that conforms to the DTD is called a *valid* document.

An example of a DTD is given as follows:

```
<!ELEMENT ITEMS (ITEM)+>
<!ELEMENT ITEM (NAME, PRICE)>
<!ELEMENT NAME (#PCDATA)>
<!ELEMENT PRICE (#PCDATA)>
```

In this example, we have declared four elements, ITEMS, ITEM, NAME, and PRICE. After specifying the element name, you specify the type of content of that element. In case of ITEMS, the content type is (ITEM)+, which means that this element can contain one or more ITEM elements. Similarly, the ITEM element contains the elements NAME and PRICE, which contain character data. This type of data is represented as (#PCDATA).

Note   DTD files have the extension .dtd.

You can attach this DTD to an XML document by including the following statement after the processing instruction:

```
<!DOCTYPE ITEMS SYSTEM  "items.dtd">
```

Consider the following XML document that uses the previous DTD statement:

```
<?xml version="1.0"?>
<!DOCTYPE ITEMS SYSTEM "ITEMS.DTD">
<ITEMS>
<ITEM>
<NAME> Chocolate </NAME>
</ITEM>
</ITEMS>
```

When you check this document using a validating parser such as MSXML, it results in an error message, because the ITEM element declared in the DTD contains two mandatory elements, NAME and PRICE. However, the PRICE element is missing in the XML document. Thus, a DTD enables you to implement consistency in the structure of data contained within XML documents.

XML namespaces

As stated earlier, XML enables you to create your own elements. It also enables you to use elements that are defined for and used by various software modules. This may lead to certain problems. For example, in case of a purchase order, you may have an element called QTY that stores the quantity of a purchase. In some other case, the same element may be used to store the quantity on hand for a particular item. In such a case, there may be a collision of elements having the same names. To prevent this from happening, W3C has recommended the use of XML *namespaces*.

XML namespaces use Uniform Resource Identifiers (URIs) to differentiate tags used in different vocabularies. With this approach, each element can be uniquely identified using the namespace. A namespace can be declared using the xmlns keyword. For example, a namespace for a purchase order could be defined in the following way:

```
xmlns:PurchaseOrder="http://www.po.com/po"
```

Now when you use the QTY element, you must prefix it with the alias "PurchaseOrder" as follows:

```
<PurchaseOrder:QTY>
```

When you specify a namespace URI, the parser does not actually search for the URI, nor does it search for any documents at the specified URI. The URI just serves as a unique identifier for tags from different vocabularies.

XML schemas

An XML schema provides a way of defining a structure of an XML document. It enables you to describe the elements and attributes that can be present in an XML document. An XML schema is similar to a DTD. However, it can be considered a superset of a DTD in terms of the functionality that it provides. An advantage of using an XML schema is that it enables you to specify the data types for elements. A DTD, on the other hand, enables you to specify whether the element can contain character data or other elements, or whether it is an empty element. It does not enable you to specify whether a particular element should contain integer, float, or string values. Another difference between an XML schema and a DTD is that an XML schema follows XML syntax. In other words, it is an application of XML, whereas a DTD has its own syntax.

The following is an example of an XML schema for the Items.xml document:

```
<xsd:schema xmlns:xsd="http://www.w3.org/2001/XMLSchema">
<!-- Declaring the root element "ITEMS" -->
<xsd:element name="ITEMS" type="ITEMDATA"/>

<!-- Declaring the complex type "ITEMSDATA" which should
contain one or more "ITEM" elements -->
<xsd:complexType name="ITEMDATA">
        <xsd:sequence>
        <!-- The "ITEM" element can occur one or more times
in the XML document. This can be specified by using the
minOccurs and maxOccurs attributes -->
        <xsd:element name="ITEM" type="DETAILS"
minOccurs="0" maxOccurs="unbounded" />
        </xsd:sequence>
</xsd:complexType>

<!-- Declaring the complex type "DETAILS" which is used in the
"ITEM" element. This type contains the elements "NAME" and
"PRICE" -->
<xsd:complexType name="DETAILS">
        <xsd:sequence>
            <xsd:element name="NAME" type="xsd:string"/>
            <xsd:element name="PRICE" type="xsd:decimal" />
        </xsd:sequence>
</xsd:complexType>
</xsd:schema>
```

As you can see from this example, you can specify the structure of elements by using an XML schema. In addition, you can specify whether the element occurs once or more than once, whether it is optional, and whether it should contain a string or a numeric value. When you validate an XML document against this schema, the parser will ensure that all the necessary elements are specified in the XML document. In addition, it will check whether the value specified in the PRICE element is a numeric value. If you add a string instead of a numeric value, the parser will give you an error message. Thus, XML schemas provide additional control over the contents in an XML document, as compared to a DTD.

Note   XML schema files have the extension .xsd. XML schemas are fully supported with MSXML 4.0, which is a validating parser from Microsoft. This parser can be freely downloaded from http://msdn.microsoft.com.

Extensible Stylesheet Language Transformations (XSL/T)

As discussed earlier, XML does not deal with the presentation of data contained within an XML document. It concentrates only on the structure and the data contained within the structure. This separation of the data and its presentation enables you to display the same data in various formats. However, because an XML document does not contain any formatting instructions for displaying data, you need some special tool that can convert an XML document into a user-viewable format.

XSL/T is a W3C specification for formatting XML documents and displaying them in the desired format. XSL/T follows XML syntax. You will be looking at the creation of an XSL/T style sheet later in this chapter in the section "XML Web server control."

XML Document Object Model

The XML Document Object Model (XML DOM) is an in-memory representation of an XML document. It represents data in the form of hierarchically organized object nodes, and enables you to programmatically access and manipulate the elements and attributes present in an XML document. W3C has provided some common DOM interfaces for accessing XML documents through a program. These standard interfaces have been implemented in different ways. Microsoft's implementation of XML DOM has the XMLDocument class, which is at the top of the document object hierarchy. It represents the complete XML document. Another example is the XMLTransform class, which has a reference to the XSL/T file that specifies how the XML data is to be transformed. You can access XML DOM classes and objects from any scripting language as well as from programming languages such as VB.NET.

Support for XML in ASP.NET

The growing popularity of XML as a common data interchange format between Web applications has resulted in an increase in the number of software platforms that support XML, and ASP.NET is no exception. ASP.NET enables you to work with XML by supporting a number of XML-related classes. Some of the features provided in ASP.NET for working with XML are as follows:

✦ System.Xml namespace

✦ XML server-side control

✦ Data conversion from a relational to XML format

✦ Data binding with XML documents

System.Xml namespace

The System.Xml namespace is a collection of classes that are used to process an XML document. This namespace supports XML-related specifications, such as DTDs, XML schemas, XML namespaces, XML DOM, and XSL/T. Some of the classes present in the System.Xml namespace are as follows:

✦ **XmlDocument:** Represents a complete XML document.

✦ **XmlDataDocument:** Derived from the XmlDocument class and enables you to store and manipulate XML and relational data into a data set.

✦ **XmlElement:** Represents a single element from an XML document.

✦ **XmlAttribute:** Represents a single attribute of an element.

✦ **XmlDocumentType:** Represents the DTD used by an XML document.

✦ **XmlTextReader:** Represents a reader that performs a fast, noncached, forward-only read operation on an XML document.

✦ **XmlTextWriter:** Represents a writer that performs a fast, noncached, forward-only generation of streams and files that contain XML data.

XML Web server control

The XML Web server control enables you to insert an XML document as a control within a Web Form. The control has the following properties:

✦ `DocumentSource`: Enables you to specify the URL to the XML document to be displayed in the Web form

✦ `TransformSource`: Enables you to specify the URL to the XSL/T file, which transforms the XML document into a desired format before it is displayed in the Web form

✦ `Document`: Enables you to specify a reference to an object of the XMLDocument class

✦ `Transform`: Enables you to specify a reference to an object of the XMLTransform class

All four properties can be changed programmatically by providing an ID to the XML server-side control. To use the XML server-side control in ASP.NET, you can use the following syntax:

```
<asp:xml DocumentSource="XML document" TransformSource="XSL/T file"
Document="XMLDocument object" Transform="XSLTransform object">
```

You can also use the toolbox to create an XML Web server control. You can drag the XML control from the Web Forms tab and then set the DocumentSource, TransformSource, Document, and Transform properties of the control.

Consider the following XML document:

```
<?xml version = "1.0"?>
<Products>
    <Product>
        <ProductId> P001 </ProductId>
        <ProductName> Baby Food </ProductName>
        <UnitPrice> 2.5 </UnitPrice>
        <QtyAvailable> 1200 </QtyAvailable>
    </Product>
    <Product>
        <ProductId> P002 </ProductId>
        <ProductName> Chocolate </ProductName>
        <UnitPrice> 1.5 </UnitPrice>
        <QtyAvailable> 1500 </QtyAvailable>
    </Product>
</Products>
```

You can transform this XML document into a desired format by creating a style sheet. The steps for creating an XSL/T style sheet are as follows:

1. XSL/T follows XML syntax. Therefore, the following is the first line in the XSL/T file:

   ```
   <?xml version="1.0"?>
   ```

2. An XSL/T file has `stylesheet` as its root element. This element also specifies the namespace for XSL/T:

   ```
   <xsl:stylesheet version = "1.0" xmlns:xsl =
   "http://www.w3.org/1999/XSL/Transform">
   ```

   The XSL/T processor provided with the MSXML parser supports the URI "http://www.w3.org/1999/XSL/Transform" for XSL/T.

3. Create a template for displaying your data in the desired format. You can create a template using the `template` element. The `match` attribute of the `template` element enables you to specify the element from which you want the template to be applied. If you want to apply the template from the root element, you provide the value "/" to the match attribute:

   ```
   <xsl:template match="/">
   ```

4. Within the template, you can use HTML tags to create an ordered list:

   ```
   <OL>
   ```

5. The data from the XML document should be fetched and displayed in the ordered list. All data from the XML document needs to be processed. You use the `for-each` element to perform a task repeatedly. The `select` attribute of the `for-each` element enables you to specify the element for which the repetitive task needs to be performed. In this example, each product needs to

be processed. The "Product" element exists within the "Products" element. Therefore, you give the following statement to process the details of each product:

```
<xsl:for-each select='Products/Product'>
```

6. Next, you need to fetch the values of various elements within the "Product" element and display the values in the list. You can fetch the values of elements from an XML document using the value-of element. The select attribute of the value-of element enables you to specify the element that needs to be fetched. The following code snippet shows how values for each product can be fetched and displayed in the list:

```
<LI>
        <b><i>
            Product Id :
              <xsl:value-of select='ProductId'/> <br />
        </i></b>
          Product Name :
            <xsl:value-of select='ProductName'/> <br />
          Unit Price :
            <xsl:value-of select='UnitPrice'/> <br />
          Quantity On Hand :
              <xsl:value-of select='QtyAvailable'/> <br />
          <hr />
</LI>
```

In this code, the <LI> tag of HTML is used to create a list item. The <BR> tag is used to insert a line break. Note that the <BR> tag has an extra / character before the closing angular bracket. Because XSL/T follows XML syntax, you must ensure that all empty elements have the / character.

7. The last step is to ensure that all the opening tags are closed:

```
</xsl:for-each>
</OL>
</xsl:template>
</xsl:stylesheet>
```

The complete XSL/T style sheet will look as follows:

```
<?xml version="1.0"?>
<xsl:stylesheet version = "1.0" xmlns:xsl =
"http://www.w3.org/1999/XSL/Transform">
    <xsl:template match="/">
        <OL>
            <xsl:for-each select='Products/Product'>
            <LI>
                <b> <i>
                    Product Id :
                    <xsl:value-of select='ProductId'/> <br />
                </i></b>
                Product Name :
                <xsl:value-of select='ProductName'/> <br />
```

```
                    Unit Price :
                    <xsl:value-of select='UnitPrice'/> <br />
                    Quantity On Hand :
                    <xsl:value-of select='QtyAvailable'/> <br />
                    <hr />
            </LI>
            </xsl:for-each>
        </OL>
    </xsl:template>
</xsl:stylesheet>
```

You can display the formatted XML document in a Web form by typing the following code in an ASPX file:

```
<html>
<body>
        <asp:xml id="MyXmlDoc" documentsource="products.xml"
transformsource="products.xsl" runat="server">
        </asp:xml>
</body>
</html>
```

When you execute the application, it will give the output shown in Figure 13-3.

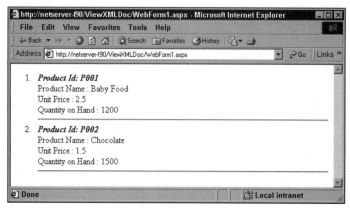

Figure 13-3: Output of the application implementing the XML server-side control

Converting Relational Data to XML Format

ASP.NET enables you to easily convert the data from a database into an XML document. ASP.NET provides the XMLDataDocument class, which enables you to load relational data as well as data from an XML document into a data set. The data loaded in XMLDataDocument can then be manipulated using the W3C Document Object Model.

The following example converts the data stored in the "Orders" table of the "Sales" database on SQL Server 7.0 into an XML document:

```
<%@ Page ContentType="text/xml" %>
<%@ Import Namespace="System.Data" %>
<%@ Import Namespace="System.Data.SqlClient" %>
<%@ Import Namespace="System.Xml" %>
<script language="VB" runat=server>
Sub Page_Load(Sender as Object, E as EventArgs)
    Dim SQLcon as New SqlConnection (
"server=localhost;uid=sa;pwd=;          database= sales")
    Dim Mycommand as New SqlDataAdapter("SELECT * FROM
Orders", SQLCon)
    Dim dsOrders As New DataSet()
    Mycommand.Fill(dsOrders, "Order")
    Dim XmlDoc as XmlDocument = New
                XmlDataDocument(dsOrders)
    MyXmlDoc.Document = XmlDoc
    Xmldoc.save ("orders.xml")
End Sub
</script>
<asp:xml id="MyXmlDoc" runat=server/>
```

In this example, you specify that the contents of the page represent an XML document by giving the following statement:

```
<%@ Page ContentType="text/xml" %>
```

You can also set the `ContentType` property to HTML to indicate that the page contains HTML elements. This statement is given to ensure that the contents of the resulting output are processed properly.

The next step is to import all the necessary namespaces. In addition to including the System.Data and System.Data.SQL namespaces, you are also required to include the System.Xml namespace, because it contains all classes required to process an XML document.

After importing the namespaces, you need to establish a connection with the SQL server and fetch the required data. This is done using the following code:

```
Dim SQLcon as New SqlClient.SqlConnection (
        "server=localhost;uid=sa;pwd=;
        database= sales")
Dim SQLcommand as New SqlClient.SqlDataAdapter("SELECT * FROM
        Orders", SQLCon)
Dim dsOrders As New DataSet()
SQLcommand.Fill(dsOrders, "Order")
```

After you have fetched the data into the data set, you can convert it into an XML document by using the following statement:

```
Dim XmlDoc as XmlDocument = New XmlDataDocument(dsOrders)
```

In this statement, the constructor of the XmlDataDocument class is invoked. The constructor takes the `DataSet` object as a parameter and loads the data set into the XmlDataDocument object. The reference to this new instance is stored in an object of the XmlDocument class.

Finally, you display the resulting XML document in the Web form. This is done by creating an XML server control with the ID "MyXmlDoc" and setting the `Document` property of the control to the XmlDocument object created in the previous step:

```
MyXmlDoc.Document = XmlDoc
```

You can save the resulting XML document in a file by using the `Save()` method of XMLDocument. The `Save()` method takes a string that specifies the name of the file as a parameter. The following statement illustrates this:

```
Xmldoc.save ("orders.xml")
```

When you view the ASPX file in a browser, it will display the output as shown in Figure 13-4.

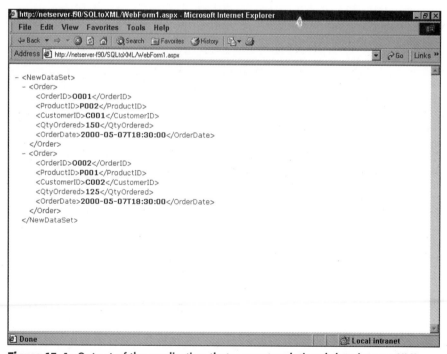

Figure 13-4: Output of the application that converts relational data into an XML document

Binding server-side controls with data in XML files

ASP.NET enables you to associate server controls with a variety of sources, including XML files. You can think of an XML file as a special data table that contains data embedded within the tags that describe the data.

You cannot bind an XML document directly to a server-side control because it contains data in a plain-text format. You must first load XML data as a data table into a data set. After loading the data into a data set, you can bind it to a server-side control. In this section, you will create a file "Products.xml" and bind a DropDownList control to the "ProductID" tag in the file. When a user selects a product ID from the DropDownList control, the details about the product will be displayed in a DataGrid control. The following are the steps involved in creating a Web application that performs the specified tasks:

1. Type the following contents in a text file and save it as "products.xml":

```
<?xml version = "1.0"?>
<Products>
<Product>
<ProductId> P001 </ProductId>
<ProductName> Baby Food </ProductName>
<UnitPrice> 2.5 </UnitPrice>
<QtyAvailable> 1200 </QtyAvailable>
</Product>
<Product>
<ProductId> P002 </ProductId>
<ProductName> Chocolate </ProductName>
<UnitPrice> 1.5 </UnitPrice>
<QtyAvailable> 1500 </QtyAvailable>
</Product>
</Products>
```

2. Create a new Web project and create a Label control in the Design view of the ASPX file. Change the Text property of the control to "Select Product Id:".

3. Create a DropDownList control in the Design view of the ASPX file. Set the values of the different properties of the DropDownList control as given in Table 13-1.

	Table 13-1	
	DropDownList control properties	
Property	**Value**	**Description**
ID	DLProdId	ID for the control.
DataTextField	ProductId (the field from the XML document)	Retrieves the data source that provides the content of the DropDownList. In this case, the value of the property is set to ProductId, which means that the control will display the ProductId from the data source.
DataValueField	ProductId	Specifies the value to be set in the data set when the selection changes.
AutoPostBack	True	Specifies whether the control posts back to the server each time a user interacts with the control. In this case, it is set to true, which means that every time a user interacts with the DropDownList, it should post back to the server. This is done so that whenever an item is selected from the DropDownList, the server retrieves details of the corresponding item.

4. Create a DataGrid control and set the ID property of the control to DGProdDetails.

5. Type the following lines in the ASPX file for importing the namespaces System.Data and System.IO:

```
<%@ Import Namespace = "System.Data" %>
<%@ Import Namespace = "System.IO" %>
```

Any class that implements the ICollection interface can be used as a data source by controls in a Web form. The ICollection interface provides the basic functionality required for accessing data. To be able to manage collections, you must import the System.Data interface. The System.IO interface contains the classes that are required for reading the XML file into a data set.

6. Write the following code within the Page_Load() function to open the products.xml file with read access permission:

```
dim ProdFile as new FileStream
(server.mappath("products.xml"), FileMode.Open,
FileAccess.Read)
```

The FileStream class is defined in the System.IO namespace and has functions for reading from and writing to the files. The constructor for the FileStream class takes three parameters, described in Table 13-2.

Table 13-2
FileStream class constructor parameters

Parameter	Type	Description
Path	String	Relative or absolute path of the file that needs to be opened
Mode	FileMode	Contains a constant that specifies how the file is to be created or opened
Access	FileAccess	Contains a constant that specifies the way in which the file can be accessed by the FileStream object

In this example, the file is opened with read access.

7. The next step is to fill the data set with XML data. This can be done by creating an object of DataSet and calling the ReadXml() method of DataSet:

```
dim dsProductsData as new DataSet
dsProductsData.ReadXml(ProdFile)
```

The ReadXml() method takes a parameter of classes derived from the Stream class and fills the DataSet object with the XML data. The DataSet object will now hold the XML data in a relational form.

8. After reading the data into the DataSet, you can work with it. In this application, the DataGrid is not to be displayed unless the user selects an item from the DropDownList control. You also need to ensure that the DropDownList control is populated only if the user has visited the first time. Therefore, you need to check whether the user is visiting the page for the first time. This can be done by using the IsPostBack() method provided in ASP.NET. In case the user is visiting the page for the first time, the DropDownList control needs to be populated with the product IDs read from the XML document. This can be done by using the following code:

```
if Not IsPostBack then
'Set the DataSource property of the DropDownList
        DLProdId.DataSource =
                dsProductsData.Tables(0).DefaultView
'Bind the data with the control
        DLProdId.DataBind()
```

In this code, the DataSource property of the DropDownList is set to the XML data read in the DataSet. Because the DataTextField property of the DropDownList has been set to ProductId, this step will result in displaying all product IDs in the DropDownList.

9. If the user is not visiting the page for the first time, the DataGrid should be populated with the details about the product selected from the DropDownList. This can be achieved by using the following code:

```
Else
   dvProductsView = new DataView(dsProductsData.Tables(0))
   dvProductsView.RowFilter = "ProductId='" +
            DLProdId.SelectedItem.Text + "'"
   DGProdDetails.DataSource = dvProductsView
   DGProdDetails.DataBind()
end if
```

In this code, a new object `dvProductsView` of type DataView is created. The constructor of the DataView class takes a DataTable as a parameter. In this example, you pass the XML data read in the data set as a parameter. Next, the `RowFilter` property of the DataView object is set to the product ID selected from the DropDownList. This limits the results of the DataView to only the rows that contain the same product ID as the one selected from the DropDownList. Then, the DataSource property of the DataGrid with the ID `DGProdDetails` is set to the DataView object. Finally, the data from the DataView is bound to the DataGrid. This code will result in displaying the details of the product selected from the DropDownList into the DataGrid.

The final code for displaying product IDs in a DropDownList and corresponding details in a DataGrid is as follows:

```
<script language="vb" runat="server">
public sub Page_Load (Sender as Object, e as EventArgs )
    dim ProdFile as new FileStream
(server.mappath("products.xml"), FileMode.Open,
FileAccess.Read)
    dim dsProductsData as new DataSet
    dsProductsData.ReadXml(ProdFile)

    if Not IsPostBack then
        DLProdId.DataSource =
dsProductsData.Tables(0).DefaultView
        DLProdId.DataBind()
    else
        dim dvProductsView as new
DataView(dsProductsData.Tables(0))
            dvProductsView.RowFilter = "ProductId='" +
DLProdId.SelectedItem.Text + "'"
            DGProdDetails.DataSource = dvProductsView
            DGProdDetails.DataBind()
    end if
end sub
</script>
```

When you execute the application, you'll find that the DropDownList control displays the product IDs stored in the XML document. When you click a particular product ID, it will display the details about the product in the DataGrid control, as shown in Figure 13-5.

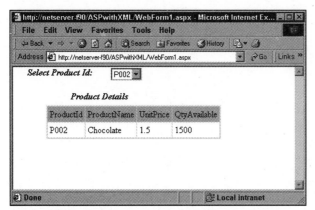

Figure 13-5: Output of the application implementing data binding with an XML file

This is one of the ways of binding XML data with ASP.NET server-side controls. You can perform many such tasks of opening an XML document, reading each element from the document, and displaying data from it using ASP.NET.

Summary

In this chapter, you were introduced to XML and its related specifications, such as DTD, XML Schema, XSL/T, namespaces, and XML DOM. You also learned about the System.Xml namespace provided in ASP.NET for working with XML documents. Then, you looked at some simple applications of using XML with ASP.NET. Finally, you learned about binding ASP.NET server controls to data from an XML document.

✦   ✦   ✦

Advanced ASP.NET

ASP.NET Application Configuration

After an application is designed and developed, it needs to be deployed on an application Web Server for launching it as a Web site on the Internet or an intranet. The deployment process includes installation and configuration of the Web application (Web site) on an application Web Server. Configuring a Web site requires implementation of settings according to the server's capabilities and requirements. Configuring a Web site might also require developers to write code. At a later stage, the site administrator might need to change the settings of the site or the server on which the site has been deployed so as to enhance the performance of the site. However, if the change in settings involves embedding values into code, it becomes very complicated and difficult for both the developer and the administrator to reconfigure the application.

The application deployment process requires a rich and flexible configuration system. The configuration system should enable developers to easily associate settings with an installable application without having to embed values into code. The system should also enable administrators to easily adjust or customize these values after the deployment of the application on the application Web Server. The ASP.NET configuration system fulfills both these requirements.

This chapter explores the ASP.NET configuration concept, the Web.config file, and the sections in the Web.config file.

ASP.NET Configuration Concepts

ASP.NET is designed to provide developers with rich support for designing, developing, and deploying Web applications. For application deployment, ASP.NET provides a rich set of configuration settings. The configuration information for the entire ASP.NET application is defined and contained in *configuration files*. These files are written in XML and are named Web.config.

ASP.NET uses a *hierarchical configuration architecture* that uses an XML format. In the hierarchical configuration architecture, whenever a client makes a request for an ASP.NET application or a specific ASP.NET resource, ASP.NET checks the settings for the URL requested by the client in a hierarchical fashion. The check is carried out using the configuration files located in the path for the requested URL. These settings are then logged or cached by the application Web Server to speed up any future requests for ASP.NET resources. To understand the hierarchical configuration architecture better, consider a Web site that has a file structure similar to that shown in Figure 14-1.

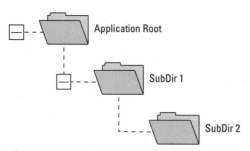

Figure 14-1: File structure of a Web site

In this file structure, suppose that the Application Root directory is the virtual directory (vdir) mapped for the site. A *virtual directory* is the main directory for the site, which contains all the files and subdirectories, including the script pages, HTML pages, programs, or any graphics for the site. Every site must have a virtual directory; the virtual directory might contain many subdirectories. The other two subdirectories within the Application Root directory are not virtual directories. This directory structure allows administrators to configure the application settings. For example, administrators can configure the application settings, such that all users are given access to the ASP.NET resources in the Application Root directory, but only selected users are given access to the ASP.NET resources in the subdirectories.

Consider a scenario wherein the Web site has only one Web.config file in the SubDir1 directory. Although the Web site has only one Web.config file in the directory structure, the Web site actually uses two Web.config files, because a file named Machine.config exists in the %windir%\Microsoft.NET\Framework\v1.0.<*buildnumber*>\ CONFIG directory. In this path, <*buildnumber*> represents 2914 for the Beta 2 release of the Microsoft .NET Framework SDK. In future releases, this build number will change, and therefore the actual name of the folder might also change. This file is at the highest level and is called the *machine-level configuration file*. This machine-level configuration file comes with the Microsoft .NET Framework and contains the default settings. All ASP.NET directories and subdirectories inherit settings from this machine-level configuration file. However, a Web.config file can also be located at the Web site level, and if it is not overridden at a lower level, it will apply to all ASP.NET resources on the Web site.

Note   A server can host multiple Web sites.

The default settings of the machine-level configuration file allow access to all users. In this scenario, there is no configuration file in the Application Root directory that modifies the default behavior of the machine-level configuration file; all users will be given access to the ASP.NET resources on the site, because the Application Root directory inherits settings from the machine-level configuration file. The configuration file located in the SubDir1 directory can have settings that specify access only to certain users. In such a case, all users can access the ASP.NET resources in the Application Root directory, but only certain users can access the ASP.NET resources in both the subdirectories.

Note   The configuration settings for virtual directories are independent of the physical directory structure, and unless the manner in which the virtual directories are organized is exclusively specified, configuration problems might result.

To summarize, the hierarchical configuration architecture provides a flexible and rich configuration system that enables extensible configuration data to be defined and used throughout the ASP.NET applications. The configuration system of ASP.NET has the following benefits in terms of deployment of Web applications:

✦ The configuration information for the ASP.NET applications is stored in XML-based configuration files, which makes it easy to read and write. Administrators and developers can use a standard text editor, XML parser, or Perl script for any kind of interpretation or updating of the configuration settings of the application.

✦ The configuration information files are stored in the same directory tree as the rest of the application files, thus making the installation of ASP.NET applications easy.

✦ The configuration system is highly flexible and allows developers to store customized configuration criteria and settings in the configuration system. This extensibility feature can then be used at run time to affect the processing of the HTTP requests.

✦ The configuration system allows the automation of any configuration updates made to the ASP. NET configuration files. The changes made are applied without requiring any user intervention.

✦ The configuration information contained in the XML file is applied hierarchically with regard to the virtual directory structure, which is provided at the time of site creation on the Application Server. Subdirectories under the virtual directory inherit or override the configuration settings from their parent directories. This allows different settings for different applications or different parts of a single application.

Now that you understand the basic concepts of the ASP.NET configuration, let us now take a closer look at the structure of the Web.config configuration files.

Web.config Configuration Files

As mentioned earlier, the configuration information for any ASP.NET application is defined and contained in configuration files named Web.config files. The following code illustrates the basic structure of an ASP.NET configuration file:

```
<configuration>
    <configSections>
        <section name="appSettings" type =
"System.Web.Configuration.NameValueSectionHandler" />
        <section name="httpModules" type =
"System.Web.Config.HttpModulesConfigHandler"/>
        <section name="httpHandlers" type = "
System.Web.Config.HttpHandlerConfigHandler " />
        <section name="sessionState" type = "
System.Web.Config.SessionStateConfigHandler " />
        <section name=" globalization " type = "
System.Web.Config.GlobalizationConfigHandler " />


        <!-- Additional configsection declarations go here -->
    </configSections>

    <appSettings>
        <!--custom application settings go here-->
    </appSettings>

    <system.web>

        <compilation defaultLanguage="vb" debug="true">
          <!-- all compiltion config is here -->
        </compilation>

        <customErrors mode="RemoteOnly">
          <!-- error config goes here -->
        </customErrors>

        <authentication mode="Windows">
          <!-- authentication settings controlled here -->
```

```
        </authentication>

        <authorization>
            <!—Allow/Deny all users , roles-->
        </authorization>

        <trace enabled="false" requestLimit="10"
pageOutput="false" traceMode="SortByTime" localOnly="true" />
            <!-- control trace settings for this web application -->

        <sessionState>
            <!-- configure session state for this web application -
->
        </sessionState>

        <httpHandlers>
            <!--configure HTTP Handlers for this web application-->
        </httpHandlers>

        <httpModules>
            <!--configure HTTP Modules for this web application-->
        </httpModules>

        <globalization/>
            <!-- configure globalization settings -->

    </system.web>

</configuration>
```

Note   This code listing is not the full description for the Web.config file; this code simply displays the basic structure of an ASP.NET configuration file.

The preceding code displays the structure of a Web.config file presented in the XML format. As you can see in the code, tags provide structure to the document. In a Web.config file, all the configuration information for an ASP.NET application must reside between the `<configuration>` and `</configuration>` tags. The file is divided into three main parts:

✦ The configuration section handler declaration part contained within the `<configSections>` and `</configSections>` tags. This is the root section, which contains the declaration of all other sections of the Web.config file.

✦ The application-specific settings in configuration variables in the appSettings section.

✦ The actual configuration sections in the system.web section. All tags defined in this section control the behavior of the ASP.NET runtime. This section is a great way to control, change, and manage the behavior of a Web application.

For each configuration section in the file, there should be one `<configSections>` declaration. Each individual declaration specifies the configuration section name and the type of the configuration section handler. The type attribute is used to specify the configuration section handler class to be associated with the element specified in the name attribute. If the name of the configuration section is other than the default name, an entry must be made in ⟨configSections⟩ to reflect the change. For example, if the Web.config file has session state information defined in a section named anything other than ⟨sessionState⟩, then an entry for this new section must be made in ⟨configSections⟩.

Note ⟨configSections⟩ entries can be made even if the default section names are being used. Of course, this is redundant.

ASP.NET Configuration Sections

The Web.config file is used to configure the ASP.NET applications and contains several configuration section handlers that are used to process the configuration settings. This section describes these configuration sections in detail.

⟨configuration⟩ section

The ⟨configuration⟩ section is the root configuration section for all the ASP.NET configuration files. This is a special tag that encapsulates all other sections in the file. The syntax is as follows:

```
<configuration>

</configuration>
```

⟨configSections⟩ section

The ⟨configSections⟩ section contains a list of the configuration section handlers associated with each configuration section. When you want to devise your own section handlers, you must declare them in the ⟨configSections⟩ section. The syntax is as follows:

```
<configSections>
    <section name="config section element name" type = "Type"/>
</configSections>
```

The two attributes Name and Type are described as follows:

✦ Name: Used to specify the name of the element that will contain the configuration data.

✦ Type: Used to specify the configuration section handler class to be associated with the element specified in the Name attribute.

Note A configuration section handler must be declared for each configuration section in the file.

An example of using the ⟨configSections⟩ section is as follows:

```
<configSections>
   <httpModules>
     <section name="System.Web.Caching.OutputCacheModule" />
     <section name="System.Web.SessionState.SessionStateModule"
/>
   </httpModules>
</configSections>
```

The ⟨httpModules⟩ section has a configuration handler that is set to System.Web.
Caching.OutputCacheModule, and the ⟨sessionState⟩ section has a configuration
handler that is set to System.Web.SessionState.SessionStateModule classes.

⟨appSettings⟩ section

The ⟨appSettings⟩ section of the Web.config file provides a way to define custom
application settings for an application. The section can have multiple ⟨add⟩ subelements. The syntax is as follows:

```
<appSettings>
  <add Key="[key]" Value="[value]"/>
</appSettings>
```

The ⟨add⟩ subelement supports two attributes:

✦ Key: Specifies the key value in an appsettings hashtable

✦ Value: Specifies the value in an appsettings hashtable

An example is as follows:

```
<appSettings>
      <add Key="dsn"
        Value="localhost;uid=user1;pwd=password"/>
</appSettings>
```

The Key value is set to dsn, and the Value is set to the name of a server, user ID,
and password.

⟨browserCaps⟩ section

The ⟨browserCaps⟩ section of the Web.config file enables you to specify the
configuration settings for the browser capabilities component.

Note   The HttpBrowserCapabilities class contains all the browser properties. These
properties can be retrieved and set in this section.

The syntax is as follows:

```
<browserCaps>
    <result type="System.Web.HttpBrowserCapabilities" />
    <use var="Environment Variable" />
            browser="type"
            version=browser version
            majorver=0
            minorver=0
            frames=false/true
            tables=false/true
    <filter>
        <case match="Name of operating systems to match">
            platform="Current OS"
        </case>
        . . .
    </filter>
</browserCaps>
```

In this syntax:

✦ The `<result>` tag specifies the class that contains all the browser capabilities.

✦ The `<use>` tag defines the environment variable, such as HTTP_USER_AGENT, which is to be matched to determine the browser being used.

✦ The `<filter>` tag specifies the operating system on which the browser is running. This tag can be used to filter the browsers that are running on specific platforms.

An example is as follows:

```
<browserCaps>
    <result type="System.Web.HttpBrowserCapabilities" />
    <use var="HTTP_USER_AGENT" >
            browser="Unknown"
            version=0.0
            majorver=0
            minorver=0
            frames=false
            tables=false />
    <filter>
        <case match="Windows 95|Win95">
            platform=Win95
        </case>
        <case match="Windows NT|WinNT">
            platform=WinNT
        </case>
    </filter>
</browserCaps>
```

This sets the result type to BrowserCapabilities and also sets certain environmental variables.

<compilation> section

The <compilation> section contains all the compilation settings used by ASP.NET. Some of the settings involve setting a default language and debug option for the application setting. The section also provides support for the <compilers>, <assemblies>, and <namespaces> subelements. The syntax is as follows:

```
<compilation debug="true/false">
 <compilers defaultLanguage="[Lang]">
      <compiler
          language="[Lang]"
          extension="[ Ext]"
          type="Type[,assemblyName]"/>
      </compiler>

      <assemblies>
          <add assembly="[Assembly] " />
          <remove assembly="[Assembly]" />
           <clear />
      </assemblies>

      <namespaces>
          <add namespace="[namespace]"/>
          <remove namespace="[namespace]"/>
          <clear/>
      </namespaces>

  </compilation>
```

The <compilation> element supports the debug attribute, which can take either a True or False value, and indicates whether compilation should be retail (False) or debug (True) binaries. The default value is False. If the value is set to True, the temporary source file is not immediately deleted from the codegen directory. This is helpful for debugging compilation and parser errors.

This syntax uses three subelements, <compilers>, <assemblies>, and <namespaces>. These elements are explained in the following sections.

<compilers> subelement

The <compilers> section can contain multiple <compiler> subelements, which are used to create a new compiler definition. The <compiler> subelement has three attributes:

✦ Language: Provides a list of languages, separated by semicolons, used in dynamic compilation files. For example, C#; VB; JScript; and PERL.

✦ Extension: Provides a list of file name extensions, separated by semicolons, used for dynamic code behind files. For example, .pl; .cls; and .js.

✦ Type: Indicates the .NET Framework class, which implements the ICompiler interface and that should be used to compile all resources that use either the specified language or the file extension.

<assemblies> subelement

The subelement `<assemblies>` is used to add or remove assembly references that need to be used during the compilation of a dynamic resource. These assemblies are also loaded at run time. Therefore, this element allows both early and late binding. This element has three attributes:

✦ `Add`: Used to add an assembly reference to be used during the compilation of a dynamic resource. ASP.NET will automatically link this assembly when compiling each code module. The value specified is an assembly name and not a DLL path. ASP.NET will first perform a lookup on the supplied assembly name to find the physical location of the DLL. A developer can optionally specify * to add every assembly within an application's private assembly cache, which is located in the bin subdirectory of an application, or in the Microsoft .NET Framework install directory (%windir%\ComPlus\Version\).

✦ `Remove`: Used to remove an assembly reference from the compile settings. The value must explicitly match a previous "add" directive. Here, wildcard selections are not supported.

✦ `Clear`: Used to remove all assembly references currently contained in or inherited by a particular Web.config file.

<namespaces> subelement

The `<namespace>` subelement is used to add or remove namespace references for assemblies that must be made available when compiling Web pages. This element has three attributes:

✦ `Add`: Used to add a namespace reference for the assemblies to be used during the compilation of an ASP.NET Web page.

✦ `Remove`: Used to remove a namespace assembly reference from the compilation settings. The value must explicitly match a previous "add" directive.

✦ `Clear`: Used to remove all the namespace assembly references currently contained in or inherited by a particular web.config file.

The following is an example:

```
<compilation debug="true">
   <compilers defaultLanguage="VB">
      <compiler language="VB"
                extension=".cls"
                type="MSVSA.dll#Microsoft.VB.Compiler" />
      <compiler language="c#"
                extension=".cs"
                type="C#.dll#Microsoft.C#.Compiler" />

   </compilers>

   <assemblies>
      <add assembly="MyCompany.MyApplication.MyFirstDLL" />
```

```
        <add assembly="ADODB System.Data.OleDb " />
        <add assembly="*" />
    </assemblies>
</compilation>
```

This sets the compilation settings for the application. The debug mode is set to True. The default language for the application is set to VB and the compilation options are set to either VB or C#.

<customErrors> section

The <customErrors> section provides a means for defining custom error messages for an ASP.NET application. The syntax is as follows:

```
<customErrors defaultRedirect="[url]"  mode="[on/off/remote]">
      <error statusCode="[statuscode]" redirect="[url]" />
</customErrors>
```

In this syntax:

- ✦ The defaultRedirect attribute is an optional attribute of the section and is used to indicate the default URL to which the client browser should be redirected if an error occurs.

- ✦ The mode attribute is used to specify if the status of the custom errors is enabled, disabled, or only shown to remote machines. This attribute takes one of three values: On, Off, RemoteOnly. On indicates that the custom errors are enabled. Off indicates that the custom errors are disabled. RemoteOnly indicates that the custom errors will be shown only to remote clients.

The <customErrors> section supports multiple <error> subelements that are used to define custom errors. Each <error> subelement supports two attributes:

- ✦ Statuscode: Specifies an error status code that causes a browser to be directed to an error page, which is not the default error page.

- ✦ Type: The URL to which the browser should be redirected in the event an error occurs.

An example is as follows:

```
<customErrors defaultRedirect="customerror.htm"
   mode="On">
     <error statusCode="500"
     redirect="CustomInternalError.htm"/>
</customErrors>
```

The custom error file for the application is set to Customerror.htm, the error code is 500, and the error-redirection file is set to CustomInternalError.htm.

`<globalization>` section

The `<globalization>` section is used to configure the globalization settings of the application. The syntax is as follows:

```
<globalization
  requestEncoding="[any valid encoding string]"
  responseEncoding="[any valid encoding string]"
  fileEncoding="[any valid encoding string]"
  culture="[any valid culture string]"
  uiCulture="[any valid culture string]"
/>
```

The `<globalization>` element supports the following attributes:

✦ `requestEncoding`: Used to check for the encoding of each incoming request. The default value for this attribute set in the machine-level Web.config file is iso-8859-1.

✦ `responseEncoding`: Used to check for the content encoding of responses. The default value for this attribute as set in the machine-level Web.config file is: iso-8859-1.

✦ `fileEncoding`: Used to check for default encoding forASPX, ASMX, and ASAX file parsing.

✦ `culture`: Used to check for the default culture used to process incoming Web requests. Valid culture strings are specified in the System.Globalization.CultureInfo class.

✦ `uiCulture`: Used to check for the default cultures that are used to lookup for resources that need to be used for the current page.

An example is as follows:

```
<globalization
  fileEncoding="utf-8"
  requestEncoding="utf-8"
  responseEncoding="utf-8"
/>
```

This section sets the `fileEncoding`, `requestEncoding`, and `responseEncoding` attributes to "utf-8".

`<httpHandlers>` section

The `<httpHandlers>` section maps the incoming URL requests to the classes that implement IHttpHandler or IHTTPHandler interfaces. The syntax is as follows:

```
<httpHandlers>
  <add verb="[verb list]"
```

```
        path="[path/wildcard]"
        type="Type[,assemblyName]" />
    <remove verb="[verb list]"
            path="[path/wildcard]" />
    <clear />
</httpHandlers>
```

The child elements supported by this section are described as follows:

✦ Add: Used to add a verb/path mapping to an IHttpHandler or IHttpHandlerFactory interface. The following are the attributes used:

- Verb: Specifies the method used for receiving the data. The verb list can be either a comma-separated list of HTTP verbs, such as GET, PUT, or POST, or a start-script mapping, such as *.

- Path: The Path attribute specifies a path from where the incoming requests are generated. The path attribute can contain either a single URL path or a simple wildcard, such as *.aspx.

- Type: Composed of an assembly and a class combination — the two values are separated by a # character. The assembly DLL is always resolved first against an application's private "bin" directory, and then against the system assembly cache.

✦ Remove: Used to remove a verb/path mapping to an IHTTPHandler or an IHTTPHandlerFactory interface. The Remove directive should match the verb/path combination of a previous add directive in order to remove an entry. The attributes in this element do not support the use of wildcards.

✦ Clear: Used for removing all the IHttpHandlerFactory mappings that are currently configured or inherited by a particular Web.config file.

Note If an identical verb/path combination is specified by two or more <add> subelements, the last <add> will override all others.

The following is an example:

```
<httpHandlers>
    <add verb="*" path="FirstApp.Mack" Type="FirstApp.Mack,
    FirstApp" />
    <add verb="*" path="FirstApp.Gaze" Type=" FirstApp.Gaze,
    FirstApp" />
</httpHandlers>
```

This section sets the verb to use all the methods along with the path and type of files.

\<httpModules\> section

The \<httpModules\> section is used for adding, removing, or clearing HTTP modules in an application. The syntax is as follows:

```
<httpModules>
    <Add Type="Type [,assemblyName]" name="module name"/>
    <Remove Type="Type [,assemblyName]" name="module name"/>
    <Clear />
</httpModules>
```

The section can be configured using the three following subtag directives:

✦ Add: Used to add HttpModule classes to an application. This element takes two attributes: Type and Name. The Type attribute is composed of an assembly and class combination. The Name attribute specifies the name used in the application to refer to this assembly. If the Name attribute is omitted, the assembly name is used to refer to the module.

✦ Remove: Used to remove an HttpModule class from an application. This subtag also takes two attributes: Type and Name.

✦ Clear: Used to remove all the HttpModules mappings that are currently configured or inherited by a particular Web.config file from the application.

An example is as follows:

```
<httpModules>
    <add Type="System.Web.State.CookielessSessionModule" />
    <add Type="System.Web.OutputCacheModule" />
    <add Type="System.Web.State.SessionStateModule" />
    <add Type="FirstClass, FirstAssembly" />
</httpModules>
```

This sets the types to three different values of the assembly class combination.

Security settings in Web.config files

ASP.NET enables you to manage the entire security configuration from the Web.config file. The security configuration is implemented by using three sections: \<authentication\>, \<authorization\>, and \<identity\>. The syntax for the three sections is as follows:

```
<configuration>
<system.web>

  <authentication mode="[Windows/Forms/Passport]">
    <Forms name="[name]" loginurl="[url]"
protection="All/None/Encryption/Validation" timeout="30"
path="/">
    <credentials passwordformat="[Clear/ SHA1/ MD5]">
```

```
    <user name="[UserName]" password="[password]"/>
    </credentials>
  </forms>
  <passport redirectUrl="url"/>
</authentication>

<authorization>
  <allow users="[comma separated list of users]"
   roles="[comma separated list of roles]"/>
  <deny users="[comma separated list of users]"
   roles="[comma separated list of roles]"/>
</authorization>

<identity>
  <impersonation enable="[true/false]"/>
</identity>
</system.web>
</configuration>
```

The three security sections have elements for which the values are set by overriding the section of the machine-level configuration file with a similar section in an application configuration file placed in the application root. All subdirectories automatically inherit the settings defined. However, subdirectories can have their own configuration files that override their parent directory's settings.

The <identity> section is used to enable or disable impersonation. *Impersonation* is the ability of a thread to execute in a security context that is different from the context of the process that owns the thread. The other two sections are described next in more detail.

<authentication> section

This element takes an attribute "mode" that controls the default authentication mode for an application. This attribute can be set to one of the following values:

- ✦ Windows: Uses IIS authentication, which can be Basic, Digest, or Windows (NTLM) authentication, or a combination of these.
- ✦ Passport: Uses the Passport cookie authentication. To set this value, the Passport SDK must be installed and the user must subscribe to the Passport service.
- ✦ Forms: Uses the ASP.NET forms-based cookie authentication.

The <authentication> section also supports one subelement <forms>, which defines cookie authentication settings. This element supports three attributes, which are described as follows:

- ✦ Name: Specifies the name of the HTTP cookie to be used for the authentication ticket. By default, the value is set to ASPXAUTH.

✦ loginUrl: Defines the URL to which the request is redirected if it doesn't contain a valid authentication ticket.

✦ Protection: Specifies the protection technique applied to safeguard the cookie data. The following are the possible values for this attribute:

- All: The cookie is protected by encrypting the cookie data as well as by validating the contents of the cookie using a message authentication code.

- None: The cookie is not protected. This value is not recommended due to security concerns. However, it can be used for the sites that do not use cookies for security, but only for personalization of information to users.

- Encryption: The contents of the cookie are encrypted by using DES encryption.

- Validation: Defines the URL to which the request is redirected, if it doesn't contain a valid authentication ticket.

✦ TimeOut: Specifies the time after which the cookie expires. If a user wishes to access the site after the timeout has expired, the user will have to reauthenticate and get a new cookie.

✦ Path: Specifies the path of the cookie issued by ASP.NET on behalf of the Web application represented by the Web.config file.

✦ Decryptionkey: Specifies a key to be used for decrypting the authentication tickets. If login and authentication are distributed across multiple machines, they all need to share the same key. The key is stored in cleartext.

The <forms> subtag optionally allows users to define name/password credentials within the <credentials> subtag. Alternatively, developers can implement their own custom password scheme wherein validation occurs from external stores, such as databases. The <credentials> child element contains an attribute, passwordformat, which defines the encryption format used to store passwords. In addition to the passwordformat attribute, the element supports multiple <user> subelements. A <user> subelement has the following attributes:

✦ name: Indicates the user login name

✦ password: Indicates the user password

<authorization> section

Authorization for an ASP.NET application can be implemented by using the <authorization> subelement. This element controls client access to the ASP.NET resources at a given URL. The settings specified in an <authorization> element are inherited by subdirectories hierarchically.

The <authorization> element is configured by using two subelements, <allow> and <deny>, which are interpreted and processed in top-down sequential order. The <allow> element enables administrators to explicitly identify a class of users to whom access should be granted. The ⟨deny⟩ element enables administrators to explicitly identify a class of users to which access is denied. The ⟨allow⟩ and ⟨deny⟩ elements take the following two attributes:

✦ Users: Contains a comma-separated list of usernames that should be granted access. The ? character allows or denies access to anonymous users, and the * character allows or denies access to all users.

✦ Roles: Contains a comma-separated list of roles that should be granted or revoked access.

While the application is running, the authorization module iterates through the ⟨allow⟩ and ⟨deny⟩ elements to search for the first access rule that is applied for a particular user. The element decides to grant or reject access to a URL resource depending on whether the first access rule satisfied is an ⟨allow⟩ or a ⟨deny⟩ rule. By default, the access is rejected if no rule is found. The following is an example:

```
<configuration>
<system.web>
  <authentication mode="Cookie">
   <forms name="401kApp" loginUrl="/Firstlogin.aspx"
     protection="All">
    <credentials passwordformat="SHA1">
      <user name="Marie" password="GAF97FSA3223NTT"/>
      <user name="Caste" password="DF^$3GFDX443BSD99"/>
      <user name="RockMen" password="IDCJMWAFSLKSTGDLS##"/>
    </credentials>
   </forms>
 </authentication>

<authorization>
  <allow roles="Admins", "Managers" />
  <allow users=" Caste, "John" />
  <deny users="Jane", " RockMen " />
 </authorization>

<identity>
 <impersonation enable="false"/>
</identity>
</ system.web>
</configuration>
```

This uses all the attributes to set the security settings for the application.

⟨processModel⟩ section

The ⟨processModel⟩ section is responsible for configuring the ASP.NET process model settings on an IIS Web server. The process model settings are used for defining how the threads within a process should work.

Note The <processModel> section can appear only in the machine-level Web.config file.

The syntax is as follows:

```
<processModel
  enable="[true/false]"
  timeout="[mins]"
  idleTimeout="[mins]"
  shutdownTimeout="[secs]"
  requestLimit="[num]"
  requestQueueLimit="[num]"
  memoryLimit="[percent]"
  cpuMask="[num]"
  webGarden="[true/false]"
  userName="username"
  password="password"
/>
```

The <processModel> element supports the following attributes:

✦ enable: Specifies a value that indicates whether or not the process model is enabled.

✦ timeout: Specifies the number of minutes after which a new worker process will be launched to take the place of the current one. The default value is set to infinite.

✦ idleTimeout: Specifies the number of minutes of inactivity after which the worker process automatically gets shut down. The default value is set to infinite.

✦ shutdownTimeout: Specifies the time, in hh:mm:ss format, the worker process is given to shut down by itself. When the timeout expires, the ASP.NET runtime will kill the worker process automatically. The default value is set to 5 seconds.

✦ requestLimit: Specifies the number of requests after which a new worker process will be launched to take the place of the current one. The default value is set to infinite.

✦ requestQueueLimit: Specifies the maximum allowed number of requests in the queue after which the worker process is considered to be in a "hung" state. Once the requestQueueLimit is reached, a new process will be launched and the requests will get reassigned. Then, no further requests will be directed toward the "hung" worker process. The default value is set to 5000.

✦ memoryLimit: Specifies a maximum allowed memory size for a worker process. The value is set as a percentage of the total system memory that the worker process consumes before it is considered as a misbehaving process. After this limit is crossed, a new process will be launched and the requests will get reassigned. The default value is set to 40 percent.

✦ cpuMask: Specifies the processors on which the ASP.NET worker processes will execute. This attribute is used when the webGarden attribute is set to True, which indicates that ASP.NET worker processes will not use all the processors on the system. When the webGarden attribute is set to False, it means that all eligible CPUs will be used.

✦ webGarden: This attribute controls the CPU affinity in conjunction with the cpuMask attribute. The default value is True, which indicates that the processes should be allocated CPUs by the operating system; there is no preferential allotment of processors to the worker processes.

The following is an example:

```
<processModel
    enable="true"
    timeout="15"
    idleTimeout="25"
    shutdownTimeout="0:01:00"
    requestLimit="1000"
    requestQueueLimit="500"
    memoryLimit="20"
    webGarden="true"
/>
```

The processModel is enabled for the Web server. After every 15 minutes, the server will launch a new worker thread. After every 25 minutes of idle time, the worker process will automatically get shut down. The worker process is given 1 minute for a graceful shutdown before it is terminated. After every 1,000 requests, a new worker thread will be launched to handle further Web requests. The maximum limit for the worker thread, after which it will be treated as a misbehaving thread, is set to 500 requests in the queue. The memory limit is set to 20 percent of the available memory on the system, and the CPU affinity is set to True.

\<sessionState> section

The \<sessionState> section provides a means to configure the session state HttpModule of the ASP.NET application. The syntax is as follows:

```
<sessionstate
 mode = "mode="Off|Inproc|StateServer|SqlServer"
 cookieless="true|false"
 timeout="number of minutes"
 connectionString="server name:port number"
 sqlConnectionString="sql connection string"/>
```

The \<sessionState> section uses five attributes, which are described as follows:

✦ Mode: Indicates where the session state is stored. These are the possible settings:

  • Off: Indicates the session state is disabled for the Web application.

- Inproc: Indicates that session state is stored by the worker process itself. In case of a crash, the session state is lost. Also, this model does not work well in a Web farm due to redirection of client requests to other Web servers.

- StateServer: Indicates that the session state information is stored in a separate ASP.NET State Service that runs out of process from the Web server. This model is safe from any crashes that might occur in the Web server. The session state will be available no matter what happens to the Web server. This is an out-of-process state management model. The Session State service can be hosted on the same server as the Web server or it can be configured on a separate physical machine. In case it is hosted on the same machine as the Web server, if a serious failure occurs, such as in the disk subsystem or CPU or power supply, it will cause the server to switch off or reboot. In such a case, the session state is lost. If this service is configured on a separate physical machine, then this problem can be avoided. But, there is no way to cluster this service to protect against failure of the state server machine.

- SqlServer: The most reliable model for storing session state information across Web server crashes and machine reboots. To improve the availability of session state information across a Web farm, the session information can be stored on a SQL Server database, which itself can be placed on a cluster.

✦ Cookieless: Takes one of the values True or False. A True value indicates that the cookieless sessions should be used to identify client sessions. On the other hand, a False value indicates that the cookie-enabled sessions should be used. The default value for the tag is set to False.

✦ Timeout: Defines the number of minutes a session can remain idle. Once this limit has passed, the session is abandoned automatically. The default value for this attribute is set to 20.

✦ ConnectionString: Specifies the server name of the remote session state store for the application, as well as the port on which the Session State service is listening. The default value is set to localhost. This attribute is used when the mode is set to StateServer (the out-of-process state service).

✦ sqlConnectionString: Specifies the connection string used to connect to the SQL Server that is running the session state database.

Note   If you wish to have a remote session state store, you must set the inproc attribute to False and specify the server name and port number (using the server and port attributes) of the machine on which state services are running.

The following is an example:

```
<sessionState mode = "InProc"
  stateConnectionString = "tcpip=127.0.0.1:42424"
  sqlConnectionString="data source=127.0.0.1;user
id=sa;password="
  cookieless="true"
  timeout="5"/>
```

This states that the application session is managed by using cookieless sessions. The URL will be encoded by the ASP.NET runtime to include a character string, which is unique for every client. The session timeout is 5 minutes. Here is a sample Web page that uses session state to record some information:

```
<%@ Page Language="vb"%>
<HTML>
  <HEAD>
   <title></title>
  </HEAD>
   <script runat="server">
     sub Page_Load()
       Session("Var1")="This is the value stored in Variable 1"
     end sub

     Sub Display(Src As Object, E As EventArgs)
       lblResult.Text = Session("Var1")
     end sub
   </script>

   <body>
     <form id="Form1" method="post" runat="server">
      <P>
        <asp:Button id="cmdDisplay" runat="server" Text="Call
Display" onclick="Display" />
      </P>
      <P>
        <asp:Label id="lblResult" runat="server" Width="270px"
Height="31px"></asp:Label>
      </P>
     </form>
   </body>
</HTML>
```

Figure 14-2 shows the output of this page.

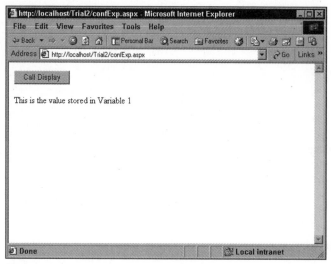

Figure 14-2: Output of the page displaying value of a Session variable

<trace> section

The <trace> section allows the configuration of the ASP.NET trace service. The syntax is as follows:

```
<trace
  enabled="[true/false]"
  requestLimit="[Integer]"
  pageOutput="[true/false]"
/>
```

The <trace> section can be configured using the following attributes:

✦ enabled: Indicates the status of the trace feature specified for the application. The default value is set to False.

✦ requestLimit: Specifies the number of trace requests to store on the server for the application. The default value for the attribute is set to 10.

✦ pageOutput: Indicates whether the trace information for the application should be displayed at the end of each page or be accessible only via the trace utility.

An example is as follows:

```
<trace
 enabled="true" requestlimit="20" pageoutput="true"
/>
```

The section sets the application-level trace to True and the number of trace requests to be stored to 20. The trace output is set to be displayed on the page.

<webServices> section

The <webServices> section is used to control the settings of the ASP.NET Web Services. An example is as follows:

```
<configuration>
 <system.web>
  <webServices>
    <protocolTypes>
      <add type="System.Web.Services.Protocols.
      SoapServerProtocol" />
      <add type="System.Web.Services.Protocols.
      HttpServerProtocol" />
      <add type="System.Web.Services.Protocols.
      DiscoveryServerProtocol" />
    </protocolTypes>

    <returnWriterTypes>
      <add type="System.Web.Services.Protocols.XmlReturnWriter"
      />
    </returnWriterTypes>

    <parameterReaderTypes>
      <add type="System.Web.Services.Protocols.
      HtmlFormParameterReader" />
      <add type="System.Web.Services.Protocols.
      UrlParameterReader" />
    </parameterReaderTypes>

    <protocolReflectorTypes>
      <add type="System.Web.Services.Description.
      SoapProtocolInfoReflector" />
      <add type="System.Web.Services.Description.
      HttpPostProtocolInfoReflector" />
      <add type="System.Web.Services.Description.
      HttpGetProtocolInfoReflector" />
    </protocolReflectorTypes>

    <mimeReflectorTypes>
      <add type="System.Web.Services.Description.
      XmlMimeInfoReflector" />
      <add type="System.Web.Services.Description.
       FormInfoReflector" />
    </mimeReflectorTypes>

    <protocolImporterTypes>
      <add type="System.Web.Services.Description.
      SoapProtocolInfoImporter" />
      <add type="System.Web.Services.Description.
      HttpPostProtocolInfoImporter" />
```

Continued

```
      <add type="System.Web.Services.Description.
       HttpGetProtocolInfoImporter" />
    </protocolImporterTypes>

    <mimeImporterTypes>
      <add type="System.Web.Services.Description.
       XmlMimeInfoImporter" />
      <add type="System.Web.Services.Description.
       FormInfoImporter" />
    </mimeImporterTypes>

    <protocolInfoTypes>
      <add type="System.Web.Services.Description.
       SoapProtocolInfo" />
      <add type="System.Web.Services.Description.
       HttpGetProtocolInfo" />
      <add type="System.Web.Services.Description.
       HttpPostProtocolInfo" />
    </protocolInfoTypes>

    <mimeInfoTypes>
     <add type="System.Web.Services.Description.HtmlFormInfo"/>
     <add type="System.Web.Services.Description.XmlMimeInfo"/>
     <add type="System.Web.Services.Description.AnyMimeInfo"/>
    </mimeInfoTypes>

    <referenceResolverTypes>
     <add type="System.Web.Services.Discovery.
      DiscoveryResolver" />
     <add type="System.Web.Services.Discovery.ServiceResolver"
      />
     <add type="System.Web.Services.Discovery.SchemaResolver"
      />
    </referenceResolverTypes>

    <discoverySearchPatternTypes>
      <add type="System.Web.Services.Discovery.
       ServiceSearchPattern" />
    </discoverySearchPatternTypes>

    <soapExtensionTypes>
    </soapExtensionTypes>

    <soapExtensionReflectorTypes>
    </soapExtensionReflectorTypes>

    <soapExtensionImporterTypes>
    </soapExtensionImporterTypes>

    <sdlHelpGenerator href="DefaultSdlHelpGenerator.aspx" />
   </webServices>
  </system.web>
</configuration>
```

The preceding example used different elements of the `<webServices>` section to set the configuration settings for the ASP.NET Web Services. Some of the settings involve setting the protocol, return type for the application, help file for the application, and the search patterns supported by the application.

Summary

This chapter explored the ASP.NET configuration concepts and the Web.config configuration files used by the ASP.NET configuration system. First, you learned the advantages offered by the ASP.NET configuration system in the process of deploying the ASP.NET applications. You saw the structure of the Web.config configuration files. Then, you learned the structure and implementation of different sections in the Web.config configuration file.

✦   ✦   ✦

Developing Business Objects

CHAPTER

15

Most modern applications are based on the client/server architecture, which divides an application into two logical parts, the client and the server. The functions performed by the client and the server can be divided into three categories: user services, business services, and data services. These services are implemented as logical layers in an application. The user service layer, also called the presentation layer, performs the task of providing an interactive user interface. The business service layer enforces the business rules that define the behavior of an organization. For example, an organization might decide that the credit limit for its clients should not exceed $2,000. The business service layer performs such validations pertaining to the business rules of an organization. The data service layer is responsible for managing and manipulating data.

Based on the methods used for implementing these three layers, client-server applications are further categorized as single-tier, two-tier, three-tier, and n-tier or multitier applications. In case of a single-tier or monolithic application, all the functions relating to the user, business, and data service layers are grouped into one logical application module, which might be a single executable file. In a two-tier application, the user and data services are located separately, either on the same machine or on separate machines. For example, you might have a Visual Basic application, which provides the user interface, and SQL Server 7.0, which manages data. In such a case, the business services might be handled by the client or by the server. In a three-tier application, all the three service layers reside separately, either on the same machine or on different machines. A multitier or n-tier application is very similar to a three-tier application. An n-tier application uses business objects for handling business rules and data access. It has multiple servers handling business services. This application architecture provides various advantages over other types of application architectures. Some of the advantages include extensibility, resilience to change, maintainability, and scalability of the application.

Most Web applications are based on the *n*-tier architecture. In case of Web applications, the browser acts as a client, which makes requests to the Web server for some data. The Web server processes the request and sends the requested data to the browser. You might implement an extra layer between the browser and the Web server for performing business rule validations. This layer can be implemented by using business objects.

In this chapter, you will learn to create and use business objects in ASP.NET. You will also learn about deploying business objects and working with business object namespaces in ASP.NET.

Introduction to Business Objects

In an *n*-tier application, the business services layer can be encapsulated in various reusable classes, known as *business object classes,* which can be combined to create precompiled components. Thus, business objects are reusable and interoperable components that perform a specific set of functions. Business objects enable you to build applications that can be easily changed as per the changing requirements of users and the organization. You can also build new applications based on existing components. This results in reduced development time and maintenance costs. You can also substitute the user and the data services layers without having a negative impact on the working of the business objects.

Business objects can be broadly categorized as follows:

✦ **User interface (UI)-centric business rule objects:** These objects concentrate on validation of user interface components. For example, you may create a UI-centric business rule object to ensure that a text box is not blank. A UI-centric business rule object may also perform some calculations on the data returned from the database.

✦ **Data-centric business rule objects:** These objects perform the functions relating to data access such as locating the source of data, sending the necessary commands for retrieving data, manipulating data, and sending the data back and forth between the database and the UI-centric business rule objects. Data-centric business rule objects run faster than UI-centric business rule objects, because the latter often depends on the former for completion of data manipulation and integration. For example, you might create a UI-centric business rule object that displays the net amount after calculating the sales tax and the discount based on the product price and order quantity. This object might depend on a data-centric object, which establishes a connection to the data server, sends the required commands to the server, and returns the prices and order quantities of products from the database to the UI-centric object. In this case, the UI-centric object has to wait until the data-centric object returns the required data for calculating the net amount.

Creating and Using Business Objects

ASP.NET enables you to easily create your own business objects and use them in Web applications. In this section, you will look at the process of creating a simple UI-centric business object that calculates the sales tax and the discount based on the price of a product. You will also learn to create a data-centric business rule object for establishing a connection and sending queries to the database server.

Creating a UI-centric business rule object

To create a business rule object, follow these steps:

1. Select File ⇨ New ⇨ Project. This invokes the New Project dialog box. Select Visual Basic Projects from the Project Types list box. Select Class Library from the Templates list box. Name the project CalcNetAmt.

2. In the Solution Explorer window, right-click the Class1.vb file and select Rename from the pop-up menu. Change the name of the Class1.vb file to CalcNetAmt.vb.

3. Create the function CalcAmt() in the class CalcNetAmt and type the following code:

```
Public Class CalcNetAmt
    Public Function CalcAmt(ByVal dPrice As Double) As Double
        Dim dNetAmt As Double
        dNetAmt = dPrice * 1.1
        If (dNetAmt > 100)
            dNetAmt = dNetAmt * 0.95
        End If
        Return dNetAmt
    End Function
End Class
```

This function takes the price of a product as a parameter. It calculates the sales tax as 10 percent of the product price. If the net price after adding the sales tax is greater than $100, a discount of 5 percent is given on net price. The function returns the net payable amount for a product.

4. Compile this class by selecting Build ⇨ Build. When you compile the class, a DLL file is created; this file can be used by other applications. Alternatively, you can compile this class by typing the following statement at the MS-DOS command prompt:

```
vbc /t:library /out:calcnetamt.dll calcnetamt.vb
```

In this statement, `vbc` is the Visual Basic compiler. You can use various command-line options with the compiler. The `/t` option is used to specify the type of output file format to be created by the compiler. You can set this option to exe (console application), library (code library), module (DLL), or winexe (Windows-based application). In this statement, the `/t:library` option instructs the compiler to create a *library assembly*.

Note Business objects created in .NET are packaged in the form of assemblies, which store all the information required for deploying and versioning a component. Assemblies are discussed in detail later in this chapter.

The `/out` option specifies the name of the output file to be created. In this case, the name of the resulting file is Calcnetamt.dll. Finally, you specify the file to be compiled as Calcnetamt.vb.

Note For more information about the command-line options used with vbc, type "vbc /?" at the command prompt.

Creating a data-centric business rule object

For creating a data-centric business rule object, the steps will be similar to those in case of UI-centric business objects. In this section, we will create a simple reusable data-centric business rule object that establishes a connection with the specified server and sends the queries to the database server.

For creating the data-centric business rule object, complete the following steps:

1. Select File ➪ New ➪ Project.

2. Select Visual Basic Projects from the Project Types list box. Select Class Library from the Templates list box. Name the project GetData.

3. In the Solution Explorer window, right-click the Class1.vb file and select the Rename option from the pop-up menu.

4. Rename the Class1.vb file GetData.vb and type the following code in the file:

```
Imports System.Data
Imports System.Data.SQLClient
Public Class DataAccessObj

    Dim sConnectionStr As String
    Dim sQryStr As String

    Public Property sConnection() As String
        Set
            sConnectionStr = value
        End Set
        Get
            Return sConnectionStr
        End Get
```

```
        End Property

        Public Property sQry() As String
            Set
                sQryStr = value
            End Set
            Get
                Return sQryStr
            End Get
        End Property

        Private Function EstablishConnection() As SQLConnection
            Dim SQLConObj As New SQLConnection(sConnectionStr)
            Return SQLConObj
        End Function

        Public Function DisplayData() As DataView
            Dim CmdObj As New SqlDataAdapter(sQryStr,
    EstablishConnection())
            Dim dsObj As New DataSet()
            CmdObj.Fill(dsObj, "DISPLAYDATA")          Return
    dsObj.Tables(0).DefaultView
        End Function
    End Class
```

This class establishes a connection with the database server and also uses DataSet and DataView objects. Therefore, you must import the System.Data and System.Data.SQLClient namespaces. The DataAccessObj class contains two data members:

✦ sConnectionStr: Used for storing connection information such as the server name, database to be used, and the username and password to be used for establishing a connection with the database server.

✦ SQryStr: Used for storing the query to be sent to the database server.

Next, you write the property procedures for returning and setting sConnectionStr and sQryStr.

In addition to the property procedures, the DataAccessObj class also includes the EstablishConnection() method for establishing a connection with the database server by using the connection string stored in sConnectionStr. This function returns an object of the type SQLConnection.

Finally, the class has the GetData() method, which sends the command stored in sQryStr to the database server by using the connection object returned by the EstablishConnection() method. The GetData() method fills a DataSet object with the data returned by the database server and returns an object of type DataView.

Compile the DataAccessObj class by selecting Build ➪ Build. Alternatively, you can compile the class from the MS-DOS command prompt by giving the following statement:

```
vbc /t:library /out:dataaccess.dll GetData.vb /r:System.dll /r:System.Data.dll
/r:System.XML.dll
```

This statement is similar to the statement we used earlier to compile the UI-centric data component. The /r option in the statement specifies the additional libraries to be used for compiling the application. The statement creates the Dataaccess.dll file, which can be included in projects to access the functions written in the DataAccessObj class.

Using business objects

In the previous section, you were introduced to the process of creating business objects. In this section, you will learn to use the business objects in an application with the help of an example. You will create an application, which will display a list of product IDs from the Products table in a DropDownList control. When a user selects a product ID from the DropDownList, the details about the product should be displayed along with the net amount payable on the product. The application should use the DataAccessObj and CalcNetAmt business objects created earlier for fetching the required data from the SQL Server and for calculating the net amount payable. For using these business objects in your application, follow these steps:

1. Create a new Web application by clicking the File ➪ New ➪ Project option. Select Visual Basic Projects from the Project types list box. Select ASP.NET Web Application from the Templates list box. Name the project UseBusinessObj.

2. Create a DropDownList control in the Design view of the Web Form and set the properties of the control as given in Table 15-1.

Table 15-1
DropDownList control properties

Property	Value
ID	LstProductId
DataTextField	ProductID
DataValueField	ProductID
AutoPostBack	True

3. Create Label controls for displaying the name and the unit price of a product. Specify the ID of these Label controls as LblProductName and LblUnitPrice. Also create an additional Label control for displaying the net amount payable on the product. Specify the ID of this Label control as LblNetAmt.

4. To use the CalcNetAmt and DataAccessObj business objects, you must add a reference to them in the project. Right-click the References tree in the Solution Explorer and select Add Reference from the pop-up menu. This invokes the Add Reference dialog box, shown in Figure 15-1.

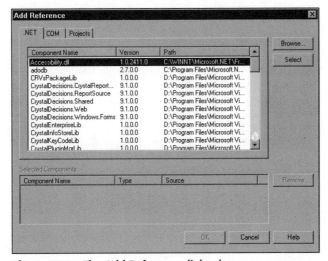

Figure 15-1: The Add Reference dialog box

Click the Browse button to invoke the Select Component dialog box. Locate the folder where you created the CalcNetAmt component. Select CalcNetAmt.dll and click Open. The Select Component dialog box closes and the control returns to the Add Reference dialog box. Notice that the dll file that you selected appears in the Selected Components list view. Add a reference for the GetData.dll file in a similar way.

5. Import the required namespaces by adding the following statements in the WebForm1.aspx file:

```
<%@ Import Namespace=System.Data %>
<%@ Import Namespace=System.Data.SqlClient %>
```

6. Create an instance of each business object by writing the following code in the Page_Load() method of theWeb Form:

```
Dim NetAmtObj As New CalcNetAmt.CalcNetAmt()
Dim daObj As New GetData.DataAccessObj()
```

Note You can write this code in the `Page_Load()` method in the VB file corresponding to the Web application instead of including it in the `Page_Load()` method of the ASPX file. If the VB file corresponding to the Web application is not visible in the Solution Explorer window, click the Display All Files icon to display the listing of all files included in the project.

7. Set the connection string and the SQL query string of the DataAccessObj instance by typing the following statements:

```
daObj.sConnection="Server=localhost;uid=sa;pwd=;
database=NorthWind"

daObj.sQry= "Select  ProductID, ProductName, UnitPrice from
Products"
```

8. If the user is visiting the Web page for the first time, the DropDownList control needs to be populated with the product IDs existing in the Products table. This can be done by invoking the `GetData()` method of DataAccessObj. This method returns an object of type DataView after executing the query. Set the `DataSource` property of the DropDownList control to the DataView object returned by the `GetData()` method by using the following code:

```
If not IsPostBack then
'Set the DataSource property of the LstProductID
'DropDownList to the DataView object returned by the
'GetData() method of DataAccessObj
      LstProductID.datasource=daObj.DisplayData()

'Bind the data in the DataView to the DropDownList
      LstProductID.DataBind()
```

9. When a user selects an item from the DropDownList control, the `AutoPostBack` property of the control causes the Web page to be reloaded. At this point, you need to display the details relating to the products in the respective Label controls. This can be done by using the following code:

```
If not IsPostBack then
       :
       :
Else
'create a dataview object
      Dim dvProducts1 as new DataView()

'Call the DisplayData() method of DataAccessObj to
'return product details and store the resulting
'DataView object in dvProducts1
      dvProducts1 = daObj.DisplayData()

'Set the RowFilter property of the dvProducts1
'DataView to the product ID selected from the
'DropDownList. This will result in displaying only the
'details about the selected product
```

```
        dvProducts1.RowFilter = "ProductId='" +
LstProductID.SelectedItem.Text + "'"

'Store the details of the selected row from the DataView
'into the myrow DataRow object
dim myrow as DataRow
myrow = dvProducts1.Table.Rows(LstProductID.SelectedIndex)

'Set the text of Label controls to the values of 'respective
columns
LblProductName.Text =
myRow(dvProducts1.Table.Columns(1)).ToString
LblUnitPrice.Text =
myRow(dvProducts1.Table.Columns(2)).ToString

'Invoke the CalcAmt() method of the CalcNetAmt object to
'calculate the net amount payable on the product
LblNetAmt.Text =
NetAmtObj.CalcAmt(CDbl(lblUnitPrice.Text)).ToStringEnd If
```

This code will result in populating the Label controls when you select a product ID from the DropDownList control. The explanation for each line of code is included in the comments inserted in the code. The complete code in the Page_Load() method of the Web Form will look as follows:

```
<script language=vb runat="server">
    sub Page_Load(Sender as Object, e as EventArgs)
        Dim NetAmtObj As New CalcNetAmt.CalcNetAmt()
        Dim daObj As New GetData.DataAccessObj()
        daObj.sConnection =
        "Server=localhost;uid=sa;pwd=;database=NorthWind"
        daObj.sQry = "Select ProductID, ProductName,
                     UnitPrice from Products"
        If Not IsPostBack Then
            LstProductID.DataSource = daObj.DisplayData
            LstProductID.DataBind()
        Else
            Dim myrow As DataRow
            Dim dvProducts1 As New DataView()
            dvProducts1 = daObj.DisplayData
            dvProducts1.RowFilter = "ProductId='" +
            LstProductID.SelectedItem.Text + "'"
            myrow =
        dvProducts1.Table.Rows(LstProductID.SelectedIndex)
            LblProductName.Text =
            myrow(dvProducts1.Table.Columns(1).ToString)
            lblUnitPrice.Text =
                myrow(dvProducts1.Table.Columns(2).ToString)
            LblNetAmt.Text =
        NetAmtObj.CalcAmt(CDbl(lblUnitPrice.Text)).ToString
        End If
End Sub
    </script>
```

LblProductName, LblUnitPrice, and LblNetAmt are not Textboxes. They are labels that are being used to display the values retrieved from the database.

10. Run the application by pressing Ctrl + F5. Sample output of the application is shown in Figure 15-2.

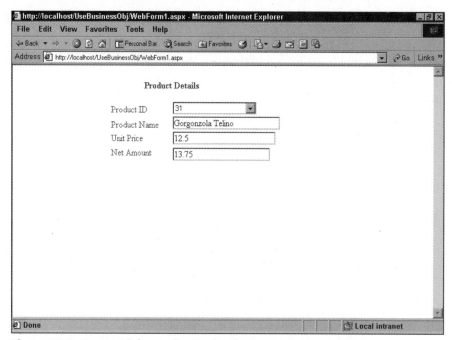

Figure 15-2: Output of the application implementing business objects

Creating a data access component by using Data controls of ASP.NET

ASP.NET provides you with Data controls that enable you to create data-centric business rule objects in an easier way without having to type the code manually. In this section, you will look at the process of creating a simple data-centric business rule object by using the Data controls provided in ASP.NET. This object will be responsible for establishing a connection with the database and returning all necessary data.

Creating a data access component

To create a data-centric business object by using Data controls, follow the steps given as follows:

1. Select File ➾ New ➾ Project. In the Project Types list box, select Visual Basic Projects. In the Templates list box, select ASP.NET Web application. Change the name of the application to DataAccessComp and click OK.

2. Select Project ➾ Add Component to open the Add New Item dialog box. In the dialog box, change the name of the file to DataAccess.vb.

3. To create a component by using the Data controls available in ASP.NET, click the Data tab on the Toolbox. The Data tab expands to display the Data controls. Point to the OleDbDataAdapter control and drag it to the component designer. The OleDbDataAdapter control enables you to create an instance of the OleDbDataAdapter classm, which represents a set of SQL statements and connection information required for getting the data from the database. It also enables you to fill a data set with the data returned by the SQL statement.

4. When you drag the OleDbDataAdapter control to the component designer, it invokes the Data Adapter Configuration Wizard, shown in Figure 15-3.

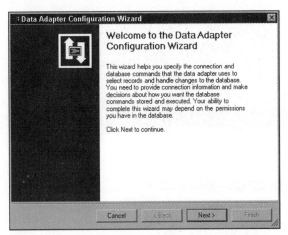

Figure 15-3: Data Adapter Configuration Wizard

This wizard guides you through various steps for establishing a connection with the database. The first step in this wizard enables you to choose the database connection. Select the name of the data server and the database from the drop-down list. If the name of the desired server does not exist in the drop-down list, click the New Connection button to open the Data Link Properties dialog box, shown in Figure 15-4.

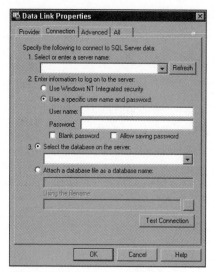

Figure 15-4: The Data Link Properties
dialog box

Select the Connection tab. Specify the data server name and the logon information for connecting to the data server. Select the NorthWind database. Click the Test Connection button to ensure that the connection to the database server is successfully established. Click the OK button to close the Data Link Properties dialog box and return to the Data Adapter Configuration Wizard.

5. The next step of the Data Adapter Configuration Wizard enables you to specify the query type for fetching the required data. This step provides three options, as shown in Figure 15-5: Use SQL Statements; Create New Stored Procedures; and Use Existing Stored Procedures.

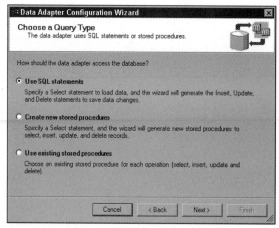

Figure 15-5: Choose a Query Type window

Select the Use SQL Statements radio button and click the Next button.

6. The next step of the Data Adapter Configuration Wizard enables you to generate the SQL statement to be used for fetching the data. You can type the SQL statement in the text area provided to you or generate it visually by clicking the SQL Builder button. Type the following SQL statement in the text area:

```
SELECT
    Orders.OrderID,
    Customers.CustomerID,
    Customers.CompanyName,
    Products.ProductName,
    Products.UnitPrice,
    [Order Details].Quantity
FROM
    Customers INNER
JOIN
    Orders ON
        Customers.CustomerID = Orders.CustomerID
INNER JOIN [Order Details]
        ON Orders.OrderID = [Order Details].OrderID
INNER JOIN Products
        ON [Order Details].ProductID = Products.ProductID
```

This step finishes the process of creating the OleDbDataAdapter control. Click the Finish button to close the Data Adapter Configuration Wizard dialog box. At the end of this process, you will see two new objects, OleDbDataAdapter1 and OleDbConnection1, added to the component tray, as shown in Figure 15-6.

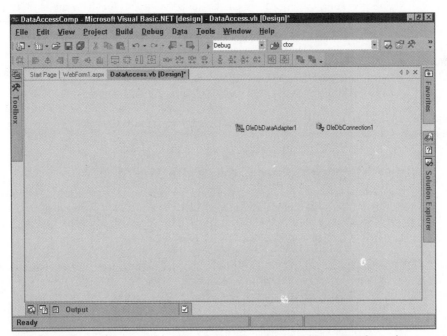

Figure 15-6: Component tray after adding the adoDataSetCommand1 and adoConnection1 objects

7. The next step is to create the DataSet class for storing the data returned by the SQL statement. For this, right-click the empty area in the component designer and select the Generate Dataset option. This results in invoking the Generate Dataset dialog box, shown in Figure 15-7.

Figure 15-7: Generate Dataset dialog box

Enter the name of the DataSet class as OrderDataSet and click the OK button. This results in generating the OrderDataSet.xsd file. The file is included in the Solution Explorer window. This file contains the XML schema definition for the resulting DataSet. Components in .NET use XML for ensuring interoperability. The XSD file defines the structure of the data in the OrderDataSet object. In addition to the XSD file, the Generate Dataset option also generates the methods required for filling and updating the OrderDataSet class. The OrderDataSet class can now be used in the Web Form.

Cross-Reference   For information on XML and XML schemas, refer to Chapter 13.

Using the data access component in a Web Form

You will now look at using the OrderDataSet class and the DataAccess class in a Web Form. You will create a DropDownList control in the Web Form to display all order IDs. When a user selects an order ID, the details about the order ID should displayed in a DataGrid control.

1. To use the OrderDataSet class in a Web Form, you need to create an instance of the OrderDataSet class. Select the DataSet control from the Data tab of the Toolbox and drag it to the Web Form. This invokes the Add DataSet dialog box, shown in Figure 15-8.

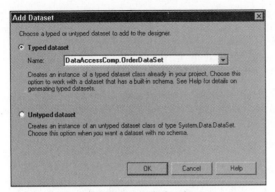

Figure 15-8: Add DataSet dialog box

This dialog box has two radio buttons, Typed Dataset and Untyped Dataset. The Typed Dataset option enables you to create a data set based on an XML schema definition. You can use the Untyped Dataset option if you do not have an XML schema definition. In this example, you have already generated the XML schema called OrderDataSet.xsd. Therefore, select the Typed Dataset option. In the drop-down list box, locate the name of the OrderDataSet class, which appears with the prefix of your project name. For example, if your project name is DataAccessComp, the class appears in the drop-down list as DataAccessComp.OrderDataSet. Selecting the OrderDataSet class and clicking the OK button results in the creation of an instance of the OrderDataSet class. This object has the name OrderDataSet1.

2. The OrderDataSet1 object needs to be filled with the required data by using the connection information and the SQL statement stored in the OleDbDataAdapter and OleDbConnection objects. To achieve this functionality, create an instance of the DataAccess component in the `Page_Load()` event of the Web application as follows:

```
Dim ordercomponent as new DataAccess()
```

This statement creates an instance of the DataAccess class in which you created the OleDbDataAdapter1 and OleDbConnection1 objects and generated the functions for filling the OrderDataSet.

3. Invoke the `Fill()` method of the OleDbDataAdapter object in the `Page_Load()` method of the Web Form, as follows:

```
If Not IsPostback Then
  ordercomponent.OleDbDataAdapter1.Fill(OrderDataSet1)
End If
```

4. After filling the DataSet, the next step is to create a DataView object. You can create a DataView object by using the DataView control provided in ASP.NET. Click the Data tab on the Toolbox. Click and drag the DataView control to the

Web Form. This will create a DataView object called DataView1. You can change the name of this object by using the Properties window. Press F4 to switch to the properties window and change the ID of the DataView object to OrderDataView1. Change the Table property of the DataView object to OrderDataSet1.customers.

5. The DataView object created in the previous step can now be used to populate controls in the Web Form. Create a DropDownList control on the Web Form. Set the properties of the control as shown in Table 15-2.

Table 15-2
DropDownList control properties

Property	Value
ID	LstOrderId
DataTextField	OrderID
DataValueField	OrderID
AutoPostBack	True
DataSource	OrderDataView1

6. Modify the `Page_Load()` method of the Web Form to include instructions for binding the order ID to the DropDownList control as follows:

```
If Not IsPostback Then
ordercomponent.OleDbDataAdapter1.Fill(OrderDataSet1)
          LstOrderId.DataBind()
    End If
```

7. Now, you need to add the functionality for displaying the details of an order when a user selects a particular order ID from the DropDownList. For this purpose, create another DataView object by clicking and dragging the DataView control from the Data tab of the Toolbox to the Web Form. Set the ID property of the DataView control to OrderDataView2 and the Tables property to OrderDataSet1.customers.

8. Create a DataGrid control on the Web Form for displaying the details of the selected order ID. Set ID of the DataGrid control to dgOrderData.

9. Click the Property Builder link in the Properties window of the DataGrid. This will invoke the dgOrderData Properties dialog box, shown in Figure 15-9.

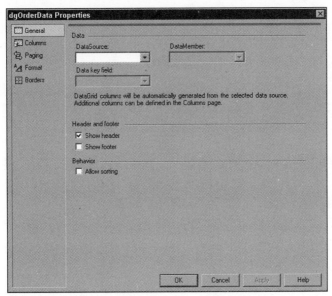

Figure 15-9: dgOrderData Properties dialog box

Specify the DataSource as OrderDataView2. Click the Columns tab and specify the columns from the DataView that should appear in the DataGrid. Ensure that the Create Columns Automatically At Runtime check box is cleared.

10. If the user is not visiting the Web page for the first time, the DataGrid should be populated with the details about the orders. This is done by modifying the Page_Load() method to include the following statements:

```
If Not IsPostback Then
    ordercomponent.OleDbDataAdapter1.Fill(OrderDataSet1)
    LstOrderId.DataBind()
Else
    ordercomponent.OleDbDataAdapter1.Fill(OrderDataSet1)
    OrderDataView2.RowFilter = "OrderID='" +
            LstOrderId.SelectedItem.Text + "'"
    dgOrderData.DataBind()
End If
```

The highlighted code in this code snippet repopulates OrderDataSet1 and sets the RowFilter of OrderDataView2 to the item selected from the DropDownList. This ensures that the details about only the selected order ID are displayed in the DataGrid control. Finally, the DataBind() method binds the DataGrid dgOrderData to the data held in the DataView OrderDataView2.

When you open this application in the browser, it will initially display a DropDownList with all the order IDs. When you select a particular order ID, the browser window will display a DataGrid containing all the details about the order as shown in Figure 15-10.

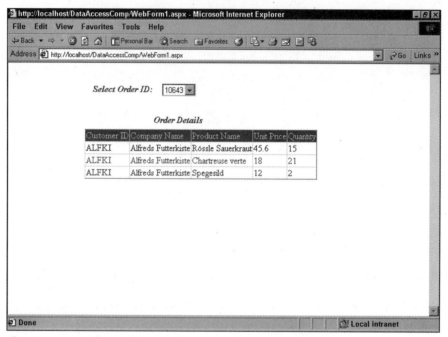

Figure 15-10: Output of the application implementing the data access component

Thus, ASP.NET enables you to easily create and use business objects in your applications. In addition, it also provides various data controls for quickly generating the code for database connectivity. This helps in reducing the development time.

Deploying Business Objects

Deployment refers to the process of distributing an application or a component for installation on other machines. The .NET Framework has introduced several new features to simplify the deployment of business objects. Until now, Microsoft's Component Object Model (COM) has been used for creating business objects. However, COM suffers from various problems relating to deployment:

✦ **Registration:** When you install a COM component on your machine, the component makes some entries that store information about the component in the Windows Registry database. This information includes the Globally

Unique Identifier (GUID) and the Class Identifier (CLSID). Thus, the process of deploying COM components involves the task of copying necessary files to the disk and making Registry entries. This separation of entries to the disk and Registry causes difficulty in the task of replicating and uninstalling applications. Moreover, the registration of components complicates the task of deploying an application, because each client machine must have appropriate entries in the Registry for using the component.

✦ **Versioning:** Often, you have various applications attempting to use the same COM component. When you install a new application, it may result in installing the newer version of the component. In this case, the newly installed application may work well. However, the existing applications that depend on the older version of the component may stop functioning. These problems occur because the system does not keep track of the versions of different components used by different applications. In addition, the applications do not specify the information about the version of a component that it uses.

To solve these problems, Microsoft has introduced assemblies in .NET. An *assembly* is a single deployable unit that includes all the information required to deploy a component. An assembly can be embedded within a single DLL. In such a case, it is called a single-file assembly. An assembly can also be made up of multiple files. In such a case, the assembly is called a multifile assembly. Assemblies are used as the basic building blocks for solving the issues relating to registration and versioning. You can think of an assembly as a logical DLL. However, a DLL is dependent on the Registry for maintaining information about it, whereas an assembly maintains all information about itself and does not depend on any Registry entries. Assemblies have the following features:

✦ **They are self-describing:** Assemblies are self-describing deployable units. .NET stores the metadata about the components in assembly manifests, which include the identity of the assembly (such as the name and the version number), security information, information about the dependencies, and the list of files that constitute the assembly. In .NET, an application is also made up of assemblies. Therefore, the information about the version of a component used by an application is also maintained in the assembly.

✦ **They record the version information and enforce it at run time:** The assembly manifest also includes the information about the dependencies between different assemblies, such as the name of the referenced assembly and its version number. This version number is used at run time to ensure that the correct version of the dependency is loaded.

✦ **They provide the ability to work with side-by-side components:** This feature allows multiple versions of a component to be installed and run simultaneously. The caller of the assembly can specify the version to be loaded. Thus, the .NET Framework allows multiple versions of a single component to coexist on a machine. This feature also isolates the application from the changes made to the system by other applications.

Creating a single-file assembly

You can create a single-file assembly by using command-line compilers such as vbc and csc. A single-file assembly includes all the information about the component. You can use the following statement to create an assembly file with the .exe extension.

C#:

```
csc filename.cs
```

VB.NET:

```
vbc filename.vb
```

These statements create an assembly that has the same name as that of the VB or CS file and with an .exe extension. To create an assembly file with a different file-name, you can use the /out: option of the compiler command, as follows:

C#:

```
csc /out:outputfile.exe sourcefile.cs
```

VB.NET:

```
vbc /out:outputfile.exe sourcefile.cs
```

In these examples, the source file must contain a single entry point, such as the Main() function. If you do not have an entry point, the compiler gives you an error message. If you do not want your source file to contain any entry point and want it to contain only other classes and methods, you must create a *library assembly*. A library assembly contains components that will be accessed by other assemblies. It is very similar to class libraries.

You can create a library assembly by typing the following command:

C#:

```
csc /t:library /out:outputfile.dll sourcefile.cs
```

VB.NET:

```
vbc /t:library /out:outputfile.dll sourcefile.cs
```

After you have created assemblies for all the files to be used in a project, you can create a deployment project.

Creating a multifile assembly

You might be required to create a multifile assembly if you want to use classes written in different languages. You might also be required to create a multifile assembly if you want to optimize the process of downloading components. For example, you might want to combine rarely used components into a single assembly.

When you create a multifile assembly, one of the files in the assembly must contain the assembly manifest. Let us look at the process of creating a multifile assembly with the help of an example. Consider the class ConnectDB:

```
'ConnectDB.VB
'-------------
Imports System.Data
Imports System.Data.SQL
Namespace DB
Public Class ConnectDB
:
    Functions for establishing connection
:
End Class
End Namespace
```

Consider another class, Calculate, which uses the class ConnectDB to connect to the sales database and returns the price of a product after calculating the discount:

```
'Calculate.VB
'-------------
Imports System.Data
Imports System.Data.SQL
Imports DB
Public Class Calculate
:
    Call functions from the ConnectDB class
    Calculate the discounted price
:
End Class
```

To create an assembly with these two files, you need to follow these steps:

1. Compile all the classes that are created within a namespace, which is referenced by other modules. In this example, the class ConnectDB is created within the namespace DB. The DB namespace is accessed in the Calculate class. Therefore, you first need to build the ConnectDB class into a module by using the following statement:

```
vbc /t:module ConnectDB.vb /r:system.dll /r:system.data.dll
```

When you want to create a module instead of a library assembly or an executable file, you need to specify the /t:module option, which instructs the compiler to create a standard DLL file that does not contain the assembly manifest. The /r option is used to specify references to other libraries. This statement creates a module called ConnectDB.mcm.

Note   The default extension for a module is .mcm. You can change the default name of the output file generated by the compiler by using the /out: option of the compiler.

2. After compiling classes that are included inside namespaces, you need to compile classes that use other modules. In the example, the Calculate class references the ConnectDB module and makes calls to functions written in the ConnectDB class. Therefore, you must compile the Calculate class file by executing the following statement at the command prompt:

```
vbc /addmodule:ConnectDB.mcm /t:module Calculate.vb
```

In this statement, the /addmodule option is included to specify the name of the module, which is referenced by the file Calculate.vb. When you give this statement from the command prompt, the compiler creates a module called Calculate.mcm, which references another module, ConnectDB.mcm.

3. After compiling various classes into modules, you can create a multifile assembly by using the Al.exe utility. Type the following statement at the command prompt to create an assembly:

```
al /out:App.dll /t:lib ConnectDB.mcm Calculate.mcm
```

In this statement, the /out option specifies the name of the output file to be produced by Al.exe. The /t option specifies the file format of the output file. You can set the option to lib (code library), exe (console application), or win (Windows-based application). Finally, you specify the names of the modules to be included in the assembly. This statement creates a library assembly called App.dll. This file contains the assembly manifest, which describes the types in other modules included in the assembly.

Creating a deployment project

A deployment project enables you to specify the files to be included in the deployment and the name of the remote machine where the application or component needs to be deployed. You can create a deployment project by completing the following steps:

1. Open the CalcNetAmt project.

2. Select File ⇨ New ⇨ Project. Select Setup and Deployment projects from the Project Types list box.

3. The Templates list box provides various options, such as Cab Project, Merge Module Project, Setup Project, Setup Wizard, and Web Setup Project, for performing different types of installations. Select Setup Wizard. Click the Add To Solution radio button.

4. The Setup Wizard guides you through various steps of creating a deployment project. It enables you to specify whether you want to deploy a client application or Web application, and the files to be included in the deployment project.

5. The first step in the Setup Wizard is to choose the project type of the deployment application. This screen provides four options: Create A Setup For Windows Application, Create A Setup For A Web Application, Create A Merge

Module For Windows Installer, and Create A Downloadable CAB File. Select Create A Setup For A Web Application.

6. The next screen asks you to specify the project output groups to be included in the setup project. Select the Project Output check box. Project output includes the EXE or DLL files in a project.

7. The last screen asks you to specify any additional files that you want to be included in the setup project. These files may include the Readme.txt file or an HTML page containing instructions for installation. Add the files that you want to be included in the setup project. Click the Finish button.

8. If you want to change any of the properties of the deployment project that you have created, right-click the project in the Solution Explorer window and select Properties from the pop-up menu. This will invoke the Setup Property Pages dialog box, shown in Figure 15-11.

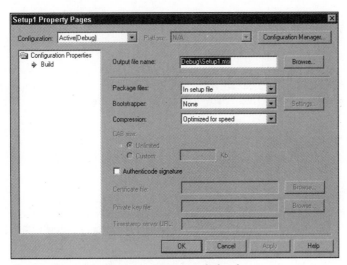

Figure 15-11: Setup Property Pages dialog box

9. If you forgot to specify some files that are required to deploy the application in the wizard while creating the setup project, you can add them by right-clicking the setup project in the Solution Explorer window and clicking Add ➪ File.

10. After you have specified all the options and the files to be included in the deployment project, right-click the project in the Solution Explorer and click the Build option. This will create a MSI (Windows Installer Package) file in the Debug folder of your project. You can now use this file to deploy your components and application.

Cross-Reference

For a detailed discussion on deploying classes and assemblies, see Chapter 21.

Working with Business Object Namespaces

Namespaces enable you to organize your classes in a hierarchical manner and organize all the classes and methods that perform related tasks. You can use namespaces to organize your business objects as well. For example, you might create a namespace called SalesData, which might contain all the components that perform the tasks of inserting, manipulating, and validating the data from the sales database.

You can create a business object namespace by using the Namespace keyword, as follows:

```
Namespace SalesData
Class AddSalesData
         :
    code for adding sales data
         :
End Class
End Namespace
```

While using this business object in your Web application, you must import the namespace SalesData by including the following statement in the ASPX file:

```
<%@ Import Namespace="SalesData" %>
```

You might alternatively include the following statement in the VB file of the Web project:

```
Imports salesdata
```

Cross-Reference   For a detailed discussion on creating and using namespaces, refer to Appendix F.

Summary

In this chapter, you learned about the business objects and the different types of business objects. You also learned to create UI-centric business rule objects and data-centric business rule objects. Next, you learned to use business objects in your application. Then, you looked at the process of deploying business objects. Finally, you learned about working with business object namespaces.

✦   ✦   ✦

Building HTTP Handlers

CHAPTER

16

◆ ◆ ◆ ◆

In This Chapter

Introduction to HTTP
Runtime and HTTP
Handlers

Creating an HTTP
Handler

◆ ◆ ◆ ◆

The World Wide Web (WWW) uses the Hypertext Transfer
Protocol (HTTP) as the underlying protocol for communication. It is an application-level protocol that is responsible
for establishing a connection between a client (browser) and
a Web server and transmitting the information requested by
the client. In fact, the day-to-day life of a Web server involves
receiving requests from clients and responding to them by
using HTTP.

ASP.NET works by dispatching the client requests to user-
defined HTTP handler objects called *HTTP handlers*. With
ASP.NET, you can create these user-defined HTTP handlers by
implementing a .NET interface named IHttpHandler. After
you've created a user-defined handler, you can bind a specific
URL request to the handler for handling specific requests. For
example, you can bind a URL request for a file, with your name
as an extension, to a user-defined handler for processing.
However, if a specific URL request is not mapped to a handler,
the default handler of ASP.NET handles it.

In this chapter, you will learn about HTTP runtime provided in
ASP.NET, which allows you to process HTTP requests coming
from clients. You will also learn about the interfaces and
classes involved in creating HTTP handlers. Finally, you will
learn to create a custom HTTP handler.

Introduction to HTTP Runtime and HTTP Handlers

When you enter a URL in a browser, the browser builds an
HTTP request and sends it to the address specified in the
URL. While building the HTTP request, various methods are
used. These methods indicate the purpose of the request.
These methods include the following:

✦ Get: Used when a request for a particular page is made. When a user enters a link in the Address box of the browser or clicks a hyperlink, the HTTP Get method is used to build the HTTP request. The Get method is usually used when the request does not alter the state of a database.

✦ Head: Used when a user wants to retrieve only the information about the document and not the document itself.

✦ Post: Used when a user requests a resource that interacts with a database.

The Web server, which contains the requested page, performs necessary processing based on the method used for sending the request, and returns the page requested by the client. In addition to these methods, you can have a lower-level control over the processing of requests on the Web server. This is possible with the help of application programming interfaces (APIs), which are covered in the next two sections.

ISAPI and HTTP Runtime

A number of APIs have been developed that enable developers to have lower-level control over the processing of requests on the Web server. For example, the Internet Services API (ISAPI) developed for IIS Web Server enables developers to create high-performance applications. At the same time, it enables developers to have low-level control over the way requests are processed by IIS.

With ISAPI, you can create your own dynamic link libraries (DLLs) that specify the tasks that need to be performed when a request is sent to the Web server. The DLLs provided in ISAPI can be of two types, filters and extensions. *Filters* enable you to write code that can receive notifications from the Web server during the processing of a request. Thus, filters are used to alter the standard behavior of the Web server. You can use filters to perform tasks such as compressing and encrypting the data to be sent and authenticating a user. On the other hand, ISAPI *extensions* accept user requests, perform tasks such as retrieving data from a database and generating an HTML page, and send a response to the client.

In ASP.NET Web applications, low-level control over client requests is achieved by using the *HTTP runtime*. The HTTP runtime is built on the Common Language Runtime (CLR) of the .NET Framework, and provides an environment for processing requests. Thus, the CLR replaces the ISAPI under IIS. The HTTP runtime performs various functions, including receiving requests from the client, resolving the address specified in the URL, and sending the request to the appropriate application for further processing of the request. The HTTP runtime is capable of receiving multiple requests simultaneously. The applications are run in separate address spaces, thereby improving reliability and preventing cross-platform chaos. Therefore, the failure of a single Web application does not affect the working of the HTTP runtime.

Just like the ISAPI extensions and ISAPI filters, the HTTP runtime enables developers to have lower-level control over processing Web requests. However, unlike ISAPI, for which developers must know C++, the HTTP runtime is a cleaner model and enables developers to program in any .NET programming language. Therefore, ASP.NET prefers the CLR of the .NET Framework to the ISAPI architecture.

Architecture of the HTTP Runtime

The architecture of the HTTP runtime is similar to that of a pipeline. It is comprised of a number of HTTP modules and handlers. In simple terms, *HTTP modules* and *HTTP handlers* are classes created by developers that implement predefined interfaces of ASP.NET. When a client makes a request that results in executing a Web application, the request passes through a pipeline of HTTP modules. HTTP modules enable a Web application to perform specific tasks, such as encrypting the data, performing custom authentication for providing access to the application, and managing the state of the client session and the application. After passing through a series of HTTP modules, the request is sent to the HTTP handler. An HTTP handler is a replacement for ISAPI extensions that receive the request, fetch the required data, and send the data in response to the request sent by the client. ASP.NET provides higher-level programming models, such as Web services and Web Forms, which are implemented as HTTP handlers. The pipeline architecture of the HTTP runtime enables you to easily implement new functionality by adding new HTTP modules and handlers. Figure 16-1 depicts the pipeline architecture of the HTTP runtime provided in ASP.NET

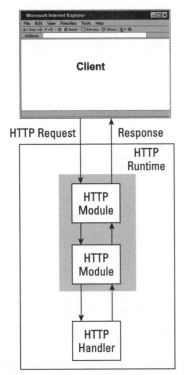

Figure 16-1: Architecture of the HTTP runtime provided in ASP.NET

ASP.NET provides various interfaces that can be implemented for creating HTTP modules and HTTP handlers. For example, it provides the IHttpModule interface, which can be used to create modules that perform tasks related to security and compression. State management functions are often implemented in HTTP modules so that they can be easily added or removed from the HTTP runtime pipeline.

In addition to the IHttpModule interface, ASP.NET has the IHttpHandler interface that can be implemented by developers to create a lower-level HTTP handler that receives the request and performs various tasks.

As you already know, HTTP is used to process requests for the ASP.NET pages. Because HTTP is a connectionless protocol, clients connect to servers only for the duration of HTTP requests. There must be a way in ASP.NET to manage connections within an application. To do so, ASP.NET generates one HttpContext object and passes it to HTTP handlers for each request that is serviced.

The HttpContext object provides a way to manage the connections within an application. This object maintains the information about the current request and also provides access to the `Request`, `Response`, and `Server` objects corresponding to a particular HTTP request. The `Request` object provides access to the values entered by a user while sending a request to the Web server. For example, you may enter values in an HTML form and send a request to the Web server to look up the value in a table stored in a database. This value can be accessed by using the `Request` object. Similarly, you can use the `Response` object to send a response from the Web server to the client. The `Server` object provides methods that are used for processing the request. For example, the `Server` object has the `HtmlDecode` method, which decodes the HTTP request sent by the client by removing the HTML characters from the request. You can use all of these built-in objects and their methods to perform different tasks in your HTTP handlers.

You learned about the HTTP runtime, HTTP modules, and HTTP handlers provided in ASP.NET. Now, you will learn to create an HTTP handler.

Interfaces and Classes Used to Create HTTP Handlers

The .NET Framework provides classes that enable you to handle HTTP requests for the ASP.NET Web pages and services. You can handle HTTP requests by creating a class that implements the IHttpHandler interface contained in the System.Web namespace. The *System.Web* namespace contains classes and interfaces that enable you to handle the communication between browsers and Web servers. Before you can use a class that implements the IHttpHandler interface, you need to write the <httpHandlers> section in the Web.config configuration file to map the class that implements IHttpHandler to a URL request.

Cross-Reference For more information on the <httpHandlers> section, refer to Chapter 14.

Before you create an HTTP Handler, let us look at the IHttpHandler and IHttpHandlerFactory interfaces, and some of the classes contained in the System.Web namespace.

IHttpHandler interface

The IHttpHandler interface must be implemented to create user-defined HTTP handlers to process Web requests. Specific instances of the classes that implement the IHttpHandler interface process the Web requests received by ASP.NET. When you create a class that implements the IHttpHandler interface, you need to implement a method and a property of this interface. The method that needs to be implemented is ProcessRequest, and the property that needs to be implemented is IsReusable.

ProcessRequest

The ProcessRequest method is called whenever an HTTP request is made and has the following Visual Basic .NET syntax:

```
Sub ProcessRequest (ByVal context As HttpContext)

End Sub
```

As you can see in the preceding syntax, the ProcessRequest method takes an object of the HttpContext class (discussed later in this section) as a parameter. You use the HttpContext object to handle all Web requests.

IsReusable

The IsReusable property is an overrideable read-only property that gets a value indicating whether the instance of the class that implements the IHttpHandler interface can be recycled and used for other Web requests. The Visual Basic .NET syntax of the IsReusable property is given as follows:

```
ReadOnly Property IsReusable As Boolean
```

As you can see in this syntax, the IsReusable property gets a Boolean value. If it gets True, the IHttpHandler instance can be reused for other Web requests. However, if the property gets False, the IHttpHandler instance cannot be reused for other Web requests.

IHttpHandlerFactory interface

As mentioned earlier, the Web requests received by ASP.NET are processed by specific IHttpHandler instances. At run time, the Web requests must be resolved to the IHttpHandler instances. This resolution of the Web requests to the IHttpHandler instances is done by the IHttpHandlerFactory interface. This interface contains two methods, GetHandler and ReleaseHandler.

GetHandler

The GetHandler method returns an IHttpHandler object that processes the Web request from the client. The Visual Basic syntax for the GetHandler method is given as follows:

```
Function GetHandler( ByVal context As HttpContext, ByVal
requesttype As String, ByVal url As String, ByVal
pathtranslated As String ) As IHttpHandler

End Function
```

The return type of the GetHandler method is IHttpHandler. The different parameters include:

✦ context: Represents the object of the HttpContext class that provides reference to built-in server objects

✦ requesttype: Represents a string value that refers to the method used for HTTP data transfer, such as Get and Post

✦ url: Represents a string value that refers to the URL that is requested by the client

✦ pathtranslated: Represents the string value that refers to the physical path of the application's root directory

ReleaseHandler

The ReleaseHandler method allows releasing an IHttpHandler instance so that it can be reused. The Visual Basic syntax for the ReleaseHandler method is given as follows.

```
Sub ReleaseHandler( ByVal handler As IHttpHandler)

End Sub
```

In this code, handler is the IHttpHandler instance that needs to be released.

HttpContext class

The HttpContext class provides reference to the built-in server objects to process Web requests. Some of the properties that retrieve the built-in server objects are described in Table 16-1.

Table 16-1
Properties of the HttpContext class

Property	Description
Application	Gets the HttpApplicationState object associated with the current HTTP request.
Session	Gets the SessionState object associated with the current HTTP request.
Request	Gets the HttpRequest object associated with the current HTTP request.
Response	Gets the HttpResponse object associated with the current HTTP request.
Server	Gets the HttpServerUtility object associated with the current HTTP request. The HttpServerUtility class provides certain utilities that can be used while processing HTTP requests. For example, the MachineName property of this class returns the name of the server machine.

HttpRequest class

The HttpRequest class enables you to handle communication from a browser to a Web server. You can use this class to access the data supplied by clients during HTTP requests. Table 16-2 describes some of the properties of this class.

Table 16-2
Properties of the HttpRequest class

Property	Description
Browser	Gets the information related to the capabilities of the browser from which the HTTP request is made. This property returns a reference to the HttpBrowserCapabilities class, which is also a member of the System.Web namespace.
RequestType	Gets the data transfer method that is used by the client.
ApplicationPath	Gets the virtual application root path of the current application that is executing on a server.
FilePath	Gets the virtual path of the current HTTP request.
PhysicalApplicationPath	Gets the physical path of the application that is executing on a server.
Url	Gets the information related to the URL of the current HTTP request.

HttpResponse class

The HttpResponse class enables you to handle communication from a Web server to a browser. This class is used to send the output from the server to the browser. Table 16-3 describes some of the properties of this class.

Table 16-3 Properties of the HttpResponse class	
Property	**Description**
ContentEncoding	Gets or sets the character set of the output from the server.
IsClientConnected	Returns a Boolean value that indicates whether or not the client is connected to the server.
Cache	Gets the policy information, such as expiration time and privacy for the current Web page.

The HttpResponse class provides the Write method to display the output in a browser. This method takes a String parameter, which indicates the value to be displayed.

Creating HTTP Handlers

After understanding the different classes and interfaces contained in the System.Web namespace, you can now implement them to handle the communication between a browser and a Web server.

The general steps to create an HTTP handler class are detailed in the sections that follow.

Creating a class that implements the IHTTPHandler interface

To create a class that implements the IHTTPHandler interface, complete the following steps:

1. Create an ASP.NET Web Application project by using either C# or Visual Basic.NET.

2. Add a class to the project.

3. In the class that you added, create a class that implements the IHttpHandler interface. Also, implement the ProcessRequest method and the IsReusable property of the IHttpHandler interface.

4. Build the project to create the DLL file for the handler class.

Note The DLL file is created in the bin directory of your project.

After the DLL file is created, you can use this handler to handle request for any ASP.NET page.

Using the handler class in a Web application

To use the handler in a Web application, you need to add an entry for the handler class in the <httpHandlers> section of the Web.config file. To do so, you use the <add> tag. The syntax is given as follows:

```
<configuration>
  <system.web>
    <httpHandlers>
      <add verb="[HTTP Verb]" path="[Request Path]" type="[.NET
Class]" />
    </httpHandlers>
  </system.web>
</configuration>
```

Note You'll find many more sections and many more <add> tags in the <httpHandlers> section of the Web.config file.

The <add> tag takes three attributes:

✦ verb: Indicates the HTTP verb type that the handler services request. This attribute takes a string value, such as verb = "Get" or verb = "Get; Head; Post". If the attribute takes an asterisk (*) as a value, it instructs the HTTP runtime to match on all HTTP verbs.

✦ path: Indicates the request path, such as /Trial/Sample.aspx, which the handler is mapped to.

Tip You can also specify any file extension, such as .Rita. But, for this to work, you must map this file extension in IIS. You can do so in the IIS Microsoft Management Console (MMC).

✦ type: Indicates the name of the .NET class that contains the HTTP handler code. This attribute takes the value in the following format: [Namespace].[Class].[Assembly name].

Next, you need to add a reference to the DLL file of the handler class. To do so, select Add Reference from the Project menu. This opens the Add Reference dialog box. In this dialog box, click Browse to select the DLL file of the handler.

After you've added the entry for the handler in the Web.config file and added its reference, when you browse the page (whose path is mentioned in the "path" attribute of the <add> tag), you'll notice that the handler automatically handles this request.

Now that you know the general steps, let's implement them to create a custom HTTP handler.

Custom HTTP Handler Example

Let us now create a simple HTTP handler that displays a hello message to the user and accesses the request and response information when an HTTP request is made for a Web page.

To implement this example, create a Web application project. In this case, the project is a Visual Basic project named SampleHTTPHandler. Then, add a class to the project. To do so, select Project ⇨ Add Class. This displays the Add New Item dialog box. In this dialog box, specify an appropriate name for the class. In this case, the name of the class is SampleHandler.vb. In case of a Visual C# project, the class would have a .cs extension. Next, add the following code to the class:

```
'Importing the System.Web namespace
Imports System.Web

'Creating a namespace
Namespace Acme

' Creating a class that implements the IHttpHandler class
    Public Class SampleHandler : Implements IHttpHandler

' Implementing the ProcessRequest method of the IHttpHandler
' interface
    Public Sub ProcessRequest(ByVal Context As HttpContext)
Implements IHttpHandler.ProcessRequest

    Dim str As String
'    retrieving the value that is passed to the Name variable '
at the time of request. To do so, you are using the
'    Request property of the object of the HttpContext class.
'    Notice that the Context object of the HTTPContext class '
is passed as an argument.

    str = Context.Request.QueryString("Name")

'    Using the Write method of the Response method to
'    display a hello message
    Context.Response.Write("<h1> Hello " + str + "</h1>")
```

```vbnet
'    Using the write method of the Response object to display '
a message in a browser. Notice that the HTML elements
'    are also used.
    Context.Response.Write("<b>This is an HTTPHandler
demo</b>")
    Context.Response.Write("<hr align=left width=205> <Br>")

'    Using the Browser property of the Request object to get
'    an object of the HttpBrowserCapabilities class
    Dim hBrC As HttpBrowserCapabilities =
Context.Request.Browser

'    Displaying the name and version of the browser
    Context.response.Write("<b>Browser capabilities:</b><br>")
    Context.Response.Write("Name = " & HBrC.Browser & "<br>")
    Context.Response.Write("Version=" & HBrC.Version & "<br>")

'    Using the PhysicalApplicationPath and the
'    Applicationpath properties of the Request object to get
'    the physical path and the virtual path of the
'    application respectively
    Dim pPath As String
    Dim vPath As String
    pPath = Context.Request.PhysicalApplicationPath
    vPath = Context.Request.ApplicationPath

'    Displaying the virtual and physical path of the
'    application
    Context.Response.Write("<Br><b>Virtual path of the
application:</b><Br>")
    Context.Response.Write(vPath & "<br>")

    Context.Response.Write("<Br><b>Physical path of the
application:</b><Br>")
    Context.Response.Write(pPath & "<Br>")

'    Using the IsClientConnected property of the Response
'    object to determine whether the client is connected to
'    the server
    Dim connect As Boolean
    Dim connectStr As String
    connect = Context.Response.IsClientConnected
    connectStr = connect.ToString

    Context.Response.Write("<Br><b>Client connection
status:</b><br>")
    Context.Response.Write(connectStr)

    End Sub
```

```
'   Implementing the IsReusable method of the IHttpHandler
'   interface

    Public ReadOnly Property IsReusable() As Boolean Implements
IHttpHandler.IsReusable
        Get
            Return True
        End Get
    End Property
  End Class

End Namespace
```

After creating this class, build the project. After the build is complete, a DLL file is created in the bin directory of the project. Now, the handler is ready, and you can use it to handle any Web request.

Next, you'll use the handler in a new Web application. To do so, create a Visual Basic ASP.NET Web Application project named HandlerTesting. In the Web.config file, in the <httpHandlers> section, add an entry for the handler to map the Web request to the handler class:

```
<httpHandlers>
    <add verb="*" path="Test.aspx"
type="SampleHTTPHandler.Acme.SampleHandler,SampleHTTPHandler"
/>
</httpHandlers>
```

In the preceding code, the path attribute is set to Test.aspx. Therefore, rename the WebForm1.aspx file to Test.aspx. The next step involves adding a reference to the DLL of the handler class.

After adding the reference, browse the Test.aspx page by passing your name in the Name variable as QueryString. The URL of the page should appear as follows:

```
.../Test.aspx?Name=Rita
```

Figure 16-2 displays the output of this page.

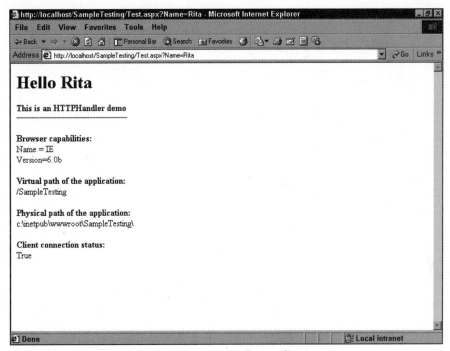

Figure 16-2: Output of the SampleHTTPHandler application

Summary

This chapter introduced you to HTTP handlers. First, you learned about the HTTP runtime provided in ASP.NET for performing low-level processing on the HTTP request sent by the client. You also learned about HTTP modules and HTTP handlers. Next, you learned about various interfaces, classes, and built-in objects provided in ASP.NET for creating your own HTTP handlers. Finally, you learned how to create an HTTP handler.

✦　　✦　　✦

Understanding Caching

Usually, Web sites (Web applications) are accessed by multiple users. On certain days, a Web site can experience an extremely low load and, as a result, provide faster access. However, in just a few hours, the load on the site can increase exponentially, resulting in slow access. Slow access is the most common problem that plagues a Web site when it is accessed by a large number of users simultaneously. However, load is not the only reason why a Web site is slow. Other physical aspects affect speed, such as the type of modem, Internet connection, and telephone line. Therefore, it might not be good business sense to invest in high-grade hardware that handles the entire load just to improve the access speed, because the heavy load is only temporary and not constant. It would be better if access speeds could be improved without investing in high-grade hardware. In such a scenario, caching provides a solution.

Caching is a technique wherein frequently used data and Web pages are stored temporarily on local hard disks for later retrieval. This technique improves the access time when multiple users access a Web site simultaneously or a single user accesses a Web site multiple times. Caching allows server-side Web applications to scale better, and improves the overall performance of the Web application. Thus, the ASP.NET code does not need to be executed every time to process the same request from multiple clients or from a single client multiple times. This saves on the CPU cycles at the Web server, resulting in improved response time.

This chapter introduces you to caching. You will also learn the concept of caching page output and caching page data for optimizing the ASP.NET Web applications.

Introduction to Caching

Caching, as a technique for improving system performance, is not a new concept. It has been used successfully in various applications, ranging from relational databases such as Microsoft SQL Server to various operating systems. ASP.NET provides a Web cache to store Web objects.

A *Web cache* is a temporary storage of Web objects, such as HTML documents, for later retrieval. You can specify the cache location to be on the client or on the server. The different locations where caching can be performed are described as follows:

✦ **Client:** To provide improved performance, client applications (like browsers) perform caching by storing data from the Web in temporary files on the hard drive or system memory of users' computers. However, these caches cannot be shared across multiple users. Figure 17-1 demonstates caching at the client side.

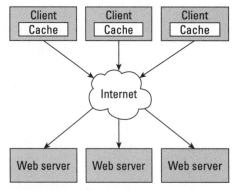

Figure 17-1: Client caching

✦ **Dedicated server:** Caching can be performed at the server side so that caches can be shared across multiple users on a network. Most administrators use proxy servers, such as Microsoft Proxy Server, to store frequently used Web pages on the hard disk of the proxy server. The proxy server fulfills all the requests for the Web page without sending out the request to the actual Web server over the Internet, resulting in faster access. Figure 17-2 shows caching at the proxy side.

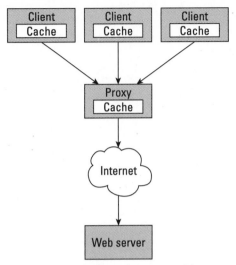

Figure 17-2: Dedicated server caching

Note Proxy caches are often located near network gateways to reduce the bandwidth required over expensive dedicated Internet connections. These systems serve many users (clients) with cached objects from many servers.

Note The Web objects that are requested by one client are stored in a cache, and can be retrieved later when another client requests the same object. For even greater performance, many proxy caches are part of cache hierarchies, in which a cache can enquire neighboring caches for a requested document, to reduce the need to fetch the object directly. Such an organization of multiple cache servers is also referred to as a cache array.

✦ **Reverse proxy:** Caches can also be placed directly in front of a particular Web server, to reduce the number of requests that they receive. This model allows the proxy server to respond to the frequently received requests and pass the other requests to the Web server. This form of proxying is called a reverse proxy, wherein the proxy server is used by the Web server to speed up request processing. This model is unique in that it caches objects for many clients, but usually from a single server. Figure 17-3 shows the reverse proxy caching.

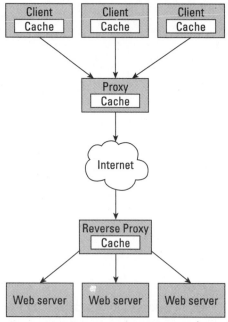

Figure 17-3: Reverse proxy caching

After discussing the various locations where caching can be performed, let us now look at some of the most significant advantages of Web caching:

✦ **Reduced bandwidth consumption:** Because the frequently used data and Web pages are cached and ASP.NET allows developers to configure the cache location to be on the client machine, most requests are fulfilled from the local cache. Therefore, fewer requests and responses need to go over the network between the client and the server. This results in reduced bandwidth consumption.

✦ **Reduced server load:** Because frequently used data and Web pages are retrieved from the cache, the server does not need to execute the same ASP.NET code multiple times to produce the same output. This saves valuable CPU time at the server end.

✦ **Reduced latency:** Because most requests do not need to go to the server for processing, the access time improves significantly.

Although Web caching provides many advantages, it is one of the most misunderstood technologies on the Internet. Webmasters, in particular, fear losing control of their sites because a cache can hide their users from them, making it difficult to see who's using the sites. In addition, the number of hits is not counted correctly, because the cache server(s) might fulfill some percentage of client requests. However, careful planning and proper location of a proxy server cache will help your Web site load faster, and reduce load on your server and the Internet link. The difference can be dramatic; a site that is difficult to cache may take several seconds to load. Users will appreciate a fast-loading site, and will visit it more often.

Another concern related to Web caching is that the caches might serve outdated content. As you'll see later in the chapter, this issue can be taken care of by configuring your server to control the expiry time for the cached content. The next section describes caching in ASP.NET in detail.

Caching in ASP.NET

ASP.NET has introduced various new features to the server-side programming model. These new features have made it easier to cache application data, and hence enhance the performance of Web applications. For example, unlike classic ASP, wherein the code is interpreted, all code in ASP.NET is compiled before execution, resulting in huge performance gains. After the code for an ASP.NET Web page is compiled, all future requests for that page are handled by the compiled code without requiring any recompilation until a change is made to the original ASP.NET page. Also, when a page is accessed for the first time, the code is compiled depending on user needs. For example, if there are 10 functions in an ASP.NET Web page, only those functions are compiled into native machine code, which are needed to respond to a user's request.

It is important to clarify that compilation is a two-stage process in the .NET Framework. First, the code is compiled into the Microsoft Intermediate Language (MSIL). Then, the MSIL is compiled into native code during execution. The entire code in an ASP.NET Web page is compiled into MSIL when the solution is built. However, during execution, only the portions of the code that are actually needed will be compiled into native code. In addition, the configuration of an ASP.NET Web site is loaded from the Web.config file and stored in a memory cache, thereby preventing expensive disk read operations when a configuration value needs to be retrieved.

Cross-Reference   For more information on the Web.config configuration file, refer to Chapter 14.

ASP.NET provides several caching mechanisms that enhance the performance of Web applications. One of the caching mechanisms involves compiling the ASP.NET page and caching the instance on the server. Afterward, the page can be directly retrieved from the cache. The page in the cache is updated only when a change occurs in the page or when the caching period expires. *Expiring* of an object from the cache refers to the object being removed from the cache. When the cache expiry for an object is reached, future requests for that object cannot be fulfilled from the cache. In such a situation, the object needs to be retrieved from the actual Web server, or the code behind file for the ASP.NET page needs to be executed again. ASP.NET supports two types of expiration policies, which determine when an object will be expired from the cache. These two policies are described as follows:

✦ **Absolute expiration:** Determines that the expirations occur at a specified time. Absolute expirations are specified in full-time format (hh:mm:ss). The object will be expired from the cache at the specified time.

✦ **Relative expiration:** Determines that expirations occur after the specified time window has passed. Relative expiration is specified in seconds. After the specified number of seconds, the item is automatically expired from the cache.

The next few sections describe the Cache API and the Cache Performance Monitor counters.

Cache API

ASP.NET uses the .NET Framework classes to control the caching services. The caching services are encapsulated in the classes contained in the System.Web. Caching namespace. For example, the Cache class is used for explicitly managing an application cache, and the CacheDependency class is used to define and track dependencies of cache objects. These classes are covered later in the chapter. Some of the classes used by ASP.NET for managing cache behavior are discussed next.

HttpCachePolicy

The complete implementation of cache policies provided by ASP.NET is encapsulated in the HttpCachePolicy class. Applications that want more control over the HTTP headers related to caching can directly use the functionality provided by the HttpCachePolicy class. This class is used to set the expiration time for cached content in relative or absolute time. This class contains methods that are used by ASP.NET to enforce any expiration policies set by the user.

Some of the public properties and methods included in the HttpCachePolicy class are described as follows:

✦ VaryByHeaders: This property represents the list of HTTP headers used to vary the cache output. The ASP.NET cache can maintain different versions of the same Web page if the HTTP headers received in the request are different. This property, therefore, is used to control the HTTP headers that should result in caching multiple versions of the same Web page.

✦ VaryByParams: This property represents the list of parameters received in a Get or Post request. ASP.NET maintains multiple versions of a Web page if the parameter(s) specified in this property vary.

✦ SetCacheability: This is an overloaded method, which sets the Cache-Control HTTP header. Further, the Cache-Control HTTP header controls how documents are to be cached on the network.

✦ SetExpires: This method sets the Expires HTTP header to an absolute date and time.

HttpCacheability

HttpCacheability is an enumeration of all the possible values for the Cache-Control HTTP header. The Cache-Control HTTP header determines whether or not the output is cached. It also determines the location, such as the Web server, proxy server, or a client machine, where the output is cached. The default cache location is the client machine. The following are the available values in the HttpCacheability enumeration:

✦ `NoCache`: Indicates that the output will not be cached at any location.

✦ `Public`: Indicates that the output can be cached on the proxy server as well as on the client side.

✦ `Private`: Indicates that the output can be cached only on the client side. This is the default value.

✦ `Server`: Indicates that the Web server will cache the output and the clients and proxy servers will receive a no-cache HTTP header value.

@OutputCache

This page-level directive in an ASP.NET page is used to control the cache duration of the page output. To control the cache behavior of an ASP.NET page, you can use either the `@OutputCache` directive or the HttpCachePolicy class. However, if the ASP.NET page is parameterized by using QueryString parameters or the `Post` method, the page cache needs to be maintained by setting the `VaryByParam` attribute.

HttpCacheVaryByParams

When the output generated by an ASP.NET page depends on the parameters passed by using QueryString or the `Post` method, it requires ASP.NET to maintain multiple versions of the same page. The HttpCacheVaryByParams class is used to maintain multiple versions of the same ASP.NET page in the cache. When the `VaryByParam` attribute is set with the `@OutputCache` directive in a page, ASP.NET internally uses the HttpCacheVaryByParams class. For example, consider that a Web server receives the following requests:

```
http://localhost/caching/displaysuppliers.aspx?city=london
http://localhost/caching/displaysuppliers.aspx?city=NY
http://localhost/caching/displaysuppliers.aspx?city=london
http://localhost/caching/displaysuppliers.aspx?city=SJ
```

If multiple requests for the Displaysuppliers.aspx page with the city parameter, "london," are to be cached, the `@OutputCache` directive must set the `VaryByParam` to city, as follows:

```
<% @OutputCache duration = "60" varybyparam = "city"%>
```

This statement will cause ASP.NET to cache the requests for the Displaysuppliers. aspx page and maintain the cache citywide. Then, the cache will contain three versions (one each for London, New York, and San Jose) of the Displaysuppliers. aspx page.

HttpCacheVaryByHeaders

The HttpCacheVaryByHeaders class is used to cache multiple versions of an ASP.NET page, depending on a particular HTTP header. Therefore, the cache will have multiple versions of the ASP.NET Web page — one for each value of the specified HTTP header. A common use for this class is when you need to generate browser-specific versions of a Web page and store that page in the cache. In such a situation, all future requests for the page from a specific section of browsers are fulfilled from the cache and do not require re-rendering of the page.

If the HTTP header has a value "User-Agent" specifying the name of the browser that requested an ASP.NET page, and if the page is browser-specific, you can set the VaryByHeaders property to "User-Agent". This makes ASP.NET maintain a browser-specific cache. To achieve this, set the @OutputCache directive as follows:

```
<%@OutputCache Duration =  "120" VaryByHeaders =  "User-Agent">
```

If the ASP.NET page is requested multiple times by the same browser, the first request will cause the ASP.NET page to be rendered and stored in the cache. The subsequent requests will then be fulfilled from the cache. However, if a different browser requests the same page, ASP.NET will re-render the page and store this version also in the cache. This way, the cache will have two versions of the same page.

Cache API Performance Monitor counters

The Performance Monitor counters can be used to determine the efficiency and performance of ASP.NET applications. To monitor the cache-specific counters in Performance Monitor, complete the following steps:

1. Select Start ⇨ Programs ⇨ Administrative Tools ⇨ Performance to start the Performance Monitor.

2. In the Performance Monitor window, use the Add counter toolbar icon to view the list of ASP.NET cache counters.

3. In the Add Counters dialog box, from the Performance Object drop-down list box, select ASP.NET Applications. Now, the various cache-related counters are displayed in the Counters list box. Figure 17-4 shows the Add Counters dialog box.

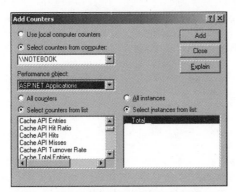

Figure 17-4: The Add Counters dialog box

Some of the cache counters are described as follows.

✦ **Cache Total Entries:** Represents the total number of items stored in the ASP.NET cache.

✦ **Cache Total Hits:** Represents the total number of items that were requested by a user and were successfully retrieved from the cache and returned to the user. This counter presents an overall picture of the "success" of the ASP.NET caching engine.

✦ **Cache Total Misses:** Represents the total number of items that were requested by users and were not retrieved from the cache (failed cache retrievals).

✦ **Cache Total Hit Ratio:** Represents the ratio of total cache hits to total cache misses for the cache. This counter gives a good overall picture of what percentage of items is retrieved from the cache.

✦ **Cache Total Turnover Rate:** Represents the number of additions and removals to the total cache per second. If there are excessive additions and removals happening from the cache, it is an area of concern, because the CPU is potentially spending a lot of time maintaining the cache. This counter is useful in determining how effectively the cache is being used. Large values for this counter indicate inefficient use of the cache.

✦ **Cache API Entries:** Represents the total number of entries made explicity in the cache by an application by using the Cache API.

✦ **Cache API Hits:** Represents the total number of items successfully found in the cache when accessed only through the external Cache API.

✦ **Cache API Misses:** Represents the total number of fetch requests made to the cache that failed. This counter is applicable only to fetch requests that are made explicitly by using the external Cache API.

✦ **Cache API Hit Ratio:** Represents the cache hit-to-miss ratio when accessed through the Cache API.

✦ **Cache API Turnover Rate:** Represents the number of additions and removals to the cache per second when used via the external Cache API, excluding the internal Cache APIs used by the ASP.NET Framework.

After understanding the Cache API and Cache Performance Monitor counters, let us now discuss page output and page data caching.

Caching Page Output

Most Web sites today use dynamic Web pages, which present information depending on user preferences. This approach requires a template page, such as an ASPX page, to be used by Web applications. When a Web page is presented to a user, the data retrieved from a data store is dynamically merged into the template and displayed to the user. Although this approach allows the same page to be tailored dynamically to incorporate user preferences, it has certain problems. These dynamic Web pages are less scalable.

Because the pages are generated each time a request is made, as shown in Figure 17-5, dynamic Web pages require more server resources. Having a background batch process that pregenerates the HTML output is one of the ways in which this problem can be circumvented. However, this approach fails when the number of user requests is unknown or the number of requests is very large. In such a case, what is needed is a smart caching solution. ASP.NET provides the output cache feature to solve this problem of scalability.

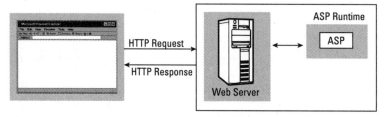

Figure 17-5: Processing a Web page in classic ASP

Page output caching allows the entire content of a given page to be stored in the cache. Thus, unlike dynamic Web pages, the cached ASP.NET pages are served statically directly from the cache, instead of dynamically executing them from a Web server for each request. Therefore, the page output–caching feature provides a huge performance enhancement on the server as compared to the dynamic Web page model.

When an ASP.NET page is accessed for the first time, the page is compiled into Intermediate Language (IL) and then into native code. This native code is cached and all future requests to the ASP.NET page are processed by this native code for the next request. This cached page code is updated and rebuilt when the source ASP.NET file is changed or the cache timeout is reached. Figure 17-6 shows the processing of a Web page in ASP.NET.

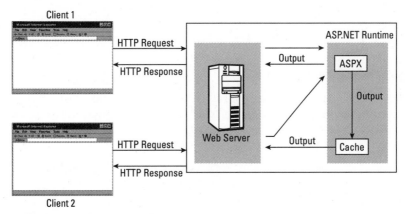

Figure 17-6: Processing a Web page in ASP.NET

You can mark the output of an ASP.NET Web page for caching by specifying the @OutputCache page directive at the beginning of the page. This directive takes a Duration parameter in seconds and causes the ASP.NET cache to store the output of the page in the cache for the specified number of seconds. For example, to cache the output of an ASP.NET page for five minutes, add the following @OutputCache directive at the beginning of an ASPX file:

```
<%@OutputCache Duration="300" VaryByParam = "none"%>
```

When the @OutputCache directive is specified at the beginning of an ASP.NET page, the ASP.NET runtime automatically invokes the cache services to store the data output by the Web page. The page output that includes all data output from the page (including any data retrieved from a database) is retrieved from this cache for all future requests made to that Web page. The first user request to the ASP.NET page will generate HTML; all future requests will then be answered with the HTML present in the cache. For example, consider an ASP.NET Web page that displays the current time on the server. The code for the page is given as follows:

```
<%'Cache the output for 300 seconds irrespective of any
parameters received in any GET or POST requests %>

<%@ OutputCache Duration="300" VaryByParam="none" %>

<html>

  <Script Language="VB" runat="Server">

    Sub Page_Load(ByVal Src As System.Object, ByVal E As
System.EventArgs) Handles MyBase.Load
```

```
        'Set the text in the label as the current server time

        lblServerTime.Text = DateTime.Now.ToString("G")

    End Sub

  </script>

  <body>

    <h3>Output Cache</h3>

    <p>This page was generated at:
<asp:Label ID=lblServerTime runat="Server"/>

  </body>

</html>
```

Figure 17-7 shows the output of this code.

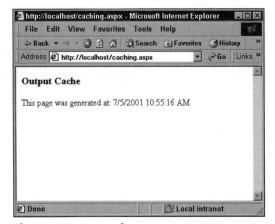

Figure 17-7: A sample output

To test the preceding code, switch to IIS and locate the file that you created. Next, right-click the file and choose Browse from the context menu. Repeat these steps after a few seconds, and take note of the time displayed. In this Web page, if the `@OutputCache` directive were not used, the page would have displayed the exact server time on receiving a client request. However, because the `@OutputCache` directive is set to cache the output data for 300 seconds, the server time displayed will be same for five minutes—all requests received within five minutes of the first request will display the same time. After five minutes, when the cache is expired, the first request received will cause the server to execute the ASP.NET page once again and cache the output data.

It is also possible to specify an absolute expiration time. To do so, you need to call the `Response.Cache.SetExpires` method and pass the absolute time as an argument. For example, to specify the absolute expiration time for an ASP.NET page at 9:00 a.m., use the following VB code:

```
Response.Cache.SetExpires ( DateTime.Parse ("9:00:00 AM"))
```

Tip   Absolute expiration is very useful for pages that do not change frequently.

Caution   Remember that creating an output cache for an application should be your final task in application development. Otherwise, when you debug your pages, instead of getting new and modified pages, you might get old pages that are stored in the output cache.

As mentioned earlier, the entire HTML output is cached by default when the `@OutputCache` directive is specified. However, if you do not want this default behavior of caching, you can apply region caching. *Region caching*, also called fragment caching, allows specific sections of the output page to be cached instead of the entire page. If an ASPX file consists of different code sections, you can set different cache settings for these different code sections. For example, if a Web page reads several database tables, processes some XML-formatted data, and also displays some customized content for a user, then the page can be cached in sections. The database table read sections can be cached for one hour, the XML portion can be cached for 10 minutes, and the user-specific data might not be cached at all.

This type of fragment caching is achieved by using user controls and setting the `@OutputCache` directives in the user control page. When the user control is instantiated in a container page, the cache settings of the control are applied along with any cache settings on the container page. Figure 17-8 shows the fragment caching.

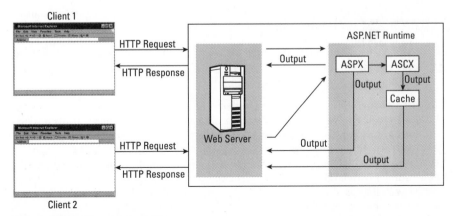

Figure 17-8: Fragment caching

If you set the cache time of a page to 60 seconds and that of a contained user control to 300 seconds, the cached output will expire and the content of the page will be refreshed after every 60 seconds. However, the contained user control will be refreshed independent of the container page.

Caching Page Data

Storing frequently requested data in memory variables on the server side is a familiar concept for ASP developers. In classic ASP, two intrinsic objects, the Session object and the Application object, are used to store application data in memory variables. The Session and Application objects are available in ASP.NET, but their functionality is not enhanced much. ASP.NET encapsulates the application data caching in the Cache class. The following sections cover the Session and Cache objects in detail.

Session object

The Session object is used to store data across multiple requests for each user. When a session begins, a unique key is assigned to the user. ASP maintains the session state for each user by providing the client with this unique key. This key is stored in an HTTP cookie that the client sends to the server on each request. The server can then read the key from the cookie and rebuild the server session state. But some limitations exist to using the ASP Session object over the ASP.NET Session object:

✦ **Process dependency:** In the case of classical ASP, the ASP Session object is process-dependent. If an ASP service on a Web server is restarted, the session state of all the users on that server is lost, and all these users are assigned new sessions. On the other hand, the ASP.NET Session object can be stored in the same memory that ASP.NET uses (in-process), in separate memory from ASP.NET (out-of-process using Windows NT Service), or in a persistent storage (in SQL Server). Since the ASP.NET Session object can be stored out-of-process, it is process-independent. ASP.NET session state can run in a separate process from the ASP.NET host process. Therefore, the session state is available irrespective of the ASP.NET process. Of course, you can still use session state in a process similar to the classic ASP.

✦ **Server farm support:** In a real-world scenario, as the load on a Web server increases, the Web administrator balances the load across multiple Web servers by replicating the Web site on multiple servers. The load balancing can be achieved by using additional hardware, such as Cisco LocalDirector, or software solutions, such as Windows Load Balancing Services. In the classic

ASP scenario, there is no guarantee that all requests from a user will always be sent to the same Web server. In such a case, the different Web servers will treat the incoming requests from the user as separate sessions. As the user moves from one Web server to another, the session state is not carried along with the user. Until the user returns to the same server, the session state cannot be accessed. This problem can be solved by using network IP–level routing solutions, which can ensure that the client IPs are routed to the originating server. However, some Internet service providers (ISPs) choose to use a proxy load-balancing solution for their clients. On the other hand, ASP.NET supports server farm configurations. The new out-of-process model allows all servers in the farm to share a session state process. You can implement this by changing the ASP.NET configuration to point to a common server. Now, the session state can be stored out of process as well as out of system by using the session state service. The session state can be recorded into a SQL Server database, which can be on a cluster for the purpose of reliability.

✦ **Cookie-dependent:** ASP sessions are cookie-dependent. As already mentioned, ASP sessions are identified with a unique Session ID cookie that is sent by a Web server to a Web browser when the session is established. The browser sends the cookie with every request made to the Web server. Clients that don't accept HTTP cookies can't take advantage of session state. Some clients believe that cookies compromise security and/or privacy and thus disable them, which in turn disables the session state on the server. ASP.NET sessions, on the other hand, can be configured to be cookie-independent. ASP.NET reduces the complexities of cookieless session state to a simple configuration setting.

State management in classic ASP

In classic ASP, when a client requests ASP scripts from a Web server, a session is established between the client and the server. During this session establishment, the Web server generates a Session ID cookie and sends it to the client. The Session ID cookie is sent to the client in HTTP header. Therefore, to identify its session data in subsequent requests, the client shares a common key (Session ID cookie) with the Web server. This state management model works well for the clients that accept HTTP cookies. However, there are certain clients who think that cookies compromise on security. This is because the Session ID cookie is the only way a browser request is identified. Any other HTTP request with a matching cookie is assumed to have come from the same browser. Thus, a hacker who succeeds in hijacking the cookie could use a user's active session. Due to these security threats, some clients disable cookies and thus disable session state on the server. Thus, the ASP scripts do not work well for the clients who do not accept HTTP cookies.

Cache object

ASP.NET provides a full-featured cache engine that can be utilized by pages to store and retrieve arbitrary objects across HTTP requests. This is a replacement to the Session and Application variables that were used in classic ASP. The ASP.NET cache is private to each application and stores objects in memory. The lifetime of the cache is equivalent to the lifetime of the application. Therefore, when the application is restarted, the cache is also re-created.

ASP.NET encapsulates the application data caching in the Cache class. The Cache class is always associated with an ASP.NET application. When an ASP.NET application starts, an instance of the Cache class is always created. The Cache object is destroyed as soon as the ASP.NET application stops. Therefore, the lifetime of this Cache object is the same as the lifetime of an ASP.NET application.

The ASP.NET cache provides a simple dictionary interface that enables programmers to easily place objects in the cache and later retrieve them from it. In the simplest case, placing an item in the cache is just like adding an item to a Session or Application object. For example, you can add a variable to the Cache object as follows:

```
Cache("myvar") = 20
```

Each cache item has a key/value pair. In this code, "myvar" is the key and 20 is the value. In addition to storing key/value pairs, the Cache object provides additional functionality to store transient data. To achieve transient data caching, you can use *dependencies,* which enable you to invalidate a particular item within the Cache object depending on the changes to the dependent keys, files, or time. For example, an item should be removed from the cache when a dependent file changes. The .NET Framework provides the CacheDependency class that encapsulates the implementation of cache dependencies. The different dependencies are described in the remaining sections.

File-based dependency

File-based dependency invalidates a particular Cache item when a file(s) on the disk changes. For example, consider the following code wherein the product data is loaded from an XML file:

```
Dim dom As XmlDocument()
dom.Load(Server.MapPath("product.xml")
Cache("ProductData") = dom
```

You can add a cache dependency to force ASP.NET to expire the "ProductData" item from the cache when the Product.xml file changes. To do so, you need to create an object of the CacheDependency class. If the Product.xml file resides in the same directory as the requesting application, write the following code:

```
Dim dependency as new
CacheDependency(Server.MapPath("product.xml"))
Cache.Insert("ProductData", dom, dependency)
```

In this code:

✦ `dependency` is an instance of a CacheDependency class

✦ The `Insert()` method of the Cache class is used to create the `ProductData` key that is dependent upon the file from which it retrieves data

You can also create a cache dependency based on multiple files. In such a case, the dependency should be built from an array of files or directories. As an example, consider a case in which an XML document arrives in a directory, immediately after which an item in the ASP.NET cache needs to be expired. In such a case, you need to add a cache dependency to the directory.

The following is the complete code of the Web page to demonstrate the implementation of the CacheDependency class:

```
<%@ Import Namespace="System.IO" %>
<%@ Import Namespace="System.Data" %>

<Html>

<Script language="VB" runat="server">

Sub Page_Load(ByVal sender As System.Object, ByVal e As
System.EventArgs) Handles MyBase.Load
    If Not IsPostBack
        GetData()
    End If
End Sub

Sub GetData()
    Dim Source As DataView

    Source = Cache("ProductCatalog")
    If Source Is Nothing
      Dim ds As DataSet
      Dim fs As FileStream
      Dim reader As StreamReader

    'Read the data from the Product.XML file
      ds = New DataSet()
      fs = New FileStream(Server.MapPath("product.xml"),
FileMode.Open,FileAccess.Read)
      reader = New StreamReader(fs)
      ds.ReadXml(reader)
```

```
        fs.Close()

        Source = New DataView(ds.Tables(0))

        'Cache it for future use and also add product.xml as a
dependency
        'Any changes to product.xml will cause us to refresh the
cache (build the cache once again)

        Cache.Insert("ProductCatalog", Source, New
CacheDependency(Server.MapPath("product.xml")))

        'Message to indicate that we created the cache
        lblMsg.Text = "Dataset created explicitly"
    Else
        lblMsg.Text = "Dataset retrieved from cache"
    End If

MyDataGrid.DataSource = Source
MyDataGrid.DataBind()
End Sub

</Script>

<Body>

<Form runat="server">

<H3><Font Face="Verdana">File Dependencies</Font></H3>

<ASP:DataGrid id="MyDataGrid" runat="server" Width="650"
BackColor="#cccfff" BorderColor="black" ShowFooter="false"
CellPadding=3 CellSpacing="0" Font-Name="Verdana" Font-
Size="8pt" HeaderStyle-BackColor="lightgreen" />

<Hr>
<P>
<I><asp:label id="lblMsg" runat="server"/></I></P>
</Form>
</Body>
</Html>
```

The code of the Product.xml file used in the preceding Web page is given as follows:

```
<Catalog>
    <Product>
      <id>1</id>
        <name> Oranges </name>
          <qty> 120 </qty>
          <price>$2.95 </price>
    </Product>
    <Product>
      <id>2</id>
```

```
        <name> Apples </name>
        <qty> 100 </qty>
        <price>$2.65 </price>
    </Product>
</Catalog>
```

The output of the preceding code is shown in Figure 17-9.

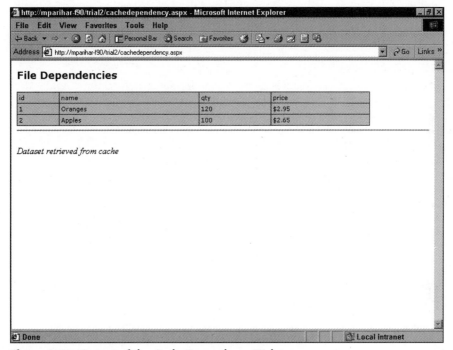

Figure 17-9: Output of the CacheDependency Web page

Note If the content of the Product.xml file is updated manually or otherwise, the Web page will automatically refresh the cache, and the message "Dataset created explicitly" will be displayed.

Key-based dependency

Key-based dependency invalidates a particular cache item when another cache item changes. For example, consider an application that adds multiple datasets to the cache, such as ProductData, SalesData, and MarketingData. If the SalesData and MarketingData datasets rely upon the ProductData dataset for data validation, you can use a key-based dependency to invalidate SalesData and MarketingData if the ProductData item changes. To do so, you need to set up this dependency when you create the cache entries for SalesData and MarketingData:

```
Dim dependencyKey(1) As String
dependencyKey(0) = "ProductData"
Dim productDataDependency As new CacheDependency(nothing,
dependencyKey)
Cache.Insert("SalesData", LoadDataSet("Sales"),
productDataDependency)
```

In this code, `productDataDependency` is the object of the CacheDependency class. The dependency key, which is set to ProductData, is passed as a parameter to instantiate the object. Now, whenever ProductData changes, SalesData will be removed from the cache. Similarly, you can extend the code to incorporate a dependency on the MarketingData dataset.

Time-based dependency

Time-based dependency causes an item to expire at a defined time. Again, the `Insert()` method of the Cache class is used to create a time-based dependency. Two options are available for the time-based dependency:

✦ **Absolute:** Sets an absolute time for a cache item to expire. This option is best suited for data that changes on a periodic basis and at a known time.

✦ **Sliding:** Resets the time for the item in the Cache to expire on each request. Therefore, an item remains in the cache for the specified time; if no requests are made for that item, it automatically expires from the cache. If requests for that item are received, the cache duration is automatically extended. Therefore, this option is useful when an item in the cache is to be kept alive so long as requests for that item are coming in from various clients.

For example, to cache the ProductData dataset for a maximum duration of 10 minutes, you can use the Sliding option:

```
'set a 10 minute time span
Dim span As New TimeSpan(0,10,0)

'Add the return data from the LoadDataSet method into the
'Cache. The item will be identified as ProductData and will 'be
stored in the cache for 10 minutes

Cache.Insert("ProductData", LoadDataSet(), nothing, nothing,
span)
```

In addition to the dependencies, ASP.NET allows the following:

✦ **Automatic expiration:** The cache items that are underused and have no dependencies are automatically expired.

✦ **Support for callback:** The Cache object can be configured to call a given piece of code that will be executed when an item is removed from the cache. This gives you an opportunity to update the cache.

For example, you can guarantee that the item (ProductData dataset) is always served from the cache. To do so, add the following code in the GetData method:

```
'Declare a callback method for notifying applications when
'a cached item is removed from the cache
Dim onRemoveItem As New CacheItemRemovedCallback(AddressOf
Me.RemovedCallback)

'Cache the item. Notice the last parameter, which is the
'callback method. Also, notice that the priority of the
'item has been kept high and the decay has been set to
'slow
Cache.Insert("ProductData",ds,nothing,DateTime.Now.AddSeconds
(5),TimeSpan.Zero,CacheItemPriority.High,CacheItemPriorityDec
ay.Slow,onRemove)

'Removing the item to invoke the callback method

Cache.Remove("ProductData")
```

Then, create the callback method that should be invoked when the cache item is removed.

```
'Define the callback method
Public Sub RemovedCallback(k as String, v as Object, r As
CacheItemRemovedReason)

'loading the item from cache
GetData()

End Sub
```

Because the Cache object is maintained by ASP.NET depending on the usage of items, it is likely that items in the cache are removed if they are not used or are underused. Hence, you must ensure that the applications that use the Cache object always check for the presence of an item in the cache before attempting to retrieve the item.

Summary

This chapter introduced you to caching in ASP.NET. First, you learned about the Cache API provided by the .NET Framework. Then, you saw the different Cache Performance Monitor counters. Finally, you learned how to use the Cache API for page output and page data caching.

✦　　✦　　✦

Building Wireless Applications with ASP.NET Mobile Controls

The Internet is constantly evolving, and has moved from the desktop to include the wireless world. As an extension of ASP.NET, Microsoft has released the Mobile Internet Toolkit (MIT). MIT is an intelligent solution to produce mobile applications that detect the browsing device and return the appropriately formatted content. Thus, MIT provides a single application that adapts to Web-enabled cell phones, pagers, and personal digital assistants (PDAs).

This chapter provides an overview of the Wireless Application Protocol (WAP) and the basics of the Wireless Markup Language (WML). After you understand how your data is transferred to your wireless devices, you will learn about the MIT controls that produce a single application that is then available to multiple devices.

Introduction to Mobile Development

There are many challenges and obstacles we need to consider when developing mobile applications. You will start by learning what some of these challenges are, and how you can deal with them using the MIT.

Challenges to Mobile Development

Many people have become reliant on the information that is available on the Internet. However, whereas people traditionally have used their desktop computer to access the Internet, they increasingly are relying upon mobile devices to access the Internet. Although the technology exists to extend your desktop applications to a mobile environment, you have to be aware of some of the limitations of mobile devices:

✦ **Smaller screen size**: A typical cell phone can only display 15 to 20 characters across and between 4 to 6 lines of text.

✦ **Power**: Most mobile devices have limited battery life, memory, and processing power, and do not carry the same capabilities as your desktop PC.

✦ **Bandwidth**: By nature, wireless applications are more costly to run and, technically, cannot provide the bandwidth found on a wired network.

Luckily, MIT will handle most of the screen size limitations that you will run into when developing wireless applications. MIT will dynamically detect the device being used and provide the appropriate output. However, you still must remember that screen real estate will be at a premium when developing your applications. Along with real estate, bandwidth is also at a premium. You must be able to compress your applications into small chunks of data. Obviously, you won't be sending streaming video down to your cell phone (at least not yet), but you may be sending images to enhance the user experience.

In spite of the difficulties previously mentioned, MIT makes it easy to deploy wireless applications, and it does so intelligently.

Wireless devices and emulators

Over 80 percent of Internet-enabled, wireless devices consist of cell phones and PDAs. Cell phones have a typical display screen of 15 to 20 characters and between 4 to 6 lines of text. PDAs are a little bit larger, and may be as wide as 20 to 25 characters, and include up to 6 to 10 lines of text. Testing your applications on wireless devices could get to be expensive over the process of building your software. Therefore, to test your applications, this chapter explains how to use two different emulators: a cell phone emulator by Openwave, and the Pocket PC emulator available from Microsoft.

Openwave is one of the world's largest providers of mobile Internet software. You can download its cell phone emulator (Openwave SDK) from `http://developer.openwave.com` . After you've installed the SDK on your system, it may look similar to Figure 18-1.

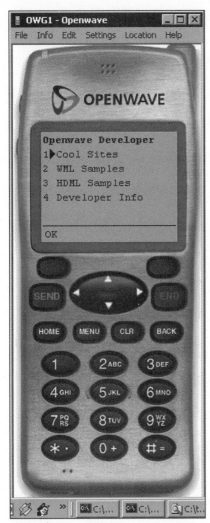

Figure 18-1: Using the Openwave
cell phone emulator

Microsoft provides an emulator for its Windows CE device. This emulator is part of
the Microsoft eMbedded Visual Tools kit. Like the Openwave SDK, both the
Openwave SDK and the PocketPC emulator are standalone Windows applications.
Figure 18-2 shows the opening screen of the Pocket PC emulator.

Figure 18-2: Using the Pocket PC emulator

WAP, WML, and a deck of cards

The Wireless Application Protocol (WAP) is used to transfer your data to your wireless devices. WAP was conceived by four companies: Ericsson, Motorola, Nokia, and Unwired Planet (now Openwave). These four companies founded the WAP Forum (http://www.wapforum.com), which has now grown to over 200 members, including operators, infrastructure suppliers, software developers, and content providers.

Because WAP is the protocol used to transfer our data, we need another protocol to format our data. That's where WML, or Wireless Markup Language, comes into play. WML is used to format pages that are delivered using WAP. WML has its roots in XML, and is in fact still XML-compliant.

Note   Because WML is XML-compliant, it is case-sensitive and must have a closing tag for every opening tag.

Each WML file is made up of a deck of cards. Just as a traditional "deck of cards" contains individual playing pieces, a WML deck of cards contains individual screens. Although a complete deck is normally sent to your mobile device at a time, only one card can be seen at a time. A card can be thought of as a single page or screen. Thus, by sending a deck of cards to your mobile device, you are actually sending multiple pages at a time. As an example, Figure 18-3 displays the layout of a deck of cards that we will use to select a bicycle.

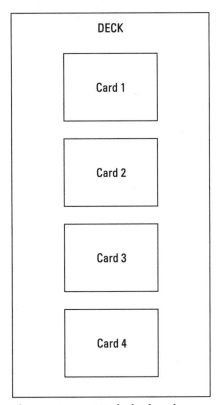

Figure 18-3: WML deck of cards

Building Your First Mobile Application

Now that you understand the foundation of mobile applications, you will build your first application. Your sample application, about bicycling, will demonstrate various techniques of displaying data, and receiving input data from the user.

Static pages

Let's take our layout and convert it to an application. However, before we start coding, we need to make sure our Internet Information Server (IIS) is set up to properly serve WML pages. To configure IIS 5.0 on Windows 2000 to serve up static WML pages, follow these steps:

1. Open Control Panel, then Administrative Tools, then IIS administrator.

2. Right-click your Web site instance and select Properties.

3. Click the HTTP Headers tab.

4. Under Mime Types, click File Types.

5. Under Registered File Types, check to see if .wml is listed.

6. If .wml is not listed, click New Type to show the File Type dialog box.

7. Enter ".wml" (without quotes) in the Associated Extension box.

8. Enter "text/vnd.wap.wml" (without quotes) in the Content Type (MIME) box. Figure 18-4 shows the File Type dialog box.

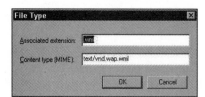

Figure 18-4: Registering .wml as a MIME type

The following code provides an example of a deck of cards. This WML deck contains 3 cards that provide links between each card.

```
<? xml version="1.0" ?>
<! DOCTYPE wml PUBLIC "-//WAPFORUM//DTD WML 1.1 //EN"
"http://www.wapforum.org/DTD/wml_1.1.xml">
<wml>
    <card id="firstcard" title="Bike Style">
        <p>
        Select a Bike Style
        <br />
        <a href="#secondcard">Road Bike</a>
        <br />
        <a href="#thirdcard">Mountain Bike</a>
        </p>
    </card>

    <card id="secondcard" title="Road Bike">
        <p>
        <b>You Selected a Road Bike!</b>
        </p>
    </card>

    <card id="thirdcard" title="Mountain Bike">
        <p>
        <b>You Selected a Mountain Bike!</b>
        </p>
    </card>
    </wml>
```

Our deck contains three cards. Based upon which bike style you select, you will be taken to a different card. This example links within the same deck. When this WML file is downloaded to the device, the entire deck will be resident in memory. Figure 18-5 shows our newly created WML file.

Figure 18-5: Bike.wml

 Note All WML files must begin with:

```
<? xml version="1.0" ?>
<! DOCTYPE wml PUBLIC "-//WAPFORUM//DTD WML 1.1 //EN"
"http://www.wapforum.org/DTD/wml_1.1.xml">
```

Note   Because <br> tags normally don't have a closing tag, it is considered an empty element, and closed with a trailing slash, like <br />.

Our example currently links cards together. Sometimes we need to link decks together. The following code demonstrates linking decks together:

```
[bike.wml]
<? xml version="1.0" ?>
<! DOCTYPE wml PUBLIC "-//WAPFORUM//DTD WML 1.1 //EN"
"http://www.wapforum.org/DTD/wml_1.1.xml">
    <wml>
          <card id="firstcard" title="Bike Style">
                  <p>
                  Select a Bike Style From a Deck
                  <br />
                  <a href="roadbike.wml">Road Bike</a>
                  <br />
                  <a href="mountainbike.wml">Mountain Bike</a>
                  </p>
          </card>
    </wml>
```

Installing the Mobile Information Toolkit

Currently, MIT is available as an additional download from `http://www.asp.net`. The installation process is straightforward and painless. After you have downloaded the EXE file, double-click the file to start the Microsoft Installer (or MSI) InstallShield Wizard. Figure 18-6 displays the start page of the InstallShield Wizard for MIT.

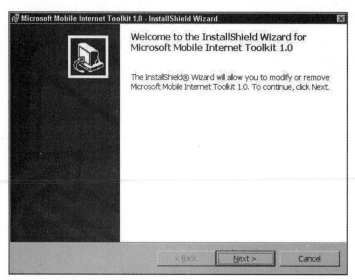

Figure 18-6: Installing MIT

Clicking the Next button provides you with several options, including Mobile QuickStart, Mobile Internet Designer for Visual Studio .NET, and Documentation, as shown in Figure 18-7. If you have the space available on your system, you should choose to install all the files.

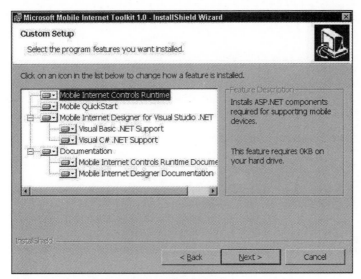

Figure 18-7: Configuring MIT installation

Clicking the Next button two more times will finish our installation. Let's build and test our first MIT form.

Building your first MIT page

MIT is considered an intelligent solution. It will detect what type of device is requesting data and will return the appropriately formatted data. For example, if a browser is requesting your mobile page, the respective HTML will be returned. If a cell phone is requesting your page, the appropriate WML will be returned. This happens because all mobile pages must inherit from System.Web.UI.MobileControls.MobilePage.

The object `MobilePage` is the outermost layer of all the containers in a mobile Web application. However, unlike a normal ASP.NET page, a `MobilePage` object can contain multiple forms, specifically multiple `<mobile:form>`...`</mobile:form>` tags. Each of these `<mobile:form>` tags will match with our cards in a deck.

Converting your WML to MIT

Now that you've installed the MIT and understand a little about mobile forms, let's convert our Bike.wml page to Bike.aspx. In all of the examples, you will be building your pages in VS.NET. VS.NET enforces the CodeBehind model, separating application logic and HTML layout in two separate files. The following code is a conversion of our original WML deck to the MIT:

```
[bike.aspx]
<%@ Register TagPrefix="mobile"
Namespace="System.Web.UI.MobileControls"
Assembly="System.Web.Mobile" %>
<%@ Page Language="vb" AutoEventWireup="false"
Codebehind="bike.aspx.vb" Inherits="wVB.bike" %>
<body
Xmlns:mobile="http://schemas.microsoft.com/Mobile/WebForm">
   <mobile:Form id="Form1" runat="server">
   <P>Select a Bike Style
       <BR>
       <mobile:Link id="Link1" NavigateUrl=#Form2
runat="server">Road Bike</mobile:Link>
       <BR>
       <mobile:Link id="Link2" NavigateUrl=#Form3
runat="server">Mountain Bike</mobile:Link>
       </P>
   </mobile:Form>

   <mobile:Form id="Form2" runat="server">
       <p>
       <b>You Selected a Road Bike!</b>
       </p>
   </mobile:Form>

   <mobile:Form id="Form3" runat="server">
       <p>
       <b>You Selected a Mountain Bike!</b>
       </p>
   </mobile:Form>
</body>
```

Notice how our <card> tags are now replaced with <mobile:Form> tags. Also, we decided to use the <mobile:Link> tag instead of the <a> tag. Using MIT will enable us to build a single page, but provide output to multiple devices. For example, Figures 18-8, 18-9, and 18-10 show our page viewed in the Openwave emulator, Pocket PC emulator, and a browser, respectively.

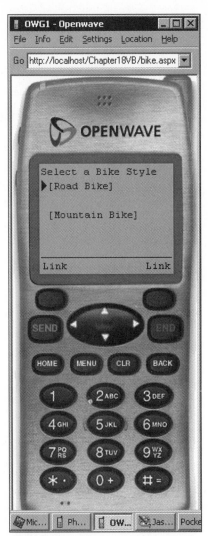

Figure 18-8: Bike.aspx displayed on a cell phone

Figure 18-9: Bike.aspx displayed on a Pocket PC

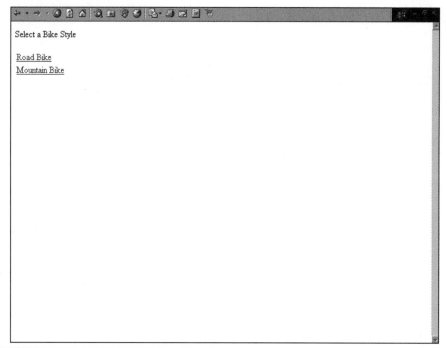

Figure 18-10: Bike.aspx displayed in a browser

Mobile Lists

Now that you've been introduced to some basic mobile controls, you will see how to use mobile lists. Mobile lists are one of the most powerful, and most popular mobile controls. They provide an easy way for the user to input data through their mobile device.

Simple lists

Let's take our example one step further and explore some other controls. In the following example code, we are going to use the <mobile:List> control. This control is much more flexible than the standard <mobile:Link>tag, because it provides special commands and formatting features.

```
[list.aspx]
<mobile:Form id="Form1" runat="server">
        <mobile:Label id="Label1" runat="server">Select a Bike
Style</mobile:Label>
        <BR>
        <mobile:List id="List1" runat="server"
OnItemCommand="SelectBike">
                <Item Text="Road Bike" Value="Road"></Item>
                <Item Text="Mountain Bike"
Value="Mountain"></Item>
        </mobile:List>
   </mobile:Form>
   <mobile:Form id="Form2" runat="server">
        <P>
                <B>You Selected a Road Bike!</B>
        </P>
   </mobile:Form>
   <mobile:Form id="Form3" runat="server">
        <P>
                <B>You Selected a Mountain Bike!</B>
        </P>
   </mobile:Form>
```

In this code, we use the <mobile:List> tag to present a few options to our users. By specifying the action of the OnItemCommand event, we can determine what mobile form we want to display. In this case, we are calling the function "SelectBike". The following code shows the code for VB.NET and C#, respectively.

VB.NET:

```
[list.aspx.vb]
Public Sub SelectBike(ByVal sender As Object, ByVal e As
ListCommandEventArgs)

        If e.ListItem.Value = "Road" Then
```

```
            ActiveForm = Form2
        Else
            ActiveForm = Form3
        End If

    End Sub
```

C#:

```
[list.aspx.cs]
        protected void SelectBike( object sender,
ListCommandEventArgs e)
        {
            if ( e.ListItem.Value=="Road")
            {
                ActiveForm = Form2;
            }
            else
            {
                ActiveForm = Form3;
            }
        }
```

In this code, we take advantage of the ListCommandEventArgs parameter, e. Based upon the value of the ListItem, we check to see if a "Road" bike or a "Mountain" bike was selected. If a "Road" bike was selected, we take advantage of setting the ActiveForm to Form2. If the "Mountain" bike was selected, we set the ActiveForm to Form3. Figure 18-11 displays the output of our list.

Figure 18-11: A simple list

Note By default, when a mobile page is first rendered, the first form is made Active. This can be overridden programmatically by setting the ActiveForm property to a different Form control, as seen in the preceding code.

Decorated lists

Lists are much more functional than just displaying data. When the device permits it, list items can be undecorated, or decorated with bullets or numbers. The following code shows how to set the `Decoration` property to `"Bulleted"` to produce a bulleted list:

```
[listdecoration.aspx]
   <mobile:Form id="Form1" runat="server">
         <mobile:Label id="Label1" runat="server">Select a Bike
Style</mobile:Label>
         <BR>
         <mobile:List id="List1" runat="server"
OnItemCommand="SelectBike" Decoration="Bulleted">
               <Item Text="Road Bike" Value="Road"></Item>
               <Item Text="Mountain Bike"
Value="Mountain"></Item>
         </mobile:List>
   </mobile:Form>
```

If we wanted a numbered list, we would have set `Decoration=" Numbered"`. Figure 18-12 shows the results.

Figure 18-12: A bulleted mobile list

ListDataBinding

Like any ASP.NET list, mobile lists also support data binding, which we will cover in the following example. To support data binding, our data source must either implement `IEnumerable` or `IListSource`. In the following example, we use an arraylist to build our data source. We could have just as easily used a datareader or datatable as our data source. The following shows the code required to build our arraylist and bind to our mobile list in VB.NET and C#, respectively.

VB.NET:

```
[listdatabinding.aspx.vb]
Private Sub Page_Load(ByVal sender As System.Object, ByVal e As
System.EventArgs) Handles MyBase.Load

        If (Not Page.IsPostBack) Then
            Dim al As New ArrayList()
            al.Add("Road Bike")
            al.Add("Mountain Bike")
            List1.DataSource = al
            List1.DataBind()
        End If
End Sub
```

C#:

```
[listdatabinding.aspx.cs]
private void Page_Load(object sender, System.EventArgs e)
{
   if (! Page.IsPostBack)  //build datalist
   {
        ArrayList al = new ArrayList();
        al.Add( "Road Bike" );
        al.Add( "Mountain Bike" );
        List1.DataSource=al;
        List1.DataBind();
   }
}
```

First, we check to see if the page has *not* been posted back to the server. In VB.NET, we actually use the word "Not" as the operator. In C#, we use the "!" as the not operator. If the page has not been posted back, then we build our arraylist. In this example, our arraylist will consist of two strings: `"Rode Bike"` and `"Mountain Bike"`. Once our arraylist is built, we use it as the list datasource. We set the list datasource by coding as follows: `List1.DataSource=al`. After we set our data-source, we bind it to the mobile list, by calling `List1.DataBind()`.

Pagination

Often times, we want to send more text to the client or device than what can fit on a single screen. After all, most cell phones are only around 15 characters wide and have 4 to 6 lines for text. Some devices have more room for display, some have less. So, how much text should you show at a time and for what device? Fortunately for us, MIT takes care of this by the way of pagination.

Pagination automatically formats the text to fit the device. By default, pagination is not turned on, or set to true. To turn pagination on, you set the `Paginate` property of the <mobile:form> control to true, as in the following example:

```
<mobile:form id=form1 Paginate="true">.
```

In the following example, we are going to link to two separate forms and display a couple of screens of text. We don't have to worry about where to end one screen and start with the next because pagination will take care of that for us. The following code shows an example of this:

```
[pagination.aspx]
<mobile:Form id="Form1" runat="server">
        <mobile:Label id="Label1" runat="server">Select a Bike
Style</mobile:Label>
        <BR>
        <mobile:List id="List1" runat="server"
OnItemCommand="SelectBike">
                <Item Text="Road Bike" Value="Road"></Item>
                <Item Text="Mountain Bike"
Value="Mountain"></Item>
        </mobile:List>
   </mobile:Form>
   <mobile:Form id="Form2" runat="server" Paginate="True">
        <mobile:TextView>
                <b>Road Biking</b>
                <br>
                Road biking is a challenging sport. There riding
on a group ride
                can bring your level of riding up a notch.
Especially when riding with experienced riders.
                If you want to increase your speed there are a
number of techniques to choose from, including,
                aero bars, drafting, intervals, and sprints.
During the winter months it is important to build a good
                base for the upcoming summer races.  Contact
your local bike shop for classes on spinning during the
                off season and group rides during the summer.
   </mobile:TextView>
   </mobile:Form>
   <mobile:Form id="Form3" runat="server" Paginate="True">
        <mobile:TextView>
        <b>Mountain Biking</b>
        <br>
        Mountain biking is technically challenging.
        Although it does not usually offer the speed that road
        biking does, it offers its own set of challenges.
        When first mountain biking, it's best to find an easy
trail and to
        follow someone that is more experienced than you.
        As you are trail riding, be careful to watch out for
rocks, dirt, roots,
        and tree branches. Any of these items can
        be an obstacle in your path and cause bodily injury.
   </mobile:TextView>
   </mobile:Form>
```

In the preceding code, we are presenting our users with our standard form to select either Road Biking or Mountain Biking. When the user makes their selection, the SelectBike function will determine which form to show next. In Figures 18-13, 18-14, and 18-15, we demonstrate this by first selecting "Road Bike" and then viewing our first page of text and then clicking to our next page of text. Pagination occurs automatically because we set Paginate="True" in our <mobile:form> tags.

Figure 18-13: Selecting road bike

Figure 18-14: Viewing your first page of text

Figure 18-15: Viewing your next
page of text

Making phone calls

Because most mobile devices are cell phones, this chapter would not be complete
without discussing how to make phone calls from your mobile application. MIT handles this easily, by making the control <mobile:PhoneCall> available to us.

The <mobile:PhoneCall> tag is an easy-to-use tag that presents the user with an
option to place a call. If the device does not support phone calls, such as a Pocket

PC, then the user can be provided with an optional link. The following code shows how to create a mobile form to make a phone call:

```
[phonecall.aspx]
<mobile:Form id="Form1" runat="server">
        <mobile:PhoneCall PhoneNumber="636-555-1213"
AlternateUrl="details.aspx?id=0"
AlternateFormat="{0}">Home</mobile:PhoneCall>
        <br>
        <mobile:PhoneCall PhoneNumber="619-555-1214"
AlternateUrl="details.aspx?id=1" AlternateFormat="{0}">Kirk
Physh</mobile:PhoneCall>
        <br>
        <mobile:PhoneCall PhoneNumber="812-555-1215"
AlternateUrl="details.aspx?id=2" AlternateFormat="{0}">Lee
Sifu</mobile:PhoneCall>
        <br>
        <mobile:PhoneCall PhoneNumber="812-555-1216"
AlternateUrl="details.aspx?id=3" AlternateFormat="{0}">Shellie
Sommers</mobile:PhoneCall>
   </mobile:Form>
```

In the preceding code, we are taking advantage various attributes of the `<mobile:PhoneCall>` tag:

✦ `PhoneNumber` is the phone number we want the cell phone to dial when the user picks that selection.

✦ `AlternateUrl` is the link that devices that are not phone call–enabled present to the user.

✦ `AlternateFormat` is the way the string will be displayed to the user, when using a device that is not phone call-enabled.

Collecting User Data

Up until this point, we've mainly been reading about how to present data to users. We've covered links, lists, bulleted lists, pagination, and dealing with phone numbers. But what about when we want to collect information from users? The remainder of this chapter deals with various input controls, from selection lists, to textboxes, to passwords, to data validation.

Selection lists

A selection list is very similar to a regular mobile control list. However, selection lists have the additional functionality of being a radio button list, drop-down list, list box, or a multiple selection list box. All of this functionality is available to the user simply by setting the `SelectType` property of the `<mobile:SelectionList>` tag. The following shows how to use the SelectionList, when the `Type` property is set to MultiSelectListBox:

```
[listselect.aspx]
<mobile:Form id="Form1" runat="server">
        <mobile:Label id="Label1" runat="server">Select a Bike
Style</mobile:Label>
        <mobile:SelectionList id="SelectList1" Runat="server"
SelectType="MultiSelectListBox">
                <Item Text="Road Bike" Value="Road"></Item>
                <Item Text="Mountain Bike"
Value="Mountain"></Item>
        </mobile:SelectionList>
        <mobile:Command id="Command1" onclick="Command1_Click"
Runat="server">Go</mobile:Command>
   </mobile:Form>
   <mobile:Form id="Form2" runat="server">
        You Selected
<mobile:Label id="lblResults" Runat="server"></mobile:Label>
bike(s).
   </mobile:Form>
```

In this code, we are presenting the user with the option to select more than one bike. In this instance, we are using the MultiSelectListBox. Again, because MIT can detect what type of device is requesting the content, it will provide a different user experience. Figures 18-16 and 18-17 show how this page looks, both on the Pocket PC emulator and on the Openwave emulator.

Figure 18-16: Listselect.aspx
on the Pocket PC emulator

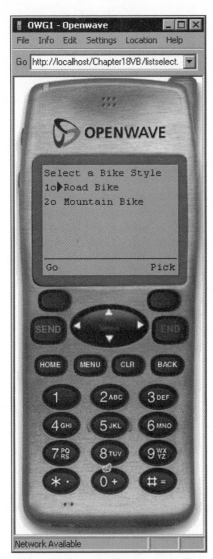

Figure 18-17: Listselect.aspx on the Openwave emulator

The code running behind these mobile forms is simple. We simply loop through each of the items in the SelectionList. If we find that an item was selected, we increment the counter for the number of items selected. The following shows this code in VB.NET and C#.

VB.NET:

```
[listselect.aspx.vb]
Public Sub Command1_Click(ByVal sender As System.Object, ByVal e As
System.EventArgs) Handles Command1.Click
        Dim count As Integer = 0
        Dim item As MobileListItem
        For Each item In SelectList1.Items
            If item.Selected Then
                count = count + 1
            End If
        Next
        lblResults.Text = count.ToString()
        ActiveForm = Form2
    End Sub
```

C#:

```
[listselect.aspx.cs]
    protected void Command1_Click(object sender, System.EventArgs e)
    {
            int count =0;
            foreach( MobileListItem item in SelectList1.Items)
            {
                    if ( item.Selected)
                    {
                            count++;
                    }
            }
            lblResults.Text = count.ToString();
            ActiveForm = Form2;
    }
```

Mobile TextBoxes

Entering text on a cell phone is one of the hardest challenges you may encounter. When building user interfaces for mobile devices, you have to remember that the user doesn't always have a full keyboard to use. Not only that, but the user may not even have keys available for certain symbols. For example, entering a ^ or a ~ isn't always available, and when it is, you may have to go through a cryptic set of keys to find these characters. The bottom line is that, if possible, you should always use or present lists as an option to the user, and only ask for typed input when needed. When you do need the user to actually enter text (for example, a name, address, credit card, or pin number), the <mobile:TextBox> handles this easily.

In the following code, we have an example to ask the user for their name. Once the user enters their name, they click the <mobile:Command> object. We take their name and write it out to Form2.

```
[textbox.aspx]
   <mobile:Form id="Form1" runat="server">
         <B>Enter Your Name:</B>
         <mobile:TextBox id="txtName"
Runat="server"></mobile:TextBox>
         <mobile:Command id="cmdGo"
Runat="server">Go</mobile:Command>
   </mobile:Form>
   <mobile:Form ID="Form2" Runat="server">
   Hi
<mobile:Label id="lblName" Runat="server"></mobile:Label>
   How are you doing today?
   </mobile:Form>
```

The following code shows how to do this in VB.NET and C#, respectively. Figures 18-18 and 18-19 show our results in the cell phone and PocketPC, respectively.

VB.NET:

```
[textbox.aspx.vb]
Private Sub cmdGo_Click(ByVal sender As System.Object, ByVal e
As System.EventArgs) Handles cmdGo.Click
      lblName.Text = txtName.Text & ","
      ActiveForm = Form2
   End Sub
```

C#:

```
[textbox.aspx.cs]
private void cmdGo_Click(object sender, System.EventArgs e)
      {
            lblName.Text = txtName.Text + ",";
            ActiveForm = Form2;
      }
```

Figure 18-18: A TextBox on a cell phone

Figure 18-19: A TextBox on a Pocket PC

Using passwords or numbers

In some instances, we need to allow the user to enter a pin number or a password. MIT understands that, more often than usual, you may only want the user to enter numbers, and that any passwords must be masked. Setting the `Password` property of the `<mobile:TextBox>` tag to true will mask the input, while setting the `Numeric` property to true will allow only numbers to be entered. We need to specify which property, in this case the password and numeric properties, we are talking about.

Note The `Numeric` property only works on devices that support a numeric mode. Cell phones will automatically place the keypad in numeric mode when they recognize the numeric properties. Browsers, however, do not.

The following displays our code to set a TextBox to password mode:

```
[password.aspx]
   <mobile:Form id="Form1" runat="server">
        <B>Enter Your Password or Pin Number:</B>
        <mobile:TextBox id="txtPassword" Password="True"
Runat="server"></mobile:TextBox>
        <mobile:Command id="cmdGo"
Runat="server">Go</mobile:Command>
   </mobile:Form>
   <mobile:Form ID="Form2" Runat="server">
        <mobile:Label id="lblResult"
Runat="server"></mobile:Label>
   </mobile:Form>
```

Validating input

Some of the most powerful features of ASP.NET are the validation controls. MIT also has its own set of validation controls; however, these validation controls are much more limited, due in part to the limitations of the mobile devices we are sending content to. In fact, validation controls can only validate <mobile:TextBox> and <mobile: SelectionList> controls.

Validation controls themselves come in four different flavors:

✦ **RangeValidator:** Validates that another control's value falls within a certain range.

✦ **RegularExpressionValiator:** Validates another control's value against a regular expression.

✦ **RequiredFieldValidator:** Makes sure the user enters a value for a control.

✦ **ValidationSummary:** Displays a summary of all validation errors that occur on a form. When using the ValidationSummary control, usually a separate form is built to display all the errors.

In the following code, we require a user to enter their name in our textbox. We do this by setting the `ControlToValidate` property to `"txtName"`, which is the name of our TextBox. If the user doesn't enter a value, we obviously want to write out an error message. The error message we chose to show is "Please Enter Your Name" and is specified with the `ErrorMessage` property.

```
[validate.aspx]
  <mobile:Form id="Form1" runat="server">
        <B>Enter Your Name:</B>
        <mobile:TextBox id="txtName"
Runat="server"></mobile:TextBox>
        <mobile:Command id="cmdGo"
Runat="server">Go</mobile:Command>
        <mobile:RequiredFieldValidator
id="RequiredFieldValidator1" runat="server"
ErrorMessage="Please Enter Your Name" Display="Dynamic"
ControlToValidate="txtName"></mobile:RequiredFieldValidator>
  </mobile:Form>
  <mobile:Form ID="Form2" Runat="server">
  Hi
<mobile:Label id="lblName" Runat="server"></mobile:Label>
  How are you doing today?
  </mobile:Form>
```

Summary

We've looked at various controls and aspects of designing mobile applications. We've looked at the simple labels and then moved on to simple lists. We've looked at decorating those by making the lists bulleted or numeric. We've also looked at other ways of presenting data to users, from pagination to selection lists. Finally, we've accepted data via the TextBox, and looked at ways of validating user input.

Developing applications for the mobile Web is a tedious process that requires a lot of forethought. We must take into account various limitations such as screen size, low bandwidth, low power, and, last but not least, the vast array of mobile devices that may be using our Web site. The Mobile Internet Toolkit (MIT) takes all of these considerations into account and provides a tool that works wonders. At the time of this writing, MIT supports over 50 different mobile devices, with many more being added. What would have taken us weeks to develop has been cut down to days or even hours.

✦   ✦   ✦

ASP.NET Security

The reasons to secure a Web site are well known and thus do not require a detailed discussion. A few of the reasons for securing a Web site include transfer of sensitive data over the Internet, exchange of sensitive data between Web applications, and risks of hack attacks.

Security is a critical issue for both Web application developers and administrators alike. It is undoubtedly one of the most confusing areas, and hence requires careful planning and designing. Web site developers and administrators must have a clear understanding of the various options, such as authentication, for securing their sites.

This chapter explores the different types of security implementations that can be used to secure an ASP.NET Web site. You'll also learn how the Microsoft .NET Framework assists in securing Web sites.

Introduction to ASP.NET Security

Security, in the context of an ASP.NET application, involves three fundamental operations. These operations are carried out during the lifetime of each secure ASP.NET Web application and are described as follows:

+ **Authentication:** This is the process of validating the identity of a user, to allow or deny a request. Typically, authentication is a process of accepting the username and password from a user, and validating the username/password combination in a security database. In addition to this typical case, the authentication process can be more sophisticated. After the identity is verified and validated, the user is considered to be legitimate, and the resource request is fulfilled. Future requests from the same user, ideally, are not subject to the authentication process, until the user logs out of the Web application.

✦ **Authorization:** This is the process of ensuring that users with valid identity are allowed to access only those resources for which they have been assigned access rights. In other words, authorization is a check that is performed at every stage of the request-processing cycle on the Web server. This check ensures that access is given only to the allowed resources.

✦ **Impersonation:** This process enables an application to assume the identity of the caller, and in turn make requests to the other resources. Access to resources will be granted or denied based on the identity that is being impersonated. If the identity being impersonated has permissions to a resource, the application that impersonates the identity will also have the access permission to that resource.

Before delving deeper into the security system that is available with ASP.NET, let us review the security system that is made available to the Web sites by the underlying Web server. For the ASP.NET applications, the underlying Web server is Microsoft Internet Information Services (IIS). Therefore, every ASP.NET Web application can continue to leverage the security options provided by the IIS server. Let us now look at the security provided by the IIS server.

IIS security

Securing a Web application involves different aspects. The best place to start securing a Web application is by looking at the security methods provided by the Web server that hosts the Web application. The IIS server has built-in support for authentication and authorization of user requests.

Authentication

The IIS server has built-in support for authenticating clients who request the Web content stored in an IIS Web site. Three different types of authentication can be implemented by using the IIS server:

✦ **Anonymous Authentication:** Allows all users to browse the Web site without prompting for a username and password. The access to the Web site resources is impersonated by the IIS server by using the IUSR_machinename account.

✦ **Basic Authentication:** Requires the users to enter a username/password combination for accessing the Web site. The major downside to this method of authentication is that the password is sent over the network in an unencrypted form, making it possible for unauthorized users to snoop the network packets and retrieve the password information easily.

✦ **Integrated Windows Authentication:** Requires the users to be valid Windows users in addition to fulfilling the basic authentication. In this mode, IIS will verify the username and password with a Windows Domain Controller. The access to the Web site is allowed only if the domain controller validates the username and password.

✦ **Digest Authentication:** Is similar to the basic authentication. However, this authentication uses a different way of transmitting the authentication credentials. This authentication sends a hash value over the network rather than the password. The hash value cannot be decrypted and hence the original text cannot be deciphered.

Authorization

The IIS server can be configured to control the resources that can be accessed by users. You can control the access permissions on an IIS Web site by marking the allowed operations on the Web site. The different permission levels include the following:

✦ **Read:** Allows users to retrieve and read the content stored in the virtual directory. This permission is assigned to most virtual directories.

✦ **Write:** Allows users to retrieve and modify the content stored in the virtual directory. If a Web site is open to receiving content over the HTTP protocol, the virtual directory used to store the received files must have the write permission. A typical example of this would be a virtual directory that stores the files that are uploaded as attachments to e-mail messages.

✦ **Script source access:** Allows users to view the source code of any server-side program.

✦ **Directory browsing:** Allows users to view the contents of the entire virtual directory. This is similar to viewing an FTP folder.

✦ **Log visits:** Keeps track of the number of users who visit the site, and records information about various details, such as the IP address of the client and the resources that are requested for.

✦ **Index:** Uses Microsoft Index Server to index the virtual directory. The contents of the directory can be retrieved in a search result using the Index Server.

In addition to the IIS permission levels, NTFS permissions can also be used to secure the files and directories on a Web server. The following are the different access permissions that can be assigned to users and groups for the files and directories on the server:

✦ **Full Control:** Allows users to have complete control on files and/or directories.

✦ **Modify:** Allows users to modify the contents of files and/or directories. However, users will not be able to delete files and/or directories.

✦ **Read & Execute:** Allows users to read the contents of the existing files and/or directories and execute any application stored in that folder. However, users will not be able to modify the contents of the files and/or directories.

✦ **List Folder Contents:** Allows users to view the contents of the folder. However, users will neither be able to read the contents of any file in the folder nor modify any contents.

✦ **Write:** Allows users to make changes to files and/or directories.

✦ **No Access:** Does not allow any access to files and/or directories.

Authentication in Web applications

Various ways exist to authenticate user access to Web applications. In intranet applications, it is possible to use Integrated Windows Authentication to authenticate user access and implement access control. But, in most of the Internet applications, it is not possible to use Windows authentication as it puts various restrictions. The following are two of these restrictions:

✦ **Number of user accounts:** Although Windows Active Directory can scale up to a large number of user accounts, managing all the user accounts for Internet applications (that involve millions of user accounts) can be a big management challenge, if not a nightmare. Therefore, most Web administrators and developers prefer an authentication mechanism that is based on databases, such as SQL databases.

✦ **Licensing issues:** If millions of users were to be authenticated against an Active Directory database, the Web site would need to procure user licenses for all the users. Thus, to say the least, it can prove to be an expensive proposition.

In classic ASP, authentication issues were addressed by security implementations that relied on cookies or client IP. This approach, typically, meant writing a lot of code and proved to be an unnecessary overhead for developers. The approach is very different from implementing security in Windows applications. In Windows, applications are developed in a way that maximizes the leverage on the services provided by the operating system. With ASP.NET, however, the days of writing tedious user validation code are gone. Developers can rely on the underlying Microsoft .NET Framework to provide security. They just need to focus on solving business problems and implementing the functionality in the Web site. Let us now explore the various authentication models that are supported by ASP.NET.

ASP.NET authentication options

The security section of the Web.config file contains the information related to the level and type of authentication services that would be provided for a Web application. The Web.config file is an XML file and is located in the root directory of a Web application. Various configuration options for an ASP.NET Web application can be controlled and configured from this XML file.

For more information on the security section of the Web.config file, refer to Chapter 14.

The system.web section of the Web.config file is used to control the various aspects of security that are provided to the Web application. An ASP.NET Web application can be provided with one of the following types of security:

✦ **Windows:** The application is secured by using Integrated Windows Authentication. In this method, access to a Web application is allowed only to those users who are able to verify their Windows credentials. Credentials can be verified against the Windows authentication database (SAM) or against Active Directory.

✦ **Passport:** The application is secured by using Microsoft Passport authentication. Passport is a single-sign-on technology developed by Microsoft for use on the Web. For more information on using Microsoft Passport, visit http://www.passport.com/business/.

✦ **Forms:** The application is secured by using a custom authentication model with cookie support.

✦ **None:** The application is not secured; access to the application does not require authentication.

The system.web section has an `<authentication>` element that is used to specify the security settings. The following is the syntax of the `<authentication>` element:

```
<authentication mode="Windows|Forms|Passport|None">
    <forms name="name" loginUrl="url"
        protection="All|None|Encryption|Validation"
        timeout="30" path="/" >

        <credentials passwordFormat="Clear|SHA1|MD5">
            <user name="username" password="password" />
        </credentials>

    </forms>
    <passport redirectUrl="internal"/>
</authentication>
```

The various attributes of the `<authentication>` element are described as follows:

✦ **Mode:** Indicates the authentication mode to be used for the ASP.NET Web application.

✦ **Forms:** Indicates the Forms-based authentication that is used. The different suboptions that are used include the following:

  • **Name:** Specifies the name of the cookie that will be issued when a user is authenticated. This is the cookie that the ASP.NET application will check before processing requests from the client. If this cookie is found and is determined to be valid, ASP.NET will process the client request.

  • **LoginURL:** Specifies the URL of the Web page to which a client will be redirected if the client is not authenticated.

  • **Protection:** Specifies the level of protection that is applied to the cookie. The default value is All, which causes the cookie to be encrypted by using the 3DES algorithm. It also validates the cookie contents to ensure that the cookie is not tampered with. The other options include None,

Encryption, and Validation. The None option specifies that the cookie is not encrypted or validated. This is as good as a nonsecure cookie access. Therefore, use this value only if the Web site has very low security requirements. The Encryption option specifies that the cookie contents are encrypted by using the 3DES algorithm, but contents of the cookie are not validated. Therefore, the contents of the cookie can be altered by someone during transmission. The Validation option specifies that the cookie is not encrypted. However, the cookie contents are validated to ensure that the cookie cannot be altered during data transmission.

- **Timeout:** Indicates the time after which the cookie will expire. If the site is visited before the timeout, the timeout value is refreshed. This is called *sliding expiration*. For example, if the timeout is 30 minutes and the user requests another document from the Web site after 10 minutes of inactivity, the timeout will occur if the user remains inactive for another 30 minutes.

- **Path:** Sets a path for the cookie. The path allows a Web page to share cookie information with other pages within the same domain. If the path is set to /mywebapp, all pages in /mywebapp and all pages in subfolders of /mywebapp can access the cookie.

✦ **Credentials:** Allows the application to specify the username and password combinations that are valid.

- **PasswordFormat:** Specifies the encryption format that is used for storing passwords. The available options include Clear, MD5, and SHA1. The Clear option indicates that no encryption is used. The MD5 option indicates that the MD5 algorithm is used. The SHA1 option indicates that the SHA1 algorithm is used.

✦ **User:** Defines the username and password combinations that are valid.

- **Name:** Defines the username.

- **Password:** Defines the password of the user.

✦ **Passport:** Specifies the configuration information if the authentication mode is set to Passport.

- **RedirectURL:** Specifies the URL to which the client will be redirected when a page requires Passport authentication, but the user has not logged on with a Passport.

Forms-based Authentication

ASP.NET includes a built-in feature, called forms-based authentication, which can be used to implement customized logic for authenticating users and authentication handlers without having to worry about session management using cookies. In forms-based authentication, when a user is determined to be unauthenticated, the user is automatically redirected to the login page. Some of the benefits of the forms-based authentication are the following:

✦ Developers can configure forms-based authentication for various parts of the Web site differently, because the Web.config file is a hierarchical XML document.

✦ Administrators and developers can change the authentication scheme quickly and easily in the Web.config file.

✦ Administration is centralized because all the authentication entries are in one place — the Web.config file.

You can enable forms-based authentication for a Web application by setting the Authentication mode property to "Forms" in the Web.config file. The following is a sample code in the Web.config file used to enable forms-based authentication:

```
<configuration>
<system.web>

<authentication mode="Forms">

    <!-- Assign a cookie named B2CBuySiteAuthCookie when user is
authenticated. The page used for validating user credentials is
userauth.aspx. Make sure the cookie is encrypted and validated
by setting the protection to All, the cookie will timeout after
10 minutes -->

    <forms name=".B2CBuySiteAuthCookie"
loginUrl="userauth.aspx" protection="All" timeout="10" />

</authentication>

<authorization>

    <!-- anonymous users will be denied access. This is needed
to force forms-authentication -->

    <deny users="?"/>

</authorization>

</system.web>
</configuration>
```

In this code:

✦ The authentication mode is forms-based authentication.

✦ The Userauth.aspx file is the Web page that is used for authenticating user credentials.

✦ The cookie protection level is set to `All`. This value causes the ASP.NET runtime to not only encrypt the cookie contents, but also validate the cookie contents to ensure that the contents have not been modified on the network.

You can also add authorization support to sections of an ASP.NET Web application. To do so, you need to add the `<location>` element in the Web.config file. Consider the following sample code that uses the `<location>` element:

```
<!-- Require Authentication for Shopping Cart -->
<location path="Default.aspx">
   <system.web>
      <authorization>
         <deny users="?" />
         <allow users="Jack,Joe"/>
      </authorization>
   </system.web>
</location>
```

In this code, when an unauthenticated user attempts to access the Default.aspx page, ASP.NET will automatically redirect the request to the userauth.aspx page. After the user provides the valid credentials, the user is redirected to the Cart.aspx page.

The usernames specified can be certain specific usernames. In addition, you can use some special characters to represent usernames:

✦ *: Refers to all users

✦ ?: Refers to all unauthenticated, anonymous users

In the previous sample code, only Jack and Joe will be allowed to access the Default.aspx page, and no unauthenticated, anonymous user will be allowed to access the Default.aspx page.

After you add the necessary code in the Web.config file for the forms-based authentication, you need to set the security configuration of the IIS virtual directory to "Allow Anonymous Access".

Let us now implement the forms-based authentication for an ASP.NET Web application. Complete the following steps:

1. Set the Authentication mode to "Forms" in the Web.config file. This file should be present in the same directory as the ASP.NET Web application.

```
<configuration>
<system.web>

<authentication mode="Forms">
<!-- Assign a cookie named B2CBuySiteAuthCookie when user is
authenticated. The page used for validating user credentials
is userauth.aspx. Make sure the cookie is encrypted and
validated by setting the protection to All, the cookie will
timeout after 10 minutes -->
```

```
<forms name=".B2CBuySiteAuthCookie" loginUrl="userauth.aspx"
protection="All" timeout="10" />

</authentication>

<authorization>
<!-- anonymous users will be denied access. This is needed to
force forms-authentication -->

<deny users="?"/>

</authorization>

</system.web>
</configuration>
```

2. The next step is to create the login page that will accept and validate user credentials before assigning the client a session cookie. The login page will then redirect the user back to the page requested by the client. Write the following code in "Userauth.aspx" file:

```
<%@ Import Namespace="System.Web.Security " %>
<html>
<script language="VB" runat=server>
' Verify credentials
Sub Login_Click(Src As Object, E As EventArgs)
' Do complex hashing and look up other data sources to
' determine validity ;)

If UserName.Value = "john" And UserPass.Value = "secret"

'Credentials are ok, redirect back to the page that forced
'authentication, pass the user name and don't persist the
cookie
FormsAuthentication.RedirectFromLoginPage(UserName.Value,Fals
e)

Else

Msg.Text = "Invalid user name or password: Please try again"

End If
End Sub
</script>

<body>
<form runat=server>
<h3><font face="Verdana">Please Sign-In</font></h3>
<table>
<tr>
<td>Login Name:</td>
<td><input id="UserName" type="text" runat=server/></td>
</tr>
```

```
<tr>
<td>Password:</td>
<td><input id="UserPass" type=password runat=server/></td>
</tr>
</table>
<asp:button text="Login" OnClick="Login_Click" runat=server/>
<asp:Label id="Msg" ForeColor="red" Font-Name="Verdana" Font-
Size="10" runat=server />
</form>
</body>
</html>
```

3. Finally, create the Default.aspx file with the following code:

```
<%@ Import Namespace="System.Web.Security " %>

<html>
<script language="VB" runat=server>
Sub Page_Load(Src As Object, E As EventArgs)

'Use the User object to retrieve information about the
current 'user
Welcome.Text = "Hello, " + User.Identity.Name

End Sub

Sub Signout_Click(Src As Object, E As EventArgs)
' logout from the web application and display login screen

FormsAuthentication.SignOut()
Response.Redirect("userauth.aspx")

End Sub
</script>

<body>
<h3><font face="Verdana">Using Forms
Authentication</font></h3>
<form runat=server>
<h3><asp:label id="Welcome" runat=server/></h3>
<asp:button text="Signout" OnClick="Signout_Click"
runat=server/>
</form>
</body>
</html>
```

Figure 19-1 and Figure 19-2 show the output of the preceding code. When a user requests the Default.aspx page, the ASP.NET run time checks for the presence of the specified cookie. If the cookie is not found, the user is prompted to sign on the form represented by the Userauth.aspx page. Once the user credentials are verified, ASP.NET makes the Default.aspx page accessible to the user by redirecting the browser to the Default.aspx page.

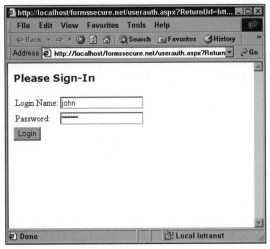

Figure 19-1: The Userauth.aspx page

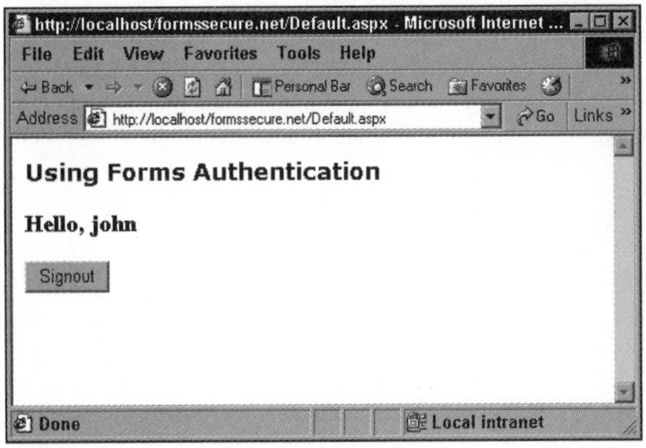

Figure 19-2: The Default.aspx page

Integrating Security Methods

In certain cases, Web applications might need to be integrated with the security provided by Windows. One such case would be an intranet Web application that provides different levels of access to users depending on the Windows credentials. In this case, the Web applications can be secured by using Windows authentication.

Configuring Windows authentication for a Web application is quite simple. To do so, the Authentication mode must be set to "Windows" in the Web.config file. Consider the following sample code:

```
<configuration>
  <system.web>
```

```
        <authentication mode="Windows" />
      </system.web>
    </configuration>
```

In addition to this setting, you also need to set Integrated authentication in the virtual directory by using the IIS administration tool for Integrated Windows Authentication to work properly. To enable Integrated Windows Authentication for a Web application, complete the following steps:

1. Start the IIS administration tool and open the Properties dialog box for the Web application.

2. Select the Directory Security tab and click the Edit button to view or change the authentication methods. The Authentication Methods dialog box displays, as shown in Figure 19-3.

3. Check the Integrated Windows Authentication check box to enable Integrated Windows Authentication.

Figure 19-3: Setting Integrated Windows Authentication for a virtual directory in IIS

You will now modify the earlier example to implement Integrated Windows Authentication.

1. Modify the code in the Web.config file to set the Authentication mode property to "Windows" as follows:

```
<configuration>
<system.web>
<authentication mode="Windows"/>
<authorization>
<!-- anonymous users will be denied access -->
<deny users="?"/>
</authorization>
</system.web>
</configuration>
```

2. Modify the page that would determine the identity of the user. In this case, modify the Default.aspx page:

```
<%@ Import Namespace="System.Web.Security " %>

<html>
<script language="VB" runat=server>
Sub Page_Load(Src As Object, E As EventArgs)

'Use the User object to retrieve info about the current user
Welcome.Text = "Hello, " + User.Identity.Name

End Sub
</script>

<body>
<h3><font face="Verdana">Using Integrated Windows
Authentication</font></h3>
<form runat=server>
<h3><asp:label id="Welcome" runat=server/></h3>
</form>
</body>

</html>
```

Figure 19-4 shows the output of this code.

Figure 19-4: The Default.aspx page using Integrated Windows Authentication

Role-based Security

The Microsoft .NET Framework security design provides support for authorization and also role-based security. As mentioned earlier, ASP.NET stores information about the current user in the User object. The User object is available in the context of the HTTP request that is received by the ASP.NET Web application. The information in this User object can be readily used for authorization decisions based on either the user identity or role membership.

A *role* is a named set of users that have the same privileges with respect to security. For example, sales agent and sales manager are two different roles. Each role has the same security privileges. A user can be a member of one or more roles. Applications can readily use role membership to determine whether or not a user is authorized to perform a requested action. Roles are like groups in the sense that multiple users can belong to a role and a user can also belong to multiple roles. Although roles are logically equivalent to security groups, there is a major difference. Roles are always specific to an application, whereas typically groups are not specific to any application—they are defined at the operating system level.

Roles are often used in Web applications to enforce security authorization policy. For example, an online banking application may impose a limit of $100,000, which cannot be exceeded by a teller in a single debit or credit transaction—only a manager can conduct this transaction. In such a situation, you can configure the application to allow the tellers to process transactions that are less than $100,000 and managers to process transactions that exceed $100,000.

Microsoft, first, introduced support for defining application roles in Microsoft Transaction Server and extended this further with the release of COM+ 1.0 in Windows 2000. With the launch of the Microsoft .NET Framework, the support for role-based security has been extended further. The .NET Framework provides role-based security support that is flexible and extensible enough to meet the needs of a wide spectrum of applications. Role-based security is particularly well suited for use in ASP.NET Web applications, which are processed primarily on a server.

The .NET implementation of role-based security is similar to the COM+ 1.0 implementation. However, there are certain differences. Table 19-1 describes some of the differences.

Table 19-1
Role-based security in COM+ 1.0 vs. role-based security in .NET Framework

COM+ 1.0	.NET Framework
Only configured applications can use role-based security; COM+ will not maintain role information for nonconfigured applications.	The run time attaches an IPrincipal object to the call context, which is always available to the current thread. The IPrincipal object contains a reference to an identity object as well as the roles to which the identity belongs. This information can be readily used inside application code to determine authorization.
Role membership is mapped to Windows user accounts; only valid Windows users can be added into application roles.	Users don't necessarily need to be associated with Windows user accounts. If a need exists, applications can use Windows user accounts. However, applications can also define custom user lists and credentials.
Relies on Windows accounts/security to identify users.	Does not rely on Windows accounts/security to identify users.
Roles are managed for each application.	Application-specific roles can be defined. The run time provides support to enable administrators to create and manage the mapping of Windows user accounts to application roles.

Let us now implement the role-based security in the teller/manager transaction limit example discussed earlier. This example allows all the users with the role "Tellers" to access the Web site. The Web.config file allows all members of the Tellers role to access the Web site. The Tellers role is a group created in the Windows Active Directory. This simplifies administration greatly because the authorization of Web users is done against the Active Directory. Also, in the Web.config, we are blocking all the anonymous users from accessing the Web site.

Modify the Web.config file as follows:

```
<configuration>
<system.web>
<authentication mode="Windows"/>
<authorization>
<!-- Tellers & anonymous users will be denied access -->
    <allow roles="Tellers"/>
    <deny users="?"/>
</authorization>
  </system.web>
</configuration>
```

Modify the Default.aspx file as follows:

```
<%@ Import Namespace="System.Web.Security " %>

<html>
  <script language="VB" runat=server>
    Sub Page_Load(Src As Object, E As EventArgs)
    'Use the User object to retrieve information about the
current user
    Welcome.Text = "Hello, " + User.Identity.Name
    End Sub
  </script>

  <body>
    <h3><font face="Verdana">Using Integrated Windows
Authentication</font></h3>
    <form runat=server>
      <h3><asp:label id="Welcome" runat=server/></h3>
    </form>
  </body>

</html>
```

Figure 19-5 shows the output of this code.

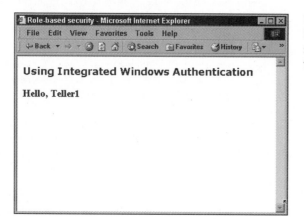

Figure 19-5: Output after implementing role-based security (Teller1 is part of the Tellers role)

Summary

In this chapter, you learned about the various aspects of security in ASP.NET applications. You learned about authentication services provided by ASP.NET and the various authentication mechanisms. Then, you learned how to enable forms-based authentication and integrated Windows-based authentication for ASP.NET Web applications. Finally, you learned how to implement role-based security in ASP.NET applications.

✦   ✦   ✦

Localizing ASP.NET Applications

People all over the world speak different languages and follow different conventions and cultures. There are cases wherein people in different regions speak the same language, but the conventions and cultures vary according to the regions. For example, people in France, Canada, and Belgium speak French, but currencies differ in these regions. Also, there are cases wherein people living in the same region speak multiple languages. Therefore, a region or a language solely does not identify a locale. A *locale* is a combination of a language and region. For example, English/US is a locale that indicates the culture specific to the English language spoken in United States. In Belgium, three languages — French, Dutch, and German are spoken. Therefore, there are three locales, French/Belgium, Dutch/Belgium, and German/Belgium associated with the region, Belgium.

When speaking in terms of applications, a locale refers to the user preferences, such as the user interface language, fonts, date/time format, and language rules for checking spelling and grammar. These different locales must be taken care of when developing applications for the international audience. Consider an application that has been developed for the English audience. Later, you realize that the German audience also requires the same application. Because the application was not developed with different locales in mind, you need to modify the application and recompile it for the German audience. This is not cost effective and might lead to inconsistencies in the two versions of the application. To solve this problem, ASP.NET provides a functional model for the development process of international applications, wherein you can create applications that can incorporate any locale required.

This chapter introduces you to localization. You'll learn how to set cultures and regions for specific locales, and use resource files.

Introduction to Localization

ASP.NET enables you to create applications that are international-ready. These applications can be used in any locale without being modified and recompiled. The process of creating international applications is called *internationalization*. When you create international applications, you should consider the following factors:

✦ The language to be used to design the user interface

✦ The locale-specific settings, such as currency formats, date/time formats, and number formats

Internationalization is further divided into three subparts: globalization, localizability, and localization. The process of designing and implementing applications that include generic coding and design considerations so that they can adapt themselves according to the locale they are used in is called *globalization*.

Localizability is an intermediate phase between globalization and localization. Localizability is a quality-assurance phase, which verifies that a globalized application is ready for localization by separating the resources (that require localization) from the rest of the application. Proper localizability results in a source code that you will not need to modify during localization.

After globalization, the process of working with resources, such as string and image representations for specific locales, is called *localization*. Localization consists primarily of translating the user interface.

Conceptually, a globalized application can be divided into two parts, a data block, and a code block. The *data block* part consists of all user interface resources and is locale-dependent. On the other hand, the *code block* part consists of the application code that can work with the data blocks irrespective of locales. Thus, localization involves working with the data blocks for specific locales.

Data can be represented in a number of ways identified as character sets. For localization, you should have a basic understanding of the different character sets.

Character sets

A *character set* is a set of characters grouped together from different languages. Each character that you input from your keyboard has a code associated with it called a *character code*. A character code is a unique number that is stored by a computer when you input the character. Thus, a character code is an internal representation of a character in a specific language. Internal tables called *code pages,* which can include numbers, punctuation marks, and other glyphs, are maintained that are used by operating systems to map keys on keyboards to the characters to be displayed. Some of the different character sets are described as follows:

✦ **American National Standards Institute (ANSI):** Consists of 256 characters and punctuation codes. Each character is represented as a single byte. This set is sufficient for English applications. However, for most other languages, the ANSI character set is not adequate.

✦ **Double Byte Character Set (DBCS):** A combination of the standard ASCII character set and alphabets from East Asian languages. An ASCII character is represented as a single byte whereas East Asian characters are represented as 2 bytes.

✦ **Unicode:** Includes characters from almost all major languages that are spoken today. Therefore, multiple code pages are not required to map characters from different languages. Unicode thus provides a single universal code page that includes characters from almost all languages. Unicode enables you to easily transfer data between different locales. In Unicode, each character is represented as 2 bytes. However, two basic problems are associated with Unicode. First, Unicode increases the file size because it has a large character set. Second, most systems do not support Unicode, which results in problems when Unicode characters are identified on a network. To address these problems, Unicode Transformation Formats (UTFs) can be used. UTFs use a technique wherein the Unicode characters are encoded as byte values so that they can be understood by systems that do not support Unicode. The most commonly used UTF is UTF-8, which encodes Unicode characters to single-byte characters.

Configuration settings

ASP.NET provides configuration settings that enable you to access locale-specific properties for the entire application. These settings are included in the `<globalization>` section of the Web.config configuration file of each ASP.NET application. The following code shows the configuration settings included in the `<globalization>` section:

```
<globalization
  requestEncoding="any valid encoding string"
  responseEncoding="any valid encoding string"
  fileEncoding="any valid encoding string"
  culture="any valid culture string"
  uiCulture="any valid culture string"
/>
```

In the `<globalization>` section:

✦ `requestEncoding` represents the way the request data is encoded.

✦ `responseEncoding` represents the way the response data is encoded.

Note The default request encoding and response encoding is specified in the `<globalization>` tag included in the Machine.config file, which is created when the .NET Framework is installed. For English-language systems, the default is iso-8859-1. If request encoding or response encoding is not specified in the Machine.config or Web.config file, the encoding defaults to the computer's Regional Options locale setting.

✦ `fileEncoding` represents the way the ASPX, ASMX, and ASAX files are encoded.

✦ `culture` represents the default culture used to process the Web requests.

✦ `uiCulture` represents the default culture used to search for resources.

Cross-Reference For more information on configuration settings, refer to Chapter 14.

You can specify the configuration settings in the `<globalization>` section in the Web.config file to control the globalization settings for the entire application. This makes it easy to develop and administer Web applications. However, you can specify the configuration settings at the page level also to set the configuration settings for a specific page. For example, the following `Page` directive specifies `responseEncoding` for the page:

```
<%@Page ... responseEncoding="UTF-8"%>
```

The page-level settings override the settings specified in the Web.config file. Most of the time, it is beneficial to use this page-level setting even if the same settings have been specified in the `<globalization>` section, because if the ASPX file is moved to a server that does not use the same settings as your application, the page-level settings will ensure that the correct encoding is done.

Setting Culture and Region

In addition to the configuration settings, you can use the classes provided by the .NET Framework to create international applications. These classes are contained in the System.Globalization namespace. In addition to these classes, you can use the Thread class of the System.Threading namespace to control the locale-specific settings for each executing instance of an application. The *Thread* class represents the threads that execute within the runtime. Let us now look at the System.Globalization namespace in detail.

System.Globalization namespace

The System.Globalization namespace contains classes that enable your applications to determine the locale at run time. This gives you the flexibility of creating applications that can automatically adapt themselves to the locale in which they run. The classes of the System.Globalization namespace define culture-related information, such as the language, the country/region, the calendars in use, the format patterns for dates, currency, and numbers, and the sort order for strings. The following sections describe the CultureInfo and RegionInfo classes of this namespace.

CultureInfo class

The *CultureInfo* class represents the information that is specific to the user language, country, region, and culture. The name of the culture follows the `<languagecode2>-<country/regioncode2>` format. The `languagecode2` represents a lowercase two-letter code for the language, whereas `country/regioncode2` represents an uppercase two-letter code for the country or region. For example, if the name of the language is English and the country/region in which the language English is spoken is United States, the name of the culture is en-US. A culture associated with a language and not with a country or region is called a *neutral culture*. On the other hand, a culture associated with both the language and the country or region is called a *specific culture*. For example, en is a neutral culture, whereas en-US is a specific culture.

Note In addition to the culture-specific culture names, such as en-US, an invariant culture exists, represented by iv. An *invariant* culture is culture-insensitive and returns results that are independent of a specific culture. An invariant culture is associated with the English language but not with any country/region. It can be used in almost any method in the Globalization namespace that requires a culture, except for sorting.

Some culture names have prefixes to specify the scripts for the cultures. For example, the prefix "Cy-" represents the "Cyrillic" script, and the prefix "Lt-" represents the "Latin" script. Therefore, the culture name "Cy-sr-SP" represents "Serbian (Cyrillic)-Serbia," and the culture name "Lt-sr-SP" represents "Serbian (Latin)-Serbia." Similarly, some cultures have suffixes to specify the sort order. For example, the suffix "-In" represents the International sort, and the suffix "-Ts" represents the Traditional sort. Table 20-1 lists some of the specific cultures.

Table 20-1	
Some specific culture names	
Culture Name	**Description**
ar-AE	Arabic-U.A.E
ar-EG	Arabic-Egypt
ar-KW	Arabic-Kuwait
bg-BG	Bulgarian-Bulgaria
cs-CZ	Czech-Czech Republic
de-DE	German-Germany
el-GR	Greek-Greece

Continued

Table 20-1 *(continued)*

Culture Name	Description
en-US	English-United States
en-NZ	English-New Zealand
es-ES	Spanish-Spain
fa-IR	Farsi-Iran
fr-FR	French-France
fr-BE	French-Belgium
hi-IN	Hindi-India
hu-HU	Hungarian-Hungary
id-ID	Indonesian-Indonesia
ja-JP	Japanese-Japan
ru-RU	Russian-Russia
sa-IN	Sanskrit-India
th-TH	Thai-Thailand
ur-PK	Urdu-Islamic Republic of Pakistan
zh-CHT or zh-CHS	Chinese (Traditional) or Chinese (Simplified)

Note   Each culture has a specific identifier associated with it. For example, the culture "en-US" has an identifier, 0x0409. To see the complete list of culture names and the corresponding culture identifiers, refer to the .NET documentation.

When you create an object of the CultureInfo class, the CultureInfo constructor is called automatically. The CultureInfo constructor takes either the culture name or the culture identifier as an argument. Use the following Visual Basic syntax to create a CultureInfo object:

```
Dim cult as CultureInfo
cult = new CultureInfo (culture name/culture identifier)
```

If you want to set the CultureInfo object to a "German-Germany" culture, use the following code:

```
Dim cult as CultureInfo
cult = new CultureInfo ("de-DE")
```

or:

```
Dim cultIdentifier As Integer
cultIdentifier = &H407
Dim cult As New CultureInfo(cultIdentifier)
```

where, "de-DE" is the culture name and "0x0407" is the culture identifier for the "German-Germany" culture.

If you do not create an object of the CultureInfo class, you can access the culture-specific information directly from the CultureInfo class. The CultureInfo class represents the information specific to the culture used by the system. Some of the properties of the CultureInfo class that can be used to access the culture-specific information are described in Table 20-2.

Table 20-2 Properties of the CultureInfo class	
Property	**Description**
Name	Returns the name of the culture in the `<languagecode2>-<country/regioncode2>` format.
DisplayName	Returns the full name of the culture in .NET Framework language in the `<language>-<country/region>` format.
NativeName	Returns the full name of the culture in the user interface language in the `<language>-<country/region>` format.
EnglishName	Returns the full name of the culture in English in the `<language>-<country/region>` format.
CurrentCulture	Returns the CultureInfo instance that represents the current culture for the current thread.
CurrentUICulture	Returns the CultureInfo instance that represents the current culture for the culture-specific resources.
LCID	Returns the culture identifier of the CultureInfo instance.

RegionInfo class

The RegionInfo class represents the information specific to a country/region. Unlike the CultureInfo class, the RegionInfo class information does not depend on the user's language or culture. The two-letter codes supported by the RegionInfo class to represent countries or regions are described in Table 20-3.

	Table 20-3 Region names	
Two-Letter Code	**Country/Region**	
AE	United Arab Emirates	
AU	Australia	
AT	Austria	
BG	Bulgaria	
BR	Brazil	
CA	Canada	
CH	Switzerland	
CZ	Czech-Republic	
DE	Germany	
EG	Egypt	
ES	Spain	
GB	United Kingdom	
GR	Greece	
HU	Hungary	
IN	India	
JP	Japan	
LB	Lebanon	
MX	Mexico	
NZ	New Zealand	
PK	Pakistan	
RU	Russia	
SG	Singapore	
TR	Turkey	
US	United States	
ZA	South Africa	

Note   The RegionInfo names are not case-sensitive. To see the complete list of region names, refer to the .NET documentation.

When you create an object of the RegionInfo class for a specific region, you need to pass the region name or the culture identifier as an argument to the RegionInfo constructor. Table 20-4 describes some of the properties of the RegionInfo class.

Table 20-4
Properties of the RegionInfo class

Property	Description
CurrentRegion	Returns the RegionInfo instance that represents the country/region for the current thread.
Name	Returns the two-letter code for the country/region of the RegionInfo instance.
EnglishName	Returns the complete name of the country/region in English.
DisplayName	Returns the complete name of the country/region in the .NET Framework language.
CurrencySymbol	Returns the currency symbol associated with the country/region.
IsMetric	Indicates whether or not the metric system of measurement is used by the country/region.

Implementing the classes

After understanding the classes involved in creating international applications, you can now implement these classes. In the example discussed here, users are prompted for a culture name. When a user enters a culture name, such as en-US or de-DE, the page displays the name of the culture in English. Also, the native name is displayed. To implement this example, create a Visual Basic Web Application and create a SampleCulture.aspx file that has the following code:

```
<%@ Page Language="vb" AutoEventWireup="false"
Codebehind="SampleCulture.aspx.vb"
Inherits="ResourceApplication.WebForm1"%>
<%@Import Namespace="System.Globalization"%>
<%@Import Namespace="System.Threading"%>
<!DOCTYPE HTML PUBLIC "-//W3C//DTD HTML 4.0 Transitional//EN">
<HTML>
  <HEAD>
     <title></title>
     <meta name="GENERATOR" content="Microsoft Visual
Studio.NET 7.0">
     <meta name="CODE_LANGUAGE" content="Visual Basic 7.0">
     <meta name="vs_defaultClientScript" content="JavaScript">
     <meta name="vs_targetSchema"
content="http://schemas.microsoft.com/intellisense/ie5">
```

```
<script language="VB" runat="server">
   Dim cult as CultureInfo

   Sub Page_Load(ByVal sender as System.Object,ByVal args
as System.EventArgs) Handles MyBase.Load

      If(IsPostBack) Then
        Try
         'Creating an instance of the CultureInfo class by
passing the value entered by a user in a text box
          cult = new CultureInfo(InputCulture.Text)
        Catch
         cult = Nothing
        End Try
       Else
         'initializing the CultureInfo instance to the
         'current culture
        cult = CultureInfo.CurrentCulture
       End If
     End Sub

     Sub DisplayButton_Click (ByVal sender as System.object,
ByVal e as System.EventArgs)

     If Not( cult is nothing) then
        'Setting the CurrentCulture property of the current
        'thread to the instance of the CultureInfo class
         Thread.CurrentThread.CurrentCulture=cult
     End If

     'Set the text on a label to display the English name
     'and native name of the culture. The Thread class is
     'also used to display the English name and native name
     'of the current culture.
     CultureInfoLabel.Text= "The English name is: " &
Cult.EnglishName.ToString & " (" &
Thread.CurrentThread.CurrentCulture.EnglishName.ToString & " )"
& "  The native name is : " & cult.NativeName.ToString & " (" &
Thread.CurrentThread.CurrentCulture.NativeName.ToString & " )"
       End Sub

   </script>
 </HEAD>

 <body MS_POSITIONING="GridLayout">
   <form id="Form1" method="post" runat="server">
     <b><i>This is a culture demo</i></b>
     <Br>
     <Br>
     <b>Enter the name of the culture</b>
     <asp:TextBox id="InputCulture" style="Z-INDEX: 101; LEFT:
228px; POSITION: absolute; TOP: 53px"
runat="server"></asp:TextBox>
```

```
        <asp:Button id="DisplayButton"
onClick="DisplayButton_Click" style="Z-INDEX: 102; LEFT: 407px;
POSITION: absolute; TOP: 52px" runat="server"
Text="Display"></asp:Button>
        <asp:Label id="CultureInfoLabel" style="Z-INDEX: 103;
LEFT: 20px; POSITION: absolute; TOP: 109px"
runat="server">Culture Information</asp:Label>
    </form>
    </body>
</HTML>
```

When a user executes this code and enters "de-DE" in the text box and clicks the button, the English name and native name of the culture are displayed, as shown in Figure 20-1.

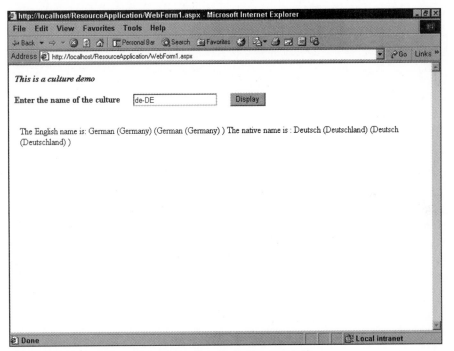

Figure 20-1: Sample output of the SampleCulture.aspx file

Using Resource Files

As mentioned earlier, a global ASP.NET application can be divided into two separate parts: data block and code block. These separate parts enable you to create localized versions of the applications without modifying the executable content. To produce the localized versions of a global ASP.NET application, you simply need to create localized versions of the data files. These files are called *resource files*, and must be persisted in a binary resource file format at run time. At run time, the appropriate resources are loaded depending on the culture settings provided by the browser.

When you make an application, it is a part of an assembly called the *main assembly*. If any change is made to this main assembly, you need to recompile the application. Because you might need to add the resources to provide support for more cultures, it is advisable to keep only the default set of resources in the main assembly. The other sets of resources can be kept in separate assemblies called *satellite assemblies,* which contain only resources. Therefore, changes made to these assemblies do not require you to recompile the application.

The first step to create the resource files is to identify the resources specific to different cultures and include them in files. For each culture, you need to include resources in a separate file. You can create a text file to do so. The text file stores a key/value pair for each resource. For example to store a value "Welcome" as a resource, you need to assign it to a key:

```
;A key/value pair
welcomeMessage = "Welcome"
```

In this sample code:

✦ The text following the semicolon represents a comment.

✦ welcomeMessage is a key.

✦ Welcome is the value assigned to the welcomeMessage key.

> **Note** The keys are case-sensitive. While retrieving values from their respective keys, if the proper case is not used, the values cannot be retrieved.

You can also include the identified resources in a ResX format, which is an XML format. In addition to the string resources, this format can also contain embedded objects. A typical ResX format is given as follows:

```
[Header]

[Entries: Strings]
key=value

[Entries: Objects]
```

The files containing resource entries must follow a specific naming convention. Otherwise, the system won't be able to find the resources at run time. For the default culture, the file should be named as Strings.txt or Strings.ResX. For any other culture, the filename must be of the form Strings.culture-name.txt or Strings.culture-name.ResX. For example, if the culture is "fr-FR", the file should be named as Strings.fr-FR.txt or Strings.fr-FR.ResX. Also, it is good practice to categorize these files in subdirectories under the application directory.

After you include all the resources in a file (text or ResX format), you need to convert it to a format that the .NET runtime can understand. To do so, you can use the Resource File Generator (ResGen.exe utility) utility. The syntax is shown as follows:

```
resgen [/compile] filename.extension [outputFilename.extension]
```

In this syntax:

✦ `filename.extension` represents a file that includes all the resource entries. The extension can be one of the following:

   • .txt: Represents a text file to be converted to a RESOURCES or RESX file. This file can contain only string resources.

   • .resx: Represents an XML-based resource file to be converted to a RESOURCES or TXT file.

   • .resources: Represents a resource file to be converted to a RESX or TXT file.

✦ `outputFilename.extension` represents the RESOURCES file that is generated after conversion.

   When converting from a TXT or RESX file, this parameter is optional. The TXT and RESX files are converted to files with the .resources extension. If you do not specify this parameter, the output file is named after the text file or the RESX file in the same directory where the input file exists.

   When converting from a RESOURCES file, this parameter is mandatory.

✦ `[/compile]` is used to specify multiple RESX or TXT files to convert to a RESOURCES file in a single bulk operation. This is optional.

Note This utility can also be used to decompile. However, when you decompile the RESOURCES file, the comments are lost.

The .NET Framework provides a set of classes that work with the resource files to produce localized versions of a global ASP.NET application. The classes are encapsulated in the System.Resources namespace.

System.Resources namespace

The .NET Framework provides a class library that uses these resource files to retrieve resources for different languages at run time. The classes that allow developers to create, store, and manage various culture-specific resources used in an application are included in the System.Resources namespace. Some of the classes of this namespace are described as follows:

✦ **ResourceManager:** Represents a set of all the resources to be used in an application at the time of execution. This class provides many constructors that you can use to create its objects. The choice of the constructors depends on the need and the scenario in which you want to use resources. For example, when you need to retrieve resources from an assembly, you can use the constructor that takes three parameters: `baseName`, `Assembly`, and `Type`.

```
Dim rm as ResourceManager
rm = New ResourceManager(baseName, Assembly, Type)
```

In the preceding syntax, `baseName` represents the root name of the resource. `Assembly` represents the main assembly for the resources. `Type` represents the ResourceSet (covered next). If "Nothing" is used, the default run-time ResourceSet is used.

The satellite assemblies are compiled into DLLs and are referenced by the main assembly. However, you do not need any specific code for this reference. This is done by the ResourceManager.

On the other hand, if you need to retrieve resources from a directory instead of an assembly, you can use the CreateFileBasedResourceManager function of the ResourceManager class. This function takes three parameters: `baseName`, `resourceDir`, and `type`.

```
Dim rm as ResourceManager
rm = ResourceManager.CreateFileBasedResourceManager(baseName,
resourceDir, type)
```

In the preceding syntax, `baseName` represents the root name of the resource, `resourceDir` represents the directory to search for the resources, and `type` represents the ResourceSet (covered next). If "Nothing" is used, the default run-time ResourceSet is used.

✦ **ResourceSet:** Represents the set of resources for a specific culture. The resources for every culture have an associated ResourceSet.

✦ **ResourceWriter:** Used to write the resources in a run-time binary resource file format. To create a resource file, you need to create a ResourceWriter object with an appropriate filename, such as CustomApplication.resource. Then, you need to call the `AddResource (key, string)` method to add each resource. Thus, to add *N* resources, you need to call the `AddResource` method *N* times. Finally, you need to call `WriteFile` to write the resources. To use the resources, you can then create an object of ResourceManager and call the `getString(key)` or `getString(key, culture)`.

Instead of the ResourceWriter class, you can use the ResGen utility to create resources in a run-time binary resource file format.

✦ **ResourceReader:** Used to read resources in a run-time binary resource file format. To create a ResourceReader, you need to pass the filename in the constructor.

Creating a resource-aware application

Let us now create an ASP.NET application that is aware of resources. Here, you'll create resources for two cultures, en-US and fr-FR. The application loads the resources depending on the selected culture while the application runs. Not only this, the application displays the localized information in a highly graphic manner. An output of this application is displayed in Figure 20-2. Notice that the output displays the localized information in French.

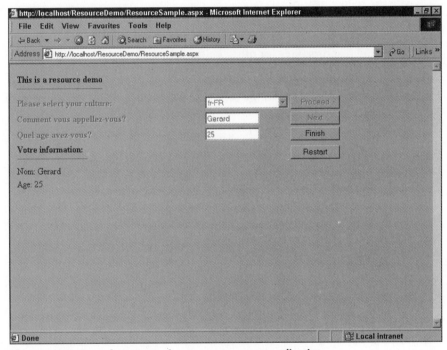

Figure 20-2: Sample output of a resource-aware application

To create this application, complete the following steps:

1. Create a directory named ResourceApplication. This directory is the application's main directory. Create a virtual directory in the Default Web site on your Web server. Specify the alias as ResourceDemo and the path of the content as the path of the ResourceApplication directory.

2. In the ResourceApplication directory, create a subdirectory called Resources. This directory will include all the resource files.

3. Create a default Strings.txt file in the Resources directory. This file contains the resources as key/value pairs. The code is shown as follows:

```
[strings]
;prompts
```

```
NameStr = What is your name?
AgeStr = What is your age?

OutputStr = Your information is:

;outputs
OuputNameStr = Name:
OutputAgeStr = Age:
```

4. Convert this text file to a RESOURCES file. To do so, use the ResGen utility with the following:

```
ResGen Strings.txt
```

5. Create the resource files for other cultures that your system supports. For example, to create a resource file for the culture fr-FR, create the Strings.fr-FR.txt file that includes all the resources. Then, use the ResGen utility to convert the file to the Strings.fr-FR.resources file. The sample code for the Strings.fr-FR.txt file is given as follows:

```
[strings]
;prompts

NameStr = Comment vous appellez-vous?
AgeStr = Quel age avez-vous?

OutputStr = Votre information:

;outputs
OuputNameStr = Nom:
outputAgeStr = Age:
```

Note   You can also create the resource files for other cultures later to add support for more cultures, without recompiling the application.

6. In the application's main directory, ResourceApplication, create the ResourceSample.aspx file. The code is given as follows:

```
<%@ Import Namespace="System" %>
<%@ Import Namespace="System.IO" %>
<%@Import Namespace="System.Globalization"%>
<%@ Import Namespace="System.Resources" %>
<%@Import Namespace="System.Threading"%>

<script runat="Server" Language="VB" >

 'Declaring shared public objects
  Public Shared rm As ResourceManager
  Public Shared cinfo As CultureInfo

Sub Page_Init(ByVal sender As System.Object, ByVal args As
System.EventArgs) Handles MyBase.Init

  'Create an instance of the ResourceManager class
```

```
    rm =
ResourceManager.CreateFileBasedResourceManager("strings",
Server.MapPath("resources") + Path.DirectorySeparatorChar, _
Nothing)

    CultureList.Items.Clear()
    'Adding the names of cultures to the drop down list
    CultureList.Items.Add("Select your language")
    CultureList.Items.Add("fr-FR")
    CultureList.Items.Add("en-US")

End Sub

Sub Proceed_Click(src As Object, E As EventArgs)

    'Create an instance of the CultureInfo class
    cinfo = New CultureInfo(CultureList.SelectedItem.Text)

    'Setting text on the Name label from the resource file
    EnterNamelabel.Text = rm.GetString("NameStr", cinfo)


    'Setting the Visible property of the Name label to true
    EnterNamelabel.Visible = true

    'Disable the Culture label, Culture list, and the
    'Proceed button
    Culturelabel.Enabled = false
    CultureList.Enabled = false
    Proceed.Enabled = false

    'Setting the Visible property of the Name Next button
    'and Name text box to true so that the user can enter
    'his/her name
    NameNextButton.Visible = true
    EnterNametextbox.Visible = true
    EnterNametextbox.Text = ""
End Sub

Sub NameNextButton_Click(src As Object, E As EventArgs)

    'setting text on the Age label from the resource file
    'and setting its Visible property to true
    EnterAgelabel.Text = rm.GetString("AgeStr", cinfo)
    EnterAgelabel.Visible = true

    'Disabling the Name label, Name text box, and the Name
    'Next button
    EnterNamelabel.Enabled = false
    EnterNametextbox.Enabled = false
    NameNextButton.Enabled = false

    'Setting the Visible property of the Age text box to
    'true so that a user can enter his/her age
```

```
    EnterAgetextbox.Visible = true
    EnterAgetextbox.Text = ""

    'Setting the Visible property of the Finish button to
    'true and enabling it. Clicking on the Finish button
    'completes the data entry.
    Finishbutton.Visible = true
    Finishbutton.Enabled = true

End Sub

Sub Finishbutton_Click(src As Object, E As EventArgs)

    Dim age As Int32 = 0
    'Converting the value entered in the Age text to Int32.
    age = Convert.ToInt32(EnterAgetextbox.Text)

    'Setting the output values from the resource file on
    'the Output label, Output Name label, and the Output
    'Age label.

    Outputlabel.Text = rm.GetString("OutputStr", cinfo) & "<hr
align=left width=130>"
    outputlabel.Visible = True

    OutputNamelabel.Text = rm.GetString("OuputNameStr", cinfo)
& " " & EnterNametextbox.Text.Trim()
    outputNamelabel.Visible = True

    OutputAgelabel.Text = rm.GetString("OutputAgeStr", cinfo)
& " " & EnterAgetextbox.Text.Trim()
    outputAgelabel.Visible = True

    'Setting the Visible property of the Output label to
    'true.
    Outputlabel.Visible = true
    EnterAgelabel.Enabled=false
    EnterAgetextbox.enabled=false

    'Setting the Visible property of the Restart button to
    'true. Clicking this button refreshes the page.
    Restartbutton.Visible = true

End Sub

Sub Restartbutton_Click(src As Object, E As EventArgs)

    'Enabling the culture list and setting the selected
    'index to 0.
    CultureList.Enabled = true
    CultureList.SelectedIndex = 0

    'Enabling the Proceed button.
    Proceed.Enabled = true
```

```
       'Enabling the Finsh button but setting its Visible
       'property to false
        Finishbutton.Enabled = true
        Finishbutton.Visible = false

       'Enabling the Name label, Name text box, and the Name
       'Next button. Also, setting their Visible property to
       'false.
        EnterNamelabel.Enabled = true
        EnterNamelabel.Visible = false
        EnterNametextbox.Enabled = true
        EnterNametextbox.Visible = false
        EnterNametextbox.Text = ""
        NameNextbutton.Enabled = true
        NameNextbutton.Visible = false

       'Enabling the Age label and Age text box and setting
       'their Visible property to false. Also, the Visible
       'property of the Output, Output Name, and Output Age
       'labels and Restart button is set to false.

        Culturelabel.Enabled = true
        EnterAgelabel.Enabled = true
        EnterAgelabel.Visible = false
        EnterAgetextbox.Enabled = true
        EnterAgetextbox.Visible = false
        EnterAgetextbox.Text = ""
        Outputlabel.Visible = false
        OutputNamelabel.Visible = false
        OutputAgelabel.Visible = false
        Restartbutton.Visible = false
End Sub

Sub ProceedEnabled(src As Object, E As EventArgs)
If CultureList.SelectedIndex > 0 Then
    Proceed.Enabled = true
End If
End Sub
</script>

<html>
<head></head>

<body bgcolor="#99cccc">

<form runat="server">
<p>

<table>
    <tr><td><b>This is a resource demo<hr>
    </td></tr> </tr>
</table>
```

```
<table width=600>
    <tr><td width=450><b><asp:label id="Culturelabel"
Text="Please select your culture:"
            visible=true runat=server/></b></td>
        <td ><asp:DropDownList id="CultureList"
AutoPostBack=true OnSelectedIndexChanged="ProceedEnabled"
runat="server"/></td>
        <td width=40><asp:button width="90px" Text="Proceed"
Enabled=false id="Proceed" onclick="Proceed_Click"
runat="server"/></td>
    </tr>

    <tr><td><b><asp:label id="EnterNamelabel" visible=false
runat=server/></b></td>
        <td><asp:textbox width="100px" id="EnterNametextbox"
visible=false runat="server"/></td>
        <td><asp:button width="90px" Text="Next"
visible=false id="NameNextbutton"
onclick="NameNextbutton_Click" runat="server"/></td>
    </tr>

    <tr><td><b><asp:label id="EnterAgelabel" visible=false
runat=server/></b></td>
        <td><asp:textbox width="100px" id="EnterAgetextbox"
visible=false runat="server"/></td>
        <td width=80><asp:button width="90px" Text="Finish"
Enabled=false id="FinishButton" onclick="FinishButton_Click"
runat="server"/></td>
    </tr>

    <tr><td colspan=2><b><asp:label id="Outputlabel"
visible=false runat=server/></b></td>
        <td><asp:button width="90px" Text="Restart"
visible=false id="Restartbutton"
onclick="Restartbutton_Click" runat="server"/></td>
    </tr>

    <tr><td><asp:label id="OutputNamelabel" visible=false
runat=server/></b></td>

    </tr>

    <tr><td><asp:label id="OutputAgelabel" visible=false
runat=server/></b></td>
    </tr>

</table>

</form>
</body>
</html>
```

This program prompts users for their name and age. After a user clicks the Finish button, the information is displayed. The text is adjusted according to the culture selected by the user. The output of this program is shown in Figure 20-2, which is displayed at the beginning of this section.

Summary

In this chapter, you learned the concepts related to international applications. First, you learned the configuration settings for global applications in the Web.config file. Next, you learned about the CultureInfo and RegionInfo classes and their implementation to access culture-specific information. Then, you learned the different classes in the System.Resources namespace. Finally, you learned how to create resource files and implement them to create localized versions of global applications.

✦   ✦   ✦

Deploying ASP.NET Applications

After a Web application is developed, it needs to
be deployed to make it available as a Web site. A
Web application may be made up of a number of files and
components. These components may be developed by the
application developer or by a third party. Therefore, while
deploying a Web application, you must determine the files
to be included in the deployment. In addition, you must
determine the method to be used for deploying an application. In this chapter, you will learn about creating deployment
projects, specifying configuration settings, and deploying
classes and assemblies in ASP.NET.

Introduction to Deployment Projects

Deployment is the process of packaging all files that make up
an application and distributing them for the purpose of installation on other computers. Deploying an ASP.NET application can
be as easy as copying the application files to the machine on
which the application needs to be deployed. When you deploy
an application by copying files, no Registry entries are made.
To deploy more complex applications, which may comprise
various components, you may create deployment projects in
Visual Studio .NET.

A deployment project enables you to specify the files to be
included in the deployment, the method by which the application files will be deployed, and the location where the
application is to be deployed. In this section, you will look
at the different types of deployment projects, the process of
creating a deployment project, adding files to the deployment
project, and building the deployment project.

Choosing the type of deployment projects

Visual Studio .NET provides different types of deployment projects. The choice of a particular type of deployment project depends upon the application or the component that you want to deploy and the mode of deployment. For example, you may want to deploy an application in the form of a collection of cabinet (CAB) files for downloading the application.

The different types of deployment projects provided in Visual Studio .NET are as follows:

✦ **Merge module project:** Creates a single package that contains all files, resources, Registry entries, and the setup logic necessary for deploying the package. A merge module is similar to a dynamic link library (DLL), which allows multiple applications to share code. The only difference in this case is that a merge module allows sharing of the setup code. A merge module project file has the extension .msm. You cannot use a merge module file by itself. You must merge the resulting .msm file with another deployment project, which creates a Windows Installer (MSI) file.

You can use a merge module project when you want to deploy a component that will be shared by multiple applications, because a merge module project identifies all the dependencies for a component and ensures that the correct versions of the components are installed. Thus, problems relating to versioning can be avoided with merge module projects. When a new version of a component needs to be deployed, you simply create a new merge module project that contains the dependencies for the new version of the component.

✦ **Setup project:** Enables you to create a Windows Installer (MSI) file for deploying an application. The resulting MSI file contains the application, dependencies, information about the Registry entries to be made, and installation instructions. A setup project can be used for deploying standard Windows-based applications. When you execute the resulting MSI file, all files related to the application are copied to the Program Files directory on the target computer.

While selecting between a merge module project and a setup project, you must consider the target audience. If the application is intended for use by an end user, you should package all the files for the application in an MSI file. On the other hand, DLLs, controls, and resources that are intended for use by developers should be packaged in a merge module, which can then be packaged by the developer in an MSI file for distribution to the end user.

✦ **Web setup project:** Is similar to a setup project. This type of project also results in the creation of an MSI file, which can be used for deploying an application. When you execute the MSI file, all files that make up the application are copied to the virtual root directory on the Web server. This type of project should be used for installing a Web application on a Web server.

✦ **Cab project:** Enables you to generate CAB files of a specific size. These CAB files can be used to download components to a Web browser. You can create a cabinet project if you want your component to run on the client instead of the Web server.

You can determine the type of deployment project to be created based on the guidelines given here.

In addition to these types of projects, Visual Studio .NET also provides the Setup Wizard, which creates a basic setup project. It guides you through the steps of creating a deployment project. During each step, the wizard collects information, such as the files to be included in the deployment project.

Creating a deployment project

After determining the type of deployment project, you can create it by following these steps:

1. Open the project that needs to be deployed.

2. Select File ⇨ New ⇨ Project.

3. Select Setup And Deployment Projects from the Project Types pane.

4. Select the type of deployment project that you want to create from the Templates pane.

5. Change the name of the deployment project to Setup1. Click the Add To Solution radio button.

6. If you select the Setup Wizard, it takes you through the various steps. Each step prompts you to enter the required information, such as the type of project (whether you want to create an MSI file or CAB files), the type of application (Windows application, Web application, merge module for Windows Installer, or downloaded CAB file), and the files to be included in the project.

   If you select one of the project types instead of the wizard, it opens the File System Editor, shown in Figure 21-1.

Working with editors in a deployment project

While creating a deployment project, you might want to specify the files to be included in a project and the Registry entries to be made when the application is deployed. You might also want to customize the user interface provided at the time of installing an application. You can easily accomplish these tasks by using one of the editors provided in a deployment project. These editors are discussed in the next sections.

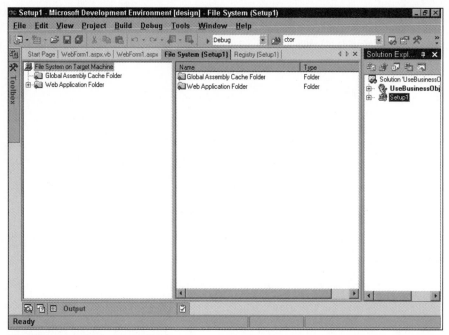

Figure 21-1: File System Editor

File System Editor

The File System Editor enables you to add or remove various files, components, and project output in the deployment project. The File System Editor displays the folders that correspond to the folder structure on the target computer.

Adding and removing folders

You can add your own folders to the deployment project by using the File System Editor. To add a folder, follow these steps:

1. If the File System Editor is not open, open it by clicking the File System Editor button in the Solution Explorer, as shown in Figure 21-2.

2. Select the File System On Target Machine node and select Action ➪ Add Special Folder ➪ Custom Folder.

3. Type the name of the folder to be created on the target computer.

To remove a folder from the File System Editor of the deployment project, click the folder and select Edit ➪ Delete.

Figure 21-2: File System Editor button in Solution Explorer

Adding and removing files

You may want to include files such as Readme.txt, a rich text file containing the license agreement, and some GIF files in a deployment project. You can include these files by following these steps:

1. Select the folder in which the file is to be included.

2. Select Action ⇨ Add ⇨ File. This invokes the Add Files dialog box.

Note You can also select the Project ⇨ Add to add files, project outputs, and components to the deployment project. However, this will result in adding the item to the application folder instead of the folder of the target computer.

3. Browse to the folder in which the file is stored and select the file.

Note You can also add an assembly file by using this procedure.

To remove a file from the File System Editor, select the file and select Edit ⇨ Delete.

Adding and removing project outputs

You can add or remove project outputs from a deployment project. Project outputs may include the EXE and DLL files that are created when you build a project and the source code of the project.

Note

To be able to add the project outputs of one or more projects, you must include the projects in the solution of the deployment project. You can do this by right-clicking the solution in Solution Explorer, selecting Add, and clicking Existing Project. Repeat this process for each project that you want to include in the deployment.

The steps for adding project outputs of one or more projects are as follows:

1. In the File System Editor, select the target folder in which the project outputs are to be included.

2. Click Action ⇨ Add ⇨ Project Output. This invokes the Add Project Output Group dialog box, shown in Figure 21-3.

Figure 21-3: Add Project Output Group dialog box

3. Select the project from the Project drop-down list.

4. Select the project output group from the list box below the Project drop-down list. These groups include Primary Output, Localized Resources, Debug Symbols, Content Files, and Source Files. When you select a group, the description for the group is displayed in the Description text box. Each of the project output group is described as follows:

   • **Primary Output:** Contains the DLL or EXE built by the project.

   • **Localized Resources:** Contains satellite assemblies for each culture's resources. This group is useful to deploy localized applications.

Cross-Reference

To learn more about localization, refer to Chapter 20.

- **Debug Symbols:** Contains the debugging files for the project.

- **Content Files:** Contains all the content files in the project.

- **Source Files:** Contains all source files in the project.

5. Click OK.

To remove a project output from the deployment project, select the project output group to be deleted and click Edit ⇨ Delete.

Registry Editor

You may want to access the Registry and set values of existing Registry keys or add new Registry keys to the target computer. The Registry Editor enables you to add your own Registry keys and their values to a deployment project. When you execute the deployment project, the Registry keys are added to the Registry of the target computer. When you open the Registry Editor, it displays a standard set of keys, which correspond to the keys in the Windows Registry of the target computer. Figure 21-4 depicts the Registry Editor.

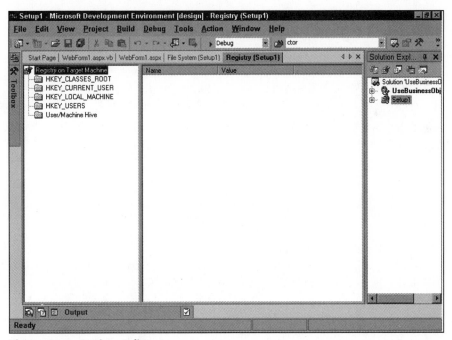

Figure 21-4: Registry Editor

Adding and removing a Registry key

To add a Registry key to the deployment project, follow these steps:

1. Open the Registry Editor by clicking the Registry Editor button in Solution
   Explorer of the deployment project, as shown in Figure 21-5.

Figure 21-5: Registry Editor button in
Solution Explorer

2. Click one of the top-level key nodes: HKEY_CLASSES_ROOT, HKEY_CUR-
   RENT_USER, HKEY_LOCAL_MACHINE, HKEY_USERS, or User/Machine Hive.

3. Select Action ➪ New Key. This adds the new key under the top-level key node
   that you selected. The new key has a default name. Change the name of the
   key by typing the new name or by changing the Name property from the
   Properties window.

You can remove a Registry key from the Registry Editor of the deployment project
simply by clicking the key and pressing the Delete key on the keyboard.

Adding and removing Registry values

You can add values to the existing or newly added keys by using the Registry Editor.
When you install the application, the Registry key value will be written to the
Registry of the target computer. You can assign a string, binary value, or DWORD
value to a Registry key. To assign a value to a Registry key, follow these steps:

1. Select the key to which the value is to be assigned.

2. Select Action ➪ New. Click the String Value, Binary Value, or DWORD value
   option based on the type of value that you want to assign to the Registry key.

3. Press F4 to switch to the Properties window and type the value for the
   Registry key in the Value property.

You can delete a Registry key value by selecting the value from the Values pane of the Registry Editor and selecting Edit ⇨ Delete.

Importing an existing Registry

The Registry Editor also enables you to import a complete Registry, thereby saving the time and effort required to create the same keys and values in a deployment project. You can import an existing Registry by following these steps:

1. Select the Registry On Target Machine node in the Registry Editor.

2. Select Action ⇨ Import. This invokes the Import Registry File dialog box. Browse to the folder that contains the Registry file (REG) to be imported to the deployment project and click the Open button.

File Types Editor

The File Types Editor enables you to associate file types and extensions with your application.

> **Note** An example of a file type is Microsoft Word Document. The extension associated with it is .doc. Windows also associates an executable file with a file type. For example, when you double-click a Microsoft Word document, Windows launches the Microsoft Word (Winword.exe) application. You can view the available file types and their associations by using Windows Explorer (selecting the View ⇨ Folder option and pressing the File Types tab).

You can also specify the actions allowed on each file type by using the File Types Editor. When you deploy your application, the file types created in the deployment project will appear in the File Types list in Windows Explorer. Figure 21-6 depicts the File Types Editor.

Adding and removing a file type

To add a file type to the deployment project, follow these steps:

1. Open the File Type Editor in the deployment project by clicking the File Types Editor button in Solution Explorer, as shown in Figure 21-7.

2. In the File Types Editor, select the File Types On Target Machine node.

3. Select Action ⇨ Add File Type. This will add the file type to the File Types On Target Machine node. You can change the name of the newly added file type by typing the new name as soon as the file type is added or by using the Properties window.

4. To associate file extensions with the file types, click the file type with which a file extension is to be associated. In the Properties window, select the Extensions property and specify the file extensions to be associated with the file type.

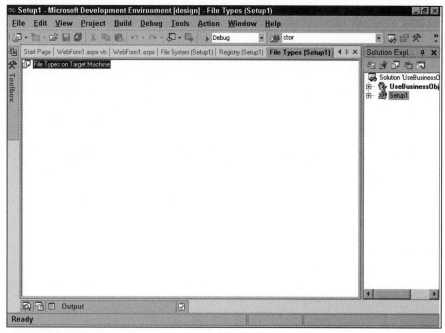

Figure 21-6: File Types Editor

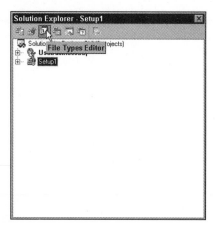

Figure 21-7: File Types Editor button in Solution Explorer

Note   You must enter the extension without a period (.). You may associate one or more extensions with a file type. You must separate the list of extensions with semi-colons (;).

5. To associate an executable file with a file type, select the file type. From the Properties window, select the Commands property and click the ellipsis (...) button. This invokes the Select Item In Project dialog box, shown in Figure 21-8.

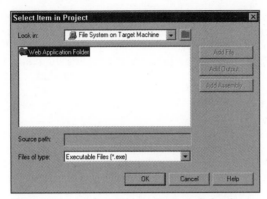

Figure 21-8: Select Item In Project dialog box

Click the Add File button and select an executable file to be associated with the file type.

To remove a file type created earlier in a deployment project, click the file type in the File Types Editor and select Edit ➪ Delete.

Adding actions

You can add actions to a file type by using the File Types Editor. You can also specify the tasks that can be performed by a user with the files of the specified file type. An action appears in the shortcut menu when a user right-clicks the file of the specified file type. You can associate actions with a file type by following these steps:

1. Select the file type to which an action is to be added. Select Action ➪ Add Action. This results in adding a New Document Action node in the File Types Editor. Specify the name of the newly added action. The name of the action appears in the shortcut menu when you right-click a file.

2. Select the Verb property from the properties window and type the verb. This verb will be used in the application code to specify the tasks to be performed when the action is selected from the shortcut menu.

You can also specify a particular action to be the default action for a file type. The default action occurs when a user double-clicks a file of the specified file type. You specify an action to be the default action by selecting an action node from the File Types Editor and selecting Action ➪ Set As Default.

User Interface Editor

When you create a deployment project, it automatically creates some dialog boxes that are displayed during the installation of the application on the target computer. The User Interface Editor displays the dialog box names and enables you to specify the properties of the dialog boxes, such as the message to be displayed in a dialog box and the name of the dialog box. In addition, the User Interface Editor enables you to add your own dialog boxes.

The User Interface Editor is divided into two sections, Install and Administrative Install. The Install section contains the dialog boxes that are displayed to the users when they start installation. The Administrative Install section contains the dialog boxes that are displayed when a network administrator moves the installer to a network location, to make it available for installation over a network.

Each section has some predefined dialog boxes, which are categorized as follows:

✦ **Start dialog boxes:** Displayed to the user before the actual installation process begins. Examples of dialog boxes in this category are the Welcome screen, the dialog box that accepts customer information such as the username and company name, and the dialog box that enables a user to specify the directory in which the files are to be copied.

✦ **Progress dialog boxes:** Used as a means of providing visual feedback to the user about the progress of the installation process. It typically depicts the progress in terms of the percentage of completion of the process.

✦ **End dialog boxes:** Used to inform the user about the success or failure of the installation process. They also include the dialog boxes that enable you to launch the newly installed application or to restart the computer.

Figure 21-9 depicts the User Interface Editor.

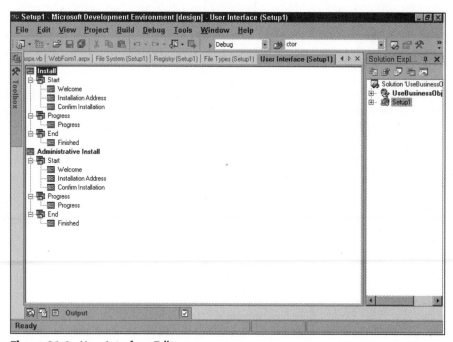

Figure 21-9: User Interface Editor

Adding installation dialog boxes

You can add your own installation dialog boxes by using the User Interface Editor. The procedure for creating custom dialog boxes is as follows:

1. Open the User Interface Editor by clicking the User Interface Editor button in the Solution Explorer window, as shown in Figure 21-10.

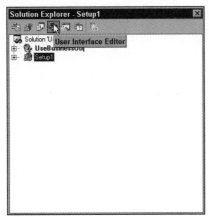

Figure 21-10: User Interface Editor button in Solution Explorer

2. In the User Interface Editor, click the Start, Progress, or End node to add a dialog box of a particular type.

3. Select Action ⇨ Add Dialog. This will invoke the Add Dialog dialog box, shown in Figure 21-11. Select the dialog box that you wish to add.

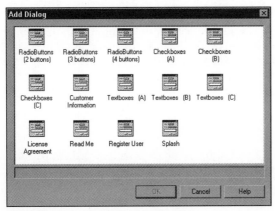

Figure 21-11: Add Dialog dialog box

For example, you may select to add the License Agreement dialog box. You can select the License Agreement dialog box from the Add Dialog dialog box. You can specify the text to be displayed in the license agreement in a file and save the file in Rich Text Format (RTF). To associate the file with the License Agreement dialog box, you need to add the file to the deployment project by using the File System Editor. After the file is included in the deployment project, you can associate it with the License Agreement dialog box by using the Properties window and specifying the name of the RTF file in the LicenceFile property. When you run the setup, it will display the standard License Agreement dialog box with the text from the RTF file.

Changing the sequence of dialog boxes

After adding the necessary dialog boxes, you might want to change the sequence in which they appear during the installation process. You can change the sequence of the dialog boxes by selecting the dialog box and selecting the Move Up or Move Down option from the Action menu.

Removing dialog boxes

To remove a dialog box from the deployment project, select the dialog box and press the Delete key. Alternatively, you may select Edit ➪ Delete.

Custom Actions Editor

You might want to perform some tasks on the target computer as soon as the installation process is complete. For example, you might want to execute a program that starts a Web service as soon as the process of installation is complete. Another example is when you want to create a database on the target computer during installation. The Custom Actions Editor enables you to specify such additional actions to be performed after the completion of the installation process. The actions that you want to perform must be compiled into a DLL or EXE file and added to the deployment project by using the File System Editor.

Figure 21-12 shows the Custom Actions Editor in a deployment project.

The Custom Actions Editor displays four folders: Install, Commit, Rollback, and Uninstall. Each folder corresponds to a phase in the installation process. The folder in which you created a particular custom action determines the sequence in which that custom action is performed.

Adding a custom action

To add a custom action to the deployment project, follow these steps:

1. Open the Custom Actions Editor in the deployment project by clicking the Custom Actions Editor button in Solution Explorer, as shown in Figure 21-13.

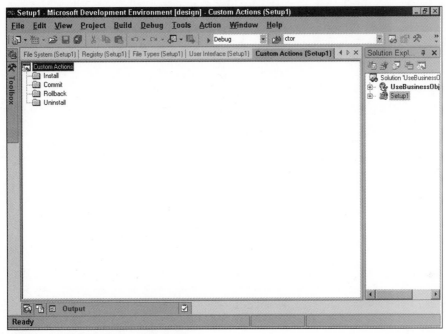

Figure 21-12: Custom Actions Editor

Figure 21-13: Custom Actions Editor button in Solution Explorer

2. Select Action ⇨ Add Custom Action. This invokes the Select Item In Project dialog box.

3. From the Select Item In Project dialog box, select the DLL or EXE file that contains the custom action to be performed during or after installation.

After you have added all custom actions, you can change the sequence of their execution by selecting the Move Up or Move Down option from the Action menu.

Removing a custom action

To remove a custom action, select the custom action in the Custom Actions Editor and press the Delete key. Alternatively, you can select Edit ⇨ Delete.

Launch Conditions Editor

Your application may be dependent on several factors, such as availability of files, the version of the operating system on the target machine, and Registry keys. Therefore, you might want to ensure that the version of the operating system on the target computer is appropriate for running your application or search the target computer for the existence of a particular file or a key in the Registry. You can perform these tasks by using the Launch Conditions Editor. Figure 21-14 depicts the Launch Conditions Editor in a deployment project.

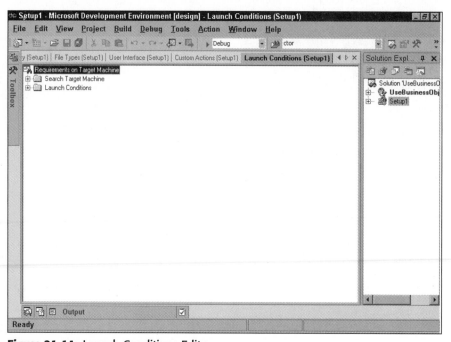

Figure 21-14: Launch Conditions Editor

Adding and removing a file search

You can search for a file to ensure that it exists at a specific location on the target computer by using the Launch Conditions Editor. To add a search for a file, follow these steps:

1. Click the Launch Conditions Editor button in Solution Explorer, as shown in Figure 21-15.

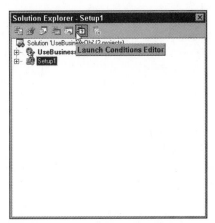

Figure 21-15: Launch Conditions Editor button in Solution Explorer

2. Click the Search Target Machine node.

3. Click the Add File Search option from the Action menu.

4. Select the FileName property from the Properties window. Set this property to the name of the file that you want to search on the target computer. In addition to the filename, you can specify the folder and attributes such as the file size and version to be searched on the target computer.

You can remove a file search by clicking the file search and selecting Edit ⇨ Delete.

Adding and removing a Registry search

To search for the existence of a specific Registry key or value, you can add a Registry search in the Launch Conditions Editor by using the following procedure:

1. Select the Search Target Machine node in the Launch Conditions Editor.

2. Select Action ⇨ Add Registry Search.

3. Select the Properties window. If you want to search for a Registry key on the target computer, set the Root and RegKey property values to the key that you want to search. If you want to search for a particular value in the Registry of the target computer, specify the value to be searched in the Value property.

To remove a Registry search, select the Registry search node from the Launch Conditions Editor and select Edit ➪ Delete.

Adding and removing a component search

At times, you may want to search for a particular component on a machine. For example, if your application uses XML, you might want to ensure that the Microsoft XML parser MSXML 3.0 exists on the computer. The MSXML parser is implemented as a DLL. To search for components, you can add a component search by using the Launch Conditions Editor. The steps for adding a component search are as follows:

1. Select the Search Target Machine node in the Launch Conditions Editor.

2. Select Action ➪ Add Windows Installer Search. This adds a Search For Component node to the Launch Condition Editor.

3. Select the Properties window and specify the GUID of the component that you want to search on the target computer in the ComponentID property.

To remove a component search, select the component search node from the Launch Conditions Editor and select Edit ➪ Delete.

Adding a launch condition

You can also ensure that certain conditions are evaluated before the installation process begins by using the Launch Conditions Editor. For example, if you want to ensure that Windows 2000 is installed on the target computer, you can add a launch condition, VersionNT>=500. When you add a condition, the installer evaluates it. If the condition is true, the process of installation continues; otherwise, it is rolled back. To add a launch condition, follow these steps:

1. Select the Launch Condition node in the Launch Conditions Editor.

2. Select Action ➪ Add Launch Condition. This will add a new launch condition. Change the name of the launch condition.

3. Select the Properties window and set the value of the Condition property to the condition that you want to check on the target computer.

You can use the editors to perform a variety of tasks; these editors help you to simplify the process of adding files, checking for various conditions, and adding Registry entries.

Building a deployment project

After you have specified the various files to be included in the deployment project, user interface screens, launch conditions, and custom actions, you can build the deployment project by selecting Build ➪ Build. When you build the deployment project, it results in creation of the CAB, MSM, or MSI file, depending on the type of the deployment project. You can use the resulting file to install your application on the target computer.

ASP.NET Configuration System

When you install a new application, you may be required to configure it. For example, you may need to provide information about the amount of memory to be used by the application. In addition, you may need to specify application-specific information, such as the path for the data source. A configuration system provides all this information for an application, which may be used at the time of or after the deployment of the application.

A Web application should provide a flexible configuration system that allows configuration settings to be easily applied to the application. It should also facilitate easy customization of configuration settings after the deployment of the application so that changes in the configuration settings can be applied to the application without having to recompile the entire code. In addition, the configuration system should provide a rich set of configuration settings to enable different types of Web clients to work with the applications.

The configuration system provided in ASP.NET meets all of these requirements. It provides a flexible configuration system, as well as a rich set of initial configuration settings. A thorough understanding of the configuration system helps you to easily specify the settings for the target computer. You can also easily change the settings after the application is deployed.

In ASP.NET, the configuration file Web.config stores the information about browser capabilities, compilation, custom error messages, security, and globalization. The Web.config file stores the configuration information in an XML format; therefore, it can be easily read and modified by developers by using any standard text editor. Developers can also use scripting languages such as Perl and VBScript to navigate, interpret, and modify the configuration settings specified in the file.

The Web.config file can have various configuration sections for specifying configuration settings. These sections have already been covered in Chapter 14. A recapitulation of the different sections is summarized in Table 21-1.

Table 21-1
Configuration sections in ASP.NET

Section	Configuration Section Handler in ASP.NET	Description
AppSettings	System.Configuration. NameValueFileSectionHandler	Enables you to specify custom configuration settings for your application. You can use one or more `<add>` elements in this section to add a new key and specify the values for the same.
Authentication	System.Web.Configuration. AuthenticationConfigHandler	Enables you to specify the default authentication mode, and specify cookie authentication settings.
Authorization	System.Web.Configuration. AuthorizationConfigHandler	Controls client access to the ASP.NET resources at a given URL.
BrowserCaps	System.Web.Configuration. HTTPCapabilitiesSectionHandler	Controls the settings of the HttpBrowser Capabilities component, which enables you to gather the information about the browser running on the client.
Compilation	System.Web.Configuration. CompilationConfigHandler	Contains the compilation settings that are used by ASP.NET for compiling a Web application.
CustomErrors	System.Web.Configuration. CustomErrorsConfigHandler	Enables you to specify the page to which the application should be redirected in the event of an error.
Globalization	System.Web.Configuration. GlobalizationConfigHandler	Specifies the globalization settings for an application.
HttpHandlers	System.Web.Configuration. HTTPHandlersConfigHandler	Maps the incoming URL requests to the classes that implement IHttpHandler or the IHTTPHandler interfaces.
httpModules	System.Web.Configuration. HTTPModulesConfigHandler	Enables you to add, remove, and clear HTTP module classes to or from your application.
httpRuntime	System.Web.Configuration. HttpRuntimeConfigurationHandler	Configures ASP.NET HTTP runtime settings.
identity	System.Web.Configuration. HttpIdentityConfigHandler	Controls the identity of the ASP.NET application.

Section	Configuration Section Handler in ASP.NET	Description
machineKey	System.Web.Configuration. MachineKeyConfigHandler	Configures the keys to use for encryption and decryption of forms authentication cookie data, and enables developers to configure a validation key that performs message authentication checks on view state data and forms authentication tickets.
pages	System.Web.Configuration. SingleTagSectionHandler	Specifies page-specific configuration settings.
processModel	System.Web.Configuration. IgnoreConfigHandler	Specifies the process model settings, such as timeout, idletimeout, and shutdowntimeout, for an ASP.NET application.
securityPolicy	System.Web.Configuration. SecurityPolicyConfigHandler	Specifies the authorization mode, and enables you to allow or deny access to specific users.
sessionState	System.Web.Configuration. SessionStateConfigHandler	Provides a means to configure the session state HttpModule of the ASP.NET application.
trace	System.Web.Configuration. TraceConfigHandler	Configures the trace service of ASP.NET.
trust	System.Web.Security. CodeAccessSecurityHandler	Enables you to configure the code access security permission set, which is used to run an ASP.NET application.
webServices	System.Web.Services.Webservices. ConfigurationSectionHandler	Configures the settings for ASP.NET Web services.

ASP.NET provides a default configuration file for the entire Web server. This file provides the default settings for an ASP.NET application. This file, called Machine.config, is located in the %windir%\Microsoft.NET\Framework*version*\CONFIG folder and is available at the machine level. In addition to this machine-level file, you can create your own Web.config file that specifies the settings for a particular application.

When a user makes a request for a resource, ASP.NET determines the configuration settings for the resources by referring to the settings in the Web.config file located in the path of the resource. In the absence of this file, ASP.NET refers to the settings in the Machine.config file.

For a detailed discussion on the different configuration sections and the working of the configuration system in ASP.NET and its benefits, refer to Chapter 14.

Deploying Classes and Assemblies

A Windows application is composed of different types of files, such as EXEs and DLLs. When you deploy a new application, it might result in the installation of all the files that comprise the application. However, this may cause a number of problems, especially in case of applications that use COM-based components. COM components need to be registered so that the system can locate them. This requires several Registry settings, in the absence of which the components do not work. In addition, if an application results in installing a newer version of a component, which is shared by a number of applications on a computer, the existing applications might not work as expected.

To overcome the problems of COM-based components and to simplify the process of deploying classes and components, .NET introduces the concept of assemblies. An *assembly* is a single logical unit of functionality. It is the fundamental unit of class deployment.

An assembly contains an assembly manifest, which contains data about the dependencies of the files that are included in the assembly, their version requirements, security information, and all other information required to resolve references to resources and classes in the assembly.

For a detailed discussion on creation of single-file and multifile assemblies, refer to Chapter 15.

After you have created an assembly, you can easily deploy it by using Windows Installer (as an MSI file), by using Internet Explorer (as CAB files), or simply by copying the assembly to the target computer. An assembly can be deployed into the local assembly cache or the global assembly cache. The local assembly cache is specific to an application. On the other hand, when you install an assembly into a global assembly cache, it can be accessed by all applications on a computer.

Usually, assemblies are deployed into the local assembly cache of the application. This ensures that the assembly can be accessed only by the code in the application. It also facilitates side-by-side versions of an application to run simultaneously, because the classes of the assemblies are private to a particular application version instance. You can deploy an assembly into the local assembly cache by copying the assembly files in the directory, which is marked as the *assembly cache location* for an application. ASP.NET applications are configured to use the bin directory specific to an application as the default local assembly cache. Therefore, you can copy the assembly files to the bin directory of the application.

You can install an assembly into the global assembly cache, using Windows Installer, when you want multiple applications to share the code in the assembly. Windows Installer 2.0 provides the reference-counting feature for assemblies that are shared by multiple applications.

Summary

In this chapter, you learned about the different types of deployment projects. You also learned about various editors that are used in deployment projects. Then, you learned about the configuration settings in ASP.NET. Finally, you learned about deploying classes and assemblies.

✦   ✦   ✦

Building Web Services

Introduction to Web Services

Web Services solve a basic, but pervasive problem experienced by many of us with today's Internet. Although literally billions of pages of useful data and information are served up by the Web, it is typically difficult to extract, examine, and use that data programmatically.

Much of this difficulty arises from the fact that the Web (at least as it exists today) is designed for human consumption. Consequently, data is presented in a form that's easy for a human to read but relatively difficult and error prone for applications to read and process reliably.

In this chapter, you will learn about some of the limitations of today's Internet as a backbone for application integration and how Web services promise to deliver an effective platform for enabling the next generation of distributed, integrated applications to the Web.

The foundational elements of Web services will be covered, providing a solid understanding of the infrastructure that enables Web services to be built and consumed. In addition, some of the Web services being planned by Microsoft will be discussed, which can be leveraged for use in your own Web service implementations.

Understanding Web Services

Web services are all about delivering distributed applications via programmable components that are accessible over the Web. As an example, many e-commerce sites need to calculate shipping charges based on a variety of shipping options. Typically, such a site might maintain a set of database tables that describe the shipping options and charges for each shipping company. Obviously, this can become a time-consuming process, because the data is likely to change often, and someone must repeatedly update the tables.

A more automated approach might incorporate a process called "screen scraping." Suppose that one of the shipping companies maintains a Web site that conveniently lists the various shipping options and associated charges. By utilizing screen scraping (essentially a process of analyzing the data in a page for certain patterns in order to extract the data you are interested in processing), a program can examine the Web page and extract the shipping information from that page.

At first glance, this might appear to be an effective solution (and, in fact, it is used relatively frequently and with some success today). But, what happens if the Webmaster at the shipping company decides to change the layout or otherwise reformat the data on the page? This might be necessary if, for example, a new shipping option is introduced. Suddenly and unexpectedly, your screen scraper may no longer be able to locate the data you need.

Now, imagine this same e-commerce site programmatically calling a Web service provided by the shipping company on its Web site that automatically calculates shipping costs based on the shipping method and package weight that you specify in your request and returns the resulting charge to you in real time.

While this is admittedly a simple example, it clearly illustrates the power and potential of Web services to transform the Web from a passive, interactive information display medium into a platform for truly distributed computing. Essentially, Web services extend the capabilities of classic distributed applications and services to the heterogeneous platform that is the Internet.

Of course, there are many other potentially valuable applications of Web services. Some of these include:

✦ Services that are either too difficult or too expensive to implement yourself. For example, credit card validation, financial account management, stock quotes, and so on.

✦ Services that provide commonly needed functionality for other services. For example, user authentication, usage billing, usage auditing, and so on.

✦ Services that aggregate distributed, discrete services into an orchestrated whole. A good example of this type of service would be travel booking.

✦ Services that integrate your business systems with your partners (or other business systems within your own organization).

No wonder so much excitement surrounds the promise that Web services offer to programmers, systems integrators, and IT professionals.

What is a Web service?

In short, a Web service is a programmable URL. Stated another way, a Web service is an application component that is remotely callable using standard Internet protocols such as HTTP and XML. Thus, any system that supports these basic, standard protocols is capable of supporting Web services.

The ability to package application code into reusable components that is callable across process and machine boundaries is not a new concept. Today, technologies are available such as the Component Object Model (COM), the Common Object Request Broker Architecture (CORBA), Internet Inter-ORB Protocol (IIOP), and Remote Method Invocation (RMI), to name a few. A key limitation of these technologies is that they are not easily interoperable amongst the tremendous number of heterogeneous systems that comprise the Internet. This is due, in part, to dependencies on particular operating systems, programming languages, or object-model-specific protocols. Consequently, this limits their effectiveness as a standard method for programming the Web. Clearly, what is needed for Web services to succeed on the Internet is a platform that does not depend on a specific operating system, object model, or programming language.

What sets Web services apart from these prior-generation component and middleware technologies is the fact that they are built upon widely accepted Internet standards that can interoperate seamlessly in the diversity of the Web. Web services use a text-based messaging model to communicate, allowing them to operate effectively on these many different platforms.

If you are familiar with creating and consuming COM components for distributed applications, you will find creating and consuming Web services a natural evolution of what you already know.

Note The remaining chapters in Part IV, "Building Web Services," will provide you with a solid introduction to the technologies that will enable you to understand, build, and consume Web services.

As this book is being written, major platform and software vendors (including Microsoft, IBM, Sun, Hewlett-Packard, and others) have all begun delivering support for Web services with technologies and tools that enable software developers to easily create Web services on these platforms. We will, of course, be concerned with creating Web services using the Microsoft .NET Framework with the VB.NET and C# programming languages.

Foundational elements of Web services

Now that you have an idea of what Web services are and how they can be used, let's examine the key technologies that you will encounter when working with Web services.

Microsoft provides an excellent platform for building and consuming Web services with the .NET Framework, which virtually eliminates the need to learn about the "plumbing" that is a part of building and consuming Web services. If things worked right all of the time and never had the opportunity to fail, there would be no need to even discuss this plumbing. But, of course, things don't always work right and, when they don't, it is both useful and practical to have a basic understanding of the working principals of the foundation upon which Web services are built. The goal is to empower you with enough knowledge that you can effectively troubleshoot any problems you might encounter when working with Web services.

The key to the broad-reach capabilities of Web services on the Internet is a foundation built on Internet standards that does not rely on any platform-specific technology. This foundation supplies standards-based services that provide the following capabilities to Web services:

✦ A standard, portable method for describing data

✦ A standard, extensible message format for communicating requests and responses

✦ A standard, extensible method for describing the capabilities of Web services

✦ A method to discover what Web services are available at any particular site

✦ A method to discover what sites provide Web services

The following sections will help you to understand why these issues are important and also introduce you to the technologies that provide these capabilities to the Web services platform.

Representing Data

Web services enable consumers to programmatically request and obtain structured data. But, how is this data encoded so that it can be exchanged between service and consumer? How do you ensure a consistent and accurate interpretation of the data when the service and consumer may reside on different platforms, operating systems, object models, and/or programming languages?

To promote the ability of Web services to communicate their data unambiguously, efficiently, and effectively, a common, portable, and standard method for describing data must be used.

The simple (and logical) answer is XML. As you will soon see, XML is used extensively in every aspect of Web services. The following is an introduction to the specific XML technologies you will encounter when building or consuming Web services.

What is XML?

XML provides a standards-based method for describing data (also known as metadata). XML has the ability to describe data using a simple grammar that is highly interoperable among the many heterogeneous systems that are connected to the Internet. Using the basic elements of the XML language, you can describe simple as well as complex data types and relationships.

XML has several key strengths that have helped it to become the de facto method for describing data (especially over HTML and other binary formats):

✦ XML is a text-based language, which makes it easily readable and more portable than binary data formats.

✦ XML gives you the ability to define your own tags to describe data and its relationships to other data (hence, the word extensible in its name).

✦ XML strictly enforces its language syntax, unlike HTML.

✦ Parsers are widely available to accurately parse and validate XML structures that you define, which means you don't have to do it yourself!

Of course, XML is not without it's weaknesses. Among these is the fact that XML can be more "wordy" than an equivalent binary format. In addition, data interoperability can be difficult to achieve due to differences in naming conventions from one application to another.

In the following sections, we will briefly examine the syntax and structure of XML documents.

XML syntax

XML is a markup language that, at first glance, looks very much like HTML. In fact, XML and HTML are both derived from the Standard Generalized Markup Language (SGML). XML (like HTML) uses a set of human-readable tags and declarations to create a document. The major difference is in the meaning implied by these tags and declarations. Whereas HTML is concerned with describing how to format information on a page, XML is concerned with describing data and its relationship to other data.

XML uses tags enclosed in < and > angle brackets to define elements that form element structures and hierarchies within an XML document.

XML document structure

An XML document consists of a prolog, document elements, and optional attributes that model a logically related set of data. An invoice is one example of such an information model. The prolog contains information that applies to the document as a whole and appears at the top of the document before the first document tag. The prolog usually contains information about the character encoding and document structure as well as other possible information. XML parsers use the prolog to correctly interpret the contents of an XML document.

The following sample illustrates the format of a simple XML document that describes the weather conditions in the city of St. Louis, Missouri:

```
<?xml version="1.0" encoding="UTF-8"?>
<weather>
   <location city="St. Louis, MO USA">
      <forecast date="2001-07-15">
         <temperature units="F">80</temperature>
         <humidity units="%">55</humidity>
         <skies>Cloudy, 40% chance of showers</skies>
      </forecast>
   </location>
</weather>
```

Note that the indentation applied to elements is not required; however, it makes reading the document and understanding the relationship between elements easier.

From this sample, we can see that the `<weather>` element is a container for a collection of city-based weather conditions (in this case, the conditions for a single city, St. Louis). The weather conditions for a specific city are contained within a `<location>` element. Within the `<location>` element are elements that describe a date-based weather forecast.

Note that several of the elements contain a `"units"` attribute. In XML, attributes are used to further describe or qualify information related to the element in which they are contained. In this example, the `"units"` attribute is used to define the numeric units of the air temperature described by the `<temperature>` element. Other examples of attributes are `"city"` and `"date"`.

As this simple example shows, XML lets you define your own tags for describing data. The XML standard does not define the meaning of the `<weather>` tag. However, it will enforce the grammatical rules, which are required to create a well-formed XML document.

Specifically, when creating an XML document, it is very important that you follow these basic rules:

✦ All elements must have an end tag.

✦ All elements must be cleanly nested (no overlapping like that which is tolerated in HTML today).

✦ All attribute values must be enclosed in quotation marks.

✦ Each document must have a unique first element (the document root).

Unlike HTML, syntax errors and other mistakes encountered in an XML document will cause the XML parser to halt processing of the document. This is important, because we are relying on XML to accurately describe our data. When dealing with data, there is no room for the ambiguities and loose interpretation that HTML allows in its syntax.

XML namespaces

When developing XML documents, it is common to refer to element and attribute names that share a common context as a vocabulary. Thus, we might say that our previous sample XML document belongs to a weather vocabulary.

Given that an XML document consists of a vocabulary that you define, the possibility arises that an element or attribute in that vocabulary may have a name that is identical to an element or attribute used by someone else in a different vocabulary. What's worse, what if someone else also defines a weather vocabulary that uses some of the same names, but whose elements mean something quite different or arranges the elements in a different hierarchy?

Let's take the case of our fictional weather example. The `<temperature>` element we used to define the current air temperature might also be used to define the temperature of a liquid or the surface temperature on Mars. How do we distinguish an air temperature from a liquid temperature or the surface temperature on Mars? Or, stated another way, how do we determine the vocabulary to which the temperature element belongs?

XML namespaces solve this ambiguity problem by associating an explicit namespace (or vocabulary) with elements and attributes in an XML document. Thus, a namespace is essentially a set of names in which all the element and attribute names can be guaranteed to be unique.

For example, we can slightly change our weather sample as follows:

```
<?xml version="1.0" encoding="UTF-8"?>
<weather xmlns="http://mydomain.com/xml/weather">
  <location city="St. Louis, MO">
    <forecast date="2001-07-15">
       <temperature units="F">80</temperature>
       <humidity units="%">55</humidity>
       <skies>Cloudy, 40% chance of showers</skies>
    </forecast>
  </location>
</weather>
```

In this example, the `<weather>` element includes a namespace declaration specified by the standard `xmlns` attribute. This defines a namespace using a URI with the name "http:// mydomain.com/xml/weather" for the `<weather>` element and all the elements contained within.

It is worth pointing out here that the URI used to define the namespace does not need to point at anything (unlike a URL). It is simply a method to uniquely identify your weather vocabulary from all others. Therefore, you will typically want to define namespaces using names that you own or have control over. Generally,

Internet domain names are used, because they are already guaranteed to be unique (and also identify the entity defining the namespace). However, when using the XML Schema Definition (XSD) language, this URI can point to the XSD file, which defines the schema for the XML document. We will cover the fundamental features of XSD in the next section.

A namespace can be declared using default declaration (as in our example) or explicit declaration. Let's take a brief look at these methods, because you'll see them frequently when examining XML documents related to Web services.

Default namespace declaration

Default declaration defines a namespace whose scope includes all elements contained within the element where the declaration was specified. Default declaration is typically used when a document contains elements from a single namespace. Our weather example used a default namespace declaration because all the elements shared the same context or vocabulary (in other words, none of the elements refers to elements from other namespaces).

Explicit namespace declaration

Explicit declaration defines a shorthand reference to an existing namespace. This method is used when referencing an element or attribute from other namespaces. For example, you could combine the elements from several namespaces into another XML document by using explicit namespace declaration as follows:

```
<weather:temperature
xmlns:weather="http://md.com/xml/weather">80</weather:temperatu
re>
<liquid:temperature
xmlns:liquid="http://md.com/xml/liquid">150</liquid:temperature
>
```

The name preceding the colon is called the prefix and serves as a shorthand notation so that references to the actual namespace URI do not have to be repeated everywhere an element or attribute is used within the document. Instead, you simply use the prefix to refer to the namespace. The only requirement for the shorthand name is that it must be unique within the context of the document that you are using.

Using namespaces in this way eliminates naming conflicts and guarantees that any two elements that have the same name must come from the same vocabulary. In our example, the weather temperature is clearly distinguished from the liquid temperature.

You will find explicit namespace declarations used in many places within the XML documents that are an integral part of the Web services architecture.

XML schemas

In our coverage of XML thus far, it was mentioned that the XML parser uses strict rules to ensure that the XML document is well formed. Recall that a well-formed XML document is one that follows the rules for properly closing tags, nesting tags, enclosing attributes in quotes, and using a unique first element.

However, this does not address the issue of validating that an XML document contains the proper assortment of elements and in valid combinations. What is needed is a language that will allow a generic XML parser to determine that the document conforms to these additional, user-defined rules.

The XSD language defines rules for describing the valid combinations and relationships of elements, attributes, and data types that can appear in an XML document. This enables authors as well as consumers to validate that the document is formed correctly according to the schema definition.

XSD syntax

An XSD schema document contains a top-level schema element. The schema element must define the XML schema namespace, as in the following:

```
<xsd:schema xmlns:xsd="http://www.w3.org/2001/XMLSchema">
```

The schema element contains type definitions and element/attribute declarations. XSD enables you to use built-in data types (such as integer and string) as well as user-defined data types when specifying the valid types of data that can be specified for particular elements in the schema definition.

In addition to the built-in data types, user-defined type definitions can be built using the simpleType and complexType elements. Element and attribute definitions are built using the element and attribute tags. The following example schema (again, using our weather forecast grammar) illustrates the use of these tags:

```
<?xml version="1.0" encoding="utf-8"?>
<xsd:schema xmlns:xsd="http://www.w3.org/2001/XMLSchema">

    <xsd:element name="skies" type="xsd:string" />
    <xsd:attribute name="city" type="xsd:string" />
    <xsd:attribute name="units" type="xsd:string" />
    <xsd:attribute name="date" type="xsd:date" />

    <xsd:element name="temperature">
        <xsd:complexType>
            <xsd:attribute ref="units" />
        </xsd:complexType>
```

```xml
        </xsd:element>

        <xsd:element name="humidity">
            <xsd:complexType>
                <xsd:attribute ref="units" />
            </xsd:complexType>
        </xsd:element>

        <xsd:element name="forecast">
            <xsd:complexType>
                <xsd:all>
                    <xsd:element ref="temperature" />
                    <xsd:element ref="humidity" />
                    <xsd:element ref="skies" />
                </xsd:all>
                <xsd:attribute ref="date" />
            </xsd:complexType>
        </xsd:element>

        <xsd:element name="location">
            <xsd:complexType>
                <xsd:all>
                    <xsd:element ref="forecast"
                        minOccurs="1" maxOccurs="unbounded" />
                </xsd:all>
                <xsd:attribute ref="city" />
            </xsd:complexType>
        </xsd:element>

        <xsd:element name="weather">
            <xsd:complexType>
                <xsd:all>
                    <xsd:element ref="location"
                        minOccurs="1" maxOccurs="unbounded" />
                </xsd:all>
            </xsd:complexType>
        </xsd:element>

    </xsd:schema>
```

The schema begins by declaring the `<xsd:schema>` root element.

The next several lines of the schema declare simple type elements and attributes, such as the `<skies>` element and the `<city>` attribute. As in regular programming, it is good practice to declare variables before they are referenced. This same practice is followed in defining XML schemas. All elements, whether simple or complex, should have their constituent types declared before they are referenced by other element declarations.

Following the simple type declarations are the complex type declarations, indicated by the `<complexType>` tag. The first of these is the `<temperature>` element declaration. Recall that any elements that contain attributes or other elements are defined as complex types. Because the `<temperature>` element has an associated `"units"` attribute, the declaration uses the `<complexType>` tag to form the declaration of this element. This same structure is used to declare the `<humidity>` element as well.

Note that this is the first use of the XSD schema `"ref"` attribute. This attribute is used to refer to a previously declared element in the schema. In this instance, you're referring to the `"units"` attribute that was declared earlier in the schema document.

The next part of the schema declares the `<forecast>` element. This is also a complex type declaration, as indicated by the `<complexType>` tag. The `<all>` tag indicates that the child elements can appear in any order within the `<forecast>` element.

The declaration of the `<location>` element closely resembles that of the `<forecast>` element. The major difference is the inclusion of the `"minOccurs"` and `"maxOccurs"` attributes in the declaration of the `<forecast>` element reference. These attributes control how many times a particular element can occur. The declaration states that at least one `<forecast>` element must appear within a `<location>` element. The term `"unbounded"` indicates that there is no upper limit to the number of `<forecast>` occurrences.

This brings us to the final declaration of the root `<weather>` element. As you can see, the `<weather>` element consists of at least one occurrence of a `<location>` element with no upper limit. This declaration is nearly identical to that of the `<location>` element preceding it.

By using the basic XML schema building blocks, you can describe the required vocabulary and structure for any arbitrary XML grammar and document derived from that grammar.

Given an XML document and a schema, an XML parser can validate the document against the schema and report any problems that it finds. This mechanism provides a simple method for determining that a particular document conforms to a specified XML grammar.

Previous to XSD, the Document Type Definition (DTD) language was used to describe the valid syntax of XML documents. Unfortunately, the DTD language had several drawbacks, which makes it unsuitable for use with Web services. Those of you who are familiar with and have used DTDs should be aware that they have been retired in favor of using XSD.

Note   To learn more about all the XML standards discussed in this book (as well as many others), you can visit the Worldwide Web Consortium at `http://www.w3.org`.

In short, XML is at the heart of Web services and, as you will soon see, is used to describe the data for many of the Web service technologies.

Exchanging Messages

Web services communicate in the form of messages. A request message delivers information about an operation to be executed and any data required to carry out that operation. Request messages flow from clients to Web services. A response message delivers information about the results of the operation execution. Response messages flow from Web services to clients.

Communication via messages is an extremely effective method for insulating Web service consumers from the implementation details of the service. Of course, it is necessary to define, in a standard way, the rules for how these messages should be formatted and what they can contain.

Message exchange with SOAP

The Simple Object Access Protocol (SOAP) is an industry-standard message format that enables message-based communication for Web services. SOAP implements a message format based on XML to exchange function requests and responses. Using XML as the basis for SOAP messages makes it possible for these messages to be understandable and transportable by any system that implements basic Internet communications services.

SOAP simply defines a message format. It does not impose a specific transport protocol for exchanging these messages. Thus, it is possible to transport SOAP messages over any one of many different and widely available transport protocols such as HTTP, SMTP, FTP, and so on. Note, however, that the HTTP POST command is the default method for transporting SOAP requests and responses.

 Tip SOAP uses the term "binding" when referring to a specific protocol that is used to transport SOAP messages.

A SOAP request is an HTTP POST request. An HTTP POST request (like all HTTP commands) consists of human-readable text that contains one or more headers followed by the command payload. The payload is separated from the headers by a blank line.

A SOAP request over HTTP uses the payload section of the HTTP POST request to contain the encoded SOAP envelope. The following code shows the structure of a simple SOAP message using HTTP POST as the transport mechanism:

```
POST /TemperatureConverter/TemperatureConverter.asmx HTTP/1.1
Host: jdc7200cte
Content-Type: text/xml; charset=utf-8
Content-Length: {length}
SOAPAction: "http://tempuri.org/ConvertTemperature"
```

```
<?xml version="1.0" encoding="utf-8"?>
<soap:Envelope xmlns:xsi="http://www.w3.org/2001/XMLSchema-
instance" xmlns:xsd="http://www.w3.org/2001/XMLSchema"
xmlns:soap="http://schemas.xmlsoap.org/soap/envelope/">
  <soap:Body>
    <ConvertTemperature xmlns="http://tempuri.org/">
      <Temperature>{decimal}</Temperature>
      <FromUnits>{string}</FromUnits>
      <ToUnits>{string}</ToUnits>
    </ConvertTemperature>
  </soap:Body>
</soap:Envelope>
```

As shown in the sample code, SOAP messages must use the `text/xml` content type. Note that named placeholders have been substituted (enclosed in { and }) where the SOAP message would normally contain the actual content length and specific argument values associated with (in this case) the request.

The example also illustrates the basic structure of a SOAP message. The outermost element in a SOAP payload is the envelope. The envelope encapsulates the various parts of a SOAP message. Within the envelope are elements that define SOAP headers (not present in this example) and the SOAP body, which defines the specific request or response message.

Because SOAP uses XML to encode commands and data, the SOAP message format can pass any kind of data that can be described in XML! This includes classic scalar and array data types as well as complex document types such as invoices, purchase orders, and so forth.

We will discuss SOAP in more detail in Chapter 24, "Understanding SOAP." To learn more about the SOAP protocol and standard, visit `http://www.soap.org` or `http://www.w3.org/soap`.

Message exchange with HTTP-GET and HTTP-POST

In addition to SOAP, Web services can also exchange messages using HTTP-GET and HTTP-POST. These verbs are standard messages of the HTTP protocol that enable the exchange of information as name/value pairs.

HTTP-GET passes name/value pairs as UUencoded text appended to the URL of a request. This method of passing parameters is referred to as a query string.

Figure 22-1 shows an example of a URL with a query string.

Figure 22-1: An HTTP-GET request with a query string

In Figure 22-1, the URL is specified as: `http://jdc7200cte/Demo/`
`TemperatureConverter.asmx/ConvertTemperature?Temperature=98.`
`6&FromUnits=F&ToUnits=C`. Note that the ? character separates the base URL
from the list of name/value pairs. Following the ? delimiter, each name/value pair
is encoded as follows:

```
Name=value
```

Multiple name/value pairs are separated by the & character. In the example from
Figure 22-1, the name/value pairs are the following:

- ✦ Temperature=98.6
- ✦ FromUnits=F
- ✦ ToUnits=C

HTTP-POST also passes name/value pairs as UUencoded text, except that the
parameters are passed within the actual HTTP request header rather than as
a query string appended to the URL. This is shown below:

```
POST /TemperatureConverter/TemperatureConverter.asmx HTTP/1.1
Host: jdc7200cte
Content-Type: text; charset=utf-8
Content-Length: {length}
```

```
Temperature=98.6
FromUnits=F
ToUnits=C
```

 Note   Because HTTP-GET and HTTP-POST utilize name/value pairs to encode data, the list of data types that can be supported is more limited than using SOAP. So, generally, using SOAP will provide for more flexibility in passing complex data types such as classes, datasets, XML documents, and so forth.

Describing Web Service Capabilities

Given a standard method to encode data (XML) and a standard method to exchange Web service requests and responses via messages (SOAP), we need a standard way to describe the specific message exchanges (or capabilities) that a Web service supports.

Recall that SOAP defines a message format based on XML to enable exchange of method requests and responses. However, SOAP does not define the specific methods and results that a Web service may offer.

Those of you familiar with COM programming know that COM components use interfaces to describe their capabilities to a potential consumer. This is done using a language called Interface Definition Language (IDL). Compiling an IDL file results in the creation of a Type Library (TLB). A Type Library in COM contains all the information necessary to query the specific capabilities of the COM component (in other words, the objects, methods, attributes, events, and so on that it supports).

Similar to the Type Library concept in COM, Web services must have a method to describe to potential consumers the specific capabilities that the service offers. Without this capability, consumers would not be able to determine how to request some functionality of the Web service or what to expect as a response.

A Web service description is an XML document (surprise!) that defines the capabilities that a Web service offers. This document provides essential information in a structured form that enables a consumer to understand how to interact with a Web service. The Web Service Description Language (WSDL) defines a standard, extensible XML grammar that is used to define these Web service descriptions in the form of an XML document.

The WSDL document defines the message formats and message exchange patterns that a Web service can process. In addition to these definitions, the WSDL document contains the address of each Web service entry point, formatted according to the protocol used to access the service (for example, a URL for HTTP or an e-mail address for SMTP).

A WSDL document defines services as a collection of network endpoints, or ports using the elements listed in Table 22-1.

Table 22-1 WSDL elements	
Types	A container for data type definitions using some type system (such as XSD)
Message	An abstract, typed definition of the data being communicated
Operation	An abstract description of an action supported by the Web service
Port Type	An abstract set of operations supported by one or more endpoints
Binding	A concrete protocol and data format specification for a particular port type
Port	A single endpoint defined as a combination of a binding and a network address
Service	A collection of related endpoints

Let's take a look at a sample WSDL document that describes the capabilities of a Web service named CTemp (we will be building this Web service in an upcoming chapter). The CTemp Web service converts temperature values between various numeric units. A partial listing of the WSDL document for this service is as follows:

```
<?xml version="1.0" encoding="utf-8" ?>
<definitions xmlns:s="http://www.w3.org/2001/XMLSchema"

xmlns:http="http://schemas.xmlsoap.org/wsdl/http/"

xmlns:mime="http://schemas.xmlsoap.org/wsdl/mime/"

xmlns:tm="http://microsoft.com/wsdl/mime/textMatching/"

xmlns:soap="http://schemas.xmlsoap.org/wsdl/soap/"

xmlns:soapenc="http://schemas.xmlsoap.org/soap/encoding/"
                   xmlns:s0="http://tempuri.org/"
                     targetNamespace="http://tempuri.org/"
                   xmlns="http://schemas.xmlsoap.org/wsdl/">
<types>
<s:schema
attributeFormDefault="qualified"elementFormDefault="qualified"
                   targetNamespace="http://tempuri.org/">
<s:element name="CTemp">
<s:complexType>
<s:sequence>
   <s:element minOccurs="1" maxOccurs="1"name="Temperature"
                      type="s:decimal" />
   <s:element minOccurs="1" maxOccurs="1"name="FromUnits"
nillable="true"
                      type="s:string" />
```

```
   <s:element minOccurs="1" maxOccurs="1"name="ToUnits"
nillable="true"
                        type="s:string" />
   </s:sequence>
   </s:complexType>
   </s:element>
<s:element name="CTempResponse">
<s:complexType>
<s:sequence>
   <s:element minOccurs="1" maxOccurs="1"name="CTempResult"
type="s:decimal" />
   </s:sequence>
   </s:complexType>
   </s:element>
   <s:element name="decimal" type="s:decimal" />
   </s:schema>
   </types>
<message name="CTempSoapIn">
   <part name="parameters" element="s0:CTemp" />
   </message>
<message name="CTempSoapOut">
   <part name="parameters" element="s0:CTempResponse" />
   </message>
<portType name="TempConverterSoap">
<operation name="CTemp">
   <input message="s0:CTempSoapIn" />
   <output message="s0:CTempSoapOut" />
   </operation>
   </portType>
<binding name="TempConverterSoap" type="s0:TempConverterSoap">
   <soap:binding
transport=http://schemas.xmlsoap.org/soap/httpstyle="document"
/>
<operation name="CTemp">
   <soap:operation soapAction=http://tempuri.org/CTemp
style="document"
/>
<input>
   <soap:body use="literal" />
   </input>
<output>
   <soap:body use="literal" />
   </output>
   </operation>
   </binding>
<service name="TempConverter">
<port name="TempConverterSoap" binding="s0:TempConverterSoap">
   <soap:address
location="http://jdc7200cte/Services/Ctemp/CTemp.asmx"
/>
   </port>
   </service>
   </definitions>
```

As shown in this example, the CTemp Web service supports a single method named CTemp that accepts the three input arguments shown in Table 22-2.

Table 22-2 CTemp method arguments and data types	
Argument	**Data Type**
Temperature	Decimal
FromUnits	String
ToUnits	String

In addition, CTemp returns a result of type Decimal. You can also see that the Web service supports the HTTP-GET, HTTP-POST, and SOAP protocols for transporting the request and response messages.

As of the writing of this book, the WSDL specification had been submitted to the World Wide Web Consortium as a Note for review. For its part, the W3C has created a group called the XML Protocol activity whose mission is to define and formalize standards around using XML for distributed applications to communicate on a peer-to-peer basis. This includes the WSDL specification as well as several others.

Note   For more information about the WSDL specification, visit `www.w3.org/TR/WSDL.html`. For more information about the XML Protocol's activity, visit `www.w3.org/2000/xp`. Finally, you can read more about SOAP messaging by visiting `http://www.w3.org/TR/2001/WD-soap12-part1-20011002/`.

Publishing and Finding Web Services

Given a standard means to describe the capabilities of a Web service via the WSDL document, we must now consider how a potential consumer of a Web service will locate a WSDL document on a target Web server. Recall that to consume a service, a client must be able to determine how to interact with that Web service, which means that it must follow the message formats and message exchange patterns described for the Web service in the WSDL document.

Of course, if you are both the author and consumer of the Web service, you probably will not need help in locating the WSDL document. However, if you will be consuming Web services from other authors, you may not know where a particular service is located on a target Web server. Web service authors use a discovery

(DISCO) document to publish their Web service. The DISCO document is an XML document that contains pointers to such things as the WSDL file for the Web service.

Web service consumers employ a discovery process to learn that a Web service exists and where to find the Web service's WSDL document. Web service consumers enact this discovery process on a target Web server by providing a URL to a discovery tool. The discovery tool attempts to locate DISCO documents on the target server and informs the consumer of the location of any available WSDL documents.

As mentioned earlier, the DISCO document is encoded as an XML document, which provides the ability to programmatically discover information about Web services. This technique has enabled the creation of tools that can be used by a consumer to locate Web services. The Microsoft .NET Framework provides a tool named `disco.exe` to enable Web service discovery. In addition, Visual Studio .NET has integrated support for Web service discovery using the concept of Web References. We will learn more about the `disco` tool and its capabilities in upcoming chapters.

The following sample illustrates the structure of a DISCO document:

```
<?xml version="1.0" ?>
<disco:discovery
xmlns:disco="http://schemas.xmlsoap.org/disco"
xmlns:wsdl="http://schemas.xmlsoap.org/disco/wsdl">
        <wsdl:contractRef
ref="http://jdc7200cte/Services/CTemp/CTemp.asmx?WSDL"/>
</disco:discovery>
```

In this sample, a pointer to the WSDL document is contained in a contractRef element, which contains the URL that points to the WSDL document.

An interesting feature of the DISCO document is that it need not physically reside alongside the Web service description document or other Web service implementation files, because the DISCO document provides information about resources such as the Web service description via pointers. Thus, it is possible to distribute DISCO documents to centralized Web service directories, which can be used to more easily locate Web services.

Note Enabling discovery of your Web service is optional. You may not wish to enable discovery if you are providing a Web service for restricted and/or private use, or you have delegated the discovery process to a dedicated directory server instead of the host Web server.

While this book was being written, the DISCO technology had been submitted to the W3C XML Protocols activity for consideration. You can find out more about DISCO in the Microsoft .NET Framework documentation and at the W3C Web site.

Finding Web Service Providers

As more and more Web services are created and deployed by numerous organizations on the Internet, it will become increasingly more difficult for consumers to find these services. This is analogous to the difficulty Web users might experience in finding a specific page of information amongst the billions of pages of information currently published on the Web were it not for Web search engines.

Similar to the search engine approach that is used to query and locate Web pages, the Universal Description, Discovery, and Integration (UDDI) specification defines a logically centralized but physically distributed, XML-based registry database and API for companies to find each other and the Web services that they offer. The UDDI registry API offers support for querying as well as updating the registry database.

The UDDI Web site (located at `http://www.uddi.org`) provides a browser-based interface for registering your company and services as well as the capability to look up potential business partners.

The true power of the UDDI business registry lies in the UDDI Web service (that's right, UDDI is itself a Web service), which provides a mechanism for ad-hoc discovery of potential business partners and dynamic integration of Web services. Visual Studio .NET has support for UDDI built into the "Web Reference" metaphor used to locate and consume Web services.

UDDI defines, classifies and stores three basic types of information:

✦ **White Pages:** Describes address, contact, and other standard business demographic information

✦ **Yellow Pages:** Describes industrial categorizations for businesses based on standard categories

✦ **Green Pages:** Describes the technical specification for Web services

Collectively, these three types of data provide a flexible and effective method for locating Web services.

In July 2001, version 2.0 of the UDDI specification was released, and several registry databases are currently operational. You can see the latest list of registries by visiting `http://www.uddi.org`. As of the writing of this book, both IBM and Microsoft had registries online and operational. These registries are available from the UDDI Web site. If you wish to find potential Web service providers, you can browse to `http://www.uddi.org/find.html` or click the Find tab on the UDDI home page. The Find page is shown in Figure 22-2.

If you wish to register your business and any Web services that you offer, you can browse to `http://www.uddi.org/register.html` or click the Register tab on the UDDI home page. The Register page is shown in Figure 22-3.

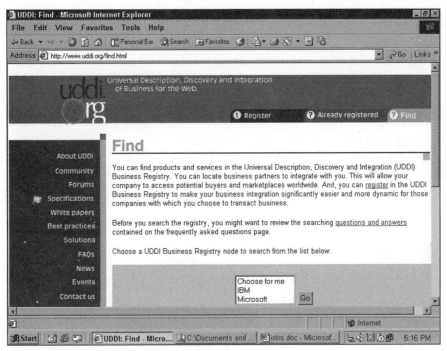

Figure 22-2: The UDDI Find page

More than 280 companies have now come on board to support the specification, and the outlook is good that UDDI will become the standard method for locating business partners and Web services on the Internet. In addition, the service is free to use.

Searching the UDDI database from the UDDI Web site is free and does not require registration or authentication. However, if you wish to register your company in the database, you must first obtain a username/password from the registry site before you can register your company. This is necessary so that you can control who is able to change your company information in the database.

For its part, Microsoft is using (or has plans to use) UDDI as a core building block in the .NET platform. It has plans to integrate UDDI into such products as Microsoft BizTalk Server, Microsoft PassPort, Microsoft bCentral, and the Microsoft .NET Framework. And, as mentioned earlier, support for UDDI is also built into Visual Studio .NET.

Note   For more information about UDDI, you can visit http://www.uddi.org.

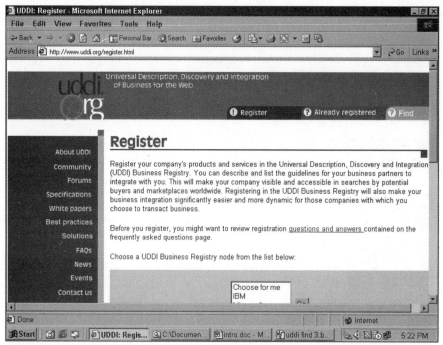

Figure 22-3: The UDDI Register page

Microsoft HailStorm

With the creation of such an important and far-reaching technology as Web services, it is not surprising that major software vendors are planning to deliver a horizontal set of useful Web services that will be needed by many next-generation Web-based applications.

Microsoft itself has announced that it will deliver a set of Web services based on the .NET technologies codenamed "HailStorm." These services collect and store personal information that can be shared with other applications and services based entirely on your consent and control.

Nearly all of us have dealt with the frustration of having multiple usernames, passwords, and profiles for the myriad sites and services that we visit on the Web. What's more, each site that retains this personal information has differing privacy policies and procedures for sharing this information with partners.

HailStorm promises to eliminate this frustration and lack of control over your personal information and replace it with a single source for this data that is under your complete control with respect to accessing this information.

Microsoft has announced that it will release the following sets of HailStorm services initially:

✦ **MyAddress:** Electronic and geographic address for an identity. For example, your mailing address and/or your e-mail address can be managed by this service.

✦ **MyProfile:** Name, nickname, special dates, pictures, and other more personal information about yourself.

✦ **MyContacts:** Electronic relationships/address book that maintains names, e-mail addresses, and other information about your personal contacts.

✦ **MyLocation:** Electronic and geographical location and rendezvous. This service provides information to help locate you electronically.

✦ **MyNotifications:** Notification subscription, management, and routing provide services that let you control automatic notifications via e-mail, paging, etc for items that are important to you.

✦ **MyInbox:** Inbox items like e-mail and voice mail, including existing mail systems enables you to centrally manage your e-mail and related information.

✦ **MyCalendar:** Time and task management services.

✦ **MyDocuments**: Raw document storage. Think of this as a virtual disk drive that exists in the Internet for storing your documents so that they are available no matter where you are.

✦ **MyApplicationSettings:** This service permits your application-specific preferences and other settings to be centrally managed and available to your applications regardless of where you use them.

✦ **MyFavoriteWebSites:** Favorite URLs and other Web identifiers are made available to you no matter where you are when browsing the Web.

✦ **MyWallet:** Receipts, payment instruments, coupons, and other transaction records are managed by this service so that they can be used by many Web applications that need this information, without having to duplicate it over and over.

✦ **MyDevices:** Device settings, capabilities, and related information about the devices that you use on your computer or network-attached devices.

✦ **MyServices**: Services provided for an identity.

✦ **MyUsage:** Usage report for services that can report what services you used how much (or how often) you used them, and so on.

Of course, one of the most important issues related to the use of these technologies is personal data security. Because all of these services store personal information of some nature, it is imperative that this data be protected according to your wishes. Consequently, interaction with your personal data will only be allowed with your explicit authorization. You will be able to do the following:

✦ Determine who or what services have access to your data

✦ Revoke or deny these privileges at will or on a timed basis

Unfortunately, not very much information was available about HailStorm when this book was being written. By the time you read this, however, a broadly available beta version of these initial HailStorm services is expected to be released. For more information about HailStorm, visit `http://www.microsoft.com/net` and `http://msdn.microsoft.com/net`.

Summary

Providing a foundation for the creation and consumption of Web services based on standards such as XML, SOAP, WSDL, DISCO, and UDDI makes Web services capable of being supported on any platform that implements XML and HTTP. What's more, having an infrastructure that supports these standards makes it possible for development tools and platforms such as the .NET Framework and Visual Studio .NET to supply these capabilities to your Web services automatically, greatly simplifying and accelerating the Web service development process. We will see the fruits of this labor as we begin working with the Microsoft .NET Framework tools to create a Web service.

✦   ✦   ✦

Web Services Infrastructure

In this chapter, you will learn about the Microsoft technologies and tools that provide the essential architectural elements for executing, creating, and consuming Web services on the Microsoft platform.

Although it is possible to build or consume Web services on a platform with support for only the core technologies (XML, TCP/IP, HTTP, and SOAP), it is certainly not a task suited for the beginning programmer or the easily intimidated.

The power of the infrastructure on which the Microsoft Web Services implementation is built is embodied in the basic design principal that Web services should be simple to create and easy to consume. Rather than waste your time writing Web service infrastructure code, you should be able to focus your time and energy on the actual functionality of your application and let the platform do the rest.

The technologies and tools provided in the Microsoft .NET Framework do just that. These technologies give you an excellent, easy-to-use platform for building and consuming Web services quickly and efficiently.

Microsoft Web Services Platform

In the last chapter, you learned that Web services are built on the foundation of XML, HTTP, and SOAP. Using these technologies, Web services enable the creation of distributed applications that can easily leverage the size and diversity of the Internet.

One of the primary motivations behind the creation of the Web services architecture was the inadequacy of existing distributed object model technologies, such as DCOM, CORBA, and IIOP, for Internet-based applications. Although each of these technologies worked well in a controlled, homogeneous environment, this obviously cannot be guaranteed for systems on the Internet.

What's more, these legacy object technologies could also be extremely large and complex (some more than others). Again, this makes it difficult to rely on these older technologies as a foundation for distributed computing on the Internet.

One of the major advantages of the Web services foundation is its simplicity as well as its reliance on existing (or emerging) Internet standards. This ensures that Web services can be implemented on and available across the diverse systems of the Internet.

Although the Web services foundation does a great job of enabling a programmable Internet composed of distributed building blocks, there's really much more to creating scalable, robust, distributed applications. Each individual platform must supply these services, because the Web services foundation does not attempt to address these issues.

The Microsoft .NET platform is specifically designed to provide these essential services, which makes it easy to create world-class Web Services. Figure 23-1 illustrates the Microsoft Web Services platform architecture.

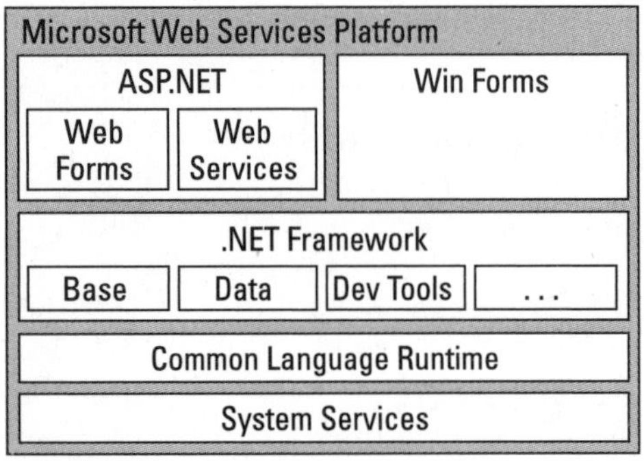

Figure 23-1: Microsoft Web Services platform architecture

The Common Language Runtime (CLR) is built on top of the system platform (such as Windows 2000). Layered on the CLR is the .NET Framework Class Library, which provides a large set of services via a hierarchically arranged collection of classes and types. On top of this base is the ASP.NET Web platform and Windows Forms environments. We will take a look at most of these architectural pieces in upcoming sections of this chapter, as they relate to the development and consumption of Web services.

One of the primary goals of the Microsoft Web Services platform is to make it easy to build Web services that can solve complex, business-critical issues. The following sections take a look at the Web Services platform features that supply critical services that not only make it possible to create these types of applications, but also make it easy.

The Microsoft .NET Framework

The .NET Framework is Microsoft's next-generation platform for building and deploying robust Web services. It has been designed specifically to address the many requirements of delivering Web services that can fulfill the vision of the programmable Internet.

Key features of the .NET Framework that provide support for Web services include:

✦ The Common Language Runtime (CLR)

✦ The .NET Framework Class Library

✦ ASP.NET

Let's examine some of the features of these key .NET Framework pieces that provide a solid environment for the creation and execution of world-class Web services.

The Common Language Runtime

The CLR provides the foundation for the .NET Framework. The CLR is responsible for managing code at execution time and provides the following services:

✦ Cross-language integration

✦ Self-describing objects

✦ Automatic memory management

✦ Thread management

✦ Remoting

✦ Code safety and security

✦ Code versioning and deployment support

Code that targets the CLR is called *managed* code. Compatible language compilers generate code that enables the CLR to manage the execution of your applications. To do this, compilers generate what is called Microsoft Intermediate Language (MSIL). This intermediate code is platform-independent; in other words, it can be hosted on any processor architecture supported by the CLR. A Just-In-Time (JIT) compiler is used to convert MSIL to processor-specific code at run time. During execution, CLR-managed code automatically receives the benefits of memory management, cross-language debugging support, security, and many other features.

Managed code is packaged into units called *assemblies*. Assemblies are the building blocks of .NET Framework applications and form the fundamental unit of deployment, version control, reuse, and security. An assembly contains all the information necessary for the CLR to provide its services.

A major design goal of the CLR (as is true of all the pieces in the Web Services architecture) is to make the development process easier. As you can see, the CLR provides an excellent execution environment for Web services, relieving developers from the responsibility of providing and managing these features themselves, thereby allowing them to easily and quickly build and deploy robust Web service applications that take advantage of the CLR.

Now that you know a little about the CLR and its contribution to the Web Services platform, let's take a few moments to look into the next layer of the architecture: the .NET Framework Class Library.

The .NET Framework Class Library

The .NET Framework Class Library is a collection of classes that are organized into a single hierarchical tree of namespaces. The Class Library provides access to system features via classes, interfaces, and value types, which greatly enhances programmer productivity and simplifies the development process. The Class Library is built on top of the CLR. Therefore, it is also managed code that receives all the benefits provided by the CLR.

At the root of the Class Library hierarchy is the System namespace, which contains over 100 core types and classes that are used by all .NET applications. In addition to the System namespace, the Class Library contains namespaces for abstract base classes and derived class implementations. This includes file I/O, messaging, networking, security, and, of course, access to the Internet. You can use these classes as is, or derive from them to create your own implementations.

The .NET Framework uses a dot-based naming scheme to represent grouped classes and types that comprise a namespace. Namespaces make it easier to search for and reference classes and types. The namespace name includes everything from the beginning of the name up to the last dot in the name. The remaining part of the name identifies the type name. For example, the System.Web namespace defines the Web type, which belongs to the System namespace.

Table 23-1 lists some of the namespaces that implement features of Web services on the .NET platform.

Table 23-1 .NET Web Service namespaces	
Namespace	**Purpose**
System.Web.Services	Contains classes that enable you to build and consume Web services.
System.Web.Services.Description	Contains classes that enable you to describe a Web service via the Web Service Description Language (WSDL).
System.Web.Services.Discovery	Contains classes that implement the discovery process used by Web service consumers to locate available Web services.
System.Web.Services.Protocols	Contains classes that implement the protocols used to exchange Web service messages between Web services and Web service consumers.

These are just the Web service–specific namespaces. As you will learn in the next section, the ASP.NET platform provides a robust framework and application environment for developing and executing Web applications (including Web services) that is built on top of the .NET Class Library and the CLR.

ASP.NET

ASP.NET is a unified Web development platform that provides advanced services for building Web applications and Web services. ASP.NET provides a new programming model and infrastructure that enables you to create powerful Web applications with unprecedented speed, flexibility, and ease. ASP.NET is fully supported by the .NET Framework, enabling you to take full advantage of the CLR, type safety, inheritance, and all the other features of that platform.

Unlike Active Server Pages (ASP), ASP.NET is a compiled, .NET-based platform. ASP.NET applications can be built using any .NET-compatible programming language. Also, because ASP.NET is built on top of the .NET Framework, your ASP.NET applications have access to the entire range of functionality provided by the framework.

Among the major advantages of the ASP.NET environment are the following:

✦ ASP.NET applications are fully compiled .NET applications, providing superior performance characteristics.

✦ ASP.NET supports WYSIWYG HTML editors and programming environments such as Visual Studio .NET. This enables you to be very productive when developing ASP.NET applications and enables you to leverage the many features of these tools.

✦ ASP.NET applications support extensive configuration capabilities based on XML configuration files.

✦ ASP.NET provides flexible, advanced, and easy-to-use application and session state management features that can be extended or replaced with custom schemes.

✦ ASP.NET implements multiple authentication and authorization schemes that can be extended or replaced with custom schemes.

ASP.NET provides two programming models that can be used to create Web applications: Web Forms and Web Services. Web Forms enable you to build forms-based Web applications using a technology called *server controls,* which enable you to create user interfaces from common UI elements such as text boxes, list boxes, and so on. Web Services, of course, are the subject of this chapter.

ASP.NET Web Services can take advantage of all ASP.NET features as well as the features of the .NET Framework and CLR. Let's take a look at some of these features, because you will likely interact with many of them when implementing your Web service applications. ASP.NET leverages the classes found in the .NET Framework Class Library to support Web services and the many other features this environment provides to developers.

As you read through the ASP.NET feature overviews found in the following sections, remember that each of these features can be leveraged by your Web service applications. As you will see, having these capabilities at your fingertips makes developing world-class Web services much easier.

ASP.NET applications

An ASP.NET application consists of all the files, pages, handlers, modules, and executable code that reside in a Web server virtual directory (and any subdirectories). Web services are also ASP.NET applications and, therefore, are governed by the same configuration rules as any other ASP.NET application.

Each ASP.NET application can include an optional Global.asax file in the root virtual directory. This file contains handlers for application-level events that can be raised by ASP.NET. For example, you can handle such events as `Application_OnStart` and `Application_OnEnd` in the Global.asax file.

In addition to these events, you have access to any events exposed by HTTPModules. An HTTPModule is a class that can process information from any HTTP requests made to your ASP.NET application. You can customize or extend modules supplied by ASP.NET or create your own. Any events raised by HTTPModules are handled within the Global.asax file.

ASP.NET applications also support a hierarchical application configuration architecture. Application configuration settings are stored in an XML file named Web.config. The settings stored in this file are applied hierarchically as follows:

✦ Web.config files supply their settings to the directory in which they are located as well as to all subdirectories.

✦ Configuration settings for a Web resource are supplied by the Web.config file located in the same directory as the resource and by all configuration files in all parent directories.

The default, global configuration file is named Machine.config and is stored at %SYSTEM_ROOT%\Microsoft.NET\Framework*version*\CONFIG. If no developer-supplied configuration files are found, the settings in this file will apply to your Web application.

State management

HTTP is a stateless protocol. This means that HTTP does not retain any information or knowledge from one request to the next even though those requests may come from the same user session and may even be related to each other. Of course, if you are building Web applications, the lack of such state information can make it extremely difficult to develop applications that require such information.

ASP.NET provides both application state and session state management capabilities for Web applications. *Application state* is used to store data that applies to the application as a whole and is available to all sessions using the application. *Session state* is used to store data that is specific to each browser session using the application. Session state is not visible across different sessions (unlike application state).

Both application and session state information is stored in key/value dictionary objects. Access to this information is supplied through an Application object (for application state) and a Session object (for session state).

Application state is essentially a global variable-storage mechanism for ASP.NET applications. Experienced developers know that global variables come with specific issues and must be considered and used sparingly. This is even more important in a server-based scenario, such as ASP.NET applications. In particular, you should be aware of the following when considering the use of application state in ASP.NET applications:

✦ Memory used by application variables is not released between requests. Thus, it can have extended effects on server memory use. Therefore, you should be a good custodian of application state memory.

✦ Application variables have concurrency and synchronization issues. Because multiple requests can be executing simultaneously, any changes to application-scoped variables must be synchronized. This can cause concurrency issues and slow down server performance.

✦ Application state is not shared across a Web farm (where an application is hosted on multiple servers) or Web garden (where an application is hosted on multiple processes on a single server).

These issues are certainly not meant to scare you away from using application state. On the contrary, used properly, application state can be a very valuable tool for Web applications. Before embarking on their use, however, you need to clearly understand the capabilities and limitations of application state within ASP.NET and the typical applications in which application state can be used effectively.

Session state permits you to automatically identify requests that come from the same browser client as well as store information specific to that session. ASP.NET session state provides the following features:

✦ Session state can survive IIS and worker-process restarts without losing session state information.

✦ Session state can be used in both Web farm and Web garden configurations.

✦ Session state can be used even if the client browser does not support cookies.

ASP.NET session state can be fully configured to meet your specific needs via the Config.web configuration files. For Web applications that require session state, ASP.NET provides excellent, reliable, and scalable support for maintaining session state.

Caching

One of the most important factors in creating highly scalable, high-performance Web applications is through the use of caching. Essentially, caching permits the Web application to supply the results of a previous request to other requests for the same information without having to involve the server in regenerating this information. This can greatly increase the performance of your Web application.

ASP.NET provides two types of caching capabilities. Output caching supplies the output of previous requests from the output cache instead of re-executing the server code necessary to generate the output a second time. The application cache is a programmatic cache that applications can use to store objects and other resources that can take a lot of time to re-create.

Transactions

A transaction is a set of related tasks that either succeed or fail as a unit. By combining a set of related operations into a unit that either completely succeeds or completely fails, you can simplify error recovery and make your application more reliable.

ASP.NET Web Services support declarative, attribute-based transactions at the method level. This means that you can specify, via a property of the `WebMethod` attribute, what, if any, type of transaction support is required for your Web service method. Subsequently, any resource managers that you interact with during the execution of the Web method (such as SQL Server, Message Queue Server, SNA Server, Oracle Server, and so on) will be transacted.

Security

ASP.NET provides a comprehensive, flexible, and extensible security framework that enables you to secure your Web services. The security framework addresses four fundamental security needs:

✦ **Authentication:** To determine that a user is who he/she claims to be

✦ **Authorization:** To control access to resources based on the identity of a user

✦ **Impersonation:** To assume the identity of the requesting user when accessing resources

✦ **Code Access Security:** To restrict the operations that a piece of code can perform (or has intentions of performing)

Fundamentally, ASP.NET uses the services of Internet Information Services (IIS) to obtain requests for pages or Web services. Thus, ASP.NET is capable of utilizing the security features of IIS. Currently, ASP.NET is hosted by IIS 5.0, which means that it relies on the basic security features provided by IIS 5.0. Three authentication mechanisms are supported by IIS 5.0: Basic, Digest, and Integrated Windows.

In addition to the authentication services provided by IIS, ASP.NET supports two additional types of authentication: Forms and Passport. Forms authentication enables custom authentication to occur via support provided by the application. For example, you may use a custom SQL Server database of defined users and passwords to identify users. Passport authentication is a centralized authentication service provided by Microsoft that offers a single sign-on feature along with basic profile services.

ASP.NET security is configured in the ASP.NET application configuration file (named Web.config). Using this configuration file, you can specify how users are authenticated, control access to resources via authorization settings, and determine impersonation settings.

Web Services Infrastructure

In the last chapter, you learned that four primary infrastructure pieces are specifically needed to support Web services:

✦ Web Service Directories, which provide a means to locate providers of Web services

✦ Web Service Discovery, which provides the capability to locate Web services

✦ Web Service Description, which enables Web service capabilities to be described

✦ Web Service Wire Formats, which allow Web services to exchange data and messages

Collectively, these technologies provide services that are essential to the creation and consumption of Web services. In the next few sections, you will learn how this Web service infrastructure is provided on the Microsoft .NET Web Services platform.

Web Service directories

Recall that Web service directories provide a centralized, Internet-accessible location that consumers can use to find Web services that have been offered for use by other companies or organizations. You can think of Web service directories as a type of Web portal or "Yellow Pages" specifically suited for listing and locating Web services.

Using Web service directories, you can search for Web services using a variety of structured criteria, such as business type, industry, type of goods produced, services offered, and so on. For example, if you were looking for a credit card validation Web service, you could search the directory using personal credit companies as the criteria.

Currently, the Universal Description, Discovery, and Integration (UDDI) specification is the de facto standard for cataloging and finding Web services. The UDDI organization (located on the Web at `http://www.uddi.org`), composed of several hundred industry participants, has created a directory schema, distributed repository, and APIs for manipulating and querying the repository.

Currently, Microsoft and IBM both have cooperating UDDI directories operational and available for general use. These sites include operational Web services, which can be called to programmatically manipulate and query the UDDI registry database.

If you are using Microsoft Visual Studio .NET to create your Web services or Web service consumer applications, the Web Reference feature of Visual Studio has the ability to search these online UDDI directories automatically. In fact, the Visual Studio .NET Web Reference feature is itself a consumer of the UDDI Web services.

Alternatively, if you are not using Visual Studio .NET, you can use the UDDI Web site to search for Web services. The Web site contains interactive forms for manipulating and querying the registry database.

If neither of these methods suits your needs, you can also download a UDDI SDK from either Microsoft or IBM, which you can use to create your own custom search tool.

We will examine in detail how to use these services in Chapter 28, "Consuming Web Services."

Web Service discovery

Web service discovery is the process of locating one or more related documents that describe a specific Web service. Recall that Web services are described in terms of the request messages they are capable of processing and the response messages (if any) that they return. These capabilities are described in a standard way using the Web Service Description Language (WSDL), which is an XML grammar specifically designed for this purpose.

Before you can submit requests to a Web service, you must know how to format requests for a particular service in the form of a message that encodes the operation requested (such as converting a temperature from one unit to another) as well as any data required to carry out the operation (such as the input temperature, the source units, and the target units). In addition, you must know whether or not to expect a response message from the Web service and what format this response will take (such as the converted temperature value).

The Web service discovery process permits a consumer to search for and locate the WSDL document for a Web service. As implied, a consumer must have possession of the WSDL document before any requests can be properly formatted and delivered to the Web service.

The DISCO specification defines an XML-based grammar and algorithm for discovering the existence of Web services and locating their WSDL document. Using DISCO, you can define search trees that are processed according to the DISCO algorithm to locate Web service descriptions. Of course, if you already know the location of the WSDL document for a specific Web service, this discovery process is not needed.

Discovery documents are XML files that have a file extension of .vsdisco. The discovery document is a container for two types of elements: pointers to WSDL documents and pointers to other discovery documents. These pointers take the form of a URL and can be absolute or relative. The `<contractRef>` element is used to link to Web Service WSDL documents, whereas the `<discoveryRef>` element is used to link to other discovery documents.

If you are using Microsoft Visual Studio .NET to create your Web services or Web service consumer applications, the Web Reference feature of Visual Studio has the ability to locate Web services automatically using the discovery process. To do this, you simply enter the URL of a discovery document in the address bar of the dialog box. This will initiate the discovery process starting at the requested URL.

Alternatively, if you are not using Visual Studio .NET, you can use the .NET Framework's *disco* tool to search for Web service description files. The *disco* tool is a command-line utility that accepts one parameter: the URL to initiate the search process. In addition, command-line switches can be used to further control the discovery process.

The *disco* tool copies the WSDL documents of any Web services that it finds and also creates several other files (including a discovery document that refers to the Web service descriptions that it found as well as a discomap file) on the hard drive from which you ran the *disco* tool. These files can be used as input to the .NET Framework's *wsdl* tool to create Web service client proxy classes.

Note
You must know at least the URL to a Web server in order to initiate the discovery process. If you do not have such a URL, you may wish to use the UDDI search mechanisms to locate Web servers that implement one or more Web services.

The implementation of the discovery process is also embodied in the .NET Framework's System.Web.Services.Discovery namespace. This namespace contains the classes that implement the .NET Web Service discovery process and can be leveraged programmatically by your applications or, if desired, replaced by your own implementation.

We will cover Web service discovery using these tools in greater detail in Chapter 28, "Consuming Web Services."

Web Service description

A Web service description is an XML document that defines the capabilities of a Web service. Using the WSDL XML grammar, you can clearly and unambiguously define the Web-addressable entry points in terms of the request messages that a Web service will accept as well as the response messages a Web service can return. Also included in this description are the supported protocol bindings and a description of the data types processed by the Web service.

Recall that the .NET Framework supports self-describing assemblies. This is accomplished by storing metadata with the assembly that describes the interfaces, data types, and other information about the classes in the assembly. Using the self-describing nature of .NET assemblies, the .NET Framework can generate WSDL documents to describe Web service capabilities from the .NET assemblies that contain ASP.NET Web service code. Much of this support is built into the System.Web.Services.Description namespace in the .NET Framework.

From the Web service perspective, ASP.NET supports the dynamic generation of WSDL documents from the Web Service assembly when it is requested. This eliminates issues related to keeping a separate WSDL document in sync with the Web Service assembly that implements the service.

In a nutshell, this process works as follows:

1. The client requests the WSDL document using a URL of the form http://server/*webservicepath*/entrypoint.asmx?WSDL.

2. The Web server maps the request for the ASMX file to the ASP.NET runtime.

3. The ASP.NET runtime uses an instance of the WebServiceHandlerFactory class (found in the System.Web.Services.Protocols namespace) to process the URL.

4. The WebServiceHandlerFactory class obtains the query string and uses classes from the System.Reflection namespace to obtain the Web Service assembly metadata.

5. The metadata is then used with classes from the System.Web.Services. Description namespace to generate and return the WSDL document to the client.

This process makes it simple for a Web service to describe its capabilities to a requesting or potential consumer. The .NET platform automatically generates the WSDL for you, relieving you of this hassle.

The standard method of interacting with a Web service is through the use of a proxy class. From the consumer perspective, Visual Studio and ASP.NET provide tools that make it easy to generate a Web service proxy class, given a Web service description. The proxy class serves as a mirror image of the actual Web service (from an interface standpoint) but does not contain the actual implementation of the service. It is a local resource (local to the consumer) that accepts method calls and then forwards them to the actual Web service via HTTP and SOAP. Results are gathered from the Web service method and returned to the consumer. This gives a Web service method call the appearance of interacting entirely with a local class.

Visual Studio .NET automatically generates proxy classes from WSDL documents when you use the Web Reference feature to locate Web services that you wish to call from within your application. After you have located a WSDL document, you can use the Add Reference button on the dialog box to generate the proxy class.

If you are not using Visual Studio .NET to develop your consumer application, the .NET Framework supplies a tool named *wsdl* that you can use to generate .NET Web service proxy classes from a supplied WSDL document. The *wsdl* tool is a command-line utility that accepts a URL that points to the WSDL document that is used to generate the proxy class. A number of switches are available that you can use to control this process, such as specifying the target language for the generated proxy class.

We will examine the use of these tools in greater detail in Chapter 28, "Consuming Web Services."

Web Service Wire Formats

The final piece of the ASP.NET Web Services infrastructure consists of the Web service wire formats. Wire formats define the method by which Web service request and response messages are encoded and transported between the Web service and any consumer. To maximize the reach of Web services on the Internet, standard Internet protocols are used.

ASP.NET Web Services support three wire formats: HTTP-GET, HTTP-POST, and HTTP-SOAP. Traditional Web applications have used HTTP-GET and HTTP-POST to deliver Web forms–based data to the Web server for processing. These same protocols are used to deliver Web service operation requests along with any necessary arguments to the Web service for processing. The HTTP-SOAP wire format is a new format that has been developed exclusively for enabling Web services to communicate very rich data types.

Caution   The HTTP-GET and HTTP-POST protocols cannot support all data types capable of being described in ASP.NET Web services. For this reason, it is recommended that HTTP-SOAP be used to call all Web service methods.

Each of these wire formats finds its implementation in the System.Web.Services. Protocols namespace of the .NET Framework Class Library. Let's take a look at how these wire formats are implemented for ASP.NET Web Services.

HTTP-GET

The HTTP-GET protocol encodes Web service operation requests and arguments in the URL to the Web service. The operation is coded as part of the URL string and any arguments are coded as query string parameters appended to the base URL. For example:

```
http://localhost/ctemp/ctemp.asmx/ctemp?Temperature=32&FromUnit
s=F&ToUnits=C
```

This URL specifies the Web-addressable entry point for the CTemp Web service (Ctemp.asxm), including the method to be called (also named `ctemp`). The arguments to the `ctemp` method are passed as query string arguments to the method request.

Similar to the way in which WSDL documents are generated and returned to requests for such information via a URL to the Web service entry point file (the ASMX file), the HTTP-GET method of calling Web service methods is handled by the WebServiceHandlerFactory class. This class takes the URL and query string parameters as input and translates this into a method call on the appropriate Web service class implementation.

.NET Proxy classes use the HttpGetClientProtocol class in the System.Web.Services. Protocols namespace to invoke Web services that support the HTTP-GET protocol.

HTTP-POST

The HTTP-POST protocol encodes Web service operation requests and arguments within the payload area of the HTTP-POST request as name/value pairs.

This technique of invoking a Web service method is identical in operation to the HTTP-GET method (from an ASP.NET perspective), except in the way in which the Web service call arguments are passed to the server.

Once again, the .NET Framework's WebServiceHandlerFactory class is responsible for extracting the method name and arguments from the request and calling the appropriate Web service method found in the Web service class implementation.

.NET Proxy classes use the HttpPostClientProtocol class in the System.Web.Services. Protocols namespace to invoke Web services that support the HTTP-POST protocol.

HTTP-SOAP

HTTP-SOAP is the default ASP.NET Web Service wire format. It is based on the SOAP specification (currently submitted to the W3C as a note) and supports the widest range of simple and complex data types (including document-oriented operations).

Web service request and response messages are encoded into SOAP messages that are included in the payload area of an HTTP-POST message. SOAP messages are encoded in XML using the SOAP vocabulary defined in the specification.

Because SOAP is really XML, it is possible to describe nearly any type of data. This makes SOAP an excellent choice for passing rich data types between Web services and their consumers. For example, it is possible to pass very complex types such as entire XML documents, such as an invoice or purchase order.

.NET Proxy classes use the HttpSimpleClientServiceProtocol class in the System. Web.Services.Protocols namespace to invoke Web services that support the HTTP-SOAP protocol.

Although these are the default wire formats, ASP.NET provides the capability to replace or add to these basic formats. For example, you can implement additional wire formats that allow Web services to communicate using FTP or SMTP.

We will cover each of these previously described Web service wire formats in greater detail in Chapter 25, "Building a Web Service."

Leveraging ASP.NET Features in Web Services

So far, we've outlined the broad support provided by the .NET platform and ASP.NET for building and consuming Web services. In the next few sections, we will look at more specific details of how to leverage some of these features within your ASP.NET Web Service applications.

Supporting transactions

ASP.NET Web Services are capable of supporting transactions, just like the automatic transaction support provided for classic COM+ components. When working with databases and other resource managers that support transactions, you will often want to use transactions to simplify and maintain the integrity of updates.

The major difference between the classic COM+ and new ASP.NET transaction support features is that ASP.NET transactions cannot be started by another application and then flow into the Web service method. In other words, Web services only support transactions that are started by the Web service method itself.

To enable transaction support for a Web service method, you must add the `TransactionOption` property to the `WebMethod` attribute that is used to identify Web-callable methods in your Web service classes. For example:

VB.NET:

```
<WebMethod(TransactionOption:=TransactionOption.Required)>
Public Function CTemp...
```

C#:

```
[WebMethod(TransactionOption=TransactionOption.Required)]
Public string CTemp...
```

The `TransactionOption` property accepts an enumerated type that specifies the type of transaction support desired for the Web method. Table 23-2 describes the supported transaction property options.

Table 23-2	
TransactionOption property values	
Option	**Description**
`Disabled`	The method does not participate in transactions.
`NotSupported`	The method does not run within the scope of a transaction, even if one is currently pending.

Option	Description
Supported	The method participates in any pending transaction. If a transaction is not pending, the method will execute without one.
Required	If a transaction is pending, the method participates in the transaction. If a transaction is not pending, a new transaction is started.
RequiresNew	Regardless of the current transaction state, a new transaction is started for the method.

The default option is Required. If you are familiar with COM+ transaction support, you know that you were required to use the SetComplete or SetAbort method to signal the completion state of the transaction. This is no longer required for ASP.NET applications. The successful completion of a method call implies a call to SetComplete, whereas if the method call raises an exception, this implies a call to SetAbort.

If a Web Service method is participating in a transaction and an exception occurs, ASP.NET automatically aborts the transaction. Likewise, if no exception occurs, then the transaction is automatically committed.

Note For more information about automatic transaction support within ASP.NET Web Services, refer to the .NET Framework online documentation.

Enabling session state

Session state allows Web service methods to maintain contextual information between calls. To use the built-in session state support provided for ASP.NET Web Services, the Web Service class must inherit from either the WebService base class or use the HttpContext class.

Session state support for Web Services is bound to the HTTP protocol because it relies on the *cookies* feature of HTTP. You may recall that the design of SOAP is purposefully transport-independent, allowing SOAP messages to be piggybacked on other transport protocols such as FTP or SMTP. However, if you rely on the HTTP transport for session state support, you can no longer bind your SOAP messages to another transport without losing session state support.

Session state support for Web Services is disabled by default because it incurs additional overhead that you may not wish or need to use. To enable session support, you must add the EnableSession property to the WebMethod attribute that is used to identify Web-callable methods in your Web Service classes. For example:

VB.NET:

```
<WebMethod(EnableSession:="true")> Public Function CTemp...
```

C#:

```
[WebMethod(EnableSession="true")] Public string CTemp...
```

This property accepts a True or False value and specifies whether or not to enable session support for the Web method. Again, the default value of this property is False.

Session state uses temporary cookies to track a session. This means that the cookie is never saved to the hard drive. So, for the session state to remain valid, the same session ID must be used between requests. The session ID is normally supplied by the proxy class and, therefore, only exists as long as the proxy class exists. This means that the lifetime of the proxy class normally determines the lifetime of the session.

If this default behavior is unacceptable, it is possible to change this such that the cookie can be persisted and, thus, survive across proxy class instances.

Note   For more information about maintaining session state with ASP.NET Web services, refer to the .NET Framework online documentation.

Web service caching

ASP.NET Web Services support output caching. This permits the result of a previous method request to be saved in a memory cache, to be recalled on subsequent requests without having to re-execute the logic of the method.

Output caching is convenient and useful in situations where the data being returned does not change often. This results in potentially large performance gains for the Web service when many consumers make requests for the same information.

To enable output caching, you must add the `CacheDuration` property to the `WebMethod` attribute that is used to identify Web-callable methods in your Web service classes. For example:

VB.NET:

```
<WebMethod(CacheDuration:=120)> Public Function CTemp...
```

C#:

```
[WebMethod(CacheDuration=120)] Public string CTemp...
```

This property accepts an integer value that specifies the length of time (in seconds) that the output will remain in the cache after the first execution of the method has returned the result the first time. Subsequent requests will immediately return the result to the call from the output cache until the specified time period expires. When this occurs, the method will be executed again, repopulating the cache and restarting the cache expiration countdown.

Output caching works correctly even if the method requires one or more arguments that can vary between requests. In this case, the output is cached for each unique combination of arguments supplied to the method. If the method has been called with identical parameters to a previous request, the response is obtained from the output cache; otherwise, the method is executed normally.

Output caching can be a very valuable tool in dramatically increasing the performance of your application. However, the effectiveness of this technique must be balanced against the memory used and the type of data being cached. If the data changes frequently or is infrequently accessed, the use of output caching will only degrade server performance. So, carefully examine your situation before deciding to use output caching as a technique to increase server performance.

Buffering server responses

Response buffering allows the Web server to return the response to the consumer all at once, after the response has been completely generated, rather than transmitting it in multiple chunks. By default, ASP.NET Web Services buffer the response before sending it. However, in some cases it may be appropriate to change this default behavior. For example, it may be beneficial for long-running methods to transmit the response as it is generated.

To disable response buffering for Web services, you must add the `BufferResponse` property to the `WebMethod` attribute that is used to identify Web-callable methods in your Web service classes. For example:

VB.NET:

```
<WebMethod(BufferResponse:=true)> Public Function CTemp...
```

C#:

```
[WebMethod(BufferResponse=true)] Public string CTemp...
```

This property accepts a true or false value that specifies whether or not output buffering is enabled. The default for this property is true, which enables output buffering.

If you choose to disable response buffering, you must balance the potential benefits of this versus the additional resources required to transmit the response in multiple requests.

Inside an ASP.NET Web Service

So far, we've spent a great deal of time talking about the motivation behind Web services and some basics about the technologies that enable us to build and consume Web services. However, we have not yet covered exactly how a Web service works.

To wrap up this chapter on Web service infrastructure, let's walk through what happens during the execution lifetime of a Web service. In this way, we can bring together all the elements of Web services that we have discussed up to now and examine how they fit together to enable the Web service execution model.

In our discussion thus far, we've revealed partial details of how an ASP.NET Web Service works. Now that we have a complete picture of the technologies and tools used to build and consume ASP.NET Web Services, let's take a conceptual, but detailed, look at the execution flow and lifetime of a fictional Web service named CTemp.

The CTemp Web service converts temperature values from one numeric unit to another. The service supports a single method that accepts three input arguments: the temperature value, the source units, and the destination units. The Web service method takes these input arguments and converts the specified temperature to the destination units and returns the new temperature value to the caller.

We will begin our walkthrough at the point where the consumer sends a properly formatted SOAP message to the target server requesting the CTemp method of the CTemp Web service.

1. The IIS Web server hosting the CTemp Web service receives the request message (technically, an HTTP-SOAP request).

2. The URL is interpreted by the Web server to determine what ISAPI filter is responsible for handling the request (based on the file type). Because the URL points to the Web service entry point file (the ASMX file), the request is passed along to the ASP.NET ISAPI filter.

3. The ASP.NET ISAPI filter passes the request to an instance of the .NET HTTPRuntime class, which is hosted within an IIS application process. The movement of the request from the ISAPI filter to the HTTPRuntime class completes a transition from unmanaged to managed code.

4. The ASP.NET HTTPRuntime class is responsible for handling all incoming HTTP requests. The runtime resolves the URL to a specific application and then dispatches the request to that application. Web services are handled by the .NET WebServiceHandlerFactory class.

5. The WebServiceHandlerFactory deserializes the SOAP payload from the request, creates an instance of the CTemp Web service implementation class, and executes the CTemp method, passing the input arguments.

6. The ASP.NET runtime takes the result of the CTemp method call and serializes it into a SOAP response message. This message is then added to the payload of an HTTP response and delivered back to the client (in this case, our proxy class).

As you can see, a lot goes on behind the scenes of a Web service method request. Although this overview gives you an idea of what happens to a Web service request while it is being processed, it is by no means a complete picture. Many details within each of these steps have been left out for brevity (and understandability). However, this short tour should make it easier to see how the various pieces of the puzzle fit together.

Summary

In this chapter, we've covered the elements of the Microsoft Web Services platform, which is based on the Common Language Runtime, the .NET Framework Class Library, and the ASP.NET Web application environment. We've seen that these architectural elements provide broad and extensive support for building and consuming world-class Web services that can incorporate advanced features offered by the platform with very little effort.

Using these architectural elements, we examined what the execution flow and lifetime of a typical Web service looks like. In upcoming chapters, we will further refine these details and drill into the step-by-step procedures for building and consuming ASP.NET Web Services.

✦   ✦   ✦

Understanding SOAP

In this chapter, you will learn more about the Simple Object Access Protocol (SOAP), which is one of the foundational elements of Web services. Although it is not necessary to have a detailed understanding of SOAP to build or consume Web services based on ASP.NET, a fundamental understanding of the technology will be useful in debugging situations as well as when dealing with specialized interoperability issues that might arise when exchanging SOAP messages with services on other platforms.

We will discuss the major parts and features of SOAP, the data types that are supported, and SOAP features provided by the .NET Framework, including capabilities for extending or modifying the behavior of SOAP-based Web services.

What Is SOAP?

SOAP is a lightweight, XML-based protocol for exchanging information in a decentralized, distributed environment, such as that offered by the Internet. In other words, SOAP enables two processes (possibly on different machines) to communicate with each other regardless of the hardware and software platforms on which they are running.

One of the greatest benefits of SOAP is that it has been created and adopted as part of an open process, which has been embraced at an unprecedented level by most of the major hardware and software vendors. The SOAP specification is an open technology (having been submitted to the W3C) that provides the basis for application-to-application integration, known as Web services.

The fundamental building block of SOAP is XML. SOAP defines a specialized, yet flexible XML grammar that standardizes the format and structure of messages. Messages are, in turn, the fundamental method for exchanging information between Web services and Web service consumers. Using XML to encode SOAP messages provides several benefits, such as these:

✦ XML is human readable, making it easier to understand and debug.

✦ XML parsers and related technologies are widely available.

✦ XML is an open standard.

✦ XML includes many related technologies that can be leveraged in SOAP.

Thus, XML is a natural choice for encoding SOAP messages and contributes to the simplicity of the specification (at least in relation to more complex binary protocols such as COM and CORBA).

Typically, a Web service consumer will send a message to a Web service, requesting a specific operation to be performed. The Web service processes this request and typically (but not necessarily) returns the results in a response message. This request/response model is conceptually akin to the Remote Procedure Call (RPC) model.

To transport SOAP messages, we need a transport protocol. The obvious choice for a transport protocol is HTTP, because it is in use on so many systems today, making it widely available. In addition, HTTP is typically allowed through most firewalls today, making it easy to get up and running without requiring administrators to open more ports through their corporate firewalls.

Although HTTP is an obvious choice for a transport protocol (and the one that most major vendors are implementing), the SOAP specification does not require a specific transport protocol. It is quite possible to transport SOAP messages over other transport mechanisms such as SMTP and FTP. However, the default transport protocol for ASP.NET Web Services based on SOAP is HTTP.

So, in a nutshell, SOAP provides the following capabilities:

✦ Enables interoperability between systems using standard, widely available protocols such as XML and HTTP.

✦ Allows systems to communicate with each other through firewalls, without having to open additional, potentially unsafe ports.

✦ SOAP fully describes each data element in the message, making it easier to understand and troubleshoot problems that may occur.

Arguably, as important as what SOAP addresses to enable interoperability is what it does *not* attempt to address. Specifically, SOAP does not do the following:

✦ Attempt to define how objects are created or destroyed

✦ Impose any specific security mechanism or implementation

✦ Define an authentication scheme

At first glance, these might seem to be serious shortcomings. However, in reality, these omissions allow each platform to address these issues in a way that best suits its needs. For example, SOAP messages can also be exchanged over Secure Sockets Layer (SSL), which is a standard Web protocol that provides a secure, encrypted HTTP connection between the client and server.

Now that you have a basic understanding of SOAP, let's take a closer look at some of the fundamental parts of the SOAP specification.

The SOAP Specification

The SOAP protocol specification is a W3C-submitted note that is now under the umbrella of the XML Protocols working group. Version 1.2 of the specification (the follow-up to version 1.1) was under development as a working draft at the beginning of October 2001. The .NET Framework and ASP.NET Web Services produce and consume SOAP messages that are compliant with version 1.1 of the SOAP protocol specification.

The SOAP protocol specification consists of four primary parts, each of which has a specific purpose:

✦ A definition for a mandatory, extensible message envelope that encapsulates all SOAP data. The SOAP envelope is the fundamental message carrier that forms the basis for SOAP message exchange between SOAP-aware endpoints. This is the only part of the SOAP specification that is mandatory.

✦ A set of data-encoding rules for representing application-defined data types and a model for serializing data that appears within the SOAP envelope.

✦ A definition for an RPC-style (in other words, request/response) message exchange pattern. SOAP does not require two-way message exchanges; however, Web services typically implement such RPC-style request/response patterns when used with HTTP as the transport protocol. Thus, the request/response RPC-style protocol is a function of HTTP and not of SOAP.

✦ A definition for a protocol binding between SOAP and HTTP. This describes how SOAP messages are transmitted using HTTP as the transport protocol.

Because the SOAP envelope is the only mandatory part of the specification, let's first take a look at the elements that comprise a SOAP message and their purpose.

SOAP Message Elements

A SOAP message is composed of three primary elements, each of which performs a special purpose. These elements are listed in Table 24-1.

Table 24-1 SOAP message elements	
Message Element	**Description**
Envelope	Serves as a container for the remaining SOAP message elements.
Header	Contains optional data a consumer may or may not be required to understand to process the message properly. This is the primary extensibility mechanism of SOAP.
Body	Contains the actual encoding of a method call and any input arguments or an encoded response that contains the results of the method call.

The following sections describe each of these elements in more detail.

The SOAP envelope

The SOAP envelope element is a required part of a SOAP message. It serves as a container for all remaining SOAP message elements. Typically, this includes the SOAP header and body elements. In addition to serving as a container for the header and body elements, the envelope defines the namespaces used by these elements. Figure 24-1 graphically depicts the structure of a complete SOAP message.

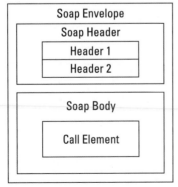

Figure 24-1: Structure of a SOAP Message

To deliver a SOAP message to an endpoint, addressing information specific to the transport protocol binding is used as a means to ensure that the message is delivered to the correct endpoint, much like the name and address on a real envelope that is used by a postal authority to deliver the mail. In the case of HTTP, a custom HTTP header named SOAPAction is used to direct the message to the proper endpoint.

One of the major reasons that message addressing is implemented in this manner is that systems administrators can configure firewall software to look for and filter traffic based on this header information, without requiring parsing of the XML.

The following sample code illustrates the format of a SOAP request message envelope:

```
<soap:Envelope xmlns:xsi="http://www.w3.org/2001/XMLSchema-
instance" xmlns:xsd="http://www.w3.org/2001/XMLSchema"
xmlns:soap="http://schemas.xmlsoap.org/soap/envelope/">
  <soap:Body>
    <!-- The Soap body elements are inserted here -->
  </soap:Body>
</soap:Envelope>
```

The SOAP envelope is identified by the `soap:Envelope` element. This particular example contains a `soap:Body` element, but no `soap:Header` element. Now that we've briefly described the SOAP envelope, let's discuss SOAP headers.

The SOAP header

The SOAP header element is an optional part of a SOAP message. It defines additional information that can be related to the method request in the body element or, more likely, information that is independent of the method request that is required or otherwise useful to your application. SOAP does not define the specific contents or semantics for a SOAP header.

SOAP headers are quite similar in concept to the META tags found in HTML documents. They define metadata that can be used to provide context to, or otherwise direct the processing of, the message. The following example shows a SOAP header named Authentication that passes user credentials as part of a Web service method request:

```
<soap:Envelope xmlns:xsi="http://www.w3.org/2001/XMLSchema-
instance" xmlns:xsd="http://www.w3.org/2001/XMLSchema"
xmlns:soap="http://schemas.xmlsoap.org/soap/envelope/">
  <soap:Header>
    <Authentication xmlns="http://tempuri.org">
      <Username>JDC</Username>
      <Password>unknown</Password>
    </Authentication>
  </soap:Header>
  <soap:Body>
```

```
      <!-- The SOAP body elements are inserted here -->
   </soap:Body>
</soap:Envelope>
```

Each direct child element of the header element is defined as a separate SOAP header. A typical use of SOAP headers is in the area of authentication (as shown in the example), where the credentials required to access the method are encoded in a SOAP header. The implementation code of the method can use the credentials obtained from the SOAP header to invoke an authentication service provided by the underlying platform, rather than having to implement this functionality itself.

If a header element is specified within a SOAP envelope, the header element must be the first element to appear after the opening envelope tag. In addition, SOAP headers (in other words, header subelements) must use XML namespaces to qualify their names, as we did with the Authentication SOAP header example.

SOAP header elements also support an optional `MustUnderstand` attribute. This attribute accepts a True or False setting, which is used to specify whether or not the message recipient must understand the data within the header. If the `MustUnderstand` attribute is set to True, the recipient must acknowledge the header by setting the `DidUnderstand` attribute on the header to True. If this is not done, a `SoapHeaderException` is generated. We will see examples of this attribute later in this chapter, when we cover the .NET support for SOAP headers.

That's enough about SOAP headers, for now. We'll look at how to use SOAP headers in more detail in an upcoming section. Let's continue our discussion of SOAP message parts by looking at the SOAP body.

The SOAP body

The SOAP body element is a required part of a SOAP message that contains the data specific to a particular method call, such as the method name and any input/output arguments or the return values produced by the method.

The contents of the SOAP body depend on whether the message is a request or a response. A request message contains method call information, whereas a response message contains method call result data.

The following example code illustrates the format of a SOAP body for a request to a temperature conversion method named CTemp:

```
<soap:Envelope xmlns:xsi="http://www.w3.org/2001/XMLSchema-
instance" xmlns:xsd="http://www.w3.org/2001/XMLSchema"
xmlns:soap="http://schemas.xmlsoap.org/soap/envelope/">
   <soap:Body>
      <CTemp xmlns="http://tempuri.org/">
         <Temperature>32</Temperature>
```

```
      <FromUnits>F</FromUnits>
      <ToUnits>C</ToUnits>
    </CTemp>
  </soap:Body>
</soap:Envelope>
```

The sample shows the method name encoded as the CTemp element. Within this element are the encoded input arguments required to call the CTemp method.

The SOAP body for the response message to the CTemp method request is as follows:

```
<soap:Envelope xmlns:xsi="http://www.w3.org/2001/XMLSchema-
instance" xmlns:xsd="http://www.w3.org/2001/XMLSchema"
xmlns:soap="http://schemas.xmlsoap.org/soap/envelope/">
  <soap:Body>
    <CTempResponse xmlns="http://tempuri.org/">
      <CTempResult>0</CTempResult>
    </CTempResponse>
  </soap:Body>
</soap:Envelope>
```

Here we can see that the body of the response message contains a single result element named CTempResult that encodes the numeric result of the temperature conversion. Of course, if the method call were to fail for some reason, the response message would not contain the results we expected, but instead would contain exception (or fault) information describing the error that occurred. We will look at this possibility in the next section.

SOAP Data Type Support

The SOAP specification defines data type support in terms of XSD, the XML Schema specification. This specification defines standards for describing primitive data types as well as complex, hierarchical structures. As you would expect, there is support for integers, strings, floats, and many other primitive types, as well as lists (or arrays) of these primitive types.

In addition to primitive types, user-defined structures can be represented. This is significant, because it paves the way for describing complex, hierarchical data relationships such as what might be found in an invoice or purchase order. The bottom line here is that it is possible to describe any type of data using XSD. Thus, SOAP is capable of supporting any data type, from the built-in primitives defined by XSD all the way to any arbitrary user-defined structure.

This is one of the primary reasons that SOAP is the preferred protocol for exchanging Web service request and response messages, because it enables Web services to accept as well as return any type of data that can be represented by an XSD schema.

The Common Language Runtime within .NET provides support for a wide variety of the common data types. All of these data types are shared equally across all of the .NET languages and also have a well-defined mapping to XSD data types, as shown in Table 24-2.

Table 24-2 XSD data types vs. CLR data types	
XML Schema Definition	**Common Language Runtime**
boolean	Boolean
byte	N/A
double	Double
datatype	N/A
decimal	Decimal
enumeration	Enum
float	Single
int	Int32
long	Int64
Qname	XmlQualifiedName
short	Int16
string	String
timeInstant	DateTime
unsignedByte	N/A
unsignedInt	UInt32
unsignedLong	UInt64
unsignedShort	UInt16

Note   The CLR specification defines the data types available to all languages. However, not all .NET languages support all of the available data types. For example, Visual Basic.NET does not directly support unsigned Ints. You should refer to your specific CLR language documentation to determine which CLR data types are supported.

In addition to complete primitive data type support, complex structures can be represented within .NET. For example, you can define a structure or class named Invoice that describes the data elements of an invoice document. The .NET

Framework and ASP.NET automatically serialize and deserialize these data structures into XML-encoded element hierarchies that can be carried in the SOAP message body. This makes it possible to pass very complex data and data relationships as a single argument to a Web service method!

As you can see, the data type support provided by XSD and SOAP is very powerful and enables the development of potentially complex applications.

Although a great deal of detail and information exists related to data types and structures as defined within XSD and SOAP, there's just not enough time or space to go into it here. What's more, you really don't have to know much about how your Web service parameters or results are serialized into XML because ASP.NET and the .NET Framework classes handle this for you automatically.

 Note If you wish to learn more about describing data, you are encouraged to examine the XML Schema Definition and SOAP specifications at the W3C Web site, located at `http://www.w3.org`. Some reference material related to this subject also is available with the .NET Framework online documentation.

SOAP Exceptions

If Web service methods were guaranteed to work at all times, we would not need any form of error notification or processing capabilities. Unfortunately, things can (and often do) go wrong. As such, errors or exceptions that occur in a Web service method call need to be communicated back to the consumer of the Web service in some manner.

This is where SOAP exceptions come into play. SOAP exceptions are used to return error or exception information to the consumer of a Web service as the result of a failed method call.

 Note The SOAP specification uses the term *faults* rather than *exceptions*. I have chosen to use the latter to maintain consistency with the terminology used within the .NET Framework, which refers to SOAP faults as exceptions. This terminology is also reflected in the SOAP classes within .NET.

SOAP exceptions can occur at various stages of processing a Web service request. For example, an error can occur at the HTTP level before the method call can actually be delivered to the Web service. In this case, an HTTP response must be returned, using the standard HTTP status code numbering conventions.

If the message makes it past the HTTP layer, it must be translated and dispatched to the actual implementation code that executes the method request. If an error occurs here, the server must return a fault message.

The following is an example of a SOAP exception message that returns an application-defined exception as the response message:

```
<soap:Envelope xmlns:xsi="http://www.w3.org/2001/XMLSchema-
instance" xmlns:xsd="http://www.w3.org/2001/XMLSchema"
xmlns:soap="http://schemas.xmlsoap.org/soap/envelope/">
  <soap:Body>
    <soap:Fault>
      <faultcode>400</faultcode>
      <faultstring>
        Divide by zero error
      </faultstring>
      <runcode>Maybe</runcode>
      <detail>
        <t:DivideByZeroException xmlns:t="http://tempuri.org">
          <expression>x = 2 / 0;</expression>
        </t:DivideByZeroException>
      </detail>
    </soap:Fault>
  </soap:Body>
</soap:Envelope>
```

As shown in the sample, the exception is contained within the `soap:Fault` element. The `faultcode` element specifies the SOAP fault that occurred. Currently, four fault codes are defined, which are listed and described in Table 24-3.

Table 24-3
SOAP fault codes

Value	Name	Meaning
100	Version Mismatch	The call used an unsupported SOAP version.
200	Must Understand	An XML element was received that contained an element with the "mustUnderstand=true" attribute, but was not understood by the receiver.
300	Invalid Request	The receiver did not process the request because it was malformed or not supported.
400	Application Faulted	The receiving application faulted when processing the request. The `detail` element contains information about the fault.

The `faultstring` element contains a string description of the error that occurred. The `runcode` element indicates whether or not the requested operation was performed before the error occurred. This must contain one of either `Yes`, `No`, or `Maybe`.

The detail element is optional and specifies an application-defined exception object (in this case, a DivideByZeroException object).

ASP.NET implements a SoapException class that can be used with the structured exception-handling capabilities built into the CLR to catch SOAP exceptions and handle them using try . . . catch blocks. This means that our ASP.NET applications have a robust, natural mechanism for handling errors within a Web service as well as within a consumer application that is identical to handling any other type of exception within the CLR. We will see specific examples of SOAP exception handling using .NET later in this chapter.

HTTP As a SOAP Transport

To deliver messages encoded as SOAP requests or responses, we need a transport protocol. This transport protocol must be widely available in order to maximize the reach of our Web services. The obvious choice of HTTP as the transport protocol makes SOAP a highly available message format. In addition, the request/response nature of HTTP gives SOAP its RPC-like behavior when piggybacking this transport protocol.

Another advantage of HTTP as the primary transport protocol is that it is human-readable, just like the SOAP message itself. Figure 24-2 graphically depicts the structure of a SOAP message within the payload section of an HTTP POST request.

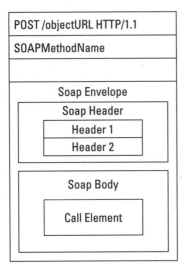

Figure 24-2: Structure of a SOAP message contained within an HTTP Post request

The POST command contains a request URI that specifies the object endpoint ID. The server is responsible both for mapping this URI to the implementation of the Web service and for activating the code that is proper for the platform on which it is running.

The SOAP request also must specify which method is to be called. This is done via a custom HTTP header (signified by SoapMethodName) and specifies the namespace-qualified method name to be invoked.

Following the HTTP header is the actual payload of the POST request. The payload is always separated from the last header by a single empty line. Now that you have an idea of what a complete SOAP message bound to the HTTP transport looks like, let's look at a specific example. The following sample code shows a complete SOAP request message in the payload section of an HTTP POST request:

```
POST /ctemp/ctemp.asmx HTTP/1.1
Host: localhost
Content-Type: text/xml; charset=utf-8
Content-Length: length
SOAPAction: "http://tempuri.org/CTemp"

<?xml version="1.0" encoding="utf-8"?>
<soap:Envelope xmlns:xsi="http://www.w3.org/2001/XMLSchema-
instance" xmlns:xsd="http://www.w3.org/2001/XMLSchema"
xmlns:soap="http://schemas.xmlsoap.org/soap/envelope/">
  <soap:Body>
    <CTemp xmlns="http://tempuri.org/">
      <Temperature>32</Temperature>
      <FromUnits>F</FromUnits>
      <ToUnits>C</ToUnits>
    </CTemp>
  </soap:Body>
</soap:Envelope>
```

Notice that the POST request URI specifies the object endpoint ID. This is used by ASP.NET to locate and activate the Web service code. The method call being requested is specified by the HTTP SoapAction header. In this instance, the CTemp method is the requested function to be called. Finally, the body of the SOAP message contains the input arguments to the CTemp method call. In this case, there are three arguments.

Similar to the SOAP request message bound to the HTTP POST command, a SOAP response message uses the HTTP response to indicate the results of the method call, as in the following HTTP response example:

```
HTTP/1.1 200 OK
Content-Type: text/xml; charset=utf-8
Content-Length: length
```

```
<?xml version="1.0" encoding="utf-8"?>
<soap:Envelope xmlns:xsi="http://www.w3.org/2001/XMLSchema-
instance" xmlns:xsd="http://www.w3.org/2001/XMLSchema"
xmlns:soap="http://schemas.xmlsoap.org/soap/envelope/">
  <soap:Body>
    <CTempResponse xmlns="http://tempuri.org/">
      <CTempResult>0</CTempResult>
    </CTempResponse>
  </soap:Body>
</soap:Envelope>
```

In this example, you can see the result of the CTemp method call returned in the payload section of the HTTP response message. The SOAP rules for encoding the response element use the same name as the call element from the request message with the `Response` suffix concatenated to it. In this case, this results in a response element named `CTempResponse`.

Although SOAP does not require HTTP as a transport binding, it is the default and preferred binding for SOAP messages. However, it is also possible to create bindings for SOAP messages over such protocols as SMTP and FTP, although the .NET framework does not yet provide this support by default. For now, ASP.NET Web Services transport SOAP messages exclusively using HTTP.

This brief overview of the SOAP specification hopefully will provide you with enough background to feel comfortable working with SOAP messages when, and if, it's necessary. Of course, if you need more information about SOAP, you should read the SOAP specification available at the W3C Web site located at `http://www.w3.org`.

Now that you have a basic understanding of SOAP, let's take a look at the SOAP support built into the .NET Framework and how you can leverage this support in building your Web service applications.

SOAP in the .NET Framework

Fortunately, everything that we have discussed related to SOAP up to this point is largely unnecessary with respect to implementing simple ASP.NET Web Services, because ASP.NET and the .NET Framework automatically generate and process SOAP messages for your Web service, leaving you to focus on writing the logic of your Web service application using a familiar object-oriented design approach.

However, more sophisticated Web services may require access to the SOAP messages in order to add custom headers, examine incoming/outgoing SOAP messages, or otherwise alter the default format of messages generated by the .NET XML serializer when interoperating with SOAP message processors on other platforms.

If SOAP message customization becomes necessary for a particular Web service that you wish to implement, the .NET Framework and ASP.NET provide the means to gain access to the SOAP messages so that you can perform the customizations that you need. In this section, we will look at some of the features provided by ASP.NET that you can use to customize the default SOAP message formats and contents.

Using SOAP headers

SOAP headers are the chief extensibility mechanism offered by the SOAP specification. This feature enables you to piggyback metadata along with a method request or response message that can be used by the receiver to control, or add additional context to, the method call.

For example, user credentials are often added as a SOAP header to enable a Web service method to authenticate a user before allowing the method call to be executed. In this example, the SOAP header is added by the consumer application and processed by the Web service method.

The SOAP specification does not define the contents of SOAP headers. The content and semantics associated with a SOAP header are completely defined by the application that adds the header and the recipient that processes it.

ASP.NET Web Services use SOAP as the default protocol for exchanging messages. This makes it possible for applications to add SOAP headers for their own use. Adding SOAP headers to ASP.NET Web Services is as simple as adding a SoapHeader attribute onto a Web service method.

.NET SoapHeader class

The .NET Framework provides a SoapHeader base class (found in the System.Web.Services.Protocols namespace), which we can inherit from to create and use a SOAP header.

An example (drawing on our previous discussion of user credentials and authentication) of a custom SOAP header class is as follows.

VB.NET:

```
Imports System.Web.Services.Protocols
Public Class AuthenticationSoapHeader
  Inherits SoapHeader
  Public Username as String
  Public Password as String
End Class
```

C#:

```
using System.Web.Services.Protocols;
public class AuthenticationSoapHeader : SoapHeader {
    public string Username;
    public string Password;
}
```

In this example, we create a class named AuthenticationSoapHeader that inherits from the SoapHeader base class. Within this class are two public member variables named Username and Password. These member variables can be set by applications that wish to pass this data within the SOAP header.

Once you have defined your SOAP header class, you can add it to your Web service implementation and reference it within the method declaration by adding an attribute to that declaration. Although we haven't covered the details of coding Web services and Web service methods, let's take a quick look at the basic syntax involved in this process.

The following code snippet shows the use of our AuthenticationSoapHeader class.

VB.NET:

```
Public Class MyWebService
    Public AuthSoapHeader As AuthenticationSoapHeader
    <WebMethod, SoapHeader("AuthSoapHeader")> Public Function
MyWebMethod() As Integer
```

C#:

```
public class MyWebService : WebService {
    public AuthenticationSoapHeader AuthSoapHeader;
[ WebMethod, SoapHeader("AuthSoapHeader")]
    public int MyWebMethod() {
    }
}
```

In this example, we have declared a class named MyWebService that is the implementation class for our Web service. Within this class, we declare a public member variable named AuthSoapHeader, which is an instance of our custom SOAP header class. This class instance is used to set the values contained in the SOAP header.

The next line in our sample decorates the MyWebMethod method declaration with two attributes. The WebMethod attribute indicates that this will be a Web-callable method. The simple addition of this attribute causes ASP.NET to add all the additional features required to make our method callable via the Web. We will examine the WebMethod attribute in much greater detail in subsequent chapters, when we build an ASP.NET Web Service.

Otherwise, our code continues to look and function like a normal class. The SoapHeader attribute is used to specify that a SOAP header should be added to the MyWebMethod method. The parameter of this attribute is used to identify the specific header information to be added to this header and is the name of the member variable we previously declared for our SOAP header instance.

The result of this work is that a SOAP header will be added to the SOAP message that contains two SOAP header elements, the Username and Password. These elements will have values that are specified by the consumer of the Web service.

As we discussed earlier in our coverage of SOAP headers, two attributes named MustUnderstand and DidUnderstand are used with a SOAP header to indicate whether it is mandatory or optional for a recipient to process the header entry. The .NET SoapHeader class implements these SOAP attributes as two Boolean properties of the base class. Therefore, you can set these properties to the desired Boolean value, which will automatically generate the appropriate SOAP attribute when the SOAP message is generated by ASP.NET.

.NET SoapHeader attribute

As we saw in our last example, the SoapHeader attribute is used to enable support for SOAP headers on specific Web service methods that are declared with the WebMethod attribute. Specifically, the SoapHeader attribute is supplied with the name of a member variable that is an instance of our custom SoapHeader class. Technically, this syntax is setting a property of the SoapHeader attribute, namely the MemberName property. The SoapHeader attribute supports three properties:

✦ MemberName

✦ Direction

✦ Required

The MemberName property of the SoapHeader attribute identifies the name of the class variable that determines the type of the SOAP header. In our example, the type of the SOAP header is obtained from the AuthSoapHeader member variable within the MyWebService class.

The Direction property of the SoapHeader attribute is used to specify in which direction the header is expected to be supplied. By default, SOAP headers are attached to method requests only and are said to be *inbound* to the Web service. Using this property, we can change this default behavior.

The Direction property accepts an enumeration named SoapHeaderDirection, which supports the three values described in Table 24-4.

Table 24-4
SOAP header direction enumeration

Name	Definition
SoapHeaderDirection.In	Declares that the SOAP header is expected to be supplied to request messages generated by the Web service consumer.
SoapHeaderDirection.Out	Declares that the SOAP header is expected to be supplied by response messages generated by the Web service.
SoapHeaderDirection.InOut	Declares that the SOAP header is expected to be supplied by both the request and response messages.

An example of the Direction property is as follows.

VB.NET:

```
<SoapHeader("AuthSoapHeader",
Direction:=SoapHeaderDirection.Out>
```

C#:

```
[SoapHeader("AuthSoapHeader",
Direction=SoapHeaderDirection.Out]
```

Finally, the Required property of the SoapHeader attribute is a Boolean property that controls whether or not the SOAP header is required. By default, this property is set to True, which means that if the header is not supplied, a SOAP exception will be raised. Setting this property to False makes the header optional, as in the following example:

VB.NET:

```
<SoapHeader("AuthSoapHeader", Required:=false)>
```

C#:

```
[SoapHeader("AuthSoapHeader", Required=false)]
```

These are the basics for using SOAP headers in ASP.NET Web Services. Up to this point, however, we have not discussed how a consumer would access the SOAP header to set the values that need to be passed via the SOAP header. Fortunately, these details are handled for us by ASP.NET when the Web service proxy class is created. This makes setting SOAP header values as simple as setting a property on the proxy class instance. You will learn all about Web service proxy classes (the primary means by which a consumer interacts with a Web service) in Chapter 28, "Consuming Web Services."

Now, let's turn our attention to a slightly more advanced feature of ASP.NET, called SOAP extensions.

Using SOAP extensions

One of the more advanced features of SOAP within the .NET Framework is the SOAP extensions technology. Using this technology, you can inspect or modify a SOAP message at specific stages in message processing on either the client (consumer of the Web service) or server (the Web service itself). Of course, this assumes that the client and server are both based on .NET.

SOAP extensions are a powerful feature, because they enable you to implement some very interesting applications that can be leveraged by Web services and/or their clients in a completely transparent manner. For example, you can create extensions that do the following:

✦ Encrypt messages to protect the contents while in transit

✦ Compress messages to reduce the size of the transmission stream

✦ Log messages for auditing or tracing message activity (especially useful in debugging)

✦ Process SOAP attachments

These are just a few examples of the many other potentially useful applications of this technology.

The .NET Framework exposes this functionality through the following base classes that you can derive from to create custom SOAP extensions:

✦ System.Web.Services.Protocols.SoapExtension

✦ System.Web.Services.Protocols.SoapExtensionAttribute

The SoapExtension class is the base class for all SOAP extensions. This class defines a method named `ProcessMessage` that is called several times at various stages of message processing. These stages are listed in Table 24-5.

Table 24-5
SOAP extension message processing stages

Name	Definition
BeforeSerialize	During SoapClientMessage processing, this stage occurs after a client calls a Web Service method, but prior to the call being serialized.
	During SoapServerMessage processing, this stage occurs after the Web Service method returns results, but prior to those results being serialized.
AfterSerialize	During SoapClientMessage processing, this stage occurs after a client call to a Web Service method is serialized, but prior to the network request for the call is made.
	During SoapServerMessage processing, this stage occurs after the results for a Web Service method are serialized, but prior to the network response sending the results to the client.
BeforeDeserialize	During SoapClientMessage processing, this stage occurs after the network response for a Web Service method has been received, but prior to the response being deserialized.
	During SoapServerMessage processing, this stage occurs after a network request for a Web Service method is received, but prior to the request being deserialized.
AfterDeserialize	During SoapClientMessage processing, this stage occurs after the network response for a Web Service method has been deserialized, but prior to the client receiving the results.
	During SoapServerMessage processing, this stage occurs after a network request for a Web Service method is deserialized, but prior to the Web Service method being called.

To create a SOAP extension, you simply derive a class from the SoapExtension class and implement your extension code in the `ProcessMessage` method. The SOAP message is supplied to you as an input argument to the method. You can examine the SOAP message to determine which stage of message processing is in effect (using the `Stage` property) and then perform the appropriate processing for that stage.

 Note   You do not have to implement code for all SOAP extension message stages.

For example, a SOAP extension that is applied to a Web service client could gain access to the SOAP request message at the AfterSerialize stage. To gain access to the SOAP response message, the extension would wait for the BeforeDeserialize stage to occur.

In addition to implementing the SoapExtension class, you must also derive a class from the SoapExtensionAttribute base class. You use this class to create and apply a custom SOAP extension attribute to a method. When the custom extension attribute is added to a Web service method or a proxy class method, the associated extension is invoked at the appropriate time.

So, in summary, to implement a SOAP extension, you must derive classes from the .NET SoapExtension and SoapExtensionAttribute base classes, and then implement the code in these derived classes to intercept SOAP messages at the message processing stages you are interested in handling.

For specific examples of SOAP extensions, you can refer to the Microsoft .NET online documentation or the Visual Studio online documentation. The MSDN library also contains information about SOAP extensions in the .NET Framework.

Handling SOAP exceptions

As we have previously discussed, SOAP defines a mechanism for Web services to return a SOAP exception message in the face of a failed method call.

Handling SOAP exceptions within .NET applications (including ASP.NET applications) is a simple, straightforward process. The .NET Framework implements a class named SoapException (contained within the System.Web.Services.protocols namespace). The ASP.NET runtime converts SOAP exceptions into instances of the .NET SoapException class. This means that you can use `try...catch` blocks within your calls to Web service methods to catch SOAP exceptions. The following example illustrates how this is done:

VB.NET:

```
Imports System.Web.Services
Public Class MyWebService
  <WebMethod()> Public Function Divide(x as Integer, y as
Integer) as Integer
    Return x / y
  End Function
End Class
```

C#:

```
using System.Web.Services;
public class MyWebService : WebService {
public int Divide(int x, int y) {
```

```
      return x / y;
    }
}
```

We can catch divide-by-zero exceptions that can occur when calling the `Divide` Web method by using code similar to the following fragment:

VB.NET:

```
Dim div As New MyWebService
Dim z as Integer
Try
   Z = div.Divide(1, 0)
Catch err As SoapException
   strError = "Web method caused an exception"
End Try
```

C#:

```
public MyWebService div = new MyWebService;
int z;
try {
z = div.Divide(1,0);
}
catch (Exception e)
{
   strError = "Web method caused an exception";
}
```

The structured exception handling offered by the CLR makes error handling efficient and effective. All we need to do is use `try ... catch` blocks to trap errors that may occur in our calls to Web service methods.

Generally speaking, you should always wrap Web service method calls in `try ... catch` blocks. Because Web method calls are at least cross-process (and typically cross-machine or even cross-network), the possibility always exists that something within the underlying network may go wrong. Unlike local procedure calls that are within a single process, many other factors could cause a remote Web method invocation to fail. So, it's better to be safe than sorry when it comes to recognizing and handling these types of errors.

Microsoft SOAP Toolkit

As you might expect, it is entirely possible to create and consume Web services without the infrastructure and services provided by the .NET Framework and Visual Studio .NET (although it is much easier to do so with their support).

Because Web services are based on XML, HTTP, and SOAP, all we need to create or consume Web services are implementations of these technologies. This is precisely what Microsoft has done with the Microsoft SOAP toolkit.

The Microsoft SOAP toolkit supplies the technologies and tools needed to build and deploy Web services using Visual Studio 6.0 as the development environment along with the familiar COM programming model. In addition to building Web services that can run on Windows NT 4.0 SP6 and Windows 2000, you can build Web service consumers that will run on Windows 98, Windows ME, Windows NT 4.0 SP6, or Windows 2000 SP1.

The toolkit is a free and fully supported SDK that you can download from the MSDN Web site. For those of you who cannot deploy .NET or wish to address legacy platforms with Web services, the Microsoft SOAP Toolkit will prove to be a valuable resource for you.

Although we won't go into great detail about the toolkit here (after all, the subject of this book is ASP.NET), we will briefly discuss the features of the toolkit in case you ever have a need to use it. If that happens, you will want to refer to the documentation that comes with the toolkit for more-detailed information on system requirements, installation instructions, code samples, and the like.

Toolkit features

The toolkit contains both client- and server-side COM components as well as development tools that enable you to build or consume Web services using Visual Studio 6.0 as the development environment. The following are the technologies and tools included in the SOAP toolkit:

✦ A server-side component that maps Web service requests to COM object method calls described by WSDL and Web Service Meta Language (WSML) documents

✦ A client-side component that enables a consumer to call Web services described by a WSDL document

✦ Components that generate, transport, and process SOAP messages

✦ A WSDL/WSML document-generator tool

✦ A Visual Basic Add-in that simplifies the processing of XML documents contained in SOAP messages

✦ Additional APIs, utilities, and sample applications that illustrate how to use the SOAP Toolkit to build Web service and consumer applications

It is worth noting here that Web service consumers created with the SOAP toolkit can invoke any Web service, whether it is based on the SOAP toolkit, ASP.NET, or some other Web service implementation. Likewise, Web services created with the SOAP toolkit can be invoked by any Web service client, regardless of implementation. This illustrates one of the most powerful features of the Web services model that we have discussed previously: implementation independence. The way in which a Web service or Web service consumer is implemented is unimportant so long as they can communicate via XML, HTTP, and SOAP and implement the standards in an equivalent manner.

Let's take a quick look at some of the SOAP Toolkit features that enable you to create Web services and Web service consumers.

Creating a Web service

To enable Web service capabilities on the server, you must first and foremost be able to listen for Web service requests (in other words, SOAP messages) that are delivered to the server. This means that the Web server must be configured to listen for and process Web service request messages.

The SOAP Toolkit provides two choices for providing a SOAP listener for the Internet Information Server (IIS) Web server: an Internet Server API (ISAPI) listener and an Active Server Pages (ASP) listener. Your choice of which listener to use depends on the following:

✦ In most cases, you can choose the ISAPI listener. The advantages of the ISAPI listener are that it is faster than the ASP listener and does not require you to implement any code. You simply need to supply the WSDL and WSML files that describe the Web service and the mappings to COM server methods. The disadvantage of the ISAPI listener lies in the fact that you have no control over the invocation of Web service methods (this is done automatically).

✦ If you need to parse or validate input arguments, perform security checks, or execute similar actions on an incoming request, you must use the ASP listener. The advantage of the ASP listener is that you can perform special message processing on the server before invoking the Web service method. The drawbacks of the ASP listener are that it is slower than the ISAPI listener and you must implement custom code in an ASP page to invoke the Web service methods.

After making your choice, you must edit the WSDL document to specify the appropriate URL of the Web service endpoint. For the ASP listener, you should specify the URL to the ASP file. To use the ISAPI listener, you specify the URL to the WSDL file.

If you are using the ISAPI listener, Web service message processing is automatic. When an incoming SOAP request is detected, the ISAPI listener is invoked to handle the message. The ISAPI listener loads the WSDL and WSML files, executes the request, and returns the results in a response message. In this scenario, you only need provide the WSDL and WSML files.

If you are using the ASP listener, you must create an ASP page that uses the SOAPServer COM component to process incoming Web request messages.

 Note   Both the ISAPI and ASP listeners use the SOAPServer component. So, regardless of listener choice, the SOAP messages are handled identically (once the SOAPServer component receives the request).

The SOAPServer component enables Web service request messages to call methods on COM components. The component exposes several properties and methods that permit an ASP page to pass a Web service request to the component for execution (via the request stream) and supply the results to the caller (via the response stream). Using this component, the ASP page does not have to understand how to process SOAP messages.

To use the SOAPServer component, you specify the WSDL and WSML documents as input arguments to the initialization method. This allows the component to create the mappings between Web service requests and COM method calls.

After you have initialized the SOAPServer object, you can call its invoke method, passing the ASP input stream and output stream as arguments to the method. When you call the `invoke` method on the SOAPServer object, the following steps occur:

1. The SOAPServer object deserializes the SOAP request message supplied to it via the invoke method.

2. The request is then examined to locate the COM component and method to be called from the WSDL and WSML documents that were loaded when the SOAPServer object was initialized.

3. An instance of the identified COM object is created and the appropriate method is called using the arguments obtained from the request message.

4. The result is obtained from the method call and serialized into a SOAP response message.

5. The SOAP response message is returned to the caller via an output argument of the invoke method.

Creating a Web service consumer

The SOAPClient COM component enables Web service consumers to call Web services. This component leverages the features of the SOAP Toolkit to provide properties and methods that a Web service consumer can use to call Web service methods without having to deal with SOAP messages directly. In this way, the SOAPClient component acts as a proxy object for the Web service.

To use the SOAPClient component, you must have access to the WSDL document that describes the Web service. When you call the initialization method on the component, you pass in the location of the WSDL document. This causes all the operations defined in the WSDL document to be dynamically bound to the SOAPClient component. Once this has been completed, you can invoke the methods defined in the WSDL document via the SOAPClient object.

When you invoke a Web service method bound to the SOAPClient object, the following steps occur:

1. The SOAPClient object serializes the method call into a SOAP request message and delivers it to the server.

2. The server deserializes the SOAP request message and processes the request.

3. The server serializes the result into a SOAP response message and delivers it to the client.

4. The SOAPClient object deserializes the SOAP response message and returns the result to the caller.

5. The SOAPClient object also exposes SOAP fault properties so that you can examine error information in case a method call fails for some reason.

To summarize, the SOAPClient object makes it easy to consume Web services in a COM-like manner. The consumer need only supply the WSDL document that describes the Web service to the SOAPClient object in order to call the operations exposed by the Web service. The SOAPClient object takes care of translating COM method calls into SOAP requests and then translating the SOAP response into a COM method return value. If an error occurs in the method call, the SOAPClient object exposes properties that allow a consumer to gain access to the SOAP fault information that is returned.

WSDL/WSML generator tool

The WSDL/WSML generator tool is used to automatically generate WSDL and WSML documents from COM type libraries. The graphical version of the tool (named Wsdlgen.exe) walks you through the process of generating these documents. It will request the type of listener you wish to use, the location of the COM type library, which methods you wish to expose from the available interfaces in the type library, the folder in which to write the WSDL and WSML documents, and a few other details. After answering these questions, the tool will generate the files for you.

If you wish to script the generation of these files, a command-line version of the tool is also supplied, named Wsdlstb.exe. You can use the /? switch on the command line to get help information on valid command parameters and switches.

The bottom line here is that the WSDL/WSML generator tool can be a great time-saver when preparing your COM components for accessibility as Web services.

SOAP trace utility

One final useful utility to point out that ships with the Microsoft SOAP Toolkit is the SOAP trace utility. Using this graphical utility, you can view SOAP request and response messages transported over HTTP between a Web service and Web service consumer.

The trace utility can be configured to run either on the client or the server. To run the trace utility on the server, you must make a small modification to the WSDL document that specifies the URL to the SOAP endpoint. Once this has been done, you can start the trace utility to begin a tracing session. To run the trace utility on the client, you must copy the WSDL document to the client machine, make a similar modification to the WSDL document, and start the trace utility. After starting the utility, you need to specify the name of the host where the actual Web service is running. After doing so, you will be able to begin a tracing session.

Summary

SOAP is a major element of the Web services infrastructure and a critical factor in the ability of Web services to reach across platforms, operating systems, object models, and programming languages. This greatly increases the interoperability of distributed computing components built on this model.

SOAP extinguishes the language and object model wars by permitting component interoperability at a message level, enabling the user to implement their Web service code in any manner that they wish, using tools and technologies that are familiar and native to the platform on which they work.

Relatively speaking, SOAP is still a young technology, and although it has been submitted to the W3C as a note, the specification has not made it through the W3C's standardization process as of yet. Rest assured, though, that the major vendors driving and implementing SOAP will keep pace with any changes that occur through the standards process and hopefully be able to insulate developers from the subtle changes that may occur.

✦   ✦   ✦

Building a Web Service

In this chapter, you will learn how to build a simple Web service using Visual Basic .NET and C#. We will go step by step through the process of creating a Web service that converts given temperatures between Fahrenheit, Celsius, Kelvin, and Rankine. Along the way, this chapter describes some of the implementation details and options available to you related to building Web services.

The Temperature Conversion Web Service

Before we begin building your first Web service, let's take a moment to briefly describe the service we intend to build. The first thing you will notice when you begin building this Web service is its simplicity. This has been done deliberately in order to focus more on the big picture of the various architectural elements of ASP.NET Web services than the details of the algorithm implemented by the code.

With this in mind, we will be building a simple, but useful Web service that converts temperature values between various numeric units.

The temperature conversion Web service will convert specified temperature values from Fahrenheit or Celsius to any one of Fahrenheit, Celsius, Kelvin, or Rankine. Each of these unit conversions is defined by a well-known arithmetic formula that can be easily represented in any programming language and does not require a lot of code.

Temperature conversion formulas

Table 25-1 shows the conversions that will be supported by the service and the corresponding formulas used to perform the conversion.

Table 25-1 Temperature conversion formulas				
From/To	**Fahrenheit (F)**	**Celsius (C)**	**Kelvin (K)**	**Rankine (R)**
Celsius	((C * 9) / 5) + 32	N/A	C + 273.15	F + 459.67
Fahrenheit	N/A	((F - 32) * 5) / 9	C + 273.15	F + 459.67

As you can see from the table, some of the conversions are specified assuming an initial conversion to another unit. For example, to convert a Celsius temperature to Rankine, the temperature value is first converted to Fahrenheit and then the remaining conversion rules are applied.

Finally, in keeping with the goal of code simplicity and brevity, the service will only support temperature conversions from Celsius or Fahrenheit to any of the other applicable units.

Method description

The temperature conversion Web service will support a single method named CTemp, which is modeled along the lines of the classic Visual Basic type conversion functions such as CBool, CLng, CDbl, and so forth. The obvious difference, of course, being that we are converting to other numeric units instead of converting to other data types.

Method arguments

The temperature conversion method will accept three arguments, summarized in Table 25-2.

Table 25-2 Temperature conversion method arguments		
Argument Name	**Data Type**	**Comments**
Temperature	Decimal	Any numeric value that can be specified by the Decimal data type
FromUnits	String	Valid values are C for Celsius or F for Fahrenheit
ToUnits	String	Valid values are C for Celsius, F for Fahrenheit, K for Kelvin, and R for Rankine

The method will return a Decimal result, which is the value of the conversion to the units specified in the `ToUnits` argument.

Method behavior

If the `FromUnits` and `ToUnits` arguments are the same, the method call will be successful and the `Temperature` argument will be returned unchanged. If the `FromUnits` and/or `ToUnits` do not specify valid unit identifiers, an `ArgumentException` exception will be thrown. Likewise, if the conversion specified by the `FromUnits` and `ToUnits` arguments is not supported, an `ArgumentException` exception will be thrown.

Creating the Web Service

Although the Visual Studio Integrated Development Environment (IDE) is a highly productive tool for building ASP.NET Web services, it is not a required tool. The .NET Framework itself comes bundled with the Visual Basic .NET and C# command-line compilers as well as other tools that you can use to build ASP.NET Web services.

ASP.NET Web services require a Web-addressable entry point file, an assembly that implements the functionality of the service, a Web Service Description (WSDL) document an optional Discovery (DISCO) document, and an optional UDDI registration. In this chapter, you will learn how to create and properly format the files required to implement a Web service.

Web services built with the .NET Framework leverage the ASP.NET infrastructure, tools, and runtime. Of course, ASP.NET itself is built upon the foundation of the .NET Framework and the Common Language Runtime (CLR), providing all the benefits of these technologies to your Web service implementation.

These relationships are also important because they affect the physical structure of Web services on the .NET platform. The power of this model is quite evident as you begin to dissect the various pieces of a Web service on the .NET platform and gain an understanding of the features that are provided by these technologies. We will cover this as we work our way through the temperature conversion Web service implementation.

Getting started

Before you start working with the .NET Framework to build a Web service application, you must consider a few environmental factors related to your software and network configuration. These considerations will directly affect how you build, debug, and deploy your ASP.NET Web services.

ASP.NET Web service development requirements

The typical development environment for an ASP.NET Web service application usually consists of the following elements:

✦ A personal workstation with the.NET Framework SDK installed

✦ A development Web server that is configured to host and run a development (nonrelease) version of your Web service

✦ A production Web server that is configured to host the final run-time (release) version of your Web service

Often, the personal workstation and development Web server are combined on a single computer. This makes design, implementation, and debugging easier during the early development stages of your Web service. This is the development environment we will use in creating and building the CTemp Web service in this chapter.

Note   If you intend to develop Web services using this configuration, you must be running Windows 2000 or later as your operating system.

If you prefer to develop Web services on a remote Web server, you should make sure that at least the runtime portion of the .NET Framework is installed and configured. With this configuration, you only need worry about copying your Web service implementation files to an appropriately configured virtual directory on the Web server.

Creating the Web service application

ASP.NET Web services are ASP.NET applications. Good practice dictates that ASP.NET applications have a Web server virtual directory defined for them. This allows more flexibility in configuring and customizing the Web service from a Web application perspective. Therefore, we will create a virtual directory for our CTemp Web service. Follow these steps:

1. Create a directory under the Web server root directory (typically inetpub/ wwwroot) named CTemp.

2. From the Microsoft Windows 2000 Start menu, choose Settings ⇨ Control Panel.

3. Double-click the Administrative Tools icon.

4. Within the Administrative Tools group, double-click the Internet Services Manager icon. This will display the Internet Information Services window.

5. In the Internet Information Services window, drill down to the default Web site on your local computer. You should see a list of virtual directories similar to that shown in Figure 25-1.

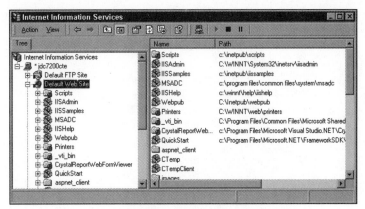

Figure 25-1: Internet Information Services window

6. From the Action menu, choose New ➪ Virtual Directory. This displays the Virtual Directory Creation Wizard, shown in Figure 25-2.

Figure 25-2: Virtual Directory Creation Wizard

7. Click the Next button to continue. This displays the Virtual Directory Alias panel.

8. Enter "CTemp" as the name for your virtual directory in the text box, as shown in Figure 25-3.

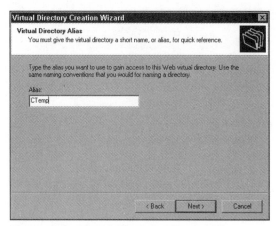

Figure 25-3: Virtual Directory Alias panel

9. Click the Next button to continue. This displays the Web Site Content Directory panel.

10. Enter in the text box the physical path to the CTemp directory you created earlier, as shown in Figure 25-4.

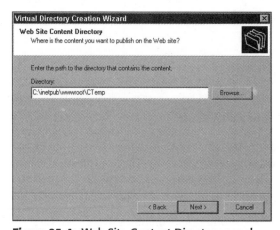

Figure 25-4: Web Site Content Directory panel

11. Click the Next button to continue. This displays the Access Permissions panel, shown in Figure 25-5.

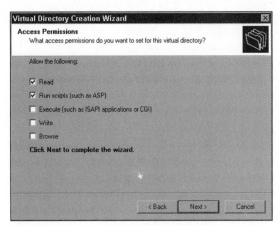

Figure 25-5: Access Permissions panel

12. This panel controls the type of access permitted to users of files referenced by the virtual directory. You can enable one or a combination of choices from the list by toggling the checkbox next to each option. The choices are as follows:

✦ Read: Enables read access to all files in the virtual directory

✦ Run scripts (such as ASP): Enables scripts to be executed from the virtual directory

✦ Execute (such as ISAPI applications or CGI): Enables executable files to be run from the virtual directory

✦ Write: Enables files to be uploaded to the virtual directory

✦ Browse: Enables files to be listed (or enumerated) in the virtual directory

Keep the default settings as shown in the permissions panel and click Next to continue. This displays the completion panel, shown in Figure 25-6.

13. Click the Finish button to complete the Virtual Directory Creation Wizard.

This process will create a Web server virtual directory named CTemp in the default Web site of your Web server.

Now that we have a directory into which to place our Web service application files, as well as a Web server virtual directory to govern how the Web server treats our application, we are ready to begin creating our first Web service.

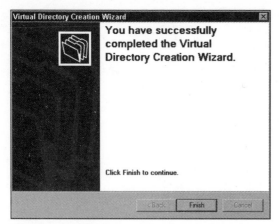

Figure 25-6: Final step of the Virtual Directory
Creation Wizard

Declaring the Web service

The first step in building the temperature conversion Web service outlined in the
beginning of this chapter is to create the Web service entry point file (CTemp.asmx)
in our application directory.

Note   You can use any text editor to create the ASMX file, such as Windows Notepad.

The ASMX file serves as the Web-addressable entry point for your Web service and
defines the class that implements the functionality of the Web service. The Web service declaration can specify that the class implementation is contained in the ASMX
file itself (referred to as "inline") or that the class is contained in an external assembly. This latter type of declaration is also called a code behind file and is the type of
Web service implementation created by Visual Studio.

To declare a Web service with an inline implementation class, add an ASP.NET
WebService directive at the top of the CTemp.asmx file, specifying the class implementing the Web Service and the programming language used for the implementation code. The following Web service declaration illustrates how this is done.

VB.NET:

```
<%@ WebService Language="VB" Class="TempConverter" %>
```

C#:

```
<%@ WebService Language="C#" Class="TempConverter" %>
```

To declare a Web service with an implementation that resides in a code behind file,
add an ASP.NET WebService directive at the top of the CTemp.asmx file, specifying

the class implementing the Web Service, the programming language used in the implementation, and, optionally, the assembly containing the implementation or the name of the code behind file. The following Web service declaration shows how this is done.

VB.NET:

```
<%@ WebService Language="VB" Codebehind="CTemp.vb"
Class="TempConverter" %>
```

C#:

```
<%@ WebService Language="C#" Codebehind="CTemp.cs"
Class="TempConverter" %>
```

Note   If you do not specify an assembly within the `WebService` directive, then ASP.NET searches through the list of assemblies in the \bin directory of the Web application hosting the Web Service.

For our CTemp Web service, we will specify an inline implementation class. We will put all of this together (the declaration and the implementation class) in the next section.

When you have finished building and testing your Web service, features of the .NET Framework make it easy to deploy your Web service to a production Web server. We will discuss this in more detail in Chapter 26, "Deploying and Publishing Web Services."

Lastly, the complete path to your new Web service is `http://localhost/CTemp/ CTemp.asmx`. This is the path that consumers of your Web service will use when calling your service (at least while it is under development).

Web service files

The simplest of ASP.NET Web services can be built using only an ASMX file in a Web application directory. However, more sophisticated and flexible Web services can be built by leveraging features of ASP.NET and the .NET Framework. In this case, you will need to include additional files in the application folder of your Web service implementation.

Table 25-3 lists the various files that may be used by an ASP.NET Web service, along with their purpose.

Tip   Many of these files are optional. A minimal ASP.NET Web service only requires the ASMX file.

Table 25-3
ASP.NET Web service files

Project File	Description
Service name.asmx	Serves as the Web-accessible entry point for the Web service. It contains the Web service processing directive, which declares information about the implementation of the Web service.
Service name.asmx.vb or *Service name*.asmx.cs	Contains the code behind class that implements the functionality of the Web service. This file is referenced by the *Service name*.asmx file in its Web service processing directive, if code behind is used.
Web.config	Contains ASP.NET application configuration information for the Web service.
Global.asax	Responsible for handling ASP.NET application-level events.
Global.asax.vb	Contains the code behind class that handles the ASP.NET application-level events. This file is referenced by the Global.asax file in its ASP.NET application directive, if code behind is used.
Service name.vsdisco	Contains the links (URLs) to the discovery (DISCO) file information that is available for the Web service.
Bin*service name*.dll	The assembly package for the class(es) that implements the functionality of the Web service. This is the location of the compiled version of the Web service code behind file.

Implementing the Web service

We are now ready to write the code that will implement our Web service. Recall that in the last section we decided to use an embedded class declaration and implementation. Thus, we will be adding our implementation code to the CTemp.asmx file. This is very much like the technique used to code ASP.NET pages.

First, let's begin by adding the Web service declaration and class definition in the CTemp.asmx file as follows.

VB.NET:

```
<%@ WebService Language="VB" Class="TempConverter" %>
Imports System
Imports System.Web.Services
```

```
Public Class TempConverter
...
End Class
```

C#:

```
<%@ WebService Language="C#" Class="TempConverter" %>
using System;
using System.Web.Services;
public class TempConverter : WebService{
...
}
```

In this code, we have added the ASP.NET `WebService` directive that declares the Web service, and the class definition that declares the class containing our Web service implementation code.

The `WebService` directive specifies the language used to implement the Web service as well as the name of the class containing the functionality of the Web service. These two pieces of information give ASP.NET essential information that it needs to identify the Web service implementation.

The class definition, as you can see, is a normal class declaration. This is one of the great features of ASP.NET Web services — writing code for Web services is essentially like writing traditional object-oriented code using the built-in support provided by the host language (in this case, VB.NET or C#).

Lastly, note the references to the System and System.Web.Services namespaces. The System namespace enables us to use exceptions in our method implementation, and the System.Web.Services namespace, of course, provides us access to the Web services features of ASP.NET.

The WebService attribute

The `WebService` attribute is an optional attribute that can be added to the Web service class declaration to configure various properties for the class. The `WebService` attribute can be added to the front of the class declaration as follows:

```
<WebService()> Public Class TempConverter
```

Table 25-4 lists the properties that you can add to the `WebService` attribute.

Table 25-4
WebService attribute properties

Property Name	Description
Description	Provides a brief description of the functionality of the Web service as a whole.
Namespace	Used to provide a unique XML namespace for the WSDL document that describes the capabilities of the Web service.
Name	Overrides the Web service name, normally taken from the class name. The name is typically used when generating proxy classes from the WSDL document of the Web service.

We will not be using these properties in our TempConverter class declaration, although we will use the Namespace property later in Chapter 26 when we cover Web service deployment and publishing.

Creating Web methods

Now that we have the skeleton of our CTemp Web service in place, we are ready to add the method declaration that will provide the implementation for our Web service.

So far, we have turned a normal class definition into a Web service simply by adding the Web service declaration to the ASMX file. This same model is used to identify a Web method. Specifically, a normal method declaration becomes a Web method by adding the WebMethod attribute to it.

The TempConverter class contains the following Web method declaration.

VB.NET:

```
    <WebMethod()> Public Function CTemp(ByVal Temperature As
Decimal, ByVal FromUnits As String, ByVal ToUnits As String) As
Decimal
...
End Function
```

C#:

```
[WebMethod]
public Decimal CTemp(Decimal Temperature, String FromUnits,
String ToUnits) {
...
}
```

Let's examine this declaration for a moment. The first thing that you should notice (and also appreciate) is that the method declaration looks quite similar to function or method declarations you are already used to writing in previous versions of Visual Basic.

But, perhaps more important than what is the same is the recognition of what is missing from this declaration. Note that no reference exists to SOAP, XML, HTTP, or any of the other technologies that are required for Web services. All of these details are buried in the plumbing provided by the ASP.NET runtime and the .NET Framework. All we have to do is mark our methods with the WebMethod attribute, and the .NET Framework takes care of the rest.

You should notice that the WebMethod syntax is similar but slightly different depending on the language in use. This reflects the personality of the language syntax itself, making the particular method of declaring the WebMethod a more natural extension of the specific language being employed.

The only part of our method declaration that is remotely different from traditional component programming in Visual Basic is the introduction of the <WebMethod()> attribute. The simple addition of this attribute to a public method declaration instructs Visual Basic or C# to make this method a Web method. This results in additional support for serialization/deserialization of XML, the mapping of all data types to XML, and the formatting/exchange of SOAP-based messages.

Note   The WebMethod attribute can also be applied to public properties of a class, making these Web-callable as well.

Notice that the WebMethod() attribute also has room (within the parentheses) for attribute properties. Attribute properties enable you to override default behavior or enable Web methods with additional functionality.

Table 25-5 lists the properties that you can add to the WebMethod attribute.

| Table 25-5 | |
| **WebMethod attribute properties** | |
Property Name	*Description*
Description	Provides a brief description of the functionality of the Web method.
EnableSession	Enables session state so that state can be maintained between method calls.
MessageName	Used to provide an alias name for Web methods. This is typically required when implementing polymorphic methods in a class.

Continued

	Table 25-5 *(continued)*	
Property Name	**Description**
TransactionOption	Allows the Web method to support transactions (similar to the transaction support provided by MTS and COM+).
CacheDuration	Enables output caching so that the results of a particular method call can be saved to a cache and reused, rather than regenerated.
BufferResponse	Permits the server to buffer the response and transmit it only after the response has been completely generated.

We won't use these optional properties in our CTemp Web service method, however, these properties are covered in Chapter 23, "Web Services Infrastruture." You can also learn more about these properties by referring to the .NET Framework online documentation.

Adding the implementation code

After you have added the Web method declaration, you are ready to insert the code that actually performs the temperature conversions. Enter the following code into the CTemp.asmx file within the CTemp Web method.

VB.NET:

```
Select Case FromUnits.ToUpper.Chars(0)
Case "F" 'Fahrenheit
   Select Case ToUnits.ToUpper.Chars(0)
     Case "F" 'No conversion necessary
       Return Temperature
     Case "C" 'Convert Fahrenheit to Celsius
       Return ((Temperature - 32) * 5) / 9
     Case "K" 'Convert Fahrenheit to Kelvin
       Return (((Temperature - 32) * 5) / 9) + 273.15
     Case "R" 'Convert Fahrenheit to Rankine
       Return Temperature + 459.67
     Case Else
       'Throw exception
       Throw New ArgumentException("Bad ToUnits arg.")
   End Select
Case "C" 'Celsius
   Select Case ToUnits.ToUpper.Chars(0)
     Case "C" 'No conversion necessary
       Return Temperature
     Case "F" 'Convert Celsius to Fahrenheit
       Return ((Temperature * 9) / 5) + 32
     Case "K" 'Convert Celsius to Kelvin
       Return Temperature + 273.15
```

```
          Case "R" 'Convert Celsius to Rankine
            Return (((Temperature * 9) / 5) + 32) + 459.67
          Case Else
            'Throw exception
            Throw New ArgumentException("Bad ToUnits arg.")
        End Select
    Case Else
      'Throw exception
      Throw New ArgumentException("Bad FromUnits arg.")
    End Select
```

C#:

```
    switch (FromUnits.ToUpper().Substring(0,1))
    {
        case "F": //Fahrenheit
            switch (ToUnits.ToUpper().Substring(0,1))
            {
            case "F": //No conversion necessary
                return Temperature;
            case "C": //Convert Fahrenheit to Celsius
                return ((Temperature - 32) * 5) / 9;
            case "K": //Convert Fahrenheit to Kelvin
                return (((Temperature - 32) * 5) / 9) +
(Decimal)273.15;
            case "R": //Convert Fahrenheit to Rankine
                return Temperature + (Decimal)459.67;
            default:
                //Throw exception
                throw new ArgumentException("Bad ToUnits arg.");
            }
        case "C": //Celsius
            switch (ToUnits.ToUpper().Substring(0,1))
            {
            case "C": //No conversion necessary
                return Temperature;
            case "F": //Convert Celsius to Fahrenheit
                return ((Temperature * 9) / 5) + (Decimal)32;
            case "K": //Convert Celsius to Kelvin
                return Temperature + (Decimal)273.15;
            case "R": //Convert Celsius to Rankine
                return (((Temperature * 9) / 5) + 32) +
(Decimal)459.67;
            default:
                //Throw exception
                throw new ArgumentException("Bad ToUnits arg.");
            }
        default:
            //Throw exception
            throw new ArgumentException("Bad FromUnits arg.");
    }
```

As noted earlier, the logic of our CTemp Web service does not change, regardless of whether or not the method is marked as a `WebMethod`.

Handling errors

The .NET Framework, via the CLR, provides excellent support for handling errors via exceptions. Applications built on the .NET Framework can throw and catch exceptions to handle all types of run-time errors. This support is also available to Web services.

Generally, you will want to use exceptions to communicate run-time errors back to Web service consumers for conditions that your service cannot handle effectively. As you can see in our implementation of the CTemp Web method, there are several cases in which we must throw exceptions based on invalid input obtained from the consumer in the method call.

Web services communicate exceptions to consumers via SOAP exception messages. A SOAP exception is represented by the SoapException class in the .NET Framework's System.Web.Services.Protocols namespace. As a Web service consumer, you can wrap calls to Web service methods within `try...catch` blocks to intercept exceptions thrown by Web services.

Referring to our CTemp implementation, arguments that cannot be processed as specified by the consumer cause the Web service to throw an `ArgumentException` exception. This exception is serialized into a SOAPException message and returned to the consumer.

Note that communicating exceptions to Web service consumers is only supported via SOAP. Therefore, if you use HTTP-GET or HTTP-POST to call a Web service method (as is the case when using a Web browser to test and invoke Web services), you cannot get exceptions transported back to the browser. In this case, the exception within the Web service is handled by the Web server, which results in the transmission of a server error page back to the consumer.

Building the Web service

Now that we've added all the implementation code to our CTemp Web service, we are ready to build it. For inline Web services (such as our CTemp Web service, where the implementation code is contained in the ASMX file), a separate build of the code is not necessary, because the ASP.NET runtime recognizes when it is necessary to compile and build the Web service automatically.

If your Web service is being invoked for the first time, ASP.NET will build the Web service and cache the application code for future reference. Each subsequent request for your Web service will then be handled by the cached executable. If the ASP.NET runtime is restarted, however, the cache is lost and the next request for your Web service will result in the build and cache process being repeated.

The automatic build capability of ASP.NET is yet another example of how ASP.NET and the .NET Framework make it easy to build Web services. In the simplest case, you can copy your Web service ASMX file to a target Web server as is. ASP.NET will take care of the rest.

Having a complete Web service in place on your Web server, you are now ready to test it. We will cover Web service testing in the next section.

Testing the Web Service

The .NET Framework provides a quick and simple method you can use to test your Web service. Specifically, you can test your Web service using a Web browser and the HTTP-GET protocol. This technique does not require developing a consumer application.

Note   This technique works only for the HTTP-GET protocol support that is provided by the browser. By default, an ASP.NET Web service supports the HTTP-GET, HTTP-POST, and HTTP-SOAP protocols.

In addition to using a Web browser with HTTP-GET, you can test your Web service using a Web browser with HTTP-POST, with a slight modification to the default ASP.NET page used to view Web services. Finally, you can test your Web service by developing a custom consumer application. We will discuss this technique in Chapter 28, "Consuming Web Services," where we will build a consumer to invoke the CTemp Web service.

The following sections describe how to use your Web browser with the HTTP-GET and HTTP-POST protocols to test your Web service.

Testing with HTTP-GET

Using a Web browser to test your Web service with the HTTP-GET protocol does not require you to develop a consumer application. Therefore, this is a quick and easy way to perform some initial testing of your Web service.

The HTTP-GET protocol encodes data (in this case, method arguments) as query string parameters when posting to the server. This encoding method is used to pass the proper method input arguments as query string arguments.

Two ways exist to invoke the HTTP-GET protocol using a Web browser to test your Web service. You can use the built-in test page offered by the ASP.NET runtime or you can encode the complete URL to your Web service using location, method name, and any input arguments as query string parameters in the Address bar of your browser. We will illustrate each of these techniques using our CTemp Web service as an example.

Using the Web service test page

The ASP.NET runtime provides excellent support for interactive viewing of Web service information and capabilities, as well as basic HTML forms for performing interactive tests using the HTTP-GET protocol support built into your browser.

ASP.NET provides this capability via a Web service help file template named DefaultWsdlHelpGenerator.aspx. By default, this file is located in the \Winnt\ Microsoft.NET\Framework*version*\CONFIG folder. Note that this is just an ordinary ASP.NET page, so you can customize this page to suit your particular needs. What's more, you can copy this file to your Web service virtual application folder to provide custom capabilities for each Web service application that you create. We will cover how to do this shortly.

Using the Web service help template to view Web service information is as simple as entering the URL to your Web service entry point file (the ASMX file) into the Address bar of your browser.

To view the help page for our CTemp Web service, type the following URL in your Web browser Address bar (this example assumes that the Web service is available on your local machine):

```
http://localhost/ctemp/ctemp.asmx
```

This will cause the Web server to execute the help file template and return a page similar to Figure 25-7.

This page shows us the name of the Web service (TempConverter), the methods that it supports (in this case, the single method named CTemp), and a link to the Web service WSDL document.

The second part of this page includes a warning regarding the use of the temporary namespace URI http://tempuri.org/ for our service. This namespace is used to uniquely identify your Web service from all others, and should be changed before deploying your Web service for public consumption. During initial development, however, it is not necessary to change this URI. We will discuss the Web service namespace URI and how to change it in Chapter 26, "Deploying and Publishing Web Services."

Let's continue our exploration of the Web service help page by following some of the links found on the page. We will begin by taking a look at the WSDL service contract.

Viewing the WSDL service contract

Let's take a quick look at the WSDL service contract document for the CTemp Web service. To view the WSDL service contract, simply click the Service Description hot link on the Web service help page. This will display the WSDL XML file contents, as shown in Figure 25-8.

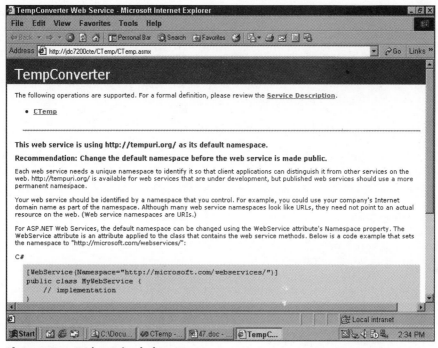

Figure 25-7: Web service help page

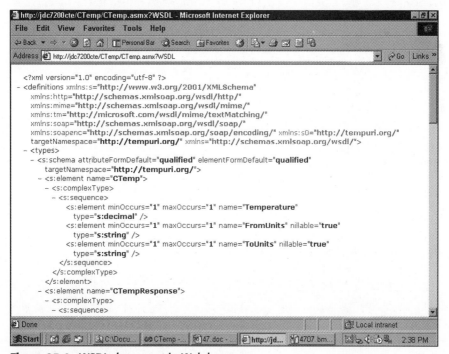

Figure 25-8: WSDL document in Web browser

Note the URL in the Address bar of the browser window. The base URL is the same (it points at our ASMX file), but the URL now also includes the following query string:

```
http://jdc7200cte/CTemp/CTemp.asmx?WSDL
```

This query string instructs the ASP.NET to generate and display the WSDL service contract for the specified Web service.

You may be wondering at this point how this process works, because no actual WSDL file is stored in the virtual directory of your Web service application. The .NET Framework supports a feature called *reflection,* which basically means that a .NET class can be queried to obtain information about the properties, methods, events, and other features it offers via its programmatic interfaces.

This is a great feature, because you don't have to worry about keeping a separate WSDL file in sync with the actual class that implements the capabilities of the Web service. Simply let ASP.NET use run-time reflection to query the Web service class and dynamically generate the WSDL contract all at once.

Now that you have had a chance to look at the WSDL service contract for your Web service, let's take a look at the help page provided for the CTemp Web method.

Viewing Web method help

If you followed the instructions in the last section to view the WSDL service contract, click the Back button in the browser window to return to the main Web service help page. Now, click the CTemp method hot link. This displays in your browser a page similar to Figure 25-9.

Note the URL that appears in the Address bar of the browser window. The base URL is again the same as before (it points at our ASMX file), but the URL now includes a new query string, as follows:

```
http://jdc7200cte/CTemp/CTemp.asmx?op=CTemp
```

This query string instructs the IIS Web server (or, more specifically, the ASP.NET runtime) to display a page that contains detailed information about the Web service method specified as the value part of the query string argument (in this case, the CTemp method).

The first part of the Web method help page contains a hot link that will return you to the main Web service documentation page. Underneath this link is a simple form that permits you to invoke the Web service method.

The second part of the Web method documentation page contains sample SOAP, HTTP-GET, and HTTP-POST request and response message definitions. These are the messages that will be exchanged between the Web service and the consumer for this method call for the three supported message transports.

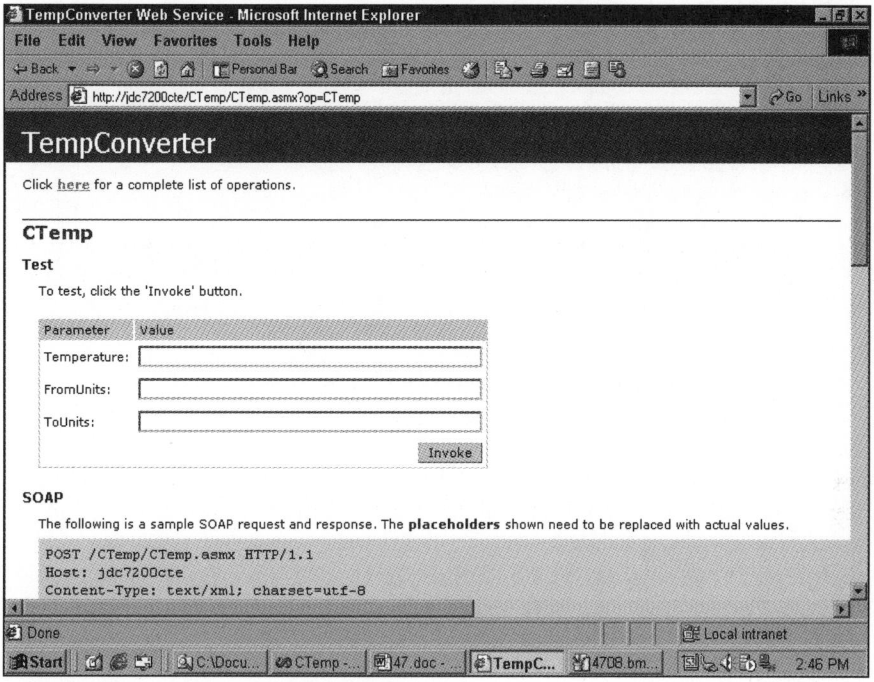

Figure 25-9: Web method help page

On this page, we have the ability to test our CTemp method by interacting with a form in our browser. Using this form, we can enter test values for the input arguments and click the Invoke button to execute the CTemp method using the HTTP-GET protocol.

Let's go ahead and test our service with some sample input. Enter the following information into the test form and click the Invoke button when you are finished:

    ✦ Temperature: 78

    ✦ FromUnits: F

    ✦ ToUnits: C

The form data is posted to the Web server using the HTTP-GET protocol. The Web server receives the URL and passes it to the ASP.NET runtime, which locates your Web service, creates an instance of the implementation class, calls the target method with the specified input arguments extracted from the query string parameter list, and returns the serialized XML result to your browser window, as shown in Figure 25-10.

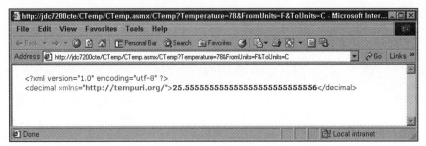

Figure 25-10: XML results returned from method execution

The XML lists the return type in the element name and displays the return value of 25.5 within this element. Note the URL that is displayed in the browser Address bar. This URL shows how the query strings are formatted to specify the input arguments required by the method that appears as the last component of the base URL.

Manually invoking a Web service method

In addition to using the Web service test page to test our CTemp method using the HTTP-GET protocol, we can manually enter a properly formatted URL into the Address bar of our browser, which encodes the method name and input arguments as query string parameters, as follows:

```
http://localhost/ctemp/ctemp.asmx/CTemp?Temperature=78&FromUnit
s=F&ToUnits=C
```

Entering this URL into your browser will result in the same XML-encoded response from the Web server as that which we obtained when testing the Web service using the test form generated by the DefaultWsdlHelpGenerator.aspx page described in the last section.

Testing with HTTP-POST

Just like the HTTP-GET protocol, we can use a Web browser to test our Web service with the HTTP-POST protocol without going to the trouble of writing a consumer application.

The HTTP-POST protocol encodes data as name/value pairs within the body of the HTTP request when posting to the server, rather than encoding data in the form of query strings, as does HTTP-GET.

With only a few minor modifications to the default Web service help page and our application configuration file, we can test our CTemp Web service using the HTTP-POST protocol. To do this, follow these steps:

1. Copy Winnt\Microsoft.NET\Framework*version*\CONFIG\ DefaultWsdlHelpGenerator.aspx to the CTemp Web service virtual directory.

2. Rename the file "CTemp.aspx."

3. Edit CTemp.aspx with your favorite text editor.

4. Change the showPost flag to True.

5. Save the changes to the file.

6. Create a text file named "Web.config" in the CTemp virtual directory with your favorite text editor (if you do not already have a Web.config file).

7. Add the following text to the Web.config file:

```
<?xml version="1.0" encoding="utf-8" ?>
<configuration>
  <system.web>
    <webServices>
      <wsdlHelpGenerator href="CTemp.aspx" />
    </webServices>
  </system.web>
</configuration>
```

8. Save the changes to the file.

You can now test your CTemp method using the HTTP-POST protocol. To do this, enter the URL to the CTemp entry point file into your browser's Address bar as follows:

```
http://localhost/ctemp/ctemp.asmx
```

When the test page is displayed, click the CTemp method link once again and enter test values into the form. Click the Invoke button, and you should see the XML-formatted results returned to a new browser window (identical to what happened when testing with the HTTP-GET protocol).

The only difference between the two methods is revealed in the URL that is displayed in the browser Address bar in the results window. Note that the method name is the last segment of the URL and no query string arguments are visible.

Debugging the Web Service

Sometimes, testing your Web service as outlined in the last section will reveal flaws in your implementation or other unexpected results. If this occurs, you may need to debug your Web service. For those of you who have experience in trying to debug prior-generation ASP applications, you will find that the .NET Framework SDK and ASP.NET have much-improved support for testing and debugging your Web service applications.

To illustrate the general debugging process, we will set a breakpoint in our CTemp method code using the .NET SDK debugger so that we can examine what happens during a call to our Web service method.

The .NET SDK debugger, named Dbgclr.exe, is located in the .NET SDK installation folder, which is typically found at Program Files\Microsoft.NET\ FrameworkSDK\ GuiDebug.

Enabling Debug mode for ASP.NET Web services

Inline ASP.NET Web service implementations rely on the ASP.NET runtime to dynamically compile the Web service at run time. To generate the symbolic debugging information required to debug a Web service, we need to instruct the ASP.NET runtime to compile the application with this additional information.

To configure a Web service to be compiled with symbols, you must include a `debug` attribute in the `<compilation>` section of the Web.config file. The following example illustrates a complete Web.config file with the required `compilation` tag and `debug` attribute:

```
<?xml version="1.0" encoding="utf-8" ?>
<configuration>
  <system.web>
    <compilation debug="true"/>
  </system.web>
</configuration>
```

If you do not already have a Web.config file in the CTemp Web service virtual directory, create one with a text editor, include the previous text, and save it. Otherwise, you can simply add the `compilation` tag to any existing Web.config file.

Starting the ASP.NET runtime

After you have enabled generation of debug symbols for your Web service, you need to request the Web service entry point file from within a Web browser window. This ensures that the ASP.NET runtime process (aspnet_wp.exe) is started and running. This is necessary because the debugger must be attached to this process to intercept the execution of your Web service code.

To start the ASP.NET runtime, open Internet Explorer and type the following URL into the Address bar:

```
http://localhost/ctemp/ctemp.asmx
```

This will activate the ASP.NET runtime and return the base documentation page for your CTemp Web service to your browser window. Keep this browser window around, because we will use it shortly to activate the debugging process.

Debugging the CTemp Web service

The .NET SDK debugger is a GUI debugging tool that, by default, can be found at Program Files\Microsoft.NET\FrameworkSDK\GuiDebug\dbgclr.exe. Starting the .NET debugger application displays the window shown in Figure 25-11.

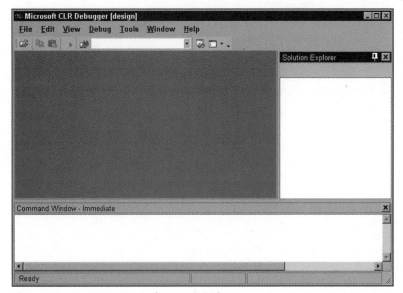

Figure 25-11: .NET SDK Debugger window

Follow these steps to begin debugging your CTemp Web service:

1. Select File ➪ Open ➪ File. This displays the Open File dialog box.

2. Navigate to the inetpub\wwwroot\ctemp folder, select the CTemp.asmx file, and click the Open button. This loads the CTemp Web service code into the main debugger window.

3. Select Tools ➪ Debug Processes. This displays the Processes dialog box, shown in Figure 25-12.

4. Check the box labeled Show System Processes, if it is not already checked.

5. Select the aspnet_wp.exe entry from the list of processes and click the Attach button.

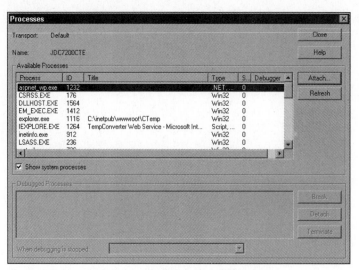

Figure 25-12: .NET Debugger Processes dialog box

6. Click the Close button to close the Processes dialog box.

The .NET debugger is now configured to debug your Web service.

Up to this point, we have simply been preparing the debugging environment so that we can interact with the Web service during run time. You are now ready to set one or more breakpoints in your Web service code and activate the debugging session. We will cover how to do this in the next section.

Setting a breakpoint

To set a breakpoint in the Web service code, simply point your mouse to the left margin of the code window in the .NET debugger application and click the line on which you would like to set a breakpoint. For the purposes of our test, set a break-point at the first line of the CTemp method, as shown in Figure 25-13.

The .NET debugger represents a breakpoint using a red circle in the code margin adjacent to the appropriate line of code. You can toggle the breakpoint on and off by clicking in the code margin repeatedly. The .NET debugger also provides menu options to manage breakpoints and other debugger features.

Having set a breakpoint in our CTemp Web service code, let's begin the debugging session.

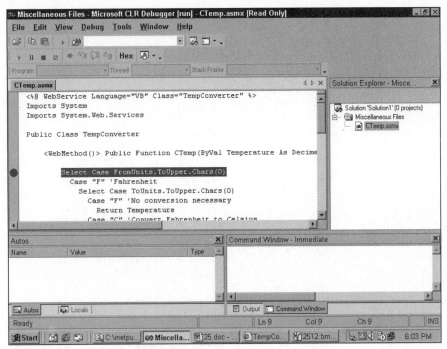

Figure 25-13: Setting a breakpoint

Testing Web service methods

To activate our Web service, we will use the testing capability built into the Web service documentation page we opened earlier in a Web browser window. This is the base documentation page for the Web service and displays, amongst other things, a link to the CTemp method (called "operations" in the page). Click the CTemp method link now to display the Web method test form.

The Web method test form displayed in your browser window contains text entry boxes for each of the input arguments defined by the CTemp method in the WSDL file. To test the functionality of the method, simply enter values in each of the input argument text boxes and click the Invoke button.

To continue with our example, enter the following argument values in the appropriate text boxes:

✦ Temperature: 32

✦ FromUnits: F

✦ ToUnits: C

After entering these values into the input boxes, click the Invoke button to execute the CTemp method. This action delivers the CTemp method request to the ASP.NET runtime. The runtime dynamically compiles the ASMX file with debugging symbols (if necessary) and then loads and executes the resulting code. This, in turn, causes the debugger to be activated.

Because we had previously set a breakpoint in our CTemp method code, the .NET debugger will be activated and halt execution at our breakpoint. If the Command window is not displayed, choose Debug ➪ Windows ➪ Immediate.

You are now ready to examine data within the method and perform other debugging operations. Let's take a quick look at how to examine program variables.

Examining program variables

You can use the Immediate window in Debug mode to quickly examine the values of variables in your Web service method. One of the first steps you will take when debugging new Web service methods is to examine the values of all input arguments.

Click your mouse in the Immediate window and type the following text:

```
? Temperature
```

Then press Enter. This causes the debugger to print the value of the input argument named Temperature. The result of these examinations is shown in Figure 25-14.

You can repeat this process to examine all the input arguments.

Resuming method execution

After you have examined program variables and performed the other actions necessary to debug your Web service, you can resume execution of the method call by choosing Debug ➪ Continue in the .NET debugger window, or by pressing the F5 key.

When the method completes execution, a new browser window is loaded and displays the results of the method call, as shown in Figure 25-15.

As mentioned previously, the Web form that is a part of the Web method documentation page uses the HTTP-GET request/response protocol to invoke the CTemp Web service method. This is evident when you examine the URL that appears in the Address bar of the browser window that displays the result of the method call. Note that the result format conforms to the sample HTTP-GET request/response protocol messages displayed in the Web method documentation page.

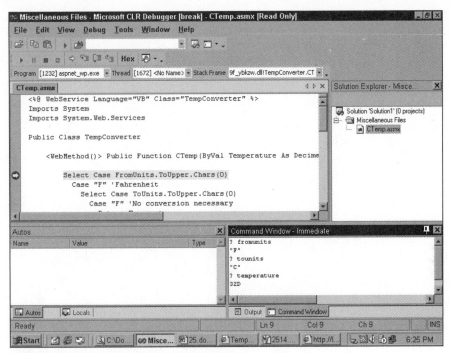

Figure 25-14: Examining input arguments

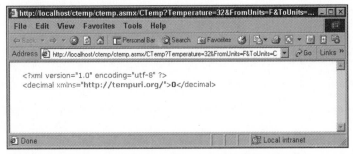

Figure 25-15: Results window of successful method call

Summary

In this chapter, you learned the basics of building an ASP.NET Web service using the features and tools of the .NET Framework SDK, including how to test and debug the service during development.

Now that you have successfully built and tested your first Web service, you are ready to learn how to deploy your service to a production-quality Web server. We will explore how to do this in the next chapter.

✦   ✦   ✦

Deploying and Publishing Web Services

In this chapter, you will learn how to deploy and publish a Web service. Deploying a Web service enables that Web service to execute on a specific host Web server, whereas publishing a Web service enables potential consumers to locate and interrogate the capabilities of the Web service before actually calling any methods of the service.

We will discuss what you need to do before deploying a Web service, the options available to you for deploying and publishing a Web service using .NET techniques, and the support built into Visual Studio .NET.

Deployment Preparation

Before you deploy a Web service, you must make sure that the Web service specifies a unique XML namespace. This namespace is used within the Web service WSDL document to uniquely identify the callable entry points of the service. As mentioned in Chapter 25, "Building a Web Service," the default Web service namespace is set to `http://tempuri.org/` when you first build your Web service. Now that you are ready to deploy and publish your Web service, you must change this temporary namespace designator to a permanent value.

Web service namespaces

The namespace that you choose to identify your Web service must be unique. In general, it is recommended that you choose a namespace URI that is owned or otherwise under your control. Typically, using your Internet domain name as part of the Web service namespace will guarantee uniqueness and also more readily identify the owner of the Web service. Therefore, it is recommended that you use this technique to supply a namespace to all Web services that you make available for Internet consumption.

ASP.NET Web Services support a Namespace property as part of the WebService attribute used to identify the class that implements the functionality of the Web service. For example, the WebService attribute for the CTemp Web service looks like this:

VB.NET:

```
<%@ WebService Language="VB" Class="TempConverter" %>
Imports System
Imports System.Web.Services

<WebService(Namespace:="http://mydomain.com/ctemp/")> Public
Class TempConverter
    ' implementation
End Class
```

C#:

```
<%@ WebService Language="C#" Class="TempConverter" %>
using System;
using System.Web.Services;

[WebService(Namespace="http://mydomain.com/ctemp/")]
public class TempConverter : WebService{
    // implementation
}
```

Changing the Web service namespace is even more important for ASP.NET Web Services, because a default namespace of http://tempuri.org/ is used. This, unfortunately, makes it even more likely that you will have namespace conflicts with other Web services, unless you change this default.

Setting the CTemp Web service namespace

Before we deploy our CTemp Web service, we need to set the namespace to a permanent value. To do this, follow these steps:

1. Open the Ctemp.asmx file in your favorite text editor.

2. Add the WebService attribute along with the Namespace property (using the appropriate language syntax) and set it to the appropriate value.

The new class declaration should look as follows:

VB.NET:

```
<WebService(Namespace:="http://mydomain.com/ctemp/")> Public
Class TempConverter
    ' implementation
End Class
```

C#:

```
[WebService(Namespace="http://mydomain.com/ctemp/")]
public class TempConverter : WebService{
    // implementation
}
```

Save the changes you have made and use a Web browser to test your Web service. The base documentation page returned to your browser should no longer warn you about the temporary namespace URI. In addition, when you link to the CTemp method test page, you will also notice that the sample SOAP messages now refer to the namespace you specified as part of the SOAPAction header.

You are now ready to deploy your Web service!

Deploying Web Services

Deploying a Web service enables the service to execute on a target Web server. Generally speaking, the deployment process for a Web service involves copying the Web service entry point file (the ASMX file), the Web service assembly (if you are using code behind) along with any dependent assemblies (excluding the .NET Framework assemblies), and related support files (such as the Web service contract file and/or Web.config file) to an appropriately configured virtual directory file structure on the target Web server.

A sharp contrast from deploying previous-generation Windows applications, ASP.NET Web Services are typically easy to deploy and do not require the complicated registration of DLLs, copying to many different target folders, and so forth.

Files deployed with a Web service

Some ASP.NET Web Services may require no more than just the ASMX file. Others (such as those built with Visual Studio) may consist of many files, including the

Web service entry point file (the ASMX file), the Global.asa application startup file, the Web.config application settings file, the .NET assembly that contains the implementation classes for the Web service (when using code behind), and any dependent assemblies that the Web service references (excluding the .NET Framework).

In the case of ASP.NET Web Services you build with the .NET Framework, you will usually copy all the files to the target Web server (unless you have created files during the development process that you are sure you do not need for production use). Our CTemp Web service only requires that you copy the ASMX file to the target Web server.

ASP.NET Web Services built with Visual Studio typically include many more files, some of which are not necessary for execution on the target server. Table 26-1 summarizes the standard file structure for deploying a Web service built with Visual Studio.

Table 26-1
Files deployed with the CTemp Web service

Folder	File	Description
\inetpub\wwwroot\ projectname	Servicename.asmx	The Web service entry point file. The folder containing this file should be configured as a Web application directory in IIS.
	Global.asax	The ASP.NET application startup file.
	Web.config	The ASP.NET application configuration file.
\inetpub\wwwroot\ projectname\bin	Servicename.dll	The Web service assembly that contains the implementation classes for the Web service as well as any dependent assemblies not a part of the .NET Framework

When creating Web services with Visual Studio, you can typically ignore the remaining files not listed in this table when it comes time to deploy your Web service.

Web service deployment tools

The following are the tools you can use to deploy a Web service, any one of which may be more appropriate depending on the complexity and circumstances of any particular Web service project:

- ✦ Visual Studio Web Setup Project
- ✦ Visual Studio Project Copy
- ✦ DOS XCOPY command

Of course, if you are not using Visual Studio to develop your application, you will not have the benefit of the tools built into this development environment for deploying your Web service.

The following sections describe these deployment options so that you can choose the proper deployment model for your ASP.NET Web Services.

Deployment using a Web Setup Project

If you have built your Web service using Visual Studio, the IDE provides a Web Setup Project template that utilizes the services of the Microsoft Windows Installer technology to create a deployment package for your Web service. A Web Setup Project in Visual Studio creates a MSI file (also called an installation package) that, when executed, creates and configures a virtual directory on the Web server, copies the files required to execute the Web service to the virtual directory, and registers any additional assemblies needed by the Web service.

One of the advantages of using a Web Setup Project is that the installation package automatically handles any registration and configuration issues that your Web service may depend upon, relieving you of this burden.

In general, the basic steps required to deploy a Web service using the Web Setup Project method are as follows:

1. Create a Web Setup Project using the Web Setup Project template in Visual Studio.
2. Build the project.
3. Copy the installation package to the target Web server.
4. Run the installation package on the target Web server.

Note
You must have administrative privileges on the target Web server computer in order to successfully install the Web service using the installation package.

If you intend to deploy your Web service to a production-quality Web server, make sure that you have built a release-quality version of your Web service using the Release configuration.

It is important to remember the following facts about the setup packages created by Web Setup Projects:

✦ The user has the opportunity to specify an alternate virtual directory target during the setup process.

✦ The setup process creates a new virtual directory and configures the virtual directory for the Web service.

In summary, although the Web Setup Project method of deployment requires more upfront work to create and configure properly, the result is a setup package that provides a solid, repeatable, and reliable installation experience that guarantees that your Web service will operate correctly.

Deployment using Project Copy

As an alternative to using a Web Setup Project to deploy a Web service built using Visual Studio, you can use the Project Copy method, because it is a simpler deployment method than using a Web Setup Project. However, copying your Web service project files does not perform such tasks as virtual directory configuration or file registrations that may be necessary for your Web service to function correctly. In more complex scenarios, the Web Setup Project method described in the previous section is a superior and more reliable choice (although somewhat more complex to set up and configure).

Be that as it may, simple Web services can be easily and successfully deployed to target Web servers with very little effort using the Project Copy feature in Visual Studio. This feature is available by choosing Project ➪ Copy Project in the Visual Studio IDE.

The following are the three options available for copying files:

✦ **Only Files Needed To Run This Application:** Copies all DLLs with references in the /bin folder as well as any files marked with a BuildAction of Content.

✦ **All Project Files:** Copies all project files created and managed by Visual Studio.

✦ **All Files In The Source Project Folder:** Copies all Visual Studio project files as well as other files that reside in the project folders.

The default option is to copy only the files needed to run the application.

Deployment using XCOPY

The DOS XCOPY command is perhaps the simplest method for deploying a Web service to a target Web server. However, as is the case with the Visual Studio Copy Project feature, XCOPY simply copies files from one location to another. It does not create or configure virtual directories for your Web service, nor does it register or configure any dependent assemblies outside of the .NET Framework.

You can type XCOPY /? at a command prompt to get help on the XCOPY command-line syntax and available options.

Publishing Web Services

Publishing a Web service enables potential consumers to locate and interrogate service descriptions that instruct the consumer on how to interact with the Web service. The process of locating and interrogating Web service descriptions is referred to as the discovery process.

The following are the two methods for enabling discovery of a Web service:

✦ DISCO

✦ UDDI

You may choose to use one or both of these methods based on the consumer audience you are trying to reach.

If your consumer population is fairly small (or well known), you could simply point them to the target Web server and deploy the DISCO file on this server. In this case, the consumers will invoke the discovery process against the URL of the target server and locate your Web service description. In this situation, you only need to deploy your DISCO documents to the proper server and inform the consumers of the URL to the server.

On the other hand, if your consumer population is relatively large or unknown (in which case it is impractical to provide them with a pointer to the target Web server where the service is located), you will need to provide a mechanism for the consumers to find where your DISCO and/or Web service descriptions are located, just as Web users utilize search engines to find Web pages. In this situation, you will need to publish your Web service through UDDI.

As mentioned in Chapter 22, "Introduction to Web Services," the DISCO document and the UDDI business registry provide the mechanisms to solve these issues. Let's explore how to use these technologies to enable potential consumers to locate the essential information they need in order to use your Web service.

Publishing with DISCO

As you may recall from our previous discussions regarding Web service discovery, consumers of Web services enact a discovery process to locate Web services. The discovery process searches for XML-encoded discovery documents that contain pointers to other resources that describe the Web service.

Encoding discovery documents in XML enables tools such as Visual Studio to programmatically discover the availability of Web services (if you know the URL to the server). This is how the Web Reference metaphor works in Visual Studio when you provide it with a specific discovery URL. For those of you not using Visual Studio, you can use the `disco.exe` tool that comes with the .NET Framework SDK to discover Web services.

Web service discovery via the Web Reference feature in Visual Studio or the `disco.exe` tool in the .NET Framework SDK is useful when a consumer knows the URL to the server hosting the Web service or the application virtual directory.

Visual Studio automatically creates a DISCO file when you create a Web service project. This file has an extension of .vsdisco and is stored in the main application virtual directory (along with the ASMX file). This file contains links to the resources that describe the Web service.

Note   If you do not wish to enable discovery for a particular Web service, simply omit the DISCO file from the deployment process.

If you are not using Visual Studio to create your Web service (or find them), you need to manually create the DISCO document. In this case, you must create an XML file containing DISCO elements that can be used to find your Web service description documents. The following is a sample DISCO document for our CTemp Web service:

```
<?xml version="1.0" ?>
<disco:discovery
xmlns:disco="http://schemas.xmlsoap.org/disco/">

xmlns:scl="http://schemas.xmlsoap.org/disco/scl">
  <scl:contractRef
ref="http://jdc7200cte/Services/CTemp/CTemp.asmx?WSDL"/>
  <disco:discoveryRef ref="SomeFolder/default.disco" />
</disco:discovery>
```

The DISCO document consists of a `discovery` element that serves as a container for `contractRef` and `discoveryRef` elements. You can specify as many `contractRef` and `discoveryRef` elements as you desire. This makes it possible to provide information for more than one Web service from within a single DISCO document.

The `contractRef` element is used to provide a pointer to the WSDL document that describes the message formats and exchanges supported by the Web service. In the preceding example, you can see that a single `contractRef` element has been included that provides a pointer to the WSDL document for the CTemp Web service. The `contractRef` element is optional.

References specified by the `ref` attribute can be absolute or relative. If you specify a relative reference, the reference is relative to the folder in which the DISCO document resides.

The `discoveryRef` element is used to provide a pointer to other DISCO documents. This allows you to logically link the discovery process to several Web services, which may have independent DISCO documents. In the preceding example, a single `discoveryRef` element has been included that provides a pointer to another DISCO document. The `discoveryRef` element is optional.

Because a DISCO document simply contains pointers to the resources that describe a Web service, you can physically deploy your DISCO documents anywhere you want (in other words, they don't have to be physically deployed with the Web services that they describe). This provides you with the capability to enable discovery of any set of Web services that may be physically distributed on your network, but allow users to browse to a single point at which to begin the discovery process to find them.

Note If you wish to deploy your DISCO documents in a different location from the Web service itself, you should be very careful when using relative references within the `discoveryRef` and `contractRef` elements.

To make it easier for consumers to find your Web service, you can create a DISCO file in the root directory of your Web server named Default.disco, which then links to the various Web service DISCO files that you have implemented. That way, a consumer can simply browse to the root directory of the server to begin the discovery process using tools such as `disco.exe`.

For more information about DISCO documents and the `disco.exe` tool, refer to the .NET Framework documentation. We will cover more details related to using the `disco.exe` tool later when we build a consumer for the CTemp Web service.

Publishing with UDDI

Discovery of Web services via DISCO is sufficient if you know the URL to the Web server or the application virtual directory that hosts the Web service. However, in cases where this information is unavailable, you must use a more generalized search tool.

Universal Description, Discovery, and Integration (UDDI) enables Web service consumers to search for and locate Web services, even if the consumer is unaware of the exact location, owner, or author of the Web service.

UDDI is to Web services what Lycos and Alta Vista are to Web pages. UDDI provides powerful features for easily locating Web services based on a logically centralized, globally available registry of businesses accessible via the Internet. UDDI consists of two basic parts:

✦ An XML schema that describes and categorizes a business as well as the Web services that it offers

✦ The business registry (or database) that contains all known information about businesses and Web services based on the XML schema

The business registry is accessible interactively via the `http://www.uddi.org` Web site as well as programmatically through the UDDI Web services. These Web services are utilized by Visual Studio's Web Reference feature for locating and creating proxy classes to interact with Web services.

Although we will not publish the CTemp Web service through UDDI, this discussion will cover the basic features and procedures for getting your Web services published to the UDDI business and Web service registry via the UDDI.org Web site.

The UDDI home page (found at `http://www.uddi.org`) is shown in Figure 26-1.

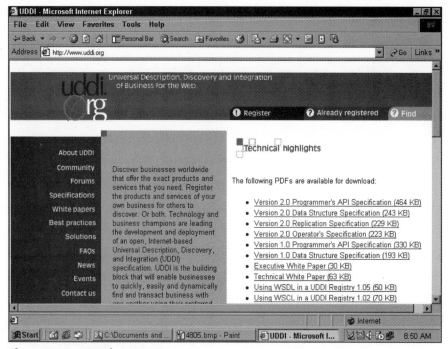

Figure 26-1: UDDI home page

From the home page, you can register your business by clicking the Register tab at the top of the page. Alternatively, you can go directly to the page by typing `http://www.uddi.org/register.html` in the Address bar of your browser.

On the other hand, if you have already registered your business and want to maintain your business and/or Web service information (including adding new Web services), click the Already Registered tab at the top of the home page. Alternatively, you can go directly to the page by typing `http://www.uddi.org/alreadyregistered.html` in the Address bar of your browser.

In either case, you will next be asked to choose which registry you wish to use to add or update your information. As of the writing of this book, IBM and Microsoft were both maintaining UDDI business registry sites. The examples presented here will use the Microsoft site, but you could just as easily use the IBM site with the exact same results.

Note   Although there are multiple distributed registries (and more expected to come online), the UDDI architecture uses replication techniques to keep all the registries synchronized. Therefore, you don't have to worry about which online registry you use to search or maintain your business information.

If you have not yet registered your business, you will be required to obtain a user-name/password before adding any information to the UDDI business registry. This is necessary so that your particular business information can be protected from any unauthorized changes. Although the specific methods for obtaining a username and password differ between the IBM and Microsoft sites, the end result is the same. In the case of Microsoft, you will be asked to create a Passport account. If you already have a Passport account, you can choose to use that account instead of creating another one.

Go ahead and choose Microsoft from the list and submit the form. You will then be requested to log in to the site using your username and password. If you don't have a username and password yet, create one and then log in.

After you have successfully logged in to the site, you will see the personal registra-tion page, similar to Figure 26-2.

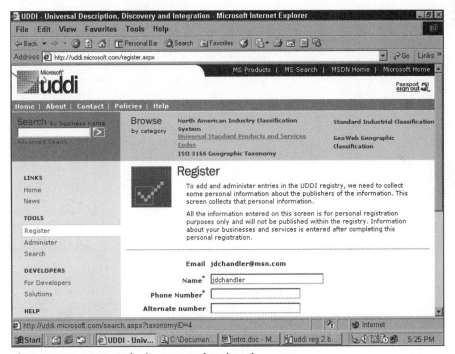

Figure 26-2: UDDI Web site personal registration page

Fill in your personal contact information here. This information is used for private registration purposes so that you can add and update entries in the business reg-istry database, and it is not published within the public business registry database.

After you have filled in your personal information and submitted the form, you are now ready to review and accept the terms and conditions of use for the site. Confirm your acceptance of the terms and conditions. After you have done so, a confirmation page is displayed. Everything up to now has been part of a one-time process that you should not have to repeat the next time you come to the UDDI site. Click the Continue button and you are ready to register your business (see Figure 26-3).

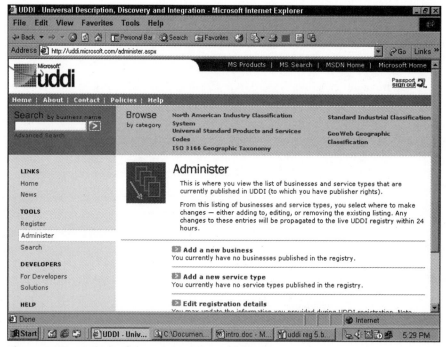

Figure 26-3: UDDI business registration administration page

Adding a new business

At this point, you will want to add a new business. Click the Add A New Business link and you will be able to enter the details regarding your business. Although we won't go into detail about these steps, the process is straightforward and easy to accomplish. You will be able to add and maintain the following categories of information about your business:

✦ **Business Detail Information:** Specifies the name, address, and other details about your company.

✦ **Contacts:** Specifies company contact information.

✦ **Services:** This is where you publish your Web services, among other things. Details include the specifics of these applications, such as location, supported bindings, and other details of the service.

✦ **Business Identifiers:** Identifiers are pieces of data that are unique to an individual business (for example, a company register listing number).

✦ **Business Classifications:** These are pieces of data that classify the field of operation of a business or a service (for example, a geographic location or an industry sector).

✦ **Discovery URLs:** Provide a location where details about a particular entity can be found.

Each of these categories can contain one or several entries. The ultimate goal of this variety of information is to make it quick and simple for consumers to find your Web services from various perspectives, such as industry, geographic location, and other taxonomies.

Note   Changes you make to your business information will typically be updated to the live registry within 24 hours of the change.

Adding a Web service to your business registration

We will finish out this chapter by walking through the process of adding a Web service to your business registration. To begin the process, complete the following steps:

1. Scroll the browser window to the Services section within the business details page. This is where all of your published Web services reside in the business registry.

2. Click the Add A Service link. Specify the name of your Web service and provide a brief description, as shown in Figure 26-4.

3. After you have entered this information and clicked the Continue button, you are ready to add the appropriate classification categories for your service as well as the bindings that your service supports (see Figure 26-5).

Although not visible in this figure, the classifications are similar to those that you specified when you registered your company information. This helps potential consumers more easily locate Web services based on these classifications. We won't go through the classification process here, but you should consider using classifications so that it is easier for consumers to find your Web services.

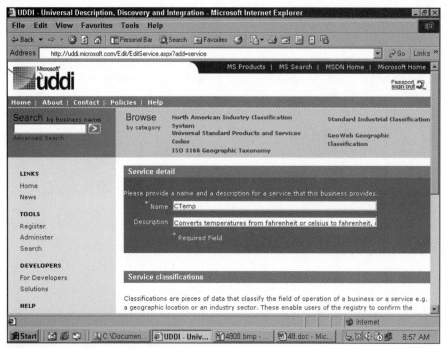

Figure 26-4: UDDI Service Registration page

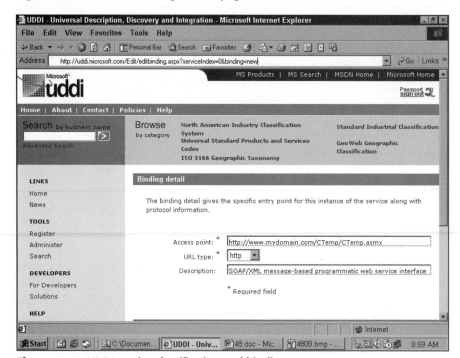

Figure 26-5: UDDI service classification and bindings page

Defining a new binding

Let's define a new binding for our Web service publication. To do this, complete the following steps:

1. Click the Define New Binding link in the Bindings section of the page. This displays the Binding Detail page, shown in Figure 26-6.

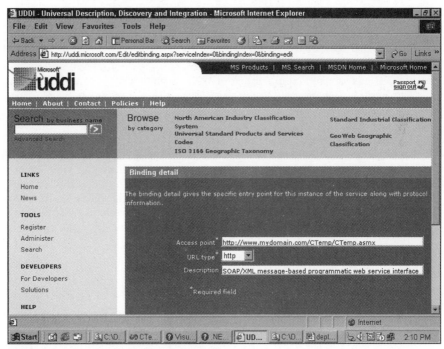

Figure 26-6: UDDI Binding Detail page

2. In the Access Point text box, enter the URL to your Web service entry point (ASMX) file. In this example, you can see the pseudo-URL for the CTemp Web service.

3. Select HTTP as the URL type from the drop-down list. In the Description text box, enter a description for the binding. Typically, you will want to mention the protocol details for the entry point you specified. For ASP.NET Web Services (which is what you build using Visual Studio or the .NET Framework), you should specify HTTP and SOAP. Note the description that was specified for the CTemp Web service.

4. After you have finished entering this information, click the Continue button. This will return you to the Service Detail page. Click the Continue button on this page and you will be returned to the Business Detail page, where you can further administer your business information.

Note   You may find it easier to supply the appropriate information for your business and Web services by first examining business registry information from other companies such as Microsoft and IBM.

That, in a nutshell, is the basic process for getting your Web services published via UDDI. You can learn a lot more about UDDI by visiting the UDDI Web site and browsing the existing registry as well as the available help information. The information you can glean from the examples will be quite useful to you in creating the necessary information that will make it easier for consumers to find your Web services.

Internal publication tools

Before we wrap up our discussion of Web service deployment and publication (which has focused on making your Web services visible to the outside world), let's spend a few moments to discuss using these tools for internal (intranet) publication.

If you are a developer in a small to medium-sized business that has a relatively small network with few developers and Web servers, you may find that discovery through DISCO is a sufficient mechanism for publishing your Web services on an intranet. Larger companies that are physically distributed and have large, possibly diverse developer groups may consider implementing their own internal UDDI registry just for company-specific Web services. At any rate, a great deal of flexibility is offered by these tools to structure the discovery process in a manner that is the most efficient for your specific needs.

Summary

In this chapter, you learned how to deploy a Web service using simple file-copying techniques (such as XCOPY) and received a short introduction to the built-in support provided by Visual Studio. In addition, this chapter covered how to publish a Web service so that potential consumers can locate the service via DISCO and/or UDDI.

You will learn more about the discovery process from a Web service consumer's perspective when we discuss this topic in Chapter 28, "Consuming Web Services."

✦   ✦   ✦

Finding Web Services

Previous chapters discussed the tools used to publish
Web services from the perspective of a Web service
author. This chapter examines the tools used to find Web
services from the perspective of a Web service consumer.
This process includes locating where a Web service resides,
as well as interrogating the WSDL document to determine
how to interact with the Web service. This chapter examines
the tools in the Microsoft .NET Framework that can be used
to locate Web services.

Web Service Discovery

In previous chapters, we have discussed the tools used to
publish Web services from the perspective of a Web service
author. In this chapter, we will examine the tools used to find
Web services from the perspective of a Web service consumer.

As you have learned in the chapter on Web service deployment and publishing, several methods are available for a consumer to locate a Web service. Visual Studio combines these
methods into a single tool via the Add Web Reference feature.
When using the .NET tools for locating Web services, the tool
you use depends on how much you know about the location
of the Web service before you start. We will examine how to
use each of these tools in this chapter.

If you have been provided with (or already know) the URL of
a Web server where one or more Web services are deployed,
you can locate these Web services using a discovery tool (if
Web service discovery has been enabled by placing one or
more discovery documents on the Web server). The .NET
Framework provides a command-line tool named `Disco.exe`
that can be used to locate discovery documents against a
specified URL.

In cases where you do not know anything about where a Web service is located (or even if it exists), you will need the services of Universal Description, Discovery, and Integration (UDDI). This technology is essentially a universal search engine for Web services that is available via the Internet as both an interactive Web site and a set of programmable Web services.

UDDI consists of two parts:

✦ An XML-based schema that describes attributes of businesses, including basic demographic information, as well as specialized information related to industry affiliations, types of goods or services provided, and other taxonomies.

✦ A Web-based distributed database consisting of multiple, synchronized nodes that can be accessed via a Web browser, as well as programmable Web services.

 Cross-Reference You can refer to Chapter 23, "Web Services Infrastructure," for a more thorough introduction to UDDI in general and Chapter 26, "Deploying and Publishing Web Services," for more information on using UDDI to publish a Web service.

As of the writing of this book, two UDDI nodes were available: one at IBM and another at Microsoft. It is expected that other nodes will come online over time. You can read more about UDDI on the UDDI Web site at http://www.uddi.org. Although there are multiple registry nodes, the UDDI architecture maintains data synchronization between all the nodes so that you do not have to worry about which particular node services your search requests.

Because UDDI supports programmable Web services, tools such as Visual Studio can provide support for finding Web services automatically. Visual Studio also supports Web service discovery via UDDI through the Add Web Reference feature.

Ultimately, we are searching for Web services because we intend to consume them programmatically. To consume a Web service, we must locate the Web service description document (the WSDL file). Therefore, once you locate a Web service, you will use the Web service description document to create one or more proxy classes from the descriptions. A proxy class is a software component that provides access to the remote Web service as if it were a local resource. Essentially, the proxy class hides from the consumer the details of the request/response protocols and underlying network transports. We will discuss Web service proxy classes later in this chapter.

Now, let's take a look at how Disco and UDDI discovery tools can be used to help you locate and consume Web services.

Finding Web services with the Disco tool

The .NET Framework provides a tool named Disco.exe to locate Web services at a given URL and copy Web service descriptions that it finds to your local hard drive. The output of the Disco tool is typically used as input to the wsdl tool to create a proxy class with which to consume the Web service. We will discuss the `wsdl` tool in more detail in the next section.

By default, the following is the location of the `Disco` tool:

```
Program Files\Microsoft.NET\FrameworkSDK\Bin
```

The `Disco` tool is a console application, so you will need to start it from within a command window.

Tip You may want to add the path to the .NET Framework Bin folder to your system's `PATH` environment variable so that the tools can be located without typing the path to them on the command line.

The general format of the `Disco` tool command line is as follows:

```
disco [options] URL
```

where *URL* specifies the HTTP address of the target Web server that you wish to search for discovery (files of type .disco) documents.

The `Disco` tool supports the command-line options listed in Table 27-1.

Table 27-1	
Disco tool command-line options	
Option	**Description**
/d[omain]:domain	Used along with the /username and /password options to specify the user credentials to a proxy server that requires authentication.
/nosave	By default, the Disco tool saves the discovery results (WSDL, XSD, DISCO, and DISCOMAP files) to disk. Use this option to throw away the results.
/nologo	Use this option to eliminate the Microsoft startup banner that is normally displayed when the tool is started.
/o[ut]:directoryName	Specifies the folder where the discovered documents will be saved. The default is the current directory from where the tool was executed.
/p[assword]:password	Specifies the password to use when connecting to a proxy server that requires authentication.
/proxy:URL	Specifies the URL of the proxy server to use for HTTP requests. By default, the system proxy settings are used.

Continued

Table 27-1 *(continued)*	
Option	*Description*
`/proxydomain:domain` `/pd:domain`	Specifies the domain to use when connecting or to a proxy server that requires authentication.
`/proxypassword:password` `/pp:password`	Specifies the password to use when connecting or to a proxy server that requires authentication.
`/proxyusername:username` `/pu:username`	Specifies the username to use when or connecting to a proxy server that requires authentication.
`/u[sername]:username`	Specifies the username to use when connecting to a proxy server that requires authentication.
`/?`	Displays command syntax and options for the tool.

The `Disco` tool copies and generates the following files into the folder where you executed the `Disco` tool or the folder specified by the `/out` option. Let's look at an example using the `Disco` tool to locate the Web service description files for our CTemp Web service.

First, let's assume for a moment that we only know the name of the Web server that is hosting our CTemp service, but would like to discover the complete URL to it. We can do this by typing the following at the command prompt:

```
disco /nosave http://localhost
```

This command will initiate the discovery process against the local Web server, searching for all discovery documents and related files that are referenced in these discovery documents. Note that we are not saving any of the results yet (using the `/nosave` option).

When dynamic discovery is enabled at the root of the Web server (the default), the `Disco` tool will search hierarchically through all Web server folders. Running the previous command against my Web server produces the results shown in Figure 27-1.

Notice that the `Disco` tool has listed all the discovery documents it found on the Web server as well as a reference to a single WSDL document for our CTemp Web service.

Now that we know the complete URL to the CTemp Web service, let's use the `Disco` tool one more time to discover information specific to the CTemp Web service. This time, we will save the results to a temporary folder, using the following command:

```
disco /out=c:\temp http://localhost/ctemp/ctemp.vsdisco
```

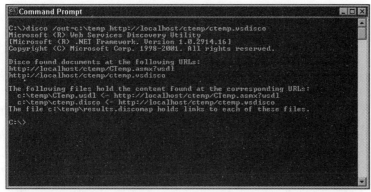

Figure 27-1: Using the Disco tool to find Web services

This will initiate the discovery process against the discovery document of the CTemp Web service located on your local Web server. Once again, executing this command on my Web server produces the results shown in Figure 27-2.

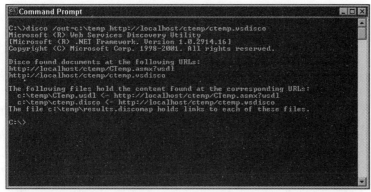

Figure 27-2: Using the Disco tool to discover information about the CTemp Web Service

Note that the Disco tool has saved three files to your local computer. These files are summarized in Table 27-2.

Table 27-2
Files created by the Disco tool

File	Description
Ctemp.wsdl	The WSDL document for the CTemp Web service
Ctemp.disco	The discovery document for the CTemp Web service
Results.discomap	A discovery document that contains references to the local copies of the Ctemp.wsdl and Ctemp.disco files

In actual practice, you would save the results of the discovery process to the project folder where you were building the client application that consumes the Web service just discovered.

Armed with the information and files copied to our system by the Disco tool, we could use the wsdl tool to generate a proxy class for the CTemp Web service, which could be used to consume the service in a client application. We will discuss this process later in this chapter in the section "Creating a proxy class with the WSDL tool."

Finding Web Services with UDDI

While the Disco tool is an effective means of locating Web service descriptions, you must know the URL to either a specific target server where the Web service is deployed or a specific Web service virtual directory on a Web server. In any case, you won't be able to find any Web services using Disco without knowing a URL.

As mentioned previously, UDDI is a more generalized search tool for locating Web services. Using UDDI, you can specify search terms that enable you to pinpoint Web services you wish to use based on company, industry, service type, and many other classifications. Using these more generalized search terms usually results in the listing of specific URLs to which you can locate information about specific Web services, including the WSDL document that you are ultimately searching for.

In this section, we will explore how to find Web services using the interactive UDDI Web site. This Web site provides search forms for locating Web services (and Web service descriptions). To illustrate the search process, we will search for Web services that are published by Microsoft.

Let's start by browsing to the UDDI Web site at http://www.uddi.org. After you get there, click the Find link at the top of the page. This displays the Find page. On this page, choose the Microsoft UDDI node from the list box and click GO. This brings you to the Microsoft UDDI node search page, as shown in Figure 27-3.

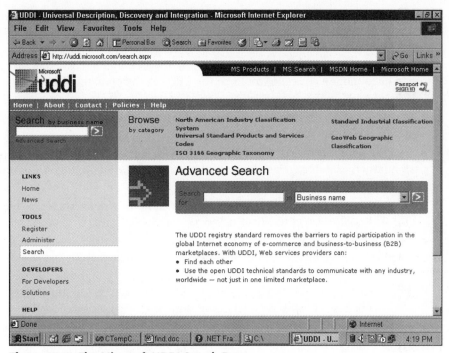

Figure 27-3: The Microsoft UDDI Search Page

Notice that the search page provides category-based browsing that enables you to locate Web services based on various company classifications, including ISO 3166 Geographic Taxonomy and Standard Industrial Classification, among others.

In the middle of the page is the Advanced Search form. From here, you can enter text in the Search For text box to perform a custom search of various fields within the database. You can locate Web services in this manner by searching any one of the following field types:

✦ **Business Name:** Use this field to search within registered business names. For example, you could search for services provided by IBM.

✦ **Business Location:** Use this field to search by geographic location. For example, you could search for companies that provide services within the St. Louis area.

✦ **Service Type By Name:** Use this field to search services submitted by a company by the service name.

✦ **Business Identifier:** Identifiers are pieces of data that are unique to an individual business, such as the standard D-U-N-S™ Number. There are several standard, as well as custom, identifiers that a company can register.

✦ **Discovery URL:** Provides a location where details about a particular entity can be found. An example would be the URL to the company Web site or a URL for a particular Web service.

✦ **GeoWeb Taxonomy:** Provides a standard, hierarchical classification of geographic locations by which to search.

✦ **NAICS Codes:** The North American Industry Classification System provides a standard, hierarchical classification of businesses based on the products or services they provide.

✦ **SIC Codes:** The Standard Industrial Classification provides a standard, hierarchical classification of businesses based on industry.

✦ **UNSPSC Codes:** Universal Standard Products and Services Codes provides a standard, hierarchical classification of businesses based on the products and services they provide.

✦ **ISO 3166 Geographic Taxonomy:** Provides a standard, hierarchical classification of businesses based on geography; similar to the GeoWeb Taxonomy.

✦ **RealNames Keyword:** RealNames is a keyword-like name, similar to AOL keywords, that are registered to specific companies.

Let's do a simple search by business name and take a look at what Microsoft has provided in terms of Web service registrations.

Choose Business Name from the drop-down list, enter "Microsoft" in the Search For text box, and then submit the form. The search facility will look for any businesses with the name Microsoft in the Business Name field and return a list of hits. In this example, you should see a single listing. Click the Microsoft Corporation link and you will see a page similar to Figure 27-4.

Scroll the page until you see the list of services offered. Here you will find an entry named Web Services for Smart Searching. Click this link and the browser will display a Service Detail page. Scroll this page until you find the Bindings section. The browser window should look similar to Figure 27-5.

The interesting information displayed here is supplied by the Access Point link. Note that the URL points to the entry point of two categorized Web service interfaces:

✦ A Vocabulary service

✦ A Best Bets service

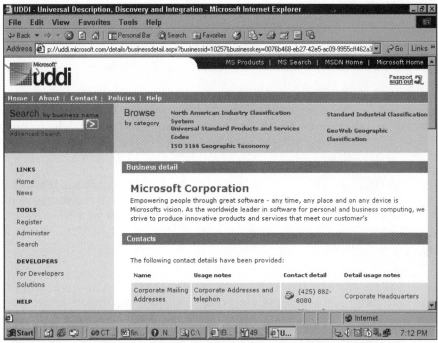

Figure 27-4: UDDI business registration information for Microsoft

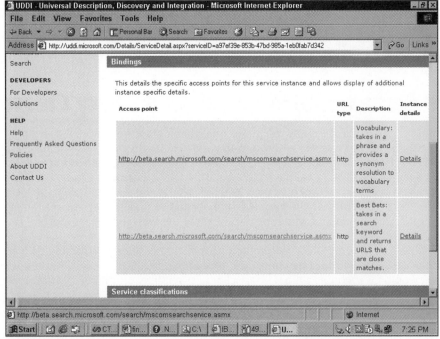

Figure 27-5: Microsoft Smart Searching Web Service bindings detail

Each service shares a common URL. Go ahead and click one of the entry point links. By now you know that pointing your browser to an ASMX file will return the ASP.NET Web Service description page. From this page, you can access the WSDL contract, which can be saved to your local hard drive and then interrogated by the `wsdl` tool to create a Web service proxy class. You will learn more about this process shortly.

Congratulations! You have just located your first Web service from the UDDI business registry! Of course, myriad ways exist to search the registry. Which one you choose depends on what you are looking for and how much information you have related to the Web service.

Caution

While this book was being written, the UDDI nodes at Microsoft and IBM were still very immature. The search capabilities on the Microsoft node had several bugs, and both sites had few businesses registered. Because this is a new technology, it appears that some patience will be required before these registries become truly useful to the average developer.

If you are not using Visual Studio to build or consume Web services, you will want to become familiar with the facilities provided by the UDDI business registry nodes. Over time, these sites will hopefully provide one-stop shopping for locating high-quality Web services that you can incorporate into your custom solutions.

Although a simple and effective solution for finding Web services, you may encounter some cases in which you cannot use Visual Studio's Web Reference feature, such as when the Web service is not accessible from the machine on which you are using Visual Studio. Under these circumstances, you can use the Web Service Description Language Tool (wsdl.exe) to generate a Web Service client proxy class. We will cover this tool in the next section.

Web Service Interrogation and Proxy Classes

Web service interrogation is the process of examining a Web service description to determine how to interact with the Web service as a consumer. As you have learned, a Web service communicates with consumers using messages encoded in XML and encapsulated in SOAP. You have also seen that these messages can be transported over one of several protocols (such as HTTP, SMTP, and so on). Lastly, the Web service description defines the message formats and exchange patterns for the particular methods, arguments, and return values that the Web service supports.

If you were required to code directly to these technologies, consuming Web services would be a time-consuming (and probably painful) process. What's worse, you would be spending time writing what is essentially plumbing code to consume a Web service, rather than focusing (and rightly so) on the actual task you were attempting to accomplish.

Fortunately, you do not have to worry about creating and formatting SOAP messages, or understanding how to exchange messages with various transport protocols. All of this plumbing is hidden from you via the Web service proxy class. Instead, you simply instantiate an instance of the proxy class and make calls to its methods in a completely object-oriented fashion.

Recall that the .NET Framework provides the wsdl tool for parsing Web service description files. But, in addition to interrogating these files, the wsdl tool is able to generate a proxy class, which provides an object-oriented interface for calling methods on the Web service and returning the results to the caller.

Visual Studio automatically creates Web service proxy classes for you when you use the Add Web Reference dialog box to create a reference to a Web service. If, however, you are unable to use Visual Studio's Web Reference feature, you can create the proxy class manually using the wsdl tool. Let's take a look at the tool and how it can be used to create Web service proxy classes that can be used by Web service consumers.

Creating a proxy class with the WSDL tool

The .NET Framework provides a tool named wsdl.exe to parse Web service descriptions and generate proxy classes, which can be used by a consumer to call methods on a Web service. The wsdl tool is capable of generating proxy classes given any one of the following types of files as input:

✦ WSDL files

✦ XSD (XML Schema Definition) files

✦ DISCO files

✦ DISCOMAP files

Note that these files are all outputs of .NET's Disco tool. By default, the wsdl tool is located in the same place as the Disco tool:

```
Program Files\Microsoft.NET\FrameworkSDK\Bin
```

The wsdl tool is a console application, so you will need to start it from within a command window just like the Disco tool discussed in the last section.

Tip　You may want to add the path to the .NET Framework Bin folder to your system's PATH environment variable so that the tools can be located without typing the path to them on the command line.

The general format of the `wsdl` command line is as follows:

```
wsdl [options] {URL | Path}
```

where *URL* specifies the HTTP address of a target Web server that you wish to search for any of the supported file types previously listed (excluding DISCOMAP files), and *Path* specifies the local file path to any of the supported file types listed.

The `wsdl` tool supports the command line options listed in Table 27-3.

<table>
<tr><td colspan="2" align="center">Table 27-3
WSDL tool command-line options</td></tr>
<tr><td>*Option*</td><td>*Description*</td></tr>
<tr><td>`/appsettingurlkey:`*key*
or
`/urlkey:`*key*</td><td>Specifies the configuration key to use to read the default value for the URL property when generating code. This enables you to obtain the URL of the Web service from the ASP.NET configuration file, rather than having it hard-coded in the proxy class.</td></tr>
<tr><td>`/appsettingbaseurl:`*baseurl*
or
`/baseurl:`*baseurl*</td><td>Specifies the base URL to use in conjunction with the `/appsettingurlkey` option. The tool calculates the URL fragment by converting the relative URL from the *baseurl* argument to the URL in the WSDL document. You must specify the `/appsettingurlkey` option with this option.</td></tr>
<tr><td>`/d[omain]:`*domain*</td><td>Specifies the domain name to use when connecting to a server that requires authentication.</td></tr>
<tr><td>`/l[anguage]:`*language*</td><td>Specifies the language to use for the generated proxy class. You can specify CS (C#; default), VB (Visual Basic), or JS (JScript) as the language argument. You can also specify the fully qualified name of a class that implements the System.CodeDom.Compiler. CodeDomProvider Class. The default language is C#.</td></tr>
<tr><td>`/n[amespace]:`*namespace*</td><td>Specifies the namespace for the generated proxy or template. The default namespace is the global namespace. As an example, setting the namespace to TempConverter would permit us to reference our CTemp proxy class as TempConverter.CTemp.</td></tr>
<tr><td>`/nologo`</td><td>Suppresses the Microsoft startup banner display.</td></tr>
<tr><td>`/o[ut]:`*filename*</td><td>Specifies the file in which to save the generated proxy code. The tool derives the default filename from the Web Service name. The tool saves generated datasets in different files.</td></tr>
</table>

Option	Description
/p[assword]:*password*	Specifies the password to use when connecting to a server that requires authentication.
/protocol:*protocol*	Specifies the protocol to implement. You can specify SOAP (default), HttpGet, HttpPost, or a custom protocol specified in the configuration file.
/proxy:*URL*	Specifies the URL of the proxy server to use for HTTP requests. The default is to use the system proxy setting.
/proxydomain:*domain* or /pd:*domain*	Specifies the domain to use when connecting to a proxy server that requires authentication.
/proxypassword:*password* or /pp:*password*	Specifies the password to use when connecting to a proxy server that requires authentication.
/proxyusername:*username* or /pu:*username*	Specifies the username to use when connecting to a proxy server that requires authentication.
/server	Generates an abstract class for a normal (server-side) Web Service based on the contracts. The default is to generate client proxy classes. This option will probably rarely be used, but is useful in cases where you have defined a standard interface for a Web service, but may wish to create several separate implementations.
/u[sername]:*username*	Specifies the username to use when connecting to a server that requires authentication.
/?	Displays command syntax and options for the tool.

The following example illustrates the use of the wsdl tool to generate a proxy class for our CTemp Web service:

```
VB.NET:
wsdl /l:vb /out:CTempProxy.vb
http://localhost/ctemp/ctemp.asmx?wsdl
C#:
wsdl /l:cs /out:CTempProxy.cs
http://localhost/ctemp/ctemp.asmx?wsdl
```

This example creates a proxy class in the specified language syntax and saves it to a file named CTempProxy.vb (or CTempProxy.cs, depending on which language you choose). The proxy is generated from the WSDL provided by the URL specified on the command line.

The output of the `wsdl` tool in the command window should look similar to Figure 27-6.

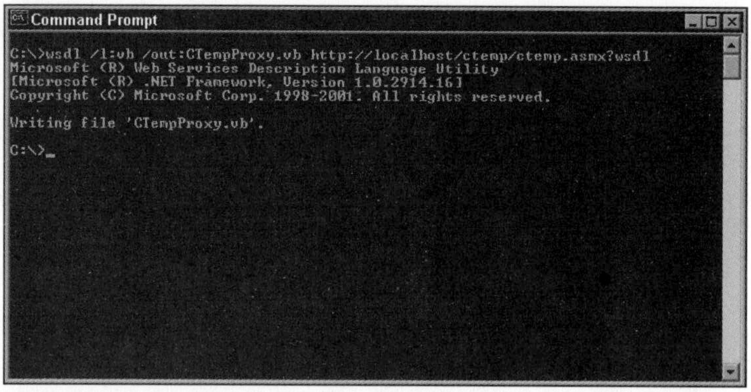

Figure 27-6: Results of executing the wsdl tool

The following proxy class source code generated by the `wsdl` tool is for VB.NET:

```
'------------------------------------------------------------
------
' <autogenerated>
'     This code was generated by a tool.
'     Runtime Version: 1.0.2914.16
'
'     Changes to this file may cause incorrect behavior and
will be lost if
'     the code is regenerated.
' </autogenerated>
'------------------------------------------------------------
------

Option Strict Off
Option Explicit On

Imports System
Imports System.Diagnostics
Imports System.Web.Services
Imports System.Web.Services.Protocols
Imports System.Xml.Serialization

'
'This source code was auto-generated by wsdl,
Version=1.0.2914.16.
'

<System.Web.Services.WebServiceBindingAttribute(Name:="TempConv
erterSoap", [Namespace]:="http://mydomain.com/ws/ctemp")> _
Public Class TempConverter
```

```
        Inherits
System.Web.Services.Protocols.SoapHttpClientProtocol

        <System.Diagnostics.DebuggerStepThroughAttribute()>  _
        Public Sub New()
            MyBase.New
            Me.Url = "http://jdc7200cte/services/ctemp/ctemp.asmx"
        End Sub

        <System.Diagnostics.DebuggerStepThroughAttribute(),  _
System.Web.Services.Protocols.SoapDocumentMethodAttribute("http
://mydomain.com/ws/ctemp/CTemp",
RequestNamespace:="http://mydomain.com/ws/ctemp",
ResponseNamespace:="http://mydomain.com/ws/ctemp",
Use:=System.Web.Services.Description.SoapBindingUse.Literal,
ParameterStyle:=System.Web.Services.Protocols.SoapParameterStyl
e.Wrapped)>  _
        Public Function CTemp(ByVal Temperature As Decimal, ByVal
FromUnits As String, ByVal ToUnits As String) As Decimal
            Dim results() As Object = Me.Invoke("CTemp", New
Object() {Temperature, FromUnits, ToUnits})
            Return CType(results(0),Decimal)
        End Function

        <System.Diagnostics.DebuggerStepThroughAttribute()>  _
        Public Function BeginCTemp(ByVal Temperature As Decimal,
ByVal FromUnits As String, ByVal ToUnits As String, ByVal
callback As System.AsyncCallback, ByVal asyncState As Object)
As System.IAsyncResult
            Return Me.BeginInvoke("CTemp", New Object()
{Temperature, FromUnits, ToUnits}, callback, asyncState)
        End Function

        <System.Diagnostics.DebuggerStepThroughAttribute()>  _
        Public Function EndCTemp(ByVal asyncResult As
System.IAsyncResult) As Decimal
            Dim results() As Object = Me.EndInvoke(asyncResult)
            Return CType(results(0),Decimal)
        End Function
End Class
```

The following proxy class source code generated by the `wsdl` tool is for C#:

```
//------------------------------------------------------------
------
// <autogenerated>
//      This code was generated by a tool.
//      Runtime Version: 1.0.2914.16
//
//      Changes to this file may cause incorrect behavior and
will be lost if
```

```
//      the code is regenerated.
// </autogenerated>
//------------------------------------------------------------
------

//
// This source code was auto-generated by wsdl,
Version=1.0.2914.16.
//
using System.Diagnostics;
using System.Xml.Serialization;
using System;
using System.Web.Services.Protocols;
using System.Web.Services;


[System.Web.Services.WebServiceBindingAttribute(Name="TempConve
rterSoap", Namespace="http://tempuri.org/")]
public class TempConverter :
System.Web.Services.Protocols.SoapHttpClientProtocol {

    [System.Diagnostics.DebuggerStepThroughAttribute()]
    public TempConverter() {
        this.Url = "http://jdc7200cte/ctemp/ctemp.asmx";
    }

    [System.Diagnostics.DebuggerStepThroughAttribute()]

[System.Web.Services.Protocols.SoapDocumentMethodAttribute("htt
p://tempuri.org/CTemp",
Use=System.Web.Services.Description.SoapBindingUse.Literal,
ParameterStyle=System.Web.Services.Protocols.SoapParameterStyle
.Wrapped)]
    public System.Decimal CTemp(System.Decimal Temperature,
string FromUnits, string ToUnits) {
        object[] results = this.Invoke("CTemp", new object[] {
                Temperature,
                FromUnits,
                ToUnits});
        return ((System.Decimal)(results[0]));
    }

    [System.Diagnostics.DebuggerStepThroughAttribute()]
    public System.IAsyncResult BeginCTemp(System.Decimal
Temperature, string FromUnits, string ToUnits,
System.AsyncCallback callback, object asyncState) {
        return this.BeginInvoke("CTemp", new object[] {
                Temperature,
                FromUnits,
                ToUnits}, callback, asyncState);
    }

    [System.Diagnostics.DebuggerStepThroughAttribute()]
```

```
    public System.Decimal EndCTemp(System.IAsyncResult
asyncResult) {
        object[] results = this.EndInvoke(asyncResult);
        return ((System.Decimal)(results[0]));
    }
}
```

At this point, you are ready to add the class to your project so that it can be compiled and used to call the methods of the Web service from a consumer application.

Creating a proxy class with Visual Studio

As mentioned previously, Visual Studio automatically creates Web service proxy classes using the Add Web Reference feature. All we need to have is the ability to locate the WSDL document for the Web service. Visual Studio silently takes care of the rest for us, locating the WSDL for a selected Web service, validating the contents, and then generating the proxy class.

Although quite easily the simplest method for obtaining a Web service proxy class, you could also use the wsdl tool in the .NET Framework to accomplish the same thing.

Summary

Finding Web services and generating proxy classes that we can use to consume them is a simple process using the tools built into .NET and Visual Studio. Instead of having to worry about the implementation details of how to communicate with a Web service, we can interact with the proxy class in an object-oriented fashion and rely on the proxy to handle the details. This greatly simplifies creating applications that consume Web services and permits us to focus on creating the application logic, rather than coding the necessary plumbing.

Now that you have learned of the techniques for creating Web service proxy classes using the wsdl tool, you are ready to create a full-fledged Web service consumer application. We will cover exactly how to do this in the next chapter.

✦   ✦   ✦

Consuming Web Services

In this chapter, you will learn how to write a consumer application for the CTemp Web service that we built in previous chapters.

Many different types of applications can consume Web services, including traditional desktop applications, Web applications, or even other Web services. The example we will build in this chapter will illustrate how to call the CTemp Web service from an ASP.NET Web forms application.

In addition to covering the details of creating Web service consumers, we will take a fairly detailed look at execution flow between our Web service and consumer applications. This will provide you with a good foundational understanding of how Web services work in ASP.NET as well as an appreciation for the great many details related to Web service implementation that are automatically handled on your behalf by the .NET Framework and the ASP.NET runtime.

Web Service Consumer Overview

A Web service *consumer* is any application that references and uses a Web service. A Web service consumer can take many forms: a client application, a server application, a component, or even another Web service. The type of the consumer does not matter as long as it has the capability to communicate with Web services using HTTP and SOAP.

To consume a Web service, we must be able to do the following:

  ✦ Find the Web service
  ✦ Obtain its WSDL service contract
  ✦ Generate a proxy class with which to call the Web service

✦ Create an instance of the proxy class

✦ Call the methods exposed by the proxy

In previous chapters, we have covered how to find Web services using various tools, including Visual Studio. We have also seen how to obtain the WSDL document and generate a proxy class using the `wsdl` tool from the .NET Framework SDK as well as Visual Studio's Add Web Reference feature. Armed with this knowledge, we are now ready to create a client application that is capable of calling the methods of any Web service that we can locate and generate a proxy class from.

Web Service Proxies

Recall that communication with a Web service is accomplished via messages that are delivered by a transport protocol. With no assistance from the platform, just to call a Web service, we would have to understand how to create and format SOAP messages as well as how to handle the delivery and receipt of these messages via HTTP.

Ideally, we would like the platform to provide this support for us. Of even greater benefit would be the ability to create an instance of a class that represented the Web service and called the methods, which in turn would carry out the necessary SOAP message generation and transportation activities required to communicate with the actual Web service.

Fortunately, this is exactly what happens when you create a Web service proxy class within the .NET Framework. The proxy class mimics the interfaces of the actual Web service and takes care of formatting appropriate SOAP messages to deliver requests to the Web service as well as process the responses that come back, such that calling a Web service is boiled down to the simple process of calling a method on a .NET class. This makes using Web services easy.

An interesting attribute of ASP.NET Web services is that they can be referenced and called both as a native .NET class and as a Web service. For example, you could build and deploy the CTemp Web service assembly to an application's \bin folder, create an instance of the class, and call its methods directly.

By generating and using a proxy class, however, we can reach our Web service via HTTP and SOAP. The benefit of the proxy class is that we can create an instance of the class and call its methods just like the native .NET assembly. The HTTP and SOAP plumbing required to call Web service methods is completely hidden from us within the proxy class (as it should be).

Why would we want to do this? Simple. We can distribute our Web service to any remote server, and all that we need is XML, HTTP, and SOAP to communicate with it. This greatly broadens the reach of our component to many different platforms, not just Windows platforms.

Let's take a look at the tools and techniques provided by ASP.NET and the .NET Framework to create an ASP.NET Web Forms application to consume our CTemp Web service.

Creating the Consumer Application

In the remaining sections of this chapter, we will build an ASP.NET Web Forms application to illustrate the techniques for consuming a Web service.

The first step in our quest to build a consumer application begins with the creation of a virtual directory on our local Web server to host our application. This process is identical to the process described in Chapter 25, "Building a Web Service," in which we created a Web server virtual directory for our CTemp Web service implementation.

If you don't recall how to create a virtual directory on your local Web server, feel free to refer to the instructions found in Chapter 25. At any rate, you will need a virtual directory named CTempClient that refers to a physical directory located at inetpub\wwwroot\CTempClient, using the same options specified in Chapter 25. When you are finished with this step, you should also create a bin folder that is a child of your Web application folder. This folder will serve as the location for storing our proxy assembly that we will create later in this chapter.

After you have done this, you are ready to begin the process of building your first Web service consumer application. This process begins with the search for the WSDL document that describes the CTemp Web service we wish to consume.

Obtaining the WSDL document

Before we can call methods of the CTemp Web service, we must locate the Web service and obtain information about its message interfaces via the WSDL document. If you have followed the examples in this book, the CTemp Web service was developed on your local Web server and will be found there.

Recall that the `disco` tool provided in the .NET Framework SDK can be used to locate Web services, given a known server URL. Using this tool, you can locate and copy DISCO and WSDL documents for discovered Web services to your local hard drive.

At this point, we have two choices for obtaining the WSDL document that describes our CTemp Web service. We can use the .NET disco tool or the Internet Explorer Web browser. Each of these methods has specific strengths and weaknesses. Your choice and the level of success you may experience will most likely depend on characteristics of the Web service you wish to consume.

The .NET disco tool is a good choice in the following situations:

✦ You know at least the URL of the target Web server on which the Web service is deployed.

✦ Web service discovery has been enabled through the use of one or more DISCO documents on the target Web server.

Internet Explorer is a good choice in the following situations:

✦ You know the exact URL of the Web service entry point.

✦ The Web service is an ASP.NET Web service (which implies that it supports discovery of the WSDL document via a properly formatted HTTP request, or obtained via the Web service help page).

✦ Web service discovery via disco is not possible because no DISCO documents are available for the service.

You may recall that ASP.NET Web services can be queried for such things as the WSDL document via Internet Explorer. You accomplish this by specifying a URL that includes a query string argument targeted at the Web service entry point file. For example, to obtain the WSDL document for our CTemp Web service, we would specify the following URL in the Address bar of our Web browser:

```
http://localhost/CTemp/CTemp.asmx?WSDL
```

This returns the WSDL for the CTemp Web service to your browser in XML format. You can then use the File ⇨ Save As option in Internet Explorer to save the WSDL to a file in your consumer application virtual directory.

Hopefully, you implemented a DISCO document for the CTemp Web service when we covered Web service deployment and publication in Chapter 26. If so, we can use the .NET disco tool to obtain the WSDL file that is the key to our ability to consume the CTemp Web service.

To obtain the WSDL document for the CTemp Web service using the .NET Framework disco tool, follow these steps:

1. Open a command prompt window.

2. At the command prompt, change the current directory to your Web application folder, as in "cd c:\inetpub\wwwroot\CTempClient," and press Enter.

3. At the command prompt, type "disco http://localhost/ctemp/ctemp.asmx" and press Enter.

Note   If you do not have the path to the .NET Framework SDK in your default path, you will have to include the complete path to the disco tool. By default, the disco tool is located at Program Files\Microsoft .NET\FrameworkSDK\Bin\disco.exe.

Tip   You can type "disco /?" at the command prompt to obtain help on the command syntax and available options for the disco tool.

Figure 28-1 shows the results of executing these commands to obtain the WSDL document for the CTemp Web service on the author's development machine.

```
Command Prompt                                                    _ □ X
Microsoft Windows 2000 [Version 5.00.2195]
(C) Copyright 1985-2000 Microsoft Corp.

C:\>cd inetpub\wwwroot\CTempClient

C:\inetpub\wwwroot\CTempClient>disco http://localhost/CTemp/CTemp.asmx
Microsoft (R) Web Services Discovery Utility
[Microsoft (R) .NET Framework, Version 1.0.2914.16]
Copyright (C) Microsoft Corp. 1998-2001. All rights reserved.

Disco found documents at the following URLs:
http://localhost/CTemp/CTemp.asmx?disco
http://localhost/CTemp/CTemp.asmx?wsdl

The following files hold the content found at the corresponding URLs:
 .\CTemp.disco <- http://localhost/CTemp/CTemp.asmx?disco
 .\CTemp.wsdl <- http://localhost/CTemp/CTemp.asmx?wsdl
The file .\results.discomap holds links to each of these files.

C:\inetpub\wwwroot\CTempClient>
```

Figure 28-1: Obtaining the WSDL document via the disco tool

Executing the disco tool with default options results in the creation of three files in the current directory. Table 28-1 describes these files.

Table 28-1
Files created by the disco tool

File	Description
CTemp.disco	Contains references to the CTemp Web service information that disco discovered at the specified target URL.
CTemp.wsdl	The actual WSDL document for the CTemp Web service.
Results.discomap	Catalogs the results obtained as a result of executing the discovery process against the specified target URL.

Now that we have the WSDL document, we can create a proxy class that can be used by our consumer application to make method calls on the CTemp Web service.

Of course, if you are using Visual Studio, you can use the Add Web Reference dialog box to locate and create references to Web services. In the specific case of the CTemp Web service, you can use the Web References On Local Web Server link in the Add Web Reference dialog box within Visual Studio to find the CTemp Web service and automatically create a Web service proxy class that can be used to interact with the service.

Generating the proxy class

The WSDL document that we obtained in the last section describes the capabilities of the CTemp Web service in terms of the data types, inputs, outputs, and message exchange patterns that it supports. In effect, this is a contract between the Web service and the consumer that documents what the Web service will provide and how it will deliver it when supplied with properly constructed messages. It is akin to the Interface Definition Language (IDL) of the RPC and COM technologies in that it describes the functionality of the service in terms of its interfaces (or, in our case, message formats and exchange patterns).

The .NET Framework SDK includes the wsdl tool that we can use to generate proxy classes from these WSDL documents. Using this tool, we can generate an ASP.NET Web service proxy class in any of the supported .NET languages when we supply the tool with a properly formatted WSDL document as input. The proxy class can then be used by our consumer application to make requests against the Web service using a local class that hides all the low-level details of the communication that takes place using HTTP and SOAP.

To generate a proxy class for the CTemp Web service from the WSDL document, follow these steps:

1. Open a command prompt window.

2. At the command prompt, change the current directory to your Web application folder, as in "cd c:\inetpub\wwwroot\CtempClient."

3. At the command prompt, type "wsdl /l:vb /o:CTempProxy.vb /n:CTempProxy CTemp.wsdl" and press Enter.

Tip   You can type "wsdl /?" at the command prompt to obtain help on the command syntax and available options for the wsdl tool. Not also that you must specify the entire path to the wsdl tool if you have not added its path to your PATH environment variable.

Figure 28-2 shows the results of executing these commands to create the CTemp proxy class on the author's development machine.

The /l (lowercase *L*) option specifies the desired source language for the proxy class, such as VB (Visual Basic), CS (C#), or JS (JavaScript). The /o (lowercase *O*) option specifies the name to be given the proxy class file. If you prefer to use C# for your proxy class, simply substitute CS for VB with the /l option. The /n option specifies the namespace to be assigned to the proxy. This will be useful when we reference the namespace in our client code using ASP.NET's @Import directive.

Before we move on to the next step in writing our Web service consumer application, let's take a brief look at the code that was generated by the wsdl tool for the CTemp proxy class. You can view the proxy class with your favorite text editor.

Figure 28-2: Generating the CTemp proxy class using the wsdl tool

The following is a partial listing of the CTemp proxy class.

VB.NET:

```
Imports System
Imports System.Diagnostics
Imports System.Web.Services
Imports System.Web.Services.Protocols
Imports System.Xml.Serialization
'
'This source code was auto-generated by wsdl,
Version=1.0.2914.16.
'
NameSpace CTempProxy

<System.Web.Services.WebServiceBindingAttribute(Name:="TempConv
erterSoap", [Namespace]:="http://mydomain.com/CTemp")>  _
Public Class TempConverter
    Inherits
System.Web.Services.Protocols.SoapHttpClientProtocol

    <System.Diagnostics.DebuggerStepThroughAttribute()>  _
    Public Sub New()
        MyBase.New
        Me.Url = "http://localhost/CTemp/CTemp.asmx"
    End Sub

    <System.Diagnostics.DebuggerStepThroughAttribute(),  _
System.Web.Services.Protocols.SoapDocumentMethodAttribute("http
://mydomain.com/CTemp/CTemp",
RequestNamespace:="http://mydomain.com/CTemp",
ResponseNamespace:="http://mydomain.com/CTemp",
Use:=System.Web.Services.Description.SoapBindingUse.Literal,
ParameterStyle:=System.Web.Services.Protocols.SoapParameterStyl
e.Wrapped)>  _
```

```
        Public Function CTemp(ByVal Temperature As Decimal, ByVal
FromUnits As String, ByVal ToUnits As String) As Decimal
            Dim results() As Object = Me.Invoke("CTemp", New
Object() {Temperature, FromUnits, ToUnits})
            Return CType(results(0),Decimal)
        End Function

        <System.Diagnostics.DebuggerStepThroughAttribute()> _
        Public Function BeginCTemp(ByVal Temperature As Decimal,
ByVal FromUnits As String, ByVal ToUnits As String, ByVal
callback As System.AsyncCallback, ByVal asyncState As Object)
As System.IAsyncResult
            Return Me.BeginInvoke("CTemp", New Object()
{Temperature, FromUnits, ToUnits}, callback, asyncState)
        End Function

        <System.Diagnostics.DebuggerStepThroughAttribute()> _
        Public Function EndCTemp(ByVal asyncResult As
System.IAsyncResult) As Decimal
            Dim results() As Object = Me.EndInvoke(asyncResult)
            Return CType(results(0),Decimal)
        End Function
End Class

End Namespace
```

C#:

```
Namespace CTempProxy {
using System.Diagnostics;
using System.Xml.Serialization;
using System;
using System.Web.Services.Protocols;
using System.Web.Services;

[System.Web.Services.WebServiceBindingAttribute(Name="TempConve
rterSoap", Namespace="http://mydomain.com/CTemp")]
public class TempConverter :
System.Web.Services.Protocols.SoapHttpClientProtocol {

    [System.Diagnostics.DebuggerStepThroughAttribute()]
    public TempConverter() {
        this.Url = "http://localhost/CTemp/CTemp.asmx";
    }

    [System.Diagnostics.DebuggerStepThroughAttribute()]

[System.Web.Services.Protocols.SoapDocumentMethodAttribute("htt
p://mydomain.com/CTemp/CTemp",
RequestNamespace="http://mydomain.com/CTemp",
ResponseNamespace="http://mydomain.com/CTemp",
Use=System.Web.Services.Description.SoapBindingUse.Literal,
ParameterStyle=System.Web.Services.Protocols.SoapParameterStyle
.Wrapped)]
```

```
       public System.Decimal CTemp(System.Decimal Temperature,
string FromUnits, string ToUnits) {
           object[] results = this.Invoke("CTemp", new object[] {
                       Temperature,
                       FromUnits,
                       ToUnits});
           return ((System.Decimal)(results[0]));
       }

       [System.Diagnostics.DebuggerStepThroughAttribute()]
       public System.IAsyncResult BeginCTemp(System.Decimal
Temperature, string FromUnits, string ToUnits,
System.AsyncCallback callback, object asyncState) {
           return this.BeginInvoke("CTemp", new object[] {
                       Temperature,
                       FromUnits,
                       ToUnits}, callback, asyncState);
       }

       [System.Diagnostics.DebuggerStepThroughAttribute()]
       public System.Decimal EndCTemp(System.IAsyncResult
asyncResult) {
           object[] results = this.EndInvoke(asyncResult);
           return ((System.Decimal)(results[0]));
       }
   }
}
```

Note that the TempConverter proxy class inherits from the .NET class named System.Web.Services.Protocols.SoapHttpClientProtocol, which implies that the TempConverter proxy uses HTTP and SOAP as the communications protocol to invoke the Web service. This is highlighted in the previous code listings.

Now, let's direct our attention to the declaration and implementation of the CTemp method in the code listing. As you can see, the proxy method declaration is identical to the CTemp Web service method, using the name, number, order, and type of arguments. However, the actual implementation is quite different. The proxy class does not perform any conversion of temperature units, as does the actual Web service. Instead, the proxy method contains just two lines of code, as follows.

VB.NET:

```
Dim results() As Object = Me.Invoke("CTemp", New Object()
    {Temperature, FromUnits, ToUnits})
Return CType(results(0),Decimal)
```

C#:

```
object[] results = this.Invoke("CTemp", new object[] {
                   Temperature,
                   FromUnits,
                   ToUnits});
return ((System.Decimal)(results[0]));
```

The first line of code calls the `Invoke` method of the proxy class to synchronously call the CTemp Web service and return the result. The second line of code converts the result to the proper type (`Decimal`) and returns this result to the caller.

Of course, our call to the CTemp proxy, which in turn calls the actual CTemp Web service method, is all marshaled on our local Web server using XML, HTTP, and SOAP. However, our proxy class could just as easily have been calling the CTemp Web service on a machine in another room, across the country, or even halfway around the world! This distinction is completely hidden from the consumer of the Web service as well as the fact that the proxy is exchanging SOAP messages with the CTemp Web service. All we have to do is create an instance of the proxy class and invoke its methods as if it were a local class. What could be easier?

Given a valid proxy class, we can now compile this class into a .NET assembly using the appropriate language compiler. Again, you will need the services of a command prompt window, because all .NET compilers have command-line interfaces. Just as we did previously, start a command prompt window and change your current directory to that of your client application folder (inetpub\wwwroot\CTempClient). After doing so, execute the following command, appropriate for the language you are using.

VB.NET:

```
vbc /t:library /out:bin\CTempProxy.dll
/r:System.Web.Services.dll
    /r:System.XML.dll /r:System.dll CTempProxy.vb
```

C#:

```
csc /t:library /out:bin\CTempProxy.dll
/r:System.Web.Services.dll
    /r:System.XML.dll /r:System.dll CTempProxy.cs
```

Tip The .NET compilers are installed in WINNT\System32\Microsoft.NET*version* by default. To reference them without a complete path prefix, you might wish to add this path to the system `PATH` environment variable on your computer. This also simplifies references to .NET assemblies using the `/r` option.

This command will compile the CTemp Web service proxy class into a .NET assembly that we can then reference from our Web Forms client application. The `/t:library` option specifies that we wish to create a DLL (rather than an executable). The `/r` option specifies the .NET assemblies that correspond to the .NET namespaces referenced by the proxy class. The `/out` option saves the assembly in the Web application's .\bin folder.

Figure 28-3 shows the results of executing the VB.NET compiler to build the CTemp proxy class assembly.

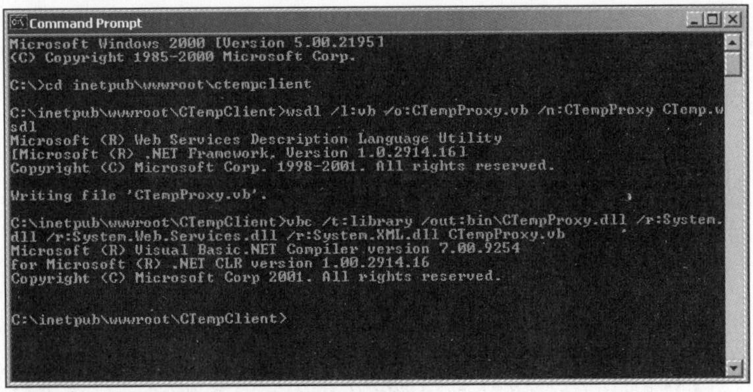

Figure 28-3: VB.NET compiler output

If you refer back to the proxy class, you will discover that the CTemp proxy class implements two additional methods named `BeginCTemp` and `EndCTemp`. These methods provide the support necessary to invoke the CTemp Web service asynchronously.

We will look at these and other features of the proxy class a little later in this chapter. For now, let's get back to building our client application by building a simple user interface form that can be used to interact with our CTemp Web service.

As mentioned earlier, you have many choices for the type of consumer application that is capable of calling methods of a Web service. In this instance, we will create an ASP.NET Web Forms Application to consume our CTemp Web service.

Building the Web form

Now that we have created a virtual directory, obtained the WSDL document, and created and built a proxy class for our consumer application, we are ready to build a form that will allow us to enter values that can be passed to the CTemp Web service and display the results after a successful call is completed.

For our ASP.NET Web Forms application, we will be using the following ASP.NET server controls:

✦ Two text boxes (one for the input temperature and one for the output temperature)

✦ Two radio button lists (one to select the input temperature units and one to select the output temperature units)

✦ One command button to initiate the units conversion

ASP.NET Web forms are contained in ASPX files. Let's begin creating our consumer application by creating a Web form based on the server controls mentioned previously. Enter the following code into your favorite text editor and save it in the Web application folder using the file name CTempClient.aspx:

```
<HTML>
  <HEAD>
    <title>CTemp Web Service Consumer Application</title>
  </HEAD>
  <body>
    <form id="frmCTemp" action="CTempClient.aspx"
runat="server">
      <asp:textbox id="txtInputTemp" style="POSITION: absolute;
TOP: 48px; LEFT: 10px;" Height="26px" Width="65px"
runat="server"></asp:textbox>
      <asp:radiobuttonlist id="optToUnits" style="POSITION:
absolute; TOP: 12px; LEFT: 347px;" runat="server">
        <asp:ListItem Value="F">Fahrenheit</asp:ListItem>
        <asp:ListItem Value="C"
Selected="True">Celsius</asp:ListItem>
        <asp:ListItem Value="K">Kelvin</asp:ListItem>
        <asp:ListItem Value="R">Rankine</asp:ListItem>
      </asp:radiobuttonlist>
      <asp:radiobuttonlist id="optFromUnits" style="POSITION:
absolute; TOP: 36px; LEFT: 76px;" runat="server">
        <asp:ListItem Value="F"
Selected="True">Fahrenheit</asp:ListItem>
        <asp:ListItem Value="C">Celsius</asp:ListItem>
      </asp:radiobuttonlist>
      <asp:button id="btnConvert" style="POSITION: absolute;
TOP: 49px; LEFT: 174px;" Text="Converts To"
OnClick="btnConvert_Click" runat="server"></asp:button>
      <asp:textbox id="txtOutputTemp" style="POSITION:
absolute; TOP: 48px; LEFT: 281px;" Height="28px" Width="66px"
ReadOnly="True" runat="server"></asp:textbox>
    </form>
  </body>
</HTML>
```

This is a simple form that will allow the user to specify a temperature value, the source units, and the desired target units. The button will allow the user to submit the request to the server for processing. Note that, so far, nothing in the form is tied to a specific implementation language. Shortly, we will be able to add our implementation code to this form using any language that we choose, without having to change our form definition at all.

Let's take a brief look at these elements of our ASP.NET form to point out some of the highlights to you.

First, note that all the server controls specify a unique ID via the id attribute. This enables us to reference these controls by name within server code, which we'll add in a moment. Also, all server controls are marked with the `runat="server"` attribute.

The `txtOutputTemp` text box will be used to display the temperature conversion value returned by a call to the CTemp Web service. This text box specifies the `ReadOnly` property, which prevents users from modifying the text in the text box (because this will be set to the appropriate value by the form after obtaining the results of the unit conversion).

The `btnConvert` button, when clicked by the user, will execute the units conversion based on the settings chosen by the user in the other controls. The `Text` property is used to display the "Converts To" string on the face of the button. Note that the `OnClick` property specifies the name of the event handler when this button is clicked. In this case, the `btnConvert_Click` procedure will be executed.

Next, we have two sets of option list controls. The `optFromUnits` control displays two entries in its list: one named `Celsius` with a value of `C` and one named `Fahrenheit` with a value of `F`. Note that the `Fahrenheit` item has been identified as the default value via the `Selected` property so that this entry is selected by default when the form is displayed for the first time.

The `optToUnits` control displays four entries in its list: one named `Fahrenheit` (value `F`), one named `Celsius` (value `C`), one named `Kelvin` (value `K`), and one named `Rankine` (value `R`). The Celsius item's `Selected` property is set to `True` so that this entry is selected by default when the form is displayed for the first time.

Now that we have our Web form created and initialized, we are ready to add the code to the form that will create an instance of the CTemp proxy class and allow us to interact with the proxy class to perform temperature unit conversions.

Creating an instance of the proxy class

To call methods of the proxy class that represents the Web service, you must create an instance of the proxy class. As it turns out, creating an instance of a Web service proxy is identical to creating an instance of any other .NET class, which, as you will see, is quite easy.

To create an instance of the CTemp proxy class, we simply reference the class definition in our declaration. Let's illustrate this process by adding some code to the Web form application we have been building.

The first step we need to complete is to import the namespace of the assembly that contains our CTemp proxy class implementation. This is done using ASP.NET's `@Import` page directive. Add the following line to the top of your CTempClient.aspx file:

```
<% @ Import Namespace="CTempProxy" %>
```

This will enable us to reference the class in our code. Recall that when we generated our proxy class using the wsdl tool, we provided a namespace for the proxy class. This is the same namespace that we have specified to the Import directive.

We are now ready to add the code that will handle the OnClick event of the btnConvert server control. Insert the following code between the <html> and <head> tags of your Web form.

VB.NET:

```
<script language="VB" runat="server">

  Sub btnConvert_Click(sender As Object, e As EventArgs)

    Dim TC As New TempConverter()

    txtOutputTemp.Text =
Format(TC.CTemp(CType(txtInputTemp.Text, _
                      Decimal),
optFromUnits.SelectedItem.Value, _
                      optToUnits.SelectedItem.Value), "Fixed")

  End Sub

</script>
```

C#:

```
<script language="CS" runat="server">

  void btnConvert_Click(Object Src, EventArgs E) {

    TempConverter TC = new TempConverter();

    txtOutputTemp.Text =
            TC.CTemp(Convert.ToDecimal(txtInputTemp.Text),
                     optFromUnits.SelectedItem.Value,
optToUnits.SelectedItem.Value).ToString("F");
  }
</script>
```

This code shows that the TC variable is declared to be an instance of the CTemp proxy class denoted by the TempConverter class declaration. Following this declaration is a single line of code that extracts the input arguments from the Web form, calls the CTemp method on the TempConverter proxy class (the synchronous form), formats the results, and inserts the value into the output text box.

Let's take a closer look at the code that actually invokes the CTemp method on the proxy class.

Calling the CTemp proxy method

ASP.NET Web services can be called both synchronously and asynchronously. A synchronous method call is characterized by the fact that the caller waits for a response from the Web service before continuing execution. An asynchronous method call, on the other hand, permits the caller to continue with other work while the call is in progress. A notification mechanism is then used to inform the consumer that the Web service call has completed.

ASP.NET Web services use HTTP and SOAP as the default transport protocol and messaging format, respectively, because it provides for the exchange of a much larger family of data types, as well as complex XML-based document types. The proxy class, of course, eliminates the details of XML serialization, SOAP message formats, and HTTP request/response exchanges from the caller, making it quick and easy to call Web service methods.

To call a Web service method on our proxy class, all we need do is specify the name of the method to call (along with any arguments) using the reference to the instance of the proxy that we declared.

In our example, we are calling the synchronous form of the CTemp Web method to convert temperature units as follows.

VB.NET:

```
txtOutputTemp.Text = Format(TC.CTemp(CType(txtInputTemp.Text,
_
                        Decimal),
optFromUnits.SelectedItem.Value, _
                    optToUnits.SelectedItem.Value), "Fixed")
```

C#:

```
TxtOutputTemp.Text =
TC.CTemp(Convert.ToDecimal(txtInputTemp.Text),
                    optFromUnits.SelectedItem.Value,

optToUnits.SelectedItem.Value).ToString("F");
```

Let's break down this statement into its fundamental parts so that we can thoroughly examine everything that is occurring in this code:

✦ The proxy object reference (TC) is used to call the CTemp method (TC.CTemp).

✦ The first argument to the CTemp method specifies the input temperature. This value is obtained from the text box on the Web form by referring to the Text property of the text box control (txtInputTemp.Text).

✦ The CTemp method expects the input temperature argument to be of type Decimal, so the text obtained from the text box control is converted into the Decimal data type.

✦ The second argument to the method specifies the source units of the temperature value. This value is obtained from the option button list by using the `SelectedItem` property to reference the currently selected option button and then referencing the `Value` property of that result (`optFromUnits. SelectedItem.Value`). This returns a single character string that encodes the source units as either F (for Fahrenheit) or C (for Celsius).

✦ The third argument to the method specifies the target units of the temperature conversion. This value is obtained from the option button list by using the `SelectedItem` property to reference the currently selected option button and then referencing the `Value` property of that result (`optToUnits.SelectedItem.Value`). This returns a single character string that encodes the target units as either F, C, K (for Kelvin), or R (for Rankine).

✦ Lastly, the `Decimal` result that is returned by the method call is converted to a formatted text string using a built-in "Fixed" numeric formatter. This results in a text string that displays at least one digit to the left of the decimal separator and two digits to the right. This string is then assigned to the `Text` property of the output text box (`txtOutputTemp.Text`).

This tiny bit of code handles the entire process of gathering the input from the Web form controls, converting this input to the proper data types expected by the `CTemp` method call, calling the method, formatting the result, and assigning it to the text box control on the Web form that displays the results of the call.

Those of you who are familiar with programming forms in Visual Basic 6 (or earlier) will notice that the programming model for ASP.NET Web Forms is strikingly similar to programming Windows Forms in previous versions of Visual Basic. What's more, interacting with Web services is very much like interacting with traditional COM automation components. This is not an accident. The designers of the .NET Framework and ASP.NET worked very hard to ensure that the skills you have gained from building traditional Windows applications can be leveraged when building the next generation of applications based on the .NET Framework.

We now have a simple, but complete Web service consumer application that is capable of collecting input from a user via a Web form and processing this input by calling our CTemp Web service. With the code in place, let's take a look at how we can test our application.

Testing the Consumer Application

Now that you have created the consumer application, designed the Web form, and added the code to the `Click` event of the button control, you are ready to test your application.

To test our application, simply start an instance of the Internet Explorer Web browser and type the following URL into the Address bar:

```
http://localhost/ctempclient/ctempclient.aspx
```

This displays our client application's Web form, as shown in Figure 28-4.

Figure 28-4: CTemp client user interface

To test the application, enter a temperature value in the first text box, select the source units, select the target units, and then click the Converts To button. The Web form is submitted to the server, where the `Click` event code of the button is executed. This code creates an instance of the CTemp proxy class, calls the `CTemp` method, and outputs the conversion results to the target temperature text box. Figure 28-5 shows the results of calling the CTemp Web service with some sample input.

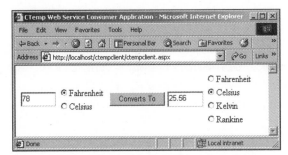

Figure 28-5: Results of temperature conversion

Having now seen our consumer application in action, let's take a look at the larger picture of what really happens when we run our application to interact with the CTemp Web service.

Application Execution Model

Seeing how simple it was to create a consumer for our CTemp Web service, you might be tempted to forget all that is actually taking place when calling a Web service method. The real value of the .NET Framework and ASP.NET is quite evident when we examine some of the details behind the operation of our simple consumer application and Web service.

Let's take a quick look at what happens during the execution lifetime of the consumer application and the Web service as it processes a single temperature conversion request.

Recall that both Web services and Web applications are really ASP.NET applications and, thus, run under the control of ASP.NET and the CLR. As such, both applications are contained in a virtual directory on a Web server, with the appropriate files for each application stored in the root of the virtual directory along with any needed assemblies, which are stored in the bin folder of the virtual directory.

The consumer application is started when a user requests the main form of the application. We will start our journey at this point.

1. A user requests the main form of the CTempClient application, such as `http://localhost/CTempClient/CTempClient.aspx`.

2. The IIS Web server on localhost receives the request (technically, an HTTP GET request) and hands it off to the ASP.NET runtime for execution of the page (because the requested page has an .aspx extension). This handoff occurs via an ISAPI filter extension that is registered within IIS to handle all of the ASP.NET file types.

3. The ASP.NET runtime creates an instance of the page class that represents the Web form and executes the page.

4. The page class generates the HTML and sends it to the browser, causing the form to be rendered in the user's browser window.

5. The page class is then destroyed by the ASP.NET runtime along with any other necessary request cleanup processing (remember, HTTP is a stateless protocol, so there is no need to keep the page class around after the HTML has been transmitted to the client).

6. The user enters information into the form and presses the Convert To button. This causes the form to be posted back to the Web server.

7. Again, the Web server hands off the request (technically, an HTTP POST request) to the ASP.NET runtime, which creates a new instance of the page class that implements the Web form and executes the page.

8. This time (because this is a postback request) the server-side button control's `Click` event code is now executed. Recall that this is where we added our code to create and call the CTemp Web service.

9. The Click event code creates an instance of the CTemp Web service proxy class. This class inherits from the System.Web.Services.Protocols. SoapHttpClientProtocol class. This provides the foundation for communicating the method request and response via SOAP messages over the HTTP transport.

10. The Click event code now calls the synchronous CTemp method on the proxy object, passing the input arguments obtained from the postback data of the form (via server-side control properties).

11. The Web service proxy calls the Invoke method, passing along the input arguments. This method serializes the CTemp method call into a SOAP message that matches the method signature defined in the WSDL document. The SOAP message is then added to the payload of an HTTP request and delivered to the Web service endpoint (the URL of the ASMX file).

12. The IIS Web server that hosts the CTemp Web service (in this specific case, localhost) receives the request (technically, a SOAP POST request) and hands it off to the ASP.NET runtime to execute the requested page.

13. The ASP.NET runtime deserializes the SOAP payload from the request, creates an instance of the CTemp Web service implementation class, and executes the CTemp method, passing the input arguments.

14. Next, the ASP.NET runtime takes the result of the CTemp method call and serializes it into a SOAP response message. This message is then added to the payload of an HTTP response and delivered back to the client (in this case, our proxy class).

15. The Invoke method of the proxy class deserializes the result from the SOAP response message into a generic .NET Object type. This type is then explicitly cast to the return data type expected by the caller (in this case, a Decimal temperature value) and returned to our consumer application.

16. The Click event code in our consumer application takes the result, converts it to the String data type, and assigns the result to the output text box in the Web form, formatted to two decimal places. The event code processing is now completed and page execution continues.

17. The page now executes through its rendering phase to generate the HTML that is returned to the user's browser. Just as before, the page class is then torn down by the ASP.NET runtime and any other cleanup processing that is necessary is executed.

Whew! That was a handful! Hopefully, this simulated flow of execution between a Web service and its consumer will give you a solid foundation for further exploration into the underpinnings of how Web services work. This information will also be useful as you build Web services and/or consumers and need to troubleshoot problems that might arise.

Summary

As we have demonstrated in this part of *ASP.NET Bible,* Web services are poised to become the programmable building blocks for the next generation of the Internet. The wide adoption of XML, HTTP, and SOAP has made it possible to create an object middleware infrastructure that is easily capable of being leveraged on the many types of systems attached to the Internet, regardless of hardware platform, operating system, or object model. Even more important, a consistent and simple way to interact with these programmable components finally exists.

Having this new level of interoperability at a programming level will enable the creation of many new and innovative solutions to problems that were once difficult, if not impossible, to address in the past. It is only a matter of time before we will have, at our fingertips, a huge library of these programmable building blocks from which to construct truly distributed applications that can interoperate with all kinds of systems.

In many respects, it is up to us, professional programmers, to create these building blocks. Web services give you a powerful tool to construct these building blocks in a way that greatly expands the potential population of consumers that can leverage these services.

✦   ✦   ✦

Building ASP.NET Applications

P A R T

V

◆ ◆ ◆ ◆

In This Part

Chapter 29
ASP.NET Blackjack

Chapter 30
Chatty Discussion
Forum

◆ ◆ ◆ ◆

ASP.NET Blackjack

Writing games is great fun. Not surprisingly, many developers originally became interested in computer programming because of their love for computer games. I know I did!

But writing games is not a trivial task. In fact, professional game programming is one of the most challenging fields in software development. But, aside from being an enjoyable pastime, why should those of us whose primary work responsibilities are business applications spend time writing games?

I've found that writing games is a great way to explore a new language or set of programming tools. Games often exercise a variety of user interface components, data structures, and programming constructs. In short, they give your brain the workout it needs to really begin to explore and understand a new development environment.

With that in mind, I've created an ASP.NET blackjack game to demonstrate a number of important ASP.NET features. Blackjack is a relatively simple card game with well-defined rules, so it's a perfect candidate for helping you to understand what all the various pieces and parts of ASP.NET do, how they fit together, and what their roles are in creating applications.

Blackjack: The Rules

If you are familiar with blackjack rules, feel free to skim or skip this section.

Blackjack, also called 21, is a card game involving one dealer and one or more players. Although any number can play, players do not play against each other. Each one plays individually against the dealer.

The goal of blackjack is to draw cards with values totaling as close to 21 as possible without going over (referred to as *busting*). In the end, if your total is higher than the dealer's, you win. If you bust or your total is less than the dealer's, you lose.

You begin with two cards. You can choose to *hit* (draw another card) or *stand* (stay with your current total). You can hit as many times as you like until you either get 21 on the nose (and win!) or choose to stand on your current total. Once you stand, the dealer plays his or her turn and has the same options.

Face cards count as 10 and aces count as either 1 or 11, whichever works best for you. All the rest of the cards are valued based on their number. When your first two cards are a face card (or a 10) and an ace, you have 21 right off the bat, called a blackjack!

When you begin, you are allowed to see what the dealer's first card is. You can use this information, if you like, to decide how aggressively or conservatively you want to play. Here's a basic strategy that is designed to play the odds to your best advantage: if the dealer's first card is a good one (7-10, face card, or an ace), you should play more aggressively and keep hitting until you get to 17 or better (or bust). If the dealer's first card is a bad one (2-6), then you should play conservatively and stop hitting when you get to 12 or better. The idea is that if the dealer's first card is bad, the dealer is more likely to bust in the end. And if the dealer busts, you win, no matter what your total is. But, again, this is just one strategy — when you play, you can choose to hit or stand whenever you like.

Playing a Hand or Two

Now that you know how to play, you are ready to walk through a demonstration of the blackjack application.

As the game begins, you have already received two cards and you can see the dealer's first card (see Figure 29-1).

At this point, you have two options: Hit or Stand, as indicated by the buttons. If you click Hit, another card is dealt (see Figure 29-2).

Figure 29-1: The game begins.

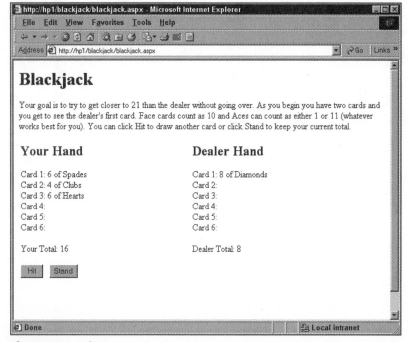

Figure 29-2: Hit me.

This continues until one of three things happens:

✦ You go over 21 — you lose. (See Figure 29-3.)

✦ You're total adds up to 21 on the nose — you win! (See Figure 29-4.)

✦ You decide to stand.

When you choose to stand, it becomes the dealer's turn. By Las Vegas rules, the dealer always draws until his total is 17 or over or he busts.

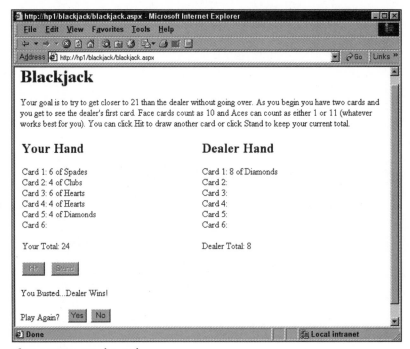

Figure 29-3: You busted.

The results are tallied and the user is informed of the result, be it good (see Figure 29-5) or bad (see Figure 29-6).

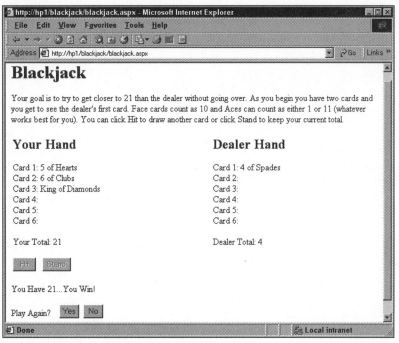

Figure 29-4: You got 21! You win!

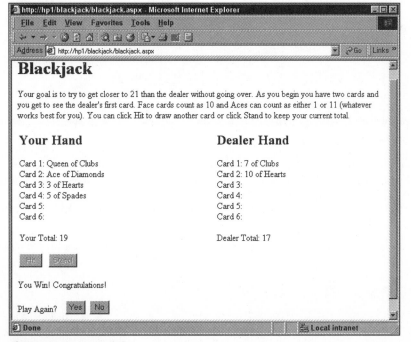

Figure 29-5: You win!

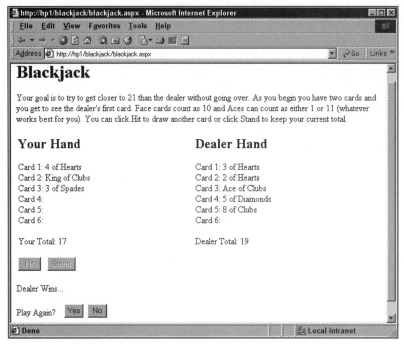

Figure 29-6: You lose.

Finally, you're asked if you'd like to play again. If you click Yes, a new game begins.

Design: The Blackjack Breakdown

The first steps in creating any software application are analysis and design. Fortunately with a game like this, if you know the rules, the analysis step is done. So on to design!

When you're developing in an object-oriented environment, design is all about compositional breakdown. That process, like most, involves asking the right questions:

✦ What is the functionality that I need to perform and the data that I need to track?

✦ How should I carve that functionality into classes, methods, and properties?

Stepping through the process

A blackjack game consists of at least one player and one dealer. So there are at least two participants. They are each going to have their own hand of cards dealt to them from a common deck. The cards themselves should be a standard deck of 52 with four suites, and so forth. You'll need to be able to shuffle those cards and draw from the top of the deck.

In addition, the user has to be able to see the cards they receive and be able to choose whether they want to hit or stand. Each time they hit, they should receive a new card and be allowed to make the decision again. Once they choose to stand, the computer will play the role of the dealer and draw cards appropriately.

Finally, when the player and dealer are done, the results should be compared and the winner declared. The user should have the option to play again, and if he or she chooses to, the process should be restarted.

Picking out the objects and dividing responsibilities

The most obvious class you need for a game like this is a Card class. It holds an individual card's identity and its value.

Further, you need a class that holds the entire deck of cards to draw from. Casinos use multiple decks and, after they are shuffled, the cards are organized into a plastic box called a *shoe*. The shoe provides an easy way to draw one card at a time from the end of the box. I call the class that holds the collection of cards Shoe. Shoe has two key capabilities in addition to holding the cards: Shuffle and Draw.

Because the player and the dealer play very similar roles, it makes sense to create one class called Participant, and then make two instances of that class — Player and Dealer. The Participant class has one important property: Hand. This is an ArrayList holding the cards that have been dealt to that person. The Participant class also has a function, `TotalValue`, which calculates the total value of the cards in the participant's hand.

The user interface

As with any game, the user interface is an important element of this application. In this application, I opted for a design that is simple rather than flashy. I did everything with little more than buttons and labels. That leaves you plenty of opportunity to dress it up as you see fit.

The player's cards appear on the left and the dealer's cards appear on the right. Each card is displayed using a label holding the name of the card, such as "Ace of Spades" or "3 of Hearts." Two buttons below the cards offer the options to Hit or Stand. After the user is done, they are asked if they'd like to play again. If they click Yes, the page is reset and a new game begins. Simple enough.

A Place to Work

The first step in the development phase is to find a place to work. You will need both access to a Web server that supports ASP.NET and the ability to create virtual folders.

If you are working on the server itself or accessing its files over a network, create a new folder under wwwroot called "blackjack." Under that folder, create a new folder called "bin." Now make the blackjack folder a *virtual folder*. (I describe how to do this in the next paragraph.) This is important, because it lets the server know that this is the root for a Web application, and it will allow you to use the bin subfolder to hold components that this Web application will use.

If you are on the server yourself, you can make blackjack a virtual folder by choosing Internet Services Manager under Administrative Tools. Then, open the server and find the Default Web Site. Under that, you should see a list of folders that includes the blackjack folder you just created. Right-click it and choose Properties. In the dialog box, on the Virtual Directory tab, under Application Settings, click the Create button. This turns the blackjack folder into a virtual folder and tells IIS that this folder contains a separate Web application. Click OK to complete the process.

If your Web site is provided by a hosting company, it may provide an administrative page or utility that enables you to identify folders and virtual folders on its Web server. If not, you may have to simply request the hosting company to do it for you.

The Card Object

With the basic organization of the game in mind, I began to search through the various data structures the .NET Framework makes available and began to think about the best ways to create my classes and their contents.

Because the Card object is really going to be very simple, I used a structure for it instead of a class. Here's the code to create it. (Don't worry about typing this code in anywhere right now. I'll show you where it goes in a future section.)

```
Public Structure Card
    Public Suit As String
    Public Name As String
    Public Value As Integer
End Structure
```

Suit holds the suit name: Hearts, Diamonds, Clubs, or Spades. Name holds the name of the card, as a string. This might be Jack, King, Ace, or 3. Value holds the value of this card in blackjack, as an integer. For numbered cards, it is the numeric equivalent of the Name. For face cards, it is 10, and aces are 1. (The potential for aces to count as 11 sometimes will be handled in the code.)

A Data Structure for the Shoe Object

Next on the agenda is the Shoe object. But before I could figure out the Shoe object itself, I had another question buzzing around in my head that I had to answer: What should I use *inside* the Shoe object to store the cards? Lots of options are available. I could use an array, an ArrayList, a stack, a queue, and so on.

I don't need to be able to directly address the individual Card objects inside the Shoe object, but I do need the ability to add new cards to it and pull cards off the top. The Stack class in the System.Collections namespace provides these capabilities, but it is missing one critical requirement: the ability to randomly rearrange the elements inside the data structure—in other words, shuffle the cards.

The randomizable stack

I decided to create my own randomizable stack. I did this by creating a namespace and a class in a text file using the Visual Basic syntax and compiling it with the command-line compiler. The beauty of this approach is that you don't have to go to the expense and complexity of using Visual Studio to do it. It's as easy as creating an ASPX page. The only difference is that you have to use the vbc command-line compiler to turn it into a DLL.

Here's what the new randomizable stack looks like. Put this code in a file named rndstk.vb.

```
Option Explicit
Option Strict

Imports System
Imports System.Collections
Imports Microsoft.VisualBasic

Namespace RandomizableStack

    Public Class RandStack

        Private StackList As ArrayList = New ArrayList

        Public ReadOnly Property Count As Integer
        Get
            Return StackList.Count
        End Get
        End Property

        Public Sub Push(Entry As Object)
            StackList.Insert(0,Entry)
        End Sub

        Public Function Pop As Object
            Dim Entry As Object
            Entry = StackList(0)
```

```
            StackList.RemoveAt(0)
            Return(Entry)
        End Function

        Public Function Peek As Object
            Dim Entry As Object
            Entry = StackList(0)
            Return(Entry)
        End Function


        Public Sub RandomizeOrder

        Dim Swaps As Integer
        Dim EntryIndex1, EntryIndex2 As Integer
        Dim NumEntries As Integer = StackList.Count
        Dim NumSwaps As Integer = NumEntries * 3
        Dim TempEntry As Object

        Randomize

        For Swaps = 1 To NumSwaps
            EntryIndex1 = CInt(Int(Rnd * NumEntries))
            EntryIndex2 = CInt(Int(Rnd * NumEntries))
            TempEntry = StackList(EntryIndex1)
            StackList(EntryIndex1) = StackList(EntryIndex2)
            StackList(EntryIndex2) = TempEntry
        Next

        End Sub

    End Class


    End Namespace
```

A new class and a place to stack your stuff

After specifying Option Strict and Explicit, I imported three namespaces to use here. Then I declared a single class inside a single namespace: RandStack. The most important part of this class is the private StackList ArrayList. This is where the stack information is actually stored.

Because an ArrayList can store anything inherited from Object (and that means *anything*), I decided to make this stack equally flexible. That means that it can be reused in any circumstance where stack-like functionality is needed along with the ability to randomly reorganize the elements. Other kinds of cards (those used in collectible card games such as Magic the Gathering, for example) can be represented with their own structures or classes and then stored in this data structure as well. Wherever possible, design for reuse!

Count is created as a read-only property that returns the number of elements in the ArrayList.

Push me, pop me

The old standby methods that are a part of every stack are Push and Pop. Push adds a value to the top of the stack and pop retrieves the value from the top of the stack. Here is the code (from the listing above) that implements these two methods.

```
Public Sub Push(Entry As Object)
    StackList.Insert(0,Entry)
End Sub

Public Function Pop As Object
    Dim Entry As Object
    Entry = StackList(0)
    StackList.RemoveAt(0)
    Return(Entry)
End Function
```

In this implementation, the Insert method of the ArrayList is used to place new elements in the very first position in the ArrayList (causing all the other elements to be pushed down a notch). Then, to retrieve an element, the object is placed in a local variable to be returned, and then the ArrayList's RemoveAt method is used to remove the very first ArrayList element (causing all the other elements to hop up a notch).

No peeking

Although I didn't need this functionality for my blackjack page, I decided to go ahead and implement another method, called Peek, from the stack in the System.Collections namespace:

```
Public Function Peek As Object
    Dim Entry As Object
    Entry = StackList(0)
    Return(Entry)
End Function
```

Peek does essentially the same thing as Pop except that the item isn't removed from the stack. Again, if this class is reused for other purposes in the future, there may be need for such a method.

Bringing order to randomness (or vice versa)

Finally, the RandomizeOrder subroutine is the reason I went to all this trouble in the first place:

```
Public Sub RandomizeOrder

Dim Swaps As Integer
Dim EntryIndex1, EntryIndex2 As Integer
Dim NumEntries As Integer = StackList.Count
Dim NumSwaps As Integer = NumEntries * 3
Dim TempEntry As Object

Randomize

For Swaps = 1 To NumSwaps
    EntryIndex1 = CInt(Int(Rnd * NumEntries))
    EntryIndex2 = CInt(Int(Rnd * NumEntries))
    TempEntry = StackList(EntryIndex1)
    StackList(EntryIndex1) = StackList(EntryIndex2)
    StackList(EntryIndex2) = TempEntry
Next

End Sub
```

How do you shuffle the entries in an ArrayList? Probably the easiest way, without creating a whole new ArrayList, is to pick two elements at random and swap them. And then do it again. And so on. How many times? Well, after trying different numbers, it seems that to really get 50 cards shuffled well, you need to do about 150 random swaps. With that ratio in mind, this routine loops for three times the number of elements in the ArrayList, picks two indexes at random, and then swaps the elements at those indexes.

Saving and compiling the new class

After I wrote this code, I saved it to a file named Rndstk.vb and put it in the black-jack/bin folder. Then, in a command window, I went to the folder and executed this command:

```
vbc /t:library rndstk.vb
```

This compiles the file using the Visual Basic command-line compiler into a DLL, the result of which is the creation of the Rndstk.dll file.

The Shoe Object

Now that I have a solid data structure to use, I'm ready to create the class for the Shoe object. This class, when it's instantiated, will actually create a deck with 52 Card objects representing the standard 52 cards (minus jokers) found in a deck of playing cards. This takes a big load off the ASP.NET page itself and allows the focus there to be on the game, not on handling the cards.

I decided to make the class for the Shoe object a separate Visual Basic component, just like the Randomized Stack. And I do it for the same reason: reusability. This is surely not the only page that could benefit from the use of a deck of standard playing cards. You might later want to create a Video Poker page, and this class would be just as useful there.

Try this on for size

The following code is what the class looks like. This code will go in its own file named playingcards.vb. I'll show you how to compile it after I describe the code.

```
Option Explicit
Option Strict

Imports System
Imports RandomizableStack

Namespace PlayingCards

    Public Structure Card
        Public Suit As String
        Public Name As String
        Public Value As Integer
    End Structure


    Public Class Shoe

        Private CardIndex As Integer
        Private CardDeck As RandStack = New RandStack

        Sub New(NumDecks As Integer)

        For CardIndex = 0 To (52 * NumDecks -1)

            Dim NewCard As Card = New Card

            Select Case (CardIndex Mod 4)
            Case 0
                NewCard.Suit = "Hearts"
            Case 1
                NewCard.Suit = "Diamonds"
            Case 2
                NewCard.Suit = "Clubs"
            Case 3
                NewCard.Suit = "Spades"
            End Select

            Select Case (CardIndex Mod 13)
            Case 0
                NewCard.Name = "Ace"
```

```
            NewCard.Value = 1
         Case 1
            NewCard.Name = "2"
            NewCard.Value = 2
         Case 2
            NewCard.Name = "3"
            NewCard.Value = 3
         Case 3
            NewCard.Name = "4"
            NewCard.Value = 4
         Case 4
            NewCard.Name = "5"
            NewCard.Value = 5
         Case 5
            NewCard.Name = "6"
            NewCard.Value = 6
         Case 6
            NewCard.Name = "7"
            NewCard.Value = 7
         Case 7
            NewCard.Name = "8"
            NewCard.Value = 8
         Case 8
            NewCard.Name = "9"
            NewCard.Value = 9
         Case 9
            NewCard.Name = "10"
            NewCard.Value = 10
         Case 10
            NewCard.Name = "Jack"
            NewCard.Value = 10
         Case 11
            NewCard.Name = "Queen"
            NewCard.Value = 10
         Case 12
            NewCard.Name = "King"
            NewCard.Value = 10
         End Select

         CardDeck.Push(NewCard)

      Next
      End Sub

      Public ReadOnly Property Count As Integer
      Get
         Return CardDeck.Count
      End Get
      End Property

      Public Sub Shuffle
      CardDeck.RandomizeOrder
```

```
    End Sub

    Public Function Draw As Card
        Return(CType(CardDeck.Pop,Card))
    End function

  End Class


End Namespace
```

Notice that this code includes an Imports statement for RandomizableStack. That's not a standard .NET namespace. That's the namespace I created with the Rndstk.vb file created in the last section. I import it here so that I can use that data structure to store the cards inside the Shoe class.

The namespace created in this file is called PlayingCards and includes two items: the Card structure, which you saw earlier in this chapter, and the Shoe class. The nice thing about doing it this way is that when this namespace is imported into an ASP.NET page, both the structure and the class that uses that structure are imported. The page can immediately begin creating and using Card objects and can receive Card objects back from methods in the Shoe class.

RandStack-ing the place

The private variable `CardDeck` holds an instance of the RandStack class and is created to hold the cards in the Shoe:

```
Private CardDeck As RandStack = New RandStack
```

The new constructor

The first and most important method of this class is one that no one will call directly. It's the constructor for the class. It is called when the class is instantiated. In Visual Basic, the constructor for a class is the subroutine that has the name New:

```
Sub New(NumDecks As Integer)
```

This constructor accepts one argument: the number of decks that should be created inside this shoe. The blackjack game page will call this constructor with 1, because I wrote it so that each new game starts off with a new, freshly shuffled deck. But it didn't have to be implemented that way. To make it more Vegas-like, you could pass a 7 in the constructor to create a seven-deck shoe, and then keep dealing one game after another out of that shoe until you get about two-thirds of the way through it and then reshuffle. If you were going to create a page that taught people how to count cards, for example, you might want to add this additional level of realism.

The other reason to offer the capability of a multideck shoe, once again, is for reusability. It makes the class much more flexible and adaptable to different applications without really adding much code at all.

Making cards

The entire contents of this subroutine are contained within a loop. This loop iterates once for each card that is to be added to the deck. It loops from 0 to 51 for a one-deck shoe, 0 to 103 for a two-deck shoe, and so on.

```
For CardIndex = 0 To (52 * NumDecks -1)

    Dim NewCard As Card = New Card
```

Each time through the loop, the second line creates a NewCard object from the Card structure. The constructor then fills that NewCard object with the appropriate information.

Mod makes it easy

I use the Mod operator to make this procedure as simple as possible. For those of you who slept through algebra, I'll briefly describe how Mod works. Mod does long division, just like you did in elementary school. But instead of giving you the answer, it gives you the *remainder*. So, for example, 11 divided by 5 is 2 with a remainder of 1. So 11 Mod 5 is 1.

Mod is a handy operator to use when you want to do something to every third element in an array or on every seventh iteration of a loop. And that's exactly what you want to do here:

```
Select Case (CardIndex Mod 4)
Case 0
   NewCard.Suit = "Hearts"
Case 1
   NewCard.Suit = "Diamonds"
Case 2
   NewCard.Suit = "Clubs"
Case 3
   NewCard.Suit = "Spades"
End Select
```

This Select Case statement uses the CardIndex Mod 4, which means that, because the loop begins at 0, the first card is hearts, the second card is diamonds, the fifth card is hearts again, and so on.

The same approach can be taken for the card Name and Value:

```
Select Case (CardIndex Mod 13)
Case 0
   NewCard.Name = "Ace"
   NewCard.Value = 1
```

```
        Case 1
          NewCard.Name = "2"
          NewCard.Value = 2
        Case 2
          NewCard.Name = "3"
          NewCard.Value = 3
        Case 3
          NewCard.Name = "4"
          NewCard.Value = 4
        Case 4
          NewCard.Name = "5"
          NewCard.Value = 5
        Case 5
          NewCard.Name = "6"
          NewCard.Value = 6
        Case 6
          NewCard.Name = "7"
          NewCard.Value = 7
        Case 7
          NewCard.Name = "8"
          NewCard.Value = 8
        Case 8
          NewCard.Name = "9"
          NewCard.Value = 9
        Case 9
          NewCard.Name = "10"
          NewCard.Value = 10
        Case 10
          NewCard.Name = "Jack"
          NewCard.Value = 10
        Case 11
          NewCard.Name = "Queen"
          NewCard.Value = 10
        Case 12
          NewCard.Name = "King"
          NewCard.Value = 10
      End Select
```

This doesn't end up organizing them the way they would be in a fresh, newly purchased deck of cards (organized first by suit and then by rank). Instead, the first
card is the Ace of Hearts followed by the 2 of Diamonds, then the 3 of Clubs, and so
on. The fourteenth card is the Ace of Diamonds, then the 2 of Clubs, and so on.

At any rate, suffice it to say that all the cards get created and assigned appropriate
values, for as many decks as were requested.

Adding the card to the shoe

The last line in the loop adds this NewCard to the CardDeck data structure:

```
CardDeck.Push(NewCard)
```

Count, shuffle, and draw

The last three items in the Shoe class are pretty straightforward. They essentially just wrap the functionality in the Randomized Stack class.

The Count property provides read-only access to the number of cards in the deck:

```
Public ReadOnly Property Count As Integer
Get
    Return CardDeck.Count
End Get
End Property
```

The Shuffle method just turns around and calls the RandomizeOrder method:

```
Public Sub Shuffle
CardDeck.RandomizeOrder
End Sub
```

The Draw method pops the top card off the deck and returns it to the calling routine. Because the objects in the CardDeck Randomized Stack are all of type object, I use the CType command to convert the object to a Card before returning it.

```
Public Function Draw As Card
    Return(CType(CardDeck.Pop,Card))
End function
```

Saving and compiling the Shoe class

This file should be saved under the name playingcards.vb in the blackjack\bin folder. And just as you did with rndstk.vb, you must compile it into a DLL. The only difference is that the class in this file makes use of classes in the rndstk.dll, so you must include a reference to it in the line you type to compile. You do that with the /r compiler option.

```
vbc /t:library /r:rndstk.dll playingcards.vb
```

Summing up the shoe

You may feel that my approach to creating the Shoe object was overly complicated. And it's true that I could easily have collapsed together the functionality of the Randomized Stack and the Shoe into one class. The main reason I didn't was to demonstrate how decoupling functionality can, in turn, make the final classes you create more reusable.

And while, in this case, how and where to do that is fairly straightforward, it isn't always that clear. When business objects are intertwined in complex and intricate ways and future plans for the software are hazy at best, it's often difficult to decide how best to decompose and decouple your classes. And you won't get it right the first time or even the fifteenth. But as you try to discover what works and what doesn't work, you'll gain the experience you need to make smaller mistakes in the future.

What's the final result? Well, now you have a handy class that you can instantiate in any page. When you do, it will automatically be holding one or more decks of standard playing cards in the shoe. Use the `Shuffle` method to mix them up and the `Draw` method to start pulling cards off the top. Pretty handy!

Now it's time to put your cards to work in a quick game of blackjack.

The Blackjack Page

The entire blackjack game takes place on a single page. This is a tribute to the dynamic nature of ASP.NET. Web Forms provide a flexible, easy-to-use environment for creating dynamic user interfaces. It's not uncommon to radically reduce the number of pages on your site when moving from static pages to ASP.NET.

Here's the complete source code for the Blackjack page. Put this in a file named blackjack.aspx and save it in the blackjack folder (not in \bin).

```
<%@ Page Language="VB" Explicit="true" Strict="true"
Debug="true" %>
<%@Import Namespace="PlayingCards" %>

<html>
<head/>

<script language="VB" runat=server>

Dim GameShoe As Shoe
Dim Player As Participant
Dim PlayerLabels As ArrayList

Dim Dealer As Participant
Dim DealerLabels As ArrayList

Class Participant
Public Hand As ArrayList

Sub New()
Hand = New ArrayList
End Sub

Function TotalValue As Integer
Dim i As Integer
Dim AceFlag As Boolean = False
Dim CurCard As Card

TotalValue = 0
```

```
For Each CurCard In Hand
    TotalValue = TotalValue + CurCard.Value
    If CurCard.Name = "Ace" Then
        AceFlag = True
    End If
Next
If AceFlag = True And TotalValue + 10 < 21 Then
    TotalValue += 10
End If
End Function

Sub UpdateLabels(CardLabels As ArrayList, TotalLabel As Label)
Dim i As Integer
Dim CurCard As Card
Dim CurLabel As Label

For i=0 To CardLabels.Count-1
    CurLabel = CType(CardLabels(i), Label)
    If i <= Hand.Count-1 Then
        CurCard = CType(Hand(i),Card)
        CurLabel.Text = CurCard.Name & " of " & CurCard.Suit
    Else
        CurLabel.Text = ""
    End If
Next
TotalLabel.Text = CStr(TotalValue)
End Sub

End Class


Sub Page_Load(sender As Object, e As EventArgs)

PlayerLabels = New ArrayList
DealerLabels = New ArrayList

PlayerLabels.Add(PCard1)
PlayerLabels.Add(PCard2)
PlayerLabels.Add(PCard3)
PlayerLabels.Add(PCard4)
PlayerLabels.Add(PCard5)
PlayerLabels.Add(PCard6)

DealerLabels.Add(DCard1)
DealerLabels.Add(DCard2)
DealerLabels.Add(DCard3)
DealerLabels.Add(DCard4)
DealerLabels.Add(DCard5)
DealerLabels.Add(DCard6)

If Not IsPostBack Then
    StartGame
Else
    GameShoe = CType(Session("GameShoe"),Shoe)
```

```
      Player = CType(Session("Player"),Participant)
      Dealer = CType(Session("Dealer"),Participant)
End If

End Sub

Sub Page_PreRender(sender As Object, e As EventArgs)
Session("GameShoe") = GameShoe
Session("Player") = Player
Session("Dealer") = Dealer
End Sub

Sub StartGame
GameShoe = Nothing
Player = Nothing
Dealer = Nothing

GameShoe = New Shoe(1)
GameShoe.Shuffle
Player = New Participant
Dealer = New Participant

Player.Hand.Add(GameShoe.Draw)
Player.Hand.Add(GameShoe.Draw)
Dealer.Hand.Add(GameShoe.Draw)

Player.UpdateLabels(PlayerLabels, PTotal)
Dealer.UpdateLabels(DealerLabels, DTotal)

Message.Text = ""
End Sub


Sub EndGame
Hit.Enabled = False
Stand.Enabled = False
PlayAgain.visible=True
Yes.visible=True
No.Visible=True
End Sub

Sub DetermineWinner
If Dealer.TotalValue = Player.TotalValue Then
   Message.Text = "A Push! No Winner..."
ElseIf Dealer.TotalValue = 21 Then
   Message.Text = "Dealer Has 21...Dealer Wins!"
ElseIf Dealer.TotalValue > 21 Then
   Message.Text = "Dealer Busted...You Win!"
ElseIf Dealer.TotalValue > Player.TotalValue Then
   Message.Text = "Dealer Wins..."
Else
   Message.Text = "You Win! Congratulations!"
End If
End Sub
```

```
Sub DealerPlay
Dealer.Hand.Add(GameShoe.Draw)

Do While Dealer.TotalValue < 17
   Dealer.Hand.Add(GameShoe.Draw)
Loop

Dealer.UpdateLabels(DealerLabels, DTotal)

DetermineWinner
EndGame
End Sub

Sub Hit_Click(Sender As Object, E As EventArgs)

Player.Hand.Add(GameShoe.Draw)
Player.UpdateLabels(PlayerLabels, PTotal)

If Player.TotalValue = 21 Then
   Message.Text = "You Have 21...You Win!"
   EndGame
ElseIf Player.TotalValue > 21
   Message.Text = "You Busted...Dealer Wins!"
   EndGame
End If
End Sub

Sub Stand_Click(Sender As Object, E As EventArgs)
Message.Text = "You decided to stand on " & _
   CStr(Player.TotalValue)
DealerPlay
End Sub


Sub Yes_Click(Sender As Object, E As EventArgs)
Yes.visible = False
No.visible = False
PlayAgain.visible = False
Hit.Enabled = True
Stand.Enabled = True
StartGame
End Sub


Sub No_Click(Sender As Object, E As EventArgs)
Yes.visible = False
No.visible = False
PlayAgain.text = "Thanks For Playing!"
End Sub

</script>
```

```
<body>
<h1>Blackjack</h1>
<p>Your goal is to try to get closer to 21 than the dealer
without going over.
As you begin you have two cards and you get to see the dealer's
first card. Face cards count as 10 and Aces can count as either
1 or 11 (whatever works best for you). You can click Hit to
draw another card or click Stand to keep your current
total.</p>

<form action="blackjack.aspx" method="post" runat="server">

<table width=100%>
<tr><td align="left" valign="top">
<h2>Your Hand</h2>
Card 1: <asp:label id="PCard1" runat="server"/><br>
Card 2: <asp:label id="PCard2" runat="server"/><br>
Card 3: <asp:label id="PCard3" runat="server"/><br>
Card 4: <asp:label id="PCard4" runat="server"/><br>
Card 5: <asp:label id="PCard5" runat="server"/><br>
Card 6: <asp:label id="PCard6" runat="server"/><br>
<br>
Your Total: <asp:label id="PTotal" runat="server"/><br><br>
<asp:button id="Hit" type=submit text="  Hit  "
OnClick="Hit_Click" runat="server"/>
 
<asp:button id="Stand" type=submit text="Stand"
OnClick="Stand_Click" runat="server"/>
</td>
<td align="left" valign="top">
<h2>Dealer Hand</h2>
Card 1: <asp:label id="DCard1" runat="server"/><br>
Card 2: <asp:label id="DCard2" runat="server"/><br>
Card 3: <asp:label id="DCard3" runat="server"/><br>
Card 4: <asp:label id="DCard4" runat="server"/><br>
Card 5: <asp:label id="DCard5" runat="server"/><br>
Card 6: <asp:label id="DCard6" runat="server"/><br>
<br>
Dealer Total: <asp:label id="DTotal" runat="server"/><br>
</td>
</tr>
</table>
<br>
<asp:label id="Message" runat="server"/>
<br><br>
<asp:label id="PlayAgain" runat="server" text="Play Again?"
visible=false />
  
<asp:button id="Yes" type=submit text="Yes" OnClick="Yes_Click"
runat="server" visible=false /> 
```

```
<asp:button id="No" type=submit text=" No " OnClick="No_Click"
runat="server" visible=false />
</form>
</center>

</body>
</html>
```

The preceding is a single page, but not a simple page! However, the page can easily be divided into its component parts, which act as building blocks for putting the whole thing together. The next several sections describe these building blocks and how they come together to create the complete game.

Getting started

The beginning of the listing has a few important things to note. First, there's an Import directive to include the PlayingCards namespace that contains both the Card structure and the Shoe class:

```
<%@Import Namespace="PlayingCards" %>
```

Then, just inside the <script> tag, some page-level variables are declared:

```
<script language="VB" runat=server>

Dim GameShoe As Shoe
Dim Player As Participant
Dim PlayerLabels As ArrayList

Dim Dealer As Participant
Dim DealerLabels As ArrayList
```

GameShoe is a variable that will hold an instance of the Shoe class and will be the collection of cards used to deal this game.

Player and Dealer are both instances of the Participant class that is created on this page. I'll discuss this class in the next section.

PlayerLabels and DealerLabels are ArrayLists that will contain all the label controls on this page used for displaying the names of the cards in the player and dealer hands. By putting the labels in an array list, they become easier to reference by index. This technique is one that is used to make up for the fact that Web Forms don't include the ability to create control arrays in the same way that you could in Visual Basic 6. You'll see how this works later when I describe the code that uses these ArrayLists.

The participant

As I began developing this page, I found myself doing the same work twice in lots of places. Both the player and the dealer share several common needs for data storage and functionality, so I decided to centralize this and thus created the Participant class. This class brings together the common functionality and data-storage needs into one place and makes the code easier to read and understand. Another big benefit of creating this class is that if, in the future, this page is extended to support multiple players, the process will be simplified, because you can just instantiate additional Participant objects.

A hand in the participant is worth . . .

If the Participant class were something I felt I could generalize to use in other games as well, I could create a DLL for it and import it as I did with the PlayingCards namespace. But for now, I've just included it within the page itself, as shown here:

```
Class Participant

Public Hand As ArrayList

Sub New()
Hand = New ArrayList
End Sub
```

The most important part of this page is the Public Hand ArrayList. It is declared and then, in the constructor for the class, instantiated.

Once the Participant-type object is created, Hand can be freely accessed and manipulated using all the standard ArrayList methods. No attempt was made here (as there was with Shoe) to hide this structure and control access to it. This approach makes it easy to implement and intuitive to use, but also limits the control you'll have over this structure. In fact, you'll have no control over this structure. But, for this use, I decided that was okay—especially because I am creating it on this page for the exclusive use in this game. If you do generalize this class in the future for other games, you definitely want to revisit the question of making Hand public.

The two methods in this class provide functionality to support the Hand ArrayList, which is assumed to contain Card-type objects.

Adding up the TotalValue

The first of these methods, TotalValue, simply loops through all the cards in the Hand, sums up their value, and returns the result:

```
Function TotalValue As Integer
Dim i As Integer
Dim AceFlag As Boolean = False
Dim CurCard As Card
```

```
TotalValue = 0
For Each CurCard In Hand
   TotalValue = TotalValue + CurCard.Value
   If CurCard.Name = "Ace" Then
      AceFlag = True
   End If
Next
If AceFlag = True And TotalValue + 10 < 21 Then
   TotalValue += 10
End If
End Function
```

Notice that this is the code that handles the ace's possible alternate values. The rule is that an ace can count as either 1 or 11 at the participant's option. But in reality, if you have two aces and count them both as 11, your total is a busting 22. So you'll only ever count, at most, one ace as 11. And, even then, you'll only do it if it doesn't cause you to bust.

With that in mind, this code adds up the total of all the cards in the hand, setting a flag to true if at least one of them is an ace. The aces are, by default, counted as 1, so the code after the loop checks to see if adding an additional 10 to the total (turning one of the aces into 11 instead of 1) causes the participant to bust. If not, 10 is added to the total.

Some user interfacing: UpdateLabels

The UpdateLabels method takes the internal data structures and shows them to the user using the labels on the page.

Typically, when you create business objects, you make a strict line of division between the user interface and the business rules. In the case of the UpdateLabels method, I cheated. I'll explain why after I describe how it works.

```
Sub UpdateLabels(CardLabels As ArrayList, TotalLabel As Label)
Dim i As Integer
Dim CurCard As Card
Dim CurLabel As Label

For i=0 To CardLabels.Count-1
   CurLabel = CType(CardLabels(i), Label)
   If i <= Hand.Count-1 Then
      CurCard = CType(Hand(i),Card)
      CurLabel.Text = CurCard.Name & " of " & CurCard.Suit
   Else
      CurLabel.Text = ""
   End If
Next
TotalLabel.Text = CStr(TotalValue)
End Sub

End Class
```

UpdateLabels accepts an ArrayList of label controls and a single label control. It then goes through all the labels in the ArrayList and fills them in with the name of the cards in this participant's Hand. Any labels that don't have corresponding cards in the Hand are set to the empty string to clear out any previous values that might be there.

Then, to top it off, UpdateLabels calls the `TotalValue` method and plots that information into the label sent in the second argument to this method.

This method is clearly designed to update the user interface with the current values stored in the business object. And, typically, that would disqualify it from being a part of the business object. But, in my mind, three mitigating factors justified making it a method:

✦ If I didn't include the subroutine in the class, I'd have two other options: I'd have to create two nearly identical subroutines on the page to update the UI for the dealer and another to update the UI for the player. That's no good. The other option is to generalize the function on the page to accept a Participant object in addition to the two other arguments and then use it to fill in the labels. That would work, but I felt this method was simpler and more straightforward.

✦ This class is a part of this page, rather than included in a DLL that may be used on other pages (with different user interface needs). This means that its scope and use is limited to begin with. In this case, the Participant class was created more for code organization and readability than for reuse. Therefore, the issue of blurring the line between business object and user interface is less significant.

✦ The method doesn't directly access the user interface. I wrote it so that it would work with any ArrayList of labels and any individual label. This means that although the method technically does a user interface task, it is not directly tied to a specific user interface implementation.

Whether you agree with the decision or not, that's the way I did it. If it bothers you, it would be relatively easy to pull the subroutine out of the class, add the Participant-type object as another argument, and tweak the code to use the Hand in the argument.

The body

I'm going to go a little out of order here. I think that when you are trying to figure out someone else's code, you should look at three things, in this order: the classes they create and use, the body of the page, and the code written to respond to page events.

The key classes, Shoe and Participant, are discussed in previous sections of this chapter. Before I dive into the event code, it's important that you take a look at the body of the page so that you can see the user interface and the controls that are likely to trigger events:

```
<body>
<h1>Blackjack</h1>
<p>Your goal is to try to get closer to 21 than the
dealer without going over. As you begin you have two cards
and you get to see the dealer's first card. Face cards count
as 10 and Aces can count as either 1 or 11 (whatever works
best for you). You can click Hit to draw another card or
click Stand to keep your current total.</p>

<form action="blackjack.aspx" method="post" runat="server">

<table width=100%>
<tr><td align="left" valign="top">
<h2>Your Hand</h2>
Card 1: <asp:label id="PCard1" runat="server"/><br>
Card 2: <asp:label id="PCard2" runat="server"/><br>
Card 3: <asp:label id="PCard3" runat="server"/><br>
Card 4: <asp:label id="PCard4" runat="server"/><br>
Card 5: <asp:label id="PCard5" runat="server"/><br>
Card 6: <asp:label id="PCard6" runat="server"/><br>
<br>
Your Total: <asp:label id="PTotal" runat="server"/><br><br>
<asp:button id="Hit" type=submit text="  Hit  "
OnClick="Hit_Click" runat="server"/>
 
<asp:button id="Stand" type=submit text="Stand"
OnClick="Stand_Click" runat="server"/>
</td>
<td align="left" valign="top">
<h2>Dealer Hand</h2>
Card 1: <asp:label id="DCard1" runat="server"/><br>
Card 2: <asp:label id="DCard2" runat="server"/><br>
Card 3: <asp:label id="DCard3" runat="server"/><br>
Card 4: <asp:label id="DCard4" runat="server"/><br>
Card 5: <asp:label id="DCard5" runat="server"/><br>
Card 6: <asp:label id="DCard6" runat="server"/><br>
<br>
Dealer Total: <asp:label id="DTotal" runat="server"/><br>
</td>
</tr>
</table>
<br>
<asp:label id="Message" runat="server"/>
<br><br>
<asp:label id="PlayAgain" runat="server" text="Play Again?"
visible=false />
  
<asp:button id="Yes" type=submit text="Yes" OnClick="Yes_Click"
runat="server" visible=false /> 
```

```
<asp:button id="No" type=submit text=" No " OnClick="No_Click"
runat="server" visible=false />
</form>
</center>

</body>
```

After displaying the header and some instructions, a table is used to organize all the pieces on this page. The table essentially divides the page into two sections vertically. On the left is the player's side, which contains labels to show the player cards and a total. In addition, buttons are included so that the player can indicate their preference to Hit or Stand. On the right is the dealer's side, and its controls are identical, with the omission of the Hit/Stand buttons.

Below the table is a label called Message, which is used to tell the user the final result of the game — whether they won or lost.

Finally, there are three controls that are initially hidden and only made visible (in code) when the game is complete. A label asks the user if they'd like to play again, and the Yes and No buttons allow the user to respond.

Initialization and object juggling

The first three subroutines on this page are designed to initialize, store, and retrieve important information that is used from one server round trip to the next. The first two subroutines are events that are triggered in the life cycle of processing the page: Page_Load and Page_PreRender. The third is a subroutine called from the Page_Load event: StartGame.

Creating an array of labels

The Page_Load event is used to initialize variables and instantiate objects. The first task in this page is to create an ArrayList to hold the label controls that display the cards in the hands of the player and dealer on the page:

```
Sub Page_Load(sender As Object, e As EventArgs)

PlayerLabels = New ArrayList
DealerLabels = New ArrayList

PlayerLabels.Add(PCard1)
PlayerLabels.Add(PCard2)
PlayerLabels.Add(PCard3)
PlayerLabels.Add(PCard4)
PlayerLabels.Add(PCard5)
PlayerLabels.Add(PCard6)

DealerLabels.Add(DCard1)
DealerLabels.Add(DCard2)
DealerLabels.Add(DCard3)
```

```
DealerLabels.Add(DCard4)
DealerLabels.Add(DCard5)
DealerLabels.Add(DCard6)
```

Most of the time, when you work with controls on a page, you simply use their name and access their properties and methods. But sometimes it is preferable to work with a set of controls in a different way.

In the section titled "The body," previously in this chapter, I pointed out that this page has six labels to show the cards of the player, and another six labels to show the cards of the dealer. And, in a section called "Some user interfacing: UpdateLabels," earlier in this chapter, I described the UpdateLabels method of the Participant class. This method updates the labels on the page with the names of the cards that are in the Participant's hand. The only catch is that this method requires that the user send the labels in the form of an ArrayList. That simplifies the updating of those labels because a loop can be used, along with an index number, to walk through each one. Here, in the Page_Load event, is where that ArrayList of labels, for both the player and the dealer, is created.

The PlayerLabels and DealerLabels ArrayLists are instantiated and promptly filled with the controls on the page, in the appropriate order. This happens the first time the page loads and on every round-trip thereafter.

Creating and initializing GameShoe, Player, and Dealer

The next piece of code, a common site in the Page_Load event, is an If...Then statement that checks Not IsPostBack. This Page property determines whether this is the first time the page has been retrieved or not.

```
If Not IsPostBack Then
    StartGame
```

In this case, if this is the first time the page has been retrieved, the StartGame subroutine is called. Here, all the objects needed for the game are instantiated and all the variables initialized:

```
Sub StartGame
GameShoe = Nothing
Player = Nothing
Dealer = Nothing

GameShoe = New Shoe(1)
GameShoe.Shuffle
Player = New Participant
Dealer = New Participant

Player.Hand.Add(GameShoe.Draw)
Player.Hand.Add(GameShoe.Draw)
Dealer.Hand.Add(GameShoe.Draw)

Player.UpdateLabels(PlayerLabels, PTotal)
```

```
Dealer.UpdateLabels(DealerLabels, DTotal)

Message.Text = ""
End Sub
```

This subroutine is called from the `Page_Load` event and then again, later, if the user wants to start over and play a new game. So, in case the GameShoe, Player, and Dealer variables already contain objects, they are set to Nothing to clear them out. Then the GameShoe is instantiated as a new Shoe class. A 1 is passed to the constructor, indicating that a one-deck shoe should be created. Then the cards in the shoe are shuffled.

Player and Dealer are each instantiated as Participants.

Next the GameShoe's `Draw` method is called three times and the result (a Card object) is added to the hands of the player and dealer.

UpdateLabels is called separately for each participant passing the appropriate ArrayList and the label control holding the card totals. This causes the labels on the page to be updated, showing the two cards in the player's hand and the single card in the dealer's hand.

Storing and retrieving the objects from Session variables

Here's a timeline of the events that will happen on this page:

1. The page is requested and loaded for the first time. The `Page_Load` event occurs and the `StartGame` subroutine is called. This subroutine creates and instantiates the GameShoe, Player, and Dealer objects, preparing them to be ready for play.

2. The `Page_PreRender` event occurs. This event happens after all the server-side code has executed and just before the final HTML is sent to the browser. It's the last opportunity to do anything. I use this event to store my key objects in `Session` variables.

3. The first server round trip occurs. The `Page_Load` event is executed. The objects are retrieved from their `Session` variables immediately so that they'll be available to any other events that occur.

4. After all events are done, the `Page_PreRender` event occurs again. And again, the objects are stored away in `Session` variables for safekeeping until the next server round trip.

The `StartGame` subroutine was discussed in the previous section. The code in the `Page_PreRender` event looks like this:

```
Sub Page_PreRender(sender As Object, e As EventArgs)
Session("GameShoe") = GameShoe
Session("Player") = Player
Session("Dealer") = Dealer
End Sub
```

The objects are placed in `Session` variables and stored in the server's memory until the page needs them again.

Then, in the `Page_Load` event, if this is a post-back, this code executes:

```
Else
    GameShoe = CType(Session("GameShoe"),Shoe)
    Player = CType(Session("Player"),Participant)
    Dealer = CType(Session("Dealer"),Participant)
End If
```

This code does just the opposite of the code in the `Page_PreRender` event — it gets the objects out of the `Session` variables. Because `Session` variables are not typed, a `CType` command is used to assure the proper conversion back into their associated classes.

This approach, using `Page_Load` and `Page_PreRender` to store and retrieve commonly used global variables and objects, is very handy and can be applied to any page that needs to remember things from one round-trip to the next. If you only need to store variable values, then you can use `ViewState` instead of `Session` and avoid taking up precious server memory. Unfortunately, you can't store objects in `ViewState` unless they implement the ISerializable interface.

Responding to events

All of the work thus far has been in an effort to get to this point: a blackjack table presented to the user and ready for them to play the game.

Now the ball is in the user's court. They look at the cards they were dealt, look at the dealer's first card, and make a decision: Hit or Stand.

Hit me

If the user has a low total, or is feeling lucky, the user is likely to click the Hit button. When the user does this, the following subroutine is executed:

```
Sub Hit_Click(Sender As Object, E As EventArgs)

Player.Hand.Add(GameShoe.Draw)
Player.UpdateLabels(PlayerLabels, PTotal)

If Player.TotalValue = 21 Then
    Message.Text = "You Have 21...You Win!"
    EndGame
ElseIf Player.TotalValue > 21 Then
    Message.Text = "You Busted...Dealer Wins!"
    EndGame
End If
End Sub
```

A card is drawn from the GameShoe and added to the player's hand. The labels on the page are updated. That's all there is to a hit!

However, after the user has a new card, there are some conditions to check. For example, does the player have 21? If so, the player wins and the game is over. Conversely, if this draw put the user over the edge and the user's total is greater than 21, then the player has busted and therefore loses.

I believe I'll stand

After the user achieves a good total, they'll click the Stand button. That event triggers this subroutine:

```
Sub Stand_Click(Sender As Object, E As EventArgs)
Message.Text = "You decided to stand on " & _
    CStr(Player.TotalValue)
DealerPlay
End Sub
```

The Message label is updated to indicate the user's decision to stand, and the value they chose to stand on. Because clicking Stand represents the end of the player's turn, the DealerPlay subroutine is called from here.

The dealer's turn

If the player gets exactly 21 or busts, the result is a forgone conclusion and there's no reason for the dealer to even play. The dealer only goes when the player decides to stand on a particular total. This is the subroutine that gets called when that happens:

```
Sub DealerPlay
Dealer.Hand.Add(GameShoe.Draw)

Do While Dealer.TotalValue < 17
    Dealer.Hand.Add(GameShoe.Draw)
Loop

Dealer.UpdateLabels(DealerLabels, DTotal)

DetermineWinner
EndGame
End Sub
```

A card is drawn from the GameShoe and added to the dealer's hand. Next, a Do While loop checks to see if the total is less than 17. If it is, the dealer keeps on drawing. This is the standard strategy that dealers are required to follow in casinos.

Once this loop completes, the labels on the page are updated to show the dealer's new cards.

The DetermineWinner subroutine is called to do just that. After the DetermineWinner subroutine executes, the EndGame subroutine is called.

Who won?

The player chose to stand and the dealer did its drawing. So what's the result? The DetermineWinner subroutine does the comparisons to see who won and displays the result in the Message label:

```
Sub DetermineWinner
If Dealer.TotalValue = Player.TotalValue Then
    Message.Text = "A Push! No Winner..."
ElseIf Dealer.TotalValue = 21 Then
    Message.Text = "Dealer Has 21...Dealer Wins!"
ElseIf Dealer.TotalValue > 21 Then
    Message.Text = "Dealer Busted...You Win!"
ElseIf Dealer.TotalValue > Player.TotalValue Then
    Message.Text = "Dealer Wins..."
Else
    Message.Text = "You Win! Congratulations!"
End If
End Sub
```

This code doesn't need to check for a player 21 or a player bust because those conditions were already handled in the Hit_Click subroutine. So here the only options are push, dealer with 21, player with 21, dealer wins, and player wins.

Ending the game

No matter who wins or loses, the game always ends in the same way:

```
Sub EndGame
Hit.Enabled = False
Stand.Enabled = False
PlayAgain.visible=True
Yes.visible=True
No.Visible=True
End Sub
```

The Hit and Stand buttons can't be used now, so they are disabled. However, the PlayAgain label along with the Yes and No buttons are made visible.

The label asks the user if they'd like to play again. If the answer is no, No_Click is called:

```
Sub No_Click(Sender As Object, E As EventArgs)
Yes.visible = False
No.visible = False
PlayAgain.text = "Thanks For Playing!"
End Sub
```

The buttons are made invisible again and the PlayAgain text is changed to thank the user for playing.

If the answer to PlayAgain is Yes, `Yes_Click` is executed:

```
Sub Yes_Click(Sender As Object, E As EventArgs)
Yes.visible = False
No.visible = False
PlayAgain.visible = False
Hit.Enabled = True
Stand.Enabled = True
StartGame
End Sub
```

All the originally invisible controls become invisible again. Hit and Stand are enabled and the `StartGame` subroutine is called to kick off the process once again.

Room to Grow

This chapter is a running start, but you certainly have lots of opportunities to take this project and make it your own. Here are some ideas for enhancing it:

✦ As already mentioned, the user interface is, well, simple. You could easily add some pizzazz by using either graphics or HTML tables to emulate the look of cards on a blackjack table.

✦ As for the game itself, it would be significantly more fun if you could track how you're doing on an ongoing basis. You could do that by showing wins and losses, but probably the better way to go to simulate a real casino is to give the user a certain amount of play money when they start and allow them to choose how much of that money they want to gamble on each hand. If they wager $10 and win, they get their original amount back plus an additional $10. You could store the user's current cash in a `Session` variable.

✦ After you implement wagering, you could add some rules to give the user more options in the game. Doubling down is an option the player has only once per hand — after being dealt the first two cards. When the player doubles down, they double their bet with the understanding that they'll receive one additional card and then stand on whatever that total is. For example, if the player is dealt a 6 and a 5, for a total of 11 with their first two cards, it is a good idea to double down and hope that the next card is a face card. This allows the player to win twice as much as they would otherwise. Of course, if the next card is a 3, the player cannot hit and is forced to stand on a very weak 14.

✦ Splitting is another popular option that is also available only after the first two cards are dealt. In addition, you can only split if the first two cards are the same, say two 8s. When you split, you put a sum of money equal to your original bet on the table beside your original bet. The two cards are split up and form the foundation for two *separate* hands. The player then chooses to hit (as many times as they like) or stand, as usual, on each hand individually, trying to get close to 21 with each hand. Remember that when you split, both hands are playing against the dealer. It's possible to win both hands, lose both, or win one and lose the other.

Summary

Blackjack is a game with just enough complexity to make a coding project interesting. For this project, I used it to demonstrate many different techniques, such as how to create a dynamic user interface with Web forms and user controls and how to use an ArrayList to create a more flexible version of the stack control. Next, I covered how to create a reusable data structure and a reusable component that encapsulates all the complexity for a particular task (in this case, initializing and handling decks of playing cards). This cleans up and simplifies the code in the main page to focus on its task—the game. Then I compiled simple Visual Basic components with the command line compiler and used them within an ASP.NET page. In addition, I used classes within a page to simplify and organize the code (as I did here with Participant) and the Mod operator to process certain iterations within a loop.

✦   ✦   ✦

Chatty Discussion Forum

Part of the promise of the Web was to open a whole new and different communications medium for people to share thoughts and ideas. And while the Web has leveled the playing field, to some degree, for small businesses, in terms of presenting themselves to the public, the average person has been left with little more than a "home page" that no one visits. Communication, to be interesting, has to be two-way, and the Web seems very entrenched in the idea of displaying information, not *sharing* information.

However, there are ways around this problem. Many sites, particularly those interested in creating more of a community-like atmosphere, have begun providing Web-based discussion forums. These forums allow people to browse categories that interest them and then read the messages other visitors have posted there. They can even post their own messages and carry on a kind of disconnected, two-way conversation. This very compelling feature can attract new visitors and is particularly effective at getting current visitors to return to your site on a very regular basis.

So is it possible to create a discussion forum in ASP.NET? You bet! In fact, you might be surprised at how easy it is. This chapter shows you how to create a simple discussion forum called Chatty, which provides a set of topics that you define and then allows users to create new threads within that topic. Then users can post messages to threads and respond to the posts from other users.

A Quick Walkthrough of Chatty

To give you a better idea of how Chatty Discussion Forum works, I'll provide you with a quick walkthrough of the application, from the user's perspective. I encourage you to pull the application off this book's companion Web site and try it out as I describe it.

The first page is called Topics (see Figure 30-1).

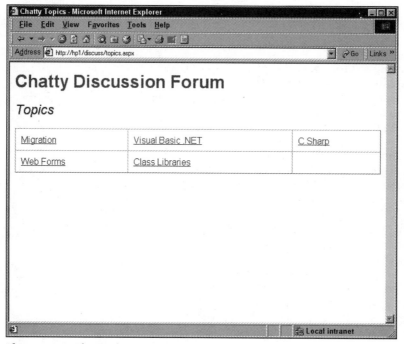

Figure 30-1: The Topics page

Topics simply presents a list of the discussion topics available, from which the user can click whatever looks interesting to them.

After choosing a topic, the user is presented with the Threads page (see Figure 30-2).

Here, all the discussion threads under the chosen topic are presented. In addition, a link is provided at the bottom of the page to create a new thread.

If the user clicks the name of an existing thread, they promptly arrive at the Messages page (see Figure 30-3).

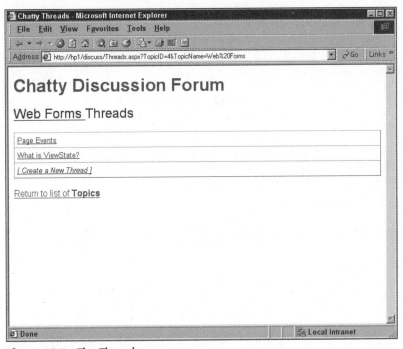

Figure 30-2: The Threads page

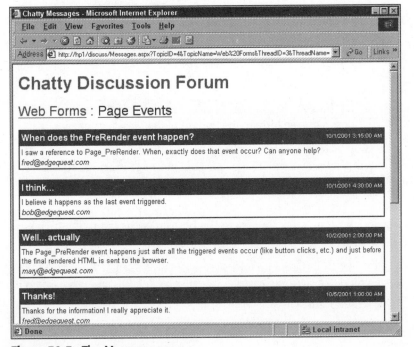

Figure 30-3: The Messages page

At the top of the Messages page, you see that the topic and thread chosen appear, so that users never loose track of exactly what messages they are looking at.

Then, each message is listed in its own tidy box, organized in chronological order from the first posting to the most recent.

At the bottom of the Messages page is a form that allows the user to post their own message to this thread (see Figure 30-4).

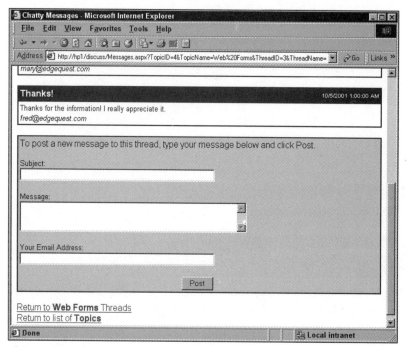

Figure 30-4: The post message form at the bottom of the Messages page

If the user enters a message and clicks Post, the message is added to the bottom of the list as the most recent posting.

Finally, if you go back to the Threads page (by clicking the link at the bottom of the Messages page), you can click the link at the bottom of the list to create a new thread. This takes you to the NewThread page (see Figure 30-5).

Here, you enter not only the name for the thread you want to create, but also the first message you'd like to appear there. When you click Post, you are taken back to the Threads page to see your new thread listed.

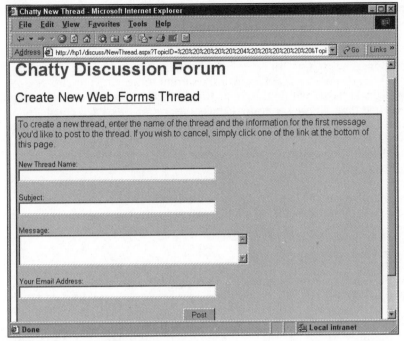

Figure 30-5: The NewThread page

Designing a Chatty Discussion Forum

When you begin to create an application like a discussion forum, it's always a good idea to go out and find similar applications on the Web and try them out. You'll find ideas for design, user interface, features you hadn't considered, and much more. You'll also be able to compare and contrast different approaches and choose which will work best for your own application.

Hierarchical or flat?

If you go out and look at discussion forums, you'll probably be surprised at the variety of different approaches and user interfaces. Some, particularly those designed for a more technical audience, are fully hierarchical. You can respond to any individual message, and your message will appear under that message. Then, other people can respond to that message and appear alongside your message, or they can respond to your message and appear under your message. This is a very detailed way of carrying on conversations and provides the most flexibility to those browsing to either follow a particular line of discussion or ignore it. The problem with a fully hierarchical approach is that it's easy to get confused and not post a message at precisely the right spot. For example, you might want to just add a message to the main discussion, but accidentally post it as a response to the last message you read.

Another approach is to go with a more flattened hierarchy. You are probably going to want to offer discussions under several different topics on your site. So that represents one level. Then, within the topic, there might be several discussions going on at the same time. These separate discussions, or *threads,* each consist of a string of messages that appears one after the other, in the order that they were posted. You can't post a response to a specific message. You simply post a new message in the same thread. This approach is really clear to the user and works for all levels of user sophistication.

After using both systems, I decided to go with the latter approach. I like it a lot better and, as a bonus, it's more straightforward to create.

Storing the discussions

The next big issue is more of a physical design question. Where do I want to store the posted messages? I could use XML. It makes sense because the data needs to be easily read and displayed but doesn't have heavy update requirements.

Another approach would be to store the information in a database. And then, of course, the question becomes, which database?

In the end, I chose to implement Chatty using an Access database. Some Web hosts have trouble with applications that create and modify text files on their servers, so using XML might limit the places where Chatty could be deployed.

Of course, if you plan to have a high volume of messages posted and users browsing, you might want to consider upgrading to SQL Server, but the bridge between the two is easy to cross in the future, and Access is an easy place to get started.

Creating the Database

Once you've decided to go with a relational database, you're going to have to figure out how you want to organize the information into tables and columns.

Chatty has two levels of organization for its messages:

✦ Topics are the highest level and are chosen by the creator of the site.

✦ Threads are essentially subtopics that the user can create.

Messages, then, are always posted by the user to a thread, which in turn is under a topic.

These storage needs can be accommodated with three tables: Topics, Threads, and Messages.

Topics is the highest level, but is also the simplest. All you have to track is the topic's name. Table 30-1 shows the columns and data types.

Table 30-1 **The Topics table**	
Field Name	*Data Type*
TopicID (Primary Key)	AutoNumber
Name	Text

The Threads table is a little more complicated, but not much (see Table 30-2).

Table 30-2 **The Threads table**	
Field Name	*Data Type*
ThreadID (Primary Key)	AutoNumber
Name	Text
Topic	Number

The Topic column holds the TopicID of the row in the Topics table with which this thread is associated.

The Name column holds the name of the thread. It should have some specific attributes set, as specified in Table 30-3.

Table 30-3 **The Thread's Name column attributes**	
Attribute	*Value*
Required	Yes
Allow Zero Length	No
Indexed	Yes (No Duplicates)

By setting these attributes, you assure that whenever a new row is added, the Name field is filled in and that it is filled in with a value that is different from any of the other names already in the table. In other words, all threads must have a unique name.

The same attributes could have been set for the Topics table's Name field, but because it's the site administrator (and not users) who will be filling that table in, you can probably assume that the administrator will assure that the topics are right.

The Messages table has the most columns (see Table 30-4).

Table 30-4 **The Messages table**	
Field Name	**Data Type**
MessageID (Primary Key)	AutoNumber
Subject	Text
Message	Memo
Author	Text
Posted	Date/Time
Thread	Number

As in an e-mail message, the Subject line is used to title and summarize the contents of the message itself. The author of the message will be stored in Chatty as the e-mail address they enter. If your site authenticates its users, then you'll be able to put their username or their chosen handle into the Author field instead.

The Posted column is important. It enables you to organize the messages in the right order within a thread.

Finally, Thread holds the ThreadID of the row in the Threads table with which this message is associated.

Seeding the Database

In order to test the pages as you create them, you'll want to put some of your own data in the database to get you started. While you're in Microsoft Access creating the tables, go ahead and add a few topics, one or more threads for each topic and a message or two for each thread. Make sure the foreign keys (like the Topic column in the Thread table and the Thread column in the Message table) refer to the primary keys in rows you've already created in the associated tables.

If you decide to use this completed application in your own Web sites, you'll have to use Microsoft Access to enter your topics. I haven't included a page to add or update topics since the discussion topics are usually created once by the Web site administrator and aren't often changed after that. Of course, if you do want easy access to update or add new topics, you can always use the code I've provided here for creating threads as a starting point for a new page that does what you want.

Picking a Topic

When a user visits Chatty, the first decision they have to make is which topic they want to browse. The Topics.aspx page, shown here, provides that opportunity:

```
<%@ Page Explicit="True" Language="VB"
Debug="True" %>
<%@ Import Namespace="System.Data" %>
<%@ Import Namespace="System.Data.OleDb" %>

<Script Runat="Server">
Sub Page_Load( s As Object, e As EventArgs )
If Not isPostBack Then
  Dim TopicConnection As OleDbConnection
  Dim TopicCommand As OleDbCommand
  TopicConnection = New OleDbConnection( _
    "Provider=Microsoft.Jet.OLEDB.4.0;" & _
    "Data Source=" & _
    "c:\inetpub\wwwroot\Discuss\DiscussDB.mdb")
  TopicCommand = New OleDbCommand( _
    "Select TopicID, Name from Topics", _
    TopicConnection )
  TopicConnection.Open()
  TopicDataList.DataSource = _
    TopicCommand.ExecuteReader()
  TopicDataList.DataBind()
  TopicConnection.Close()
End If
End Sub

Sub SelectTopic(s As Object, _
  e As DataListCommandEventArgs)
Dim TopicID,TopicName As String
TopicName = e.CommandArgument
TopicID = _
  TopicDataList.DataKeys.Item( _
    e.Item.ItemIndex).toString()
Response.Redirect("Threads.aspx?TopicID=" & _
  TopicID & "&TopicName=" & TopicName)
End Sub

</Script>

<html>
```

```
<head><title>Chatty Topics</title></head>
<body>
<font face="arial">
<h1><font color="DarkRed">
Chatty Discussion Forum</font></h1>
<font size=5><i>Topics</i></font>
<form Runat="Server">

<asp:DataList id="TopicDataList"
cellpadding=10 cellspacing=0
gridlines="both" RepeatColumns="3"
RepeatDirection="Horizontal"
Width="100%" DataKeyField="TopicID"
OnItemCommand="SelectTopic"
Runat="Server">

<ItemTemplate>
  <asp:LinkButton
  id="TopicLink"
  Text='<%# Container.DataItem("Name") %>'
  CommandArgument='<%# Container.DataItem("Name") %>'
  Runat="Server"/>
</Itemtemplate>

</asp:DataList>
</font>
</form>
</body>
</html>
```

Retrieving the topics

When the page is first retrieved, a connection is made to the Access database, and a command object is created with a Select statement that retrieves the topic information:

```
If Not isPostBack Then
  Dim TopicConnection As OleDbConnection
  Dim TopicCommand As OleDbCommand
  TopicConnection = New OleDbConnection( _
    "Provider=Microsoft.Jet.OLEDB.4.0;" & _
    "Data Source=" & _
    "c:\inetpub\wwwroot\Discuss\DiscussDB.mdb")
  TopicCommand = New OleDbCommand( _
    "Select TopicID, Name from Topics", _
    TopicConnection )
  TopicConnection.Open()
```

The Command object's ExecuteReader method is called, which executes the Select statement and then returns the results in the form of a DataReader object. This object is immediately assigned to the DataSource property of the TopicDataList control on this page. Calling the `DataBind` method of that control assures that the topics retrieved will appear there:

```
TopicDataList.DataSource = _
  TopicCommand.ExecuteReader()
TopicDataList.DataBind()
```

Displaying the topics

The DataList control is used to quickly and easily display and format the information retrieved from the database:

```
<asp:DataList id="TopicDataList"
cellpadding=10 cellspacing=0
gridlines="both" RepeatColumns="3"
RepeatDirection="Horizontal"
Width="100%" DataKeyField="TopicID"
OnItemCommand="SelectTopic"
Runat="Server">

<ItemTemplate>
  <asp:LinkButton
  id="TopicLink"
  Text='<%# Container.DataItem("Name") %>'
  CommandArgument='<%# Container.DataItem("Name") %>'
  Runat="Server"/>
</Itemtemplate>

</asp:DataList>
```

Most of the attributes specified for the DataList are concerned with how the data will be formatted. There are two important attributes that are not concerned with formatting: `DataKeyField` and `OnItemCommand`. I'll discuss `OnItemCommand` in the next section.

The DataList expects to be associated with a result set, like that retrieved from a Select statement. The `DataKeyField` attribute identifies the column in the result set that is the key.

The `ItemTemplate` tag is used to identify how individual items in this list should be displayed. In this case, I only want to display one item, the name of the topic. But I want to display it as a link. The LinkButton control makes this easy. The text is set to the value of the Container's "Name" data item. The container, in this case, is the DataList, and because it is bound to the Topics table result set, this will display the name of the topic. The `CommandArgument` is set to the same value. This assures that the Topic name is passed to the appropriate subroutine when the user clicks a topic.

Handling topic selection

When the user clicks a topic, the DataList's `OnItemCommand` attribute tells the control what to do. In this case, it tells it to call the `SelectTopic` subroutine:

```
Sub SelectTopic(s As Object, _
  e As DataListCommandEventArgs)
Dim TopicID, TopicName As String
TopicName = e.CommandArgument
TopicID =__
  TopicDataList.DataKeys.Item( _
    e.Item.ItemIndex).toString()
Response.Redirect("Threads.aspx?TopicID=" & _
  TopicID & "&TopicName=" & TopicName)
End Sub
```

The topic name was passed as an argument, which comes in through the e object. That's easy enough to retrieve. The topic ID is a little tougher. The topic ID is in the list of DataKeys (because that column was specified as the `DataKeyField` for the DataList). So I use that list to retrieve the DataKey at the current ItemIndex. With the topic ID and name in hand, I'm ready to pass control on to another page, Threads.aspx.

The Threads page is used to display the list of threads within the selected topic. But to do that, it must know which topic was chosen. I pass the topic ID and the topic name as arguments on the URL line. This makes them available to be accessed by name in the Threads page by using Request.QueryString.

Picking a Thread

Once the user has picked a topic that they're interested in, the Threads page enables them to see all the threads that have been created in that topic. It also provides a link that allows the user to go to a page and create a whole new thread, as show in here:

```
<%@ Page Explicit="True" Language="VB"
Debug="True" %>
<%@ Import Namespace="System.Data" %>
<%@ Import Namespace="System.Data.OleDb" %>

<Script Runat="Server">
Sub Page_Load( s As Object, e As EventArgs )
If Not isPostBack Then
  Dim ThreadConnection As OleDbConnection
  Dim ThreadCommand As OleDbCommand
  ThreadConnection = New OleDbConnection( _
    "Provider=Microsoft.Jet.OLEDB.4.0;" & _
    "Data Source=" & _
    "c:\inetpub\wwwroot\Discuss\DiscussDB.mdb")
```

```
      ThreadCommand = New OleDbCommand( _
         "Select ThreadID, Name from Threads " & _
         "Where Topic=" & _
         Request.QueryString("TopicID"), _
         ThreadConnection )
      ThreadConnection.Open()
      ThreadDataList.DataSource = _
        ThreadCommand.ExecuteReader()
      ThreadDataList.DataBind()
      ThreadConnection.Close()
End If
End Sub

Sub SelectThread( s As Object, _
  e As DataListCommandEventArgs )
Dim ThreadID, ThreadName As String
ThreadDataList.SelectedIndex = e.Item.ItemIndex
ThreadName = e.CommandArgument
ThreadID = _
  ThreadDataList.DataKeys.Item( _
    e.Item.ItemIndex).toString()
Response.Redirect("Messages.aspx?TopicID=" & _
  Request.QueryString("TopicID") & _
  "&TopicName=" & Request.QueryString("TopicName") & _
  "&ThreadID=" & ThreadID & _
  "&ThreadName=" & ThreadName)
End Sub

</Script>

<html>
<head><title>Chatty Threads</title></head>
<body>
<font face="arial">
<h1><font color="DarkRed">
Chatty Discussion Forum</font></h1>
<font size="5"><u>
<%=Request.QueryString("TopicName") %>
</u> Threads</font>
<form Runat="Server">

<asp:DataList
id="ThreadDataList"
cellpadding=5 cellspacing=0
gridlines="both" Width="100%"
DataKeyField="ThreadID"
OnItemCommand="SelectThread"
Runat="Server">

  <ItemTemplate>
    <font size="2">
    <asp:LinkButton
    id="ThreadLink"
    Text='<%# Container.DataItem("Name") %>'
```

```
        CommandArgument='<%# Container.DataItem("Name") %>'
        Runat="Server"/>
        </font>
      </Itemtemplate>

      <FooterTemplate>
        <font size="2">
        <a href="NewThread.aspx?TopicID=
          <%=Request.QueryString("TopicID") %>
          &TopicName=
          <%=Request.QueryString("TopicName")%>">
        <i>[ Create a New Thread ]</i></a>
        </font>
      </FooterTemplate>

</asp:DataList>
<br/>
<a href="topics.aspx">
Return to list of <b>Topics</b></a>
</form>
</font>
</body>
</html>
```

This page is actually very similar to the Topics page. It retrieves a list of threads and displays them in a DataList as LinkButtons, and the user may click any of the thread names to go to the Messages page.

Using TopicID as selection criteria

There are a few differences between this page and the Topics page. This page uses the TopicID in the query to get only the threads associated with the topic the user requested:

```
ThreadCommand = New OleDbCommand( _
    "Select ThreadID, Name from Threads " & _
    "Where Topic=" & _
    Request.QueryString("TopicID"), _
    ThreadConnection )
```

I do this simply by concatenating the information from the QueryString into my Select statement. I could have, instead, used a parameter and filled in the parameter with the TopicID. I decided not to in this case because it would have made the code more complicated and wouldn't really add any value. I do use parameters in both the Messages and the NewThread pages, and I'll explain why in a section called "Using parameters" later in this chapter.

The Thread DataList

Another difference from the Topics page is the DataList:

```
<asp:DataList
id="ThreadDataList"
cellpadding=5 cellspacing=0
gridlines="both" Width="100%"
DataKeyField="ThreadID"
OnItemCommand="SelectTopic"
Runat="Server">
```

This list isn't three columns. Instead, it's a single column, which means that each row stretches across the page, allowing for long thread names.

More importantly, there's a new tag inside the DataList after the ItemTemplate tag: FooterTemplate.

```
<FooterTemplate>
  <font size="2">
  <a href="NewThread.aspx?TopicID=
    <%=Request.QueryString("TopicID") %>
    &TopicName=
    <%=Request.QueryString("TopicName")%>">
  <i>[ Create a New Thread ]</i></a>
  </font>
</FooterTemplate>
```

The footer template appears as the last item in the DataList. This is the perfect spot to provide a link to a page that will allow the user to add their own thread. I pass the TopicID and TopicName to the NewThread page.

Selecting a thread

When the user clicks one of the threads in the DataList, the SelectThread subroutine is called. Again, this works much the same as the SelectTopic subroutine does in the Topics page. The only real difference is that it passes the thread ID and name to the Messages page as well as the topic ID and name as you can see here:

```
Response.Redirect("Messages.aspx?TopicID=" & _
  Request.QueryString("TopicID") & _
  "&TopicName=" & Request.QueryString("TopicName") & _
  "&ThreadID=" & ThreadID & _
  "&ThreadName=" & ThreadName)
```

Browsing Messages

The Messages page displays all the messages posted for a particular topic and thread:

```
<%@ Page Explicit="True" Language="VB" Debug="True" %>
<%@ Import Namespace="System.Data" %>
<%@ Import Namespace="System.Data.OleDb" %>

<Script Runat="Server">
Sub Page_Load( s As Object, e As EventArgs )
If Not isPostBack Then
  BindData
End If
End Sub

Sub BindData
Dim MessageConnection As OleDbConnection
Dim MessageCommand As OleDbCommand
MessageConnection = New OleDbConnection( _
  "Provider=Microsoft.Jet.OLEDB.4.0;" & _
  "Data Source=c:\inetpub\wwwroot\Discuss\DiscussDB.mdb")
MessageConnection.Open()

MessageCommand = New OleDbCommand( _
  "Select MessageID, Subject, Message, " & _
  "Author, Posted From Messages Where " & _
  "Thread=@ThreadID Order By Posted", _
  MessageConnection )
MessageCommand.Parameters.Add( _
  New OleDbParameter("@ThreadID", OleDbType.Integer))
MessageCommand.Parameters("@ThreadID").Value = _
  CInt(Request.QueryString("ThreadID"))

MessageRepeater.DataSource = _
  MessageCommand.ExecuteReader()
MessageRepeater.DataBind()
MessageConnection.Close()
End Sub

Sub PostClick( obj As Object, e As EventArgs )
Dim MessageConnection As OleDbConnection
Dim MessageCommand As OleDbCommand
Dim InsertString as string
Dim Message As String
MessageConnection = _
  New OleDbConnection("Provider=Microsoft.Jet.OLEDB.4.0;" & _
  "Data Source=c:\inetpub\wwwroot\Discuss\DiscussDB.mdb")
InsertString = "Insert Into Messages (Subject, Message, " & _
  "Author, Posted, Thread) VALUES (@Subject, @Message, " & _
  "@Author, @Posted, @ThreadID)"
MessageCommand = _
  New OleDbCommand(InsertString, MessageConnection)
```

```
MessageCommand.Parameters.Add( _
  New OleDbParameter("@Subject", OleDbType.Varchar,50))
MessageCommand.Parameters.Add( _
  New OleDbParameter("@Message", OleDbType.LongVarchar))
MessageCommand.Parameters.Add( _
  New OleDbParameter("@Author", OleDbType.Varchar,50))
MessageCommand.Parameters.Add( _
  New OleDbParameter("@Posted", OleDbType.Varchar,50))
MessageCommand.Parameters.Add( _
  New OleDbParameter("@ThreadID", OleDbType.Varchar,50))

Message = MessageText.Text
Message = Replace(Message, CStr(chr(13)), "<br>")

MessageCommand.Parameters("@Subject").Value = _
  SubjectText.Text
MessageCommand.Parameters("@Message").Value = Message
MessageCommand.Parameters("@Author").Value = AuthorText.Text
MessageCommand.Parameters("@Posted").Value = CStr(Now)
MessageCommand.Parameters("@ThreadID").Value = _
  CInt(Request.QueryString("ThreadID"))

MessageConnection.Open()
MessageCommand.ExecuteNonQuery
MessageConnection.Close()

SubjectText.Text = ""
MessageText.Text = ""
AuthorText.Text = ""

BindData
End Sub

</Script>

<html>
<head><title>Chatty Messages</title></head>
<body>
<font face="arial">
<h1><font color="DarkRed">
Chatty Discussion Forum</font></h1>
<a href="threads.aspx?TopicID=
<%=Request.QueryString("TopicID")%>
&TopicName=<%=Request.QueryString("TopicName")%>">
<font size="5"><u>
<%=Request.QueryString("TopicName") & _
  "</a></u> : <u>" & _
  Request.QueryString("ThreadName") %>
</font></u>
<form Runat="Server">

<asp:Repeater
  id="MessageRepeater"
```

```
      Runat="Server">
      <ItemTemplate>
        <table width="100%" border="1" cellspacing="0"
        cellpadding="3" bordercolor="DarkBlue">
        <tr bgcolor="DarkBlue"><td>
           <font color="White" face="arial"><b>
           <%# Container.DataItem("Subject") %></b></font>
        </td>
        <td align="right" >
           <font color="White" face="arial" size="1">
           <%# Container.DataItem("Posted") %></font><br/>
        </td></tr><tr><td colspan="2">
           <font face="arial" size="2">
           <%# Container.DataItem("Message") %><br />
           <i><%# Container.DataItem("Author") %></i></font>
        </td></tr>
        </table><br>
      </ItemTemplate>
    </asp:Repeater>

    <table width="100%" border="1" cellspacing="0"
    cellpadding="3" bordercolor="DarkBlue">
    <tr><td bgcolor="LightGrey">
    <p>To post a new message to this thread, type your
    message below and click Post.</p>

    <p><font size="2">Subject:</font><br/>
    <asp:textbox id="SubjectText" runat="server"
    columns="50"/></p>
    <p><font size="2">Message:</font><br />
    <asp:textbox id="MessageText" runat="server"
    textmode="multiline"
    columns="50" rows="3"/></p>
    <p><font size="2">Your Email Address:</font><br />
    <asp:textbox id="AuthorText" runat="server"
    columns="50"/></p>
    <center>
    <asp:button runat="server" text="  Post  "
    onclick="PostClick" /><br />
    </center>
    </td></tr></table>
    <br />
    <a href="threads.aspx?TopicID=
      <%=Request.QueryString("TopicID")%>
      &TopicName=<%=Request.QueryString("TopicName")%>">
    Return to <b><%=Request.QueryString("TopicName") %>
    </b> Threads</a><br>
    <a href="topics.aspx">
    Return to list of <b>Topics</b></a>
    </form>
    </font>
    </body>
    </html>
```

This page retrieves the messages and displays them. The user is free to browse through and read them. At the bottom of the page is a form to fill out, if the user wishes to post his or her own messages.

Retrieving the messages

All the messages for all the topics and threads are stored in the same table. So to retrieve only the appropriate messages for this page, I concatenate the ThreadID sent as a QueryString to this page:

```
MessageCommand = New OleDbCommand( _
  "Select MessageID, Subject, Message, " & _
  "Author, Posted From Messages Where " & _
  "Thread=" & Request.QueryString("ThreadID") & _
  " Order By Posted", MessageConnection )

MessageRepeater.DataSource = _
  MessageCommand.ExecuteReader()
MessageRepeater.DataBind()
MessageConnection.Close()
```

The results are associated with the MessageRepeater.

The header

At the top of the page, after the standard Chatty header, I placed the topic name and the thread name, separated by a colon. This tells the user exactly what messages they are looking at, as you can see here:

```
<body>
<font face="arial">
<h1><font color="DarkRed">
Chatty Discussion Forum</font></h1>
<a href="threads.aspx?TopicID=
<%=Request.QueryString("TopicID")%>
&TopicName=<%=Request.QueryString("TopicName")%>">
<font size="5"><u>
<%=Request.QueryString("TopicName") & _
  "</a></u> : <u>" & _
  Request.QueryString("ThreadName") %>
</font></u>
```

In addition, I made the topic name a link. When you click it, you are returned to the Threads page, showing the threads for this topic.

Displaying the messages

I use a Repeater to display the messages retrieved from the database:

```
<asp:Repeater
  id="MessageRepeater"
  Runat="Server">
  <ItemTemplate>
    <table width="100%" border="1" cellspacing="0"
    cellpadding="3" bordercolor="DarkBlue">
    <tr bgcolor="DarkBlue"><td>
       <font color="White" face="arial"><b>
       <%# Container.DataItem("Subject") %></b></font>
    </td>
    <td align="right" >
       <font color="White" face="arial" size="1">
       <%# Container.DataItem("Posted") %></font><br/>
    </td></tr><tr><td colspan="2">
       <font face="arial" size="2">
       <%# Container.DataItem("Message") %><br />
       <i><%# Container.DataItem("Author") %></i></font>
    </td></tr>
    </table><br>
  </ItemTemplate>
</asp:Repeater>
```

This page is different from the Topics and Threads pages. I don't need to respond to user interaction as I did on those pages. And I need to have more flexibility in the layout to make the messages look presentable and easy to read. So I decide a Repeater would be a better choice than the DataList.

Each message appears inside its own table. The table is as wide as the page and has a border all the way around it. The Subject line appears white on dark blue, while the message appears below it as the standard black text on a white background. The author's e-mail address appears after the message.

Links to threads and topics

Typically, the user will come to the Messages page, read through the messages, and then click one of the links at the bottom of the page to go to either the Topics page or back to the Threads page. That's what this code provides:

```
<a href="threads.aspx?TopicID=
  <%=Request.QueryString("TopicID")%>
  &TopicName=<%=Request.QueryString("TopicName")%>">
Return to <b><%=Request.QueryString("TopicName") %>
</b> Threads</a><br>
<a href="topics.aspx">
Return to list of <b>Topics</b></a>
```

The new message form

However, sometimes, the reader will decide to add a message to the forum. For this, I've provided a form at the bottom of the page.

The form itself

I could have placed a link here at the bottom of the Messages page, instead, and put the form on a different page. But I decided that having the form readily available would make people more likely to post and be active in the conversations.

```
<table width="100%" border="1" cellspacing="0"
cellpadding="3" bordercolor="DarkBlue">
<tr><td bgcolor="LightGrey">
<p>To post a new message to this thread, type your
message below and click Post.</p>

<p><font size="2">Subject:</font><br/>
<asp:textbox id="SubjectText" runat="server"
columns="50"/></p>
<p><font size="2">Message:</font><br />
<asp:textbox id="MessageText" runat="server"
textmode="multiline"
columns="50" rows="3"/></p>
<p><font size="2">Your Email Address:</font><br />
<asp:textbox id="AuthorText" runat="server"
columns="50"/></p>
<center>
<asp:button runat="server" text=" Post "
onclick="PostClick" /><br />
</center>
</td></tr></table>
```

Calling PostClick

After the user has filled in the subject, message, and e-mail address textboxes, they click the Post button, which sends back the result to the server and executes the PostClick subroutine:

```
Sub PostClick( obj As Object, e As EventArgs )
Dim MessageConnection As OleDbConnection
Dim MessageCommand As OleDbCommand
Dim InsertString as string
Dim Message As String
```

The SQL Insert statement

PostClick inserts a new row in the Message table with the information entered by the user. A connection to the database is made, just as you normally would:

```
MessageConnection = _
  New OleDbConnection("Provider=Microsoft.Jet.OLEDB.4.0;" & _
  "Data Source=c:\inetpub\wwwroot\Discuss\DiscussDB.mdb")
```

In addition, a command object that holds a SQL Insert statement is created:

```
InsertString = "Insert Into Messages (Subject, Message, " & _
  "Author, Posted, Thread) VALUES (@Subject, @Message, " & _
  "@Author, @Posted, @ThreadID)"
MessageCommand = _
  New OleDbCommand(InsertString, MessageConnection)
```

However, you'll notice that the data to be filled in isn't concatenated to the string that contains the Insert statement. Instead of using concatenation as I did in the Select statement of the BindData subroutine (and in the Select statement used in the Threads page), I decided, here, to use parameters.

Using parameters

Parameters enable you to identify several placeholders in your SQL statement that are to be filled in later. The placeholders always begin with an @ sign so that you don't miss them or confuse them with columns from your table.

After the command object is created, you add new OleDbParameter objects to the Parameters collection of the command — one for each placeholder in your SQL statement:

```
MessageCommand.Parameters.Add( _
  New OleDbParameter("@Subject", OleDbType.Varchar,50))
MessageCommand.Parameters.Add( _
  New OleDbParameter("@Message", OleDbType.LongVarchar))
MessageCommand.Parameters.Add( _
  New OleDbParameter("@Author", OleDbType.Varchar,50))
MessageCommand.Parameters.Add( _
  New OleDbParameter("@Posted", OleDbType.Varchar,50))
MessageCommand.Parameters.Add( _
  New OleDbParameter("@ThreadID", OleDbType.Varchar,50))
```

When you instantiate the OleDbParameter, you pass the name of the placeholder and the data type of the information (using the OleDbType enumeration object).

Finally, after you have created all the parameters, you can fill them in with their appropriate values:

```
MessageCommand.Parameters("@Subject").Value = _
  SubjectText.Text
MessageCommand.Parameters("@Message").Value = Message
MessageCommand.Parameters("@Author").Value = AuthorText.Text
MessageCommand.Parameters("@Posted").Value = CStr(Now)
MessageCommand.Parameters("@ThreadID").Value = _
  CInt(Request.QueryString("ThreadID"))
```

```
...

MessageConnection.Open()
MessageCommand.ExecuteNonQuery
MessageConnection.Close()
```

Why did I go to all of this trouble? Wouldn't it be simpler to just concatenate the values into an Insert statement? Well, with this many parameters, the concatenation code would get pretty confusing. So although this may take a little more code, it is, in the end, easier to read and understand.

But that's not the best reason to use parameters. Suppose the user enters a subject that looks like this:

```
Can't afford the migration cost...
```

Notice the apostrophe in *Can't*. When you concatenate strings, VB.NET will interpret any apostrophes as a single quote and will think you are starting a substring, which you didn't finish. Double quotes in the string cause even worse problems. Fortunately, using parameters to fill in your SQL statement avoids all of these problems. Your quotes will come out looking just as they were typed.

Getting hard returns right

There's a couple of lines I skipped as I was describing the Messages page in the previous sections:

```
Message = MessageText.Text
Message = Replace(Message, CStr(chr(13)), "<br>")
```

When the user presses the return key inside the multiline edit box, it creates a hard return in the text, just as you'd expect it to. This is a valid character and it is saved along with the rest of the message in the database just fine. But when it is retrieved and displayed, the browser ignores hard returns. So, to be sure the text displayed in the browser looks like the text the user entered, it's necessary to do a little replacement. That's what the preceding lines do.

Preparing to return the updated page

After the user has entered a new message, and clicked Post, the new message is added to the database and the updated Messages page appears. To make that happen, you have to do two things: clear out the form fields and re-retrieve the messages from the database:

```
SubjectText.Text = ""
MessageText.Text = ""
AuthorText.Text = ""

BindData
```

Creating a New Thread

One more page is needed to make this application complete: a link from the Threads page that allows the user to create a new thread. This link sends them to the NewThread page.

```
<%@ Page Explicit="True" Language="VB" Debug="True" %>
<%@ Import Namespace="System.Data" %>
<%@ Import Namespace="System.Data.OleDb" %>

<Script Runat="Server">
Sub PostClick( obj As Object, e As EventArgs )
Dim Connection As OleDbConnection
Dim ThreadCommand As OleDbCommand
Dim GetThreadCommand As OleDbCommand
Dim MessageCommand As OleDbCommand
Dim ThreadReader As OleDbDataReader
Dim InsertThread, InsertMessage As String
Dim GetThread, Message as string
Dim ThreadID As Long
Dim ThreadResult As Integer
Connection = New OleDbConnection( _
  "Provider=Microsoft.Jet.OLEDB.4.0;" & _
  "Data Source=c:\inetpub\wwwroot\Discuss\DiscussDB.mdb")

Feedback.Text = ""

InsertThread = "Insert Into Threads (Name, Topic) " & _
  "VALUES (@ThreadName,@TopicID)"
ThreadCommand = New OleDbCommand(InsertThread, Connection)

ThreadCommand.Parameters.Add( _
  New OleDbParameter("@ThreadName", OleDbType.Varchar,50))
ThreadCommand.Parameters.Add( _
  New OleDbParameter("@TopicID", OleDbType.Integer))

ThreadCommand.Parameters("@ThreadName").Value = _
  ThreadText.Text
ThreadCommand.Parameters("@TopicID").Value = _
  Request.QueryString("TopicID")

Try
  Connection.Open()
  ThreadResult = ThreadCommand.ExecuteNonQuery
Catch excp As System.Data.OleDb.OleDbException
  If excp.Errors(0).NativeError = -105121349 Then
    Feedback.Text = "<font color=red>*** There " & _
      "is already a thread with the name <b>" & _
      ThreadText.Text & "</b>. Please choose a " & _
      "different name and click Post.</font><br><br>"
  Else
    Feedback.Text = "<font color=red>*** " & _
      excp.Errors(0).Message & "<br><br>"
```

```
   End If
End Try

GetThread = "Select ThreadID from Threads Where Name='" & _
   ThreadText.Text & "'"
GetThreadCommand = New OleDbCommand( GetThread,Connection)

ThreadReader = GetThreadCommand.ExecuteReader()
ThreadReader.Read
ThreadID = ThreadReader.Item("ThreadID")
ThreadReader.Close

InsertMessage = "Insert Into Messages (Subject, " & _
   "Message, Author, Posted, Thread) VALUES (@Subject, " & _
   "@Message, @Author, @Posted, @ThreadID)"
MessageCommand = _
   New OleDbCommand(InsertMessage, Connection)

MessageCommand.Parameters.Add( _
   New OleDbParameter("@Subject", OleDbType.Varchar,50))
MessageCommand.Parameters.Add( _
   New OleDbParameter("@Message", OleDbType.LongVarchar))
MessageCommand.Parameters.Add( _
   New OleDbParameter("@Author", OleDbType.Varchar,50))
MessageCommand.Parameters.Add( _
   New OleDbParameter("@Posted", OleDbType.Varchar,50))
MessageCommand.Parameters.Add( _
   New OleDbParameter("@ThreadID", OleDbType.Varchar,50))

Message = MessageText.Text
Message = Replace(Message, CStr(chr(13)), "<br>")

MessageCommand.Parameters("@Subject").Value = _
   SubjectText.Text
MessageCommand.Parameters("@Message").Value = Message
MessageCommand.Parameters("@Author").Value = AuthorText.Text
MessageCommand.Parameters("@Posted").Value = CStr(Now)
MessageCommand.Parameters("@ThreadID").Value = ThreadID

MessageCommand.ExecuteNonQuery

Connection.Close()

Response.Redirect("Threads.aspx?TopicID=" & _
   Request.QueryString("TopicID") & _
   "&TopicName=" & Request.QueryString("TopicName"))
End Sub
</Script>

<html>
<head><title>Chatty New Thread</title></head>
<body>
<font face="arial">
<h1><font color="DarkRed">Chatty Discussion Forum</font></h1>
```

```
<font size="5">Create New <u>
<%=Request.QueryString("TopicName") %></u> Thread</font>
<form Runat="Server">

<table width="100%" border="1" cellspacing="0" cellpadding="3"

bordercolor="DarkBlue">
<tr><td bgcolor="LightGrey">
<p>To create a new thread, enter the name of the thread
and the information for the first message you'd like
to post to the thread. If you wish to cancel, simply click
one of the links at the bottom of this page.</p>

<asp:label id="Feedback" runat="server" />
<p><font size="2">New Thread Name:</font><br/>
<asp:textbox id="ThreadText" runat="server"
columns="50"/></p>
<p><font size="2">Subject:</font><br/>
<asp:textbox id="SubjectText" runat="server"
columns="50"/></p>
<p><font size="2">Message:</font><br />
<asp:textbox id="MessageText" runat="server"
textmode="multiline"
columns="50" rows="3"/></p>
<p><font size="2">Your Email Address:</font><br />
<asp:textbox id="AuthorText" runat="server"
columns="50"/></p>
<center>
<asp:button runat="server" text="  Post   "
onclick="PostClick" />
</center>
</td></tr></table>
<br />
<a href="threads.aspx?TopicID=
<%=Request.QueryString("TopicID")%>
&TopicName=<%=Request.QueryString("TopicName")%>">
Return to <b><%=Request.QueryString("TopicName") %>
</b> Threads</a><br>
<a href="topics.aspx">
Return to list of <b>Topics</b></a>
</form>
</font>
</body>
</html>
```

The NewThread form

Unlike the other pages in this application, NewThread does not retrieve anything from the database when it is first opened. Instead, it presents the user with a form that looks very much like the form at the bottom of the Messages page:

```
<asp:label id="Feedback" runat="server" />
<p><font size="2">New Thread Name:</font><br/>
```

```
<asp:textbox id="ThreadText" runat="server"
columns="50"/></p>
<p><font size="2">Subject:</font><br/>
<asp:textbox id="SubjectText" runat="server"
columns="50"/></p>
<p><font size="2">Message:</font><br />
<asp:textbox id="MessageText" runat="server"
textmode="multiline"
columns="50" rows="3"/></p>
<p><font size="2">Your Email Address:</font><br />
<asp:textbox id="AuthorText" runat="server"
columns="50"/></p>
<center>
<asp:button runat="server" text="  Post  "
onclick="PostClick" />
</center>
```

The user is here to create a new thread. However, it doesn't make much sense to create a new thread without also posting a message to it. So to save the user the trouble, this page allows the user to do both at once.

NewThread's PostClick: a big job

After the user has entered the thread name and the first message for the thread, he or she clicks the Post button. The Post button causes the page to return to the server and execute the `PostClick` subroutine.

`PostClick` has a number of responsibilities. It must do the following:

✦ Open a connection to the database.

✦ Insert a new row in the Threads table using the name the user entered and associating it with the current topic.

✦ Retrieve the newly created thread's ThreadID (which is assigned to it automatically by Microsoft Access).

✦ Insert a new row in the Message table using the rest of the information the user entered in the form. That message must be associated with the newly created thread, using the retrieved ThreadID.

Threading a new row

Aside from the primary key, the Threads table has only two columns: the thread name and the topic the thread is associated with. I use parameters to fill in these values:

```
InsertThread = "Insert Into Threads (Name, Topic) " & _
  "VALUES (@ThreadName,@TopicID)"
ThreadCommand = New OleDbCommand(InsertThread, Connection)
```

```
ThreadCommand.Parameters.Add( _
  New OleDbParameter("@ThreadName", OleDbType.Varchar,50))
ThreadCommand.Parameters.Add( _
  New OleDbParameter("@TopicID", OleDbType.Integer))

ThreadCommand.Parameters("@ThreadName").Value = _
  ThreadText.Text
ThreadCommand.Parameters("@TopicID").Value = _
  Request.QueryString("TopicID")
```

Watch for duplicates

When I created this database, I didn't want the user creating threads with the same name, so I created an index on the Threads table's Name column that didn't allow duplicates. But because I did that, I now have to check for that possibility in my code. That's made relatively painless with VB.NET's new error-trapping capabilities:

```
Try
  Connection.Open()
  ThreadResult = ThreadCommand.ExecuteNonQuery
Catch excp As System.Data.OleDb.OleDbException
  If excp.Errors(0).NativeError = -105121349 Then
    Feedback.Text = "<font color=red>*** There " & _
      "is already a thread with the name <b>" & _
      ThreadText.Text & "</b>. Please choose a " & _
      "different name and click Post.</font><br><br>"
  Else
    Feedback.Text = "<font color=red>*** " & _
      excp.Errors(0).Message & "<br><br>"
  End If
End Try
```

The Try block opens the connection and executes the query. If a database exception is raised, I check to see if the error is because a duplicate row exists. I use the NativeError property to see the raw error number returned from the database.

If that is the problem, I use the Feedback label to provide the user with a simple message informing them of the problem and asking them to change the name of the thread.

If there's some other problem, I simply drop the error message into the Feedback label.

Getting the ThreadID

When you use the AutoNumber data type with a primary key column in an Access table, Access knows to automatically generate a new, unique number for any newly inserted rows.

But to post the first message to this thread, you're going to need the ThreadID. How do you get it? Just query for the unique thread name:

```
GetThread = "Select ThreadID from Threads Where Name='" & _
  ThreadText.Text & "'"
GetThreadCommand = New OleDbCommand( GetThread,Connection)

ThreadReader = GetThreadCommand.ExecuteReader()
ThreadReader.Read
ThreadID = ThreadReader.Item("ThreadID")
ThreadReader.Close
```

Posting the message

Now that you have all the information you need, posting the message works much like it did in the Messages page:

```
InsertMessage = "Insert Into Messages (Subject, " & _
  "Message, Author, Posted, Thread) VALUES (@Subject, " & _
  "@Message, @Author, @Posted, @ThreadID)"
MessageCommand = _
  New OleDbCommand(InsertMessage, Connection)

MessageCommand.Parameters.Add( _
  New OleDbParameter("@Subject", OleDbType.Varchar,50))
MessageCommand.Parameters.Add( _
  New OleDbParameter("@Message", OleDbType.LongVarchar))
MessageCommand.Parameters.Add( _
  New OleDbParameter("@Author", OleDbType.Varchar,50))
MessageCommand.Parameters.Add( _
  New OleDbParameter("@Posted", OleDbType.Varchar,50))
MessageCommand.Parameters.Add( _
  New OleDbParameter("@ThreadID", OleDbType.Varchar,50))

Message = MessageText.Text
Message = Replace(Message, CStr(chr(13)), "<br>")

MessageCommand.Parameters("@Subject").Value = _
  SubjectText.Text
MessageCommand.Parameters("@Message").Value = Message
MessageCommand.Parameters("@Author").Value = AuthorText.Text
MessageCommand.Parameters("@Posted").Value = CStr(Now)
MessageCommand.Parameters("@ThreadID").Value = ThreadID

MessageCommand.ExecuteNonQuery

Connection.Close()

Response.Redirect("Threads.aspx?TopicID=" & _
  Request.QueryString("TopicID") & _
  "&TopicName=" & Request.QueryString("TopicName"))
End Sub
```

After the thread is created and the message is posted, the user is sent back to the Threads page so that they can see the newly created thread in the list. If they prefer, they can click the thread and see their message at the top of the list.

Ideas for Enhancement

The Chatty Discussion Forum is a simple application. It could be enhanced or expanded to meet your needs in many ways. Here are a few ideas that I thought of:

✦ In its current form, Chatty offers no way to add, update, or delete topics. Because this is a site administrator task, it's assumed that they'll simply use Microsoft Access to go in and add the topics they want when they first begin using the application. But it would be handy if there was a topic maintenance page that simplified the task. Keep in mind that deleting a topic means you need to delete all the threads and all the threads' messages!

✦ Likewise, Chatty has no way to delete or archive old threads and messages. Again, this can be done by hand in Access, but if you begin to have a lot of active discussions going on, it'd be nice if there were maintenance pages that made the task even easier.

✦ While you're making maintenance easier, you might want to consider automating some of the tasks. For example, you might want to automatically archive any thread and its messages that hasn't been posted to in over a month.

✦ If you have trouble with people posting off-topic or inappropriate messages, you might want to put newly entered messages into a holding bin to be approved by a site administrator before they are posted.

✦ Another way to combat the problem of inappropriate postings is to require users to log in to your site or at least log in to the discussion forum application before they post a new message. This provides you with more information on who the user is and enables you to cancel their account if they act antisocially.

✦ Provide a new page (or modify the Threads page) so that you can see all the Subject lines of all the messages in a thread. Then, allow the user to click one of the Subject lines to jump directly to that message on the Messages page.

Summary

A discussion forum is a very practical application. It can be used on virtually any Web site where you want to enhance the sense of community. In addition, this application has demonstrated a number of important ASP.NET techniques. Some of the techniques are creating a hierarchical relationship among tables in a relational database; connecting to and retrieving data from a database using ADO.NET; displaying data with the Repeater and DataList server controls using data-binding; using an ItemTemplate inside a repeater to format repeating data; creating new rows in a database table; connecting new rows to an exiting row in another table using appropriate foreign keys; and using parameters in queries — as well as when and why it's important.

✦   ✦   ✦

Visual Basic Syntax

Welcome to the start of a whole new adventure for both Microsoft and yourself. The .NET series of application development tools and its accompanying office suite has the potential to take you much further and much faster in productivity than you have gone before. The integration of these tools has become much tighter and thus more efficient than in the past. Because this is a book on Web application development with ASP.NET supplemented by VB.NET, you will first be taken on a tour through the VB.NET development environment. This will give you the foundation required for you to be a top-notch .NET developer. Then you will be taken on a tour of all the pieces of the construction of an application, from designing an MDI (Multiple Document Interface) application to understanding data types and defining variables, and finally to controlling the logical flow of an application.

Brief Tour of the GUI

As an application developer, it is the world of the GUI IDE (graphical user interface, integrated development environment) in which you will spend most of your time. VB.NET, although new and improved over VB 6.0, is still a GUI IDE and therefore will take some getting used to if you are new to software development. You will now take a brief tour of this IDE. You will see the highlights along the way of what is new or may have changed in look, feel, or functionality. The IDE, for the most part, looks similar to that of VB 6.0, so for those developers who are seasoned in VB 6.0, finding your way around this IDE shouldn't be very difficult.

It is assumed here that you have successfully installed at least the basic feature set of the VB portion of the .NET development suite.

Note   For more detail on the installation process, refer to this book's introduction.

As you take this tour through the IDE, you will build a small mailing list system, which will enable you to see VB.NET's productivity at an early stage.

Figure A-1 shows the first screen of the VB.NET GUI upon startup, with the major parts identified.

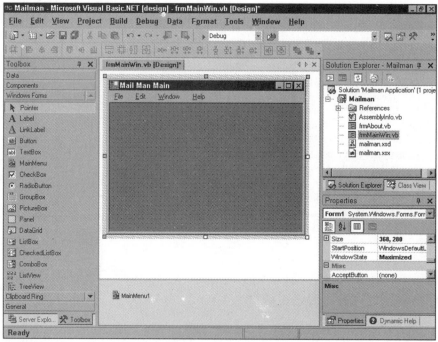

Figure A-1: The VB.NET GUI with the major sections highlighted

If you are new to IDE development or to VB.NET, then take a few minutes to try out some of these features:

◆ **Menu:** Usually context-sensitive, gives you a pull-down approach to many commands and environment options.

◆ **Toolbar:** Also context-sensitive, the toolbar is a subset of the commands that you will find on the menu. This is a way to quickly call commands, such as Save, Print, and Run, that are used more frequently than other commands.

✦ **Layout bar:** This is another kind of toolbar that supplies many of the layout features used in designing a form. Features like aligning controls to the left, making controls the same size, and making controls equidistant are among the options available. Many other context-sensitive toolbars are available for your use, too; simply right-click any toolbar in a vacant slot and you will see the list of the other available toolbars.

✦ **Solution Explorer:** This is a tree-view-style interface that shows you all the pieces to your application, or solution. This shows you all the windows and modules, and any other items of that nature, that are part of the solution and that you may want to edit.

✦ **Properties window:** This is where you will spend a lot of time fine-tuning the behaviors of your application. You set the individual features of a particular object (always the one in focus) so that it appears the way you desire. Some examples are push button text value and size, text label values, form background colors, and so on.

✦ **Toolbox:** The selection area for the controls that you want to place on a form you may be designing. Push buttons, drop-down lists, picture buttons, single-line edits, radio buttons, and check boxes are among the many tools in the toolbox at your disposal.

✦ **Development area:** This is the area used to lay out your forms, to see how they will appear. Grouping controls together, aligning them to the left, right, or top, and sizing the form are among the functions you can perform here.

Now that the major areas have been pointed out and briefly explained, you can start building the small mailing list system mentioned earlier.

Creating a Mailing List Project

The first thing you need to do is to start a new project. Complete the following steps to do so:

1. Either select New Project from the File menu or click the New Project button on the toolbar. The New Project dialog box will appear, as shown in Figure A-2. Here you are presented with quite a few options as to what kind of project you want to create.

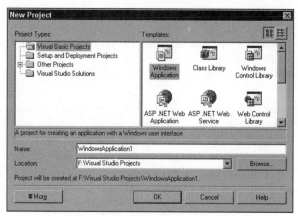

Figure A-2: The New Project dialog box options

2. Select Visual Basic Projects from the available Project Types, if it is not already highlighted. Then, select from the available Templates. For the purposes of this example, you will be creating a new Windows application, so be sure that the Windows Application icon is selected. Ignore all the other options for now, or if you are interested in them click on the help button in this window and read up on these additional features.

3. Name the project "Mailman" or something appropriate, and indicate the correct Location for your project.

4. Click OK to create the new project.

The new window will appear in the development area. With the new window in focus, click its properties tab on the right side of the display and name the new form. You can also set its Window Style to an MDI parent by making the IsMdiContainer equal to True (see Figure A-3).

Many types of Windows are available to the developer. VB.NET is based on a few interface styles and GUI presentation needs. MDI (Multiple Document Interface), SDI (Single Document Interface), and Web interface styles are a few of the most common that you will see. This example application will be an MDI application; however, to keep things small and simple, it will only have a few windows.

Tip   New to VB.NET is the disappearing sidebar feature. If you have ever seen the Windows taskbar as it is set to autohide, you'll be familiar with this feature as well. It is designed to save screen space and it is a great feature to have enabled. On the top of the toolbox, for example, you'll see a small icon that looks like a stickpin; click this pin to activate the feature. The toolbox will move off to the left and reveal more of the design surface.

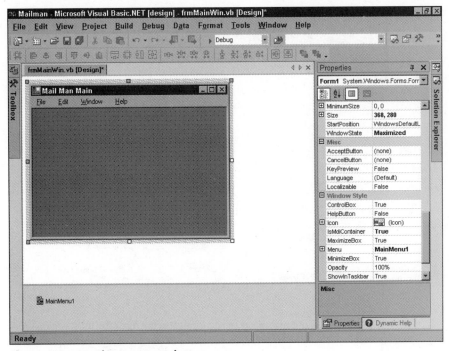

Figure A-3: Creating a new project

Setting the data elements

The mailing list system will have a small menu control, a data entry screen, and a Help About window. It will also have a small database behind it and therefore will consist of the following features:

✦ Address entry

✦ Help About window

✦ Application shutdown and exit

The database will consist of the data elements defined in Table A-1.

Table A-1 Data element items for mailing list database			
Field Name	**Field Description**	**Data Type**	**Data Size**
Mail_id	Identifying number for the database (Primary Key)	Autonumber	Auto
FName	First name	Text	25
LName	Last name	Text	20
Address	Mailing address	Text	25
City	City name	Text	15
Postal	ZIP or postal code	Text	9
Province	Province or state	Text	2
Phone	Telephone number	Text	8
E_mail	Internet e-mail address	Text	25

Note   There is a database file located on the companion Web site for this book. A further reference will be made to this file later in the appendix when it will actually be used.

Adding menu controls

The menu designer is the interface that enables you to define the actions or commands available in your application. Commands such as Print, Copy, Edit, Window Tile, and Help About are some of the common ones.

Note   The mailing list system project is going to have only a few menu items, so that you can see some of the functionality of VB.NET. Feel free to add more functionality when you are ready to do so.

To add a menu control to the main form, complete the following steps:

1. Find the MainMenu control on the toolbox window. You may have to reveal the toolbox on the left of the display, depending on how you have your IDE configured.

2. Drag the MainMenu control to the main window and drop it anywhere on the form that is being worked on.

3. After the MainMenu control is attached to the form, you can begin to build your menu structure. The menu design structure will appear on the top of the form, and you can add the menu items by typing directly into the menu option

slots that are presented to you. This is a marked difference to the menu designer that VB 6.0 developers are used to. The menu designer has the following main areas, which are accessed in different portions of the IDE:

- **Text:** The portion of the menu that the user of the application actually sees while working with it. This is accessed simply by typing the caption in the area on the menu designer; alternately, you can set this value in the properties tab.

- **Name:** The "internal" name that is assigned to the menu item. If a menu item is to be referenced in programming code, this is how it will be addressed. Typically, menu names are prefixed with "mnu" as in mnuFilePrint. This is done to visually cue the software programmer as to what type of entity is being referenced in the code. This name item is accessed in the menu's property page on the right side of the IDE.

- **Short Cut:** This is the menu shortcut that can be assigned to each item. Take a look at most Microsoft applications and you see that a shortcut for saving information is usually the Ctrl + S keystroke combination. You can have similar shortcuts assigned to your menu items, but be sure to track the ones you use so that you don't have two or more menu items assigned with the same shortcut.

- **Enabled & Visible:** These two attributes to a menu item are the most commonly used of the remaining properties. Enabled means that the menu item will trigger its supporting code if selected from a running application. The opposite of this, to have Enabled turned off, would be similar to a grayed-out option on a menu. It is visible, but because of the context that the application is in, it is inoperable. An example would be an Edit menu with Paste grayed out because nothing is in the computer memory's clipboard to paste. The other popular option, Visible, has similar functionality except that it is based on the visual aspect of the menu item. You may have also noticed that certain menu items in applications appear and disappear depending on the part of the program you're working in. This is the Visibility option at work.

4. Now build the menu structure for the application using the information and properties from Table A-2. Keep the following tips in mind when creating the menus:

- To define shortcut keys, simply place an ampersand (&) in front of the letter in the menu name that will work in conjunction with the alternate (Alt) key. For example, &File would appear as File and would open the File menu with the Alt + F keystroke combination. This functionality is triggered simply by the ampersand being in the caption field; you do not need to also define it in the shortcut property.

- To define menu options as options under, or belonging to, a top-level menu item (for example, File ⇨ Exit), simply use the space underneath the menu option to enter the value. Also, for lateral menu growth (for example, View ⇨ Toolbars ⇨ Standard), use the entry point on the right side of an existing menu item.

- To define a menu separator bar, simply enter a single dash character in the caption field and name the item accordingly.

Note

Some items in Table A-2 are not yet enabled, and enabling them doesn't make sense until the correct situation arises. The programming code that follows in this example will address such a situation.

Table A-2
Menu information and properties table

Menu Caption	Name	Shortcut	Enable	Visible
&File	mnuFile		(	(
&Open Address Form	mnuOpenAddr	Alt + o	(	(
- (Separator)	mnuFileSep1		(	(
E&xit Program	mnuExit	Alt + x	(	(
&Edit	mnuEdit		(	(
Cut	mnuCut	Ctrl + x		(
Copy	mnuCopy	Ctrl + c		(
Paste	mnuPaste	Ctrl + v		(
&Window	mnuWindow			(
Tile Horizontally	mnuTileHoriz			(
Tile Vertically	mnuTileVert			(
Cascade	mnuCascade			(
&Help	mnuHelp			(
About	mnuAbout			(

Your completed menu structure should look like the one shown in Figure A-4.

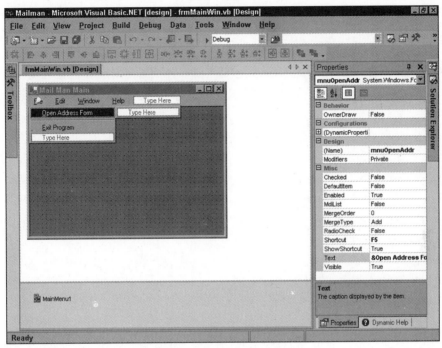

Figure A-4: The completed menu structure in MDI Form

Next you will write the programming code to make these menus active.

Activating the menu controls

The programming editor will look a little different to the one in previous versions of Visual Basic on at least two fronts. First, you will notice that a lot more code is visible to you, which is generated by .NET. Because this product strives to get closer to true object orientation, it defines more class style code and makes that code visible to the developer. This enables you to see what .NET has already generated for you in case you want your code to interact with the generated code. Also, and this is a personal opinion only, the visible code is there to impress you with the technical skills of Microsoft's .NET development team.

The other thing that you may notice as different from previous versions of Visual Basic is that the editor has a cleaner look and feel with some visual improvements. Take a look at the code editor as it is accessed within the menu editor. To do this, simply double-click a menu item. Figure A-5 shows the code editor for the File ⇨ Exit menu option.

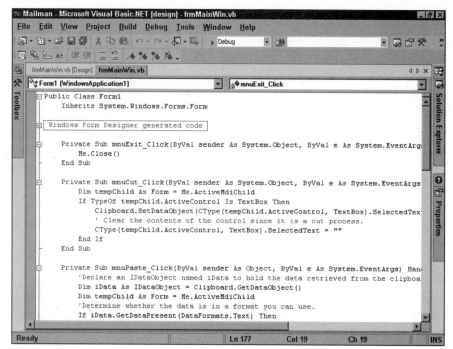

Figure A-5: The code editor for the File ⇨ Exit option

Enter the following code after the `Sub` statement and before the `End Sub` statement. The cursor should be at the correct location, but be sure it is in the right place just the same.

```
Me.Close()
```

This simple command tells the menu to close its owner, which happens to be the main application window. This is not a command instructing the menu to be unloaded as is often confused, rather it is telling the application to close. Keep in mind that the form owns any controls, including menus that are placed on it. After you have entered that code, you can close the code editor whenever you're ready. Again, this would be a good chance to look around this particular editor to get a feel for how it works and operates.

Enter the following code for the other listed menu items. Notice that .NET already has some functionality built in for these more common menu options, like the window tiling actions. Simply implement the commands in the right place.

Tip

If you are already in the code editor and want to edit code for multiple events (like the code listings that follow), then simply choose the control entity from the drop-down control on the top left of the code editor. Next, select the event of the entity from the drop-down list on the top right of the code editor. The surrounding code will be generated for you, if it has not already been done, and you can continue with writing code.

Insert the following code to activate the Edit ⇨ Copy command:

```
Dim tempChild As Form = Me.ActiveMdiChild
If TypeOf tempChild.ActiveControl Is TextBox Then
Clipboard.SetDataObject(CType(tempChild.ActiveControl,
TextBox).SelectedText)
  End If
```

Insert the following code to activate the Edit ⇨ Cut command:

```
Dim tempChild As Form = Me.ActiveMdiChild
If TypeOf tempChild.ActiveControl Is TextBox Then
Clipboard.SetDataObject(CType(tempChild.ActiveControl,
TextBox).SelectedText)
' Clear the contents of the control since it is a cut process.
CType(tempChild.ActiveControl, TextBox).SelectedText = ""
End If
```

Insert the following code to activate the Edit ⇨ Paste command:

```
'Declare an IDataObject named iData to hold the data retrieved
from the clipboard.
Dim iData As IDataObject = Clipboard.GetDataObject()
Dim tempChild As Form = Me.ActiveMdiChild
'Determine whether the data is in a format you can use.
If iData.GetDataPresent(DataFormats.Text) Then
'Yes it can be used, so paste it to the active control
tempChild.ActiveControl.Text =
CType(iData.GetData(DataFormats.Text), String)
Else
'No it is not.
MsgBox("Data on clipboard is not retrievable.",
MsgBoxStyle.Exclamation, "Clipboard error")
End If
```

Insert the following code to activate the Window ⇨ Tile Horizontal command:

```
Me.LayoutMdi(MdiLayout.TileHorizontal)
```

Insert the following code to activate the Window ⇨ Tile Vertically command:

```
Me.LayoutMdi(MdiLayout.TileVertical)
```

Insert the following code to activate the Window ⇨ Cascade command:

```
Me.LayoutMdi(MdiLayout.Cascade)
```

Insert the following code to activate the Help ⇨ About command:

```
Dim frmAbout As New frmAbout()
'Set the Parent Form of the Child window.
frmAbout.MdiParent = Me
frmAbout.Show()
```

Insert the following code to activate the File ⇨ Open Address command:

```
Dim frmAdd1 As New frmAddress()
' enable menu items now that a window will be opened...
mnuCopy.Enabled = True
mnuPaste.Enabled = True
mnuCut.Enabled = True
mnuTileHoriz.Enabled = True
mnuTileVert.Enabled = True
mnuCascade.Enabled = True

'Set the Parent Form of the Child window.
frmAdd1.MdiParent = Me
frmAdd1.Show()
```

Notice in this code that there is an assignment of Me to the MdiParent property of the frmAdd1 form. This is done to be sure that the window that will be shown at the end of this event will belong to the entity known as "me"; in this case, the controlling application object. Also, while you are working on the main form window, be sure to set the IsMDIContainer property to True (if not already done), so that the MDI functionality will also be set on the parent window of the application.

Tip   While you are looking at the properties of the main form window, you may also want to set the WindowState property to Maximized, so that when you test-run your application, it will take up your whole computer screen, for a better presentation of what you are designing.

Designing the Help About window

Next, design the Help About window that is referenced in the code, naming the form frmAbout when you are finished. To create a new form, complete the following steps:

1. Right-click the application name in the Solution Explorer and choose Add ➪ Add Windows Form.

2. Select the default Windows Form template and enter the form Name in the bottom half of the form definition window, as shown in Figure A-6.

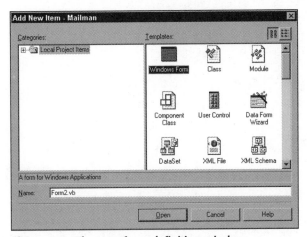

Figure A-6: The new form definition window

Tip

Be sure to leave the .vb extension on the forms that you create. This is a "feature" of VB.NET that helps the IDE and compiler to know what parts of the solution are for a particular purpose. If you change a form's name, the form may become useless to you, because .NET will not necessarily know what to do with it.

3. Click the OK button, and the new design surface of the window will be shown as having focus in the design area of the IDE, and you can begin to construct the window as you like. The Help About window can be designed as shown in Figure A-7, or you can suit it to your own taste. Figure A-7 has two Label controls, a Picture control, and a PushButton control. The code behind the push button is as follows:

```
Me.Close ()
```

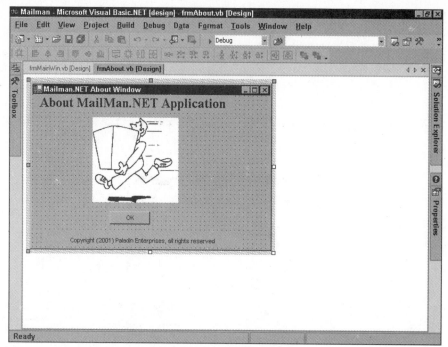

Figure A-7: The completed Help About window design

4. Change the `Text` property of the push button to OK, or something similar, to prompt your application users to eventually close this Help About window.

Be sure to save your application often for peace of mind. Now that you have all of the menu code written, you can test your Help About window. Click the Run icon (little blue triangle with point facing to the right icon on the toolbar), and Visual Basic .NET will perform a build and then try to run your application. The example shown in Figure A-8 has the Help About window showing and an active menu pulled down.

Note   You will have a build warning message that tells you that frmAddress does not exist, with the following message: "type not defined: frmAddress." This message appears simply because frmAddress has not been defined in the application yet, but you are making reference to it in the menu code. You have two ways around this situation. First, you can resolve it by actually defining a form with that name. Even though it is simply a blank form, it will at least exist. Second, you can comment out the code in the menu editor that makes reference to this form until you define it at a later time.

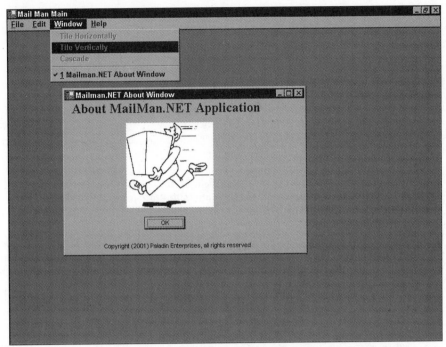

Figure A-8: Running Mailman application showing Help About window open

Looking at MDI applications

As mentioned previously, there are ways in which your application's forms will "own" other windows that are opened within the program. For example, the name of the window "Mailman.NET About Window" in Figure A-8 appears to be listed on the Window menu as a "switch to"-type command, thus showing that the application has control and actually owns the form. If additional windows were open, they too would be listed on the Window menu.

Make sure as you define new forms in the Mailman application that you set the form's isMDIContainer property to False. This should be the default anyway, but just make sure that it is set as such. Then, every time that this form is opened within the application (through the previously written menu code), it will be "owned" by the application and contained within its visual boundaries. The isMDIContainer property enables the application to know how to add the window names to the available list under the Window menu, and it also allows the application to be able to employ the tile and cascade features that you have coded a little earlier.

The next thing that you need to do is to create another form that allows the user of your application to navigate through your database tables, adding, editing, or deleting the records as they see fit.

Creating data-aware forms

Creating data-aware forms involves two stages. First, you need to make VB.NET aware that a data source is available to it. Second, you need to build the form with the Data Form Wizard. Thankfully, both of these stages are combined through the use of the Data Form Wizard.

Note The database file for this appendix is located on the companion Web site for this book. Copy the Mailman.mdb file from the site onto your system. This is done to save you time in creating a database.

Note You will also have to create a system DSN entry in your computer's ODBC management center. To do this, select Start ⇨ Settings ⇨ Control Panel and double-click ODBC Data Sources to open the ODBC definition window. Make an entry in the System DSN tab by clicking the Add PushButton and fill in the appropriate values. For the application that is being designed, the name was given as mailman, and the database was named the same.

Specifying the database and tables

To establish the database connection and designate the tables to be used, complete the following steps:

1. On the Solution Explorer pane, right-click the application name and select the add windows form menu item that appears in the pop-up menu after you click the first-level add option. As before (refer to Figure A-6), you will select the add new windows form option. However, this time, in the subsequent window, you will select the Data Form Wizard option rather than the default of Windows form.

2. Name the new form frmAddress for the purposes of this exercise, and then click the Open button. This will start the wizard process.

3. After clicking the Next button on the first informational screen, you will be presented with a window similar to that shown in Figure A-9, which asks you to either create a new dataset or use an existing one. Because a dataset doesn't already exist in this project, you are going to create a new dataset called mailman.

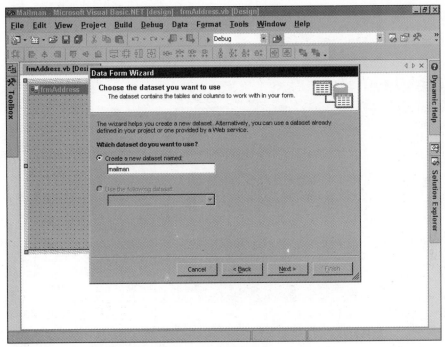

Figure A-9: Second step of the Data Form Wizard

4. After you type the "mailman" dataset name, click the Next button to continue through the Data Form Wizard.

5. Next you are asked for a connection to use. If a connection to this database already exists, use it; however, if one does not exists, then click the New Connection button and select the correct driver (which is "Microsoft Jet 4.0 OLE DB Provider" for MS-Access tables) on the Provider tab.

6. After selecting the appropriate provider you will need to click on the Next pushbutton to move the wizard to the connection tab. Here you should click on the Browse PushButton (signified by the ellipses ...) and locate the mailman.mdb file that you should have moved onto your own system.

7. The completed Connection tab should look similar to that shown in Figure A-10. If you are not sure whether you have set up the ODBC settings properly, or the other options that had to be set to use the Mailman.mdb database and file, be sure to test the connection by clicking the Test Connection button at the bottom of this Connection tab.

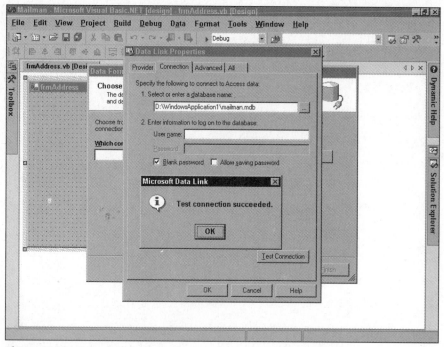

Figure A-10: Completed connection portion of Data Form Wizard

8. After obtaining a successful connection to the database, the wizard process will ask what parts of the database structures you will be accessing: tables, views, or stored procedures. For the purposes of this application, simply select the table called addresses under the tables list and click the button between the two panes that moves the selection from the left pane to the right pane. Click the Next button to move to the next stage of the Data Form Wizard.

Now that you have connected to the database and told the wizard what table(s) you want to use from that database, the next step is to tell the wizard what fields you want to use on the form that will eventually be built.

Specifying the form fields

To establish the fields to be used on the forms you are building, complete the following steps:

1. After clicking Next in the Data Form Wizard at the end of the previous section, you would have been presented with a window asking you what data columns you want to display on the subsequent form. Figure A-11 shows the column selection page of the wizard with a few of the columns selected. Select the columns that you want and click the Next button.

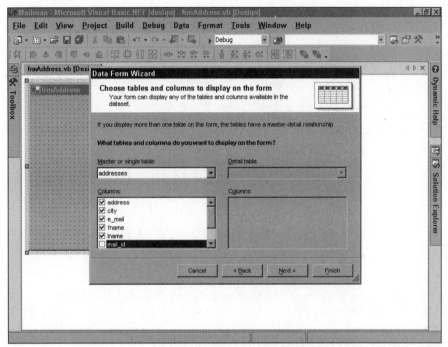

Figure A-11: The field selection page of the Data Form Wizard

2. Click on the Next button to be taken to the Display Style page of this wizard. Here you can select how the form will automatically present the information to you when the application is running. The options are self-explanatory, so simply select the options you want. To see how it has been done in this example, review the options selected in Figure A-12. The options chosen here are to show one data record at a time and to have the offered controls included on the created form.

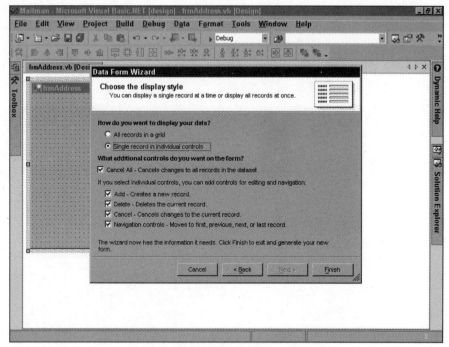

Figure A-12: Data display page of the Data Form Wizard

3. Because this is the last option in the wizard, click the Finish button to complete the process.

The new form will be created and added to your solution. Feel free to rename the text labels that are created for you to something more descriptive, and to lay out the other controls to suit your own design. As you will be able to see, the controls are arranged alphabetically rather than how they are defined in the database table, so you probably will always need to rearrange the forms that are generated by the Data Form Wizard.

Also, if earlier in the process you commented out the menu code that references this form, be sure to return to that code and reactivate it. Then, build your solution and run it to see what it looks like. The running application should look similar to that shown in Figure A-13.

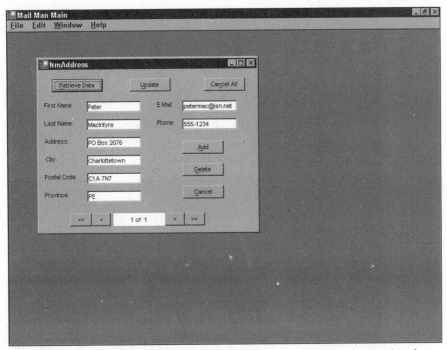

Figure A-13: Running application with the Address form open and operational

Data Types and Variables

Some fundamental logical features make up a programming language. The way data is handled and processed within the memory of the computer is accomplished through entities known as variables. Variables are defined in a way that describes the data that is contained within them, both in name and in content. For example, if you are trying to decide whether something is on or off or true or false, then you use the Boolean variable data type to house the information and may call it lCompleted. If you were trying to store somebody's address, you typically store that in a String data type variable.

Because many of these variables take up memory space, you should follow some simple guidelines for resource conservation. Although it seems like a trivial matter to be concerned with 2 bytes of space instead of 8 bytes of space on 128MB of RAM, it would not take too long to use up a fair portion of your computer's resources. The best rule to follow here is not to be too casual in your variable definitions. Don't use a Long data type when a Single data type will do the job. But also try to keep in mind what the upper limits of the variable is expected to reach, and make allowances for it. Don't sell yourself short either, because you can bet that you will be revisiting code in about a year when your computer application fails because some variables are running out of resource space.

Table A-3 is the complete list of variable data types; however, this discussion focuses only on the more commonly used data types. Check the VB.NET product manual or online help for details on the other available data types if you think you may need to use them.

Table A-3 Visual Basic data types		
Data Type Name	**Memory Storage Requirements**	**Value Range**
Boolean	1 byte	True or False
Byte	1 byte	0 to 255 (unsigned)
Char	2 bytes	0 to 65,535 (unsigned)
Date	8 bytes	January 1, 1 AD to December 31, 9999
Decimal	12 bytes	+/ 79,228,162,514,264,337,593,543,950,335 with no decimal point; +/-7.9228162514264337593543950335 with 28 places to the right of the decimal; smallest non-zero number is +/-0.0000000000000000000000000001
Double (double-values; precision floating-point)	8 bytes	-1.79769313486231E308 to -4.94065645841247E-324 for negative 4.94065645841247E-324 to 1.79769313486232E308 for positive values
Integer	4 bytes	-2,147,483,648 to 2,147,483,647
Long (long integer)	8 bytes	-9,223,372,036,854,775,808 to 9,223,372,036,854,775,807
Object	4 bytes	Any type can be stored in a variable of type Object
Short	2 bytes	-32,768 to 32,767
Single (single-precision floating-point)	4 bytes	-3.402823E38 to -1.401298E-45 for negative values; 1.401298E-45 to 3.402823E38 for positive values
String (variable-length)	10 bytes + (2 * string length)	0 to approximately 2 billion Unicode characters
User-Defined Type (structure)	Sum of the sizes of its members	Each member of the structure has a range determined by its data type and independent of the ranges of the other members

Boolean

Boolean is typically used for continuation testing or simple On/Off, True/False conditions. You can use a Boolean variable to continue a programming loop until a certain condition becomes true. The following code is an example of this:

```
Dim lFinished as Boolean
lFinished = FALSE
While lFinished = FALSE
    'Code...
    'Code...
    If X = Y then
        lFinished = TRUE
        End if
Wend
```

The preceding program will run in a continuous loop until either lFinished becomes something other than False or your computer hangs because of the loss of resources.

String

The String data type is as simple as it sounds. It is used to store strings of text (alphabetic, numeric, and special characters) in memory until it is accessed. For example, when e-mail address information is saved to a database, it is usually processed through a String data type variable. Strings can be names, addresses, phone numbers, Web addresses, and the like. The following code is an example:

```
Dim strFirstName as String
strFirstName = "Peter"
```

Date

Date, too, is straightforward. This data type is used to store date information that is to be processed by a program. For example, the date that an entry is made to a database is quite often used for audit-trail purposes, and this information would be processed with a Date data type. The system time is also stored as part of this data type and can be drawn out separately if desired through the use of built-in functions. The following code is an example:

```
Dim dRightNow as Date
dRightNow = Today()
```

Integer

Integer is the data type for whole numbers. Numbers are used in programming for such things as counting iterations in a For Next loop, storing phone numbers, and counting the number of employees you have. The Integer data type is ideal for these situations. It should not be used, however, for financial or detailed math processes in which remainders or decimals are to be used. The following code is an example of the Integer data type in use:

```
Dim iCounting as Integer
iCounting = 1
```

Single

The Single data type is typically used for financial calculations or any other math functions that require the use of a decimal. Other decimal-handling data types exist, but this one seems to be the most predominantly used. The following code is an example of the Single data type in use:

```
Dim sMyCash as Single
sMyCash = 1000.02
```

Note   As you may notice in some of the code written so far is following a naming convention known as modified Hungarian. It was named after the programmer who devised it, he worked for Microsoft his nationality happen to be Hungarian. In this naming convention variables are named with a prefix denoting their data type and with capital letters for the major name sections. For example, a variable named strFirstName is obviously a string variable (with the str prefix), and it holds a string that happens to be a first name value. The initial caps on the major named portions are used for readability. When scanning through code one can visually see much better how a variable is named and how it is defined. Perform a Web search for this topic to gather more information on naming conventions for variables, and check out http://msdn.microsoft.com/library/default.asp?url=/library/en-us/dnw98bk/html/variablenameshungariannotation.asp.

Understanding DIM statements

As in the previous sections, there is a certain way to actually define a variable in memory space. By using the DIM command followed with a variable name and its designated data type, you can reserve memory space for a variable. Following is the complete syntax of the DIM command. For now, however, the previous examples are sufficient for getting started using this command.

```
DIM [WithEvents] varname[([subscripts])]  [As [New] type]
[= initexpr]
```

Although this syntax looks complex, you really need to concern yourself only with the DIM keyword itself, a variable name, and the data type that you want the variable to be. Optionally, you can set the variables initial value at the same time as you define it. Consider the following DIM statement:

```
Dim sMySalary as Single = 100000.02
```

The variable is called sMySalary and it is being defined as a Single data type. The initial value of $100,000.02 is being assigned to it. You can also define multiple variables with the same DIM command. The following statement defines three variables within the same statement, all with different data type assignments:

```
Dim iCounter as Integer, strFirstName as String, dRightNow as Date
```

Variable scope

The life expectancy of a variable is another matter to be considered when one is to be defined. Does a variable exist through the life of the running program, within a certain module of the application, or only within a certain subroutine of a particular form? Designating the answer to this is called *defining the scope of a variable.*

Visual Basic .NET enables you to define variables on at least three different levels. Variables defined at the application level exist in memory for the life of the application (while it is running). Programmers have to be conservative here (as well with the use of memory and system resources), because if they define a number of variables to be globally accessible and yet do not use them efficiently, then they are wasting system resources in the holding of variables and memory space when only being used under certain conditions.

Defining a phone number variable as globally accessible, for example, would be a great waste of system resources, whereas defining it at the module level would make sense. If you define a variable at the module level (in the open script of a form, for example), then that variable is accessible to any subprocedures within that form. And finally, if a variable is defined within a subprocedure or function (the code behind a push button, for example), then that variable only exists and is only accessible to that subprocedure that called it into existence.

Some ways around this limitation exist, by passing and returning variables to a routine. These variable scopes, as discussed, are sometimes called global, private, and local, respectively. It is a common programming "best practice" to define variables with as limited a scope as possible.

Operators

Two major categories are involved in the decision processes of computer languages, and VB.NET is no exception. The first category is that of operators and the second one is know as logical flow (discussed in the next section).

Operators are well known in the world of math. Table A-4 shows each operator's symbol with a brief description of its function. This table goes from the simplest operator to the more complex, and typically more powerful, operators. So, after you have mastered the more general operators, you should be able to employ the more complex ones relatively easily. Following the table are some specific examples of operators and how they are used in programming code.

Table A-4
VB.NET operators

Symbol	Name of Operator	Description
+	Plus (addition)	Used in adding two or more values together
-	Minus (subtraction)	Used in subtracting two or more values from each other
/	Division	Used in dividing one value into another
*	Multiplication	Used in multiplying two or more values together
=	Equals	Used in assigning the results of a calculation to a variable
>	Greater than	Used in determining if one variable's value is larger than another's
<	Less than	Used in determining if one variable's value is smaller than another's
>=	Greater than or equal to	Used in determining if one variable's value is larger than or equal to another's
<=	Less than or equal to	Used in determining if one variable's value is smaller than or equal to another's
<>	Not equal	Used in determining if one variable's value is not equal to another's

Performing math on variables

Here are some basic examples of math functions as they are implemented in
VB.NET code:

```
Dim iSubTotal as Integer, iTax as Single, iTotal as Single

iTax = iSubTotal * 1.10
iTotal = iSubTotal + iTax
```

The first line of code simply defines the variables to be used. The second line uses
the multiplication operator and the equals operator, multiplying the integer value in
iSubTotal by 1.10 (10 percent), and then assigns the result to the iTax variable.
The next line of code uses the addition operator to simply add two variables
together and assign the result to the iTotal variable.

Some math operations do not require the use of the equals operator. Consider the
following code example:

```
Dim iCounter as integer
iCounter = 1
```

```
Do until iCounter > 50
    'more code
    'more code
    iCounter = iCounter + 1
loop
```

This code is quite powerful if you need to repeat a process 50 times and no more.

Logical Flow

Our discussion now moves into the next category of how programs can flow based on simple decision processes. You thought I forgot about the other category that was mentioned in the previous section, but here it is now. There is usually a need for programs to repeat a process for a certain length of time, or indefinitely, and VB.NET has these features built in. There are also many times when decisions must be based on the context of the code at a moment in time and that context can change depending on the application users decisions.

If Then Else Endif Decision Construct

This is a coding construct that allows the code to perform one of two or more possible steps depending on the logical evaluation of an expression. The If...Then...Else programming construct has the following syntax:

```
If condition [ Then ]
    [ statements  ]
[ ElseIf elseifcondition [ Then ]
    [ elseifstatements ] ]
[ Else
    [ elsestatements ] ]
End If
```

Simplified, the syntax looks like this:

```
IF lExpression [THEN]
    Commands
[ELSE
    Commands]
END IF
```

Here is a simple example of the If...Then...Else command structure in operation:

```
If strA = strB then
    intCounter++
Else
    intOtherNumber++
End If
```

The process here is to test the equality of strA and strB; if they are equal in value, then increase the variable called intCounter by 1. However, if strA is not equal to strB, then the Else portion of the construct is handed the controls and is processed, increasing the value of intOtherNumber by 1. So if strA has the value of "ABC", strB has the value of "ABC", intCounter has the value of 10, and intOtherNumber has the value of 15, stepping through this code once would leave intCounter holding the value of 11, and all other values would remain the same. This should give you the general idea of the use of this construct. This theme has many variations, though, so you should look into the different applications of the construct, because some of the options available could increase the efficiency of your applications.

While Loops

The While...Wend set of commands is very powerful, yet can be dangerous at the same time, because it allows for a series of other commands to run indefinitely unless an escape route is planned for it. This is also known as a programming loop, because the code loops around and around until told to stop or the computer runs out of available resources. If not controlled properly the latter can occur causing what is known as an infinite loop, which is a bad thing.

The syntax of this command allows for a few escape routes, and it is usually good to use the first one available, that being the condition that controls the start of the While loop. First, take a look at the official syntax:

```
While condition
    'statements
End While
```

Now look at a practical example of how this While...Wend programming structure can be used in the real world:

```
Dim lContinue as Boolean, intCounter as Integer
lContinue = TRUE
intCounter = 1
While lContinue = TRUE
    MsgBox("Welcome to my .NET world !",
MsgBoxStyle.Exclamation, "Welcome Message" & str(intCounter))
    if intCounter > 10 then
        lContinue = FALSE
        end if
    intCounter = IntCounter + 1
End While
'Other code continues here...
```

This code tests for a few conditions. The first one is to run the While loop until the lContinue variable becomes something other than True. The code then sends out a message box to the screen, welcoming the user to the new world of .NET. Then, another control structure is used within the While loop; this is called program nesting.

Note You will find that many of these logical decision programming constructs will work in concert with each other to make an application flow smoothly. There are many combinations of "nesting" these commands within others. In the preceding code example, the While construct leverages on the answer of a nested If...Then...Else statement. Don't be surprised if you see nested Ifs and nested Whiles used repeatedly in programming code.

The loop is being tested for how many times it has run by interrogating the value of intCounter. If it is found to be greater than 10, then the logical variable lContinue is set to a value of False. The code then continues to flow, adding 1 to the intCounter variable and then returning to the top of the loop, where the value of lContinue is tested one more time. This time it is tested as being False (not True), and the While loop is terminated with the programming code continuing to run at the next command that follows the End While command.

For Next Loops

Another logical construct that is available to the .NET developer is the controlled looping commands of the For...Next loop. This looping structure is very similar to that of the While loop, except that it is only concerned with a certain number of iterations and does not depend on the value of another variable. Although there are some variations on this construct, flexibility is built in, as shown later in this section. The complete syntax follows:

```
For counter = start To end [ Step step ]
    ' Statement block to be executed for each value of counter.
Next [ counter ]
```

Here is a practical example of a For...Next loop:

```
Dim intLoopCount
For intLoopCount = 1 to 25
    'Debug.WriteLine  exports the given values to the debug
window...
    Debug.WriteLine ("Current Value of intLoopCount:" &
intLoopCount)
Next intLoopCount
'More code...
```

This example will repeat the code of displaying text in the debug window 25 times. When the loop is concluded, the program continues its operation on the next line of code following the Next command. The For...Next loop increases the value of intLoopCount automatically, so you don't need to increment it yourself. Another feature of the For...Next loop construct is that you can set the amount by which the loop counter is counted. This is accomplished with the Step addition. Consider the following example:

```
Dim intLoopCount
For intLoopCount = 1 to 25 Step 5
```

```
    'Debug. WriteLine exports the given values to the debug
window...
Debug. WriteLine("Current Value of intLoopCount:" &
intLoopCount)
Next intLoopCount
'More code...
```

Again, this code repeats until the intLoopCount reaches the number 25; however, in this case, it will only loop a total of five times, because intLoopCount is being increased by 5 each iteration of the loop rather than the default of 1. Step can also be used to count backward. The following example of the For portion of the construct is also valid:

```
For intLoopCount = 500 to 25 Step -50
```

Select Case Construct

The last major decision construct is that of Select Case. This construct is used when more than two paths need to be considered. Its use replaces the need for multiple If...Then commands, and it is easier to code, understand, and follow logically. For example, if you were trying to determine in what category to place someone's information based on the number of toes they have on each foot (sorry, that's all I could think of), and you were trying to do that with one long If statement, you would have to write this code:

```
If intToes = 1 then
   ' some code...
elseif intToes = 2 then
   ' some more code
elseif intToes = 3 then
   ' some more code
elseif intToes = 4 then
   ' some more code
elseif intToes = 5 then
   ' some more code
elseif intToes = 6 then
   ' it is possible !
end if
```

As you can see, even from this lame example, it is programmatically difficult to catch all the possibilities with this kind of coding scheme. Also, consider what would have to be changed if you had to start counting toes on both feet and then fingers too! This is where the Select Case construct can help. The full syntax follows:

```
Select [ Case ] testexpression
   [ Case expressionlist
      [ statements ] ]
   [ Case Else
      [ elsestatements ] ]
End Select
```

Here is a practical example:

```
Select Case intToes
Case 1
    ' some code...
Case 2
' some more code
Case 3
    ' some more code
Case 4
    ' some more code
Case 5
    ' some more code
Case 6
    ' it is possible !
End Select
```

This is close to the other example, except that it looks cleaner and is easier to read. This alone is worth using it if you have a lot of similar coding decisions to make. The `Select Case` construct also has a "catch all" at the end that is very beneficial, which is the `Case Else` portion. Consider the preceding example. If you have to code for all the previous conditions and then also consider the situation in which there may be more toes to count, you have the option of using `Case Else`. You could write the preceding example as follows:

```
Select Case intToes
Case 1
    ' some code...
Case 2
    ' some more code
Case 3
    ' some more code
Case 4
    ' some more code
Case 5
    ' some more code
Case 6
    ' it is possible !
Case Else
    ' more code to catch all the other possibilities.
End Select
```

As you can see, the `Case Else` portion of the command can be used to catch any other situations that are not specifically being trapped. Even if you think that all the situations are covered in the detailed `Case` condition lines, it is always a good idea to use `Case Else`, in the event that you may have missed a possible situation in the application.

Summary

This has been a very cursory overview of the VB.NET development environment. You have been introduced to the IDE as well as some coding standards. You have seen some of the basic building blocks of the whole .NET environment, and if you followed the sample mailing list project, you should have an application up and running.

✦   ✦   ✦

Visual Basic Functions and Features

In Appendix A, "Visual Basic Syntax," you developed a small application, or solution, in the .NET environment. You were introduced to some of the basic code structures and decision-making constructs. As well, you were introduced to some of the more common IDE tools. All in all, you were given the first part of the foundation of the .NET environment. In this appendix, you will look at the second portion of the foundation, that of functions and subroutines.

Functions and Subroutines

First you need some definitions to lay the groundwork and set the stage for what will be covered in this appendix. A function is almost the same as a subroutine, except that the function is programmed to return a value to the calling code. A subroutine is a smaller portion of programming code that is defined to perform a specific task. Upon completion, subroutines do not return a data value to the calling code. Functions and subroutines also share the following attributes:

✦ Usually small blocks or sections of programming code

✦ Code is generally reusable in many contexts (if written well)

✦ Entities can have different scopes of use depending on how they are defined

To illustrate the differences between these two types of coding entities, a messenger analogy will be employed. A function is like a real-life messenger whom you send to the store for groceries. You give the messenger some money and a list of items to purchase. The messenger performs the task and returns with the goods. A subroutine is another type of messenger, except that this type of messenger is sent to a bank with money to deposit. The cash is given to the messenger and off he goes to perform the task. Eventually, and hopefully, your messenger returns with the good news that all has been accomplished. In effect, he only returns with the news that the task is completed. In both situations, you, as the sender, have to wait for the messenger to return (because you are hungry and want to know your new bank balance).

Subroutines and functions act in a similar fashion. Your code makes reference to them by name, and then you have to wait for the process to finish before your calling code can continue.

Now that you have been introduced to the definitions, you are ready to look at the syntax, with some code examples thrown in. Here is the official syntax for defining a subroutine:

```
[ <attrlist> ] [{ Overloads | Overrides | Overridable |
NotOverridable | MustOverride | Shadows | Shared }]
[{ Public | Protected | Friend | Protected Friend | Private }]
Sub name [(arglist)]
    [ statements ]
    [ Exit Sub ]
 @code: @code: @code:[@code:
@code:s@code:t@code:a@code:t@code:e@code:m@code:e@code:n@code:t
@code:s@code: @code:]@code:

End Sub
```

The following is a more concrete example:

```
Private Sub MySubRoutine(OptionalVariable as DataType)
    'Code here
    'Code here
End Sub
```

Every subroutine uses the key word Sub to indicate to the compiler that it is a subroutine. Also, to denote the conclusion of the subroutine, the key words End Sub are required. Any programming code between these "book ends" is considered part of the subroutine. The parentheses after the subroutine's name are used optionally to send data into it for processing.

Note   The key word Private is used to denote the program scope of the defined subroutine or function. The scope of the defined routine is also determined by *where* it is created — more on that later in the section titled "Defining functions and scope."

Here is an example of a subroutine that receives data and uses that data within its contained code:

```
Private Sub MySubRoutine (strValue as String)
    Dim strMessage as String
    StrMessage = "This is the passed in value: " & strValue

    Debug.WriteLine(strMessage)
End Sub
```

You can see the variable called `strValue` being given to the subroutine via the parentheses. Then, within the routine, the `strValue` variable is concatenated to the hard-coded string and sent as output to the debug window.

Now look at the programming animal called a function — again, you will be shown the syntax first, followed by some practical examples:

```
[ <attrlist> ] [{ Overloads | Overrides | Overridable |
NotOverridable | MustOverride | Shadows | Shared }]
[{ Public | Protected | Friend | Protected Friend | Private }]
Function name[(arglist)] [ As type ]
    [ statements ]
    [ Exit Function ]
    [ statements ]
End Function
```

The following is a more reasonable example of the basic syntax:

```
Private Function MyNextFunc(strValue as String) as String
    'code here
    'code here
    MyNextFunc = "Hello My Name is Dawn Etta Riley"
End Function
```

Notice the differences here in relation to a subroutine:

✦ The `Function` keyword is used instead of `Sub`

✦ After the parentheses, a data definition is used

✦ `End Function` is used instead of `End Sub`

✦ The returned value is the name of the function as it is assigned within the function itself

And now for your practical example of a working function:

```
Private Function MyValue (intGiven as Integer) as Integer
    Dim intCounter as integer, I as integer
    Dim intHolder as Integer
    IntCounter = intGiven * 5
    IntHolder = 0
    For I = 1 to intCounter
```

```
        IntHolder += I
    Next I
    MyValue = intHolder
End Function
```

In this example, the function is defined as an integer function, and it will accept into it a value of an Integer data type called `intGiven`. Some variables are defined for use inside the function, and the counter variable is multiplied by 5 (just because). Then, a `For...Next` loop is employed to run `intCounter` times and during that loop another command is increasing the `intHolder` variable by the value of the counter (I).

You may find it helpful to "walk through" this code with some actual values. Let's pretend that `intGiven` is equal to 2. `IntCounter` becomes equal to 10, so the loop will then run 10 times. The first time through, the loop `intHolder` equals 1, the next time through `intHolder` is 1 + 2 = 3, next time 3 + 3 = 6, then 6 + 4 = 10, and so on. At the end of this process, `intHolder` finally equals 55. `MyValue` is assigned `intHolder`'s value and is returned to the line of code that originally called the function.

This brings up a few other issues that you may have been wondering about:

✦ How do you call or invoke a function in code?

✦ What holds the value of the function once it is returned to the invoking code?

To help you understand the answers to these questions, consider the following code:

```
Dim intReturnedValue as Integer
IntReturnedValue = MyValue(2)
Debug.Write( intReturnedValue )
```

The second line of code performs two steps in one line. On the right side of the equal sign, the function called `MyValue` is triggered or called, passing it the value of 2. When the function is completed (remember that it should return the value of 55 in this case), the answer is assigned to `intReturnedValue`.

Defining functions and scope

Now that you see how to call a function, the next step to putting this puzzle together is to see *where* the function is defined. So far, all you have been exposed to in .NET is programming code being associated with a form or a window. .NET has the ability, and the need, to define programming code independently of a window or form. This is done by creating a *module* in which to house your code. A module is a nonvisual component of .NET. In this section, you will be using the solution coded in Appendix A called Mailman. It is on the companion Web site for this book. To define an empty module, do the following:

1. Select the solution name in the Solution Explorer.

2. Right-click the solution name.

3. Select Add Item from the resulting pop-up menu.

4. Select Module and name it "GlobalCode.vb."

5. Click OK.

The module selection window looks like that shown in Figure B-1. The module has been named GlobalCode, but you can call it whatever you wish. The new module should appear in the Solution Explorer list.

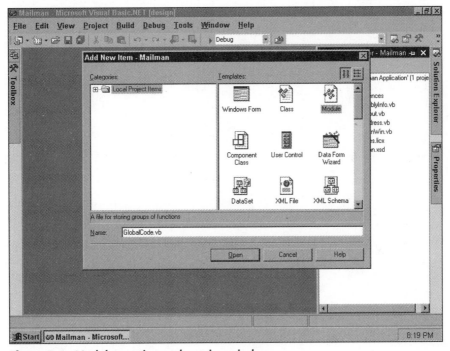

Figure B-1: Module creation and naming window

This brings up the discussion of subroutine and function scope. Because this particular module is not part of any specific form or window, it can be referenced on a global or application-wide level. If a subroutine or function were to be created within this module, then any other entity within the application could use it by default. If, for example, a special date routine is defined in this module and it is needed throughout the entire solution, you could call it from any window or routine that needed it.

With the new module in the Solution Explorer in focus, double-click it to open the code editor for it. It may already be open in the design area for you, so simply click that area to give it focus. Define the following subroutine, which will be used to send information to the debug window whenever a menu item is clicked. This can be a helpful routine to use when tracing program action.

```
Sub MenuCheck(ByVal RoutineName As String)
    Debug.Write("you are in the " & RoutineName & " menu code")
End Sub
```

Now you need to tell the subroutine how to start. With the Mailman solution open, create another module using the same process as before; this time call the module MainMod.

Launching programs

VB.NET has a neat way to launch the programs that you create in it. If you create a MDI application, such as the Mailman program, then .NET knows to launch that window upon program execution simply because it is a MDI application. But what happens if you want to do some processing before the main MDI form appears? What if you want to make a splash screen (welcome screen) or accept a user login request for system security needs? If either of the preceding is the case, then you have to do an additional two steps:

✦ Step 1: Create a special subroutine named Main().

✦ Step 2: Inform .NET that you now have a main module that you want to start the application with.

You can create a special subroutine named Main() in the new module you just defined called MainMod, or you can create it in another module of your choice.

Note

You should not call any other subroutine in your application by the special moniker of Main. This is a "reserved" subroutine name used specifically for program launch issues. There are some ways around this, but it is highly recommended that you toe the Microsoft line on this one.

Consider the following Main() subroutine code and see if you can follow what is happening. After the code listing, it will be explained for you.

```
Sub Main()

    Dim TimerEvent As New System.Threading.AutoResetEvent(False)

    Dim Start, Finish
    Dim frmMainForm As New frmMainWin()

    ' wait 6 seconds by calling dummyevent and giving the
milliseconds.
    TimerEvent.WaitOne(6000, False)
    ' close the event handle
    TimerEvent.Close()

    frmMainForm.Show()
End Sub
```

Note   The splash screen code is not yet included in the preceding code because the frmSplash window itself has not yet been defined within the solution.

After defining some variables in memory with the DIM command, the Start variable is stored with the Timer object's current value. Adding five seconds to the value of the Timer object and storing the value in the variable called Finish is what happens next. Then, a simple "dummy" loop is run until the current value of the Timer object (which updates itself constantly with the value of the system clock) is less than the value stored in the Finish variable. This is done to keep the computer "busy" while the splash screen is showing and needed. After the loop has finished, the main MDI form is loaded and displayed. Then, control of the application is released to the new form because this subroutine is finished.

The second step that you are required to perform to have a Main() module in operation is to inform .NET that you now have a main module that you want to start the application with. You want this new module to take precedence during program launch. Under the Project Tools menu, after selecting the project name, you should see a menu item named Project Properties. Click this menu item to open the form shown in Figure B-2.

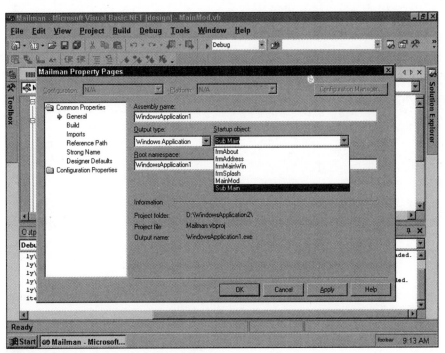

Figure B-2: Compiler options window

Here you tell the compiler what object to use for application launching. You should see in the Startup Object drop-down list all system objects (forms and modules) that you have defined so far. Select Sub Main to tell the compiler to use this subroutine to begin the application.

Note   Other options are available here that you can explore yourself. Different ways to make the compiler act are among some of the additional options. Take a few minutes to explore through these options.

Now that you have set up the start module and written the main subroutine, make a simple splash screen similar to that shown in Figure B-3 and name it frmSplash.

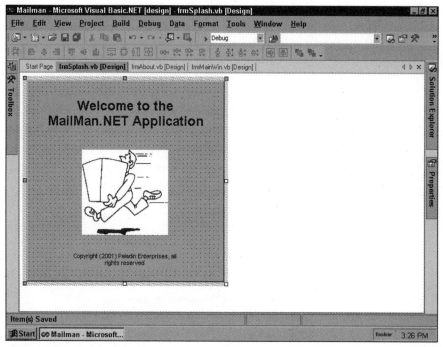

Figure B-3: Sample splash window

Now, go back to your main code module and add the line of code shown in bold in the following code. This was left out previously because the code would not have compiled if it made reference to an entity that did not exist.

```
Sub Main()

    Dim TimerEvent As New System.Threading.AutoResetEvent(False)

    Dim Start, Finish

    Dim frmSplashNew As New frmSplash()
```

```
    Dim frmMainForm As New frmMainWin()

    frmSplashNew.Show()

    ' wait 6 seconds by calling dummyevent and giving the
milliseconds.
    TimerEvent.WaitOne(6000, False)
    ' close the event handle
    TimerEvent.Close()

    frmSplashNew.Close()
    frmMainForm.Show()
End Sub

End Sub
```

Let's get back to the point of this whole section, which is to call the subroutine that was created in the module called "GlobalCode." Open the main form named frmMainWin and access the menu code for the address form. It should look like the code in the following listing:

```
Dim frmAdd1 As New frmAddress()
' enable menu items now that a window will be opened...
mnuCopy.Enabled = True
mnuPaste.Enabled = True
mnuCut.Enabled = True
mnuTileHoriz.Enabled = True
mnuTileVert.Enabled = True
mnuCascade.Enabled = True

'Set the Parent Form of the Child window.
frmAdd1.MdiParent = Me
frmAdd1.Show()
```

Add the following code that is in bold text, which will call the MenuCheck subroutine defined earlier in this appendix .

```
Dim frmAdd1 As New frmAddress()
' enable menu items now that a window will be opened...
mnuCopy.Enabled = True
mnuPaste.Enabled = True
mnuCut.Enabled = True
mnuTileHoriz.Enabled = True
mnuTileVert.Enabled = True
mnuCascade.Enabled = True
MenuCheck("Open Address")

'Set the Parent Form of the Child window.
frmAdd1.MdiParent = Me
frmAdd1.Show()
```

Build the application before you run it this time, because a lot of changes have occurred in different areas of the solution. If all goes well, when you run the program, you should see the splash screen followed by the MDI main form. Then, open the address window to see the subroutine being called. If you have successfully written this project, the debug window should appear as shown in Figure B-4.

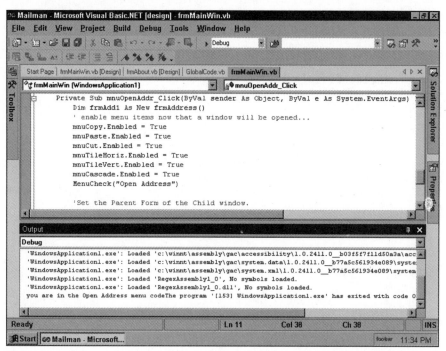

Figure B-4: Debug window showing results of the `MenuCheck` subroutine

Now, every time your system users select that menu item, the message will go to the debug window. Of course, this example is not the most practical of all examples, but it should have at least brought the point home that some subroutines or functions can be used in a generic way, and in a way that is independent of the overall application solution.

Built-in Functions

This section looks at some of the built-in functions that are provided with .NET. This product is so vast that it would almost take an entire book just to cover all the built-in functions that are provided. So, the scope here will certainly be much more narrow. The point of this section is to provide a general introduction to these tools and to help you become comfortable enough using some of them that you are confident enough to explore and discover more of the provided functions when the need arises in your applications.

A *built-in function,* as its name suggests, is a function that is built into the .NET compiler and that always performs the same task. You, as an application developer, generally cannot change or alter the actions of a function that is provided with .NET, but you have this plethora of tools at your disposal whenever you need them. These functions come in many different categories, and, as mentioned before, you will only be shown a few of the more common ones at this time, namely some of the data conversion functions.

Data conversion functions

One of the most common tasks a program needs to do is to convert data between variables of different data types. For example, suppose you are handling data from an external source over which you have no control regarding the format in which it provides the data, and you want to save that information in your own, different format. You would be faced with a data conversion issue. Consider the following code example:

```
Dim strPassedInValue as String, dConvertedDate as Date
StrPassedinValue = "June 16, 1966"
DConvertedDate = CDate( strPassedinValue )
If isDate (dConvertedDate)
    Debug.Write("This is a valid date: " & dConvertedDate )
Else
    Debug.Write("This is an invalid Date: " & dConvertedDate )
End IF
```

This code uses the CDate built-in function, which converts the data passed to it into a date format, checking it as it is processed. Another built-in function, isDate, checks the date for validity and returns a True or False Boolean answer based on its findings.

Now consider this code, which converts a String value into an Integer value so that it can be used in mathematical equations:

```
Dim StrValue as string, intValue as Integer
StrValue = "123456"
IntValue = Val(strValue) * 5
' should return the value of 617280
Debug.Write intValue
```

Val converts the string of numbers into actual numeric data so that the compiler knows what to do when performing the math operation.

The following example includes a neat conversion function called CType, which will convert any valid information passed to it to any specified data type, as long as it can be converted properly.

```
Dim lngNumber As Long, sngNewValue As Single
lngNumber = 5500
' sngNewValue is set to 5500.0
sngNewValue = CType(lngNumber, Single)
```

Available .NET functions

To complete this discussion of built-in functions, Table B-1 provides a list of all the currently available .NET functions. Be sure to look up any of these functions in the online help so that you can be sure of their uses. These functions go well beyond simple data conversion techniques to include such things as record-locking functions, string-trimming functions, date-manipulation functions, and so on.

Table B-1 Complete list of .NET built-in functions				
Abs	AppActivate	Asc	AscW	Atn
Beep	CallByName	CBool	CByte	CChar
CDate	CDbl	CDec	ChDir	ChDrive
Choose	Chr	Cint	CLng	CObj
Command	Conversions	Cos	CreateObject	CShort
CStr	CType	CurDir	DateAdd	DateDiff
DatePart	DateSerial	DateValue	Day	DDB
DeleteSetting	Derived Math	Dir	Environ	EOF
ErrorToString	Exp	FileAttr	FileClose	FileCopy
FileDateTime	FileLen	FileOpen	FileWidth	Filter
Fix	Format	FormatCurrency	FormatDateTime	FormatNumber
FormatPercent	FreeFile	FV	GetAllSettings	GetAttr
GetChar	GetException	GetObject	GetSetting	Hex
Hour	Iif	Input	InputBox	InputString
InStr	InStrRev	Int	IPmt	IRR
IsArray	IsDate	IsDbNull	IsError	IsNothing
IsNumeric	IsReference	Join	Kill	LBound
LCase	Left	Len	LineInput	Loc
Lock	LOF	Log	LSet	LTrim
Mid	Minute	MIRR	MkDir	Month
MonthName	MsgBox	Nper	NPV	Oct

Partition	Pmt	PPmt	Print	Printline
PV	QBColor	Rate	Rename	Replace
Reset	RGB	Right	RmDir	Round
Rnd	Rset	RTrim	SaveSetting	Second
Seek	SetAttr	Sgn	Shell	Sin
SLN	Space	Spc	Split	Sqr
Str	StrComp	StrConv	StrDup	StrReverse
Switch	SYD	Tab	Tan	TimeSerial
TimeValue	Trim	TypeName	UBound	UCase
Unlock	Val	Weekday	WeekdayName	Write
WriteLine	Year			

Built-in Objects

Just as .NET has many built-in functions, it also has many built-in objects. Once again, a few definitions will be helpful before we get into the meat of built-in objects:

✦ **Object**: A programming entity that can have both state (known as properties) and actions (known as methods) associated with it. A real-world example of an object would be a rubber ball. A .NET example of an object would be a clickable push button on a window form.

✦ **Property**: Something that an object owns or that describes its characteristics in such a way that it can be uniquely identified within its object. Taking the rubber ball as an example of an object, one of its properties would be its color. Taking the .NET example of an object, a push button on a form, a property of that push button would be its text label, typically OK or Cancel.

✦ **Method**: An action that can occur that affects an object. In the example of the ball, an action that can be performed against it is to roll it. An example here could be the printing action of a window or form.

So, with these definitions in mind, let's take a deeper look at what a method of an object is and then see some more examples of actual methods . If you have read through the previous section, then you should have a pretty good handle on what a function is. A method, then, is basically a function that is specific to an object. You have already coded one rather large section of code in the Mailman solution, and apart from the subroutine that is being called, it is all code that sets object properties and calls object methods.

Take a look at this code:

```
Private Sub mnuOpenAddr_Click(ByVal sender As Object, ByVal e
As System.EventArgs) Handles mnuOpenAddr.Click
        Dim frmAdd1 As New frmAddress()
        ' enable menu items now that a window will be opened...
        mnuCopy.Enabled = True
        mnuPaste.Enabled = True
        mnuCut.Enabled = True
        mnuTileHoriz.Enabled = True
        mnuTileVert.Enabled = True
        mnuCascade.Enabled = True
        MenuCheck("Open Address")

        'Set the Parent Form of the Child window.
        frmAdd1.MdiParent = Me
        frmAdd1.Show()
    End Sub
```

`MnuCopy.Enabled = True` is an example of an object's property being set. This enabled property is for a menu object, and it can either be True or False. `FrmAdd1.MdiParent = Me` is another example of another object, `frmAdd1`, having its `MdiParent` property set to another object called `Me`. This is an example of an object's property being given the value of another object. The `frmAdd1.Show()` command line is telling the compiler to run the method (it does kind of look like a function doesn't it?) called `Show` in the object called `frmAdd1`.

Figure B-5 shows the Properties page of a simple form object that is a push button. Consider all the properties of this one object and then think of all the other design tools alone that have similar and/or varying properties and methods.

 Note   System.Windows.Forms.Button also posses an interesting observation. This series of objects, separated by periods, is actually the object hierarchy of object owner-ship to the push button object. The `Button` object is owned by the `Forms` object (the button is placed on the form), which in turn is owned by the `Windows` object, which in turn is controlled by the `System` object.

As you can see from the preceding code example and Figure B-5, a .NET solution involves a lot of object manipulation. After you become more familiar with the coding style of the .NET environment, you will notice that most of the code is either calling functions (built-in or handmade) or subroutines and manipulating an object's properties or methods. There are variations of course and you will also find that your code will be doing a fair amount of employing variables to hold temporary data, but you will come to see that the code is usually focused in one of these main veins.

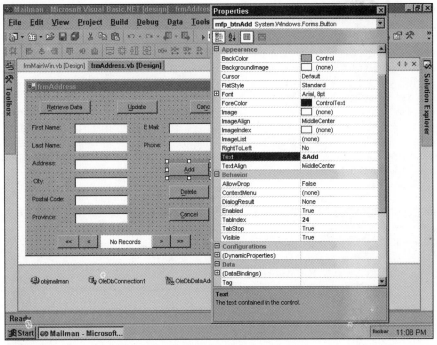

Figure B-5: The Properties page of a push button object

Brief Tour of the Debugger

This section completes the overall tour of the VB.NET product. So far in Appendix A and Appendix B, you have looked at the IDE of VB.NET and have written a fair amount of code. The code has dealt a lot with variables, functions, and objects at varying levels. If you look back over the previous pages, you will see that a lot of information was covered and that you have actually learned quite a lot about the product and how to manage it.

But soon you will begin to write applications to suit your own needs. You have the basic skills to get by, but what happens when you hit that first wall? You have checked all of your code and the logic looks good, yet when you launch your application, it performs sporadically. Where do you go for help? What can be done to rectify a wayward application? Enter the debugger!

The application debugger is a tool that ships with the VB.NET product and is set up for your use as soon as you install it. Debugging code involves two major levels: compile-time debugging and run-time debugging. These are discussed next.

Using the compiler

Compile-time debugging occurs on two smaller levels of its own. One level is the simple debugging of code that you perform when you are writing the application code. You know just by reading through it that it is not likely to work as you want it, or that you have noticed a design flaw in your code during its writing, so you make the needed adjustments. You have also used the second aspect of this first line of defense against badly performing code, and that is the compiler's build feature. When you select Build ⇨ Build in the .NET environment, you are instructing the compiler to look through your code and inform you of any glaring programming mistakes. If you have a successful build, then the Output window will display a message similar to that shown in Figure B-6.

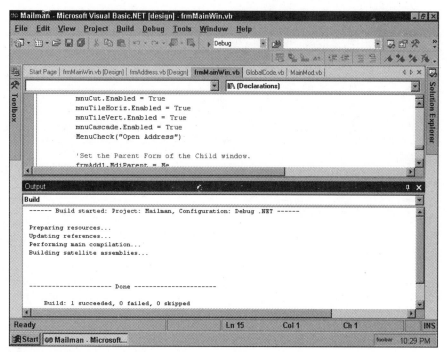

Figure B-6: Successful build results in the Output window

The IDE code editor helps you out with flagging any compiler issues as well by highlighting any erroneous code as you write it. For example, if you leave out the End Sub command when defining a subroutine, the code editor will either suggest a solution to you or flag the code as problematic. But when you actually invoke the build process, you are telling the compiler to take another complete pass through your whole application, to look for any programming errors. If the build process passes, then you are ready to run the application. If, however, you are presented with a report showing some errors, you may not be able to run your application at all (depending on the severity of the error).

Using the debugger

After you actually have finished the building and scanning of your code and are ready to run the application, you may still be faced with some bugs that are more of a challenge to ferret out. This is where the run-time debugger becomes very helpful. As you can see in Figure B-7, few options are presented to you on the Debug menu before the solution is actually executed. The debugger is invoked in either of two ways. One is to select Debug ⇨ Start (or pressing F5). The second way is to place a break point in the code close to where you suspect the bug to be. Setting of break points is discussed a bit later.

Note To jump between the debugging session and the running application, simply use the Windows task bar to switch between any running applications.

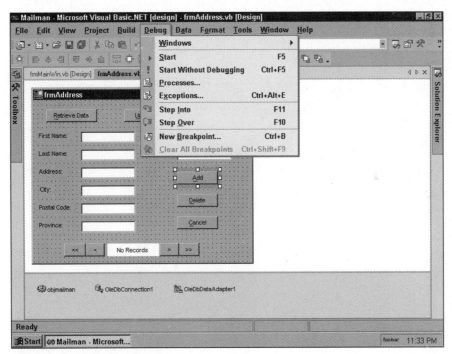

Figure B-7: Debug menu items

Stepping into and over

The Debug menu has a few options that you will want to learn to use (as well as their corresponding hot keys). The first menu item that you should become familiar with is Debug ⇨ Step Into (which also can be invoked by pressing F11 after the debugger is active). This menu item will run each line of code for you in a step-by-step process. It enables you to look at the state of the running application in many different ways. For example, if you are tracking down a programming error and want to examine the code and the actions of the application as it runs, you can use this option (after the debugger is running) to step into each line of code. Another neat feature of this option is that if a function or subroutine is about to be called in a subsequent line of code, you can press F11 to step down into that function so that you can follow the application as it travels from function to function.

If, however, you know that a certain function is bug free, you can use the other most common Debug menu item, Debug ⇨ Step Over. The code in the function that you want to step over is still executed, but the debugger does not take the time to show you each line of code in that function as it executes.

Figure B-8 shows you a debugging session of the MenuCheck subroutine that was created earlier in this appendix (refer to the section, "Defining functions and scope"). During the debug session, the Write function also ran, the output of which is shown in the little window at the bottom right. In addition, a watch [Watch?] variable was set, instructing the debugger to specifically watch and report on the state of the frmAdd1 object. As shown in the bottom-left window of Figure B-8, the debugger reported that the frmAdd1 object has not been declared.

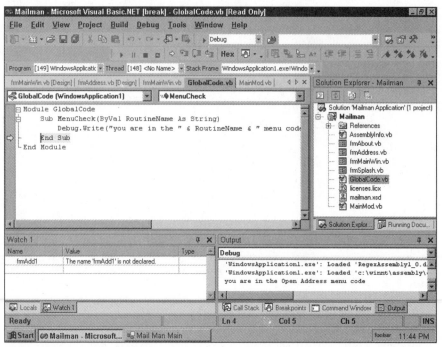

Figure B-8: Debugging session showing the current line of code with a watch variable set

Setting break points

Setting a break point is one of the best features to use in a debugging session. This feature stops the processing of the program code at a location specified by the programmer. This enables you to run your application through all the working parts and to stop just before the area where a bug may be happening. Then, after the code is stopped and displayed to you, you can use the F11 and F10 hot keys to fine-tune the bug hunt.

To set a break point, simply open the code in question in the code editor and click the mouse button on the empty gray bar to the left of the line of code that you want to break on. This invokes the break point holder, shown in Figure B-9. The line of code is highlighted in red and a large red dot appears in the gray band on the left.

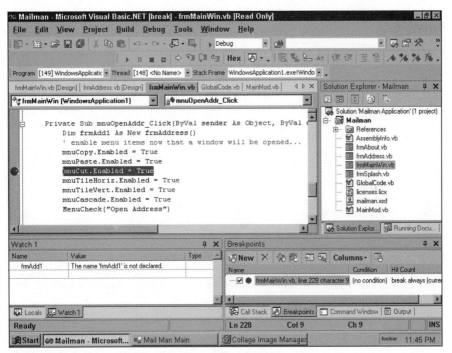

Figure B-9: Debug window showing set break point

This was, as promised, a very brief tour of the VB.NET debugger. Many aspects of it were not covered here. You are encouraged to take some time to explore this application troubleshooting tool and see what else it can do for you.

Summary

This appendix has shown you how to create your own functions and subroutines, and how to use and invoke a built-in function. You have been introduced to the basic object-oriented concepts of methods and properties. You have also been shown how to use the VB.NET debugger.

✦   ✦   ✦

Visual Basic Object-Oriented Programming

VB.NET is based on the concept of object-oriented programming (OOP). Therefore, it is essential to understand the meaning of OOP and how it is used in VB.NET. While the concept of OOP remains the same for most programming languages, its usage with regard to VB.NET has a slight difference.

In versions prior to VB 4.0, forms, controls, and databases were nothing but objects. Logically speaking, the next question that should come to mind is what in the world are "objects" and why are the variables that you declare not categorized as objects. Basically, it would be correct to state that any version of VB before VB 4.0 was not object oriented — in spite of the fact that while programming with VB, you are actually using objects. This might sound funny and ambiguous, but when you complete reading the contents of this appendix, you will have a thorough understanding of the concepts of OOP.

In addition, you will also learn the concept of classes and how they are created. Finally, you will learn how to create an object hierarchy by using the concept of inheritance. These concepts have a logical link amongst themselves, which is why these concepts are covered one after another.

Introduction to Object-Oriented Programming

To begin understanding the concept of object-oriented programming with respect to VB.NET, it is essential to understand OOP in the generic sense. A generic definition of OOP would be something along the lines of, "A collection of independent objects, which represent instances of a class and can be bound by the relationship of inheritance." To have a clearer understanding of this definition, let's split it into three parts:

✦ **A collection of objects:** This suggests that object-oriented programs use objects. Objects are the logical building blocks of a program.

✦ **Represented by an instance of a class:** This part of the definition suggests that an object is an instance of a class.

✦ **Bound by the relationship of inheritance:** This part of the definition suggests that the classes can be bound together and have a relationship. This relationship is nothing but inheritance.

An object-oriented program is one that is capable of satisfying each of these three conditions. If even one of the conditions is not applicable to a programming language, it cannot be considered an OOP language. Programming languages that do not use inheritance should consciously not be categorized as object-oriented languages. To understand the concept of OOP, you need to understand classes and objects.

Classes and objects

While working in VB.NET, you would have already worked with classes and objects, though you never knew it. The question that arises now is how to create your own classes and their objects. Just observe the toolbox that you use to put controls on your form. All the controls present on the toolbox actually represent classes, and you create an object of these classes by dragging and dropping a control on the form. You can now define an *object* as an instance of a class. A *class* defines the fields, properties, methods, and events of an object. If you take the example of birds as a class, then the objects that will fall under it will be peacock, sparrow, and kingfisher. An object can also be defined as an independent unit that consists of data and methods that are used to manipulate this data.

You can create multiple objects (instances) of a class. All of these objects share the same set of characteristics, such as properties, methods, and events that are provided by the class. However, the property values for each object might be different. For example, you can create multiple buttons on your form. By doing so, you are creating multiple instances of the Button class. All the buttons have similar sets of properties, such as Name and Text, which are defined in the Button class. However, you will specify a different name for each button.

You create an object of a class by using the `Dim` statement. For example:

```
Dim emp As Employee
```

The preceding statement creates an object named emp of the Employee class. You need to use the New keyword to assign memory to this object. For doing so, consider the following statement:

```
Dim emp As New Employee
```

Properties

Objects, in Visual Basic, have certain attributes that describe them. These attributes are nothing but *properties*. Just as credibility, goodwill, and size are attributes that describe an organization, properties describe objects.

You can set or retrieve values from these properties as you do with variables. For doing so, first you need to access the property and then assign the value. To access the property of an object, you use the following syntax:

```
Object.Property
```

In the preceding syntax, *Object* refers to the name of the object and *Property* refers to the name of the property that is to be accessed.

The following syntax explains assigning or retrieving values from a property:

```
Object.Property = value
Result = Object.Property
```

Consider the following example that returns the value stored in a text box and then assigns a new value to the text box:

```
'Declare a string variable
Dim strName As String

'Retrieve the value stored
StrName = txtName.Text

'Assign a new value
txtName.Text = "John"
```

In this code sample, txtName is an object of class TextBox.

Methods

Objects perform tasks on the data they contain. The tasks that are performed on the data are undertaken by procedures and functions that are specified in the class definition. In OOP, these procedures and functions are called *methods*. You can access the methods of an object like you access the properties.

For example:

```
Object.Method
```

In the preceding syntax, *Object* refers to the name of the object and *Method* refers to the method that you need to access.

> **Note**
>
> You might not want the properties and methods of an object to be accessed by the code outside the class. For this you declare the members of a class by using the `Private` statement. However, if you want the properties and methods to be accessible outside the class, use the `Public` statement to declare them. Public members become part of an object's interface.

Events

In addition to properties and methods, an object can have an event associated with it. *Events* are actions or occurrences that are detected by a program. They are responsible for giving indications to other objects and code about what is going on. An action, such as a user clicking the mouse or pressing a key on the keyboard, can be an event. System occurrences, such as a system running out of memory, can also be categorized as an event. The following statements and keywords help you in raising and handling events:

✦ The `Event` keyword helps you to declare an event. The following syntax is used to declare an event:

```
'Declare an event
Event MyEvent
```

✦ The `RaiseEvent` statement is used to generate or raise an event. The following syntax is used to raise an event:

```
'Raise the event
RaiseEvent MyEvent
```

✦ The `WithEvents` statement is used to declare a reference to an object that may be raising events:

```
'Declare an object of the class employee
Dim WithEvents EmpObj As Employee
```

✦ The `Handles` statement specifies the event handled by an *event handler*. An event handler (or event procedure as used with VB6 terminology) is a procedure that is invoked when the event occurs:

```
'Declare an event handler
Sub MyEventHandler() Handles EmpObj.MyEvent
```

VB.NET provides you with a set of classes that you can use to accomplish various tasks in your application. However, there might be certain tasks, which cannot be accomplished with the already existing classes. For example, consider a situation wherein you want to develop an application that handles all transactions related to salary, leave, and performance assessment of employees in an organization. In such a situation, you are required to create your own class to achieve the desired functionality. VB.NET gives developers the opportunity to put their creative and logical brains to the best use by allowing them to create their own classes instead of using the existing ones. Let us now look at some of the features of OOP.

Features of object-oriented programming

The objects in an object-oriented program support encapsulation, polymorphism, and reuse. In VB.NET, the best way to accomplish reuse is by inheritance. In VB6, reuse was partially implemented with delegation. Let us now look at the concepts related to object-oriented programming.

Encapsulation

Encapsulation is a key concept in OOP. Encapsulation means data hiding, which implies that methods and properties of an object cannot be accessed directly by any code outside the class. Objects prevent this code from accessing the data unless the data has been made available using properties or methods. The calling code isn't aware of how the data is being stored in the object.

To understand encapsulation better, consider a class named Employee. The Employee class contains two properties, EmpCode and EmpName. In your application, you need to write code to manipulate the details of employees. To do so, you need to create an object of the Employee class. The object then retrieves the data for the code, and the code acts upon it. But the code simply doesn't know from where and how the data was retrieved.

Polymorphism

Polymorphism is the ability to define multiple classes having similar methods or properties. These methods or properties might perform different functions and can be used interchangeably by the client code.

To understand polymorphism better, consider a class named Employee, which contains a method named Department. If you create a new class, FullTimeEmployee, derived from the Employee class, you can override the method Department. However, this method might be completely different from the method in the base class.

Let us now implement the concept of polymorphism in the following example. Best Products, Inc. needs to calculate bonuses for its team members and team leaders based on their monthly salaries. The bonus for team members and team leaders is 5 percent and 10 percent of their monthly salary, respectively. Now, we will create one class each for team members and team leaders, and one wrapper class that will calculate the amount of bonus for both team members and team leaders. To do so, you will use the following code:

```
'Class : clsTeamMembers

Const BonusRate As Double = .05
```

```
Public Function CalcBonus ( dblSalaryValue as Double) as Double
       CalcBonus = BonusRate * dblSalaryValue
End Function

'Class : clsTeamLeaders

Const BonusRate As Double = .10

Public Function CalcBonus ( dblSalaryValue as Double) as Double
    CalcBonus = BonusRate * dblSalaryValue
End Function

'Class : clsBonus

'The private member variables
Private strDesignation As String
Private oTeamMembers As clsTeamMembers
Private oTeamLeaders As clsTeamLeaders

Public Sub New ()
    Dim oTeamMembers As New clsTeamMembers ()
    Dim oTeamleaders As New clsTeamLeaders ()
End Sub

Public Function calcBonus (dblSalaryValue as Double) as Double
'Calculate Bonus based on designation of the employee

If strDesignation = "TM" then

    CalcBonus = oTeamMembers.CalcBonus (dblSalaryValue)

Else

    CalcBonus = oTeamLeaders.CalcBonus (dblSalaryValue)

End If

End Function
```

In the preceding code, the following classes appear:

- clsTeamMembers: Calculates the bonus for team members. The bonus rate has been specified as 0.05 (5 percent).

- clsTeamLeaders: Calculates the bonus for team leaders. The bonus rate has been specified as 0.1 (10 percent).

- clsConveyance: Used as a wrapper class, wherein you just need to specify the designation, and the amount of bonus will calculate automatically. This class references both the previously created clsTeamMembers and clsTeamLeaders classes.

The method used in the clsBonus class gives different results based on the designation. Instead of creating separate objects for the clsTeamMembers and clsTeamLeaders classes to calculate the bonus, you simply need to create one object of the clsBonus class and it will give results based on the designation. Hence, the object of the clsBonus class is a good example of using polymorphism.

Inheritance

Inheritance includes the concept of base class and derived class. The *base class* is the existing class and the *derived class* is the new class that is derived from the base class. Derived classes are also called *child classes*. Inheritance saves you time and effort by reusing the existing code.

Inheritance is transitive in nature. In other words, consider a class called Employee derived from a class called Individual, which in turn is derived from a class called Human Being (see Figure C-1). In this case, the class Employee will inherit the members (methods and properties) declared in the class Individual as well as the class Human Beings. The Employee class can also override the inherited members. Overriding inherited members means that the definition of these members can be changed in the child class depending on the requirement. In addition, the Employee class can create its own members.

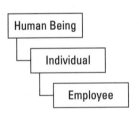

Figure C-1: The class hierarchy

In Visual Basic .NET, the following statements and modifiers have been introduced to support inheritance:

✦ Inherits: This statement is used to specify the class (base class) from which the current class inherits. The following code illustrates the use of the Inherits statement:

```
'Declare a class named Employee
Class Employee

'Specify the base class as Individual
    Inherits Individual
```

✦ NotInheritable: This modifier is used to specify that the class cannot be used as a base class. In other words, classes cannot be derived from a class. The following code statement illustrates the use of the NotInheritable modifier:

```
'Declare a class named Employee
NotInheritable Class Employee
```

This statement declares the class Employee as NotInheritable, which means that you cannot derive a class from this class.

✦ MustInherit: This modifier is used to specify that the instances of the class cannot be created. You can use the class only when you inherit from it:

```
'Declare a class named Employee
MustInherit Class HumanBeing
```

This statement declares the class HumanBeing as MustInherit, which means that you cannot create instances of this class and you need to create classes derived from this class.

Developers often get confused about when to use inheritance and when to avoid using it. Though inheritance is a very useful concept in Visual Basic programming, developers should know when to use it. The following list gives a brief description of the situations in which you can use inheritance:

✦ When the code can be reused from the base classes.

✦ When you need to apply an existing class and methods to different data types.

✦ When you want the global changes to be reflected in child classes when you change a base class.

Creating and Using Classes

In the previous section, you learned the concepts of OOP. You will now learn how to create and use classes. The six steps to create and use classes are explained in the sections that follow.

Step 1: Develop a VB Web application

To begin creating a class, you first need to have a new Visual Basic application in place. In this case, you will develop a Visual Basic Web application. To do so, complete the following steps:

1. Select File ⇨ New ⇨ Project to open the New Project dialog box.

2. In the New Project dialog box, select Visual Basic Project in the left pane and select ASP.NET Web Application in the right pane.

3. Specify a name for the new project, if necessary, and click OK.

4. Change the File Name property of the form WebForm1.aspx to EmployeeDetails.aspx.

Step 2: Design the form

Design the form as shown in Figure C-2 and name the controls on the form as shown in Table C-1.

Employee Code		Employee Category [Employee ▼]
Employee Name		Employee Details
Designation		[lblInfo]
Department		
Salary		
		Deductions for the employee
Show Details		[lblDedn]
Calculate Deduction		

Figure C-2: A sample Web application form

Table C-1
Name of the controls on the EmployeeDetails form

Control	Contains	Name
TextBox	Employee Code	TxtEmpCode
TextBox	Employee Name	TxtEmpName
TextBox	Designation	TxtDesg
TextBox	Department	TxtDept
TextBox	Salary	TxtSalary
Button	Show Details	BtnShow
Button	Calculate Deduction	BtnCalc
DropDownList	Employee Category	LstCategory

Note Also add the items Employee and Trainee to lstCategory. You can do so by using the `Items` property of the control.

Step 3: Create a class

Now you need to create a class named Employee. To do so, complete the following steps:

1. Select Project ⇨ Add Class.

2. Specify the name of the class as Employee. This will open a code window (Employee.vb).

3. In this code window, you can add your own code to specify properties and methods of this class. The class appears as shown in Figure C-3.

Figure C-3: A newly created class

Step 4: Add properties to the class

An employee will be having a number of properties, such as name, designation, and department. Therefore, the next thing you need to do is to add properties to the Employee class. Adding properties is one of the simplest things you can do in Visual Basic. For the sample form created in our example, the different employee details include Employee Code, Employee Name, Employee Designation, Employee Department, and Employee Salary. You can use these as the properties of the Employee class.

Before proceeding further, let's first understand the steps involved in creating a property.

1. You need to declare the property. You do this by using the Property statement. The Property statement also declares the procedure to assign and read values to and from a property. These procedures are referred to as *property* procedures. The following is the syntax of the Property statement:

```
'Declare a property along with its data type
Property PropertyName () As DataType
```

2. You need to assign values to a property. To do so, you use the Set statement, which declares the Set property procedure. This procedure is called whenever a change in property value occurs. The Set procedure takes the value (of the property) to be set as a parameter. The syntax is as follows:

```
'Use the Set statement to return the property value
   Set (ByVal value As Type)
      ClassVariable = value
   End Set
```

3. You need to read value stored in a property. To do so, you use the Get statement, which declares the Get property procedure. This procedure can return the value of a property either by using the Return keyword or by assigning the value to the property:

```
'Use the Get statement to return the property value
    Get
        PropertyName = ClassVariable

        'The above statement can be replaced by following
statement
        Return ClassVariable

    End Get
```

Now that you know the steps involved in creating a property, you need to create properties for the Employee class that you created. To create the properties, type the following code in the Employee.vb page between Class and End Class statements:

```
'Declare the variables used in the class
Dim EmpCode, EmpName, EmpDept, EmpDesg, EmpSal As String

Property EmployeeCode() As String
Get
    EmployeeCode = EmpCode
End Get
Set(ByVal Value As String)
    EmpCode = value
End Set
End Property

Property EmployeeName() As String
Get
    EmployeeName = EmpName
End Get
Set(ByVal Value As String)
    EmpName = value
End Set
End Property

Property EmployeeDesig() As String
Get
    EmployeeDesig = EmpDesg
End Get
Set(ByVal Value As String)
    EmpDesg = value
End Set
End Property

Property EmployeeDept() As String
Get
```

```
        EmployeeDept = EmpDept
End Get
Set(ByVal Value As String)
        EmpDept = value
End Set
End Property

Property EmployeeSal() As String
Get
        EmployeeSal = EmpSal
End Get
Set(ByVal Value As String)
        EmpSal = value
End Set
End Property
```

Note   Notice the code to create properties. Here, you create a property by using the Get and Set assessors within the Property. So, the separate Get, Set, and Let statements to create a property in VB6 are gone with the release of VB.NET.

In this code, the properties EmployeeCode, EmployeeName, EmployeeDesig, EmployeeDept, and EmployeeSal have been created.

Step 5: Create methods

After creating properties of a class, you might need to perform certain operations on these properties, such as displaying data. For this, you create methods in your class. In the Employee class, you need to add a method that displays the values stored in the properties. To do so, add the following code to the class:

```
Public Function Display(ByVal strCode As String, ByVal strName
As String, ByVal strDesig As String, ByVal strDepart As String,
ByVal strSal As String) As String

Dim strDetail As String
strDetail = "Employee code " + strCode + "  Name " + strName +
"  Designation " + strDesig + "  Department " + strDepart + "
Salary " + strSal

Return strDetail
End Sub
```

In the following code, the function `DisplayDeduction` calculates the deduction based on salary. When the user enters his/her salary in the txtSalary text box, the amount of deduction will be automatically calculated and displayed on the screen.

The DisplayDeduction method takes a String argument, which is the value entered in the txtSalary text box. The value passed as argument (a String value) is converted to Integer datatype. Then, the deduction is calculated and is stored in a variable of Double datatype. Finally, the method returns the calculated deduction.

```
Public Function DisplayDeduction(ByVal strSal As String) As
Double
    Dim intSal As Integer
    intSal = CType(strSal, Integer)
    Dim dblDedn As Double
    dblDedn = intSal * 0.1
    DisplayDeduction = dblDedn
End Function
```

Step 6: Implement the class functionality

After creating the Employee class, you need to implement the functionality of this class in your form. This step instructs you on using the methods of the Employee class in your form. As shown in Figure C-2, the form has two buttons with captions Show Details and Calculate Deduction. To associate the desired functionality with the button labeled Show Details, you'll use the Display method of the Employee class. To do so, double-click the Show Details button. This displays the Click event of the button.

Now, type the following code in this event:

```
'Declaring and initializing the object of the Employee class

Dim Emp As New Employee()

'Setting the properties of the Employee class

Emp.EmployeeCode = txtEmpCode.Text
Emp.EmployeeName = txtEmpName.Text
Emp.EmployeeDesig = txtDesg.Text
Emp.EmployeeDept = txtDept.Text
Emp.EmployeeSal = txtSalary.Text

'Calling the Display method of the Employee class

lblInfo.Text = Emp.Display(Emp.EmployeeCode, Emp.EmployeeName,
Emp.EmployeeDesig, Emp.EmployeeDept, Emp.EmployeeSal)
```

In this code:

✦ Emp is the object of the Employee class.

✦ The properties of the object have been set to values entered by a user in the different text boxes in the form.

✦ While calling the Display method, the different properties have been passed as parameters.

Similarly, double-click the Calculate Deduction button on your form to edit the code in the Click event of this button. Now, type the following code to add functionality to this button:

```
'Declaring and initializing the object of the Employee class
```

```
Dim Emp As New Employee()

'Declaring a String variable

Dim strSal As String

'Declaring a variable of Double data type to hold the value
returned from the DisplayDeduction method

Dim dblRetValue As Double

'Initializing the String value with the value entered in a text
box

strSal = txtSalary.Text

'Calling the method of the Employee class

dblRetValue = Emp.DisplayDeduction(strSal)

'Displaying the return value of the method in the label

lblDedn.Text = CType(dblRetValue, String)
```

After doing all six steps, you need to test the application you created. For this, execute the code and enter any values you want. Now, click the Show Details button, and the details of the employee appear in the label lblInfo. Then, click the Calculate Deductions button, and the deduction for the employee appears in the label lblDedn, as shown in Figure C-4.

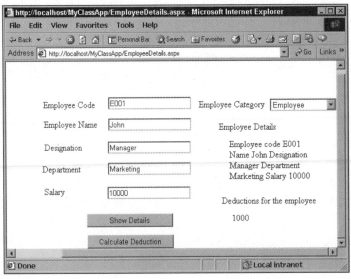

Figure C-4: The sample output

Creating an Object Hierarchy with Inheritance

We have already discussed the concept of inheritance in the earlier section. In this section, you will learn how to implement inheritance. The steps for creating an object hierarchy with inheritance are simple:

1. Create the base class with all the required members.

2. Create a child class that inherits from the base class.

3. In the child class, you can use the members of the existing class, override these members, or declare new members.

Consider the application that you created earlier. You had created a class called Employee. Now, you will create another class called Trainee. You will treat the Employee class as the base class and use inheritance to override its methods. The four steps to achieve this are provided in the following sections.

Step 1: Create a child class

In our example, the first step would be to create a child class, because the base class already exists. To create a new class, complete the following steps.

1. Select Project ⇨ Add Class.

2. Specify the name of the class as Trainee. A new code window (Trainee.vb) opens.

3. Inherit the Trainee class from the base class Employee. To do so, add the following code to the Trainee class.

```
Public Class Trainee

     Inherits Employee

End Class
```

Notice that the Inherits keyword is used to inherit the Trainee class from the Employee class.

Step 2: Specify the override

The next step would be to override the methods of the Employee class. Before doing this, you need to specify that the child classes can override the methods of the Employee class. The Overridable modifier helps you in doing so. To do this, open the Employee.vb page and edit the declaration of the DisplayDeduction function as shown here:

```
Public Overridable Function DisplayDeduction(ByVal strSal As
String) As Double
```

In this code snippet, the keyword `Overridable` indicates that the method can be overridden in derived classes.

Step 3: Override the methods of the base class

Now, you need to add code to the Trainee class so that it can override the methods of the base class. To do so, add the following code to the Trainee class (open the Trainee.vb page). This method is slightly different from the one used in the base class. It calculates deduction as 5 percent of the earnings.

```
Public Overrides Function DisplayDeduction(ByVal strSal As
String) As Double
        Dim intsal As Integer
        intSal = CType(strSal, Integer)
        Dim dblDedn As Double
        dblDedn = intSal * 0.05
        DisplayDeduction = dblDedn

End Function

End Class
```

Step 4: Use the child class methods in the form

After creating the child class, you need to use its methods in the form. To do so, switch to the EmployeeDetails.Aspx page and open its code window. Add the following code to the code window:

```
Public Sub CallMethod(ByVal EmpCat As Employee, ByVal salary As
String)
    lblDedn.Text = EmpCat.DisplayDeduction(salary)
End Sub
```

The preceding code accepts an object of the Employee class and the salary of the employee as parameters. However, you can also pass an object of any class derived from the Employee class, such as Trainee, and the method then calls the `DisplayDeduction` method of the appropriate class. This is an example of polymorphism. Now, switch to the EmployeeDetails.Aspx page and double-click the Calculate Deduction button to open the code window containing the `Click` event of the button. Edit the existing code to read as follows:

```
If lstCategory.SelectedItem.Text = "Employee" Then

    Dim emp As New Employee()
'Pass the object of the Employee class
    CallMethod(emp, txtSalary.Text)
Else

    Dim trn As New Trainee()
'Pass the object of Trainee class
```

```
        CallMethod(trn, txtSalary.Text)
    End If
```

This code uses a simple if...then...else statement. This code helps calculate the deduction on the salary on a different rate for an employee or a trainee. The code invokes the method CallMethod by passing either the Employee or the Trainee object along with the salary. CallMethod in turn calls the DisplayDeduction method of the appropriate class.

This way, we develop a simple application that accepts data from the user and performs certain calculations on it. After the user enters the information, the Show Details button displays the information entered by the user in the form. The Calculate Deduction button calculates the deduction based on the employee category selected from the Employee Category drop down list.

Summary

In this appendix, you learned the concept of object-oriented programming. You also learned the concepts of objects and classes, and the context in which they are used in Visual Basic. The concepts of encapsulation, polymorphism, and inheritance were also covered. Next, you learned to create and use classes. Finally, you learned how to create an object hierarchy by using inheritance.

✦ ✦ ✦

C# Syntax

C#, pronounced "C sharp," is the latest offering from Microsoft. This programming language is set to revolutionize the concept of object-oriented programming (OOP), because, according to Microsoft, it offers the power of C and C++ along with the simplicity of Visual Basic. In other words, it is easy to write and understand like Visual Basic. However, it has the functionality of C++. For this reason, it is being touted in the programming world as "the biggest shake up in the programming environment since the advent of Windows." In addition to Visual Basic, Visual C++, and Visual FoxPro, Microsoft ships C# as a part of Microsoft Visual Studio 7.0.

Note   Microsoft Visual Studio 7.0 also supports scripting languages, such as VBScript and JScript.

Although a little bit of C++ functionality has been compromised in C#, it offers various advantages. These include:

+ Simplicity of coding.

+ Consistency in treating everything from classes, structures, arrays, and data types as objects.

+ Automatic garbage collection, as in Java.

Note   Although the automatic garbage collection feature makes it easier to perform memory-related operations in coding, it can also cause problems, such as stray pointers and unsafe casts.

+ Type-safety, which doesn't allow a programmer to create invalid references and overwrite unallocated memory.

+ Convenience of splitting source files and compiling these scattered files, irrespective of where they are stored.

+ Exclusion of cumbersome header files.

All of these features make the C# programming language a force to be reckoned with.

In this appendix, you will learn about the various data types and variables that are supported by C#. You'll learn about the looping structures, such as `while`, `do`, `for`, and `foreach`, that cause a program to run repeatedly to perform a specified task. You'll learn about decision structures that help an application to determine the action to be taken under different circumstances. These include the `if...else` and `switch...case` constructors. You'll also learn to handle unexpected events that can cause your program or your computer to behave abnormally. You'll learn to use the `try`, `catch`, and `finally` blocks for this purpose.

Writing C# Code in the ASP.NET Framework

You'll find writing the C# code in VS.NET an easy task. You won't need to remember the complete set of functions and classes because of the pop-up IntelliSense menu, from which you can choose the required classes, methods, or functions. The key words are depicted in blue so that you can read and understand the codes with ease. Moreover, you won't have to struggle with missing or extra braces that can cause big headaches.

In the ASP.NET Framework, you need to write the C# code in a C# project. The following are the steps to create a C# project in the ASP.NET Framework:

1. Select File ⇨ New ⇨ Project, to open the New Project dialog box.

Tip

You can also press Ctrl + Shift + N to open the New Project dialog box.

2. Select Visual C# Projects from the Project Types list.

3. From the Templates pane, select Empty Project.

4. In the Name Box, specify the name of the project, say HW. In the Location box, specify the location, say C:\WorkArea, where you want to create your project. The completed dialog box is shown in Figure D-1.

Note

The Name and Location boxes contain a default project name and the location, respectively. You can either accept the default values or edit these boxes to specify the name of the project and the location.

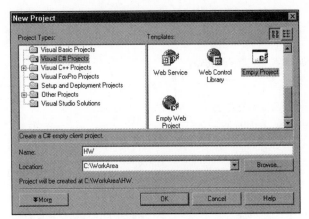

Figure D-1: The completed New Project dialog box

5. Click OK. A new project is created and indicated in the Solution Explorer window (see Figure D-2).

Note

You might have to wait for some time while ASP.NET creates the project.

Figure D-2: The Solution Explorer window depicting the new project

6. Because the project you created is empty, you need to add a class to it. To do so, select Project ➪ Add Class. The Add New Item dialog box appears.

7. Under Categories, verify that Local Project Items is selected. From the Templates pane, select C# Class.

8. In the Name box, type "HelloWorld." Click Open to create the class HelloWorld.cs. Notice that some preliminary code already is written in the class.

9. Highlight the code as shown in Figure D-3 and delete it. You'll add your own code.

Figure D-3: Code that you need to delete to be able to add your code

10. Type as follows:

```
public static void Main()
{
    Console.WriteLine("Hello World!!");
}
```

This code represents typical C# code. The code contains the following elements:

- using System: Represents that the namespace called System is being referenced, which contains the Console class used in the Main method. A namespace is used to organize the elements of a class library in a hierarchical manner. The keyword using allows you to use the specified namespace and its members.

Note C# does not have its own class library in the ASP.NET Framework. It uses the same class library used by other languages, such as Visual Basic and Visual C++.

- class HelloWorld: Represents a user-defined class called HelloWorld.

- public static void Main: Represents the Main method. Like C++, the compiler searches for the Main method in the entire code (or project) and begins the program execution by executing the statements in it. The access specifier public represents that the Main method can be accessed from anywhere in this project. The keyword static represents that there can be just one copy of the method, which would be available to all the members of the HelloWorld class. The keyword void means that the Main method does not return anything.

Cross-Reference For more information on classes and access specifiers, refer to Appendix E, "C# Classes."

- Console.WriteLine("Hello World!!"): Represents the member class of the namespace System called Console, whose method called WriteLine is being used to display the message "Hello World!!" on the console.

11. The completed code should resemble the code shown in Figure D-4. Select File ⇨ Save All to save the changes you've made to the project.

```
namespace HW
{
    using System;

    /// <summary>
    ///     Summary description for HelloWorld.
    /// </summary>
    public class HelloWorld
    {
        public static void Main()
        {
            Console.WriteLine("Hello World!!");
        }
    }
}
```

Figure D-4: The complete code of the HelloWorld.cs class

 Tip You can also press Ctrl + Shift + S to save the changes.

12. Select Build ➪ Build (or press Ctrl + Shift + B). If no errors were detected in the code, the result of the code would also be displayed. If errors are reported, you'll need to check the project for syntax errors.

13. If there were no build errors, run the application by pressing F5. The output of the application is displayed at the console.

Variables

A programming language uses *variables* to store results of calculations and data inputs from the users, functions (or methods), other programs, or subprograms. As opposed to the constants that never change their value, you can perform various operations, such as +, ++, -, −, and so forth, on the variables during an operation and change the values of the data stored by them.

 Note Variables are also commonly referred to as *fields* in C#.

C# supports seven categories of variables:

✦ **Static variables**: When a variable is declared using the keyword `static`, the variable is known as the static variable. A static variable is initialized when the class in which the static variable is declared is loaded. The following is the syntax to declare static variables:

```
access_specifier static datatype variable_name;

public static char Reply;
```

In this statement:

- *access specifier* can be `public`, `private`, `protected`, `internal`, or `protectedinternal`.
- *datatype* can be `int`, `char`, `string`, `float`, `decimal`, `double`, and so on. For more information on data types, refer to the section "Data Types" in this chapter.
- *variable_name* specifies the name of the variable.

✦ **Instance variables**: When a variable is declared without the keyword `static`, it is known as an instance variable. An instance variable is instantiated (or comes into existence) when an object of the class to which it belongs is created. Such variables cease to exist when the object is destroyed. The following is the syntax to declare instance variables:

```
datatype variable_name;

int Sum;
```

✦ **Array elements**: When a variable is stored in an array, it is known as an array element. An *array* is a contiguous block of memory allocated to the variables that have similar data types. These elements are referred by the array index, which starts from zero. The array elements are instantiated when the array to which they belong comes into existence, and are destroyed when the array is removed from the memory. The following is the syntax to declare an array:

```
datatype array_name[array_size];

int Month[12] = {Jan, Feb, Mar, Apr, May, Jun, Jul, Aug,
Sept, Oct, Nov, Dec};
```

In this statement, 12 represents the size of the array called Month. This means the Months array can hold a maximum of 12 elements. Jan can be referred to as `Month[0]`, and Dec as `Month[11]`.

✦ **Value parameters**: When a variable is declared without the keyword `out` or `ref`, it is called a value parameter. These variables are instantiated when the method to which they belong is invoked. After the method returns a value, the value parameters cease to exist. The following is the syntax for declaration of value parameters:

```
datatype variable_name;

int Result;
```

✦ **Reference parameters**: When a variable is declared with the keyword `ref`, it is called a reference parameter. These variables are instantiated when the method to which they belong is invoked. After the method returns a value, the output parameters cease to exist. The following is the syntax for declaration of value parameters:

```
ref datatype variable_name;

ref int DayNumber;
```

✦ **Output parameters**: When a variable is declared with the keyword `out`, it is called an output parameter. These variables are instantiated when the method to which they belong is invoked. After the method returns a value, they cease to exist. The following is the syntax for declaration of value parameters:

```
out datatype variable_name;

out int DayNumber;
```

Note The difference between reference and output parameters is that the reference parameters must be assigned a value before they are passed to a function. Conversely, the output parameters need not be assigned a value before they are passed as an output parameter to a function.

✦ **Local variables**: When a variable is declared within a `for` loop, a `switch` or `using` statement, or a similar block, it is called a local variable. The local variables are instantiated and exist until the block, `for` loop, `switch`, or `using` statement holds the control.

Static variables, instance variables, and array elements are automatically initialized to their default values after they are instantiated. The default value of reference type variables is `null`. The value parameters are initialized by the default constructor, if any. These variable types are known as initially assigned variables. The output parameters and the local variables, on the other hand, belong to the category of initially unassigned variables.

Data Types

In a programming language, every variable is associated with a *data type*. A data type defines the type of values that can be stored in a variable. C# supports three categories of data types:

✦ **Value type**: Variables of this data type actually store the data. In other words, each variable contains its own copy of this data. As a result, operation on one variable does not affect the other variable, even if they happen to contain the same data value. Simple data types, such as `char`, `int`, and `float`, belong to this category. In addition, `enum` and `struct` data types also belong to this category.

✦ **Reference type**: Instead of storing the data directly, variables of this data type store the reference to it. As a result, two variables might point to the same data. If an operation is performed on one variable, it might also affect the other variable that is referencing the same data. The `class`, `delegate`, `array`, and `interface` data types belong to this category.

♦ **Pointers**: Variables of this data type store the memory address of other variables. However, this data type is used in *unsafe codes* only. In C#, the code using pointer operations is known as unsafe code. Programmers can write and perform pointer operations and convert pointer types to other data types.

Note   C# differs from its predecessors by virtue of the omission of pointer operations in normal coding, apart from unsafe codes. Instead, most of the pointer operations are managed by the *garbage collector*. The garbage collector is a mechanism that periodically searches for unused memory and references and frees the memory so that it can be used by other applications that require the memory urgently.

In C#, the value of any data type is treated as an object. As a result, every data type is derived from the Object class, which serves as the ultimate base class for all the data types. In the case of reference data types, the data being referenced also belongs to the Object type.

Value type

The value data type can be further subdivided into the two categories — *struct type* and *enumeration type*.

Struct type

Struct types can be used to declare constants, variables, methods, and properties. They can also be used to declare nested type variables and operators. The C# environment provides a set of predefined struct types known as *simple types*, which are listed in Table D-1.

Table D-1 Simple data types	
Type	*Description*
Object	Serves as the base type for the rest of the types
String	Represents a set of Unicode characters
Int	Represents 32-bit signed integers
Char	Represents a single Unicode character
Float	Represents a single-precision floating-point decimal value
Decimal	Represents a decimal number with 28 significant digits; i.e., 28 decimal places
Double	Represents a double-precision floating-point value
Bool	Represents the Boolean data type, whose value can either be True or False
Long	Represents the 64-bit signed integer

Type	Description
Ulong	Represents the 64-bit unsigned integer
Short	Represents the 16-bit signed integer
Ushort	Represents the 16-bit unsigned integer
Uint	Represents the 32-bit unsigned integer
Byte	Represents the 8-bit unsigned integer
Sbyte	Represents the 8-bit signed integer

The simple data types can be further divided into four subcategories — *Boolean type*, *numeric type*, *floating-point type*, and *integral type*.

Boolean type

The Boolean data type is represented by the `bool` type, which can take either of the two Boolean logical values — True or False. The Boolean data types cannot be converted to other data types, and vice versa.

Numeric type

The numeric type is represented by the `decimal` type, which is a 128-bit data type. This data type is used for financial calculations. The `decimal` type variables can hold values that range from 1.0×10^{28} to 7.9×10^{28}. The `decimal` type operations are precise to the 28-29 significant digits.

Note   In an operation, if a `decimal` value is too small after rounding off, it is treated as 0. On the other hand, if the value is too large for the `decimal` format, `OverFlowException` is thrown.

Floating-point type

`float` and `double` are the two types that belong to the floating-point type category. The range of `float` type values is from 1.5×10^{45} to 3.4×10^{38}. For example, 2.5675 is a valid float type value. The range of `double` type values is from 5.0×10^{324} to 1.7×10^{308}. In the operations involving floating-point data type variables, the following values are valid:

- ✦ *Not a Number*, which is generated by invalid floating-point operations such as dividing infinity by infinity or zero by zero.

- ✦ *Positive and negative infinity*, which are generated by dividing a non-zero number by zero. For example, -2/0 generates negative infinity, and 2/0 generates positive infinity.

- ✦ *Positive and negative zero.*

- ✦ *Finite set of non-zero values in the form of* $X \times Y \times 2^e$, where X = 1 or –1 and Y and e are determined by the floating point.

Integral types

Nine integral types are supported by C#:

- ✦ int: Represents signed 32-bit integer values that can range from −2,147,483,648 to 2,147,483,648

- ✦ uint: Represents unsigned 32-bit integer values that can range from 0 to 4,294,967,295

- ✦ char: Represents unsigned 16-bit integer values that can range from 0 to 65,535

- ✦ byte: Represents unsigned 8-bit integer values that can range from 0 to 255

- ✦ sbyte: Represents signed 8-bit integer values that can range from -128 to 127

- ✦ long: Represents signed 64-bit integer values that can range from -9,223,372,036,854,775,808 to 9,223,372,036,854,775,808

- ✦ ulong: Represents unsigned 64-bit integer values that can range from 0 to 18,446,744,073,709,551,615

- ✦ short: Represents signed 16-bit integer values that can range from -32,768 to 32,767

- ✦ ushort: Represents unsigned 16-bit integer values that can range from 0 to 65,535

Enumeration types

The enumeration data types are represented by named constants. Every enumeration data type must have an underlying integral data type, such as short, ushort, int, uint, byte, sbyte, long, and ulong. char cannot be used as the underlying type of the enumeration type.

Reference data types

The reference data types do not store the data itself. Rather, they store the reference to the intended data. The following are the four reference data types:

- ✦ **Class type:** This reference data type represents a data structure. A data structure can contain data members, such as constants, methods, variables, fields, constructors, destructors, and events. As in C and C++, the class types support *inheritance*. Inheritance is the mechanism by which a class derives its properties and functionality from a parent class, also known as a *base class*. In C#, two class types are used most frequently:

    - • **Object type:** This class serves as the base (or parent) type for the rest of the data types, because every data type is derived from this data type—directly or indirectly.

Note

Actually, the object keyword is just an alias for the System.Object class. You can use object or System.Object interchangeably.

- **String type**: Like all the other classes and types in C#, this class is directly inherited from the `object` (or `System.Object`) class. It represents a set of Unicode characters. The `string` keyword is merely an alias of the `System.String` class. You can use `string` or `System.String` interchangeably.

✦ **Interface type**: Interfaces are special classes that can be inherited by other classes that are not directly related to them. They contain member functions, but these member functions do not have bodies (in other words, these functions are empty). The class or struct that inherits from an interface must implement these functions without renaming them. However, the inheriting class or struct can implement these functions, as they like.

✦ **Array type**: An array is a contiguous memory allocation to variables of similar data type. The variables that are stored in an array are also known as array elements. Each array element can be accessed individually by using its index.

✦ **Delegate type**: The delegate data types reference either to a static method or an object instance method.

Note

To an extent, you can compare the delegate data type to a function pointer in C or C++.

Looping Structures

You can use the *looping statements* to repeatedly execute a section of a program as long as the specified condition remains `true`. When the condition becomes `false`, the loop ends and the control is passed to the statement immediately following the loop.

Note

The looping structures are also commonly referred to as *iteration statements*.

Most of the looping structures offered by C# are similar to those available earlier in C or C++. These include:

✦ `while` statement

✦ `do` statement

✦ `for` statement

✦ `foreach` statement

while statement

The `while` statement executes a set of statements conditionally until the evaluating condition becomes false. As a result, these statements can either be executed *n* number of times or never be executed. The evaluating condition is a logical

(Boolean) expression that returns either false or true. The syntax of the `while` statement is as follows:

Caution   In ASP.NET, you need to create a new project to write this class. If you would like to continue using the project you created earlier for the HelloWorld class, you would have to make the entire HelloWorld class commented. This is because, the HelloWorld class already has a `Main` method, and in a project, there can be only one `Main` method.

```
while (Boolean_expression)
{

    statements;

}
```

For example:

```
using System;

class eval
{
    static void Main()
    {
      int Num = 0;
      while (Num < 100)
      {
        Console.WriteLine("{0}", Num);
        Num = Num + 10;
      }
      Console.WriteLine("We are out of the while loop.");
      string s1;
      s1=Console.ReadLine();
    }
}
```

In this code, `Num` is an `int` type variable, which has been initialized to zero. The evaluating expression, `Num < 100`, checks whether the value of `Num` is less than 100. If the value of `Num` is less than 100, the condition returns true and the `while` loop is executed. `Console.WriteLine ("{0}", Num)` displays the value of `Num`. The next line increments the current value of `Num` by ten and the loop restarts. This continues until `Num`'s value becomes 100. Here, the loop stops executing because 100 is not less than 100. After the execution of the loop stops, the control is transferred to the statement immediately next to the loop, which is `Console.WriteLine ("We are out of the while loop.")`. The last statement `s1=Console.ReadLine()` waits for user input. This way, you can pause the execution of the console in the Command line. The result of the execution of the code is shown in Figure D-5.

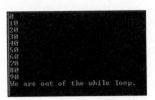

Figure D-5: Output of the while code

do...while statement

The execution of the do...while structure is similar to the while structure. It is repeatedly executed until the evaluating condition becomes false. The main difference between the while and the do...while structures is that the while loop may never be executed if the evaluating condition returns false the first time it is tested. In that case, the loop is ignored and the control is passed to the statement immediately next to the loop. However, the do...while loop is executed at least once, even if the evaluating condition returns false the first time it is tested. The syntax of the do...while structure is as follows:

```
do
{

    statements;

} while(Boolean_expression);
```

For example:

```
using System;

class eval
{
    static void Main()
    {
      int Num = 11;
      do
      {
        Console.WriteLine("{0}", Num);
        Num = Num + 1;
      } while (Num < 10);
      Console.WriteLine("We are out of the loop.");
    }
}
```

In this code, the loop has already been executed once before the condition is checked. Therefore, even though the value of the variable Num is 11, the loop will display its value. After the value of Num is displayed for the first time, when the condition is evaluated, it returns false and the loop is not executed again. The output of the code is shown in Figure D-6.

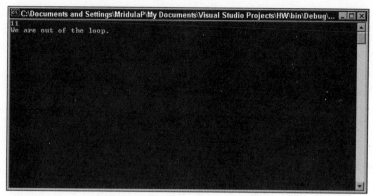

Figure D-6: Output of the do...while code

for statement

You can use this looping structure to compactly specify the statements that control the repeated execution of a loop. In this looping structure, the control statements (initialization expression, test expression, and change expression) are not specified within the loop. Rather, they are specified right at the beginning of the loop. Programmers use the for statement for easy readability and understandability. The syntax for the for looping structure is as follows:

```
for(initialization_expr, test_expr, change_expr)
{

    statements;

}
```

For example:

```
using System;

class eval
{
    static void Main()
    {
        int Num;
        for(Num = 0; Num < 10; Num++)
        {
            Console.WriteLine("{0}", Num);
        }
        Console.WriteLine("We are out of the for loop.");
    }
}
```

In this code, the variable Num is initialized to 0 and its value is checked before the for block statements are executed. If the evaluating condition returns true (the value of Num is less than 10), the value of Num is displayed on the console. The execution of the loop is repeated until the value of Num becomes 10, after which the evaluating condition returns false and the message "We are out of the for loop." is displayed on the console. The output of the execution of the code is shown in Figure D-7.

Figure D-7: Output of the for code

Note   The initialization expression is executed only once, when the control is passed to the loop for the first time. The test expression is executed each time the loop runs. The statements in the loop's body are executed only if the test expression returns true. The change expression is always executed when the control returns to the beginning of the loop.

foreach statement

You can use the foreach structure to repeatedly execute a set of statements for each number of array elements or a collection of objects. In other words, the statements of the foreach block are executed for each element in the array or collection. In this way, you can use the foreach structure to count (or enumerate) the elements of a collection or an array. After all the elements of the collection or the array are traversed, the control is transferred to the statement immediately following the foreach block. The syntax of the foreach structure is as follows:

```
foreach(datatype variable_name in expression)
{

    statements;

}
```

For example:

```
using System;

class eval
{
    static void Main()
    {
        int counter = 0;
        int [] Numbers = new int []{9, 8, 16, 11, 4, 0, 3, 15,
35,2};
        foreach(int Num in Numbers)
```

```
      {
        if(Num < 5)
           counter++;
      }
      Console.WriteLine("{0} numbers less than 5 were found.",
   counter);
      }
   }
```

This code counts the number of elements in the Numbers array that are less than 5. The foreach loop continues to run until it traverses to the last element of the Numbers array. Whenever it finds a number less than 5, the counter is incremented by one. The Console.WriteLine statement in the end displays the number of characters found that are less than 5. Figure D-8 displays the output of the code.

Figure D-8: Output of the foreach code

 Note You can use the break and continue statements in a loop. The break statement causes the execution of a loop to abruptly end and pass the control to the statement immediately next to the loop. The continue statement in a loop, on the other hand, returns the control to the beginning of the loop. Both statements cause the loop statements after them to be skipped.

Decision Structures

In addition to making decisions in daily life, you can incorporate the ability of decision making in the C# codes by using *decision structures*. The decision structures determine the sequence in which the statements of a program are executed. Hence, you can control the flow of a program, because they selectively execute the program statements depending on the value of expressions either associated with them or passed to them.

 Note The decision structures are also known as *conditional constructs*.

The decision structures are quite similar to those available in C or C++. These include:

✦ if...else statement
✦ switch...case statement

if...else statement

In the if...else decision structure, the if construct is always followed by an evaluating condition. This evaluating condition is a Boolean expression, which always involves comparison of data. Any decision is made based on the result of this comparison. If the evaluating expression after if returns true (the value is non-zero), the statements in the immediate block are executed. However, if the evaluating expression returns false, the control is then transferred to the block immediately after the else construct. The syntax of this decision structure is as follows:

```
if(Boolean_expression)
{

    statements;

}
else
{

    statements;

}
```

For example:

```
using System;

class eval
{
    static void Main()
    {
      int Num = 11;
      if (Num > 10)
      {
        Console.WriteLine("{0}", Num);
        Console.WriteLine("You are in the if block.");
      }
      else
      {
        Console.WriteLine("{0}", Num);
        Console.WriteLine("You are in the else block.");
      }
    }
}
```

In this code, Num is initialized to 11. In the if construct, when the value of Num is evaluated, it returns true because 11 is greater than 10. As a result, the statements of the if block are executed and 11 is displayed. A line is also displayed to the effect that "You are in the if block." Figure D-9 displays the output of the code.

Figure D-9: Output of
the if...else code

Note

In the preceding code, initialize the value of Num to 0. Save the code and build it. Because 0 is not greater than 10, the evaluating expression returns false and the control is transferred to the else block. As a result of this, 0 is displayed on the console. A line is also displayed to the effect that "You are in the else block."

switch...case statement

You can use the switch...case structure if a variable can have multiple values. When the switch statement is executed, the condition-variable is evaluated and compared with each constant specified with the case statement. If the variable value is equal to any of the case constants, control is passed to the block following that case statement. If no match is found for the condition-variable value, control is passed to the block following the default label. However, if no case matches and there is no default label, then all the statements in the switch block are ignored and the control is passed to the statement immediately next to the switch block. The syntax of the switch...case structure is as follows:

```
switch(condition_variable)
{
    case constant_expression_1:
        statements;
        break;

    case constant_expression_2:
        statements;
        break;

    ...........

    case constant_expression_n:
        statements;
        break;

    default:
        statements;
        break;

}
```

For example:

```
using System;

class eval
{
    static void Main()
    {
      char Reply;
      Console.WriteLine("Enter an alphabet in lower case.");
      String s = Console.ReadLine();
      Reply = char.Parse(s);
      switch(Reply)
      {
        case 'a':
          Console.WriteLine("You entered the vowel a.");
          break;

        case 'e':
          Console.WriteLine("You entered the vowel e.");
          break;

        case 'i':
          Console.WriteLine("You entered the vowel i.");
          break;

        case 'o':
          Console.WriteLine("You entered the vowel o.");
          break;

        case 'u':
          Console.WriteLine("You entered the vowel u.");
          break;

        default:
          Console.WriteLine("You entered a consonant.");
          break;
      }
    }
}
```

In this code, the user is prompted to enter a character in lowercase. When the user enters the character, it is read using `Console.ReadLine()` and is stored in the string variable s. `Reply = char.FromString(s)` converts the read character back to `char` type and stores it in the variable, `Reply`. This character is then matched with a, e, i, o, or u. If the character entered is a vowel, the message "`You entered the vowel vowel_name.`" is displayed on the console. If the entered character was a consonant (b, c, d, f, and so on), the message "`You entered a consonant.`" is displayed. The output of the code is displayed in Figure D-10.

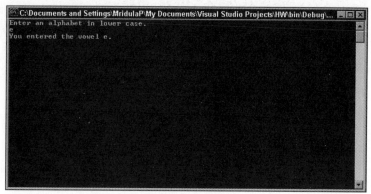

Figure D-10: Output of the switch...case code

Exception Handling

Exceptions are exceptional or abnormal events (or occurrences) that may take place while a program is executing and disrupt the normal flow of the program. These unexpected situations may include:

✦ An application running out of memory

✦ Errors in resource allocation

✦ Inability to find a class or file

✦ Problems regarding the network connectivity

Such situations can cause an application to stop functioning or to go in a hang. In the worst cases, these situations can result in crashing of the computer as well. To prevent this, you need to handle such errors so that neither the application nor the computer goes in a hang and you can exit from the application without much trouble.

Handling exceptions in C# is much like handling exceptions in C++. However, there are minor variations that are not available in C++:

✦ In C#, you need to represent all the exceptions as an instance of the class type derived from the System.Exception class.

Note   In C++, you can use any value of any type to represent an exception.

✦ You can use the finally block to write code to terminate a program in C#. This block would function normally, both in exceptional as well as in normal situations.

✦ System-level exceptions, such as overflow, null references, and division by zero, are represented by well-defined exception classes.

Whenever an unexpected error occurs in C#, an object of the appropriate exception class is created. This object contains the information about the type of error and the state of the program when the exception occurred. This object is then passed to the program, by *throwing an exception.* As the programmer, you need to handle this exception and process it. You can implement exception handling by using the try, catch, or finally blocks.

The try block

The try block contains the statements that may cause an exception. If an exception occurs within the try block, the appropriate exception handler that is associated with the try block handles the exception.

Caution

A try block must have at least one catch block following it.

The following is the syntax of the try block:

```
try
{

    statements;

}
```

The catch block

You associate an exception handler to the try block by providing one or more catch blocks immediately after the try block. The catch statement of the catch block takes an object of an exception class as a parameter. If an exception is thrown during program execution, the statements of the catch block are executed. The syntax of the catch block is as follows:

```
try
{

    statements( that may cause an exception);

}

catch( exception object)
{

    statements (error-handling code);

}
```

The finally block

When an exception is thrown, the rest of the statements in the `try` block are ignored. Sometimes, it is imperative that certain statements are processed irrespective of whether or not an exception was raised. For example, you might open a file for writing to it. However, when you write to the file, it throws an exception. In this case, you must close the file regardless of whether or not an exception was raised. You can use the `finally` block for this purpose, which follows the `catch` block. The code in the `finally` block is executed regardless of the occurrence of an exception. You can have only one `finally` block for an exception handler. However, it is not mandatory to have a `finally` block. The syntax of the `finally` block is as follows:

```
try
{

    statements;

}

catch( exception object)
{

    statements;

}

finally
{

    statements (that need to be executed whether or not an
exception was raised);

}
```

For example:

```
using System;

class eval
{
    static void Main()
    {
        int Num1, Num2, Result;
        Console.WriteLine("Enter any Number.");
        String s1 = Console.ReadLine();
        Num1 = int.Parse(s1);
        Console.WriteLine("Enter another Number.");
        String s2 = Console.ReadLine();
        Num2 = int.Parse(s2);
        try
        {
```

```
        Result = Num1/Num2;
        Console.WriteLine("The result of the division is:{0}",
    Result);
        }
    catch (Exception e)
    {
        Console.WriteLine("You tried division by zero!!");
    }
    finally
    {
        Console.WriteLine("You will definitely see this
    sentence.");
    }
    }
}
```

In this code, the user needs to enter two numbers, Num1 and Num2. The result of division of Num1 by Num2 is stored in the variable Result. The user might enter the value of Num2 as 0. This is an exception and needs to be handled. Therefore, the expression Result = Num1/Num2 has been placed in the try block. In case an exception is raised (a user enters 0 as the value of Num2), the control is transferred to the catch block, which displays the message "You tried division by zero!!" You also view another message "You will definitely see this sentence." because it is a part of the finally block. The output of the code is shown in Figure D-11.

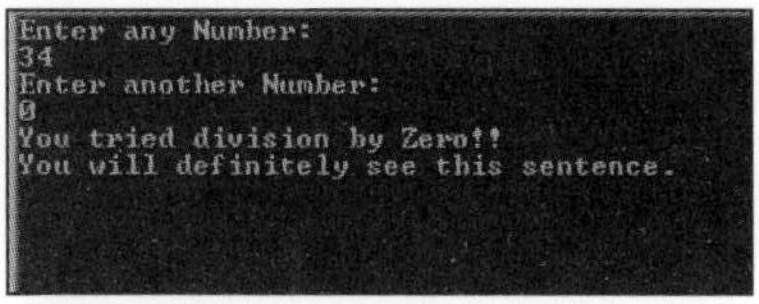

Figure D-11: Output of the exception-handling code

Summary

In this appendix, you learned about the various data types and variables that are supported by C#. You also learned about the various looping structures, such as while, do, for, and foreach. Then, you learned about the decision structures that help an application to determine the action to be taken under different circumstances. These decision structures in C# include the if...else and switch...case structures. Finally, you learned to handle unexpected events that can cause your program or your computer to behave abnormally by using the try, catch, and finally blocks.

✦   ✦   ✦

C# Classes

C# is an object-oriented programming (OOP) language and it uses classes like any other OOP language. A class is a set of defined behaviors using primitive data types such as int, float, and char. In other words, a class defines the operations that its objects can perform, and defines a value that holds the state of its objects. Here, you must note that although CLR defines these primitive data types, their usage does not guarantee portability. For example, C# supports unsigned int, but VB does not. Thus, a class created in C# that uses unsigned int, will be difficult to use in VB.

Some of the members of a typical class are constants, methods, properties, indexers, and events. These class members have associated access specifiers, such as `private` or `public`, which define the scope of the members. This appendix explains how to create and use classes. It also covers the concepts and implementation of indexers and events.

Creating and Using Classes

Classes are an integral part of an object-oriented language. An object is defined as an instance of a class. When you create a class, you need to decide the members of the class and their accessibility. You specify the accessibility of the members of a class by using the access specifiers. Table E-1 describes various access specifiers that can be used for the members in a class.

Table E-1
Access specifiers

Access Specifier	Description
public	Indicates that the class member can be accessed from anywhere in the application.
private	Indicates that the class members cannot be accessed from outside the containing class.
protected	Indicates that the class member can be accessed from within the containing class or from the derived class.
internal	Indicates that the class member can be accessed from anywhere within the program that has the containing class.
protected internal	Indicates that the class member can be accessed from anywhere within the program that has the containing class or from the derived class.

Cross-Reference

To learn more about the concept of classes and objects, refer to Appendix C, "Visual Basic Object-Oriented Programming."

You use the keyword `class` to declare a class. To declare a typical class, the following syntax is used:

```
[modifier] class <class name>
{
class body
}
```

The following list describes the elements in this syntax:

✦ `[modifier]` refers to modifiers, such as `abstract` and `sealed`, and access specifiers, such as `public` and `private`. This attribute is optional.

Note

An abstract class is a class that cannot be instantiated and is intended to act only as a base class for other classes. While declaring an abstract class, you need to use the `abstract` modifier. The sealed class prevents other classes from inheriting it.

✦ `class` is the keyword used to declare the class.

✦ `<class name>` refers to the name of the class.

✦ `class body` refers to the body of the class. You declare the class members in this part of the class declaration.

While deciding on the name of a class, keep in mind the following naming guidelines:

✦ Use a noun or a noun phrase as a class name.

✦ Use PascalCasing notation in a class name. In PascalCasing notation, the first character of every noun is capitalized. For example, a class named EmployeeDetails uses the PascalCasing notation.

✦ Do not use abbreviations in a class name.

✦ Do not use underscores in a class name.

You can use various members in a class depending on the requirement. Some class members are described in the following sections.

Constants

These class members refer to a constant value that can be assigned when the program is compiled. A constant in a class can depend on another constant only if no circular dependency exists. You can declare a constant by using the following code:

```
const int X;
```

In this code, the keyword `const` indicates that X is a constant. The data type of the constant X is integer.

 To learn more about constants, refer to Appendix A, "Visual Basic Syntax."

Properties

These class members refer to the attributes of a class. For example, color and size can be the properties for a class named Cloth. When you define and declare a property, you use accessors. *Accessors* are a set of executable statements that are used to read or write a property. In a property declaration, you use the `get` and/or the `set` accessor, depending on the requirement. A `get` accessor is used to read the property, whereas a `set` accessor is used to write the property. The syntax for `get` and `set` accessors is given as follows:

```
get
{
    statements
}
set
{
    statements
}
```

Usually, the get and set accessors are used in pairs when declaring a property. When used in pairs, the accessors allow a property to be read as well as written. However, if you want a property to be read-only, you use only the get accessor. To declare a write-only property, you use only the set accessor.

The following code declares a property called EmployeeCode, which uses both the get and set accessors. Therefore, you can read as well as write this property.

```
public class Employee
{
    private string ECode;
    public string EmployeeCode
    {
    get
    {
        return ECode;
    }
    set
    {
        ECode=value;
    }
    }
}
```

One thing to notice in the preceding code (the set accessor) is the keyword value, a variable that stores the latest value assigned to the property. Thus, the private member ECode is set to the value stored in the keyword value. After declaring the property in the class, you can use it to read the property or write a value to the property:

```
Employee emp;
string code;
// setting the property
emp.EmployeeCode="E001";
// reading the property
code=emp.EmployeeCode;
```

While choosing a property name, keep in mind the following naming guidelines:

✦ Use a noun or noun phrase as a property name.

✦ Use PascalCasing in a property name.

Methods

These class members are used to implement functionality, such as calculations and actions in a class. Methods might take parameters and return a value. However, if a method does not return a value, you need to specify it using the keyword void. The following syntax is used to declare a method:

```
[modifier] <return type> <method name>([parameter list])
{
    statements
}
```

This following list describes the elements in this syntax:

✦ [modifier] refers to the method modifiers, such as abstract, public, and private and is optional.

✦ <return type> indicates the data type of the value that the method would return. In case the method does not return a value, <return type> is specified as void.

✦ <method name> refers to the name of the method.

✦ [parameter list] refers to the list of the input and output parameters of the method. The parameters in the parameter list are separated by commas.

✦ statements refers to the statement or statements that would be executed when the method is invoked.

You should keep the following naming guidelines in mind while choosing a method name:

✦ Use a verb or verb phrase that suggests the functionality of the method as the method name. For example, you can name a method that calculates salary for employees as CalculateSalary.

✦ Use PascalCasing in a method name.

Cross-Reference   To learn more about the concept of properties and methods, refer to Appendix C.

To understand methods better, let us look at the following code snippet that declares a method called GetDetails in the Employee class. This method prompts users for the employee code and employee name.

```
public class Employee
{
    private string EmpCode;
    private string EmpName;
    public void GetDetails()
    {
        Console.WriteLine("Please enter the employee code");
        EmpCode=Console.ReadLine();
        Console.WriteLine("Please enter the employee name");
        EmpName=Console.ReadLine();
    }
}
```

Then, you can access the `GetDetails` method by creating the object of the Employee class:

```
Employee emp;
emp=new Employee();
emp.GetDetails();
```

Constructor

A *constructor* is a class member that is used to initialize the data members of a class. A constructor always has the same name as the class. However, it does not have a return type. Here, it is important to mention that constructors are not the same as methods with a return type of `void`. A constructor does not have a return type, whereas a method must have a return type. In case a method does not return a value, the return type is specified as `void`. Also, a method is called explicitly, whereas a constructor is called automatically as soon as the object is created. A constructor may or may not take parameters. C# has three types of constructors, described next: default constructors, instance constructors, and static constructors.

Default constructor

The default constructor does not take any parameters. If you do not specify a constructor in a class, the default constructor is automatically provided. The following is the syntax to declare a default constructor for a class:

```
[modifier] <classname>()
{
}
```

This following list describes the elements in this syntax:

✦ `[modifier]` refers to the constructor modifier, which can be `public`, `private`, `internal`, or `protected`. This is optional. By default, it is public. However, if the class is abstract, the default constructor is protected.

✦ `<classname>` refers to the name of the constructor, which is always the name of the class.

Instance constructor

This constructor is invoked for every instance of the class. An instance constructor is invoked as soon as the object of the class to which it belongs is created. It defines the actions that are required to initialize an object of the class. Unlike the default constructor, the instance constructor takes parameters. The following is the syntax to declare an instance constructor for a class:

```
[modifier] <classname>([parameter list])
{
<instance member>= <value>;

}
```

In this syntax:

+ [modifier] refers to the constructor modifier, which can be public, private, internal, or protected. This is optional.

+ <classname> refers to the name of the constructor, which is always the name of the class.

+ [parameter list] specifies the parameters that the constructor takes. This parameter list is optional. The parameters in the parameter list are separated by commas.

+ <instance member> = <value> assigns the specified value to the instance members that have been defined in the class.

Static constructor

This constructor is invoked only once for a class regardless of the number of instances of the class. A static constructor defines the actions that are required to initialize the static members of a class. A static constructor does not take any parameters and it cannot be invoked explicitly. The following is the syntax to declare a typical static constructor:

```
static <classname>()
{
< static member>= value;
}
```

In this syntax:

+ static is the keyword that is used to specify that the constructor is static.

+ <classname> refers to the name of the constructor, which is always the name of the class.

+ <static member> = <value> assigns the specified value to the static members that have been defined in the class.

Destructor

This class member defines the actions that need to be performed to destroy an instance (object) of the class. In a destructor, the data members are deinitialized. A destructor is called automatically when the instance of a class goes out of scope. A destructor cannot be called explicitly and it does not take parameters. A destructor of the base class is not inherited by the derived class. A destructor has the same name as the class and is preceded by a tilde (~). The following is the syntax used to declare a destructor:

```
~<class name>()
{
statements;
}
```

Where:

✦ ~<classname> refers to the name of the destructor.

✦ statements refer to the statements that would be executed when the instance of the class is destroyed.

Console applications

Using C#, you can create Console, Windows, and Web applications. The following sections discuss the procedure of creating Console applications using Notepad and Visual Studio .NET.

You can create a Console application by using Notepad or Visual Studio .NET. Irrespective of the way it is created, the output of a Console application is always displayed on the console.

Creating a Console application using Notepad

You can use the following steps to create a Console application using Notepad:

1. Type the code for the application in Notepad. For example, to create a Console application that displays "Hello World!!" on the console, type the following code in Notepad:

```
using System;


public class HelloWorld
{
    public static void Main()
    {
        Console.WriteLine("Hello World!!");
    }
}
```

In this code, a public class HelloWorld is created. It has a Main() method, which is the entry point in the application. Here, Main() is a static member of the class HelloWorld and has no return type. The WriteLine() method of the Console class is used to display the text specified in the parentheses on the command prompt.

2. Save the file with the extension .cs. For example, you would save the file that contains class HelloWorld as HelloWorld.cs.

3. Go to the command prompt.

4. Navigate to the folder in which you have saved the CS file.

5. At the command prompt, type the following:

```
csc <filename>.cs
```

The preceding command is used to compile the file <filename>.cs. If there are no compilation errors, <filename>.exe is created.

Note

During compilation, if any errors are displayed on the command prompt, you need to debug the code, save it, and then recompile it before moving to the next step.

6. At the command prompt, type the following:

```
<filename>.exe
```

This command displays the output of the application on the console.

Creating a Console application using Visual Studio .NET

If you decide to use Visual Studio .NET to create a Console application, you need to proceed as follows:

1. Select File ➪ New ➪ Project to open the New Project dialog box.

2. In the New Project dialog box, select Visual C# Project in the left pane and select Console Application in the right pane.

3. Specify a name and path for the new project, if necessary, and click OK.

4. The code window that contains the basic structure of the class opens.

5. Create a class with the required class members.

6. After typing the code, save the code and build it. If no errors are detected during compilation, the output is displayed on the console. However, if errors are detected, you need to debug the code, save it, and again build it to view the output.

For example, to create a class Employee that takes the employee name and sales made by the employee as input, and calculates a commission on the basis of the sales, you can use the following code:

```
using System;

public class Employee
{
    public Employee()
    {
    }
    public void Print(string str)
    {
      Console.WriteLine("The employee name is: {0}",str);
    }
    public void Calculate(int x)
```

```
        {
          double SalesValue;
          if (x<2000)
            {
              SalesValue =x*.15;
            }
          else
            {
              SalesValue =x*.20;
            }
          Console.WriteLine("The commission is: {0}",
    SalesValue);
        }
        static void Main(string[] args)
        {
          Employee emp1;
          emp1 = new Employee();
          string EmployeeName;
          string Sales;
          int x;
          Console.WriteLine("Enter the employee name");
          EmployeeName=Console.ReadLine();
          Console.WriteLine("Enter the employee sales");
          Sales=Console.ReadLine();
          x=int.Parse(Sales);
          emp1.Print(EmployeeName);
          emp1.Calculate(x);
        }
      }
```

In the preceding code, a class Employee has been created. It has a default constructor, Employee(). In the class, two methods, Print() and Calculate(), have been defined. The Main() method is the entry point of the application. Notice the declaration of the Main() method, which is generated by VS.NET automatically. In this declaration, the Main() method takes a string array that is used to pass command-line arguments to invoke the program. An object emp1 of the Employee class is created and initialized. The Main() method takes the employee name and sales from the user as input.

To read the user input from the console, you use the ReadLine() method of the Console class. The user input is then stored in the variables, EmployeeName and Sales. The int.Parse() method is used to convert the string value in the variable Sales to an integer value, which is then stored in an integer type variable x. After taking the user input, the Print() method is called, using the statement emp1.Print(EmployeeName). The value in the variable EmployeeName is passed as a parameter to the method Print(). This method prints the employee name entered by the user on the console. The return type of this method is void.

The Calculate() method is called using the statement emp1.Calculate(x). This method takes the integer value of sales stored in the variable x as a parameter. The Calculate() method uses the value stored in x to calculate the commission for the employee. The `Calculate()` method includes an `if...else` decision structure that tests whether the value of x (sales made) is less than 2,000. If the value is less than 2,000, commission is calculated as 15 percent of the value. However, if the value is greater than 2,000, the commission is calculated as 20 percent of the value. This calculated commission is then displayed on the screen using the `Console.WriteLine()` method.

When you build and run the code specified, "Enter the Employee Name" is displayed on the console. When you enter the employee name and press Enter, "Enter the Employee Sales" is displayed on the console. The values that you enter are used by `Print()` and `Calculate()` methods to display the employee name and the commission. A sample output of the code is shown in Figure E-1.

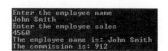

Figure E-1: A sample output
of a Console application

Windows applications

Windows applications are created using Visual Studio .NET. Windows applications have a form that is used to take user input and display the output.

Generalized steps to create Windows applications

To create a Windows application, you need to proceed as follows:

1. Select File ➪ New ➪ Project to open the New Project dialog box.

2. In the New Project dialog box, select Visual C# Project in the left pane and select Windows Application in the right pane.

3. Specify a name and path for the new project, if necessary, and click OK.

Note   The Name and the Location boxes in the New Project dialog box contain the default project name and default location. You can change the entries in the Name and Location boxes to specify a different name and location of the project.

4. The Project window opens. It has a default form in the Design mode. In this mode, you design the form by adding controls to take input and display output. Also, a class called Form1.cs, which is a class for this form, is automatically added to the project. However, you need to add a class to this project, before you can write the code for the class to add the desired functionality to your application.

5. To add a class to the project, select Project ➪ Add Class. The Add New Item dialog box opens.

6. Under Categories, verify that Local Project Items is selected. From the Templates pane, select C# Class. Notice that in the Name box, the default class name, Class1.cs, appears. Change this default class name to the class name that you want, and then click Open.

7. The code window opens that contains the basic structure of the class.

8. Enter the code in this window to add the desired functionality to your application.

9. Save and build the class.

Before you start creating your own C# Windows application, you first need to understand the C# code that is automatically generated by VS.NET in the Form1.cs class file.

When you open the Form1.cs file, you'll notice that a number of namespaces have been used. Some of the namespaces include System and System.Windows.Forms. The System namespace contains the classes that define commonly used data types, events, event handlers, interfaces, attributes, and processing exceptions. The System.Windows.Forms namespace contains classes that are required for creating Windows Forms.

The Form1.cs file also contains a namespace that has the same name as the name of the Windows application project. Within this namespace, the Form1 class is declared:

```
public class Form1 : System.Windows.Forms.Form
```

As you can see in the preceding declaration, Form1 is a class that is derived from the Form class of the System.Windows.Forms namespace.

The Form1 class contains the constructor, which is called automatically when the instance of the Form1 class is created. You can write any initialization code, such as setting a value in a variable or opening a file, in the constructor:

```
public Form1()
{
//
// Required for Windows Form Designer support
//
InitializeComponent();

//
// TODO: Add any constructor code after InitializeComponent
// call
//
}
```

As you can see in the preceding code, the constructor calls another method named InitializeComponent(), which initializes the form and all the components in the form. The code for the InitializeComponent() method is contained within "Windows Forms Designer generated code."

When objects are destroyed (set to Nothing) or are no longer in scope, the .NET Framework automatically calls the Finalize destructor, which is called implicitly and is not included in the code that is automatically generated by VS.NET. However, the only drawback with this destructor is that you do not know when the destructor is called. Also, certain objects might remain active for longer than necessary. To manage your application resources well, VS.NET automatically generates code for the destructor named Dispose. The automatically generated code for the Dispose() method is given as follows:

```
protected override void Dispose( bool disposing )
{
  if( disposing )
    {
      if (components != null)
        {
          components.Dispose();
        }
    }
  base.Dispose( disposing );
}
```

As you can see in the preceding code, the Dispose() method takes a Boolean parameter. If the Boolean parameter is True and the components are not deinitialized, the Dispose() method is called for the components. On the other hand, if the Boolean parameter of the Dispose() method is False, the Dispose() method of the base class is called.

The code that is automatically generated for the Main() method is given as follows:

```
static void Main()
{
Application.Run(new Form1());
}
```

As you can see in the preceding code, the object of the Form1 class is passed as an argument to the Run() method of the Application class.

An example to illustrate Windows applications

Now that you know the steps involved in creating a Windows application and the code that is automatically generated by VS.NET, let's create a Windows application that takes the employee code, employee name, and sales made by the employee and calculates and displays the commission earned.

The first step is to create a new project. After creating a new project, design the form, as shown in Figure E-2. Table E-2 lists the Name property of the different text boxes and buttons used in the form.

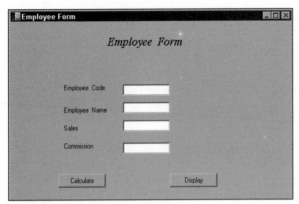

Figure E-2: A sample Windows form

Table E-2 Names of the controls on the sample form		
Control	**Contains**	**Name**
TextBox	Employee code	CodeBox
TextBox	Employee name	NameBox
TextBox	Sales	SalesBox
TextBox	Commission	CommissionBox
Button	Calculate	CalculateButton
Button	Display	DisplayButton

Add a class called Employee to this project. Notice that the default constructor appears in the basic code structure. In the code section, add the variables, as follows:

```
using System;
    ///Summary description for Employee.
    public class Employee
    {
        private string code;
        private string name;
        private string sales;
    /// Default constructor for class Employee
```

```
public Employee()
{

}
```

In this code, `code`, `name`, and `sales` are the three private string variables that have been declared.

Now add the properties for the class Employee. For the sample form created in the preceding example, the different employee details include Employee Code, Employee Name, and Sales. You can use these as the properties of the Employee class. To create these properties, you use the `get` and `set` accessors. To do so, type the following code in the Employee class (in the Employee.cs file):

```
/// Adding properties to the class Employee
/// Adding the EmpName property
public string EmpName
{
    get
    {
        return name;
    }
    set
    {
        name=value;
    }
}
/// Adding the EmpCode property
public string EmpCode
{
    get
    {
        return code;
    }
    set
    {
        code=value;
    }
}
/// Adding the EmpSales property
public string EmpSales
{
    get
    {
        return sales;
    }
    set
    {
        sales=value;
    }
}
```

In the preceding code snippet, the properties named EmpCode, EmpName, and EmpSales have been created, using the get and set accessors.

The next step is to add methods to the Employee class. To add a method that takes sales as a parameter and calculates the commission, type the following code in the Employee class (in the Employee.cs file):

```
/// Adding a method to calculate the commission
public double Commission(string sales)
{
    int z=0;
    double CommValue =0;
    z=int.Parse(sales);
    CommValue=(0.15)*z;
    return CommValue;
}
```

After adding the Commission() method, add the Display() method in the Employee class. The Display() method takes three parameters: strname, strcode, and strsales. Next, this method stores the values, passed as parameters, into a String variable, strdetail. Finally, it returns the value stored in the variable named strdetail.

```
/// Adding a method to display the name, code, and sales
    public string Display(string strname, string strcode,
string strsal)
    {
        string strdetail;
        strdetail=("Employee Name: "+strname+" Employee
Code: "+strcode+" Sales: "+strsal);
        return strdetail;
    }
```

After you've created the Employee class and added properties and methods to this class, the next step is to create the object of the Employee class and use its properties. To do so, switch to the form that you designed earlier. Next, you'll need to associate code with the Click() event of the buttons on the form. First, associate the code to calculate commission with the Click() event of the Calculate button. To do so, double-click the button labeled Calculate. The code window opens automatically. In the code window, the event handler for the Click() event of the button with name CalculateButton is displayed. The code in the CalculateButton_Click() method is given as follows:

```
private void CalculateButton_Click(object sender,
System.EventArgs e)
    {
        Employee emp1;
        emp1= new Employee();
        string strsales;
        double CommissionValue;
        strsales=SalesBox.Text;
```

```
            CommissionValue=emp1.Commission(strsales);
CommissionBox.Text= CommissionValue.ToString();
        }
```

In the preceding code, an object emp1 of class Employee is created. A string variable, strsales, is used to store the value entered in the text box, SalesBox. This string variable is passed as a parameter to the method Commission(). The method Commission() calculates the commission, which is stored in a variable CommissionValue. Because a text box can only contain strings, you need to convert the value in the double type variable CommissionValue to string. To do this CommissionValue.ToString() is used.

Next, you'll associate code with the Click() event of the button labeled Display. To do so, double-click the Display button on the form. The event handler for this button is displayed in the code window. The following code is used to call the method Display() that takes the employee code, name, and sales as parameters and stores them in a variable. A message box that displays these details appears when you click the Display button.

```
private void DisplayButton_Click(object sender,
System.EventArgs e)
      {
          Employee emp1;
          emp1= new Employee();
          emp1.EmpName=NameBox.Text;
          emp1.EmpCode=CodeBox.Text;
          emp1.EmpSales=SalesBox.Text;
          string strval;

strval=emp1.Display(emp1.EmpName,emp1.EmpCode,emp1.EmpSales);
          MessageBox.Show(strval);
      }
```

After associating code with the Click() event of the buttons labeled Calculate and Display, the last step is to add code in the Main() method of the form, which would act as the entry point of the application. Notice that the basic structure of the Main() method is already defined. You just need to create an object of class Employee and initialize it. To do so, edit the code in the Main() method as follows:

```
static void Main()
      {
          Application.Run(new Form1());
          Employee emp1;
          emp1= new Employee();
      }
```

In this way, you have developed a Windows application that accepts data from the user and performs certain calculations on it. The Display button on the form is used to display the information entered by the user in the form. The Calculate button calculates the commission based on the sales made by the employee.

ASP.NET Web applications

In addition to Visual Basic .NET, you can also use C# to create ASP.NET Web applications. In this section, you'll create an ASP.NET Web application that uses the Employee class that you created in the Windows application. To create an ASP.NET Web application by using C#, follow these steps:

1. Select File ⇨ New ⇨ Project to open the New Project dialog box.

2. In the New Project dialog box, select Visual C# Project in the left pane and select ASP.NET Web Application in the right pane.

3. In the Name box, specify the name of the application. In the Location box, specify the URL of the computer on which the IIS server is installed.

4. Click OK to create the Visual C# ASP.NET Web application. Solution Explorer displays the list of all the files generated by VS.NET. Currently, WebForm1.aspx file is selected. The VS.NET window displays the WebForm1.aspx file in Design mode.

If you click the Show All Files icon in Solution Explorer and expand the WebForm1.aspx file, you'll notice that the WebForm1.aspx.cs file is also listed under the WebForm1.aspx file. The WebForm1.aspx.cs file is the code behind file that is created by default. When you open this file, you'll notice that a number of namespaces are used. Some of the namespaces include System, System.Web, and System.Web.UI. The System.Web namespace contains classes that are required for browser/server communication. The System.Web.UI namespace is used to create Web Form pages.

The WebForm1.aspx.cs file automatically declares a namespace whose name is the same as the name of the ASP.NET Web Application project. Within the namespace, the WebForm1 class is declared:

```
public class WebForm1 : System.Web.UI.Page
```

As you can see in this declaration, WebForm1 is a class that is derived from the Page class in the System.Web.UI namespace. The WebForm1 class contains the constructor and the `Page_Load()` and `Page_Init()` methods. The following is the code for the constructor:

```
public WebForm1()
{
    Page.Init += new System.EventHandler(Page_Init);
}
```

The constructor associates the `Page_Init` event handler with the `Init` event of the Page class, which is generated when the page is requested from the server. In the preceding code, the += operator is used to add the `Page_Init` event handler to the `Init` event. This is a powerful feature of C# for associating an event handler with an event at run time based on conditions.

VS.NET generates the following code for the `Page_Init` event handler:

```
private void Page_Init(object sender, EventArgs e)
{
    //
    // CODEGEN: This call is required by the ASP.NET Web Form
    //Designer.
    //
    InitializeComponent();
}
```

The `Page_Init()` method calls the `InitializeComponent()` method, which initializes all the components on the form.

Also, VS.NET declares the `Page_Load` method that you can use to write any code, such as initializing a variable, which you want to get executed as soon as the page is loaded.

Now that you have a basic understanding of the C# code that is automatically generated by VS.NET, it is time to design the user interface for your application. You design the user interface by placing controls directly on the Web Form. Or, you can design the user interface by switching to the HTML view of the Web Form and writing the ASP.NET code. To design Web Forms, you use Web server controls instead of the Windows controls.

Note   When you open the Toolbox, the Web Forms tab lists all the Web server controls. Notice that the Windows controls are not available in the Toolbox, because you have created an ASP.NET Web application and not a Windows application.

Cross-Reference   For detailed information on Web Forms technology and Web server controls, refer to Chapter 3, "Building Forms with Web Controls."

For the current ASP.NET Web application, design the Web Form similar to the Windows Form shown in Figure E-2. To do so, use the Label, TextBox, and Button server controls. In Web Forms, the controls have an `ID` property instead of the `Name` property (used in Windows Forms). You can use Table E-1 to specify the `ID` property of the controls on the Web Form. In addition to the existing controls on this form, place one more Label server control and set its `ID` to `DisplayLabel`.

After you finish designing the Web Form, you need to associate the programming logic with it, to obtain the desired functionality. To do so, add a class to your project. Because this Web application is intended to implement the same functionality as used for the Windows application, you can add a class that has the same code as in the Employee.cs class file, which you created for the Windows application. Thus, add a new class called Employee.cs and write the following code:

```
using System;

namespace EmployeeApplication
{
```

```
/// <summary>
/// Summary description for Employee.
/// </summary>
  public class Employee
  {
   private string code;
   private string name;
   private string sales;

   public Employee()
   {
     //
     // TODO: Add constructor logic here
     //
   }
   /// Adding properties to the class Employee
/// Adding the EmpName property
   public string EmpName
   {
     get
     {
      return name;
     }
     set
     {
      name=value;
     }
   }
   /// Adding the EmpCode property
   public string EmpCode
   {
     get
     {
      return code;
     }
     set
     {
      code=value;
     }
   }
   /// Adding the EmpSales property
   public string EmpSales
   {
     get
     {
      return sales;
     }
     set
     {
      sales=value;
     }
   }
```

```
/// Adding a method to the calculate the commission
public double Commission(string sales)
{
  int z=0;
  double CommValue =0;
  z=int.Parse(sales);
  CommValue=(0.15)*z;
  return CommValue;
}

/// Adding a method to display the name, code, and sales
public string Display(string strname, string strcode, string
strsal)
{
  string strdetail;
  strdetail=("Employee Name: "+strname+" Employee Code:
"+strcode+" Sales: "+strsal);
  return strdetail;
}

}
}
```

Next, you'll need to associate code with the `Click()` event of the buttons on the Web Form. To do so, first switch to the WebForm1.aspx file in Design mode. Then, to associate code with the `Click()` event of the button labeled Calculate, double-click this button. The event handler is automatically created for you. Then, write the following code:

```
private void CalculateButton_Click(object sender,
System.EventArgs e)
{
Employee emp1;
emp1= new Employee();
string strsales;
double CommissionValue;
strsales=SalesBox.Text;
CommissionValue=emp1.Commission(strsales);
CommissionBox.Text= CommissionValue.ToString();

}
```

Also, associate the following code with the button labeled Display:

```
private void DisplayButton_Click(object sender,
System.EventArgs e)
{
Employee emp1;
emp1= new Employee();
emp1.EmpName=NameBox.Text;
emp1.EmpCode=CodeBox.Text;
emp1.EmpSales=SalesBox.Text;
string strval;
```

```
strval=emp1.Display(emp1.EmpName,emp1.EmpCode,emp1.EmpSales);
DisplayLabel.Text=strval;

}
```

When you build and run this application, the output is displayed in a browser. Figure E-3 shows the output when a user enters the employee code, employee name, and sales value, clicks the Calculate button, and then clicks the Display button.

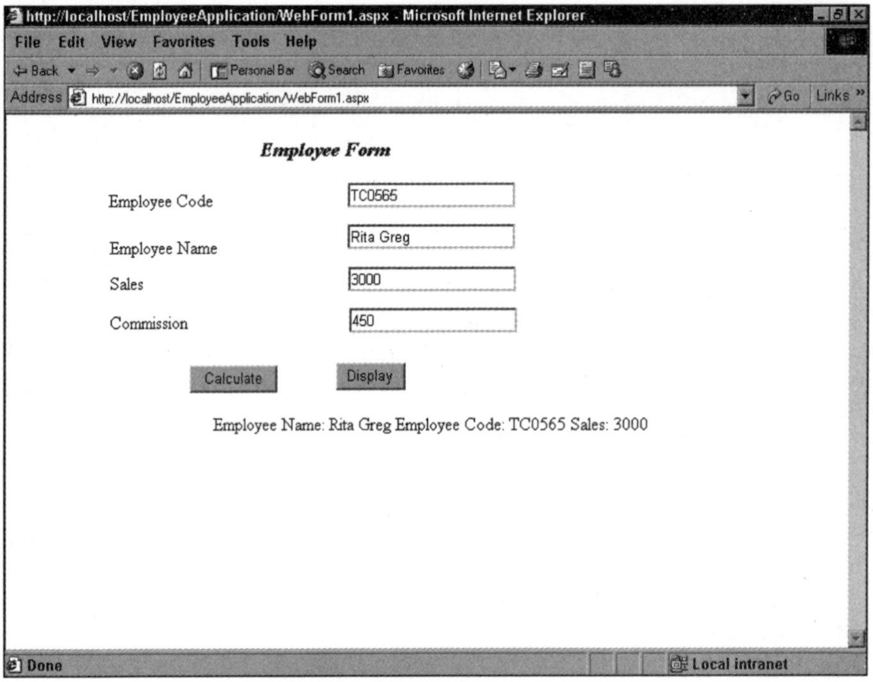

Figure E-3: Output of the ASP.NET Web application

Indexers

Indexers are the class members that allow the objects of a class to be indexed in a manner that is similar to arrays. Indexers are accessed the same way as the arrays, using the [] array access operator. The following is the syntax used to declare a typical indexer:

```
modifier datatype this[parameter list]
{
    get
    {
        statements
```

```
    }
    set
    {
        statements
    }
}
```

The modifiers that can be used while declaring an indexer are new, public, protected, internal, and private. While declaring an indexer, you also need to specify the data type of the indexer. The data type is followed by the keyword this. Indexers do not have a name, and the keyword this is used to implement indexers. The [parameter list] refers to the list of parameters that the indexer takes. The parameters in the parameter list are separated by commas. You need to specify at least one parameter in the parameter list. The number and the data type of the parameters specified in the parameter list while declaring the indexer constitute the *signature* of the indexer. An indexer is identified by its signature. You can declare more than one indexer in a class. However, these indexers should have different signatures.

Indexer declaration also includes specifying the accessors, which contain the statements that need to be executed to read and write the indexer elements. The get and set accessors are used in the indexer declaration to read and write the indexer's elements. The get accessor uses the same parameter list as the indexer. The set accessor also uses the same parameter list as the indexer, along with the parameter value. Ideally, an indexer should have both get and the set accessors.

Indexers are similar to properties, although some significant differences exist between indexers and properties:

✦ An indexer is identified by its signature, whereas a property is identified by its name.

✦ An indexer is accessed using array-like access, whereas a property is accessed using member access.

✦ An indexer must be an instance member, whereas a property can be either an instance or a static member.

✦ The get accessor of an indexer takes the same parameter list as the indexer, whereas the get accessor of a property does not take a parameter.

✦ The set accessor of an indexer takes the same parameter list as the indexer along with the parameter value, whereas the set accessor of a property takes a single parameter called value.

Consider the following code:

```
using System;

class EmpIndexer
{
    private int[] Leave;
```

```
public EmpIndexer(int size)
{
    Leave = new int[size];
    for (int i=0; i<size; i++)
    {
        Leave[i]=15;
    }
}

public int this[int elementnumber]
{
    get
    {
        return Leave[elementnumber];
    }
    set
    {
        Leave[elementnumber]=value;
    }
}
static void Main(string[] args)
{
    int size=10;
    EmpIndexer eInd =new EmpIndexer(size);
    eInd[9]=24;
    eInd[3]=18;
    eInd[5]=21;
    Console.WriteLine("EmpIndexer Output");
    for(int i=0; i<size;i++)
    {
        Console.WriteLine("eInd[{0}]:{1}",i,eInd[i]);
    }
}
}
```

The code shows the implementation of an indexer in the EmpIndexer class. In this class, an integer type private array Leave is declared. This private array is initialized in the constructor EmpIndexer that takes an integer type variable size. In this constructor, all elements in the Leave array are assigned a value, 15. The indexer, which is identified by the keyword this, takes the elementnumber as a parameter. The get and set accessors are used to read and write the elementnumber. The Main() method instantiates an object of the class EmpIndexer. Also, in the Main() method, the values of index elements 3, 5, and 9 are changed. The output of the code is shown in Figure E-4.

Figure E-4: Sample output of the application using an indexer

Events

An event is a class member that is used to provide notifications when an action occurs. In a class, an event is declared by using *delegates*. Delegates are the reference types that are derived from System.Delegate base class. A delegate encapsulates the reference to a method. Using a delegate, the encapsulated method can be invoked without knowing the identity of the method. Hence, delegates enable "anonymous" invocation. A delegate is independent of the type of method that it references. However, the signature of the method and the delegate should match. Also, the return type of the delegate should match the return type of the method.

Note   Delegates can be compared to function pointers in C++. Though you can have multiple delegates.

When declaring an event, you need to specify the modifier for it. You also need to declare a delegate type for it. This delegate type defines the parameters that need to be passed to the encapsulated method, which would be handling the event. More than one event can have the same delegate type. Consider an example in which you want to internally calculate the salary hike based on the points entered by the user. However, as soon as the salary hike is calculated, you want to notify the user that the salary hike has been calculated. To do this, you need to use the following code (in the class file) to declare an event that would notify the user when the salary hike is calculated:

```
public delegate void PointHandler (int newPoint, ref bool
cancel);

public class Employee
{
    public event PointHandler PointChange;
    int point;
    public int Point
    {
        get
        {
            return point;
        }
        set
        {
            if (point != value)
            {
                bool cancel = false;
                PointChange (value, ref cancel);
                if (! cancel)
                point = value;
            }
        }
    }
}

public class Trainer
```

```
{
    public Trainer (Employee emp1)
      {
        emp1.PointChange += new PointHandler(EmpPointChange);
      }
    private void EmpPointChange (int newPoint, ref bool cancel)
      {
        if (newPoint > 250 )
          {
            System.Console.WriteLine ("Change event fired");
            System.Console.WriteLine ("Salary Hike
Calculated",newPoint);
          }
        else
          {
            cancel = true;
          }
      }
}
public class Assessment
{
      public static void Main ()
      {
          int i=0;
          string s;
          System.Console.WriteLine("Enter the Points");
          s=System.Console.ReadLine();
          i= int.Parse(s);
          Employee emp1 = new Employee ();
          Trainer t1 = new Trainer (emp1);

          emp1.Point = i * 250;
      }
}
}
```

In this code, a delegate called PointHandler is declared, which takes two parameters. In class Employee, an event called PointChange() of delegate type PointHandler is declared using the keyword event. In the Employee class, a property, Point, is created that reads and writes an integer type variable, point. The event is handled by the Trainer class. To monitor the change of points into salary hike, the emp1.PointChange += new PointHandler(empPointChange) statement is used. In the Trainer class, a method called EmpPointChange() is created. This method checks the value in the newPoint variable and displays an appropriate message. Class Assessment contains the Main() method that is the entry point of the application. In this method, the instances of the Employee and the Trainer class are created. The points are accepted from the user and stored in a variable i. The salary hike is calculated and is passed to the property Point. When the salary hike is calculated, the event is fired. A message appears stating that the change event is fired. Also, the value of the salary hike is displayed, as shown in Figure E-5.

Figure E-5: Sample output of the application using an event

Summary

In this appendix, you learned how to create and use classes. You also learned about various class members, such as properties, methods, constructors, and destructors. Then, you learned about indexers. You also saw how indexers could be used to provide array-like access of instances of a class. Finally, you learned to create events.

✦　　✦　　✦

C# Components

A component is a reusable piece of code that, once developed, can be used across multiple applications. For example, the spell-check utility is a component that can be used by multiple applications, such as Microsoft Word and Microsoft Excel. In addition, components find a large implementation in database-based applications.

All database-based applications take data as input, process it, and provide output. Based on this mechanism of operation, all the database-based applications have the following:

+ A user interface, which is used to accept the input.

+ A business rule, which is used to perform operations on the input data.

+ A data management element, which is used to manage the stored data.

These are also known as the elements, or tiers, of an application. You can create applications based on a single-tier, two-tier, or multitier architecture, depending on how the applications would be used.

Applications that are based on the single-tier architecture have all three elements put in a single executable file. However, for large applications, the single-tier architecture is not preferred, because every time you want to fix bugs and add more functionality to these applications, you need to recompile and redistribute the entire application.

In an application that is based on the two-tier architecture, the functionality of the application is split between the *client application* and the *server application*. While the client application handles the user input and user interface, the server application handles the business rules and the data management issues. This increases the load on the network, because a large amount of data travels between the client and the server. It also increases the load on the server, because all validations on the input data are performed at the server end. Ideally, all two-tiered applications should follow this architecture. However, there are two-tiered applications, which implement business logic at the client side. Such clients are called fat clients.

A logical solution to the problems faced in the two-tier architecture is the three-tier architecture, where an application is divided into three logical parts: *user services, business services,* and *data services.* In this architecture, you validate data at the client side. Also, you can revalidate data in the middle tier to minimize round trips to the server. The database-based applications created using Web Forms, based on the ASP.NET technology, automatically implement the three-tier application architecture. Web Forms present information to users in any browser by using any markup language. The application logic for the page is implemented by using code on a Web server. This way, Web Forms segregate presentation from application logic. Also, the data services are segregated from the presentation and application logic.

Because the business services layer is separate from the user services and the data services layer in the three-tiered architecture, it is important that any change in the coding of business services should not entail changes in the user and data services modules. Also, the code modules should be flexible enough to be reused by multiple applications across various programming languages, whenever similar functionality is required. Both of these issues can be taken care of by using *components.*

A component is an executable chunk of code that provides functionality, and can be used in multiple applications across various platforms that support the Component Object Model (COM). Components provide functionality by exposing interfaces via COM. COM defines a set of standards for component interactions and interoperability and protocol standards. The following are the features of COM:

+ It specifies the blueprint for creating components.

+ It supports the concept of objects.

+ It allows seamless customization and upgrading of applications.

+ It is independent of programming languages and is available on multiple platforms.

+ It defines the standards for locating the components and their functionality.

COM provides code reusability. Also, COM-based components are self-versioning, which means that new functionality can be added to the components without affecting the applications that are already using these components. The applications that use these components are called *clients.*

This appendix deals with C# components: how to create a component, the concept of namespaces, and integrating code and role security.

Creating a Component

A component is nothing but a class that follows the standards for component interaction. In C#, you can implement the concept of components by creating Dynamic Link Libraries (DLLs).

Note   DLLs are the modules that are attached to the calling application at run time.

You can use the code in a component class in multiple applications by creating the objects of the component class and calling its methods and properties. For example, you can create a component class that has a function that searches for a word or a phrase in the text, and use that function in various applications that need to incorporate the same functionality. This not only would reduce the programming cycle time, because the component is reused, but would also reduce the possibility of errors, because the component is prebuilt and tested.

In C#, you can create a component class by using either Notepad or Visual Studio .NET. While declaring a component class, you need to specify the access modifier for the component class. Like any class, a component class has a constructor and has other class members, such as methods, properties, and events.

The component classes can be used by any of the Console, Windows, or ASP.NET Web applications. The component classes and their usage in Web applications are covered later in detail. But, let us first look at how to create a component class in Notepad and use it in a Console application.

Creating a component class using Notepad

The following steps are involved in creating a component class using Notepad:

1. Start Notepad.

2. Type the code for the component class in Notepad. For example, to create a component class CalculateAmount, type the following code in Notepad:

```
using System;
// Creating the CalculateAmount class
public class CalculateAmount
{
// Creating the Multiply() Method
    public static double Multiply(double price, double
quantity)
    {
        double Amount;
        Amount=price*quantity;
        return Amount;
    }
}
```

In this code, a class called CalculateAmount has been created. This class has a method, `Multiply()`, that takes two parameters, `price` and `quantity`. The product of `price` and `quantity` is calculated and stored in a variable called `Amount`.

3. Save the file with the extension .cs. For example, save the file as CalculateAmount.cs.

4. Go to the command prompt.

5. Navigate to the folder in which you had saved the CS file.

6. At the command prompt, type the following:

```
csc /t:library <filename>.cs
```

The /t option of the csc command is used to compile the CS file and create a DLL file. If there are no compilation errors, <filename>.dll is created. For example, to create the DLL of the CalculateAmount.cs file, at the command prompt, type the following:

```
csc /t:library CalculateAmount.cs
```

Note During compilation, if any errors are displayed on the command prompt, you need to debug the code, save it, and then recompile it.

After you have created the DLL file, you can import this file as a component in other applications. To use the CalculateAmount.dll file as a component in another class, Calculate, create a new file in Notepad and type the following code:

```
using System;
class Calculate
{
    public static void Main()
    {
        double AmountValue;
        string ProductName;
        string tempPrice;
        string tempQuantity;
        double Price;
        double Quantity;
        Console.WriteLine("Enter the product name");
        ProductName=Console.ReadLine();
        Console.WriteLine("Enter the price");
        tempPrice=Console.ReadLine();
        Price=double.Parse(tempPrice);
        Console.WriteLine("Enter the quantity");
        tempQuantity=Console.ReadLine();
        Quantity=double.Parse(tempQuantity);
// Calling the Multiply() method of the CalculateAmount class
        AmountValue= CalculateAmount.Multiply(Price,Quantity);
        Console.WriteLine(ProductName);
        Console.WriteLine(AmountValue);
    }
}
```

In this code, a class called Calculate has been created. This class uses the `Multiply()` method of CalculateAmount.dll. The variables are defined in the `Main()` method. The application accepts the product name, price, and quantity as input. The `Multiply()` method of the component class CalculateAmount is called in the `Main()` method. The product of `price` and `quantity` calculated by the `Multiply()` method of the component class is returned in the variable called `AmountValue`, which is then displayed on the console.

To compile the console client application that uses a component, you use the `/r` option of the `csc` command. For example, to compile the Calculate.cs file that uses CalculateAmount.dll as a component, you need to type the following command at the command prompt:

```
csc /r:CalculateAmount.dll Calculate.cs
```

After you have compiled the client application, you can execute it. Figure F-1 shows the sample output of the Calculate class.

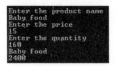

Figure F-1: Sample output of the Calculate class that uses CalculateAmount.dll as a component

Creating a component class using Visual Studio.NET

You can also create a component class using Visual Studio.NET. To create CalculateAmount.dll and use it in an ASP.NET Web application, proceed as follows:

1. Select File < New > Project to open the New Project dialog box.

2. In the New Project dialog box, select Visual C# Project in the left pane and select Class Library in the right pane.

3. Specify the name of the project as CalculateAmount and click OK. The Project window opens. The Solution Explorer window contains a starter file called Class1.cs. This file is displayed in the Visual Studio .NET window. Notice that some preliminary code along with the default constructor is already written in the class.

4. In the Solution Explorer window, right-click the file Class1.cs and select Rename. Rename the file MyCalculateAmount.cs. Also, in the class file, rename the class and the constructor from Class1 to MyCalculateAmount.

5. In the MyCalculateAmount class, write the code to create a method called `Multiply()` after the default constructor:

```
public class MyCalculateAmount
{
    public MyCalculateAmount()
    {
        //
```

```
        // TODO: Add constructor logic here
        //
    }
  public double Multiply(double price, double quantity)
    {
      double Amount;
      Amount=price*quantity;
      return Amount;
    }
}
```

6. Save and build the project.

Once the component class is created, you can use it in the client applications. To create an ASP.NET Web application called Calculate that uses the DLL CalculateAmount as a component, follow these steps:

1. Select File > New > Project to open the New Project dialog box.

2. In the New Project dialog box, select Visual C# Project in the left pane and select ASP.NET Web Application in the right pane.

3. Specify the name of the project as Calculate and click OK. The Project window opens. The default Web Form, WebForm1.aspx, is displayed in Design mode. The class file for this Web Form is WebForm1.aspx.cs. You now need to design the form to accept the product name, price, and quantity. The form should have a button that, when clicked, shows the calculated amount in a text box.

 Note You can open the class file by selecting View>Code or by pressing F7.

4. Design the form, as shown in Figure F-2. Specify the names of the controls as given in Table F-1.

5. Now, you need to add the reference of the DLL CalculateAmount to this project. To do so, select Project > Add Reference. The Add Reference dialog box opens, as shown in Figure F-3.

6. Click the Browse button. The Select Component dialog box opens. Browse for CalculateAmount.dll and click OK to add its reference to this project.

Note The CalculateAmount.dll file is located in \\CalculateAmount\bin\debug.

7. In the WebForm1.aspx.cs file, import CalculateAmount.dll. To do so, type the following statement above the Calculate class declaration:

```
using CalculateAmount;
```

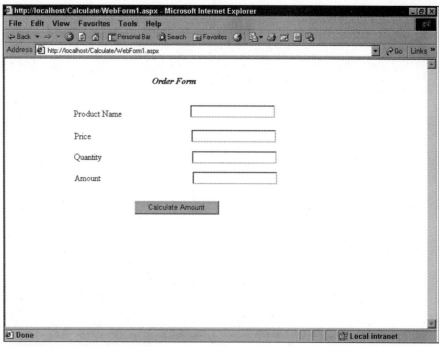

Figure F-2: Sample Order Form

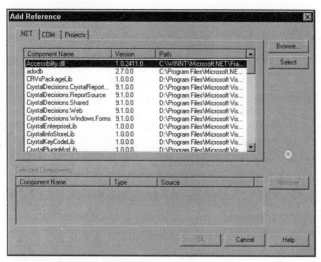

Figure F-3: The Add Reference dialog box

8. In the Click event of the button labeled Calculate Amount, type the following code:

```
// Creating an object of MyCalculateAmount class
MyCalculateAmount MyComponent= new MyCalculateAmount();
double AmountValue;
double Price;
double Quantity;
// Accepting the string type value from the text box and
// converting it into double type
Price= double.Parse(PriceBox.Text);
Quantity=double.Parse(QuantityBox.Text);
// Calling the Multiply() method of MyCalculateAmount class
AmountValue= MyComponent.Multiply(Price,Quantity);
// Changing the double type value in the variable
//AmountValue
AmountBox.Text=AmountValue.ToString();
```

Table F-1
IDs of text boxes and button in the sample form

Control	Contains	ID
TextBox	Product Name	NameBox
TextBox	Price	PriceBox
TextBox	Quantity	QuantityBox
TextBox	Amount	AmountBox
Button	CalculateAmount	CalculateButton

When the Calculate Amount button is clicked, the Multiply() method of MyCalculateAmount class is called. Notice that MyCalculateAmount is a class in the DLL CalculateAmount. This method takes two parameters, Price and Quantity, which have the data type double. The Multiply() method calculates the product of Price and Quantity. This calculated value is stored in the variable AmountValue and is then displayed in the textbox, AmountBox.

After writing the code, build and execute the application. Figure F-4 shows the sample output of the Web application.

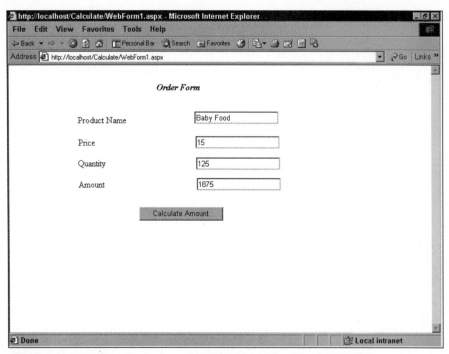

Figure F-4: Sample output of an ASP.NET Web application that uses
CalculateAmount.dll

Working with Namespaces

Now that you know the benefits of reusing code, you will be able to appreciate the
concept of *namespaces*. Namespaces are one of the ways of reusing code. You
would have noticed that when you create a Visual C# ASP.NET Web application, the
class file for the default Web Form displays a preliminary structure of the class. In
this structure, a namespace appears by default, as shown in Figure F-5.

A namespace is used to organize the elements in a *class library* in a hierarchical
manner. Consider a situation in which a team of programmers has been given the
task of developing applications to computerize the working of an organization.
Obviously, this would involve creating classes, which would in turn have numerous
methods. Also, a strong possibility exists that some of these methods can be
reused. You'll agree that the programmers would go crazy trying to recollect the
names of all the classes and the methods created in these classes. It becomes all
the more difficult when more than one programmer is working on an application.
Hence, it makes a lot of sense to organize these classes and their methods in a logical and hierarchical manner. For example, all functions that perform calculations
can be organized together. And this is exactly what a namespace does.

```
namespace NamespaceExample
{
    /// <summary>
    /// Summary description for WebForm1.
    /// </summary>
    public class WebForm1 : System.Web.UI.Page
    {
        public WebForm1()
        {
            Page.Init += new System.EventHandler(Page_Init);
        }

        private void Page_Load(object sender, System.EventArgs e)
        {
            // Put user code to initialize the page here
        }

        private void Page_Init(object sender, EventArgs e)
        {
            // CODEGEN: This call is required by the ASP.NET Web Form Designer.
            InitializeComponent();
        }

        Web Form Designer generated code
    }
}
```

Figure F-5: The preliminary structure of a class with a namespace

When you declare a namespace, you need to specify the keyword `namespace` before its name. When you create an application, by default, the name of the application is taken as the name of the namespace. However, you can change it later. The name of a namespace can be any legal identifier. However, you must be cautious about the names of namespaces, because they are case-sensitive. If you declare a namespace in lowercase, and while importing the namespace you use the namespace in uppercase, the C# application refuses to recognize the namespace.

A namespace contains members, such as classes and methods. Once you have declared a namespace for an application, you can use the classes and methods of this namespace in other applications. To use a namespace in an application, you use the following syntax:

```
using <namespace name>;
```

Note   When you import more than one namespace in an application by using this syntax, the members contained in these namespaces need to be unique. If you refer to the member names that are not unique, the reference is considered ambiguous and you'll get an error. To avoid this, use fully qualified names of namespaces.

Namespaces are implicitly public and hence the modifiers cannot be specified during namespace declaration. You can declare one or more namespaces in an application. However, within an application, the names of the namespaces need to be unique. If more than one namespaces is declared in an application, the namespace declared as the top-level declaration is referred to as the *outer namespace,* while the other namespace becomes the *inner namespace*. This is known as *nesting*. Consider the following example:

```
namespace Calculate
{
namespace Add
{
class Addition
{
statements
}
}
}
```

In this example, Calculate is the outer namespace, while Add is the inner namespace. The namespace declaration in the previous example can be alternatively done as follows:

```
namespace Calculate.Add
{
class Addition
{
}
}
```

Notice that in the namespace declaration, a period (.) is used to separate the outer and the inner namespaces. While declaring and using namespaces, one thing that you need to keep in mind is the hierarchy of the namespaces. You can use the namespace declared in the preceding code in another application by using the following statement:

```
using Calculate.Add;
```

In this example, single-level nesting of namespaces occurs. However, when there are multiple levels of nesting, using namespaces becomes cumbersome, because you have to remember the names of all the namespaces and their hierarchy. This problem can be solved by using aliases for the namespaces. You can create an alias by using the *alias directive.* To create an alias for Calculate.Add, use the following statement:

```
using c1=Calculate.Add;
```

After defining the alias c1, you can use it anywhere in the application, instead of specifying Calculate.Add. For example, to call a method called AddValues() in the class Addition, which is in the namespace Calculate.Add, you use the following statement:

```
c1.Addition.AddValues();
```

Notice that a hierarchy is followed while calling the method name. Starting from the left, the alias name of the namespace is followed by the class name, which is then followed by the method name.

Now that you know the concept of namespaces, let us look at an example that implements namespaces. To implement namespaces, create a Visual C# ASP.NET Web Application project. Design a Web Form as shown in Figure F-6. Specify the names of the controls as given in Table F-2.

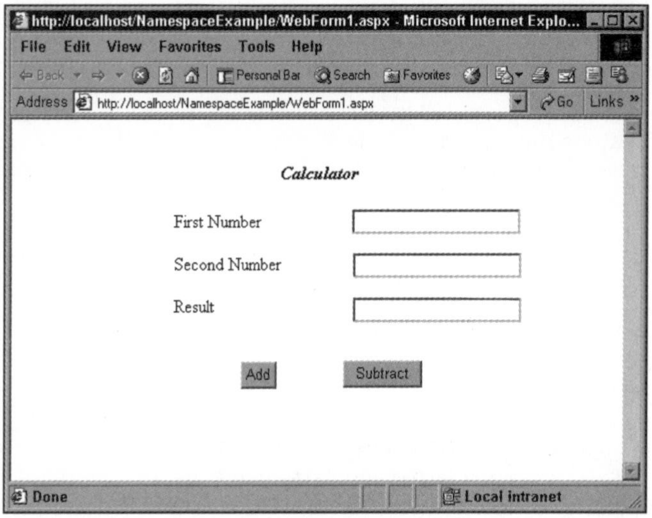

Figure F-6: A sample Calculator form

Table F-2		
IDs of text boxes and buttons in the sample form		
Control	*Contains*	*ID*
TextBox	First Number	FnumBox
TextBox	Second Number	SnumBox
TextBox	Result	ResultBox
Button	Add	AddButton
Button	Subtract	SubtractButton

After designing the Web Form, add a class called Calculator.cs to the project. Delete the preliminary class structure, as you will be creating your own namespace. Now, add the following code to this class file:

```
// Declaring the namespace, arithmetic
namespace arithmetic
{
```

```
        using System;


// Creating the class CalculateSum
    public class CalculateSum
    {
        public CalculateSum()
        {


        }
// Creating a method called Add that takes two parameters and
//calculates their sum
        public static int Add(int x,int y)
        {
            int AddNums=0;
            AddNums =x+y;
            return AddNums;
        }
    }

// Creating the class CalculateSub
    public class CalculateSub
    {
        public CalculateSub()
        {


        }
// Creating a method called Subtract that takes two
// parameters and calculates their difference
        public static int Subtract(int x,int y)
        {
            int SubNums=0;
            SubNums =x-y;
            return SubNums;
        }
    }

}
```

In this code, a namespace called arithmetic has been defined. This namespace contains two classes, CalculateSum and CalculateSub. The class CalculateSum has a static method called Add() that takes two integers as parameters and calculates their sum. The class CalculateSub has a static method called Subtract() that takes two integer parameters and calculates their sum.

Next, you'll use the methods Add() and Subtract() of the classes within the arithmetic namespace in your Web Form. To do so, the first step involves importing the namespace. In the class file of the Web Form, write the following line of code to import the arithmetic namespace:

```
using arithmetic;
```

Note Notice that the names of namepaces are case sensitive.

Then, in the `Click` event of the Add button, write the following code to call the `Add()` method of the CalculateSum class and display the result:

```
int FirstNum=int.Parse(FnumBox.Text);
int SecondNum=int.Parse(SnumBox.Text);

int Result=CalculateSum.Add(FirstNum,SecondNum);
ResultBox.Text=Result.ToString();
```

Similarly, in the `Click` event of the Subtract button, write the following code to call the `Subtract()` method of the CalculateSub class and display the result:

```
int FirstNum=int.Parse(FnumBox.Text);
int SecondNum=int.Parse(SnumBox.Text);

int Result=CalculateSub.Subtract(FirstNum,SecondNum);
ResultBox.Text=Result.ToString();
```

When you execute the application, the result is displayed in the text box with ID ResultBox when you click the Add or Subtract button.

This application is designed to accept two numbers from the user and calculate the sum as well as the difference of these two numbers. The `Add()` method, which is used to calculate the sum, exists in the namespace, arithmetic, while the `Subtract()` method, which calculates the difference, exists in the CalculateSub class of the same namespace, arithmetic.

Integrating Code and Role Security

Most Web sites are accessed by numerous users across the globe. Some portions of Web sites can be made available to almost anybody. However, most Web sites have some portions that should be accessed only by selected users. For example, the information regarding a company's achievements and milestones is available to any user who visits that company's Web site. But, the information regarding the customers' credit card cannot and should not be accessed by any user who visits the site. The Web site must secure this information from public access. ASP.NET provides security features that you can use to develop secure Web applications.

ASP.NET works in conjunction with the .NET Framework and Internet Information Server (IIS) 5.0 to provide security to Web applications. ASP.NET provides security in the following three key areas:

✦ **Authentication:** This is the process of determining the identity of the user requesting a Web page. It requires the user to enter credentials, such as a user-name and password. The credentials are then validated against some authority. If the credentials are valid, the user is considered an authenticated user.

✦ **Authorization:** After a user is authenticated, he/she can access only those resources that he/she is authorized to access. Authorization is the process of determining whether or not the authenticated user can access a given resource.

✦ **Impersonation:** When an application executes by using the identity of the requesting entity, it is called impersonation.

Cross-Reference For more information on ASP.NET security, see Chapter 19, "ASP.NET Security."

Because ASP.NET is based on the .NET Framework, the developers can access all the security features of the Common Language Runtime (CLR). The security fea-tures can be implemented by using the classes in the System.Web.Security names-pace. This section introduces you to the security features, such as code access and role-based security, that are provided by the CLR.

Before proceeding to the details, let us first understand what is meant by code access and role-based security.

✦ **Code access security:** A mechanism to provide security from malicious mobile code, which damages the computer systems and data. In today's world of the Internet, computer systems are more exposed to mobile code from varied sources, such as attachments to e-mail, documents, and Internet downloads. Therefore, code access security becomes all the more important. Code access security allows mobile code to run safely on a computer even if the computer has no trust relationship with the computer from which the code originated.

The runtime uses the security policy, which is a configurable set of rules, to decide what a code is allowed to do. A security policy is set by administrators and enforced by the runtime. Thus, the security policy ensures that the code can access only those resources and call only the code that is allowed in the security policy.

✦ **Role-based security:** The users accessing a Web site can be categorized into a set of roles. A *role* refers to a group of users who have similar rights with respect to security. For example, suppose you have developed an application that accepts points earned by an employee. Based on these points, the appli-cation calculates the salary hike and reflects the changes in the salary of the employee. Logically speaking, only supervisors should be allowed to enter the points for their subordinates. However, the application should allow the employees to view the changes in their salary. To accomplish this, you can create a role that includes all the supervisors and another role that includes the subordinates.

Web sites should be able to tailor content dynamically depending on the role to which the user belongs. To perform this authorization, the server hosting the application should have access to the information about the authenticated user. Role-based security makes available the information about the authenticated users, and hence provides support for user authorization.

You can prevent the misuse of sensitive data or applications by other applications by restricting access to the sensitive data or application. This can be implemented by using the concept of *permissions,* the rights that an application has for accessing sensitive data or another application. When the sensitive data or the application that needs to be protected receives an access request, it checks the permissions of the requesting applications. In C#, you can use the permission classes or the permission attributes to modify the security permissions. The permissions can be broadly classified into three categories: identity permissions, code access permissions, and role-based security permissions.

Identity permissions

These permissions ensure that the code is qualified to support an identity, such as a Web site or a digital signature. Some of the permission classes included in this category are the following:

✦ SiteIdentityPermission: Identifies the Web site from which the code originated.

✦ URLIdentityPermission: Identifies the URL from which the code originated. The entire URL, including the protocol, is checked.

Code access permissions

These permissions refer to rights of code to access or use protected data or resources. Some of the permission classes included in this category are the following:

✦ **FileDialogPermission:** Represents the access rights for a file that is selected using the Open dialog box.

✦ **FileIOPermission:** Represents the rights on the input and output functions that can be performed on the file.

✦ **EnvironmentPermission:** Represents the rights for reading or writing the environment variables.

Although you can use the permission classes provided by C# to ensure code security, sometimes you might want to create your own code access permissions. To create customized code access permissions, you need to follow these basic steps:

1. Design the permission class. You need to decide on the functionality of the permission class that you want to create. You also need to decide which resources need to be protected by the permission class.

2. Implement the IPermission and IUnrestrictedPermission interfaces. An interface is similar to a class, but it cannot be instantiated. Also, an interface consists of just function declarations.

3. Demand a custom permission. This would perform security checks on applications that try to access the code, or resources that your customized code access permission is meant to protect.

4. Also, you should update the security policy to include the custom permission.

Role-based security permissions

These permissions, as the name suggests, check the identity or role of the user. This permission category has only one class, PrincipalPermission, which is used to check the identity of the user. The PrincipalPermission class cannot be inherited. You can custom create and use the PrincipalPermission class in your application to implement role-based security. While custom creating the PrincipalPermission class, you need to implement the IPermission interface. You also need to include the System.Security.Permissions namespace.

By using all three categories of permissions, you can ensure the security of your code and data. This becomes all the more important when the use of Internet and Web-based applications is increasing by leaps and bounds.

Summary

In this appendix, you learned the concept of the Component Object Model (COM). You also learned about single-tier, two-tier, and multitier architecture. Then, you learned to reuse code by creating and using components. You also learned how to work with namespaces. Finally, you learned the concept of code and role security.

✦   ✦   ✦

Index

Continued

Continued